06

PARIS

Where to Stay and Eat
for All Budgets

Must-See Sights
and Local Secrets

Ratings You Can Trust

Fodor's Travel Publications   New York, Toronto, London, Sydney, Auckland
www.fodors.com

FODOR'S PARIS 2006

Editors: Andrew Collins, Jennifer Paull

Editorial Production: Linda K. Schmidt
Editorial Contributors: David Allan, Linda Cabasin, Nancy Coons, Jennifer Ditsler-Ladonne, Roger Grody, Simon Hewitt, Satu Hummasti, Rosa Jackson, Lisa Pasold, Mathew Schwartz, Heather Stimmler-Hall, Caroline Trefler
Maps: David Lindroth, *cartographer;* Bob Blake and Rebecca Baer, *map editors*
Design: Fabrizio La Rocca, *creative director;* Guido Caroti, *art director;* Moon Sun Kim, *cover designer;* Melanie Marin, *senior picture editor*
Production/Manufacturing: Colleen Ziemba
Cover Photo (Eiffel Tower): Bruno Perousse/Age Fotostock

SPECIAL SALES

This book is available for special discounts for bulk purchases for sales promotions or premiums. Special editions, including personalized covers, excerpts of existing books, and corporate imprints, can be created in large quantities for special needs. For more information, write to Special Markets/Premium Sales, 1745 Broadway, MD 6-2, New York, New York 10019, or e-mail specialmarkets@randomhouse.com.

AN IMPORTANT TIP & AN INVITATION

Although all prices, opening times, and other details in this book are based on information supplied to us at press time, changes occur all the time in the travel world, and Fodor's cannot accept responsibility for facts that become outdated or for inadvertent errors or omissions. So **always confirm information when it matters,** especially if you're making a detour to visit a specific place. Your experiences—positive and negative—matter to us. If we have missed or misstated something, **please write to us.** We follow up on all suggestions. Contact the Paris editor at editors@fodors.com or c/o Fodor's at 1745 Broadway, New York, New York 10019.

PRINTED IN THE UNITED STATES OF AMERICA

10 9 8 7 6 5 4 3 2 1

Be a Fodor's Correspondent

Your opinion matters. It matters to us. It matters to your fellow Fodor's travelers, too. And we'd like to hear it. In fact, we *need* to hear it.

When you share your experiences and opinions, you become an active member of the Fodor's community. That means we'll not only use your feedback to make our books better, but we'll publish your names and comments whenever possible. Throughout our guides, look for "Word of Mouth," excerpts of your unvarnished feedback.

Here's how you can help improve Fodor's for all of us.

Tell us when we're right. We rely on local writers to give you an insider's perspective. But our writers and staff editors—who are the best in the business—depend on you. Your positive feedback is a vote to renew our recommendations for the next edition.

Tell us when we're wrong. We're proud that we update most of our guides every year. But we're not perfect. Things change. Hotels cut services. Museums change hours. Charming cafés lose charm. If our writer didn't quite capture the essence of a place, tell us how you'd do it differently. If any of our descriptions are inaccurate or inadequate, we'll incorporate your changes in the next edition and will correct factual errors at fodors.com *immediately*.

Tell us what to include. You probably have had fantastic travel experiences that aren't yet in Fodor's. Why not share them with a community of like-minded travelers? Maybe you chanced upon a beach or bistro or B&B that you don't want to keep to yourself. Tell us why we should include it. And share your discoveries and experiences with everyone directly at fodors.com. Your input may lead us to add a new listing or highlight a place we cover with a "Highly Recommended" star or with our highest rating, "Fodor's Choice."

Give us your opinion instantly at our feedback center at www.fodors.com/feedback. You may also e-mail editors@fodors.com with the subject line "Paris Editor." Or send your nominations, comments, and complaints by mail to Paris Editor, Fodor's, 1745 Broadway, New York, NY 10019.

You and travelers like you are the heart of the Fodor's community. Make our community richer by sharing your experiences. Be a Fodor's correspondent.

Bon voyage!

Tim Jarrell, Publisher

CONTENTS

1 Exploring Paris
1

2 Where to Eat
140

3 Where to Stay
196

4 Nightlife & the Arts
243

5 Sports & the Outdoors
272

6 Shopping
283

7 Side Trips from Paris
320

Understanding Paris
346

Index
365

Maps

CloseUps

ABOUT OUR WRITERS

Nancy Coons has lived in France for many years and has written many books for Fodor's, including *Provence and the Côte d'Azur, Escape to Provence,* and *Escape to the Riviera.*

When writer/editor Jennifer Ditsler-Ladonne decided it was time to leave her longtime home of Manhattan, there was only one place to go: Paris. Her insatiable curiosity—which earned her the reputation in New York of knowing just the right place to get just the right anything—has found the perfect home in the inexhaustible streets of Paris. If you're looking for rare medieval arcana or Paris's wild edible mushrooms, she's the person to call, as we did for our Paris shopping update.

Simon Hewitt headed to Paris straight from studying French and art history at Oxford. It was a return to base; his grandmother was French, as is his daughter. Now living northwest of Paris, he explores the area around the capital for our Side Trips chapter. He has been working for Fodor's since 1987 and is the Paris correspondent for several art-market magazines. An accomplished cricketer, he captained France from 1990 to 2001 and is now national coach.

Rosa Jackson's love affair with French pastries began at age four, when she spent her first year in Paris before returning to the Canadian north. Early experiments with eclairs and croissants led her to enroll in the Paris Cordon Bleu, where she learned that even great chefs make mistakes. A food writer for more than a decade and a Parisian since 1995, Rosa also creates personalized food itineraries via www.rosajackson.com. She has eaten in hundreds of Paris restaurants—and always has room for dessert.

Exploring updater Lisa Pasold first fell in love with Paris architecture and atmosphere in 1989, while dragging her suitcase up seven flights of stairs to a *chambre de bonne.* She writes on travel, food, and architecture for papers like the *Chicago Tribune* and *The Globe and Mail.* She also recently published a book of poetry, *Weave.* As a travel writer, she has been thrown off a train in Belarus and has mushed huskies in the Yukon, but her favorite place to explore remains the fabulous tangle of streets that surrounds her Paris home.

Mathew Schwartz followed his wife to Paris, where he is a freelance freelance writer for such publications as the *The Times* of London and *Wired News.* When not working at home or in adopted cafés, he escapes to the outdoors to do street photography, peruse the open-air markets, and visit the city's arcades, museums, and parks. He applied those interests to this year's Exploring and Sports & the Outdoors chapters.

Heather Stimmler-Hall came to Paris as a university student in 1995 and was almost immediately put to work by family and friends back home asking for hotel recommendations. A decade later she's made a career out of reading between the lines of glossy hotel brochures and talking even the grumpiest front desk receptionist into letting her poke around their rooms. She's reviewed hundreds of hotels for *The Times* of London, *ELLE,* and her own monthly e-newsletter, www.secretsofparis.com. While not too jaded to appreciate the city's gorgeous five-star palace and design boutique hotels, what really gets her excited are the hidden budget hotels with a uniquely Parisian character.

ABOUT THIS BOOK

Our Ratings

Sometimes you find terrific travel experiences and sometimes they just find you. But usually the burden is on you to select the right combination of experiences. That's where our ratings come in.

As travelers we've all discovered a place so wonderful that its worthiness is obvious. And sometimes that place is so experiential that superlatives don't do it justice: you just have to be there to know. These sights, properties, and experiences get our highest rating, **Fodor's Choice,** indicated by orange stars throughout this book.

Black stars highlight sights and properties we deem **Highly Recommended,** places that our writers, editors, and readers praise again and again for consistency and excellence.

By default, there's another category: any place we include in this book is by definition worth your time, unless we say otherwise. And we will.

Disagree with any of our choices? Care to nominate a place or suggest that we rate one more highly? Visit our feedback center at www. fodors.com/feedback.

Budget Well

Hotel and restaurant price categories from ¢ to $$$$ are defined in the opening pages of each chapter. For attractions, we always give standard adult admission fees; reductions are usually available for children, students, and senior citizens. Want to pay with plastic? **AE, D, DC, MC, V** following restaurant and hotel listings indicate if American Express, Discover, Diner's Club, MasterCard, and Visa are accepted.

Restaurants

Unless we state otherwise, restaurants are open for lunch and dinner daily. We mention dress only when there's a specific requirement and reservations only when they're essential or not accepted—it's always best to book ahead.

Hotels

Hotels have private bath, phone, TV, and air-conditioning and operate on the European Plan (a.k.a. EP, meaning without meals), unless we specify that they use the Continental Plan (CP, with a Continental breakfast), Breakfast Plan (BP, with a full breakfast), or Modified American Plan (MAP, with breakfast and dinner) or are all-inclusive (including all meals and

most activities). We always list facilities but not whether you'll be charged an extra fee to use them, so when pricing accommodations, find out what's included.

Many Listings
- ★ Fodor's Choice
- ★ Highly recommended
- ⊠ Physical address
- ✦ Directions
- ⊕ Mailing address
- ☎ Telephone
- ☐ Fax
- ⊕ On the Web
- ✎ E-mail
- 💲 Admission fee
- ⊘ Open/closed times
- ► Start of walk/itinerary
- Ⓜ Metro stations
- ▭ Credit cards

Hotels & Restaurants
- ⊡ Hotel
- ⇴ Number of rooms
- ⚷ Facilities
- ⦿ Meal plans
- ✕ Restaurant
- ⤺ Reservations
- ⌂ Dress code
- ⟍ Smoking
- ⚹ BYOB
- ✕⊡ Hotel with restaurant that warrants a visit

Other
- ☺ Family-friendly
- ▤ Contact information
- ⇨ See also
- ⊠ Branch address
- ☞ Take note

The first thing you need to do is learn the difference between the Rive Droite (Right Bank, north of the Seine) and the Rive Gauche (Left Bank, south of the Seine). In the most stereotypical terms, the Rive Droite is traditionally more elegant and commercial, though its less central areas are the hip places of the moment. The Rive Gauche, on the other hand, is the artistic area; the Sorbonne and the Quartier Latin are here, along with the haunts of literary greats and fashion designers. Between the two banks you have the Île de la Cité, where you'll find Notre-Dame, and the smaller Île St-Louis.

Île de la Cité & Île St-Louis
1ᵉʳ & 4ᵉ Arrondissements

The Île de la Cité is the cradle of Paris; some 2,300 years ago the island was the strategic stronghold of a Gallic tribe called the Parisii. Today three buildings here—**Notre-Dame,** the **Conciergerie,** and **Sainte-Chapelle**—still awe through their sheer scale and unadulterated historical and architectural grandeur. Although large tracts of the island were bulldozed by Baron Haussmann in the mid-19th century, there are still enchanting corners. Just over the bridge behind the cathedral is the Île St-Louis, the smaller of the two islands, still home to some of the most charming streets in Paris and, at Berthillon, to its best ice cream.

The Louvre, Tuileries & Faubourg St-Honoré
1ᵉʳ, 2ᵉ & 8ᵉ Arrondissements

For most people the **Louvre** remains the greatest museum, period. Extending west is a welcoming green space, the majestic **Jardin des Tuileries.** Just north of the rue de Rivoli are the serene courtyard gardens of the **Palais-Royal,** where the Comédie Française is the permanent playground for the ghosts of Great French Theater. After being seduced by the luxe boutiques of the Palais-Royal arcades (Thomas Jefferson was a frequent customer here back when), spend some time window-shopping along rue St-Honoré and rue du Faubourg St-Honoré. This posh shopping strip skirts **place Vendôme,** the mecca of *haute joaillerie* (fancy jewelry) and the Ritz.

The Opéra & the Grands Boulevards
2ᵉ, 8ᵉ & 9ᵉ Arrondissements

Tap into your inner *boulevardier* in this part of town. The term *Grands Boulevards* refers to the broad avenue that cuts across the Rive Droite; the name changes several times along the way, so Parisians refer to it in the plural form. It starts at the Madeleine church with boulevard de la Madeleine, then stretches east to boulevard des Capucines, which crosses in front of the 19th-century gilded confection that is the **Opéra Garnier.** Behind the Opéra loom a couple of mammoth department stores: Galeries Lafayette and Au Printemps. The avenue morphs into boulevard des Italiens, once the address of glittering cafés. When it hits boulevard Haussmann, it becomes boulevard Montmartre for a few blocks; a couple of 19th-century *passages* (glass-roofed shopping arcades) branch off here. The avenue curves and continues on all the way to Bastille.

The Marais & Les Halles
1er, 3e & 4e Arrondissements

Le Marais translates as "the swamp." Although this appellation refers to the formerly overwhelming presence of the Seine in this area, this lively neighborhood is anything but stuck in the mud. Some of the chicest people in Paris made the Marais the home of the hip by renovating the multitude of 17th- and 18th-century mansions in the quarter, opening gorgeous shops, and transforming several *hôtels particuliers* (mansions) into museums, including the **Musée Carnavalet** and **Musée Picasso.** At the end of boutique-busy rue des Francs-Bourgeois is the Marais's showplace, the eternally elegant **place des Vosges.** The narrow, labyrinthine streets also include the venerable Jewish quarter, centered around rue des Rosiers, and rue Ste-Croix-de-la-Bretonnerie and rue Vieille-du-Temple, the lifelines of gay life in Paris. To the west of the Marais lies the **Centre Georges Pompidou**; its sloping plaza is among Paris's best people-watching spots. (Parisians call this area Beaubourg.) The adjacent Les Halles was once the city's main market, but since the 1970s a modern mall, the Forum des Halles, and a park have stood in its place.

The Quartier Latin
5e Arrondissement

The backbone of French intellectual life for more than 700 years, the Quartier Latin has always attracted the intellectually restless, the politically discontented, the artistically inspired, and those who like to hang out with them to its universities, cafés, garrets, and alleys. Home to most of the country's major centers of learning (the **Sorbonne,** the École Normale Supérieure, the École Polytechnique, the Collège de France), the Quartier Latin has also been the site of the city's fiercest street battles: in 1871 against the state, in 1945 against the Germans, and in 1968 against everyone over 30. The medieval labyrinth of streets surrounding rue de la Huchette gives a sense of what the city was like before Haussmann and the automobile transformed everything. Artistic treasures can be found in the **Musée-National du Moyen-Age,** housed in the Cluny mansion, and the sleek **Institut du Monde Arabe.** French luminaries are enshrined in the **Panthéon.**

St-Germain-des-Prés
6e Arrondissement

One of the chicest (yet most tourist-friendly) neighborhoods in Paris, this quarter is centered around the venerable tower of the **church of St-Germain-des-Prés,** the oldest house of worship in Paris. Aswarm with bookstores and cafés, St-Germain has been gentrified nearly to the hilt. But wander off traffic-clogged boulevard St-Germain, and you'll find ancient facades, antiques shops and hidden courtyards. A stroll a little farther south brings you to the sylvan **Jardin du Luxembourg.**

Invalides & the Tour Eiffel
7ᵉ Arrondissement

Home of government ministries, foreign embassies, and magnificent hô-tels particuliers, the 7ᵉ arrondissement is blueblood central. The area at-tracts tourists for three good reasons: the impressive collections of late 19th-century art at the **Musée d'Orsay,** the **Tour Eiffel,** and Napoléon's final resting spot at the **Invalides.** Yet the district offers much more, in-cluding the **Musée Rodin** and the fabulous Le Bon Marché, the city's old-est and poshest department store.

Champs-Élysées & Trocadéro
8ᵉ & 16ᵉ Arrondissements

Majestic with a capital M, Napoléon's **Arc de Triomphe** crowns the Étoile, a star of the first magnitude with 12 streams of light; by day you'll see these are avenues, the leading ray of which is the **Champs-Élysées.** The Champs was once an aristocratic pleasure park; pricey cafés and bland international chains have made their inroads, but a face-lift (broader sidewalks, fresh street furnishings) and glossy boutiques have restored some of its lost grandeur. Avenue Montaigne, thick with haute-couture shops, branches off the Champs. Crossing avenue Marceau into the 16ᵉ arrondissement brings you to cultural riches. Museums clus-ter in these decorous streets; the Asian collections of the **Musée Guimet** and the avant-garde **Palais de Tokyo** lead the pack.

East of Bastille
11ᵉ & 12ᵉ Arrondissements

The only folks storming the Bastille these days are opera-goers lining up for seats at the **Opéra Bastille** and young Parisians bent on painting the town rouge. The area around the former (now-vanished) prison has been gentrified, as an artsy crowd joined blue-collar locals. Behind the Opéra, stroll down the redbrick **Viaduc des Arts,** a stylish walkway with flowers and benches above and artisans' shops below. Place de la Na-tion, east of place de la Bastille, was the site of public guillotinings dur-ing the Revolution; now it's a major subway transfer point. From here it's a short métro ride to **Père-Lachaise Cemetery,** final resting place for dozens of luminaries, from Frédéric Chopin to Jim Morrison, Molière to Marcel Proust. Following the Seine southeast of Bastille, on the other hand, brings you to the **Bercy** district. Once the Paris center of the wine trade, it's now the domain of modern architecture; the new Cinémath-èque is due to open here in 2005. Just across the river stand the four bookish towers of the **Bibliothèque Nationale François-Mitterrand.**

Montparnasse
14ᵉ Arrondissement

Ernest Hemingway, Henry Miller, Picasso, and Sartre all did their time in the cafés, boulevards, and villas of Montparnasse. Something of them remains in the cemetery, on plaques in front of houses, and chiseled into the tables of bars they frequented, but little elsewhere. The rest of the neighborhood looks much as it did in the 1920s, were it not for the oppressive shadow of the Tour Montparnasse, Continental Europe's tallest office tower. For cutting-edge contemporary art, Jean Nouvel's glass-cubed **Fondation Cartier** is a must-see. Hit the **Fondation Henri Cartier-Bresson** for a dose of photography and the **catacombs** to get up close and personal with mortality.

Passy, Auteuil & the Bois de Boulogne
16ᵉ Arrondissement

The Passy and Auteuil neighborhoods, on the far west side, form one of the city's largest, most elegant wards. On one side Passy and Auteuil are bordered by the Seine, on the other by the **Bois de Boulogne,** an extensive wooded park. Both Passy and Auteuil have some of Paris's choicest architecture, from Art Nouveau buildings by Hector Guimard to the stark lines of the Fondation Le Corbusier. Impressionist paintings, especially masterworks by Claude Monet, will draw you to the **Musée Marmottan–Claude Monet.**

Montmartre
18ᵉ Arrondissement

Rising above the city on the highest hill in Paris is Montmartre, which maintains a fiercely independent spirit in the face of thousands of tourists seeking a whiff of its bohemian past—or of the *Amélie* movie. The beacon of the "Butte" is the icy-white **Basilique du Sacré-Coeur.** Get beyond the easel-packed place du Tertre to experience the true allure of this neighborhood: the steep stairways with great views of Paris, pocket parks, and busy cafés. At the bottom of the hill, is the netherworld of **Pigalle,** which still cashes in on its reputation as the sin center of Paris. Steer clear of the portholed "bars américaines," but the Musée de l'Érotisme and the Moulin Rouge remain safe, sexy bets.

Northeast Paris
10ᵉ, 11ᵉ & 20ᵉ Arrondissements

Princes of the Paris night will tell you that the real happening scene has retreated northeast, to the edges of the 11th arrondissement and beyond. **Oberkampf** has been the nocturnal center of things for a few years now, but the areas around are catching up quickly. Particularly thriving is the area around République and the **Canal St-Martin,** whose locks, bridges, and waterside cafés conjure up an unexpected flavor of Amsterdam. Farther north along the canal brings you to **Parc de la Villette,** once Paris's largest complex of slaughterhouses and stockyards, now a giant park with loads of high-tech buildings. Belleville, too, long a center of immigrant, working-class Paris, has become a focal point; not to be missed is the **Parc des Buttes-Chaumont.**

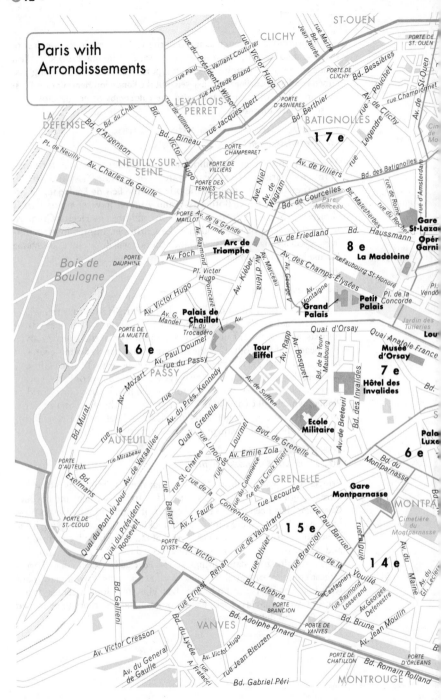

Paris with
Arrondissements

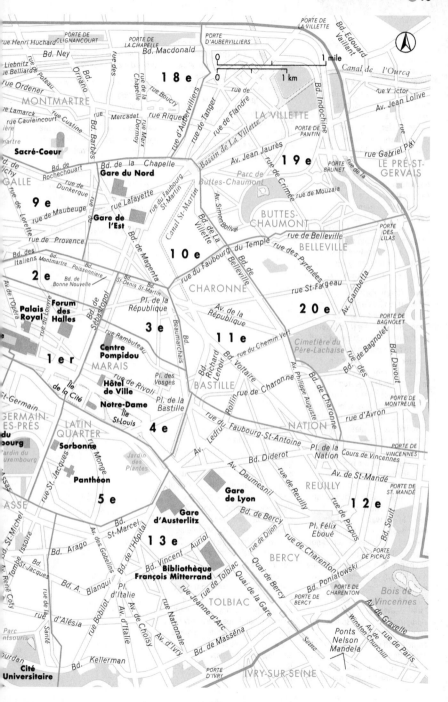

Paris in 5 Days

A visit to Paris is never quite as simple as a quick look at a few landmarks. Each neighborhood has its own treasures, so be ready to explore—a pleasant prospect in this most elegant of cities. So that you don't show up somewhere and find the doors locked, shuffle the itinerary segments with closing days in mind. To avoid crowds, go to museums and major sights early in the day. Some museums have extended evening hours one day a week, and these late times are less crowded, too. Note that some museums and major sights have reduced entrance fees on Sunday and that many museums are closed early in the week.

Day 1. Start in Paris's chronological heart, on Île de la Cité. Climb up Notre-Dame's tower for a panoramic city view (and helpful landmark orientation); then head over to neighboring Île St-Louis to wander the atmospheric streets and drink in the back view of the mighty cathedral. (A stop for Berthillon ice cream is also inevitable, even if it is before lunch.) Go back to Île de la Cité to see the stunning stained glass in Sainte-Chapelle. For a Seine-level view of the city, go to place du Pont Neuf at the far end of the island to catch the Vedettes du Pont Neuf boat tour. Cross the Pont au Change to the Châtelet métro station to catch Line 1 to the Champs-Élysées; if you'd like to walk most of the broad avenue, get off at the Franklin-D.-Roosevelt stop. If not, get off at George V (near the top) or Charles de Gaulle Étoile (by the roundabout) and head to the Arc de Triomphe. From the top of the arch there's a great view of the "star" of avenues. If platinum-card shopping is on your list, head to avenue Montaigne, which branches off the Champs. Otherwise, hop back on the métro at the Charles de Gaulle Étoile station and take Line 6 to the Champs de

Mars Tour Eiffel station to see one more monument. The graceful iron giant is especially romantic at twilight or after dark, when the tower is illuminated and the city view from the top becomes a sea of twinkling lights. Be here on the hour to see the extra-bright light display.
All the major sights on this tour are open daily.

Day 2. It's time to brave the Louvre; start early to avoid the worst of the crowds. After lunch dip into the Tuileries park, then double back on rue de Rivoli and stroll through the arcades and garden of the Palais-Royal. Next take rue St-Honoré west, window-shopping on your way past the place Vendôme, toward the Madeleine church. Catch the métro's Line 12 at the Madeleine stop and zip north to the Abbesses station. Take the elevator up to ground level, step out from underneath the Art Nouveau canopy, and you'll be in Montmartre—a funky, lively neighborhood that'll clear away any remaining museum fatigue. Explore the winding, hilly streets, catch the city view from the plaza in front of the Sacré-Coeur Basilica, and settle into a bistro or café.

This is fine any day but Tuesday, when the Louvre is closed. Many shops are closed Sunday.

Day 3. Start the morning admiring the Impressionists in the Musée d'Orsay; arrive early to avoid the crowds. In the afternoon head west along the quais, passing the Assemblée Nationale (the French parliament), to the Pont Alexandre-III, an ornate Belle Époque bridge. Above you gleams the dome of the Église du Dôme in the Hôtel des Invalides; this is where Napoléon's buried (in half-a-dozen coffins). From the Invalides it's just a short walk to the Musée Rodin, where you can pair sculpture viewing with time in the

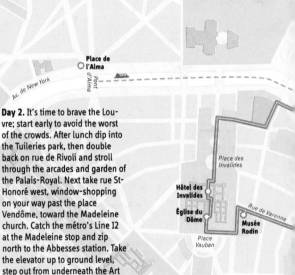

Place Charles de Gaulle

Arc de Triomphe

Av. des Champs-Élysées

Rue du Faubourg St-Honoré

Palais de l'Élyseé

Rond Point des Champs Élysées

Place de l'Alma

Pont d'Alma

Av. de New York

Place des Invalides

Hôtel des Invalides

Église du Dôme

Rue de Varenne

Musée Rodin

Place Vauban

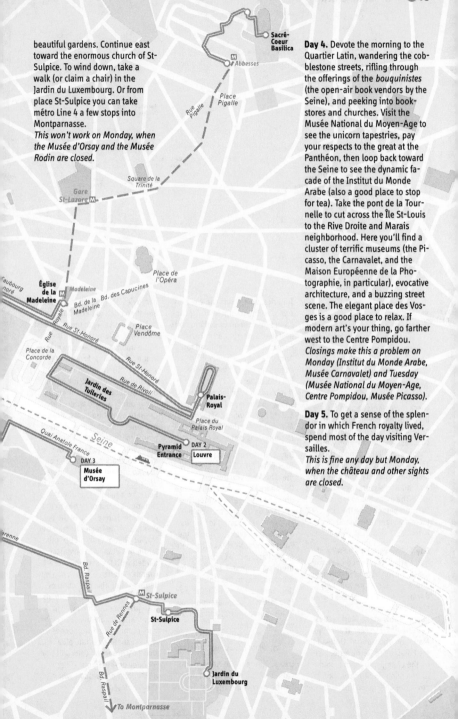

beautiful gardens. Continue east toward the enormous church of St-Sulpice. To wind down, take a walk (or claim a chair) in the Jardin du Luxembourg. Or from place St-Sulpice you can take métro Line 4 a few stops into Montparnasse.

This won't work on Monday, when the Musée d'Orsay and the Musée Rodin are closed.

Day 4. Devote the morning to the Quartier Latin, wandering the cobblestone streets, rifling through the offerings of the *bouquinistes* (the open-air book vendors by the Seine), and peeking into bookstores and churches. Visit the Musée National du Moyen-Age to see the unicorn tapestries, pay your respects to the great at the Panthéon, then loop back toward the Seine to see the dynamic facade of the Institut du Monde Arabe (also a good place to stop for tea). Take the pont de la Tournelle to cut across the Île St-Louis to the Rive Droite and Marais neighborhood. Here you'll find a cluster of terrific museums (the Picasso, the Carnavalet, and the Maison Européenne de la Photographie, in particular), evocative architecture, and a buzzing street scene. The elegant place des Vosges is a good place to relax. If modern art's your thing, go farther west to the Centre Pompidou.

Closings make this a problem on Monday (Institut du Monde Arabe, Musée Carnavalet) and Tuesday (Musée National du Moyen-Age, Centre Pompidou, Musée Picasso).

Day 5. To get a sense of the splendor in which French royalty lived, spend most of the day visiting Versailles.

This is fine any day but Monday, when the château and other sights are closed.

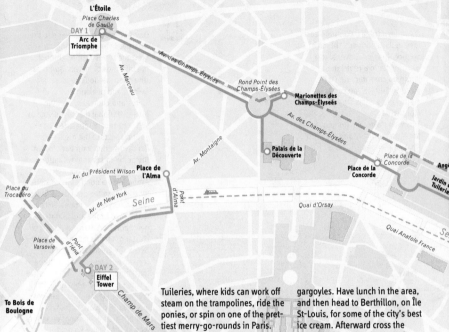

Paris with Kids

Be sure to buy a *Pariscope* and check the *enfants* section for a list of current events for children, including children's theater, circuses, special museum workshops, and all the puppet shows. Time your stints in the major museums carefully, and look into any children's tours they might offer. The ideas below focus on Paris proper; outside the city there's always Disneyland Paris . . .

Day 1. Give your kids an idea of how Paris was planned by climbing to the top of the Arc de Triomphe. From here work your way down the Champs-Élysées toward place de la Concorde. Stop for a puppet show at the Marionettes des Champs-Élysées, at avenues Matignon and Gabriel. Or head to the Palais de la Découverte, just off the Champs, to catch a planetarium show. Continue walking down the Champs to the Jardin des

Tuileries, where kids can work off steam on the trampolines, ride the ponies, or spin on one of the prettiest merry-go-rounds in Paris. For an afternoon treat head for Angélina (on rue de Rivoli), a tearoom famous for its thick hot chocolate.

If you want to see the puppet show, do this on a Wednesday, Saturday, or Sunday. Skip this on Monday, when the Palais de la Découverte is closed.

Day 2. In the morning head to the Tour Eiffel for a bird's-eye view of the city. After you descend, give the nearby carousel a whirl; ride on one of the Bateaux Mouches at place de l'Alma; or, for older kids who are looking for a grossout factor, brave Les Égouts, the Paris sewers. Next take the métro to the Parc André-Citroën, where there's a computerized "dancing fountain, " or to the Bois de Boulogne, where you'll find a zoo (the Jardin d'Acclimatation), rowboats, bumper cars, and plenty of wide-open space.

This won't work on Thursday or Friday, when Les Égouts are closed.

Day 3. Start early at Notre-Dame Cathédral, climbing up the tower for the view of the city and the

gargoyles. Have lunch in the area, and then head to Berthillon, on Île St-Louis, for some of the city's best ice cream. Afterward cross the Seine and walk or take the métro to the Odéon stop. From there walk around the colonnaded Théâtre de l'Odéon to the Jardin du Luxembourg, where there's a playground, a pond where kids can rent miniature boats, a café, a marionette theater, and plenty of places to sit. If you think your children would like to see the bustle of a local market, try the one on rue Mouffetard. Ready for more? Walk to the Centre de la Mer et des Eaux, an aquarium nearby, then continue on foot or by bus to the Arènes de Lutèce, one of the few vestiges of the former Roman city. Not far on foot or by métro is the Jardin des Plantes, a botanical garden with the state-of-the-art Grande Galerie d'Évolution, a museum exhibiting a collection of taxidermy of all kinds of animals. Also just a métro ride away in Montparnasse are the catacombs, dark tunnels filled with bones, which usually fascinate older kids. *Don't try to see the Catacombs on Monday or the Grande Galerie d'Évolution on Tuesday, when they're closed.*

Day 4. Take a walk through the Marais, stopping early on at the Musée Picasso and keeping your eyes peeled for storybook architectural details. Nearby, pick up a sandwich to eat on a bench on the place des Vosges. Next, head over to the Centre Pompidou; either see an exhibit (often there are special kids' programs related to the shows) or simply ride the escalator to the top for a great view of Paris.

Around the corner, on square Igor-Stravinsky, watch the imaginative, moving sculptures in the fountain. Another option is to take the métro from the Châtelet–Les-Halles station to the Porte de La Villette stop; in the whimsical park of the same name are an interactive science museum, a museum of musical instruments, an IMAX theater, and various innovative structures to play on and in.

Because of closings, do this between Wednesday and Sunday: the Parc de La Villette is closed Monday and the Centre Pompidou and Musée Picasso Tuesday.

WHEN TO GO

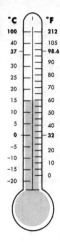

°C		°F
100		212
40		105
37		98.6
30		90
25		80
20		70
15		60
10		50
5		40
0		32
-5		20
-10		10
-15		0
-20		

The major tourist season in France stretches from Easter to mid-September, but Paris has much to offer in every season. If you're dreaming of Paris in the springtime, May is your best bet, not rainy March and April—regardless of what some songs say about the latter. Paris in the early spring can be disappointingly damp, though it's relatively tourist-free; May and June are delightful, with good weather and plenty of cultural and other attractions. (There are lots of holiday weekends in May, though, which can cut down significantly on opening hours.) July and August can be sultry, stuffy, and uncomfortable, intensified by pollution that has been getting worse each year. Moreover, many theaters and some of the smaller restaurants and shops close for the entire month of August. If you're undeterred by the hot weather, you'll notice a fairly relaxed atmosphere around the city, as this is the month when most Parisians are on vacation and the city is pleasantly deserted. Early autumn is ideal. Cultural life revives after the summer break, and sunny weather often continues through the first half of October. The ballet and theater are in full swing in November. The weather is part wet and cold, part bright and sunny. December is dominated by the *fêtes de fin d'année* (end-of-year festivities) and a busy theater, ballet, and opera season into January. Throughout the winter months, especially February, skies are usually gray, and the weather is windy and damp, although there's very little snow. When the couture fashion shows come around, usually for a few days in early July and mid-January, the chicest addresses in town get extremely crowded. Whenever you go, you can usually count on some rain—August is the wettest month, but sudden showers occur in September and in January through April.

Forecasts AccuWeather ⊕ www.accuweather.com. **CNN Weather** ⊕ www.cnn.com/weather. **Weather Channel Connection** ☎ 900/932-8437, 95¢ per minute from a Touch-Tone phone ⊕ www.weather.com. **Yahoo Weather** ⊕ weather.yahoo.com.

The following are the average daily maximum and minimum temperatures for Paris.

Jan.	43F	6C	May	68F	20C	Sept.	70F	21C
	34	1		49	10		53	12
Feb.	45F	7C	June	73F	23C	Oct.	60F	16C
	34	1		55	13		46	8
Mar.	54F	12C	July	76F	25C	Nov.	50F	10C
	39	4		58	14		40	5
Apr.	60F	16C	Aug.	75F	24C	Dec.	44F	7C
	43	6		58	14		36	2

For further details on the events listed below, contact the Office du Tourisme de la Ville de Paris (☎ 08–92–68–30–00, € 0.34 per minute ⊕ www.parisinfo.com). Another helpful resource is the Web site of the Ministry of Culture (⊕ www.culture.fr), which covers cultural events throughout France. In addition to the selections below, look for special events tied in to a cultural theme. For instance, 2005 was the year of Brazilian culture, with the city hosting Brazilian cultural activities from traditional Amazonian dance performances to contemporary Brazilian literature and arts exhibitions.

ONGOING	
Apr.–early Oct.	The Grandes Eaux Musicales turn on the fountains for a spectacular display at the Château de Versailles (weekends only).
Late May–early June	The French Open Tennis Championships (⊕ www.fft.fr/rolandgarros) takes place at Roland Garros Stadium. The Grand Steeple Chase (☎ 0821–213–213 ⊕ www.france-galop.com) takes place at the Porte D'Auteuil racetrack.
Late July–mid-Sept.	The Festival Classique au Vert (☎ for information hotline, dial 3975 from any Paris land line, or 01–55–94–20–20) is a series of free classical music concerts performed every weekend under the Delta grandstand of the Parc Floral (✉ Bois de Vincennes, 12ᵉ); entrance to the park itself is €1.50–€3.
Late Sept.–mid-Dec.	The Festival d'Automne (Autumn Festival; ☎ 01–53–45–17–00 ⊕ www.festival-automne.com) has been going strong since 1972, bringing all sorts of arts events to the capital. The fine-arts exhibits and dance, theater, and music performances all focus on emerging and international artists.
WINTER	
Late Nov.–late Dec.	Marchés de Noel Christmas markets are set up throughout the city–usually at St-Germain-des-Prés, Les Halles, and Gare de l'Est–with crafts, gifts, and toys from every region of France.
Late Dec.	Christmas is highlighted by illuminations throughout the city, particularly on the Champs-Élysées, avenue Montaigne, and boulevard Haussmann. Many churches open their doors with free Sunday-afternoon concerts. Free ice-skating rinks are set up outside the Hôtel de Ville and Garde de Montparnasse.
Dec. 31–Jan. 1	On New Year's Eve check out the spectacular fireworks illuminating the Tour Eiffel.
Jan. 6	Epiphany is when *galettes des rois* (kings' pastries)—deliciously light almond cakes available in all bakeries—are traditionally served. Whoever gets the porcelain charm embedded in each is king or queen for the day.

Mid-Jan.– late Jan.	Couture and menswear fashion shows are usually held for a few days in the third week of the month; check the Web site www.modeaparis.com for exact dates.
Feb.	The Salon d'Agriculture (⊕ www.salon-agriculture.com), an agricultural smorgasbord and a favorite with some Parisians, is held mid-month at the Porte de Versailles.

SPRING

Mar.	Salon du Livre (⊕ www.salondulivreparis.com), a fantastic international book exposition, is held annually at the end of the month.
Mar.–Apr.	Foire du Trône, an amusement park, is set up in the Bois de Vincennes.
	The Prix du Président de la République takes place at Auteuil Racecourse. The film festival Le Festival de Paris Île-de-France (⊕ www.festivaldeparisidf.com) is held at the Cinema Gaumont Matignan, on the Champs Élysées.
Late Apr.	The International Marathon of Paris (⊕ www.parismarathon.com) runs through the city and large parks on the outskirts.
Early May	At the Foire de Paris (⊕ www.comexpo-paris.com) hundreds of booths display everything from crafts to wines. The Novotel-Perrier French Open (☎ 08–25–83–48–12 ⊕ www.opendefrance.fr) takes place at Le Golf National course in Les Yvelines, just outside Paris.

SUMMER

June	The Paris Air Show (⊕ www.paris-air-show.com) is a display of old and new planes at Le Bourget Airport. The colorful Gay Pride Parade takes place midmonth.
Early June– late July	The free Paris Jazz Festival (☎ 01–45–45–05–00 ⊕ parcfloraldeparis.com) includes an afternoon of free concerts weekends at the Parc Floral (⊠ Bois de Vincennes, 12e); entrance to the park itself is €1.50–€3.
June 21	During the Fête de la Musique (Music Festival; ⊕ www.fetedelamusique.culture.fr) the city booms with free performances by international, national, and not-yet-known musicians.
Late June	The annual Jazz à Montmartre Festival (⊕ www.festival-jazz-montmartre.com) features live concerts throughout the quarter's brasseries, restaurants, cafés, squares, and gardens.
	The Grand Prix de Paris is held on the flat at Longchamp Racecourse (☎ 0821–213–213 ⊕ www.france-galop.com).
	Opéra en Plein Air (⊕ www.akouna.com/operaenpleinair) brings arias to the outdoors; in 2005, for instance, operas were held in the Jardin du Luxembourg.

Late June–early July	During the Foire Saint-Germain (⊕ www.foiresaintgermain.org) the St-Germain neighborhood hosts free music and theater performances, an antiques and brocante market, children's events, and more.
	A newish film festival, Paris Cinema (⊕ www.pariscinema.org), celebrates specific directors and actors, debuts movies, screens documentaries, and more.
Early July	Couture and menswear fashion shows are usually held for a few days early in the month; check the Web site www.modeaparis.com for exact dates.
July 13	Bals des Sapeurs-Pompiers (Firemen's Balls), held to celebrate the eve of Bastille Day, spill into the streets of every arrondissement. Head to any caserne (fire station) in Paris and dance the night away to live music; spectacular party locations also include historic landmarks in the Marais and a barge on the Seine.
July 14	Bastille Day celebrates the storming of the Bastille prison in 1789. There's a military parade along the Champs-Élysées in the morning and fireworks at night at Trocadéro.
Mid-July–mid-Aug.	Paris Plage puts 3, 000 tons of sand on the banks of the Seine for one month in the summer, creating a virtual beach for those who can't leave town for the traditional holiday. There are all kinds of thoughtful additions: hammocks, picnic tables, lounge chairs, live music, beach volleyball, tai chi in the morning, and a library that loans out books.
Late July	The Tour de France (⊕ www.letour.com), the world's leading bicycle race, speeds to a Sunday finish on the Champs-Élysées.
Late July–Aug.	The Parc de la Villette hosts the Cinéma en Plein Air (⊕ www.villette.com); crowds flock to the park with picnics to watch movies outdoors. The films range from classics to fresh American releases. The Fête Musique en l'Île (☎ 01–45–23–18–25 for details) is a series of concerts held in the picturesque 17th-century Église St-Louis on Île St-Louis.

FALL

| Late Sept. | On the Journée du Patrimoine, the third weekend in September, normally closed historic buildings—such as the state residences of the president and prime minister—are open to the public. The world-class (second only to Tokyo's) Salon Mondial de l'Automobile (auto show) takes place this month. The (very) loud Techno Parade winds its way through the streets of Paris to finish at Trocadéro. |
| Early Oct. | Nuit Blanche is a godsend for insomniacs, as the city stays open for one all-night cultural blowout, usually in the first week of the month. State-run museums stay open and music performances keep the energy up. See the Mona Lisa at midnight or walk through the Hôtel de Ville at 2 AM. Check with the city's tourist office for this year's schedule. |

	The Montmartre Grape Harvest (⊕ www.commanderiemont.com), held the first Saturday of October, celebrates the grape harvest in the Montmartre vineyard, at the corner of rue des Saules and rue St-Vincent. FIAC (International Fair of Contemporary Art; ⊕ www.fiac-online.com) takes place at Porte de Versailles. The Prix de l'Arc de Triomphe, Europe's top flat race, is the first Sunday of the month at Longchamp Racecourse (☎ 0821–213–213 ⊕ www.france-galop.com).
Oct.–Nov.	The Fête d'Art Sacré (☎ 01–42–77–92–26 for information) is a series of concerts and exhibitions held in churches throughout the city.
Nov.	Galleries and museums open their doors for Le Mois de la Photo, a month-long photography festival organized by the Maison Européenne de la Photographie (⊕ www.mep-fr.org) in even-numbered years. The Carrousel du Louvre hosts an international photography show, Paris Photo (⊕ www.paris-photo.fr).
Nov. 11	Armistice Day ceremonies at the Arc de Triomphe include a military parade down the Champs-Élysées.
Third Thurs. in Nov.	Beaujolais Nouveau, that light, fruity wine from the Beaujolais region of France, is officially released at midnight on Wednesday; its arrival is celebrated in true Dionysian form in cafés and restaurants around the city.
Late Nov.	Salon des Caves Particulières brings French producers to the exhibition center at Porte de Versailles for a wine-tasting jamboree.

PLEASURES & PASTIMES

Architectural Innovations

It may be due to a heightened sense of aesthetics or just Gallic devil's advocacy, but Parisians always seem to view with skepticism the architectural innovations continually rising in their midst—all the while assembling the most beautiful city on earth. "C'est magnifique," say some Parisians of the grandiose glass pyramid by architect I. M. Pei that sprouted in 1989 from the Cour Napoléon at their beloved Louvre. "C'est horrible, " say others. The Grand Palais was tolerated only as a frothy oddity when it went up as a temporary pavilion for the World's Fair of 1900, but it's still there, a reassuring glass-and-iron presence on the bank of the Seine. The inside-out Centre Georges Pompidou was described by its co-designer, Renzo Piano, as an "insolent, irreverent provocation." And some Parisians sniffingly refer to the high-rise complex of La Défense as "Houston on the Seine, " though this futuristic area and such other glassy creations as the Institut du Monde Arabe, completed in 1988, continue to provide the visual theatrics with which Paris astonishes. Even the Tour Eiffel wasn't spared Parisian scorn: when the city's graceful icon first appeared above the rooftops in 1889, naysayers quipped that they enjoyed ascending to the top because it was the only place they didn't have to look at the darn thing. The Tour Eiffel's new neighbor, the Musée du Quai Branly, currently under construction, will surely spark debate when it opens in 2006.

Bon Appétit! The Pleasures of Eating

"Animals feed, men eat, but only wise men know the art of dining, " wrote the French gastronome Anthelme Brillat-Savarin. Join them in the pursuit of this art and don't feel guilty if you spend as much time during your stay in Paris in its restaurants as in its museums. Eating is the heart and soul of French culture. Give yourself over to the leisurely meal; two hours for a three-course menu is par for the course, and after relaxing into the routine you may begin to feel pressed at less than three. Whether your dream meal is savoring truffle-studded foie gras served on Limoges china or sharing a baguette with *jambon* (ham) and Brie *sur l'herbe* (on the grass), eating in Paris can be a memorable experience. Needless to say, it's well worth splurging on a dinner of outstanding haute cuisine in formal splendor (and many of those restaurants feature historically dazzling interiors, worthy of any museum). But also keep in mind that many famous chefs have opened bistro annexes where you can sample their cooking for less. In addition, younger chefs are setting up shop in more affordable, outlying parts of Paris, where they are serving their own innovative versions of bistro classics. Some of these locations can mean a long métro or cab ride, but it will give you the opportunity to discover restaurants in neighborhoods that you might not otherwise see. End any proper meal with a sublime cheese course, then dessert, then an *express* (espresso; taken black, with sugar). *See* A Cheese Primer *in* Chapter 2 for some *fromage* guidelines.

The best introductions to French food are the open-air street markets. The biggest is on boulevard de Reuilly between rue de Charenton and place Félix-Eboué (12e, métro: Dugommier), open Tuesday and Friday; while others are the south end of rue Mouffetard (5e, métro: Monge); rue de Buci (6e, métro: Odéon, in the heart of St-Germain-des-Prés); rue Daguerre (14e, métro: Denfert-Rocothereau) in Montparnasse; and rue Lepic (18e, métro: Blanche or Abbesses) in Montmartre. Or head instead to the delightful grocery stores of Paris. Whether you shop at the *boulangerie* (bakery) for fine sandwiches or the baguettes lined up soldier style, at the pâtisserie for seductively displayed pastries, at the *charcuteries* where butchers sell cold cuts, at an *épicerie*—the French equivalent of a deli—or at a *fromagerie* (cheese shop), you'll find it easy to create the fixings for a pique-nique in one of the city's parks. As you'll discover, who needs to pay a fortune to dine amid the Art Nouveau splendors of Maxim's when you can enjoy a peach on a bench in that even more gorgeous showplace, the 17th-century place des Vosges? There are no "open container" laws in Paris, so bring along a bottle of wine to accompany your picnic—but don't forget the corkscrew.

Café Society Along with air, water, and wine, the café remains one of the basic necessities of life in Paris. You may prefer a posh perch at a renowned spot such as the Deux Magots on boulevard St-Germain or opt for a tiny *café du coin* (corner café) where you can have a quick cup of coffee at the counter. Those on the major boulevards (such as boulevard St-Michel, boulevard St-Germain, and the Champs-Élysées) and in the big tourist spots (near the Louvre, the Opéra, and the Tour Eiffel, for example) will almost always be the most expensive and the least interesting. The more modest establishments (look for nonchalant locals) are the places to really get a feeling for French café culture. And we do mean culture—not only the practical rituals of the experience (perusing the posted menu, choosing a table, unwrapping your sugar cube) but an intellectual spur as well. You'll see businessmen, students, and pensive types pulling out notebooks for intent scribblings. Landmarks like the Café de Flore host readings; the Flore awards an annual literary prize to boot. Several years ago, a trend for *cafés philos* (philosophy cafés) took off; these spots regularly host discussions on various, often conceptual, topics. And there's always the frisson of history available at places like La Closerie des Lilas, where an expensive drink allows you to rest your derriere on the spots once favored by Baudelaire, Apollinaire, and Hemingway. Finally, there's people-watching, which goes hand in glove with the café lifestyle—what better excuse to linger over your *café crème* or Lillet?

Rues with a View The French have a word for it: *flâner*, which means to stroll, and this is the way to best appraise Paris. Ignore any urges to hurry—just relax and let the *esprit de Paris* take over. It's hard to get utterly lost, thanks to very visible monuments that serve as landmarks. Some favorite walks are from place St-Michel through the Latin Quarter to the Panthéon and down rue Mouffetard; along the banks of Canal St-Martin and Canal de l'Ourcq up to Parc de la Villette; through the small, winding streets of the Marais from place de la Bastille to the Pompidou Center; along busy rue Faubourg St-Honoré; from the Élysée Palace to the Madeleine; place Vendôme and the gardens of the Palais-Royal; and along the streets and riverbanks of Île St-Louis from east to west, ending at Pont St-Louis for a classic view of the Seine and Notre-Dame.

Shopping: Bon Chic, Bon Genre

Quotidian activities are elevated to high art in Paris, and shopping is no exception. Sophisticated urbanites that they are—many natives live by the motto *bon chic, bon genre* (well dressed, well bred)—Parisians approach this exercise as a ritual, and an elaborate ritual at that. Whether roaming the open-air produce markets or searching for designer finds at Jean-Paul Gaultier or a secret vintage dealer, they cast a discerning eye on the smallest detail and demand the highest quality. They show practicality, a sense of economy, and inimitable élan in their ability to turn even a piece of junk into an inventive treasure. You can get in on the game at any level, from the classic *grands magasins* (department stores) to the sprawling flea market, the Marché aux Puces St-Ouen. Join the *bobos* (bourgeois bohemians) at the organic produce market in Raspail or at the counter of an essential-oils boutique. Eye cashmeres and leather ballerina flats alongside a *no no* (someone who shuns obvious labels, seeking out discreet luxury). Or simply browse through the vintage paperbacks, 1960s magazines, and intriguing old maps in the open-air secondhand book stands on the quais near the Île de la Cité, listening to the *bouquinistes* bargaining and trading stories. Keep your eyes and ears open, and shopping will net you not only souvenirs, but priceless slices of life.

Where Art Comes First

Paris's museums range from the ostentatiously grand to the delightfully obscure—the French seem bent on documenting everything any of its citizens has ever done. Not just repositories of masterworks, the city's museums also reveal the endlessly fascinating nuances of French culture. It is fitting that the Musée d'Orsay, a Belle Époque former train station, houses the city's legacy of art from 1848 to 1914: railroads and other everyday phenomena were—shockingly so at the time—favorite subjects of the period's artists, especially the Impressionists. And it was the French Revolution that opened the Louvre to the masses, so that all can now view the extraordinary collection amassed in good part by seven centuries of monarchs, while imagining the history-shaping intrigues that once fermented in these same salons. A proletarian spirit also dominates the Centre Pompidou, where the world's largest collection of modern art is displayed. Its train-station-like lobby teems with people visiting not only the artwork but also a language laboratory, movie theaters, a musical research center, and a chic rooftop restaurant.

In addition to these big three, other favorites include museums that began life not as museums but as sumptuous houses. Many of these gilded time machines are filled with salons shining with boiserie (carved wood panels) and chandeliers. For these unique peeps into yesteryear, top bets include the decorative arts treasures found at the Musée Nissim de Camondo, the Musée Jacquemart-André, and the Musée Carnavalet. Skip through the centuries at some modern art museums, as both the Musée Rodin and the Musée Picasso are housed in historic *hôtels particuliers* (mansions). For a true trip back to the 17th, 18th, or 19th centuries, discover overlooked jewels like the Atelier Delacroix, on place Furstenberg, and the Musée de la Vie Romantique (where the likes of Chopin and Georges Sand once rendezvoused), at the foot of Montmartre.

Luxury goods are getting the museum treatment too. The Maison de Baccarat glitters with fine crystal in a curious-and-curiouser interior by Philippe Starck. The atelier of fashion genius Yves Saint Laurent went public in 2004, showing rotating exhibits of the designer's work. And another major museum is taking shape: the Musée des Arts Premiers, a.k.a. the Musée du Quai Branly, slated to open in 2006. This newcomer, designed by star architect Jean Nouvel, will consolidate the state's collections of African, Asian, Oceanic, and Latin American art.

FODOR'S CHOICE

RESTAURANTS

$$$$	**Astrance.** Paris has gone wild over this cool and contemporary spot, thanks to the kitchen's fusion fireworks—anyone for coconut-curry mousseline of scallops studded with tiny green-apple ice cubes?
$$$$	**Les Élysées du Vernet.** Chef Eric Briffard deftly combines ingredients prosaic and rarefied; tear your eyes from your plate to look up at the glass ceiling by Gustave Eiffel.
$$$$	**Taillevent.** Perhaps the most traditional of all Paris luxury restaurants, this grande dame is still the city's finest representative of French *haute cuisine*.
$$$-$$$$	**L'Atelier de Joël Robuchon.** Robuchon has reappeared as a restaurateur on his own (delicious) terms, serving exquisite small plates and overturning some entrenched Parisian dining habits while he's at it.
$$$-$$$$	**La Table du Lancaster.** This stylish boutique-hotel restaurant run by the Troisgros clan is the perfect setting for stellar cosmopolitan cuisine made with humble ingredients.
$$-$$$$	**La Table de Joël Robuchon.** Another sublime dining option from Robuchon; this one has a conventional dining room layout and accepts standard reservations—but remember to book weeks in advance.
$$-$$$	**Aux Lyonnais.** The *bouchon* (the Lyonnais word for "bistro") template gets the magic Ducasse touch. Old-school choices like pork sausage and quenelles never tasted so good.
$-$$$	**Chez Savy.** A 1930s time warp serves note-perfect, rib-sticking dishes such as lentil salad with bacon, and lamb with featherlight fries.
$$	**L'Ardoise.** Just because this contemporary bistro is making waves in Paris doesn't mean you'll have to get a second mortgage to sample dishes such as crab flan in a creamy parsley emulsion.
$-$$	**Mon Vieil Ami.** Come here for a stylish "Modern Alsatian" dining experience in an updated medieval dining room.
$-$$	**Le Pré Verre.** Timeworn French dishes get a new lease on life with creative Asian and Mediterranean influences.

LODGING

$$$$	**Four Seasons Hôtel George V Paris.** Period Art Deco details and opulent room decor are matched with a fantastic restaurant.
$$$$	**L'Hôtel.** When Oscar Wilde lay dying here at the turn of the 20th century, he quipped "either this wallpaper goes or I do"—wonder what he'd say about the current over-the-top style? Baroque mirrors, shimmering murals, and a stunning atrium mean there's never a dull moment.
$$$$	**Hôtel Plaza Athenée.** A palace hotel to the hilt. Choose a Regency-, Louis XVI-, or deco-style room; Alain Ducasse helms the restaurant.
$$$$	**Murano Urban Resort.** Amid the trendy galleries and tearooms of the Marais, this hotel that calls itself a resort combines Austin Powers playfulness with serious 007-inspired gadgetry. The stylish vodka bar and restaurant attracts Parisians and out-of-towners.
$$$–$$$$	**Hôtel Saint Merry.** A Gothic hideaway, this hotel was once the presbytery of the neighboring church. The rooms have an ecclesiastical look; one is bisected by the church's stone buttresses.
$$$	**Hôtel Queen Mary.** This cheerful, cozy hotel with regal architectural details has sunny yellow walls and thoughtful extras such as trouser presses.
$$$	**Hôtel Relais Saint-Sulpice.** On a dead-quiet street near place St-Sulpice is this tiny find, a thoughtfully decorated hideaway whose decor combines Jazz Age Shanghai with treasures from your grandfather's African safari.
$–$$$	**Les Degrés de Notre Dame.** A small, quiet budget hotel a few yards from the Seine is appealingly decorated with the owner's flea-market finds.
$$	**Hôtel La Manufacture.** This hotel has a mellow style (Arts-and-Crafts-inspired decor, soft color scheme) and a quiet location near the daily rue Mouffetard market.
$–$$	**Hôtel Langlois.** Its starring role in a recent Hollywood film hasn't gone to its head—the Langlois still offers impeccably well-kept rooms with Art Nouveau and Belle Époque settings, easily competing with hotels double the price.
¢	**Hôtel Eldorado.** It's the perfect place to lie low without room phones, TVs, or an elevator. The decor is distressed-chic and many rooms face the garden courtyard, where artsy bohemian types from the hotel's wine bistro hang out in summer.

MUSEUMS & MASTERPIECES

	Centre Georges Pompidou. A hot roster of temporary exhibits has drawn ever more visitors to this brash complex. Come for the rich

modern and contemporary art holdings, the trendy restaurant with a panoramic view, or just for a ride up the external escalator.

The Louvre. Incomparable. The sprawling former palace is the address for the *Mona Lisa,* the *Venus de Milo,* the *Winged Victory,* and more than 800,000 other artworks and antiquities. This is, no question, the biggest and best museum in the world.

Musée Carnavalet. Take a fascinating crash course in Parisian history here. The thousands of artifacts and re-created interiors include everything from Proust's bedroom to Louis XVI's razor.

Musée d'Orsay. Once a Belle Époque train station, now a trove of late-19th-century art. The impressive Impressionist and Postimpressionist section includes exquisite works by van Gogh, Monet, Manet, and Gauguin.

Musée National du Moyen-Age. A 15th-century abbot's mansion makes the perfect setting for priceless medieval sculpture and tapestries, including the famous *Lady and the Unicorn* series. A bonus: remnants of ancient Roman baths.

Musée Nissim de Camondo. Built in the 19th century by an art-loving millionaire, this mansion showcases the crème de la crème of rococo and neoclassical decorative arts—and remains a moving tribute to Count Camondo's family.

Musée Rodin. Rodin's hôtel particulier and its gardens house the sculptor's greatest works, including *The Kiss, Burghers of Calais,* and *The Thinker,* as well as paintings by van Gogh, Monet, and Renoir. Devote extra time to the marble sculptures of Rodin's mistress-pupil Camille Claudel.

QUINTESSENTIAL PARIS

Ancien Cloître Quartier. Just steps from Notre-Dame you'll find this quiet tangle of streets lined with medieval buildings. Unbeatable atmosphere.

Café de Flore. The St-Germain neighborhood's gone to the fashion dogs, but this is still an essential gathering place. Neophytes like the café's wraparound terrace, but insiders go upstairs.

Canal St-Martin. One of the city's most picturesque spots, slightly off the beaten track. A barge ride takes you through the canal's nine locks, a perfect way to enjoy the pretty bridges and leafy plane trees that border the water.

Cour du Commerce St-André. This cobbled pedestrian arcade exudes 18th-century graciousness—but it's also steeped in Revolutionary history.

Jardin du Luxembourg. Children riding ponies or vying for brass rings on the merry-go-round, students reading under the shady plane trees or napping in the green metal chairs around the fountain: this is as picture-perfect Parisian as it gets.

Au Lapin Agile. The avant-garde cabaret of 19th-century Montmartre bohemia still draws a night crowd. The decor has hardly changed since the composer Erik Satie jammed on the house piano back in the 1880s.

Marché aux Puces St-Ouen. Otherwise known as the Clignancourt flea market—the epicenter for the hard-core bargain hunter, vintage clothing enthusiast, and astute antiques connoisseur.

Opéra Garnier. A gleaming gold dome heralds this über-opulent Second Empire opera house, which fairly bursts with gilding, sculptures, marble, and paintings. The Paris Ballet now commands the world's largest stage.

La Pagode. This fantastic, 19th-century pagoda-esque building was saved from demolition by determined locals; now it's the city's coolest cinema.

The Ritz's Hemingway Bar. Colin Field's bartending skills are truly mesmerizing; raise a glass to the namesake Papa who "liberated" the bar at the end of World War II.

Tour Eiffel. There is perhaps no other sight more closely associated with Paris than the magnificent steel structure of the Eiffel Tower. Come at night for a particularly illuminating view of the City of Light.

SACRED PLACES

Les Invalides's Église du Dôme. Under the dome of this commanding Baroque church, Napoléon rests in imperial splendor.

Notre-Dame Cathédral. After seeing the spectacular interior, head up to the towers to visit the gargoyles and see the 13-ton bell, which still rings on special occasions.

Sainte-Chapelle. The walls of this 13th-century chapel seem to melt into shimmering panels of colored light. The incredible stained glass, held up by delicate painted stonework, turns the space into a giant magic lantern.

SMART TRAVEL TIPS

Finding out about your destination before you leave home means you won't squander time organizing everyday minutiae once you've arrived. You'll be more streetwise when you hit the ground as well, better prepared to explore the aspects of Paris that drew you here in the first place. The organizations in this section can provide information to supplement this guide; contact them for up-to-the-minute details. Happy landings!

ADDRESSES

Addresses in Paris are fairly straightforward: there's the number, the street name, and the zip code designating one of Paris's 20 arrondissements (districts); for instance, Paris 75010 (the last two digits, "10") indicates that the address is in the 10th. The large 16ᵉ arrondissement has two numbers assigned to it: 75016 and 75116. For the layout of Paris's arrondissements, consult the map at the end of this section. They are laid out in a spiral, beginning from the area around the Louvre (1ᵉʳ arrondissement), then moving clockwise through the Marais, the Quartier Latin, St-Germain, and then out from the city center to the outskirts to Ménilmontant/Père-Lachaise (20ᵉ arrondissement). Occasionally you may see an address with a number plus *bis*—for instance, 20 bis, rue Vavin. This indicates the next entrance or door down from 20 rue Vavin. Note that in France you enter a building on the ground floor, or *rez-de-chaussée* (RC or 0), and go up one floor to the first floor, or *premier étage*. General address terms used in this book are: *av.* (avenue), *bd.* (boulevard), *carrefour* (crossway), *cours* (promenade), *passage* (passageway), pl. (place), *quai* (quay/wharf/pier), *rue* (street), *sq.* (square).

AIR TRAVEL TO & FROM PARIS

As one of the premier destinations in the world, Paris is serviced by a great many international carriers and a surprisingly large number of U.S.-based airlines. Air France (which partners with Delta) is the French flag carrier and offers numerous direct flights (often several per day) between Paris's Charles de Gaulle Airport and New

York City's JFK Airport; Newark, New Jersey; Washington's Dulles Airport; as well as the cities of Boston, Atlanta, Cincinnati, Miami, Chicago, Houston, San Francisco, Los Angeles, Toronto, Montréal, and Mexico City. Most other North American cities are served through Air France partnerships with Delta and Continental Airlines. American-based carriers are usually less expensive but offer, on the whole, fewer nonstop direct flights. United Airlines has nonstop flights to Paris from Chicago, Denver, Los Angeles, Miami, Philadelphia, Washington, and San Francisco. American Airlines offers daily nonstop flights to Paris's Charles de Gaulle Airport from numerous cities, including New York City's JFK, Miami, Chicago, and Dallas/Fort Worth. Northwest has a daily departure to Paris from its hub in Detroit. In Canada, Air France and Air Canada are the leading choices for departures from Toronto and Montréal; in peak season departures are often daily. The relatively new carrier Zoom offers discount long-haul flights from Toronto and Montréal twice weekly. From London, Air France, British Airways, and British Midland are the leading carriers, with up to 15 flights daily in peak season. In addition, direct routes link Manchester, Edinburgh, and Southampton with Paris. A number of discount carriers are cornering the market to numerous European destinations. Ryanair, Easyjet, and BMI Baby offer direct service from Paris to Dublin, London, Glasgow, Amsterdam, Cardiff, and Brussels, to name just a few. Tickets are available on the Web only and need to be booked well in advance to get the best prices—a one-way ticket from Paris to Dublin costs a mere €30, for example.

BOOKING

When you book, look for nonstop flights and remember that "direct" flights stop at least once. Try to avoid connecting flights, which require a change of plane. Two airlines may operate a connecting flight jointly, so ask whether your airline operates every segment of the trip; you may find that the carrier you prefer flies you only part of the way. To find more booking tips and to check prices and make online flight reservations, log on to www.fodors.com.

CARRIERS

📶 To & From Paris **Air Canada** 🕾 888/247-2262 in the U.S. and Canada, 08-25-88-08-81 in France 🌐 www.aircanada.com. **Air France** 🕾 800/237-2747 in the U.S., 08-20-82-08-20 in France 🌐 www.airfrance.com. **American Airlines** 🕾 800/433-7300 in the U.S., 01-55-17-43-41 in Paris, 08-10-87-28-72 elsewhere in France 🌐 www.aa.com. **British Airways** 🕾 800/247-9297 in the U.S., 0870/8509-850 in the U.K., 08-25-82-50-40 in France 🌐 www.britishairways.com. **Continental** 🕾 800/231-0856 in the U.S., 01-71-23-03-35 in France 🌐 www.continental.com. **Delta** 🕾 800/241-4141 in the U.S., 08-00-30-13-01 in France 🌐 www.delta.com. **Northwest** 🕾 800/447-4747 in the U.S., 08-90-71-07-10 in France 🌐 www.nwa.com. **United** 🕾 800/538-2929 in the U.S., 08-10-72-72-72 in France 🌐 www.unitedairlines.com. **US Airways** 🕾 800/622-1015 in the U.S., 08-10-63-22-22 in France 🌐 www.usairways.com. **Zoom** 🕾 866/359-9666 in North America 🌐 www.flyzoom.com.
📶 Within Europe **Air France** 🕾 0845/0845-111 in the U.K., 08-02-80-28-02 in France 🌐 www.airfrance.com. **British Airways** 🕾 0870/8509-850 in the U.K., 08-25-82-50-40 in France 🌐 www.britishairways.com. **British Midland** 🕾 0870/6070-222, 0133/285-4854 in the U.K., 01-55-69-83-06 in France 🌐 www.flybmi.com.
📶 Discount Airlines **BMI Baby** 🕾 08-90-71-00-81 in France 🌐 www.bmibaby.com. **Easyjet** 🕾 08-25-08-25-08 in France 🌐 www.easyjet.com. **Ryan Air** 🕾 08-92-55-55-66 in France 🌐 www.ryanair.com.

CHECK-IN & BOARDING

Always **find out your carrier's check-in policy.** Plan to arrive at the airport about two hours before your scheduled departure time for domestic flights and 2½ to 3 hours before international flights. You may need to arrive earlier if you're flying from one of the busier airports or during peak air-traffic times. The French are notoriously stringent about security, particularly for international flights. Don't be surprised by the armed security officers patrolling the airports, and be prepared for very long check-in lines. Peak travel times in France are between mid-July and September, during the Christmas/New Year's holidays in late December and early January, and during the February school break. During these periods airports are especially crowded, so allow plenty of extra time. Never leave your baggage unattended, even for a moment. Unattended baggage is considered a security risk and may be destroyed. To avoid delays at airport-security checkpoints, try not to wear any metal. Jewelry, belt and other buckles, steel-toe shoes, barrettes, and underwire bras are among the items that can set off detectors.

Assuming that not everyone with a ticket will show up, airlines routinely overbook planes. When everyone does, airlines ask for volunteers to give up their seats. In return, these volunteers usually get a several-hundred-dollar flight voucher, which can be used toward the purchase of another ticket, and are rebooked on the next flight out. If there are not enough volunteers, the airline must choose who will be denied boarding. The first to get bumped are passengers who checked in late and those flying on discounted tickets, so get to the gate and check in as early as possible, especially during peak periods.

Always **bring a government-issued photo I.D.** to the airport; even when it's not required, a passport is best.

CUTTING COSTS
The least expensive airfares to Paris are priced for round-trip travel and must usually be purchased in advance. Airlines generally allow you to change your return date for a fee; most low-fare tickets, however, are nonrefundable. It's smart to call a number of airlines and check the Internet; when you are quoted a good price, book it on the spot—the same fare may not be available the next day, or even the next hour. Always check different routings and look into using alternate airports. Also, price off-peak and red-eye flights, which may be significantly less expensive than others. Travel agents, especially low-fare specialists (⇨ Discounts & Deals), are helpful.

Consolidators are another good source. They buy tickets for scheduled flights at reduced rates from the airlines, then sell them at prices that beat the best fare available directly from the airlines. (Many also offer reduced car-rental and hotel rates.) Sometimes you can even get your money back if you need to return the ticket. Carefully read the fine print detailing penalties for changes and cancellations, purchase the ticket with a credit card, and confirm your consolidator reservation with the airline.

When you fly as a courier, you trade your checked-luggage space for a ticket deeply subsidized by a courier service. There are restrictions on when you can book and how long you can stay. Some courier companies list with membership organizations, such as the Air Courier Association and the International Association of Air Travel Couriers; these require you to become a member before you can book a flight.

You can save on air travel within Europe if you plan on traveling to and from Paris aboard Air France. If you sign up for Air France's Euro Flyer program, you can buy coupons that enable you to travel to any Air France destination. Rates are calculated by season: each coupon purchased November–March costs $90; coupons purchased April–October cost $120. You can purchase a minimum of three or maximum of nine coupons, and all must be used within two months. You can only purchase these coupons in the United States, and you must ask for them specifically. These coupons are a great deal for those who are planning on traveling from city to city and don't want to worry about the cost of one-way travel.

🚹 **Consolidators AirlineConsolidator.com** ☎ 888/468-5385 ⊕ www.airlineconsolidator.com; for international tickets. **Best Fares** ☎ 800/880-1234 ⊕ www.bestfares.com; $59.90 annual membership. **Cheap Tickets** ☎ 800/377-1000 or 800/652-4327 ⊕ www.cheaptickets.com. **Expedia** ☎ 800/397-3342 or 404/728-8787 ⊕ www.expedia.com. **Hotwire** ☎ 866/468-9473 or 920/330-9418 ⊕ www.hotwire.com. **Now Voyager Travel** ✉ 45 W. 21st St., Suite 5A New York, NY 10010 ☎ 212/459-1616 🖷 212/243-2711 ⊕ www.nowvoyagertravel. com. **Onetravel.com** ⊕ www.onetravel.com. **Orbitz**

☎ 888/656-4546 ⊕ www.orbitz.com. **Priceline. com** ⊕ www.priceline.com. **Travelocity** ☎ 888/709-5983, 877/282-2925 in Canada, 0870/111-7061 in the U.K. ⊕ www.travelocity.com.

🖪 Courier Resources **Air Courier Association/ Cheaptrips.com** ☎ 800/280-5973 or 800/282-1202 ⊕ www.aircourier.org or www.cheaptrips.com; $20 annual membership. **Courier Travel** ☎ 303/570-7586 🖷 313/625-6106 ⊕ www.couriertravel.org; $50 annual membership. **International Association of Air Travel Couriers** ☎ 308/632-3273 🖷 308/632-8267 ⊕ www.courier.org; $45 annual membership. **Now Voyager Travel** ✉ 45 W. 21st St., Suite 5A, New York, NY 10010 ☎ 212/459-1616 🖷 212/243-2711 ⊕ www.nowvoyagertravel.com.

ENJOYING THE FLIGHT

State your seat preference when purchasing your ticket, and then repeat it when you confirm and when you check in. For more legroom, you can request one of the few emergency-aisle seats at check-in, if you're capable of moving obstacles comparable in weight to an airplane exit door (usually between 35 pounds and 60 pounds)—a Federal Aviation Administration requirement of passengers in these seats. Seats behind a bulkhead also offer more legroom, but they don't have underseat storage. Don't sit in the row in front of the emergency aisle or in front of a bulkhead, where seats may not recline. SeatGuru.com has more information about specific seat configurations, which vary by aircraft.

Ask the airline whether a snack or meal is served on the flight. If you have dietary concerns, request special meals when booking. These can be vegetarian, low-cholesterol, or kosher, for example. It's a good idea to pack some healthful snacks and a small (plastic) bottle of water in your carry-on bag. On long flights, try to maintain a normal routine, to help fight jet lag. At night, get some sleep. By day, eat light meals, drink water (not alcohol), and **move around the cabin** to stretch your legs. For additional jet-lag tips consult *Fodor's FYI: Travel Fit & Healthy* (available at bookstores everywhere).

Smoking policies vary from carrier to carrier. Many airlines prohibit smoking on all of their flights; others allow smoking only on certain routes or certain departures. Ask your carrier about its policy.

FLYING TIMES

Flying time to Paris is seven hours from New York, 9½ hours from Chicago, and 11 hours from Los Angeles. Flying time from London to Paris is 1½ hours.

HOW TO COMPLAIN

If your baggage goes astray or your flight goes awry, complain right away. Most carriers require that you **file a claim immediately.** The Aviation Consumer Protection Division of the Department of Transportation publishes *Fly-Rights,* which discusses airlines and consumer issues and is available online. You can also find articles and information on mytravelrights.com, the Web site of the nonprofit Consumer Travel Rights Center.

🖪 Airline Complaints **Aviation Consumer Protection Division** ✉ U.S. Department of Transportation, Office of Aviation Enforcement and Proceedings, C-75, Room 4107, 400 7th St. SW, Washington, DC 20590 ☎ 202/366-2220 ⊕ airconsumer.ost.dot.gov. **Federal Aviation Administration Consumer Hotline** ✉ for inquiries: FAA, 800 Independence Ave. SW, Washington, DC 20591 ☎ 800/322-7873 ⊕ www.faa.gov.

RECONFIRMING

Check the status of your flight before you leave for the airport. You can do this on your carrier's Web site, by linking to a flight-status checker (many Web booking services offer these), or by calling your carrier or travel agent. Always confirm international flights at least 72 hours ahead of the scheduled departure time.

AIRPORTS & TRANSFERS

The major airports are Charles de Gaulle (CDG, also known as Roissy), 26 km (16 mi) northeast of Paris, and Orly (ORY), 16 km (10 mi) south of Paris. Both are easily accessible from Paris. Whether you take a car or bus to travel from Paris to the airport on your departure, always allot an extra hour due to the often horrendous traffic tie-ups within the airports proper (especially in peak seasons and at peak hours): once you arrive at the airports, you'll often need to take the interairport buses to shuttle you from one terminal to another, and if this bus is held up due to traffic congestion (often the case), a serious case of nail biting will result.

🖥 Airport Information **Charles de Gaulle/Roissy** ☎ 01-48-62-22-80 in English ⊕ www.adp.fr. **Orly** ☎ 01-49-75-15-15 ⊕ www.adp.fr.

AIRPORT TRANSFERS

By bus from CDG/Roissy: Roissybus, operated by the RATP (Paris Transit Authority), runs between Charles de Gaulle and the Opéra every 20 minutes from 6 AM to 11 PM; the cost is €8.30. The trip takes about 45 minutes in regular traffic, about 90 minutes in rush-hour traffic.

By shuttle from CDG/Roissy: The Air France shuttle service is a comfortable option to get to and from the city—you don't need to have flown the carrier to use this. Line 2 goes from the airport to Paris's Charles de Gaulle Étoile and Porte Maillot from 5:45 AM to 11 PM. It leaves every 15 minutes and costs €12, which you can pay on board. Passengers arriving in Terminal 1 need to take Exit 34; Terminals 2B and 2D, Exit 6; Terminals 2E and 2F, Exit 3. Line 4 goes to Montparnasse and the Gare de Lyon from 7 AM to 9 PM. Buses run every 30 minutes and cost €12. Passengers arriving in Terminal 1 need to look for Exit 34, Terminals 2A and 2C need to take Exit C2, Terminals 2B and 2D Exit B1, and Terminals 2E and 2F Exit 3.

A number of van services serve both Charles de Gaulle and Orly airports. Prices are set so there are no surprises even if traffic is a snail-pace nightmare. To make a reservation, call or fax your flight details at least one week in advance to the shuttle company and an air-conditioned van with a bilingual chauffeur will be waiting for you upon your arrival. Confirm the day before. These vans sometimes pick up more than one party, though, so you may have to share the shuttle with other passengers. Likewise, when taking people to the airport these shuttles usually pick up a couple of groups of passengers. This adds at least 20 minutes to the trip.

By taxi from CDG/Roissy: Taxis are generally your least desirable mode of transportation into the city. If you are traveling at peak times, you may have to stand in a very long line with a lot of other disgruntled travelers. Therefore, journey times and, as a consequence, prices are unpredictable. At best, the journey takes 30 minutes, but it can take as long as one hour.

By train from CDG/Roissy: The least expensive way to get into Paris from CDG is the RER-B line, the suburban express train, which runs from 5 AM to 11:30 PM daily. Each terminal has an exit where the free RER shuttle bus (a white-and-yellow bus with the letters ADP in gray) passes by every 7–15 minutes to take you on the short ride to the nearby RER station: at Terminals 2A and 2C, it's Exit 8; at Terminals 2B and 2D, Exit 6; at Terminal 2E, Exit 2.06; and at Terminal 2F, Exit 2.08. Or you can walk easily from many terminals to the train station—just look for the signs. Trains to central Paris (Les Halles, St-Michel, Luxembourg) depart every 15 minutes. The fare (including métro connection) is €7.85, and journey time is about 30 minutes.

By bus from Orly: Air France buses run from Orly to Les Invalides and Montparnasse; these run every 15 minutes from 6 AM to 11 PM. (You need not have flown on Air France to use this service.) The fare is €8, and journey time is between 30 and 45 minutes, depending on traffic. To find the bus, take Exit K if you've arrived in Orly South, or Exit D from Orly West. RATP's Orlybus is yet another option; buses leave every 15 minutes for the Denfert-Rochereau métro station in Montparnasse; the cost is €5.80. For a cheaper bus ride, take Jet Bus, which shuttles you from the airport to Villejuif Louis Aragon station, on métro line 7, for under €5. It operates daily from 6 AM to 10 PM; at Orly South look for Exit H, quai 2; from Orly West head for Exit C. The downside is that the Villejuif Louis Aragon station is far from the city center.

By train from Orly: The cheapest way to get into Paris is to take the RER-C or Orlyrail line; catch the free shuttle bus from the terminal to the train station. Trains to Paris leave every 15 minutes. Passengers arriving in either the South or West Terminal need to use Exit G. The fare is €5.45, and journey time is about 35 minutes. Another option is to take RATP's monorail service, Orlyval, which runs between the Antony RER-B station and Orly Airport daily every 4–8 minutes from 6 AM to 11 PM. Passengers arriving in the South Terminal should use Exit K; take Exit W if you've arrived in the West Terminal. The fare to downtown Paris is €8.85 and includes the RER transfer.

🚕 Taxis & Shuttles **Air France Bus** ☎ 08-92-35-08-20 recorded information in English, €.35 per minute ⊕ www.cars-airfrance.com. **Airport Connection** ☎ 01-43-65-55-55 🖷 01-43-65-55-57 ⊕ www.airport-connection.com. **Paris Airports Services** ☎ 01-55-98-10-80 🖷 01-55-98-10-89 ⊕ www.parisairportservice.com. **RATP (including Roissybus, Orlybus, Orlyval)** ☎ 08-92-68-41-14, €.35 per minute ⊕ www.ratp.com.

DUTY-FREE SHOPPING

Duty-free shopping is no longer possible when you are traveling within the European Union; you will benefit from duty-free prices only when you are leaving European territory.

BIKE TRAVEL

See the Sports & the Outdoors chapter for information on bicycle rentals and biking within the city.

BIKES IN FLIGHT

Most airlines accommodate bikes as luggage, provided they are dismantled and boxed; check with individual airlines about packing requirements. Some airlines sell bike boxes, which are often free at bike shops, for about $20 (bike bags can be considerably more expensive). International travelers often can substitute a bike for a piece of checked luggage at no charge; otherwise, the cost is about $100. Most U.S. and Canadian airlines charge $40–$80 each way.

BOAT & FERRY TRAVEL

Linking France and the United Kingdom, a boat or ferry trip across the Channel can range from a mere 35 minutes (via hovercraft) to 95 minutes (via ferryboat). Trip length also depends on your departure point: popular routes link Boulogne and Folkestone, Le Havre and Portsmouth,

and, the most booked passage, Calais and Dover.

Hoverspeed travels the route from Dover, England, to Calais, France, up to nine times a day by hovercraft. The crossings take an hour. They also link New Haven, England, with Dieppe, France, with a pair of two-hour crossings per day. P&O European Ferries links Portsmouth, England with Le Havre (6½ hours), and Dover, England, with Calais (75 minutes). P&O has up to three sailings a day. Seafrance operates up to 15 sailings a day from Dover to Calais; the crossing takes 70 or 90 minutes depending on the ship.

Driving distances from the French ports to Paris are as follows: from Calais, 290 km (180 mi); from Dieppe or Le Havre, 195 km (122 mi). The fastest routes to Paris from each port are via N43, A26, and A1 from Calais and the Channel Tunnel; via N1 from Boulogne; and via N15 from Le Havre.

🚢 Boat & Ferry Information **Hoverspeed** ✉ International Hoverport, Marine Parade, Dover, Kent CT17 9TG England ☎ 0870/460-7157 ⊕ www.hoverspeed.fr. **P&O European Ferries** ✉ Channel House, Channel View Rd., Dover, Kent CT17 9TJ England ☎ 0870/598-0333 ⊕ www.poportsmouth.com. **Seafrance** ✉ Eastern Docks, Dover, Kent, CT16 1JA England ☎ 0870/5711-711 ⊕ www.seafrance.net.

BUSINESS HOURS

BANKS & OFFICES

On weekdays banks are open generally 9–5 (note that the Banque de France closes at 3:30), and some banks are also open Saturday 9–5 as well. In general, government offices and businesses are open 9–5. *See* Mail & Shipping, *below,* for post office hours.

GAS STATIONS

Gas stations in the city are generally open 7:30 AM–8 PM, though those near the city's *portes* (or principal entranceways) and near the *périphérique* (beltway) are open 24 hours a day.

MUSEUMS & SIGHTS

Most museums are closed one day a week—usually either Monday or Tuesday—and on national holidays. Generally, museums and national monuments are open from 10 to 5 or 6. A few close for lunch (noon–2) and on Sunday are open only in the afternoon. Many of the large museums have one *nocturne* (nighttime) opening per week, when they are open until 9:30 or 10. The Louvre is closed Tuesday and stays open late Wednesday and Friday until 9:45. The Centre Pompidou is closed Tuesday and has late opening hours Thursday and Friday until 11. The Musée d'Orsay is closed Monday and stays open until 9:30 Thursday.

PHARMACIES

Pharmacies are generally open Monday–Saturday 8:30–8. Nearby pharmacies that stay open late, for 24 hours, or Sunday, are listed on the door.

SHOPS

Generally, large shops are open from 9:30 or 10 to 7 or 8 Monday to Saturday and remain open through lunchtime. Many of the large department stores stay open until 10 Wednesday or Thursday. Smaller shops and many supermarkets often open earlier (8 AM) but take a lengthy lunch break (1–3) and generally close around 8 PM; small food shops are often open Sunday morning 9–1. There is typically a small corner grocery store that stays open late, usually until 11, if you're in a bind for basic necessities like diapers, bread, cheese, and fruit. Note that prices are substantially higher in such outlets than in the larger supermarkets. Most shops close all day Sunday, except in the Marais, where shops that stand side by side on rue des Francs Bourgeois, from antiques dealers to chic little designers, open their doors to welcome hordes of Sunday browsers. The Bastille, the Quartier Latin, the Champs-Elysées, Île St-Louis, and the Île de la Cité also have shops that open Sunday.

BUS TRAVEL TO & FROM PARIS

The excellent national train service in France means that long-distance bus service in the country is practically nonexistent; regional buses are found where train service is spotty. Local bus information to the rare rural areas where trains do not have access can be obtained from the SNCF (*see* Train Travel, *below*).

The largest international operator is Eurolines France, whose main terminal is in the Parisian suburb of Bagnolet (a half-hour métro ride from central Paris, at the end of métro line 3). Eurolines runs international routes to more than 1,500 cities in Europe.

FARES & SCHEDULES

It is possible to take a bus (via ferry) to Paris from the United Kingdom; just be aware that what you save in money will almost certainly cost you in time—the bus trip takes about seven hours—as opposed to the three it takes on the Eurostar train line (Victoria Station–Gare du Nord). In general, the price of a round-trip bus ticket is 50% less than that of a plane ticket and 25% less than that of a train ticket, so if you have the time and the energy, this is a good way to cut the cost of travel. Eurolines also offers a 15-day (€285), 30-day (€425), or 60-day (€490) pass if you're planning on doing the grand European tour. Ask about one of the Circle tours that depart from Paris (for example, via London, Amsterdam, then back to Paris again). Eurolines operates a service from London's Victoria Coach Station, via the Dover–Calais ferry, to Paris's Porte de Bagnolet. There is an 8:30 AM departure that arrives in Paris at 5:30 PM, a noon departure that arrives at 9 PM, and the overnight trip at 9 PM, which arrives in Paris at 7:30 AM. Fares are €68 round-trip (an under-25 youth pass is €57). Other Eurolines routes include Amsterdam (7 hours, €70), Barcelona (15 hours, €160), and Berlin (10 hours, €140). There are also international-only arrivals and departures from Avignon, Bordeaux, Lille, Lyon, Toulouse, and Tours.

PAYING

Eurolines accepts all major credit cards but does not accept traveler's checks.

RESERVATIONS

Reservations for an international bus trip are essential. Be sure to check the Eurolines Web site for special discounts or incentives. Avoid buying your ticket at the last minute, when prices are highest.

🚌 Bus Information **Eurolines** ✉ 28 av. Général-de-Gaulle, Bagnolet 93541 ☎ 08-92-89-90-91 in France, 020/7730-3499 in the U.K. ⊕ www.eurolines.fr.

BUS TRAVEL WITHIN PARIS

With dedicated bus lanes now in place throughout the city—allowing buses and taxis to whiz past other traffic mired in tedious jams—taking the bus is now an appealing option. Although nothing can beat the métro for speed, the buses offer great city views, and the new ones are equipped with air-conditioning—something to think about on those sweltering August days.

Paris buses are green and white; route number and destination are marked in front, major stopping places along the sides. The brown bus shelters contain timetables and route maps; note that buses must be hailed at these larger bus shelters, as they service multiple lines and routes. Smaller stops are designated simply by a pole bearing bus numbers.

More than 200 bus routes run throughout Paris, reaching virtually every nook and cranny of the city. On weekdays and Saturday, buses run every five minutes (as opposed to the 15- to 20-minute wait you'll have on Sunday and national holidays). One ticket will take you anywhere within the city; once you get off at any point, that ticket is no longer valid. Bus transport is ideal for the elderly, women with children (easy access with strollers), and anyone who likes to take the scenic route. Needless to say, seats are more difficult to find during rush hours.

A map of the bus system is on the flip side of every métro map, in all métro stations, and at all bus stops. Maps are also found in each bus. A recorded message announces the name of the next stop. To get off, press one of the red buttons mounted on the silver poles that run the length of the bus, and the *arrêt demandé* (stop requested) light directly behind the driver will light up. Use the rear door to exit.

The Balabus, an orange-and-white public bus that runs between mid-April and September, gives an interesting 50-minute tour around the major sights. You can use your Paris-Visite, Carte Orange, or Mobilis pass (⇨ Métro), or 1–3 bus tickets depending on how far you ride. The route runs from La Défense to the Gare de Lyon.

The RATP has also introduced aboveground tram lines: two (T-1 and T-2) operate in the suburbs, and the new T-3 tram, slated to commence in fall 2006, will connect the 13ᵉ, 14ᵉ, and 15ᵉ arrondissements, running from the Porte d'Ivry (Chinatown) to the Parc Montsouris, Porte d'Orléans, and the Porte de Versailles. Trams take the same tickets as buses and the métro, with one ticket good for the entire line.

FARES & SCHEDULES

Regular buses accept métro tickets. Your best bet is to buy a *carnet* of 10 tickets for €10.50 at any métro station, or you can buy a single ticket on board (exact change appreciated) for €1.40. If you have individual tickets, you should be prepared to **punch your ticket in the red-and-gray machines at the entrance of the bus.** You need to show (but not punch) weekly, monthly, and Paris-Visite/Mobilis tickets to the driver. Tickets can be bought on buses, in the métro, or in any bar/tabac store displaying the lime-green métro symbol above its street sign.

Most routes operate from 7 AM to 8:30 PM; some continue to midnight. After 8:30 PM you must either take the métro or one of the 18 Noctambus lines (indicated by a brown owl symbol at bus stops). These bus lines operate hourly (1:30 AM–5:30 AM) between Châtelet and various nearby suburbs; they can be stopped by hailing them at any point on their route. Paris-Visite/Mobilis passes are accepted on the Noctambus. A regular ticket costs €2.70 and allows for one transfer.

🚌 **Bus Information** RATP ☒ 54 quai de la Rapée, 75012 Paris ☎ 08-92-68-77-14, €.35 per minute ⊕ www.ratp.com.

CAMERAS & PHOTOGRAPHY

Not only is Paris one of the most photogenic places in the world, it's also the birthplace of photography itself—it would be almost criminal not to snap some pictures. **Take advantage of all sorts of vantage points,** from the sunken level of the Seine to sweeping city views from high points such as the tower of Notre-Dame, the dome of Sacré-Coeur, and the tops of the Eiffel Tower or Arc de Triomphe.

You'll usually get the best light if you **shoot early or late in the day**; the hours just before or after a storm are a good time for dramatic lighting. Paris certainly gets its share of rain; use it to your advantage by shooting the reflections of lights, monuments, or greenery in puddles or drenched pavements.

When photographing monumental sights, don't forget to **capture some close-up details as well as the larger view.** Think creatively; it's easy to get a standard head-on picture of the Eiffel Tower, but an extreme angle or a striking juxtaposition in the setting could give you a memorably fresh image. Pursue the incredible illuminations of major sights, bridges, fountains, and streets with a tripod and long exposures.

When photographing houses of worship, you may need a wide-angle lens to fit in the exterior—or you could angle your camera up, which makes the building look as though it's falling away. Once inside, always ask whether photography's permitted. Flashes don't work in large indoor spaces, so dark interiors call for high-speed film and often a tripod. For stained-glass windows try to **visit on a bright but slightly overcast day**; this kind of light will yield the most intense colors. Make sure you **turn off your flash.**

If you're snapping a formal garden, such as the Tuileries or the park of Versailles, choose your position carefully or try to get a position on higher ground to reveal the patterns of the landscaping. The *Kodak Guide to Shooting Great Travel Pictures* (available at bookstores everywhere) is loaded with more tips.

 Camera Repair & Photo Developing **FNAC** ✉ 26–30 av. des Ternes, 17ᵉ ☎ 01-44-09-18-00 ✉ in Forum des Halles ✉ 1–7 rue Pierre-Lescot, 1ᵉʳ ☎ 01-40-41-40-00 ✉ 136 rue de Rennes, 6ᵉ, Montparnasse ☎ 01-49-54-30-00 ✉ 157 rue du Faubourg St-Antoine, 11ᵉ ☎ 01-43-46-54-78.
 Photo Help **Kodak Information Center** ☎ 800/242-2424 ⊕ www.kodak.com.

EQUIPMENT PRECAUTIONS

Don't pack film or equipment in checked luggage, where it is much more susceptible to damage. X-ray machines used to view checked luggage are extremely powerful and therefore are likely to ruin your film. Try to ask for hand inspection of film, which becomes clouded after repeated exposure to airport X-ray machines, and keep videotapes and computer disks away from metal detectors. Always keep film, tape, and computer disks out of the sun. Carry an extra supply of batteries, and be prepared to turn on your camera, camcorder, or laptop to prove to airport security personnel that the device is real.

FILM & DEVELOPING

The easiest place to get film developed and printed is at one of the various FNAC stores around the city. Keep in mind that it is expensive to have film developed and printed in Paris—around US$20 per 36-exposure roll.

VIDEOS

Video systems are not the same all over the world. The United States, for instance, uses NTSC and France uses SECAM. Other European countries, including the United Kingdom, use PAL. This means that you probably won't be able to play videotapes from the United States in France. You should also **bring extra blank videotapes with you from home** for your camcorder, as you may not be able to find compatible tapes in France.

CAR RENTAL

An unlimited third-party liability insurance policy is mandatory for all automobiles driven in France; the documents for this policy will be issued to you automatically as part of your car rental agreement. While an international driver's permit is not required, it's recommended (*See* Requirements & Restrictions, *below*).

Thanks to competition among Internet sites, rental rates start as low as $35 a day and $200 a week for an economy car with air-conditioning, manual transmission, and unlimited mileage. This does not include tax on car rentals, which is 19.6% or, if you pick up a car at the airport, the airport tax. **Make reservations before you go**; you can generally get a much better deal. Note that driving in Paris is best avoided, and parking is very difficult to find. You're better off renting a car only when you want to take excursions out of the city.

Renting a car through a local French agency has a number of disadvantages, the biggest being price, as they simply cannot compete with the larger international companies. These giants combine bilingual service, the security of name recognition, extensive services (such as 24-hour hot-lines), and fully automatic vehicles. However, there are a couple of exceptions. Easycar, an Internet-only rental service, offers the Smartcar, a tiny Mercedes-built two-seater perfect for zipping around the city. Rentacar Prestige can be useful if you are interested in luxury cars (convertible BMWs) or large family vans (a Renault Espace, for example).

🚗 Major Agencies **Alamo** ☎ 800/522-9696 ⊕ www.alamo.com. **Avis** ☎ 800/331-1084, 800/879-2847 in Canada, 0870/606-0100 in the U.K., 02/9353-9000 in Australia, 09/526-2847 in New Zealand ⊕ www.avis.com. **Budget** ☎ 800/527-0700 ⊕ www.budget.com. **Dollar** ☎ 800/800-6000, 0800/085-4578 in the U.K. ⊕ www.dollar.com. **Hertz** ☎ 800/654-3001, 800/263-0600 in Canada, 0870/844-8844 in the U.K., 02/9669-2444 in Australia, 09/256-8690 in New Zealand ⊕ www.hertz.com. **National Car Rental** ☎ 800/227-7368 ⊕ www.nationalcar.com.

CUTTING COSTS

For a good deal, book through a travel agent who will shop around. Do look into wholesalers, companies that do not own fleets but rent in bulk from those that do and often offer better rates than traditional car-rental operations. Prices are best during off-peak periods. Rentals booked through wholesalers often must be paid for before you leave home.

🚗 Local Agencies **Easycar** ⊕ www.easycar.com. **Rentacar Prestige** ✉ 15 rue des Pyramides, 75001 ☎ 01-42-96-95-95 ⊕ www.rentacar.fr. 🚗 Wholesalers **Auto Europe** ☎ 207/842-2000 or 800/223-5555 🖷 207/842-2222 ⊕ www.autoeurope.com. **Destination Europe Resources** (DER) ✉ 9501 W. Devon Ave., Rosemont, IL 60018 ☎ 800/782-2424 🖷 800/282-7474. **Europe by Car** ☎ 212/581-3040 or 800/223-1516 🖷 212/246-1458 ⊕ www.europebycar.com. **Kemwel** ☎ 877/820-0668 or 800/678-0678 🖷 207/842-2147 ⊕ www.kemwel.com.

INSURANCE

When driving a rented car you are generally responsible for any damage to or loss of the vehicle. Collision policies that car-rental companies sell for European rentals typically do not cover stolen vehicles. Before you rent—and purchase collision or theft coverage—see what coverage you already have under the terms of your personal auto-insurance policy and credit cards.

REQUIREMENTS & RESTRICTIONS

Drivers in France must be over 18 years old, but there is no top age limit (if your faculties are intact). To rent a car, however, you must be 21 or older and have a major credit card. If you're under 25, there's a €17-per-day supplementary charge.

SURCHARGES

Before you pick up a car in one city and leave it in another, ask about drop-off charges or one-way service fees, which can be substantial. Also inquire about early-return policies; some rental agencies charge extra if you return the car before the time specified in your contract while others give you a refund for the days not used. Most agencies note the tank's fuel level on your contract; to avoid a hefty refueling fee, return the car with the same tank level. If the tank was full, refill it just before you turn in the car, but be aware that gas stations near the rental outlet may overcharge. It's almost never a deal to prepurchase a tank of gas with the car when you rent it; the understanding is that you'll return it empty, but some fuel usually remains.

CAR TRAVEL

Unless you have a special, compelling reason, do yourself a favor and **avoid driving in Paris.** The pleasures of walking and the thorough, reliable public transit system should see you through most situations—and why mar your day with the stress of navigating narrow, one-way streets while surrounded by breakneck drivers in mosquito-size cars? You're better off driving only on trips out of the city.

Your driver's license may not be recognized outside your home country. International driving permits (IDPs) are available from the American and Canadian automobile associations and, in the United Kingdom, from the Automobile Association and Royal Automobile Club. These international permits, valid only in conjunction with your regular driver's license, are universally recognized; having one may save you a problem with local authorities.

France's roads are classified into five types; they are numbered and have letter prefixes: A (autoroute, expressways), N (route nationale), D (route départmentale), and the smaller C or V. There are excellent links between Paris and most French cities. When trying to get around Île-de-France, it is often difficult to avoid Paris—just try to **steer clear of rush hours** (7–9:30 and 4:30–7:30). A péage (toll) must be paid on most expressways outside Île-de-France: the rate varies but can be steep. Certain booths allow you to pay with a credit card.

The major ring road encircling Paris is called the périphérique, with the périphérique intérieur going counterclockwise around the city, and the périphérique extérieur, or the outside ring, going clockwise. Up to five lanes wide, the périphérique is a major highway from which portes (gates) connect Paris to the major highways of France. The names of these highways function on the same principle as the métro, with the final destination as the determining point in the direction you must take.

Heading north, look for Porte de la Chapelle (direction Lille and Charles de Gaulle Airport); east, for Porte de Bagnolet (direction Metz and Nancy); south, for Porte d'Orléans (direction Lyon and Bordeaux); and west, for Porte d'Auteuil (direction Rouen and Chartres) or Porte de St-Cloud.

EMERGENCY SERVICES

If your car breaks down on an expressway, pull your car as far off the road as quickly as possible, set your emergency indicators, and, if possible, take the emergency triangle from the car's trunk and put it at least 30 yards behind your car to warn oncoming traffic; then **go to a roadside emergency telephone.** These phones put you in direct contact with the police, automatically indicating your exact location, and are available every 3 km (2 mi). If you

have a breakdown anywhere else, find the nearest garage or contact the police. There are also 24-hour assistance hotlines valid throughout France (available through rental agencies and supplied to you when you rent the car), but do not hesitate to call the police in case of any roadside emergency, for they are quick and reliable and the phone call is free.

🚔 **Police** ☎ 17.

GASOLINE

There are gas stations throughout the city but they can be difficult to spot; you'll often find them in the underground tunnels that cross the city and in larger parking garages. Gas is expensive and prices vary enormously, ranging from about €1 to €1.50 per liter. If you're on your way out of Paris, save money by waiting until you've left the city to fill up. All gas stations accept credit cards.

PARKING

Finding parking in Paris is tough. Both meters and parking ticket machines use parking cards (cartes de stationnements), which you can purchase at any café posting the red TABAC sign; they're sold in three denominations: €10, €20, or €30. Parking in the capital runs €2 per hour. Insert your card into the nearest meter, choose the approximate amount of time you expect to stay, and receive a green receipt. Place it on the dashboard on the passenger side; **make sure the receipt's clearly visible to the meter patrol.** Parking tickets are expensive, and there is no shortage of blue-uniformed parking police. Parking lots, indicated by a blue sign with a white P, are usually underground and are generally expensive (charging €1.20 to €3 per hour, or €9 to €23 per day). One bright spot: you can **park for free on Sunday, national holidays, and in certain residential areas in August.** Parking meters marked with yellow circles indicate a free parking zone during the month of August.

ROAD CONDITIONS

Chaotic traffic is a way of life in Paris. Some streets in the city center can seem impossibly narrow; street signs are often hard to spot; and jaded city drivers often make erratic, last-minute maneuvers without signalling. Pay particular attention to motorcycles, which often weave around traffic. Priority is given to drivers coming from the right, so **watch out for drivers coming from the right**; they can come barrelling out of small streets and surprise you. Traffic lights are placed to the left and right of crosswalks, not above, so they may be blocked from your view by vehicles ahead of you—keep a sharp eye out for them.

There are a few major roundabouts at the most congested intersections, notably at L'Étoile (around the Arc de Triomphe), the place de la Bastille, and the place de la Concorde. Watch oncoming cars carefully and stick to the outer lane to make your exit. The *périphériques* (ring roads) are generally easier to use, and the quais that parallel the Seine can be a downright pleasure to drive when there's no traffic. Electronic signs on the périphériques and highways post traffic conditions: *fluide* (clear) or *bouchon* (jammed).

Some important traffic terms and signs to note: *sortie* (exit), *sens unique* (one-way), *stationnement interdite* (no parking), *impasse* (dead end). Blue rectangular signs indicate a highway; triangles carry illustrations of a particular traffic hazard; speed limits are indicated in a circle with the maximum speed circled in red.

ROAD MAPS

For the best, most detailed directional information, do what the French do and invest in a Michelin or IGN road map—available at almost any gas station or bookstore. You can buy either regional or national maps for approximately €6.

RULES OF THE ROAD

You must **always carry vehicle registration documents and your personal identification.** The French police are entitled to stop you at will to verify your ID and your car—such spot checks are frequent, especially at peak holiday times. In France you drive on the right and **give priority to drivers coming from the right** (this rule is called *priorité à droite*).

You must **wear your seat belt,** and children under 12 may not travel in the front

seat. Speed limits are designated by the type of road you're driving on: 130 kph (80 mph) on expressways (*autoroutes*), 110 kph (70 mph) on divided highways (*routes nationales*), 90 kph (55 mph) on other roads (*routes*), 50 kph (30 mph) in cities and towns (*villes et villages*). These limits are reduced by 10 kph (6 mph) in rainy, snowy, and foggy conditions. Drivers are expected to know these limits, so signs are generally only posted when there are exceptions to these rules. Right-hand turns are not allowed on a red light.

The use of hand-held cellular phones while driving is forbidden; the penalty is a €60 fine. Alcohol laws have become quite tough—a 0.05% blood alcohol limit (a lower limit than in the United States).

THE CHANNEL TUNNEL

Short of flying, taking the "Chunnel" is the fastest way to cross the English Channel: 35 minutes from Folkestone to Calais, 60 minutes from motorway to motorway, or 2 hours and 40 minutes from London's Waterloo Station to Paris's Gare du Nord.

🚗 Car Transport Eurotunnel ☎ 0870/535-3535 in the U.K., 070/223210 in Belgium, 03-21-00-61-00 in France ⊕ www.eurotunnel.com. French Motorail/ Rail Europe ☎ 0870/241-5415 ⊕ www.raileurope. co.uk/frenchmotorail.

🚃 Passenger Service Eurostar ☎ 1233/617575 or 0870/518-6186, in the U.K. ⊕ www.eurostar.co.uk. Rail Europe ☎ 800/942-4866 or 800/274-8724, 0870/584-8848 U.K. inquiries and credit-card bookings ⊕ www.raileurope.com.

CHILDREN IN PARIS

Fodor's Around Paris with Kids (available in bookstores everywhere) can help you plan your days together.

If you are renting a car, don't forget to arrange for a car seat when you reserve. For general advice about traveling with children, consult *Fodor's FYI: Travel with Your Baby* (available in bookstores everywhere).

BABYSITTING

Agencies can provide English-speaking babysitters with just a few hours' notice. The hourly rate is approximately €6 (three-hour minimum) plus an agency fee of €10. Many hotels offer babysitting services as well.

Agencies **Allo Assistance BabyChou** ☎ 01-43-13-33-23 ⊕ www.babychou.com. **Baby sitting services** ✉ 4 rue Nationale, Boulogne Billan ☎ 01-46-21-33-16 ⊕ www.babysittingservices.com.

FLYING

When booking, confirm carry-on allowances if you're traveling with infants. In general, for babies charged 10% to 50% of the adult fare you are allowed one carry-on bag and a collapsible stroller; if the flight is full, the stroller may have to be checked or you may be limited to less.

Experts agree that it's a good idea to use safety seats aloft for children weighing less than 40 pounds. Airlines set their own policies: if you use a safety seat, U.S. carriers usually require that the child be ticketed, even if he or she is young enough to ride free, because the seats must be strapped into regular seats. And even if you pay the full adult fare for the seat, it may be worth it, especially on longer trips. Do **check your airline's policy about using safety seats during takeoff and landing.** Safety seats are not allowed everywhere in the plane, so get your seat assignments as early as possible.

When reserving, request children's meals or a freestanding bassinet (not available at all airlines) if you need them. But note that bulkhead seats, where you must sit to use the bassinet, may lack an overhead bin or storage space on the floor.

FOOD

Most French children supplement their three meals a day with a *goûter* (snack) after school. This traditional afternoon snack might be a fresh baguette with a couple of squares of chocolate, a *pain au chocolat*, or occasionally *bonbons* (candies) sold by the gram at bakeries or small grocery stores. In cafés try an *orange pressé* or *citron pressé*, fresh-squeezed orange or lemon juice, respectively, served in a tall glass with a long spoon; sugar comes on the side, so you can add it to taste. Or while the grownups are sipping their *café crèmes*, kids can order a *chocolat chaud* (hot chocolate).

Hit the supermarkets for snacks or the makings of an impromptu meal. You'll usually find an entire aisle for *gâteaux* (cakes) and *biscuits* (cookies), stocked with everything from jam-filled cookies to individually wrapped lemon tarts. You can find juice in small portable boxes with straws. In the refrigerator cases there are plenty of kid-friendly cheeses—individual servings wrapped in red wax or packaged with crackers—and all types of yogurt. For milk there's *lait entier* (whole milk), *lait demi-écremé* (a bit richer than 2%), and *lait écremé* (skim). In restaurants milk is generally not served with meals, but you can ask for it even if you don't see it on the menu.

Don't limit yourself to supermarkets, though—let your kids help choose bread or pastries from a bakery, fresh fruit from an outdoor market. This is a wonderful city for picnics—some of the nicest places for a bite are behind Notre-Dame, in the Luxembourg or Tuileries gardens, on the hills in the Parc des Buttes-Chaumont, and near the water fountains at Trocadéro.

For tips on restaurant dining with kids, *see* "With Children?" *in* the Where to Eat chapter.

LODGING

Some Paris hotels allow children under a certain age to sleep in the same room with their parents for free. This can vary from age 5 up to age 16, so be sure to ask in advance. Most hotels have baby cots (free) or extra fold-out beds for children (usually a supplemental fee), but this can depend on availability and the size of the room, so be sure to ask when reserving. Not all hotels are baby/child-friendly for lack of space and services. Only the large palace hotels have their own children's programs; other hotels can usually arrange for babysitting services through a local agency.

SIGHTS & ATTRACTIONS

Places that are especially appealing to children are indicated by a rubber-duckie icon (🦆) in the margin. For details on Guignol shows, *see* Puppet Shows *in* Nightlife & the Arts. Almost all museums and movie theaters offer discounted rates to children.

The Centre d'Information et de Documentation pour la Jeunesse (CIDJ, Center for Information and Documentation for Young People), has information about activities and events for youngsters in Paris. If you read French, pick up *Paris Môme*, a supplement of the newspaper *Libération*, published every four months, for its listings of children's activities, including special events, films, theater productions, and puppet shows. It's available free at any tourist office.

SUPPLIES & EQUIPMENT

Supermarkets carry several major brands of diapers (*couches*), universally referred to as Pampers (pronounced "pawm-paires"). Junior sizes are hard to come by, as the French toilet-train early. Baby formula is available in grocery stores or pharmacies. There are two types of formula: *lait premier age*, for infants 0–4 months, and *lait deuxième age*, for 4 months or older. French formulas come in powder form and need to be mixed with a pure, low-mineral-content bottled water like Evian or Volvic (the French *never* mix baby formula with tap water). American formulas are not found in France. If you're looking for treats for your little ones, some items to keep in mind are *coloriage* (coloring books); *crayons de couleur* (crayons); *pâte à modeler* (modeling clay); and *feutres* (markers).

COMPUTERS ON THE ROAD

If you use a major Internet provider, getting online in Paris shouldn't be difficult. Call your Internet provider to get the local access number in Paris. Many hotels have business services with Internet access, in-room modem lines, and even high-speed wireless access. You will, however, need an adapter for your computer for the European-style plugs. If you're traveling with a laptop, carry a spare battery and adapter. **Never plug your computer into any socket before asking about surge protection.** IBM sells a pen-size modem tester that plugs into a telephone jack to check if the line is safe to use.

🔳 Access Numbers in Paris **AOL** ☎ 01-41-45-81-00. **Compuserve** ☎ 08-03-00-60-00, 08-03-00-80-00, or 08-03-00-90-00.

🔳 Internet Cafés **Access Academy** ✉ 60/62 rue St-André des Arts, 6ᵉ, Quartier Latin ☎ 01-43-25-25-80 ⊕ www.accessacademy.com. **La Baguenaude** ✉ 30 rue Grande-Truanderie, 1ᵉʳ, Beaubourg/Les Halles ☎ 01-40-26-27-74 ⊕ http://perso.wanadoo.fr/baguenaude.cafe. **Cybersquare** ✉ 1 pl. République, 3ᵉ, République ☎ 01-48-87-82-36 ⊕ www.cybersquare-paris.com. **XS Arena Saint Michel** ✉ 53 rue de la Harpe, 5ᵉ, Quartier Latin ☎ 01-44-07-38-89 ⊕ www.xsarena.com.

CONCIERGES

Concierges, found in many hotels, can help you with theater tickets and dinner reservations: a good one with connections may be able to get you seats for a hot show or prime-time dinner reservations at the restaurant of the moment. You can also turn to your hotel's concierge for help with travel arrangements, sightseeing plans, services ranging from aromatherapy to zipper repair, and emergencies. **Always tip** a concierge who has been of assistance (⇨ Tipping).

There's another type of concierge who's considered a quintessential if fading part of Paris life: the *concierge* or *gardien,* stereotyped as a watchdog type who has all the gossip on the building's residents. These caretakers work in some nicer residential buildings, and you may encounter them if you're renting an apartment or visiting a Parisian friend. They pick up mail, accept packages, clean entrances and stairways, and monitor the building's comings and goings. When you enter the building, be prepared to be questioned and just state your business courteously. The concierges aren't being inappropriately nosy—they're just doing their job.

CONSUMER PROTECTION

Whether you're shopping for gifts or purchasing travel services, **pay with a major credit card** whenever possible, so you can cancel payment or get reimbursed if there's a problem (and you can provide documentation). If you're doing business with a particular company for the first time, contact your local Better Business Bureau and the attorney general's offices in your state and (for U.S. businesses) the company's home state as well. Have any complaints been filed? Finally, if you're buying a package or tour, always consider travel insurance that includes default coverage (⇨ Insurance).

BBBs Council of Better Business Bureaus ✉ 4200 Wilson Blvd., Suite 800, Arlington, VA 22203 ☎ 703/276-0100 📠 703/525-8277 🌐 www.bbb.org.

CUSTOMS & DUTIES

When shopping abroad, keep receipts for all purchases. Upon reentering the country, **be ready to show customs officials what you've bought.** Pack purchases together in an easily accessible place. If you think a duty is incorrect, appeal the assessment. If you object to the way your clearance was handled, note the inspector's badge number. In either case, first ask to see a supervisor. If the problem isn't resolved, write to the appropriate authorities, beginning with the port director at your point of entry.

IN AUSTRALIA

Australian residents who are 18 or older may bring home A$400 worth of souvenirs and gifts (including jewelry), 250 cigarettes or 250 grams of cigars or other tobacco products, and 1, 125 ml of alcohol (including wine, beer, and spirits). Residents under 18 may bring back A$200 worth of goods. Members of the same family traveling together may pool their allowances. Prohibited items include meat products. Seeds, plants, and fruits need to be declared upon arrival.

Australian Customs Service 📫 Regional Director, Box 8, Sydney, NSW 2001 ☎ 02/9213-2000 or 1300/363-263, 02/8334-7444 or 1800/020-504 quarantine-inquiry line 📠 02/9213-4043 🌐 www.customs.gov.au.

IN CANADA

Canadian residents who have been out of Canada for at least seven days may bring in C$750 worth of goods duty-free. If you've been away fewer than seven days but more than 48 hours, the duty-free allowance drops to C$200. If your trip lasts 24 to 48 hours, the allowance is C$50. You may not pool allowances with family members. Goods claimed under the C$750 exemption may follow you by mail; those claimed under the lesser exemptions must accompany you. Alcohol and tobacco products may be included in the seven-day and 48-hour exemptions but not in the 24-hour exemption. If you meet the age requirements of the province or territory through which you reenter Canada, you may bring in, duty-free, 1.5 liters of wine *or* 1.14 liters (40 imperial ounces) of liquor *or* 24 12-ounce cans or bottles of beer or ale. Also, if you meet the local age requirement for tobacco products, you may bring in, duty-free, 200 cigarettes, 50 cigars or cigarillos, and 200 grams of tobacco. You may have to pay a minimum duty on tobacco products, regardless of whether or not you exceed your personal exemption. Check ahead of time with the Canada Customs and Revenue Agency or the Department of Agriculture for policies regarding meat products, seeds, plants, and fruits.

You may send an unlimited number of gifts (only one gift per recipient, however) worth up to C$60 each duty-free to Canada. Label the package UNSOLICITED GIFT—VALUE UNDER $60. Alcohol and tobacco are excluded.

Canada Border Services Agency ✉ Customs Information Services, 191 Laurier Ave. W, 15th floor, Ottawa, Ontario K1A 0L5 ☎ 800/461-9999 in Canada, 204/983-3500, 506/636-5064 🌐 www.cbsa.gc.ca.

IN FRANCE

If you're coming from outside the European Union (EU), you may import duty-free: (1) 200 cigarettes or 100 cigarillos or 50 cigars or 250 grams of tobacco; (2) 2 liters of wine and, in addition, (a) 1 liter of alcohol over 22% volume (most spirits) or (b) 2 liters of alcohol under 22% volume (fortified or sparkling wine) or (c) 2 more liters of table wine; (3) 50 ml of perfume and 250 ml of toilet water; (4) 200 grams of coffee, 100 grams of tea; and (5) other goods to the value of about €182 (€91 for ages 14 and under).

If you're arriving from an EU country, you may be required to declare all goods and prove that anything over the standard limit is for personal consumption.

But there is no limit or customs tariff imposed on goods carried within the EU except on tobacco (800 cigarettes, 200 cigars, 1 kg of tobacco) and alcohol (10 liters of spirits, 90 liters of wine, with a maximum of 60 liters of sparkling wine, 110 liters of beer).

Any amount of euros or foreign currency may be brought into France, but foreign currencies converted into euros may be reconverted into a foreign currency only up to the equivalent of €769.

📶 **Direction des Douanes** ✉ 16 rue Yves Toudic, 10ᵉ ☎ 01-40-40-39-00 ⊕ www.douane.gouv.fr.

IN NEW ZEALAND

All homeward-bound residents may bring back NZ$700 worth of souvenirs and gifts; passengers may not pool their allowances, and children can claim only the concession on goods intended for their own use. For those 17 or older, the duty-free allowance also includes 4.5 liters of wine or beer; one 1, 125-ml bottle of spirits; and either 200 cigarettes, 250 grams of tobacco, 50 cigars, *or* a combination of the three up to 250 grams. Meat products, seeds, plants, and fruits must be declared upon arrival to the Agricultural Services Department.

📶 **New Zealand Customs** ✉ Head office: The Customhouse, 17–21 Whitmore St., Box 2218, Wellington ☎ 09/300–5399 or 0800/428–786 ⊕ www.customs.govt.nz.

IN THE U.K.

If you are a U.K. resident and your journey was wholly within the European Union, you probably won't have to pass through customs when you return to the United Kingdom. If you plan to bring back large quantities of alcohol or tobacco, check EU limits beforehand. In most cases, if you bring back more than 200 cigars, 3,200 cigarettes, 400 cigarillos, 3 kilograms of tobacco, 10 liters of spirits, 110 liters of beer, 20 liters of fortified wine, and/or 90 liters of wine, you have to declare the goods upon return.

📶 **HM Customs and Excise** ✉ Portcullis House, 21 Cowbridge Rd. E, Cardiff CF11 9SS ☎ 0845/010–9000 or 0208/929–0152 advice service, 0208/929–6731 or 0208/910–3602 complaints ⊕ www.hmce.gov.uk.

IN THE U.S.

U.S. residents who have been out of the country for at least 48 hours may bring home, for personal use, $800 worth of foreign goods duty-free, as long as they haven't used the $800 allowance or any part of it in the past 30 days. This exemption may include 1 liter of alcohol (for travelers 21 and older), 200 cigarettes, and 100 non-Cuban cigars. Family members from the same household who are traveling together may pool their $800 personal exemptions. For fewer than 48 hours, the duty-free allowance drops to $200, which may include 50 cigarettes, 10 non-Cuban cigars, and 150 ml of alcohol (or 150 ml of perfume containing alcohol). The $200 allowance cannot be combined with other individuals' exemptions, and if you exceed it, the full value of all the goods will be taxed. Antiques, which U.S. Customs and Border Protection defines as objects more than 100 years old, enter duty-free, as do original works of art done entirely by hand, including paintings, drawings, and sculptures. This doesn't apply to folk art or handicrafts, which are in general dutiable.

You may also send packages home duty-free, with a limit of one parcel per addressee per day (except alcohol or tobacco products or perfume worth more than $5). You can mail up to $200 worth of goods for personal use; label the package PERSONAL USE and attach a list of its contents and their retail value. If the package contains your used personal belongings, mark it AMERICAN GOODS RETURNED to avoid paying duties. You may send up to $100 worth of goods as a gift; mark the package UNSOLICITED GIFT. Mailed items do not affect your duty-free allowance on your return.

To avoid paying duty on foreign-made high-ticket items you already own and will take on your trip, register them with a local customs office before you leave the country. Consider filing a Certificate of Registration for laptops, cameras, watches, and other digital devices identified with serial numbers or other permanent markings; you can keep the certificate for other trips. Otherwise, bring a sales receipt or insurance form to show that you owned the item before you left the United States.

For more about duties, restricted items, and other information about international travel, check out U.S. Customs and Border Protection's online brochure, *Know Before You Go.*

🚩 **U.S. Customs and Border Protection** ✉ for inquiries, 1300 Pennsylvania Ave. NW, Washington, DC 20229 ⊕ www.cbp.gov ☎ 877/287-8667, 202/354-1000 ✉ for complaints, Customer Satisfaction Unit, 1300 Pennsylvania Ave. NW, Room 5.4D, Washington, DC 20229.

DISABILITIES & ACCESSIBILITY

Although the city of Paris is doing much to ensure that public facilities accommodate people with mobility difficulties, it still has a long way to go. Some sidewalks now have low curbs, and many arrondissements have public restrooms and telephone boxes that are accessible to travelers using wheelchairs. Association des Paralysés de France, a helpful, private nonprofit organization, offers extensive English-language information about accessibility in France (although the staff may not speak much English). The Paris Office of Tourism distributes a list of hotels, restaurants, and sights around Paris that have received the "Tourism & Handicap" label.

🚩 **Local Resources Association des Paralysés de France** ✉ 22 rue de Pére Guerin, 75013 Paris ☎ 01-44-16-83-83 ⊕ www.apf.asso.fr. **Paris Office of Tourism** ⊕ www.parisinfo.com.

RESERVATIONS

When discussing accessibility with an operator or reservations agent, ask hard questions. Are there any stairs, inside *or* out? Are there grab bars next to the toilet *and* in the shower/tub? How wide is the doorway to the room? To the bathroom? For the most extensive facilities meeting the latest legal specifications, opt for newer accommodations. If you reserve through a toll-free number, consider also calling the hotel's local number to confirm the information from the central reservations office. Get confirmation in writing when you can.

TRANSPORTATION

The Paris métro is a labyrinth of winding stairs, malfunctioning doors, and hordes of scurrying Parisians, all of which makes it a less-than-ideal mode of transport for travelers with disabilities. In addition, very few métro and RER stations are wheelchair accessible, with the exception of the fully automated line Météor. For those with walking difficulties, all stairs have handrails, and nearly two-thirds of the stations have at least one escalator. Avoid peak hours between 8 and 9 and 6 and 7. Almost all buses are wheelchair accessible, but note that you will be more comfortable traveling with someone who can help you. For information about accessibility, **get the RER and métro access guide,** available at most stations and from the Paris Transit Authority. The SNCF has special accommodations in the first-class compartments of trains that are reserved exclusively for people using wheelchairs (and are available for the second-class price). It is essential to **reserve special train tickets in advance**—this not only assures a comfortable seat but guarantees assistance at the station. Taxi drivers are required by law to assist travelers with disabilities in and out of their vehicles.

The Airhop shuttle company runs adapted vehicles to and from the airports; Orly–Paris costs €35 and Charles de Gaulle–Paris costs €45; this service is available weekdays only. Reservations (in French) must be made in advance. Note that you must pay €2.50 for every 15 minutes there is a delay.

🚩 **Local Resources Airhop** ☎ 01-41-29-01-29. **RATP (Paris Transit Authority)** ✉ 54 quai de la Rapée, 75599, Cedex 12 ☎ 08-92-68-77-14, €.35 per minute ⊕ www.ratp.com.

🚩 **Complaints Aviation Consumer Protection Division** (⇨ Air Travel) for airline-related problems. **Departmental Office of Civil Rights** ✉ for general inquiries, U.S. Department of Transportation, S-30, 400 7th St. SW, Room 10215, Washington, DC 20590 ☎ 202/366-4648 🖶 202/366-9371 ⊕ www.dotcr.ost.dot.gov. **Disability Rights Section** ✉ NYAV, U.S. Department of Justice, Civil Rights Division, 950 Pennsylvania Ave. NW, Washington, DC 20530 ☎ ADA information line 202/514-0301, 800/514-0301, 202/514-0383 TTY, 800/514-0383 TTY ⊕ www.

ada.gov. **U.S. Department of Transportation Hotline** ☎ for disability-related air-travel problems, 800/778-4838 or 800/455-9880 TTY.

TRAVEL AGENCIES

In the United States, the Americans with Disabilities Act requires that travel firms serve the needs of all travelers. Some agencies specialize in working with people with disabilities.

🛈 Travelers with Mobility Problems **Access Adventures/B. Roberts Travel** ✉ 1876 East Ave., Rochester, NY 14610 ☎ 800/444-6540 ⊕ www. brobertstravel.com, run by a former physical-rehabilitation counselor. **CareVacations** ✉ No. 5, 5110-50 Ave., Leduc, Alberta, Canada, T9E 6V4 ☎ 780/986-6404 or 877/478-7827 ⊜ 780/986-8332 ⊕ www.carevacations.com, for group tours and cruise vacations. **Flying Wheels Travel** ✉ 143 W. Bridge St., Box 382, Owatonna, MN 55060 ☎ 507/451-5005 ⊜ 507/451-1685 ⊕ www. flyingwheelstravel.com.

DISCOUNTS & DEALS

Be a smart shopper and compare all your options before making decisions. A plane ticket bought with a promotional coupon from travel clubs, coupon books, and direct-mail offers or purchased on the Internet may not be cheaper than the least expensive fare from a discount ticket agency. And always keep in mind that what you get is just as important as what you save.

Paris Tourist Offices, railroad stations, major métro stations, and participating museums sell the Carte Musées et Monuments (Museums and Monuments Pass), which offers unlimited access over a set number of consecutive days to 74 museums and monuments in Paris, including the Louvre, Musée d'Orsay, Sainte-Chapelle, and Versailles (but not the Eiffel Tower, temporary exhibits, or guided tours). One-, three-, and five-day passes cost €18, €36, and €54, respectively. From the looks of it, only the most rabid museumgoer will benefit from this pass: you'd have to do three museums in one day, or six in three days, to reap any real savings—and it's even less of an attractive proposition now that the museums owned by the city of Paris are free. However, the pass also allows access to museums and monuments without having to wait in line (something to consider if you're going to make the Louvre your home away from home). If you don't plan on seeing that many museums or monuments, you may be better off paying at each site.

Also look into the Club France card offered by the Maison de la France, a branch of the French ministry of tourism. The Club France card is available for an annual $25 fee and it gives a 10–50% discount at select hotels, tour companies, and other tourist-oriented businesses. You'll also get invitations to France-related events in your home country.

🛈 Museum Passes **Association InterMusées** ✉ 4 rue Brantôme, 75003 Paris ☎ 01-44-61-96-60 ⊕ www.intermusees.com. **Maison de la France** ☎ 02/9231-5244 in Australia, 514/876-9881 in Canada, 09068/244-123 in the U.K., 60p per minute, 410/286-8310 in the U.S. ⊕ www.franceguide.com.

DISCOUNT RESERVATIONS

To save money, look into discount reservations services with Web sites and toll-free numbers, which use their buying power to get a better price on hotels, airline tickets (⇨ Air Travel), even car rentals. When booking a room, always **call the hotel's local toll-free number** (if one is available) rather than the central reservations number—you'll often get a better price. Always ask about special packages or corporate rates.

When shopping for the best deal on hotels and car rentals, look for guaranteed exchange rates, which protect you against a falling dollar. With your rate locked in, you won't pay more, even if the price goes up in the local currency.

🛈 Hotel Rooms **Accommodations Express** ☎ 800/444-7666 or 800/277-1064. **Hotels.com** ☎ 800/246-8357 ⊕ www.hotels.com. **International Marketing & Travel Concepts** ☎ 800/790-4682 ⊕ www.imtc-travel.com. **Steigenberger Reservation Service** ☎ 800/223-5652 ⊕ www.srs-worldhotels.com. **Turbotrip.com** ☎ 800/473-7829 ⊕ w3.turbotrip.com.

PACKAGE DEALS

Don't confuse packages and guided tours. When you buy a package, you travel on your own, just as though you had planned the trip yourself. Fly/drive packages, which combine airfare and car rental, are often a good deal. In cities, ask the local visitor's bureau about hotel and local transportation packages that include tickets to major museum exhibits or other special events. If you **buy a rail/drive pass,** you may save on train tickets and car rentals. All Eurailpass holders get a discount on Eurostar fares through the Channel Tunnel and often receive reduced rates for buses, hotels, ferries, sightseeing cruises, and car rentals.

ELECTRICITY

To use electric-powered equipment purchased in the U.S. or Canada, **bring a converter and adapter.** The electrical current in Paris is 220 volts, 50 cycles alternating current (AC); wall outlets take continental-type plugs, with two round prongs.

If your appliances are dual-voltage, you'll need only an adapter. Don't use 110-volt outlets marked FOR SHAVERS ONLY for high-wattage appliances such as blow-dryers. Most laptops operate equally well on 110 and 220 volts and so require only an adapter.

EMBASSIES

🇦🇺 Australia **Australian Consulate** ✉ 4 rue Jean-Rey, 15ᵉ, Paris ☎ 01-40-59-33-00 ⊘ Weekdays 9:15–12:15 Ⓜ Bir-Hakeim

🇨🇦 Canada **Canadian Embassy** ✉ 35 av. Montaigne, 8ᵉ, Paris ☎ 01-44-43-29-02 ⊘ Weekdays 9–noon and 2-4:30 Ⓜ Franklin-D.-Roosevelt

🇳🇿 New Zealand **New Zealand Consulate** ✉ 7 ter rue Léonardo da Vinci, 16ᵉ, Paris ☎ 01-45-01-43-43 ⊘ Mon.-Thurs. 9-1 and 2-5.30; Fri. 9-1 and 2-4 Ⓜ Victor-Hugo

🇬🇧 United Kingdom **United Kingdom Consulate** ✉ 18 bis, rue d'Anjou, 8ᵉ, Paris ☎ 01-44-51-31-00 ⊘ Weekdays 9:30–12:30 and 2:30-5 Ⓜ Madeleine

🇺🇸 United States **United States Consulate** ✉ 2 rue St-Florentin, 1ᵉʳ, Paris ☎ 01-43-12-22-22 in English ⊘ Weekdays 9-1 Ⓜ Concorde.

EMERGENCIES

The French National Health Care system has been organized to provide fully equipped, fully staffed hospitals within 30 minutes of every resident in Paris. A sign of a white cross within a rectangular blue box appears on all hospitals. This guidebook does not list the major Paris hospitals, as the French government prefers an emergency operator to make the judgment call and assign you the best and most convenient option for your emergency. Note that if you are able to walk into a hospital emergency room by yourself you are often considered "low priority, " and the wait can be interminable. So if time is of the essence, it's best to call the fire department (☎ 18); a fully trained team of paramedics will usually arrive within five minutes. You may also dial for a Samu ambulance (☎ 15); there is usually an English-speaking physician available who will help you to assess the situation and either dispatch an ambulance immediately or advise you as to your best course of action. Be sure to **check with your insurance company before your trip** to verify that you are covered for medical care in other countries.

In a less urgent situation, do what the French do and call SOS Doctor or SOS Dental services; like magic, in under an hour a certified, experienced doctor or dentist arrives at the door, armed with an old leather doctor case filled with the essentials for diagnosis and treatment (at an average cost of €65). The doctor or dentist may or may not be bilingual but, at worst, will have a rudimentary understanding of English. This is a very helpful 24-hour service to use for common symptoms of benign illnesses that need to be treated quickly for comfort, such as high fever, toothache, or upset stomachs (which seem to have the unfortunate habit of announcing themselves late at night).

The American Hospital and the Hertford British Hospital both have 24-hour emergency hotlines with bilingual doctors and nurses who can provide advice. For small problems go to a pharmacy, marked by a green neon cross. Pharmacists are authorized to administer first aid and recommend over-the-counter drugs, and they can be very helpful in advising you in English or sending you to the nearest English-speaking pharmacist.

Call the police (☎ 17) if there has been a crime or an act of violence. On the street, some French phrases that may be needed in an emergency are: *Au secours!* (Help!), *urgence* (emergency), *samu* (ambulance), *pompiers* (firemen), *poste de station* (police station), *médecin* (doctor), and *hôpital* (hospital).

A hotline of note is SOS Help for English-language crisis information, open daily 3 PM–11 PM.

📞 Doctors & Dentists **SOS Dentiste** ☎ 01-43-37-51-00. **SOS Médecin** ☎ 01-47-07-77-77.

📞 Emergency Services **Ambulance** ☎ 15. **Fire Department** ☎ 18. **Police** ☎ 17. These numbers are toll-free and can be dialed from any phone.

📞 Hospitals **The American Hospital** ✉ 63 bd. Victor-Hugo, Neuilly ☎ 01-46-41-25-25. **The Hertford British Hospital** ✉ 3 rue Barbès, Levallois-Perret ☎ 01-46-39-22-22.

📞 Hotline **SOS Help** ☎ 01-46-21-46-46.

📞 Late-Night & 24-Hour Pharmacies **Dhéry** ✉ Galerie des Champs, 84 ave. des Champs-Élysées, 8e ☎ 01-45-62-02-41 is open 24 hours. **Pharmacie des Arts** ✉ 106 bd. Montparnasse, 14e is open daily until midnight. **Pharmacie Internationale** ✉ 5 pl. Pigalle, 9e ☎ 01-48-78-38-12 is open daily until midnight. **Pharmacie Matignon** ✉ 2 rue Jean-Mermoz, at the Rond-Point de Champs-Élysées, 8e ☎ 01-45-62-79-16 is open daily until 2 AM.

ENGLISH-LANGUAGE MEDIA

BOOKS

For information about bookstores in Paris, *see* Specialty Shops *in* Chapter 6. The American Library in Paris is another resource for English-language books; it's open Tuesday–Saturday 10–7.

NEWSPAPERS & MAGAZINES

A number of free magazines in English, with all kinds of listings, including events, bars, restaurants, shops, films, and museums, are available in Paris. Look for them in the tourist offices and in all Anglo-American restaurants, bars, and bookshops. *Time Out Paris,* published every summer, dishes up a host of information about hot spots, good hotels, trendy music, new museum exhibits, cool bars, and other hip happenings. *FUSAC,* France USA Contacts, is published every six weeks and is popular for its listing of short- and long-term rentals. The *Paris Voice* is a small monthly magazine with arts and entertainment listings and snappy restaurant reviews. *Irish Eyes,* a monthly magazine that targets the growing Irish community in Paris, lists cultural events, movie reviews, recipes, and postings for affordable weekends in Ireland.

Besides a large selection of French newspapers and magazines, all kinds of English-language newspapers and magazines can be found at newsstands, especially in major tourist areas, including the *International Herald Tribune, USA Today,* the *New York Times,* the *European Financial Times,* the *Times* of London, *Newsweek, The Economist, Vogue,* and *Elle.* The weekend edition of the French daily paper *Le Monde* carries a *New York Times* supplement in English.

RADIO & TELEVISION

Although most TV stations dub English-language shows, Canal Jimmy (channel 8) shows American shows in their original, undubbed format. On cable TV you can find English-language programming including CNN, BBC World, and BBC Prime. Every morning at 7:05 AM, ABC News (from the night before) is aired on Canal Plus, channel 4. Most radio stations broadcast in French.

ETIQUETTE & BEHAVIOR

When meeting someone for the first time, whether in a social or a professional setting, it is appropriate to shake hands. Other than that, the French like to kiss. For the Parisians, it's two *bisous,* which are more like air kisses with your cheeks touching lightly–don't actually smack your lips onto the person's face!

The French like to look at people—that's half the point of cafés and fashion. **Get used to being looked at**; it's as natural as breathing here. They'll look at your shoes or your watch, check out what you're wearing or reading. What they will not do is maintain steady eye contact or smile. If a stranger of the opposite sex smiles at you, it is best to do as the French do and return only a blank look before turning away. If you smile back, you might find yourself in a Pepé Le Pew–type situation.

Visitors' exuberance—and accompanying loud voices—may cause discreet Parisians to raise their eyebrows or give a deep chesty sigh. They're not being rude, but they're telling you that they think you are. Be aware of your surroundings and **lower your voice** accordingly, especially in churches, museums, restaurants, theaters, cinemas, and the métro.

When entering and leaving a shop, **greet and say goodbye to the staff.** A simple *bonjour, monsieur/madame* and *au revoir, merci* are considered a virtual necessity for politeness. Other basic pleasantries in French include: *bonne journée* (have a nice day); *bonne soirée* (have a nice evening); *enchanté* (nice to meet you); *s'il vous plaît* (please); and *je vous en prie* (you're welcome). When asking for directions or other help, be sure to **preface your request with a polite phrase** such as *excusez-moi de vous déranger, madame/monsieur* (excuse me for bothering you, ma'am/sir).

When visiting a French home, don't expect to be invited into the kitchen or to take a house tour. The French have a very definite sense of personal space, and you'll be escorted to what are considered the guest areas. If you're invited to dinner be sure to bring a gift, such as wine, champagne, flowers, or chocolates.

Table manners are often considered a litmus test of your character or upbringing. When dining out, note that the French only fill wineglasses until they are half full—it's considered bad manners to fill it to the brim. They never serve themselves before serving the rest of the table. During a meal, **keep both hands above the table,** and keep your elbows off the table. Bread is broken, never cut, and is placed next to the plate, never on the plate. When slicing a cheese, don't cut off the point (or "nose"). Coffee or tea are ordered after dessert, instead of with dessert. (In fact, coffee and tea usually aren't ordered with any courses during meals, except breakfast.) Checks are often split evenly between couples or individuals, even if someone only ordered a salad and others had a full meal. Eating on the street is generally frowned on.

BUSINESS ETIQUETTE

In a business situation greetings are typically made with a friendly handshake. A suit is appropriate for business meetings for both men and women. Professional presentation is extremely important: casual Fridays are unheard of, sneakers saved for weekends. The French don't like overfamiliarity in any form; use formal surname greetings unless a mutual decision has been made to use first names.

GAY & LESBIAN TRAVEL

Though Paris's popular mayor Bertrand Delanoë is openly gay, this fact doesn't cause a stir—for Paris, in general, is not only tolerant of its homosexual community but notably laissez faire. Most Parisians consider sexuality, of any type, to be an individual's own affair.

The epicenter of the city's large gay community is the Marais—also one of the city's hippest areas, no matter who you are. It's characteristic of the city that straight families, orthodox Jews, and gay and lesbian couples share the neighborhood with perfect unconcern on such matters.

Several gay and lesbian organizations provide information on events and medical care. Association des Médecins Gais and Écoute Gaie run crisis hotlines that give advice over the phone (although limited English is spoken). Centre Gai et Lesbien is a great source of information, assembled from a multitude of associations, and can respond to most questions. Les Mots à la Bouche is Paris's largest gay bookstore and is always a rich resource for current happenings and literature.

A number of informative newspapers and magazines that cover the Parisian gay-lesbian scene, including *TETU* and *Lesbia* magazines, are available at stores and kiosks around the city.

⁊ Gay- & Lesbian-Friendly Travel Agencies
Different Roads Travel ⊠ 1017 N. LaCienega Blvd., Suite 308, West Hollywood, CA 90069 ☎ 310/289-6000 or 800/429-8747 (Ext. 14 for both) 🖷 310/855-0323 ✉ lgernert@tzell.com. **Kennedy Travel** ⊠ 130 W. 42nd St., Suite 401, New York, NY 10036 ☎ 212/840-8659 or 800/237-7433 🖷 212/730-2269 ⊕ www.kennedytravel.com. **Now, Voyager** ⊠ 4406 18th St., San Francisco, CA 94114 ☎ 415/626-1169

or 800/255-6951 🖶 415/626-8626 ⊕ www.
nowvoyager.com. **Skylink Travel and Tour/Flying
Dutchmen Travel** ✉ 1455 N. Dutton Ave., Suite A,
Santa Rosa, CA 95401 ☎ 707/546-9888 or 800/225-
5759 🖶 707/636-0951; serving lesbian travelers.

HOLIDAYS

With 11 national holidays (*jours feriés*)
and five weeks of paid vacation, the
French have their share of repose. In May
there is a holiday nearly every week, so be
prepared for stores, banks, and museums
to shut their doors for days at a time. If a
holiday falls on a Tuesday or Thursday,
many businesses *font le pont* (make the
bridge) and close on that Monday or Friday as well. But some exchange booths in
tourist areas, small grocery stores, restaurants, cafés, and bakeries usually remain
open. Bastille Day (July 14) is observed in
true French form. Celebrations begin on
the evening of the 13th, when city firemen
open the doors to their stations, often
classed as historical monuments, to host
their much-acclaimed all-night balls and
finish the next day with the annual military parade and air show.

Note that these dates are for the calendar
year 2006: January 1 (New Year's Day);
April 16–17 (Easter Sunday/Monday);
May 1 (Labor Day); May 8 (VE Day);
May 25 (Ascension); June 4–5 (Pentecost
Sunday/Monday); July 14 (Bastille Day);
August 15 (Assumption); November 1 (All
Saints' Day); November 11 (Armistice);
December 25 (Christmas).

INSURANCE

The most useful travel-insurance plan is a
comprehensive policy that includes coverage for trip cancellation and interruption,
default, trip delay, and medical expenses
(with a waiver for preexisting conditions).

Without insurance you'll lose all or most
of your money if you cancel your trip, regardless of the reason. Default insurance
covers you if your tour operator, airline,
or cruise line goes out of business—the
chances of which have been increasing.
Trip-delay covers expenses that arise because of bad weather or mechanical delays. Study the fine print when comparing
policies.

If you're traveling internationally, a key
component of travel insurance is coverage
for medical bills incurred if you get sick on
the road. Such expenses aren't generally
covered by Medicare or private policies.
U.K. residents can buy a travel-insurance
policy valid for most vacations taken during the year in which it's purchased (but
check preexisting-condition coverage).
British and Australian citizens need extra
medical coverage when traveling overseas.

Always **buy travel policies directly from
the insurance company**; if you buy them
from a cruise line, airline, or tour operator
that goes out of business you probably
won't be covered for the agency or operator's default, a major risk. Before making
any purchase, review your existing health
and home-owner's policies to find what
they cover away from home.

🛈 Travel Insurers In the U.S.: **Access America**
✉ 2805 N. Parham Rd., Richmond, VA 23294
☎ 800/284-8300 🖶 804/673-1491 or 800/346-
9265 ⊕ www.accessamerica.com. **Travel Guard International** ✉ 1145 Clark St., Stevens Point, WI
54481 ☎ 800/826-1300 or 715/345-1041 🖶 800/
955-8785 ⊕ www.travelguard.com.
🛈 In the U.K.: **Association of British Insurers**
✉ 51 Gresham St., London EC2V 7HQ ☎ 020/
7600-3333 🖶 020/7696-8999 ⊕ www.abi.org.uk. In
Canada: **RBC Insurance** ✉ 6880 Financial Dr., Mis-
sissauga, Ontario L5N 7Y5 ☎ 800/668-4342 or 905/
816-2559 🖶 905/813-4704 ⊕ www.rbcinsurance.
com. In Australia: **Insurance Council of Australia**
✉ Insurance Enquiries and Complaints, Box 561,
Collins St. W, Melbourne, VIC 8007 ☎ 1300/780-808
or 03/9629-4109 🖶 03/9621-2060 ⊕ www.iecltd.
com.au. In New Zealand: **Insurance Council of New
Zealand** ✉ Level 7, 111-115 Customhouse Quay, Box
474, Wellington ☎ 04/472-5230 🖶 04/473-3011
⊕ www.icnz.org.nz.

LANGUAGE

The French may appear a little prickly at
first to English-speaking visitors, but it
usually helps if you **make an effort to
speak a little French.** A simple, friendly
bonjour (hello) will do, as will asking if
the person you are greeting speaks English
(*parlez-vous anglais?*). Be patient, and
speak English slowly—but *not* loudly. *See*
the French Vocabulary and Menu Guide at
the back of the book for more suggestions.

LANGUAGES FOR TRAVELERS

A phrase book and language-tape set can help get you started. *Fodor's French for Travelers* (available at bookstores everywhere) is excellent.

MAIL & SHIPPING

Post offices, or PTT, are scattered throughout every arrondissement and are recognizable by a yellow LA POSTE sign. They are usually open weekdays 8–7, Saturday 8–noon. Airmail letters or postcards usually take at least five days to reach North America, three days to arrive in the U.K., and seven to nine days to reach Australia and New Zealand. When shipping home antiques or art, it's prudent to request assistance from the dealer, who can usually handle the customs paperwork for you or recommend a licensed shipping company.

🛈 Post Offices **Main office** ✉ 52 rue du Louvre, 1er, open 24 hours seven days a week. **Champs-Élysées office** ✉ 10 rue Balzar, 8e, Monday to Saturday, open until 7 PM.

OVERNIGHT SERVICES

Sending overnight mail from Paris is relatively easy. Besides DHL, Federal Express, and UPS, the French post office has an overnight mail service called Chronopost that has special prepaid boxes for international use (and also boxes specifically made to mail wine). All agencies listed can be used as drop-off points, and all have information in English.

🛈 Major Services **DHL** ✉ 6 rue des Colonnes, 2e ☎ 01-55-35-30-30 ⊕ www.dhl.com ✉ 59 ave. Iéna, 16e ☎ 01-45-01-91-00. **Federal Express** ✉ 63 bd. Haussmann, 8e ☎ 01-40-06-90-16 ⊕ www.fedex.com/fr. **UPS** ✉ 34 bd. Malesherbes, 8e ☎ 08-00-87-78-77 ✉ 107 rue Réaumur, 2e ☎ 08-00-87-78-77 ⊕ www.ups.com.

POSTAL RATES

Airmail letters to the United States and Canada cost €.90 for 20 grams, €1.80 for 40 grams, and €2.40 for 60 grams. Letters to the United Kingdom cost €.53 for up to 20 grams, as they do within France. Postcards cost €.55 within France and EU countries and €.90 to the United States and Canada. Stamps can be bought in post offices and cafés displaying a red TABAC sign.

RECEIVING MAIL

If you're uncertain where you'll be staying, have mail sent to American Express (if you're a card member) or to "poste restante" at any post office.

MEDIA

NEWSPAPERS & MAGAZINES

Parisians like their newspapers; kiosks throughout the city are packed with daily papers for every political perspective. French dailies include the right-leaning *Figaro*; the left-leaning *Libération*, often called simply *Libé*; *Équipe*, for the sports lover; and *Le Parisian*, for a *USA Today*-like overview of local and world events. *Le Monde*, one of the most respected newspapers in France, publishes a thick weekend edition, complete with a lifestyle weekly magazine insert and an English-language *New York Times* supplement. Two free general-interest newspapers, *A Nous Paris* and *20 Minutes*, are distributed weekly in larger métro stations. For many Parisians Sunday morning is traditionally reserved for reading; you'll see a casually clad *monsieur* heading home with a bag of croissants in one hand and a weighty stack of magazines and thick Sunday newspapers in the other.

Fashion-centric *Elle* magazine is published weekly here; French *Vogue* and *Numéro* are glam monthly mags. For interior design and lifestyle coverage, check out *Côte Sud, Côte Ouest, Marie Claire Maison,* and *Elle Maison.* Gossip anyone? *Gala* and *Paris Match* have the best of the worst.

RADIO & TELEVISION

Radio in France is an eclectic mix, with a broad variety of music. Most stations broadcast in French. A number of them play Top 40 music, including Cherie FM (91.3), Skyrock (96), NRJ (100.3), Radio Nova (101.5), and Le Mouv' (92). A wide range of music can be found on FIP (105.1); classical on Radio Classique (101.1); '60s–'90s on Nostalgie (90.4); techno on Radio FG (98.2); and the news (in French) on France Info (105.5).

Turn on the television, and you'll find many American shows dubbed into

French. France has both national stations (TF1, France 2, France 3, La Cinq/Arte, and M6) and cable stations, most notably CanalPlus, France's version of HBO.

MÉTRO

Taking the métro is the most efficient way to get around Paris. Métro stations are recognizable either by a large yellow *M* within a circle or by the distinctive curly green Art Nouveau railings and archway bearing the full title (Métropolitain). *See the Métro map, below.*

Fourteen métro and five RER (Réseau Express Régional, or the Regional Express Network) lines crisscross Paris and the suburbs, and you are seldom more than 500 yards from the nearest station. The métro network connects at several points in Paris with the RER, the commuter trains that go from the city center to the suburbs. RER trains crossing Paris on their way from suburb to suburb can be great time-savers because they make only a few stops in the city (you can use the same tickets for the métro and the RER within Paris).

It's essential to know the name of the last station on the line you take, as this name appears on all signs. A connection (you can make as many as you like on one ticket) is called a *correspondance*. At junction stations, illuminated orange signs bearing the name of the line terminus appear over the correct corridors for each correspondance. Illuminated blue signs marked *sortie* indicate the station exit. Note that tickets are valid only inside the gates, or *limites*.

Access to métro and RER platforms is through an automatic ticket barrier. Slide your ticket in and pick it up as it pops out. Be certain to **keep your ticket during your journey;** you'll need it to leave the RER system and in case you run into any green-clad ticket inspectors, who will impose a hefty fine if you can't produce your ticket.

Métro service starts at 5:30 AM and continues until 1 AM, when the last train on each line reaches its terminus. Some lines and stations in Paris are a bit risky at night, in particular Lines 2 and 13, and the mazelike stations at Les Halles and République. But in general, the métro is relatively safe throughout, providing you don't travel alone late at night or walk around with your wallet hanging out of your back pocket.

FARES & SCHEDULES

All métro tickets and passes are valid not only for the métro but also for all RER, tram, and bus travel within Paris. Métro tickets cost €1.40 each; a *carnet* (10 tickets for €10.50) is a better value. The best deal is the unlimited usage *Carte Orange* ticket, sold according to zone. Zones 1 and 2 cover the entire métro network; tickets cost €15.40 a week or €50.40 a month. If you plan to take suburban trains to visit places in Île-de-France, consider a four-zone (Versailles, St-Germain-en-Laye; €25.20 a week) or six-zone (Rambouillet, Fontainebleau; €34 a week) ticket. For these weekly/monthly tickets, you need a pass (available from rail and major métro stations) and a passport-size photograph (many stations have photo booths).

One-day (Mobilis) and two- to five-day (Paris-Visite) tickets assure unlimited travel on the entire RATP (Paris transit authority) network: métro, RER, bus, tram, funicular (Montmartre), and Noctambus (night bus). Unlike the Carte Orange (a weekly pass for unlimited travel which is good from Monday morning to Sunday evening), Mobilis and Paris-Visite passes are valid starting any day of the week. Paris-Visite also gives you discounts on a few museums and attractions. Mobilis tickets cost €5.30. Paris-Visite is €8.35 (one day), €13.70 (two days), €18.25 (three days), and €26.65 (five days) for Paris only. Children ages 4–11 receive approximately 50% off.

🚇 Métro Information **RATP** ⊠ 54 quai de la Rapée, 12ᵉ ⊕ www.ratp.fr, open daily 9–5.

MONEY MATTERS

Although a stay in Paris is far from cheap, you can find plenty of affordable places to eat and shop, particularly if you avoid the obvious tourist traps. Prices tend to reflect the standing of an area in the eyes of Parisians; the touristy area where value is most difficult to find is the 8ᵉ arrondissement, on and around the Champs-Élysées. Places where you can generally be certain to shop, eat, and stay without overpaying include the St-Michel/Sorbonne area on the Left Bank; the mazelike streets around Les Halles and the Marais in central Paris; in Montparnasse south of the boulevard; and in the Bastille, République, and Belleville areas of eastern Paris.

In cafés, bars, and some restaurants you can **save money by eating or drinking at the counter instead of sitting at a table.** Two prices are listed—*au comptoir* (at the counter) and *à salle* (at a table)—and sometimes a third for the terrace. A cup of coffee, standing at a bar, costs from €1.50; if you sit, it will cost €2 to €7. A glass of beer costs from €2 standing and from €2.50 to €7 sitting; a soft drink costs between €2 and €4. A ham sandwich will cost between €3 and €5.

Expect to pay €7–€10 for a short taxi ride. Museum entry is usually between €3.50 and €9.50, though there are hours or days of the week when admission is reduced or free.

Prices throughout this guide are given for adults. Substantially reduced fees are almost always available for children, students, and senior citizens. For information on taxes, *see* Taxes.

ATMS

ATMs are one of the easiest ways to get euros. Although transaction fees may be higher abroad than at home, banks usually offer excellent wholesale exchange rates through ATMs. You may, however, have to look around for Cirrus and Plus locations; it's a good idea to get a list of locations from your bank before you go. Note, too, that you may have better luck with ATMs if you're using a credit card or debit card that is also a Visa or MasterCard rather than just your bank card.

To get cash at ATMs in Paris, **your PIN must be four digits long.** If you are having trouble remembering your PIN, do not try more than twice, because at the third attempt the machine will eat your card, and you will have to go back the next morning

to retrieve it. Note, too, that you may be charged by your bank for using ATMs overseas; inquire at your bank about charges.

CREDIT CARDS

Throughout this guide, the following abbreviations are used: **AE,** American Express; **DC,** Diners Club; **MC,** MasterCard; and **V,** Visa.

📆 Reporting Lost Cards **American Express** ☎ 336/393–1111; call collect. **Diners Club** ☎ 303/799–1504; call collect. **MasterCard** ☎ 0800/90–1387. **Visa** ☎ 0800/90–1179, 410/581–9994 collect.

CURRENCY

In 2002 the single European Union (EU) currency, the euro, became the official currency of the 12 countries participating in the European Monetary Union (with the notable exceptions of Great Britain, Denmark, and Sweden). The euro system has eight coins: 1 and 2 euros, plus 1, 2, 5, 10, 20, and 50 cents. All coins have one side that has the value of the euro on it, while the opposite side is adorned with each country's own unique national symbol. There are seven colorful notes: 5, 10, 20, 50, 100, 200, and 500 euros. Notes have the principal architectural styles from antiquity onward on one side and the map and the flag of Europe on the other and are the same for all countries. When you first change your money, **memorize the coins as soon as you can** (notes are much easier to distinguish). Also be aware that due to their high nickel content euro coins can pose problems for people with an allergic sensitivity to the metal. If you're sensitive to nickel, try to handle the coins as little as possible, and when you do handle them, rinse your hands as soon as you can.

If you've brought some rumpled francs from home this trip, you can still exchange them. You have until midnight February 17, 2012, to change notes at the Banque de France. A fixed rate of exchange was established: 1 euro equaling 6.55957 French francs. After this date, however, you may as well frame those remaining francs and hang them on the wall for posterity, not prosperity.

CURRENCY EXCHANGE

At this writing, 1 euro equaled approximately U.S.$1.30, 1.60 Canadian dollars, 1.65 Australian dollars, 1.75 New Zealand dollars, and 0.68 pound sterling.

The easiest way to get euros is through ATMs; you can find them in airports, train stations, and throughout the city. ATM rates are excellent because they are based on wholesale rates offered only by major banks. It's a good idea, however, to bring some euros with you from home and always to have some cash and traveler's checks as backup. For the best deal when exchanging currencies not within the Monetary Union purview (the U.S. dollar, the yen, and the English pound are examples), compare rates at banks (which usually have the most favorable rates) and booths, and look for exchange booths that clearly state "no commission." At exchange booths always confirm the rate with the teller before exchanging money. You won't do as well at exchange booths in airports or rail and bus stations, in hotels, in restaurants, or in stores. Of all the banks in Paris, the Banque de France has the best rates. To avoid lines at airport exchange booths, **get enough euros before you leave home to cover any immediate necessity.**

🗂 Exchange Services **International Currency Express** ✉ 427 N. Camden Dr., Suite F, Beverly Hills, CA 90210 ☎ 888/278-6628 orders 🖷 310/278-6410 ⊕ www.foreignmoney.com. **Travel Ex Currency Services** ☎ 800/287-7362 orders and retail locations ⊕ www.travelex.com.

TRAVELER'S CHECKS

Do you need traveler's checks? It depends on where you're headed. If you're going to rural areas and small towns, go with cash; traveler's checks are best used in cities. Lost or stolen checks can usually then be replaced within 24 hours. To ensure a speedy refund, buy your own traveler's checks—don't let someone else pay for them: irregularities like this can cause delays. The person who bought the checks should make the call to request a refund.

PACKING

You'll notice it right away: the women dress well to go shopping, to go to the cinema, to have a drink; the men look good

when they are fixing their cars. The Parisians are a people who still wear hats to the races and well-cut clothes for fine meals; you will not see them in sweats unless they are doing something *sportif*. **Don't wear shorts, sweats, or sneakers if you want to blend in.** Good food in good settings deserves good clothing—not necessarily a suit and tie, but a long-sleeved shirt and pants for him, something nice for her. Trendy nightclubs usually refuse entrance to men who are wearing sandals.

Be sure to **bring rain gear, a comfortable pair of walking shoes, and a sweater** or shawl for cool churches and museums. If you'd like to scrutinize stained glass, bring a pair of small binoculars. A small package of tissues is always a good idea for the occasional rustic bathroom in cafés, airports, and train stations.

In your carry-on luggage, pack an extra pair of eyeglasses or contact lenses and enough of any medication you take to last a few days longer than the entire trip. You may also ask your doctor to write a spare prescription using the drug's generic name, as brand names may vary from country to country. In luggage to be checked, **never pack prescription drugs, valuables, or undeveloped film.** And don't forget to carry with you the addresses of offices that handle refunds of lost traveler's checks. Check *Fodor's How to Pack* (available at online retailers and bookstores everywhere) for more tips.

To avoid customs and security delays, carry medications in their original packaging. Don't pack any sharp objects in your carry-on luggage, including knives of any size or material, scissors, nail clippers, and corkscrews, or anything else that might arouse suspicion.

To avoid having your checked luggage chosen for hand inspection, don't cram bags full. The U.S. Transportation Security Administration suggests packing shoes on top and placing personal items you don't want touched in clear plastic bags.

CHECKING LUGGAGE

You're allowed to carry aboard one bag and one personal article, such as a purse or a laptop computer. Make sure what you carry on fits under your seat or in the overhead bin. Get to the gate early, so you can board as soon as possible, before the overhead bins fill up.

Baggage allowances vary by carrier, destination, and ticket class. On international flights, you're usually allowed to check two bags weighing up to 70 pounds (32 kilograms) each, although a few airlines allow checked bags of up to 88 pounds (40 kilograms) in first class. Some international carriers don't allow more than 66 pounds (30 kilograms) per bag in business class and 44 pounds (20 kilograms) in economy. If you're flying to or through the United Kingdom, your luggage cannot exceed 70 pounds (32 kilograms) per bag. On domestic flights, the limit is usually 50 to 70 pounds (23 to 32 kilograms) per bag. In general, carry-on bags shouldn't exceed 40 pounds (18 kilograms). Most airlines won't accept bags that weigh more than 100 pounds (45 kilograms) on domestic or international flights. Expect to pay a fee for baggage that exceeds weight limits. Check baggage restrictions with your carrier before you pack.

Airline liability for baggage is limited to $2, 500 per person on flights within the United States. On international flights it amounts to $9.07 per pound or $20 per kilogram for checked baggage (roughly $640 per 70-pound bag), with a maximum of $634.90 per piece, and $400 per passenger for unchecked baggage. You can buy additional coverage at check-in for about $10 per $1, 000 of coverage, but it often excludes a rather extensive list of items, shown on your airline ticket.

Before departure, itemize your bags' contents and their worth, and label the bags with your name, address, and phone number. (If you use your home address, cover it so potential thieves can't see it readily.) Include a label inside each bag and **pack a copy of your itinerary.** At check-in, make sure each bag is correctly tagged with the destination airport's three-letter code. Because some checked bags will be opened for hand inspection, the U.S. Transportation Security Administration recommends

that you leave luggage unlocked or use the plastic locks offered at check-in. TSA screeners place an inspection notice inside searched bags, which are re-sealed with a special lock.

If your bag has been searched and contents are missing or damaged, file a claim with the TSA Consumer Response Center as soon as possible. If your bags arrive damaged or fail to arrive at all, file a written report with the airline before leaving the airport.

⏏ Complaints U.S. Transportation Security Administration Contact Center ☎ 866/289-9673 ⊕ www.tsa.gov.

PASSPORTS & VISAS

When traveling internationally, carry your passport even if you don't need one (it's always the best form of I.D.) and **make two photocopies of the data page** (one for someone at home and another for you, carried separately from your passport). If you lose your passport, promptly call the nearest embassy or consulate and the local police.

U.S. passport applications for children under age 14 require consent from both parents or legal guardians; both parents must appear together to sign the application. If only one parent appears, he or she must submit a written statement from the other parent authorizing passport issuance for the child. A parent with sole authority must present evidence of it when applying; acceptable documentation includes the child's certified birth certificate listing only the applying parent, a court order specifically permitting this parent's travel with the child, or a death certificate for the nonapplying parent. Application forms and instructions are available on the Web site of the U.S. State Department's Bureau of Consular Affairs (⊕ travel.state.gov).

ENTERING FRANCE

All citizens of Australia, Canada, New Zealand, the United States, and the United Kingdom, even infants, need only a valid passport to enter France for stays of up to 90 days. If you lose your passport, promptly call the nearest embassy or consulate and the local police.

PASSPORT OFFICES

The best time to apply for a passport or to renew is in fall and winter. Before any trip, check your passport's expiration date, and, if necessary, renew it as soon as possible.

🌠 Australian Citizens **Passports Australia** Australian Department of Foreign Affairs and Trade ☎ 131-232 ⊕ www.passports.gov.au.

🌠 Canadian Citizens **Passport Office** ✉ to mail in applications: 70 Cremazie St., Gatineau, Québec J8Y 3P2 ☎ 819/994-3500 or 800/567-6868 ⊕ www.ppt.gc.ca.

🌠 New Zealand Citizens **New Zealand Passports Office** ☎ 0800/22-5050 or 04/474-8100 ⊕ www.passports.govt.nz.

🌠 U.K. Citizens **U.K. Passport Service** ☎ 0870/521-0410 ⊕ www.passport.gov.uk.

🌠 U.S. Citizens **National Passport Information Center** ☎ 877/487-2778, 888/874-7793 TDD/TTY ⊕ travel.state.gov.

RESTROOMS

Use of public toilet facilities in cafés and bars is usually reserved for customers, so you may need to buy a little something first. Bathrooms are often downstairs and are usually unisex, which may mean walking by a men's urinal to reach the cubicle. Turkish-style toilets—holes in the ground surrounded by porcelain pads for your feet—are still found (though becoming scarcer). Stand as far away as possible when you press the flushing mechanism in order to avoid water damage to your shoes. In certain cafés the lights will not come on in the bathroom until the cubicle door is locked. These lights work on a three-minute timer to save electricity. Simply press the button again if the lights go out. Clean public toilets are available in fast-food chains, department stores, and public parks. You can also find pay-per-use toilet units on the street, which require €.40. There are bathrooms in the larger métro stations, town halls, and in all train stations, too.

There are restroom attendants in train and métro stations and some of the nicer restaurants and clubs, so always **bring some coins to the bathroom.** In train and métro stations you'll pay the attendant €.50–€2 for use of the public facility;

generally you'll drop your money in a saucer near the entrance or sinks. Attendants in restaurants and the like are in charge of cleaning the bathrooms and perhaps handing you a clean towel; slip some small change into the prominently placed saucer.

SAFETY

Paris is one of the safest big cities in the world, but as in any giant metropolis it's always best to **be streetwise and alert.** Certain neighborhoods are more seedy than dangerous, thanks to the night trade that goes on around Les Halles and St-Denis and on boulevard Clichy in Pigalle. Some off-the-beaten-path neighborhoods— particularly the outlying suburban communities around Paris–may warrant extra precaution. When in doubt stick to the boulevards and well-lit, populated streets, but keep in mind that even the Champs-Elysées is a haven for pickpockets.

The métro is quite safe overall, though some lines and stations, in particular Lines 2 and 13, get dodgy late at night. Try not to travel alone late at night, memorize the time of the last métro train to your station, ride in the first car by the conductor, and just use your common sense. Pickpocketing is the main problem, day or night. **Be wary of anyone crowding you unnecessarily** or distracting you. Pickpockets often work in groups; on the métro they usually strike just before a stop so that they can leap off the train as it pulls into the station. Be especially careful if taking the RER from Charles de Gaulle/Roissy airport into town; disoriented or jet-lagged travelers are vulnerable to sticky fingers. Pickpockets often target laptop bags, so keep your valuables on your person.

Don't wear a money belt or a waist pack, both of which peg you as a tourist. Distribute your cash and any valuables (including your credit cards and passport) between a deep front pocket, an inside jacket or vest pocket, and a hidden money pouch. Do not reach for the money pouch once you're in public.

A tremendous number of protest demonstrations are held in Paris—scarcely a week goes by without some kind of march or public gathering. Most protests are peaceful, but it's best to avoid them. The CRS (French riot police) carefully guard all major demonstrations, directing traffic and preventing violence. They are armed and use tear gas when and if they see fit. **Report any thefts or other problems to the police** as soon as possible. There are three or four police stations in every arrondissement in Paris and one police station in every train station; go to the police station in the area where the event occurred. In the case of pickpocketing or other theft, the police will give you a Déclaration de Perte ou de Vol (receipt for theft or loss). Police reports must be made in person but the process is generally quite streamlined. In the case of theft, valuables are usually unrecoverable but identity documents have been known to resurface. You may need a receipt of theft or loss to replace stolen train or plane tickets, passports, or traveler's checks; the receipts may also be useful for filing insurance claims.

WOMEN IN PARIS

Although women traveling alone sometimes encounter troublesome comments and the like, *dragueurs* (men who persistently profess their undying love to hapless female passersby) are a dying breed in this increasingly politically correct world. Note that smiling automatically out of politeness is not part of French culture and can be quickly misinterpreted. If you encounter a problem, don't be afraid to show your irritation. Completely ignoring the *dragueur* should be discouragement enough; if the hassling doesn't let up, don't hesitate to move quickly away.

If you carry a purse, choose one with a zipper and a thick strap that you can drape across your body; adjust the length so that the purse sits in front of you at or above hip level. (Don't wear a money belt or a waist pack.) Store only enough money in the purse to cover casual spending. Distribute the rest of your cash and any valuables between deep front pockets, inside jacket or vest pockets, and a concealed money pouch.

SENIOR-CITIZEN TRAVEL

Travelers to Paris 60 years or older can take advantage of many discounts, such as reduced admissions of 20%–50% to museums and movie theaters. For rail travel outside Paris, the Carte Senior entitles travelers 60 years and older to discounts (⇨ Train Travel).

To qualify for age-related discounts, mention your senior-citizen status up front when booking hotel reservations (not when checking out) and before you're seated in restaurants (not when paying the bill). Be sure to have identification on hand. When renting a car, ask about promotional car-rental discounts, which can be cheaper than senior-citizen rates.

🖪 **Educational Programs Elderhostel** ✉ 11 Ave. de Lafayette, Boston, MA 02111-1746 ☎ 877/426-8056, 978/323-4141 international callers, 877/426-2167 TTY 🖷 877/426-2166 ⊕ www.elderhostel.org. **Interhostel** ✉ University of New Hampshire, 6 Garrison Ave., Durham, NH 03824 ☎ 603/862-1147 or 800/733-9753 🖷 603/862-1113 ⊕ www.learn.unh.edu.

SIGHTSEEING TOURS

BIKE & SEGWAY TOURS

Cycling is a wonderful way to get a different view of Paris and work off all those three-course "snacks." A number of companies organize bike tours around Paris and its environs (Versailles, Chantilly, and Fontainebleau); these tours always include bikes, helmets, and an English-speaking guide. Costs start at around €25 for a half-day; reservations are strongly recommended. *See* Sports & the Outdoors for more information.

Fat Tire Bike Tours, formerly known as Mike's Bike Tours, is the best-known anglophone group. In addition to a general orientation bike tour, they organize a nighttime cycling trip that includes a boat cruise on the Seine. They also offer Segway tours around the city; these are considerably more expensive, at €70. Maison Roue Libre runs both city-center and countryside tours; request an English guide when you call. Paris à Vélo, C'est Sympa offers thematic tours; the Paris Wakes Up tour, for instance, is a unique spin through Montmartre at 6 AM. **Fat Tire Bike Tours** ✉ 24 rue Edgar Faure, 15ᵉ ☎ 01-56-58-10-54 ⊕ www. FatTireBikeToursParis.com. **Maison Roue Libre** ✉ 1 passage Mondétour, 1ᵉʳ ☎ 01-48-15-28-88 ⊕ www. ratp.fr. **Paris à Vélo, C'est Sympa** ✉ 37 bd. Bourdon, 4ᵉ ☎ 01-48-87-60-01 ⊕ www.parisvelosympa.com.

BOAT TOURS

Boat trips along the Seine run throughout the day and evening for a cost of €6–€15. Many of the tours include lunch or dinner for an average cost of €50–€100, although the scenery is usually more impressive than the cuisine. Reservations for meals are usually essential, and some require jacket and tie.

The massive, double-decker Bateaux Mouches depart from the Pont de l'Alma (Right Bank); from April to September they leave daily every half hour from 10 AM to 11 PM and from October through March they sail daily approximately every three hours from 11 to 9. Recorded commentary plays in seven languages. The large, glass-roofed Bateaux Parisiens depart from the foot of the Eiffel Tower every half hour from 10 AM to 11 PM April through November and hourly from 10 to 10 the rest of the year. The live or recorded commentary is in four languages. Some travelers may prefer the smaller Vedettes du Pont Neuf, which offer one-hour trips with live commentary in French and English; boats depart daily from square du Vert Galant every 30–60 minutes from 10 AM to 10:30 PM (with a lunch break from noon to 1:30) March through October, and from 10:30 to 10 with a noon-to-2 lunch break November through February.

The quietest Seine cruise is the commentary-free Batobus, a boat-bus service used by Parisians to get from one end of town to the other with the advantage that you can get on and off at any one of eight stops along the river, including the Eiffel Tower, Musée d'Orsay, St. Germain-des-Prés, the Louvre, Notre-Dame, and the Champs-Élysées. Get a one-day pass for €11, or buy a two-consecutive-days pass for €13. It operates every half hour from 10:30 to 4:30 early February through

mid-March and early November through early January; from 10 to 7 mid-March through April and October through early November; and from 10 to 10 May through September. There's no service early January through early February. Ask about the combined Batobus and L'Open-Tour bus packages.

Canauxrama organizes leisurely canal tours year-round in flat-bottom barges along the Canal St-Martin in east Paris. There are four daily departures; the trips last about 2½ hours and have live commentary in both French and English. Reservations are required. Paris Canal runs 2½-hour trips with live bilingual commentary between the Musée d'Orsay and the Parc de La Villette from April to mid-November. Reservations are required. Yachts de Paris organizes romantic 2½-hour "gourmand cruises" (for about €165) year-round. Yachts set off every evening at 7:45; you'll be served a three-course meal while you skim along the Seine.

Bateaux Mouches ✉ Pont de l'Alma, 8ᵉ ☎ 01-42-25-96-10 ⊕ www.bateauxmouches.com. **Bateaux Parisiens-Tour Eiffel** ✉ Port de la Bourdonnais, 7ᵉ ☎ 08-25-01-01-01 ⊕ www. bateauxparisiens.com. **Batobus** ✉ Port de la Bourdonnais, 7ᵉ ☎ 01-44-11-33-99 ⊕ www.batobus. com. **Canauxrama** ✉ 13 quai de la Loire, 19ᵉ ✉ Bassin de l'Arsenal, 12ᵉ ☎ 01-42-39-15-00 ⊕ www.canauxrama.com. **Paris Canal** ✉ 19 quai de la Loire, 19ᵉ ☎ 01-42-40-96-97 ⊕ www.pariscanal. com. **Vedettes du Pont Neuf** ✉ Île de la Cité, 1ᵉʳ ☎ 01-46-33-98-38 ⊕ www.vedettesdupontneuf. com. **Yachts de Paris** ✉ Port de Javel, 4ᵉ ☎ 01-44-54-14-70 ⊕ www.yachtsdeparis.com.

BUS TOURS

The two largest bus-tour operators are Cityrama, with 90-minute double-decker tours for €15, and Paris Vision, a two-hour luxury coach tour for €19. Both have headsets for commentary in more than a dozen languages. For a more intimate—albeit expensive—tour of the city, Paris Vision also runs minibus excursions with a multilingual tour operator from €49. Paris L'OpenTour gives tours in a London-style double-decker bus with English or French commentary piped over individual headsets. You can catch the bus at any of 50 pickup points; tickets cost €24 for one day, €27 for unlimited use for two days. Les Cars Rouges also has hop-on/hop-off tours on double-decker London-style buses, but with only nine stops. A ticket good for two consecutive days costs €22.

For a more economical and commentary-free trip, why not take a regular Parisian bus for a mere €1.40 per ticket? A special Montmartrobus (€1.40) runs from the Anvers métro station to the top of Montmartre's winding streets. The RATP's Balabus goes from Gare du Lyon to the Grand Arche de la Défense, passing by dozens of major sights on the way. The Balabus runs from mid-April through September; tickets are €1.40 each, with one to three tickets required depending on how far you travel.

🚌 **Les Cars Rouge** ☎ 01-53-95-39-53 ⊕ www. carsrouges.com. **Cityrama** ✉ 4 pl. des Pyramides, 1ᵉʳ ☎ 01-44-55-61-00 ⊕ www.cityrama.com. **Paris L'OpenTour** ☎ 01-42-66-56-56 ⊕ www.paris-opentour.com. **Paris Vision** ✉ 214 rue de Rivoli, 1ᵉʳ ☎ 01-42-60-30-01 ⊕ www.parisvision.com. **RATP** ☎ 08-92-68-41-14, €.35 per minute ⊕ www.ratp.fr.

HELICOPTER TOURS
For a spectacular aerial view of Paris, Hélifrance offers a helicopter tour; it takes off from Paris Le Bourget airport (20 minutes from Paris). Tours last 25–35 minutes and cost €122–€149 per person.

🚁 **Hélifrance** ☎ 01-48-35-90-44 ⊕ www. helifrance.fr.

MINIBUS TOURS
Paris Trip and Paris Major Limousine organize tours of Paris and environs by limousine, Mercedes, or minibus (for 4–15 passengers) for a minimum of four hours. Chauffers are bilingual. The price varies from €260 to €400. Reservations are essential.

🚐 **Paris Major Limousine** ✉ 6 pl. de la Madeleine, 8ᵉ ☎ 01-44-52-50-00 ⊕ www.1st-limousine-services.com. **Paris Trip** ✉ 2 Cité de Pusy, Vincennes ☎ 01-43-65-55-55 ⊕ www.paris-trip.com.

SPECIAL-INTEREST TOURS
Has it been a while since Art History 101? Paris Muse can help guide you through the city's museums; with its staff of art historians (all native English-speakers) you can crack the Da Vinci code or gain a new understanding of Hell in front of Rodin's sculpted gates. Rates run from €60 to €120, including museum admission.

If you'd like a bit of guidance flexing your own artistic muscles, catch a themed photography tour with Paris Photo Tours. Run by the transplanted Texan Linda Mathieu, these relaxed tours are perfect for first-time visitors and anyone hoping to improve their vacation photography abilities.

Sign up with Chic Shopping Paris to smoothly navigate the city's shopping scene. You can choose a set tour, such as Shabby Chic (vintage/secondhand places) or Made in France (unique French products), or ask for an itinerary tailor-made to your interests. Tours start at €100.

Edible Paris, the brainchild of food writer and Fodor's updater Rosa Jackson, is a customized itinerary service for food-oriented visitors. Submit a wish list of your interests and guidelines for your tastes, and you'll receive a personalized itinerary, maps, and restaurant reservations on request. Prices start around $200. If you'd like a behind-the-scenes look at food in the capital, contact Culinary Concepts; Stephanie Curtis's tours will take you to Rungis, the gigantic professional food market on the outskirts of Paris at €120 per person. The Rungis trip starts at 5 AM and needs to be booked a month in advance with a minimum of three people. Or try the bread, cheese, and wine walking tour for €120, which takes you into cheese and wine cellars and to the wood-burning ovens at the celebrated Poîlane bakery.

🛍 **Chic Shopping Paris** ☎ 06-14-56-23-11 ⊕ www.chicshoppingparis.com. **Culinary Concepts** ✉ 10 rue Poussin, 75016 ☎ 01-45-27-09-09 ✏ stecurtis@aol.com. **Edible Paris** ⊕ www. edible-paris.com. **Paris Muse** ☎ 06-73-77-33-52 ⊕ www.parismuse.com. **Paris Photo Tours** ☎ 01-44-75-83-80 ⊕ http://parisphototours.com.

WALKING TOURS
The team at Paris Walking Tours offers a wide selection of tours, from neighborhood

visits to museum tours and theme tours such as the Hemingway's Paris, The Marais, Montmartre, and The Latin Quarter itineraries. The guides are very knowledgeable, taking you into less trammeled streets and divulging interesting stories about even the most unprepossessing spots. A two-hour group tour costs €10. For a more intimate experience, Context Paris offers specialized in-depth tours of the city's art and architecture by English-speaking architects and art historians. Prices range from €150 per group (maximum five people) for a two-hour Introductory Paris walk, to €200 for a three-hour Gothic Paris tour.

Black Paris Tours offers tours exploring the places made famous by African-American musicians, writers, artists, and political exiles. Tours include a 4- to 5-hour walking-bus-métro tour (€80) that offers first-time visitors a city orientation and a primer on the history of African-Americans in Paris.

The English-speaking guides at Paris Gardens give specialized tours of the city's many green spaces, from 17th-century royal gardens to 21st-century parks. Walking tours start at €15 per person, or contact Director Robin Watson for information on custom tours for Paris and the Île-de-France.

A list of walking tours is also available from the Caisse Nationale des Monuments Historiques, in the weekly magazine *Pariscope,* and in *L'Officiel des Spectacles,* which lists walking tours under the heading "*Conférences*" (most are in French, unless otherwise noted). The magazines are available at press kiosks.

🎌 **Black Paris Tours** ☎ 01-46-37-03-96. **Caisse Nationale des Monuments Historiques** ✉ Bureau des Visites/Conférences, Hôtel de Sully, 62 rue St-Antoine, 4ᵉ ☎ 01-44-61-21-70. **Context Paris** ☎ 06-13-09-67-11 ⊕ www.contextparis.com. **Paris Gardens** ☎ 01-47-41-21-59 ⊕ www.parisgardens. info. **Paris Walking Tours** ☎ 01-48-09-21-40 ⊕ www.paris-walks.com.

STUDENTS IN PARIS

Students of any age armed with an international student ID card are eligible for various discounts, from 10% off the price of movie tickets to reduced train fares. For a detailed listing of deals for students in Paris, ask for the brochure *Jeunes à Paris* from the main tourist office.

🎌 **I.D.s & Services STA Travel** ✉ 10 Downing St., New York, NY 10014 ☎ 212/627-3111, 800/777-0112 24-hr service center 🖷 212/627-3387 ⊕ www.sta. com. **Travel Cuts** ✉ 187 College St., Toronto, Ontario M5T 1P7, Canada ☎ 800/592-2887 in the U.S., 416/979-2406 or 866/246-9762 in Canada 🖷 416/979-8167 ⊕ www.travelcuts.com.

TAXES

All taxes must be included in affixed prices in France. Prices in **restaurants and hotel prices must by law include taxes and service charges:** If these appear as additional items on your bill, you should complain.

VALUE-ADDED TAX

V.A.T. (value-added tax, known in France as TVA), at a standard rate of 19.6% (33% for luxury goods), is included in the price of many goods, but foreigners are often entitled to a refund. To be eligible for V.A.T. refund, the item (or items) that you have purchased must have been bought in a single day in a single place and must equal or exceed €182. The V.A.T. for services (restaurants/theater, etc.) is not refundable.

When making a purchase, **ask for a V.A.T. refund form** and find out whether the merchant gives refunds—not all stores do, nor are they required to. Have the form stamped like any customs form by customs officials when you leave the country or, if you're visiting several European Union countries, when you leave the EU. Be ready to show customs officials what you've bought (pack purchases together, in your carry-on luggage); budget extra time for this. After you're through passport control, take the form to a refund-service counter for an on-the-spot refund, or mail it to the address on the form (or the envelope with it) after you arrive home.

A service processes refunds for most shops. You receive the total refund stated on the form. Global Refund is a Europewide service with 210, 000 affiliated stores and more than 700 refund counters—located at major airports and border crossings. Its refund form is called a Tax Free Check. The service issues refunds in the form of cash, check, or credit-card adjustment. If you don't have time to wait at the refund counter, you can mail in the form instead.

⊟ V.A.T. Refunds Global Refund ⊠ 99 Main St., Suite 307, Nyack, NY 10960 ☎ 800/566-9828 ⌂ 845/348-1549 ⊕ www.globalrefund.com.

TAXIS

Taxi rates are based on location and time. Daytime rates, denoted A (7 AM–7 PM), within Paris are €.62 per kilometer (½ mi), and nighttime rates, B, are €1.06 per kilometer. Suburban zones and airports, C, are €1.24 per kilometer. There is a basic hire charge of €2 for all rides, a €1 supplement per piece of luggage, and a €.75 supplement if you're picked up at an SNCF station. Waiting time is charged at €26.23 per hour. The easiest way to get a taxi is to **ask your hotel or a restaurant to call a taxi for you, or go to the nearest taxi stand** (you can find one every couple of blocks). Taxi stands are marked by a square dark blue sign with a white T in the middle. People waiting for cabs often form a line but will jump at any available taxi; be firm and don't let people cut in front of you. Cabs with their signs lighted can be hailed but are annoyingly difficult to spot (and they are not all a single uniform color). Chauffeurs take a fourth passenger for an average supplement of €2.60. It is customary to tip the driver about 10% (⇨ Tipping).

⊟ Taxi Companies Airport Taxi ☎ 08-25-16-66-66. **Taxis Bleus** ☎ 08-25-16-10-10. **Taxi G7** ☎ 01-47-39-47-39.

TELEPHONES
AREA & COUNTRY CODES

The country code for France is 33. The first two digits of French numbers are a prefix determined by zone: Paris and Île-de-France, 01; the northwest, 02; the northeast, 03; the southeast, 04; and the southwest, 05. Pay close attention to numbers beginning with 08. Calls that begin with 08 followed by 00 are toll-free, but calls that begin with 08 followed by 36—like the information lines for the SNCF for example—cost €.35 per minute, so be

careful. Numbers that begin with 06 are reserved for cell phones.

Note that **when dialing France from abroad, drop the initial 0 from the telephone number** (all numbers listed in this book include the initial 0, which is used for calling numbers *from within* France). To call a telephone number in Paris from the United States, dial 011–33 plus the phone number, but minus the initial 0 listed for the specific number in Paris. In other words, the local number for the Louvre is 01–40–20–51–51. To call this number from New York City, dial 011–33–1–40–20–51–51. To call this number from within Paris, dial 01–40–20–51–51. To call France from the United Kingdom, dial 00–33, then dial the number in France minus the initial 0 of the specific number.

CELL PHONES

Cell phones are called *portables* and most Parisians have one. British standard cell phones work in Paris, but for North Americans only tri-band phones work. If you'd like to rent a cell phone for your trip, reserve one at least four days before your departure, as most companies will ship it to you before you travel. CellularAbroad rents cell phones packaged with prepaid SIM cards that give you a French cell-phone number and calling rates. Planetfone rents GSM phones, which can be used in more than 100 countries.

⊟ Cell Phone Rentals CellularAbroad ☎ 800/287-3020 ⊕ www.cellularabroad.com. **Planetfone** ☎ 888/988-4777 ⊕ www.planetfone.com.

DIRECTORY & OPERATOR ASSISTANCE

To find a number in France, **dial 12 for information.** For international inquiries dial 08–36–59–32–12 for a bilingual (French/English) operator; you can request two numbers per call for a service charge of €3.

INTERNATIONAL CALLS

To make a direct international call out of France, dial 00 and wait for the tone; then dial the country code (1 for the United States and Canada, 44 for the United Kingdom, 61 for Australia, and 64 for New Zealand) and the area code (minus any initial 0) and number.

Good news—telephone rates are actually decreasing in France because the France Telecom monopoly now has some stringent competition. As in most countries, the highest rates fall between 8 AM and 7 PM and average out to a hefty €.22 per minute to the United States, Canada, and the closer European countries including Germany and Great Britain. Rates are greatly reduced from 7 PM to 8 AM, costing an average of €.10 per minute.

To call home with the help of an operator, dial the toll-free number 08–00–99–00 plus the last two digits of the country code. Dial 08–00–99–00–11 for the United States and Canada, 08–00–99–00–44 for England, and 08–00–99–00–61 for Australia.

Telephone cards are sold that enable you to make long-distance and international calls from any phone. Don't hesitate to invest in one if you plan on making calls from your hotel, as hotels often accumulate service charges and also have the most expensive rates.

LOCAL CALLS

Since all local numbers in Paris and the Île-de-France begin with a 01, you must dial the full 10-digit number, including the initial 0. A local call costs €.11 for every three minutes.

LONG-DISTANCE CALLS

To call from region to region within France, dial the full 10-digit number, including the initial 0.

LONG-DISTANCE SERVICES

AT&T, MCI, and Sprint access codes make calling long-distance relatively convenient, but you may find the local access number blocked in many hotel rooms. First ask the hotel operator to connect you. If the hotel operator balks, ask for an international operator, or dial the international operator yourself. One way to improve your odds of getting connected to your long-distance carrier is to travel with more than one company's calling card (a hotel may block Sprint, for example, but not MCI). If all else fails, call from a pay phone.

Access Codes AT&T Direct ☎ 08-00-99-00-11 or 08-00-99-01-11, 800/222-0300 for information. **MCI WorldPhone** ☎ 08-00-99-00-19, 800/444-4444 for information. **Sprint International Access** ☎ 08-00-99-00-87, 800/793-1153 for information.

PHONE CARDS

All French pay phones are operated by *télé-cartes* (phone cards), which you can buy from post offices, tabacs, magazine kiosks, and any métro station. There are as many phone cards these days as bakeries, so to be safe, request the *télécarte international*, which, despite its name, allows you to make either local or international calls and offers greatly reduced rates. Instructions are in English, and the cost is €8 for 60 units and €16 for 120 units. You may also request the simple *télécarte*, which allows you to make calls in France (the cost is €9 for 50 units, €16.25 for 120 units). You can also use your credit card in much the same way as a télécarte, but there's a minimum €20 charge. You have thirty days after the first call on your credit card to use up the €20 credit.

PUBLIC PHONES

Public telephone booths can almost always be found in post offices, métro stations, bus stops, and in most cafés, as well as on the street.

TIME

The time difference between New York and Paris is 6 hours (so when it's 1 PM in New York, it's 7 PM in Paris). The time difference between London and Paris is one hour; between Sydney and Paris, 8–9 hours; and between Auckland and Paris, 12 hours.

All schedules, whether train, plane, or theater, work on a 24-hour, or "continual, " clock in France, which means that 8 AM is 8h00, but 8 PM is 20h00. Midnight is 24h00. The European format for abbreviating dates is day/month/year, so 7/5/05 means May 7, not July 5.

TIPPING

Bills in bars and restaurants must, by law, include service, but it is customary to round out your bill with some small change unless you're dissatisfied. The amount varies—from €.20 for a beer to €1–€2 after a meal. In expensive restaurants it's common to leave an additional 5% of the bill on the table.

Tip taxi drivers and hairdressers about 10% of the bill. Give theater ushers €.50. In some theaters and hotels cloakroom attendants may expect nothing (watch for signs that say *pourboire interdit*—tipping forbidden); otherwise, give them €.75. Washroom attendants usually get €.30, though the sum is often posted.

If you stay more than two or three days in a hotel, it is customary to leave something for the chambermaid—about €1.50 per day. Expect to pay about €1.50 (€.75 in a moderately priced hotel) to the person who carries your bags or who hails you a taxi. In hotels providing room service, give €1 to the waiter (this does not apply if breakfast is routinely served in your room). If the chambermaid does some pressing or laundering for you, give her €1.50–€2 on top of the bill. If the concierge has been very helpful, it is customary to leave a tip of €8–€16, depending on the type of hotel and the level of service.

Service-station attendants get nothing for pumping gas or checking oil but €.75 or €1.50 for checking tires. Train and airport porters get a fixed sum (€1–€1.50) per bag. Museum guides should get €1.50–€3 after a guided tour. It is standard practice to tip bus drivers about €2 after an excursion.

TOURS & PACKAGES

Because everything is prearranged on a prepackaged tour or independent vacation, you spend less time planning—and often get it all at a good price.

BOOKING WITH AN AGENT

Travel agents are excellent resources. But it's a good idea to collect brochures from several agencies, as some agents' suggestions may be influenced by relationships with tour and package firms that reward them for volume sales. If you have a special interest, find an agent with expertise in that area; the American Society of Travel Agents (ASTA; ⇨ Travel Agencies) has a database of specialists worldwide. You can log on to the group's Web site to find an ASTA travel agent in your neighborhood.

Make sure your travel agent knows the accommodations and other services of the place being recommended. Ask about the hotel's location, room size, beds, and whether it has a pool, room service, or programs for children, if you care about these. Has your agent been there in person or sent others whom you can contact?

Do some homework on your own, too: local tourism boards can provide information about lesser-known and small-niche operators, some of which may sell only direct.

BUYER BEWARE

Each year consumers are stranded or lose their money when tour operators—even large ones with excellent reputations—go out of business. So check out the operator. Ask several travel agents about its reputation, and try to **book with a company that has a consumer-protection program.** (Look for information in the company's brochure.) In the United States, members of the United States Tour Operators Association are required to set aside funds (up to $1 million) to help eligible customers cover payments and travel arrangements in the event that the company defaults. It's also a good idea to choose a company that participates in the American Society of Travel Agents' Tour Operator Program; ASTA will act as mediator in any disputes between you and your tour operator.

Remember that the more your package or tour includes, the better you can predict the ultimate cost of your vacation. Make sure you know exactly what is covered, and beware of hidden costs. Are taxes, tips, and transfers included? Entertainment and excursions? These can add up.

F Tour-Operator Recommendations **American Society of Travel Agents** (⇨ Travel Agencies). **National Tour Association (NTA)** ✉ 546 E. Main St., Lexington, KY 40508 ☎ 859/226-4444 or 800/682-8886 🖷 859/226-4404 ⊕ www.ntaonline.com. **United States Tour Operators Association (USTOA)** ✉ 275 Madison Ave., Suite 2014, New York, NY 10016 ☎ 212/599-6599 🖷 212/599-6744 ⊕ www.ustoa.com.

TRAIN TRAVEL

The SNCF, France's rail system, is fast, punctual, comfortable, and comprehensive. There are various options: local trains, overnight trains with sleeping accommodations, and the high-speed TGV, or Trains à Grande Vitesse (averaging 255 kph [160 mph] on the Lyon/southeast line and 300 kph [190 mph] on the Lille and Bordeaux/southwest lines).

The TGVs, the fastest way to get around the country, operate between Paris and Lille/Calais, Paris and Lyon/Switzerland/Provence, Paris and Angers/Nantes, Paris and Tours/Poitiers/Bordeaux, Paris and Brussels, and Paris and Amsterdam. As with other main-line trains, a small supplement may be assessed at peak hours.

Paris has six international rail stations: Gare du Nord (northern France, northern Europe, and England via Calais or Boulogne); Gare St-Lazare (Normandy, England via Dieppe); Gare de l'Est (Strasbourg, Luxembourg, Basel, and central Europe); Gare de Lyon (Lyon, Marseille, Provence, Geneva, Italy); Gare d'Austerlitz (Loire Valley, southwest France, Spain); and Gare Montparnasse (Brittany, Aquitaine, TGV-Atlantique service to the west and south of France, Spain).

BETWEEN THE U.K. & FRANCE

Short of flying, taking the sleek Eurostar through the "Chunnel" is the fastest way to cross the English Channel: three hours from London's central Waterloo Station to Paris's central Gare du Nord, 35 minutes from Folkestone to Calais, and 60 minutes from motorway to motorway. There is a vast range of prices for Eurostar—round-trip tickets range from €415 for first class (with access to the Philippe Starck–designed Première Class lounge) to €70 for second class depending on when you travel. It's a good idea to **make a reservation if you're traveling with your car on a Chunnel train**; cars without reservations, if they can get on at all, are charged 20% extra.

British Rail also has four daily departures from London's Victoria Station, all linking with the Dover–Calais/Boulogne ferry services through to Paris. There is also an overnight service on the Newhaven–Dieppe ferry. Journey time is about eight hours. Credit-card bookings are accepted by phone or in person at a British Rail Travel Centre.

⚄ Car Transport Eurotunnel ☎ 0870/535-3535 in the U.K., 070/223210 in Belgium, 08-10-63-03-04 in France ⊕ ww2.eurotunnel.com.

⚄ Passenger Service BritRail Travel ☎ 866/274-8724 in the U.S. ⊕ www.britrail.com. **Eurostar** ☎ 08-36-35-35-39 in France, 1233/617-575 or 0870/518-6186 in the U.K. ⊕ www.eurostar.com. **Rail Europe** ☎ 800/942-4866 or 800/274-8724, 0870/584-8848 U.K. credit-card bookings ⊕ www.raileurope.com.

CLASSES

There are two classes of train service in France: *première* (first-class) or *deuxième* (second). First-class seats have 50% more legroom and nicer upholstery than those in second class, and the first-class cars tend to be quieter. First-class seats on the TGV have computer connections. First-class fares are nearly twice as much as those for second-class seats.

CUTTING COSTS

To save money, **look into rail passes.** But be aware that if you don't plan to cover many miles, you may come out ahead by buying individual tickets. Fares are somewhat cheaper if you avoid traveling at peak times (around holidays and weekends), purchase tickets at least 15 days in advance (look for the *billet Prem's*), or find your destination among the last-minute offers online every Tuesday.

FARES & SCHEDULES

You can call for train information or reserve tickets in any Paris station, irrespective of destination. If you know what station you'll depart from, you can get a free schedule there, or you can access the multilingual computerized schedule information network at any Paris station. You can also make reservations and buy your ticket while at the computer. Go to the Grandes Lignes counter for travel within France and to the Billets Internationaux desk if you're heading out of the country. Note that calling the SNCF's 08 number costs €.35 per minute, which quickly adds up; to save this cost, either go to the nearest station and make the reservations in person or visit the SNCF Web site, ⊕ www.sncf.fr.

📰 Train Information **Rail Europe** ☎ 800/942–4866 in the U.S. ⊕ www.raileurope.com. **SNCF** ✉ 88 rue St-Lazare, 75009 Paris ☎ 08–92–35–35–35, €.35 per minute ⊕ www.sncf.fr.

RAIL PASSES

If you plan to travel outside Paris by train, consider purchasing a France Rail Pass, which allows four days of unlimited train travel in a one-month period. If you travel solo, first class will run you $263, while second class is $229: you can add up to six days on this pass for $34 a day for first class, $30 a day for second class. For two people traveling together on a Saver Pass, the cost is $225, while in second class it is $195; additional days (up to six) cost $29 each for first class, $25 each for second class. Other options include the France Rail 'n Drive Pass (combining rail and rental car).

France is one of 17 countries in which you can use EurailPasses, which provide unlimited first-class rail travel in all the participating countries for the duration of the pass. If you plan to rack up the miles, get a standard pass. These are available for 15 days ($588), 21 days ($762), one month ($946), two months ($1,338), and three months ($1,654). If your travels will be more limited, look into the Eurail Selectpass, which gives you first-class rail travel over a two-month period in three to five bordering countries in 22 Eurail network countries. The Selectpass starts at $370 for 5 days of travel within three countries. Another option is the 2-Country Pass, introduced in 2004, which covers rail travel in and between pairs of bordering countries over a two-month period. Unlike most Eurail passes, 2-Country Passes are available for either first- or second-class travel. Costs begin at $299 (first class) and $200 (second class) for four days of travel; up to six extra travel days can be purchased.

In addition to standard EurailPasses, ask about special rail-pass plans. Among these are the Eurail Youthpass (for those under age 26, with second-class travel), the Eurail Saver Pass (which gives a discount for two or more people traveling together), the Eurail Flexipass (which allows a certain number of travel days within a set period), and the Euraildrive Pass (train and rental car).

Whichever of the above passes you choose, remember that **you must purchase your Eurail passes at home before leaving for France.** You can purchase Eurail passes through the Eurail Web site as well as through travel agents.

Another option is to purchase one of the discount rail passes available only for sale in France from SNCF.

When traveling together, two people (who don't have to be a couple) can save money with the Prix Découverte à Deux. You'll get a 25% discount during *périodes bleus* (blue periods: weekdays and periods not on or near any holidays). Note that you have to be with the person you said you would be traveling with.

You can get a reduced fare if you're a senior citizen (over 60). There are two options: for the Prix Découverte Senior, all you have to do is show a valid ID with your age, and you're entitled to up to a 25% reduction in fares in first and second class. The second, the Carte Senior, is better if you're planning on spending a lot of time traveling; it costs €49, is valid for one year, and entitles you to up to a 50% reduction on most trains, with a guaranteed minimum reduction of 25%. It also entitles you to a 30% discount on trips outside France.

With the Carte Enfant Plus, for €65 children under 12 and up to four accompanying adults can get up to 50% off on most trains for an unlimited number of trips. This card is perfect if you're planning on spending a lot of time traveling in France with your children, as it's valid for one year. You can also opt for the Prix Découverte Enfant Plus: when you buy your ticket, simply show a valid ID with your child's age, and you can get a significant discount for your child and a 25% reduction for up to four accompanying adults.

If you purchase an individual ticket from SNCF in France and you're under 26, you automatically get a 25% reduction (a valid ID such as an ISIC card or your passport is necessary). If you're going to be using the train quite a bit during your stay in France and if you're under 26, consider buying the Carte 12–25 (€48), which offers unlimited 50% reductions for one year (provided that there's space available at that price; otherwise you'll just get the standard 25% discount).

If you don't benefit from any of these reductions and if you plan on traveling at least 200 km (132 mi) round-trip and don't mind staying over a Saturday night, look into the Prix Découverte Séjour. This ticket gives you a 25% reduction.

Don't assume that your rail pass guarantees you a seat on the train you wish to ride. You need to **book seats ahead even if you're using a rail pass.**

🚆 Rail Pass Information **Eurail** ⊕ www.eurail.com. **Rail Europe** ☎ 800/942–4866 in the U.S. ⊕ www.raileurope.com.

RESERVATIONS

Seat reservations are required on TGVs and are a good idea on trains that may be crowded—particularly in summer and during holidays on popular routes. You also need a reservation for sleeping accommodations.

TRAVEL AGENCIES

A good travel agent puts your needs first. Look for an agency that has been in business at least five years, emphasizes customer service, and has someone on staff who specializes in your destination. In addition, **make sure the agency belongs to a professional trade organization.** The American Society of Travel Agents (ASTA)—the largest and most influential in the field with more than 20, 000 members in some 140 countries—maintains and enforces a strict code of ethics and will step in to help mediate any agent-client disputes involving ASTA members if necessary. ASTA (whose motto is "Without a travel agent, you're on your own") also maintains a Web site that includes a directory of agents. (If a travel agency is

also acting as your tour operator, *see* Buyer Beware *in* Tours & Packages.)

🚆 Local Agent Referrals **American Society of Travel Agents (ASTA)** ⊠ 1101 King St., Suite 200, Alexandria, VA 22314 ☎ 703/739–2782 or 800/965–2782 24-hr hotline 🖷 703/684–8319 ⊕ www.astanet.com. **Association of British Travel Agents** ⊠ 68–71 Newman St., London W1T 3AH ☎ 020/7637–2444 🖷 020/7637–0713 ⊕ www.abta.com. **Association of Canadian Travel Agencies** ⊠ 130 Albert St., Suite 1705, Ottawa, Ontario K1P 5G4 ☎ 613/237–3657 🖷 613/237–7052 ⊕ www.acta.ca. **Australian Federation of Travel Agents** ⊠ Level 3, 309 Pitt St., Sydney, NSW 2000 ☎ 02/9264–3299 or 1300/363–416 🖷 02/9264–1085 ⊕ www.afta.com.au. **Travel Agents' Association of New Zealand** ⊠ Level 5, Tourism and Travel House, 79 Boulcott St., Box 1888, Wellington 6001 ☎ 04/499–0104 🖷 04/499–0786 ⊕ www.taanz.org.nz.

VISITOR INFORMATION

Learn more about foreign destinations by checking government-issued travel advisories and country information. For a broader picture, consider information from more than one country.

The Maison de la France is the international arm of the French tourism ministry; through its newsletters, brochures, and Web site, you can pick up plenty of information on Paris attractions, special events, promotions, and more.

Once you're in Paris you can turn to the branches of the tourist information office. The longtime main tourist office that had been on the Champs-Élysées moved to Rue des Pyramides (near the Opéra) in 2004, and a half-dozen visitor bureaus are stationed at the city's most popular tourist sights. It's often easier to visit one of these branches in person rather than calling the hotline, as on the phone you'll have to wait through long stretches of generic recorded information at €.34 per minute. Most are open daily; the Gare de Lyon and Opéra–Grands Magasins branches, however, are open Monday through Saturday. The tourism bureaus have friendly, efficient, and multilingual staff. You can gather info on special events, local transit, hotels, tours, excursions, and discount passes. The branch in the Carrousel du Louvre specializes in information on the

Île-de-France (the region around Paris). The general tourist office Web site is ⊕ www.parisinfo.com.

Subscribe to the newsletter *Paris Notes* for an outstanding, all-in-one resource for Paris-centric news, a cultural events calendar, and in-depth articles on everything from current trends to overlooked historic sights. The newsletter is published 10 times a year; its Web site includes article archives, plus special sections on hotels, restaurants, and architecture. Though not entirely dedicated to Paris, the journal *France Today* often covers Paris-related news, arts events, and the like. It's also published 10 times a year.

🇫🇷 France Tourist Information **Los Angeles** ✉ 9454 Wilshire Blvd., Suite 715, Beverly Hills, CA 90212 ☎ 310/271-6665 🖷 310/276-2835. **Maison de la France** ☎ 02/9231-5244 in Australia, 514/876-9881 in Canada, 09068/244-123 in the U.K., 60p per minute, 410/286-8310 in the U.S. ⊕ www. franceguide.com. **New York City** ✉ 444 Madison Ave., 16th fl., New York, NY 10022 ☎ 410/286-8310 🖷 212/838-7855. **Canada** ✉ 1981 av. McGill College, Suite 490, Montréal, Québec H3A 2W9 ☎ 514/288-4264 🖷 514/845-4868 ✑ mfrance@mtl.net. **U.K.** ✉ 178 Piccadilly, London W1V OAL ☎ 09068/244-123, 60p per minute 🖷 020/7493-6594. **Australia** ✉ 25 Bligh St., Sydney NSW 2000 ☎ 02/9231-5244 🖷 02/9221-8682.

🇫🇷 Local Tourism Information **Espace du Tourisme d'Île-de-France** ✉ Carrousel du Louvre, 99 rue de Rivoli, 75001 ☎ 08-26-16-66-66 ⊕ www.pidf.com Ⓜ Palais-Royal Musée du Louvre. **Office du Tourisme de la Ville de Paris Pyramides** ✉ 25 rue des Pyramides, 75001 ☎ 08-92-68-30-00, €.34 per minute Ⓜ Pyramides. **Office du Tourisme de la Ville de Paris Gare du Lyon** ✉ Arrivals, 20 bd. Diderot, 75012 Ⓜ Gare du Lyon. **Office du Tourisme de la Ville de Paris Gare du Nord** ✉ 18 rue de Dunkerque, 75010 Ⓜ Gare du Nord. **Office du Tourisme de la Ville de Paris Opéra–Grands Magasins** ✉ 11 rue Scribe, 75009 Ⓜ Opéra. **Office du Tourisme de la Ville de Paris Tour Eiffel** ✉ between the east and north legs of the Eiffel Tower Ⓜ Champs de Mars/Tour Eiffel.

🇫🇷 Publications **France Today** ✆ Box 15758, North Hollywood, CA 91615 ☎ 800/232-1549 in the U.S. ⊕ www.francetoday.com. **Paris Notes** ✆ Box 15818, North Hollywood, CA 91615 ☎ 800/677-9660 in the U.S. ⊕ www.parisnotes.com.

🇫🇷 Government Advisories **U.S. Department of State** ✉ Bureau of Consular Affairs, Overseas Citizens Services Office, 2201 C St. NW Washington, DC 20520 ☎ 202/647-5225, 888/407-4747 or 317/472-2328 for interactive hotline ⊕ www.travel.state.gov. **Consular Affairs Bureau of Canada** ☎ 800/267-6788 or 613/944-6788 ⊕ www.voyage.gc.ca. **U.K. Foreign and Commonwealth Office** ✉ Travel Advice Unit, Consular Directorate, Old Admiralty Building, London SW1A 2PA ☎ 0870/606-0290 or 020/7008-1500 ⊕ www.fco.gov.uk/travel. **Australian Department of Foreign Affairs and Trade** ☎ 300/139-281 travel advisories, 02/6261-1299 Consular Travel Advice Faxback Service ⊕ www.dfat.gov.au. **New Zealand Ministry of Foreign Affairs and Trade** ☎ 04/439-8000 ⊕ www.mft.govt.nz.

WEB SITES

Do check out the World Wide Web when planning your trip. You'll find everything from weather forecasts to virtual tours of famous cities. Be sure to visit Fodors.com (⊕ www.fodors.com), a complete travel-planning site. You can research prices and book plane tickets, hotel rooms, rental cars, vacation packages, and more. In addition, you can post your pressing questions in the Travel Talk section. Other planning tools include a currency converter and weather reports, and there are loads of links to travel resources.

Besides the tourist office Web site (Visitor Information, *above*), there are a couple of other helpful government-sponsored sites. The Paris mayor's office site, ⊕ www. paris.fr, covers all kinds of public cultural attractions, student resources, park and market info, and more. On the French Ministry of Culture's site, ⊕ www.culture. fr, you can search by theme (contemporary art, cinema, music, theater, and so on) or by region (Paris is in the Île-de-France). The Réunion des Musées Nationaux (RMN), a consortium of public museums, hosts a group site for 32 national institutions: ⊕ www.rmn.fr. Fourteen of these museums are in Paris proper, including the Louvre, the Musé Rodin, and the Musée d'Orsay. The site includes detailed visitor info and an exhibition calendar for current and upcoming shows.

The Web site of the *International Herald Tribune* (⊕ www.iht.com) is a good source for articles on Paris.

Want to see exactly where you'll be staying? Check the online phone and address directory, **Les Pages Jaunes** (⊕ www.pagesjaunes.fr). Go to the photos section, input a specific address, and a street map plus a photo of the building appears.

For food-related info, make a beeline for **Patricia Wells**'s site, ⊕ www.patriciawells.com. This covers Wells's recent restaurant reviews (mostly for places in Paris), other food-related news, and a terrific glossary of French food terms. **Dininginfrance.com** (⊕ www.dininginfrance.com) has a special section on Paris, with a selection of recent newspaper and magazine articles published on the capital's food scene.

On its site, ⊕ www.associationdesgaleries.org, the **Association des Galeries** lists exhibits in over 100 galleries throughout the city. **Paris-art.com** (⊕ www.paris-art.com) focuses on contemporary art, with reviews, exhibition calendars, and interviews, in French only. **Parissi.com** (⊕ www.parissi.com) racks up club and concert listings, but it's in French only. **Secrets of Paris** (⊕ www.secretsofparis.com) is a free online newsletter of insider tips on drinking, dining, nightlife, accommodations, and sightseeing off-the-beaten-path put together by Fodor's updater Heather Stimmler-Hall.

ThinkParis.com (⊕ www.thinkparis.com) posts a Paris events calendar, a handful of lifestyle articles, a Q&A for expats in Paris, and the like. **Paris-Anglo.com** (⊕ www.paris-anglo.com) includes directories of cooking schools, galleries, language classes, and more, plus a biweekly column on various *la vie parisienne* topics.

Exploring
Paris

WORD OF MOUTH

"We started by walking through the 6th to the Latin Quarter and then across the bridge to Sainte Chappelle . . . This was probably one of the highlights of our trip . . .Pictures cannot capture the incredible beauty of the stained glass windows."

—Smyling

"Pick a favorite bridge and stand there around sunset as they turn on the lights on all the bridges in succession before finally turning on the lights on the Eiffel Tower. It's absolutely magical."

—missymay

"[We went] to the Louvre, just for the highlights, and my kids really liked the part which shows the foundations of the Louvre . . ."

—eclair

Introduction by
Nancy Coons
Revised and
updated by
Lisa Pasold
and Mat
Schwartz

YOU'LL ALWAYS HAVE PARIS. Like the champagne-frosted idyll Bogie and Bergman reminisced about in *Casablanca,* the time you spend in this endlessly resonant city will remain a lifelong reference point. Over and over, as in a reverie, you'll conjure up its sensory assault—the sting in the nostril of a freshly lighted Gitane cigarette, the rippling of lights on the misty Seine, the confetti flutter of antique prints over the stand of a *bouquiniste* (bookseller), the aromatic bedlam of a street food market, the waves battering the prow of the *Medusa* in Géricault's epic canvas at the Louvre. And you'll get starry-eyed all over again.

Whether weaned on Hemingway or Henry James, Doisneau or Cartier-Bresson, Brassaï or Cecil Beaton, Westerners share an image of Paris as the city of lovers, from Rodin's brawny duo to *La Bohème*'s Mimi and Rodolfo weeping in a chilly garret to Anaïs Nin's flappers naked under fur. The Hollywood propaganda machine melted the hearts of any stubborn holdouts: who could stand firm in the face of Leslie Caron's blushes as she danced in Gene Kelly's arms along the Seine in *An American in Paris,* Audrey Hepburn's fine-boned take on the *Winged Victory* in *Funny Face,* or the punched-in-the-gut look on Bogie's face when he remembered the German tanks rolling in?

The real love affair is with the city of Paris itself, and it can play you like a violin. Around every corner, down every *ruelle,* or little street, lies a resonance-in-waiting. You can stand on rue du Faubourg St-Honoré at the very spot where Edmond Rostand set Ragueneau's pastry shop in *Cyrano de Bergerac.* You can peruse the letters of Madame de Sévigné in her erstwhile mansion, now the Musée Carnavalet. You can hear the words of Racine resound in the hair-raising diction of the Comédie Française. You can breathe in the fumes of hubris before the extravagant tomb of Napoléon at Les Invalides. You can gaze through the gate at the Île St-Louis mansion where Voltaire honed his wit and then lay a garland on Oscar Wilde's grave.

No matter which way you head, any trip through Paris will be a voyage of discovery. But choosing the Paris of your dreams is a bit like choosing a perfume or cologne. Do you prefer young and dashing, or elegant and worldly? Something sporty, or divinely glamorous? No matter—beneath touristy Paris, historic Paris, fashion-conscious Paris, pretentious-bourgeois Paris, practical working-class Paris, or the legendary bohemian Paris, you will find your own Paris, and it will be vivid, exciting, unforgettable. Veterans know that Paris is a city of regal perspectives and ramshackle streets, of formal *espaces vertes,* or green open spaces, and quiet squares; and this combination of the pompous and the private is one of the secrets of its perennial lure.

Another draw is its scale: Paris is relatively small as capitals go, with distances between many of its major sights and museums easily walkable. In a span of just a few miles, the landmarks come thick and fast, and the river makes basic orientation easy, dividing the city into the Rive Droite (Right Bank) and Rive Gauche (Left Bank). In fact, the best way to get to know Paris is on foot, although public transportation—particularly the *métro* (subway system)—is excellent. Arm yourself with the city map *Plan de Paris* (a handy booklet with a complete street-name and métro index, easily found in bookstores and *tabacs*) and simply stroll to your heart's delight. (Métro stations also have a detailed neighborhood map just inside the entrance.)

For the first-timer, there will always be several musts at the top of the list—the Louvre, Notre-Dame, and the Eiffel Tower, among them—but a visit to Paris will never be quite as simple as a quick look at a few landmarks. Every *quartier*, or neighborhood, has its own personality and unsuspected treasures, and you should be ready to explore. Ultimately, your route will depend on your own preferences, stamina, and curiosity. The city can seem like a living art gallery: broad perspectives flashing from gold to pink to silver under scudding Impressionist clouds, a misty street straight out of Brassaï, a woman's abstracted stare over a glass of green liqueur at a Montmartre café. You can wander for hours without getting bored—though not, perhaps, without getting lost.

By the time you have seen only a few neighborhoods, you should not only be culturally replete but downright exhausted—and hungry, too. Again, take your cue from the Parisians and plan your next stop at a sidewalk café. So you've heard stories of a friend of a friend who paid $6 for a coffee at a famous café? Take it in stride. What you're paying for is time, and the opportunity to watch the intricate drama of Parisian street life unfold. There's no rush to get you to pay your bill. Hemingway knew the rules: he'd be just another sportswriter if the café waiters of Paris had hovered around him impatiently.

You'll learn it's all so familiar and all so terribly . . . Parisian. *Rillettes* (preserved pork spread) and *poilâne* (the ubiquitous chewy sourdough bread from Poilâne bakery) and Beaujolais. Ranks of posters plastered on the domed green Morris towers. The discreet hiss of the métro's rubber wheels and a waft of accordion music. The street sweeper guiding rags along the rain gutters with a twig broom. The coins in the saucer by the *pissoir*. The shriek of the espresso machine as it steams the milk for your café crème, the flip-lid sugar bowl on the zinc bar. The illuminated monuments looming like Mayan idols. The lovers buried in each others' necks along the banks of the Seine.

To paraphrase Stendhal, to know Paris is the work of a lifetime. So what are you waiting for?

FROM NOTRE-DAME TO PLACE DE LA CONCORDE

No matter how you approach Paris—historically, geographically, emotionally—it is the Seine River that beckons you. The city owes both its development and much of its visual appeal to the Seine. Each bank of the river has its own personality; the Rive Droite (Right Bank), with its spacious boulevards and formal buildings, traditionally has a more sober and genteel feel than the carefree Rive Gauche (Left Bank). In between, the river harbors two islands that stand at the center of the city—the Île de la Cité and the Île St-Louis. Both seem to be gliding downriver, as if the latter were being towed by the former.

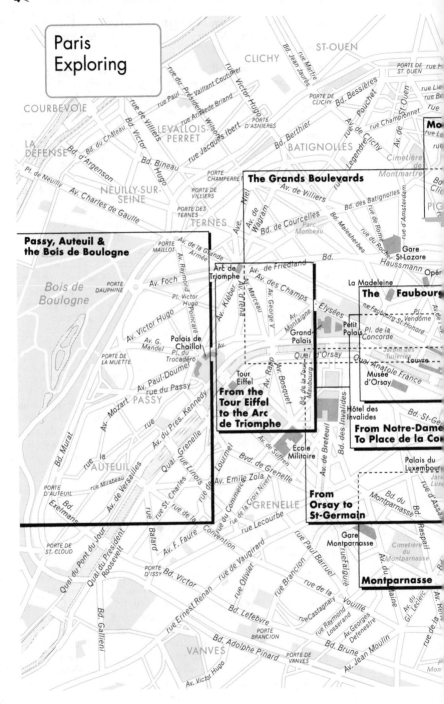

Paris
Exploring

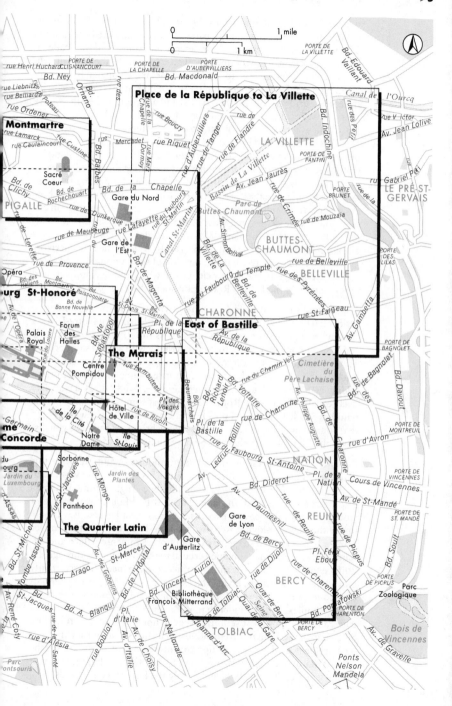

It is the Île de la Cité that forms the city's historic center. The earliest inhabitants of Paris, the Gaulish tribe of the Parisii, settled here around 250 BC. The location was ideal for defense and trade, and they called it Lutetia, "settlement surrounded by water." In 52 BC the Roman general Labienus captured the town during Caesar's campaign to conquer Gaul. Under this new power Lutetia was rebuilt in Roman style, with streets in a grid pattern, thermal baths, and a forum. In the 6th century AD the first royal palace was built at the prow of the Île de la Cité; at the island's stern grew the great brooding cathedral of Notre-Dame. Napoléon was crowned here, kings and queens exchanged marriage vows before its altar, and during the Revolution, inhabitants of the island literally linked arms to fight off a mob intent on tearing the cathedral down. Notre-Dame is the symbolic heart of the city, and for many the symbolic heart of France itself. From the cathedral's tower you can see how Paris—like the trunk of a tree developing new rings—has grown in circles from the Île de la Cité. Most of the island's other medieval buildings fell victim to town planner Baron Georges-Eugène Haussmann's ambitious rebuilding program of the 1860s. Among the rare survivors are the jewel-like Sainte-Chapelle, a vision of shimmering stained glass, and the Conciergerie, the former city prison where Marie-Antoinette and other victims of the French Revolution spent their last days.

The rarified island of Île St-Louis, meanwhile, is the smaller and more residential of the two islands. This dignified little island in Notre-Dame's shadow retains the romance and loveliness of *le Paris traditionnel*. It can feel like a tiny universe unto itself, overhung with ancient stone houses; at night its streets can become so hushed you'd almost expect to hear crickets chirping. These have long comprised some of the most prized addresses in Paris—Voltaire, Daumier, Cézanne, Baudelaire, Chagall, Helena Rubenstein, and the Rothschilds are just some of the lucky people who have called the Île St-Louis home. Until the 1800s it was reputed that some island residents never crossed the bridges—and once you discover the island's quiet charm, you may understand why.

If Notre-Dame represents the Church, another major sight on this walk—the Louvre—symbolizes the State. This royal palace was begun at the turn of the 13th century, when Philippe-Auguste built a fortress to protect the city's western flank. This fortified Louvre was used as a storehouse for valuable manuscripts, weaponry, and jewels. It was only under the pleasure-loving Renaissance king François I that a grander Louvre began to take shape, growing into an immense palace and administrative center that remained crucial to the French state through the 20th century. The last government office, the Finance Ministry, finally moved out in the 1990s, giving the Louvre more space for its phenomenal collections. Today I. M. Pei's glass pyramid shimmers at the core of the complex, as a reminder that although Parisians take their role as cultural custodians most seriously, they're not hidebound by tradition. Since seeing the Louvre's tremendous collections is a journey in itself, we have dedicated another section to a museum visit. ⇨ Please see the separate Louvre coverage that follows this section for full information on the galleries. This walk includes only the Louvre's courtyards.

Numbers in the text correspond to numbers in the margin and on the From Notre-Dame to the Place de la Concorde map.

a good walk

The most dramatic approach to the regal cathedral of **Notre-Dame** ❶ is from the Rive Gauche, crossing at the Pont au Double from quai de Montebello (St-Michel métro or RER stop). This bridge leads to the large pedestrian place du Parvis, a great square cleared by Haussmann in the 19th century; the cathedral originally loomed over a medieval huddle of buildings. Place du Parvis is *kilomètre zéro,* the spot from which all distances to and from the city are officially measured. A well-polished brass circle set in the ground, about 20 yards in front of the cathedral's main entrance, marks the exact spot, and folk tradition claims that if you close your eyes and spin clockwise three times, your wish will come true. But don't get too dizzy spinning around—you'll want a clear head to appreciate the phenomenal Gothic workmanship in Notre-Dame. Study the magnificent facade, explore the interior, then head to the special entrance on the left-hand side of the facade to climb the towers for a gargoyle-framed view of the heart of Paris. In peak season there can be a block-long line to do this, so budget your time accordingly.

To escape the crowds, relief is just a short—and magical—stroll away. Few people venture to the **Ancien Cloître Quartier** ❷, a nook of medieval Paris that's tucked behind the northern (or left-hand side as you face the cathedral) buttresses of Notre-Dame. History and art buffs will want to visit the **Musée de Notre-Dame** ❸, on rue du Cloître-Notre-Dame, where you can imagine the medieval quarter as it once was, filled with seminary students and church canons. Next, go left on any one of the adjoining side streets and head north toward the Seine to reach rue Chanoinesse. Turn left on this pretty former cloister walk, pass the police station, then turn right onto rue de Colombe. This small street slopes toward the river; near No. 5 you'll notice a change in the cobblestone pattern underfoot. Beneath your feet are ruins from the original defensive Roman wall around the city of Lutetia. The building at No. 5 includes fragments from the medieval chapel of St-Aignan. Make a right immediately onto rue des Ursins. This lovely street leads you to a remarkable medieval mansion. Stone steps lead up to the river, since over the centuries the quays have risen to protect inhabitants from floods. Just around the mansion's corner is rue des Chantres, where you'll see a green *crue* (flood height) sign marking the water's height during the great flood of 1910. Notre-Dame's spire is strikingly framed here, and its shadow falls on the house where fabled lovers Abelard and Héloïse once studied and sinned so famously. The building at 10 rue Chanoinesse has a plaque commemorating their tragic love affair. Cross the street into the well-groomed gardens of **Square Jean-XXIII** ❹, where if you're lucky you'll catch sight of the churchyard's sleek six-toe black cats, fed by generations of elderly Parisians. Also at this eastern tip of the island lies evidence of a grimmer history: the **Mémorial de la Déportation** ❺, a starkly moving modern crypt dedicated to the 200,000 people from France who died in Nazi concentration camps.

Next, cross the Pont St-Louis (a favorite for musicians and other buskers) to the Île St-Louis. There's a sharp contrast between the islands: whereas

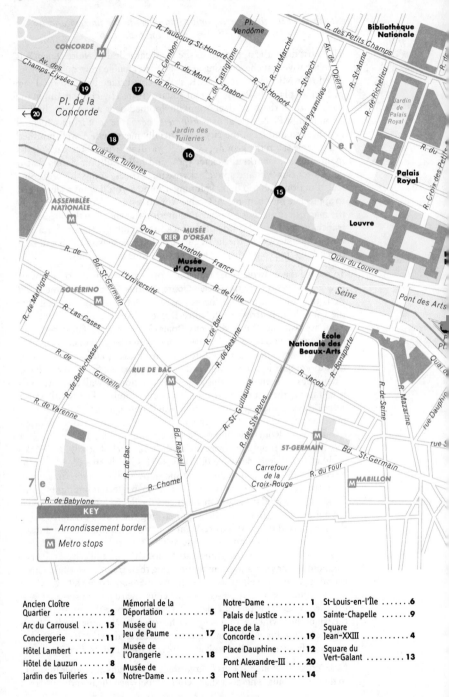

KEY

— Arrondissement border

Ⓜ Metro stops

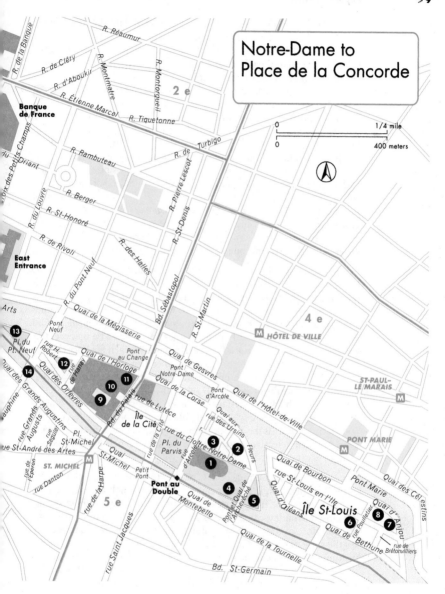

Notre-Dame to Place de la Concorde

the Île de la Cité is steeped in history and dotted with dignified public buildings, the Île St-Louis is a discreet residential district. Walk straight ahead down rue St-Louis-en-l'Île, the main shopping street running the length of the island, pausing to admire the pierced spire of **St-Louis-en-l'Île** ⑥, and pick up an ice cream at Berthillon (No. 31). There's a magnetic architectural unity here that stems from the efforts of a group of early-17th-century property speculators. At that time there were two islands here, the Île Notre-Dame and the Île aux Vaches (Cow Island, a reference to its use as grazing land), both owned by the Church. Speculators bought the two islands, joined them together, and divided the newly formed Île St-Louis into building plots. Baroque architect Louis Le Vau was commissioned to erect a series of imposing town houses, and by 1664 the project was largely complete. At the end of rue St-Louis-en-l'Île, hang a left and curve around the quai d'Anjou to pass two of the most majestic mansions, the **Hôtel Lambert** ⑦ and the **Hôtel de Lauzun** ⑧. Continue on and quai d'Anjou becomes the quai de Bourbon; you'll be facing Notre-Dame again. The quay here is one of the best picnic spots in the city and one of the most romantic places at sunset.

Going back across the Pont St-Louis, make a hard left to cross Pont de l'Archevêché for the best view of all, with Notre-Dame's flying buttresses (archlike structural supports enabling the walls to soar heavenward) lending the heavy apse a magical lightness. Once you've reached the other bank, turn left and go down the stairs onto quai de la Tournelle. Old iron rings in the walls testify to the barges that used to tie up here; this was the main unloading dock for wood in the days when fireplaces heated the city. Step underneath the bridge for another magnificent view of Notre-Dame, which seems to be a boat herself, sailing downstream. Walk beneath the black ribs of Pont au Double, then go upstairs at the TICKET sign. Crossing back to the island on the Petit Pont, you'll see the Haussmann monolith of the city's central police station on your left. (Just beyond the prefecture is the quai des Orfèvres, a street that appears in almost every Parisian detective mystery. Its name is the French symbolic equivalent of Scotland Yard.)

As you walk straight up rue de la Cité, the Hôtel Dieu hospital, founded in the Middle Ages, is to your right. When you reach an open square, turn left; this is the flower market, a pretty detour, especially in spring, but closed Monday. Straight ahead of you is what used to be the royal palace. Most of the medieval buildings have disappeared, but you can see the spire of the late-Gothic **Sainte-Chapelle** ⑨, which many consider the most beautiful church in the world. Around the chapel (entrance is to the left of the big gold gates) stretches the imposing 1860s **Palais de Justice** ⑩; if you want, you can wander around the buildings among the black-robed lawyers or attend a court hearing. To the right (going north) is the quai de l'Horloge, named for the oldest *horloge* (clock) in Paris, marking time since 1370 from high up on the **Conciergerie** ⑪, the prison where Marie-Antoinette and other bluebloods awaited their slice of history at the guillotine. Quai de l'Horloge leads left to rue de Harlay and historic **place Dauphine** ⑫. Cross this old-fashioned square onto Pont Neuf; in front of you is **square du Vert-Galant** ⑬, with its impressive equestrian statue of Henri IV. Steps on the right lead down to the water, where Vedette tour boats set off for their routes along the Seine.

Cross **Pont Neuf** ⑭ to the Rive Droite and turn left along quai du Louvre. The lidded stalls of the *bouquinistes* (booksellers) line the river side of the sidewalk, luring browsers with secondhand books, vintage magazines, and postcards. The bouquinistes have plied their trade here since 1752 and were allowed permanent stalls in the late 1800s. Walk past the art deco Samaritaine department store to reach the great **Louvre** museum. Cross at the traffic light to enter the Louvre through the elegant south front, which leads into the Cour Carrée. This square courtyard once represented a chance for the public to communicate with the king; as the ruler stepped from his coach, suppliants pressed around him extending letters and petitions. (If you pass nearby after dark, check out the courtyard's spectacular lighting.) Through the archway of the Pavillon de l'Horloge, you can see the museum's controversial 20th-century entrance: I. M. Pei's glass pyramid. Just beyond the pyramid stands the **Arc du Carrousel** ⑮—a small relation to the distant Arc de Triomphe— where you can gaze at the grand vista (aligned *almost* perfectly) that leads to the Concorde obelisk, the Champs-Élysées, the Arc de Triomphe, and the shadowy towers of La Défense just visible behind.

Continue west to the **Jardin des Tuileries** ⑯, with its manicured lawns, fountains, rows of trees, and regiments of statues old and new. On the north side is arcaded rue de Rivoli, built for Napoléon to commemorate his Italian conquests. Two smallish buildings stand sentinel at the far end of the Tuileries overlooking place de la Concorde. Nearest rue de Rivoli is the **Musée du Jeu de Paume** ⑰, host to splashy exhibits of contemporary art. The almost identical building nearer the Seine is the **Musée de l'Orangerie** ⑱, containing the largest versions of Claude Monet's *Water Lilies*, but closed for renovation.

The two museums gaze down the expansive **place de la Concorde** ⑲, centered by its gilt-tipped Egyptian obelisk, with the Seine to the south, the Champs-Élysées and Arc de Triomphe to the west, and the Madeleine church to the north. You may want to end your walk in the Tuileries, but if you'd rather squeeze in one more scenic view, follow the Seine on cours de la Reine to the **Pont Alexandre-III** ⑳. With luck, by the time you reach this exuberant Belle Époque bridge you'll be greeted with a memorable sunset to set off the gleaming, gold-leaf Invalides dome up ahead.

TIMING   Allowing for toiling up towers and ambling down quays, this 6-km (4-mi) walk will take a full day—enabling you to reach Pont Alexandre-III just before the seductive *heure bleue,* the blue hour of dusk. The Louvre collections are immense, so we've treated them as a separate tour (*see* The Louvre, *below*); this walk is geared to being out in the parks, squares, and streets.

What to See

❷ **Ancien Cloître Quartier.** Hidden in the shadows of Notre-Dame is this magical, often overlooked nook of Paris. Thankfully, when Baron Haussmann knocked down much of the Île de la Cité in the 19th century he spared this sector. Through the years lucky folk including composer Pierre

Fodor'sChoice
★

du Bellay, Ludwig Bemelmans, who created the beloved *Madeleine* series of books, and the Islamic spiritual leader the Aga Khan have called these narrow streets home. Back in the Middle Ages this was the quarter where canons boarded students of the cathedral seminary, one of whom was the celebrated Peter Abelard (1079–1142)—questioner of the faith, philosopher, and scandalizer of the civilized world for his penchant for *les femmes*. Abelard boarded with Notre-Dame's canon, Fulbert, whose niece, Héloïse, was first his student, then his lover. She became pregnant, he was castrated (but survived), the lovers took refuge in a monastery and a nunnery, and all of Parisian society turned against the canon. The poetic, passionate letters between the two cemented their fame as thwarted lovers, and their story has been a subject for artists ever since. The canon's house at 10 rue Chanoinesse was redone in the 1800s, but a plaque commemorates the lovers. In the Ancien Cloître there are no other famous sights per se, just a spellbinding warren of streets where time seems to be holding its breath. ⊠ *Rue du Cloître-Notre-Dame north to quai des Fleurs, Île de la Cité* Ⓜ *Cité.*

⑮ Arc du Carrousel. Often the setting for fashion-magazine photo spreads, this small triumphal arch between the Louvre and the Tuileries was erected by Napoléon between 1806 and 1808. The four bronze horses on top were originally the famous gilded horses that Napoléon looted from Venice; when these were returned in 1815, Bosio designed four new ones harnessed to a chariot driven by a goddess symbolizing the Restoration (of the monarchy). Ⓜ *Palais-Royal.*

> **need a break?**
>
> Settle in at **Le Fumoir** (☎ 01–42–92–00–24), a cozy, book-lined bar on rue du Louvre, just across from the eastern exit of the Louvre. The cosmopolitan crowd is drawn here by the beautiful staff, racks of international newspapers, and the best club sandwich in the city. Hot dishes are served from noon until past midnight.

⑪ Conciergerie. Built by Philip IV in the 13th and 14th centuries, these walls imprisoned dukes and duchesses, lords and ladies, and, most famously, Queen Marie-Antoinette during the French Revolution, the last stop before her fatal trip to the guillotine. By the end of the Reign of Terror (1793–95), countless others fell foul of the revolutionaries, including their own leaders Danton and Robespierre. This turreted, medieval building, originally part of the royal palace on the Île de la Cité, holds Marie-Antoinette's cell (with some of the ill-fated queen's possessions). The chapel's stained glass is emblazoned with the initials M. A.; it was commissioned after the queen's death by her daughter. Outside, in the courtyard, victims of the Terror spent their final days playing piquet, writing letters to loved ones, and waiting for the dreaded climb up the staircase to the Chamber of the Revolutionary Council to hear its final verdict. You can also visit the Gothic guardroom, with its intricately carved columns, and the atmospheric Salle des Gens d'Armes (officers' room); a short corridor leads to the kitchen and its four vast fireplaces. The building takes its name from the palace's *concierge,* or governor, whose considerable income was swollen by the privilege he enjoyed of renting out shops and workshops. ⊠ *1 quai de l'Horloge, Louvre/Tuileries*

JUMP TO THE HEAD OF THE LINE

Consider this time-versus-money equation: the Carte Musées et Monuments (Museums and Monuments Pass) offers unlimited access to more than 60 museums and monuments in the greater Paris region. Passes cover one-, three-, or five-consecutive-day periods, costing €18, €36, and €54 respectively. Since most Paris museums charge under €10, you have to be serious about museum-going to make this pay off, but one major plus is jumping to the head of most lines—a coup when the Musée d'Orsay line is 600 people long. Buy the pass at Paris's tourist offices, métro stations, and at all participating museums; it comes with a handy list of eligible attractions. Remember that most museums admit under-18s for free, give discounts to students under 26, and most open for free the first Sunday of each month, though they'll be especially crowded. Will the pass still be a good deal for you? Do your personal equation and decide.

☎ 01–53–40–60–93 ⊕ *www.monum.fr* ✉ *€7.50, joint ticket with Sainte-Chapelle €10.40* ⊙ *Daily 9:30–5* Ⓜ *Cité.*

❼ **Hôtel Lambert.** Without this house—one of the most famous in Paris—Versailles probably wouldn't exist in all its glory. Sitting on the eastern end of the Île St-Louis, it was created by the three great *Le*s of the French baroque: architect Louis Le Vau (1612–70), decorator Charles Le Brun, and painter Eustache Le Sieur. Built for the banker Lambert *le riche,* the mansion was so impressive that Nicolas Fouquet ordered the team to build his château of Vaux-le-Vicomte, which, in turn, inspired Louis XIV to commission them to create Versailles. Voltaire was the most famous occupant of the Lambert, then owned by his lover, the Marquise du Châtelet. Here, many of Paris's most famous costume balls were held; guests included everyone from Frédéric Chopin to Empress Eugénie. The house is private and has been restored by the Barons Rothschild. ✉ *2 rue St-Louis-en-l'Île, Île St-Louis* Ⓜ *Pont Marie.*

❽ **Hôtel de Lauzun.** The gilded salons here are important examples of Parisian baroque style, making the mansion a must-see for art historians, once it reopens after renovation, that is. (At this writing, the hôtel was due to reopen in January 2006.) The city now owns the mansion, built by Louis Le Vau in 1657, with decorations by Le Brun. Despite the house's name, however, it was built for Charles Gruyn, a supplier of goods to the French army, who accumulated an immense fortune but landed in jail before the house was finished. In 1848 poet Théophile Gautier (1811–72) moved in, making it the meeting place of the Club des Haschischines (Hashish Eaters' Club); novelist Alexandre Dumas and painter Eugène Delacroix were members. The club came to represent more than just a den of drug takers and gossips, for these men believed passionately in the purity of art and the crucial role of the artist as sole interpreter of the chaos of life. Art for art's sake—the more refined and exotic the better—was their creed. Anything that helped the artist to reach heightened states of perception was applauded. Somewhat later the revolutionary critic and visionary poet Charles Baudelaire (1821–67) had an apartment here, where he kept a cache of stuffed snakes and crocodiles and where he wrote a large chunk of his masterpiece, *Les Fleurs du Mal* (*The Flowers of Evil*). ⊠ *17 quai d'Anjou, Île St-Louis* ☏ *01–43–54–27–14* Ⓜ *Pont Marie.*

Ⓒ ⑯ **Jardin des Tuileries.** Claude Monet and Auguste Renoir captured this gracious garden with paint and brush and all Parisians know it as a lovely place to stroll and survey the surrounding cityscape. A palace once stood here—somehow, 16th-century rulers felt the need for yet another royal residence—on the site of a clay pit that supplied material for many of the city's tile roofs. (Hence the name *tuileries,* or tile works.) During the Revolution Louis XVI and his family were kept in the Tuileries under house arrest. The palace was repeatedly swarmed by angry mobs, and in one gruesome incident hundreds of Swiss Guards were killed. This history didn't deter either Napoléon or Louis-Philippe from living there, but the palace was burned during the 1871 Communard uprising. Now the Tuileries is a typically French garden: formal and neatly patterned, with statues, rows of trees, fountains with gaping fish, and gravel paths. No wonder the Impressionists liked it here—the gray, austere light of Paris makes green trees look even greener. ⊠ *Bordered by quai des Tuileries, pl. de la Concorde, rue de Rivoli, and the Louvre, Louvre/Tuileries* Ⓜ *Tuileries.*

> **need a break?** Stop off for a snack or lunch at **Dame Tartine** (☏ 01–47–03–94–84), on the left as you arrive from the place de la Concorde. It has a good-value, creative, seasonal menu. In fine weather choose a seat outside in the shade.

❺ **Mémorial de la Déportation** (Memorial of the Deportation). On the eastern tip of the Île de la Cité in what was once a city morgue lies a starkly moving modern monument to the 200,000 French men, women, and children who died in Nazi concentration camps during World War II. The memorial was intentionally designed to be claustrophobic; it's a shattering testament to those lost. ☏ *01–46–33–87–56* ▱ *Free* ☉ *Mar.–Oct., daily 10–noon and 2–7; Nov.–Feb., daily 10–noon and 2–5* Ⓜ *Maubert Mutualité.*

⑰ **Musée du Jeu de Paume.** At the entrance to the Jardin des Tuileries stands a 19th-century building used for *jeu de paume* (literally, "palm game," a forerunner of tennis) that has gotten another lease on life. It has been transformed into an ultramodern, white-walled photography showcase. The museum's holdings include some national photography archives, but the real standouts are the temporary shows, which change every few months and often incorporate video and multimedia installations. Basement rooms are dedicated full-time to photograpy-themed videos and movies. ⊠ *1 pl. de la Concorde, Louvre/Tuileries* ☏ *01–47–03–12–51* ⊕ *www.jeudepaume.org* ▱ *€6* ☉ *Tues.–Wed. and Fri. noon–7, Thurs. noon–9:30, weekends 10–7* Ⓜ *Concorde.*

⑱ **Musée de l'Orangerie.** Claude Monet's largest *Water Lilies* canvases filled two oval rooms here, but unfortunately this museum has been undergoing a repeatedly delayed renovation. Though it was due to open in fall 2004, workers discovered the ruins of a medieval wall underneath the building, and at this writing the project has been put on pause while the area is being excavated. When it finally reopens it will display its selection of early-20th-century paintings, with works by Renoir, Paul Cézanne, Henri Matisse, and Marie Laurencin, among other masters. The museum's name, by the way, isn't misleading; the building was originally used to store the Tuileries' citrus trees over the winter. ✉ *Pl. de la Concorde, Louvre/Tuileries* Ⓜ *Concorde.*

❶ Notre-Dame. Looming above place du Parvis on the Île de la Cité is the
FodorśChoice Cathédrale de Notre-Dame, the most enduring symbol of Paris. Begun
★ in 1163, completed in 1345, badly damaged during the Revolution, and restored by Viollet-le-Duc in the 19th century, Notre-Dame may not be France's oldest or largest cathedral, but in beauty and architectural harmony it has few peers—as you can see by studying the facade from the open square. The doorways seem like hands joined in prayer, the sculpted kings form a noble procession, and the rose windows gleam with what seems like divine light. Above, the gallery breaks the lines of the stone vaults, and between the two high towers the spire soars above the transept crossing. Seen from the front, the cathedral gives an impression of strength, dignity, and majestic serenity; seen from the Pont de l'Archevêché, it has all the proud grace of a seagoing vessel, the cross on its steeple borne like the flag on a tall mast.

The cathedral was conceived by Bishop de Sully, who claimed he had seen the building in a vision. More pragmatically, Sully needed a cathedral in Paris so that he could compete with Abbot Suger's phenomenal cathedral in St-Denis, just north of the city. An army of stonemasons, carpenters, and sculptors came to work and live on the site, which had already seen a Roman temple, an early Christian basilica, and a Romanesque church. The chancel and altar were consecrated in 1182, but the magnificent sculptures surrounding the main doors were not put into position until 1240. The north tower was finished 10 years later. If both towers seem a bit top-heavy, that's because two needlelike spires were originally conceived to top them but were never built. The tower on the left is a tiny bit wider than the one on the right.

Despite various changes in the 17th century, the cathedral remained substantially unaltered until the French Revolution, when it was transformed into a Temple of Reason—busts of Voltaire and Rousseau replaced those of saints. The statues of the kings of Israel were hacked down by the mob because they were thought to represent the despised royal line of France. An interesting postscript to this destruction occurred in 1977, when some of the heads of these statues were discovered buried beneath a bank on boulevard Haussmann. An ardent royalist had once owned that land; he salvaged the broken heads and buried them in his garden. The heads are now displayed in the Musée National du Moyen-Age.

By the early 19th century the excesses of the Revolution were over, but the reconsecrated cathedral was in dreadful condition. Napoléon crowned himself emperor here, seizing the crown from the pope and placing it on his own head in December 1804. (See Jacques-Louis David's epic painting of the lavish ceremony in the Louvre.) It was only after the publication of Victor Hugo's immensely popular novel featuring the hunchback Quasimodo that Parisians took notice of the cathedral's shabby condition. Architect Viollet-le-Duc began a renovation project that lasted through much of the 19th century. The spire is his invention; at the same time, Haussmann demolished the warren of little buildings in front of the cathedral, creating place du Parvis.

The facade divides neatly into three levels. On the first-floor level are the three main entrances: the Portal of the Virgin, on the left; the Portal of the Last Judgment, in the center; and the Portal of St. Anne (the oldest of the three), on the right. All are surmounted by magnificent carvings—most of them 19th-century copies of the originals—of figures, foliage, and biblical scenes. Above these are the restored statues of the kings of Israel, the Galerie des Rois. Above the gallery is the great rose window, and above that, the Galerie, at the base of the towers. The south tower houses the bell of Notre-Dame, as tolled by Quasimodo. Take a cue from Victor Hugo and climb all the way up the 387 steps of the tower (through the separate entrance, which is to the left of the facade as you face it). You'll be rewarded with the classic view of Paris, unforgettably framed by stone gargoyles designed by Viollet-le-Duc. To the north is Montmartre; to the west, the Arc de Triomphe, at the head of the Champs-Élysées; to the south, the towers of St-Sulpice and the Panthéon.

As you enter the nave, the faith of the early builders permeates all. The quiet, persuasive interior contrasts gracefully with the triumphant glory of the exterior, with the soft glow of the stained-glass windows replacing the statues of saints, virgins, prophets, and apostles. The best time to visit is early in the morning, when the cathedral is at its brightest and least crowded. At the entrance are the massive 12th-century columns supporting the twin towers. Look down the nave to the transepts—the arms of the church—where, at the south (right) entrance to the chancel, you'll glimpse the haunting 12th-century statue of Notre-Dame de Paris, *Our Lady of Paris*. The chancel itself owes parts of its decoration to a vow taken by Louis XIII in 1638. Still without an heir after 23 years of marriage, he promised to dedicate the entire country to the Virgin Mary if his queen produced a son. When this apparently miraculous event came to pass, Louis set about redecorating the chancel and choir. On the south side of the chancel is the **Trésor** (treasury), with a passable collection of garments, reliquaries, and silver and gold plate.

Under the square in front of the cathedral is the **Crypte Archéologique,** Notre-Dame's archaeological museum. It contains remains of previous churches on the site, scale models charting the district's development, and relics and artifacts dating from the Parisii, who lived here 2,000 years ago, unearthed during excavations in the 1960s. The foundations of the 3rd-century Gallo-Roman rampart and of the 6th-century Merovingian church can also be seen.

❸ If your interest in the cathedral is not yet sated, duck into the **Musée de Notre-Dame** (✉ 10 rue du Cloître-Notre-Dame, Île de la Cité), across the street opposite the north door. The museum's paintings, engravings, medallions, and other objects and documents chart the history of the cathedral. ⊠ *Pl. du Parvis, Île de la Cité* ☎ *01–53–10–07–00* ⊕ *www. monum.fr* 🖃 *Cathedral free, towers €7, crypt €3.30, treasury €2.50, museum €2.50* ☉ *Cathedral daily 8–7. Towers Apr.–June and Sept., daily 9:30–7:30; July–Aug., weekdays 9–7:30, weekends 9 AM–11 PM; Oct.–Mar., daily 10–5:30. Treasury Mon.–Sat. 9:30–11:30 and 1–5:30. Crypt Tues.–Sun. 10–6. Museum Wed. and weekends 2:30–6* Ⓜ *Cité.*

🔟 **Palais de Justice** (Law Courts). The city's law courts were built by Baron Haussmann in his characteristically weighty neoclassical style in about 1860. You can wander around the buildings, watch the bustle of the lawyers, or attend a court hearing. The solidity of Haussmann's buildings seems to emphasize the finesse of two important sights enclosed within the complex spared by Haussmann: La Conciergerie and Sainte-Chapelle. ⊠ *Bd. du Palais, Île de la Cité* ☉ *Mon.–Sat. 8–6* Ⓜ *Cité.*

⑲ **Place de la Concorde.** This majestic square at the foot of the Champs-Élysées was originally consecrated to the glory of Louis XV, but there was no peace or concord in its early years. Laid out in the 1770s, it was first called place Louis-XV; unlike traditional squares such as the place Royale, it was not fully hemmed in by buildings. But the great open space became a theater of punishment, as it was here that crowds watched as Louis XVI and Marie-Antoinette, like more than 2,000 others between 1793 and 1795, were guillotined. And it was here that Madame Roland cried, "Liberty, what crimes are committed in thy name!" When the blood of the victims had been washed away and the yells of the *sans culottes* extremists had died down, the square was renamed Concorde. In place of a statue of Louis XV, a politically neutral monument was put up in 1833: a 107-foot obelisk originally quarried in the 8th century BC and a present from the viceroy of Egypt (its gilded cap was restored in 1998). The square continues to have politically symbolic weight. Demonstrations gather here, as the Assemblée Nationale is right across the river and the Palais de l'Élysée (the French presidential palace) and the U.S. Embassy are just around the corner. Among the handsome 18th-century buildings facing the square is the Hôtel Crillon, originally built by Gabriel—architect of the Petit Trianon—as an 18th-century home for three of France's wealthiest families. ⊠ *Champs-Élysées* Ⓜ *Concorde.*

⑫ **Place Dauphine.** The Surrealists loved place Dauphine, which they called "le sexe de Paris" because of its suggestive V shape. Its origins were much more proper: built by Henri IV, the king named the place in homage to his successor, called the dauphin, who grew up to become Louis XIII. The triangular place is lined with some 17th-century houses that writer André Maurois believed were the quintessence of Paris and France. Take a seat on the park bench, enjoy a picnic, and see if you agree. ⊠ *Île de la Cité* Ⓜ *Cité.*

⑳ **Pont Alexandre-III.** No other bridge over the Seine epitomizes the fin-de-siècle frivolity of the Belle Époque (or Paris itself) like the exuberant, bronze lamp–lined Pont Alexandre-III. An urban masterstroke that seems as much created of cake frosting and sugar sculptures as of stone and iron, it makes an alluring backdrop for fashion shoots and the surrounding Parisian landmarks. The bridge was built, like the Grand Palais and Petit Palais nearby, for the 1900 world's fair; it was inaugurated by the visiting Russian czar, the ill-fated Nicholas II, and ingratiatingly named in honor of his father. ⊠ *Invalides* Ⓜ *Invalides.*

⑭ **Pont Neuf.** Crossing the Île de la Cité, just behind square du Vert-Galant, is the oldest bridge in Paris, confusingly called the New Bridge. It was completed in 1607 and was the first bridge in the city to be built without houses lining either side—allegedly because Henri IV wanted a clear view of Notre-Dame from his windows at the Louvre. It's a romantic spot to take in a view of the Seine. ⊠ *Île de la Cité* Ⓜ *Cité.*

❾ **Sainte-Chapelle.** This fragile Gothic jewel is home to the most ancient
Fodor'sChoice stained-glass windows in Paris. Built by the obsessively pious Louis IX
★ (1226–70), this chapel was constructed in less than three years to house the king's collection of relics acquired from the impoverished emperor of Constantinople at phenomenal expense (and that even in Louis's time were considered of questionable authenticity). Some of these relics have survived and can be seen in the treasury of Notre-Dame, but most were lost during the Revolution.

The building is actually two chapels in one. The plain first-floor chapel, made gloomy by insensitive mid-19th-century restorations (which could do with restoration themselves), is dedicated to the Virgin Mary, whose statue stands on the pier of the entrance. Today you might be startled to see a souvenir stand taking up much of the space, but look up at the low vaulted ceiling, decorated with fleurs-de-lis and cleverly arranged Ls for Louis. Up a dark spiral staircase near the entrance, you'll find the king's chapel, which he accessed through the main upstairs door, directly across from his royal bedroom.

Here the famous beauty of Sainte-Chapelle comes alive: instead of walls, all you see are 6,458 square feet of stained glass, delicately supported by painted stonework that seems to disappear in the colorful light streaming through the windows. The lowest section of the windows was restored in the mid-1800s, but otherwise this chapel presents intact incredibly rare stained glass. Deep reds and blues dominate the background glass here, noticeably different from later, lighter medieval styles such as those in Notre-Dame's rose window. The chapel is essentially an enormous magic lantern illuminating the 1,130 figures from the Bible, to create—as one writer poetically put it—"the most marvelous colored and moving air ever held within four walls." Originally, the king's holy relics were displayed in the raised apse and shown to the faithful on Good Friday. Today the magic of the chapel comes alive during the regular concerts held here; call to check the schedule. ⊠ *4 bd. du Palais, Île de la Cité* ☎ *01–53–73–78–51* ⊕ *www.monum.fr* ✆ *€6.10, joint ticket with Conciergerie €10.40* ⊗ *Daily 9:30–6, last entry at 5:30 Mar.–Oct., 4:30 Nov.–Feb.* Ⓜ *Cité.*

❻ **St-Louis-en-l'Île.** You can't miss the unusual lacey spire of this church as you approach the Île St-Louis; there are no other steeples to compete with it, as St-Louis is the only church on the island. The church was built from 1652 to 1765 to the baroque designs of architect François Le Vau, brother of the more famous Louis, who designed several mansions nearby. St-Louis's interior was essentially stripped during the Revolution, as happened to so many French churches. Look for the bizarre outdoor iron clock, which dates from 1741. ⊠ *Rue St-Louis-en-l'Île, Île St-Louis* Ⓜ *Pont Marie.*

need a break? Cafés all over sell the haute couture of ice cream, but **Berthillon** (⊠ 31 rue St-Louis-en-l'Île, Île St-Louis ☎ 01–43–54–31–61) itself is the place to come for this amazing treat. More than 30 flavors are served, including Grand Marnier and the mouth-puckering *cassis* (black currant); expect to wait in line. The shop is open Wednesday–Sunday but closes for part of August.

❹ **Square Jean-XXIII.** When it comes to views of Notre-Dame, no visit to the great cathedral is complete without a riverside walk past the cathedral through square Jean-XXIII. It offers a breathtaking sight of the east end of the cathedral. ⊠ *Île de la Cité* Ⓜ *Cité.*

⓭ **Square du Vert-Galant.** The equestrian statue of the Vert Galant himself—amorous adventurer Henri IV—surveys this leafy square at the western end of the Île de la Cité. Henri, king of France from 1589 until his assassination in 1610, was something of a dashing figure, by turns ruthless and charming, a stern upholder of the absolute rights of monarchy, and a notorious womanizer. He is probably best remembered for his cynical remark that *"Paris vaut bien une messe"* ("Paris is worth a mass"), a reference to his readiness to renounce Protestantism to gain the throne of predominantly Catholic France. To ease his conscience, he issued the Edict of Nantes in 1598, according French Protestants (almost) equal rights with their Catholic countrymen. The square itself is a fine spot to linger on a sunny afternoon and is the departure point for the glass-topped Vedette tour boats on the Seine (at the bottom of the steps to the right). ⊠ *Île de la Cité* Ⓜ *Pont Neuf.*

THE LOUVRE

Fodor'sChoice ★ The most recognized symbol of Paris is the Tour Eiffel, but the ultimate traveler's prize is the Louvre. This is the world's greatest art museum—and the largest, with representative examples from almost every civilization on earth. Along with Leonardo da Vinci's eternally inscrutable *Mona Lisa,* you can see works by virtually every major pre-20th-century Western painter, heart tuggers such as Delacroix's *Liberty Guiding the People,* and entire wings devoted to French decorative arts, Iranian treasures, and classical fragments. There's a not unfounded stereotype of Americans racing through the building, timing each other as they jog past the Big Three (the *Venus de Milo,* the *Winged Victory,* and the *Mona Lisa*) before collapsing into a waiting taxi. It's far more enjoyable to take your time, but pace yourself: thousands of treasures are on display, and despite well-located benches, it's easy to get tired as you wander through rooms crowded with Botticellis, Caravaggios, Poussins, and Géricaults. The Louvre is a coherent, unified structure, but it can be overwhelming. Instead of trying to see everything, focus on highlights that interest you personally—and don't despair if you get lost, for you're bound to stumble onto something fascinating.

The Louvre is much more than a museum—it is a saga that started centuries ago. Begun as a fortress by Philippe-Auguste at the turn of the 13th century, it became a royal residence under Charles V, who moved into the Louvre in 1364 after a bloody revolt on Île de la Cité. Parts of the medieval building have been excavated and can be seen during your visit. It was not until the 16th century, under François I, that today's Louvre began to take shape. Successive rulers expanded and adapted the palace, trying to make it both more comfortable and more impressive. In 1572 Henri de Navarre, who became Henri IV, narrowly escaped assassination here, while his retinue was slaughtered and the St. Bartholomew's Day Massacre raged through the capital. In 1594 he returned to the palace to outline a sweeping expansion plan. Through the years Louis XIII, Louis XIV, Napoléon I, and Napoléon III all contributed to its construction.

The construction of the stately **Cour Carrée** (Square Court), mainly during the reign of Louis XIII, marked the beginning of the Louvre as you see it today. When a competition for architects to design a suitably imposing east facade was held in 1668, a young draftsman named Claude Perrault teamed up with the seasoned illustrator and painter Charles Le Brun to produce the winning proposal. You'd have thought its muscular rhythms would have wowed the Sun King, but he left the city for Versailles in 1682, making only rare visits to the Louvre, which unsurprisingly fell into disrepair. After the Revolution, part of the Louvre was opened as a public museum, its galleries stocked with nationalized art taken from the Church, the royal family, and the nobility. Napoléon Bonaparte's military campaigns at the turn of the 19th century brought a new influx of holdings, as his soldiers carried off treasures from each invaded country. Vivant Denon, known as "the eye of Napoléon," directed the particularly astonishing acquisitions of art from Italy and Egypt. But Parisians had a limited time to enjoy the new collection: with Napoléon's fall in 1815, the museum was forced to return many of its works to the original owners. Three more French kings, Louis XVIII, Charles X, and Louis-Philippe, followed by Emperor Napoléon III, all used the Louvre as their power base. During World War II some of the most precious artworks were hidden, while the remainder was looted; German occupiers used the Louvre's rooms as office space. Most of the stolen pieces were recovered after the liberation of Paris. No large-scale changes were made until François Mitterrand was elected President in 1981.

Mitterrand viewed Paris the way a king might consider his palace: the city was to be an architectural reflection of his power and taste. His *Grands Projects* plan to stamp Paris with new and updated monuments kicked off with the renovation of the Louvre. Mitterrand commissioned I. M. Pei's **Pyramide,** the giant glass pyramid surrounded by three smaller pyramids in the Cour Napoléon. Unveiled in March 1989, it's more than just a grandiloquent gesture; the pyramid provided a new, much-needed museum entrance. Moreover, it acts as the originating point for the majestic vista stretching through the Arc du Carrousel, the Jardin des Tuileries, across place de la Concorde, up the Champs-Élysées to the towering Arc de Triomphe, and ending at the giant modern arch at La Défense, 4 km (2½ mi) farther west.

Numbers in the text correspond to numbers on the Louvre map.

Practicalities

The Pyramide is now the museum's main entry point. To get into the Louvre, you may have to wait in two long lines: one outside the Pyramide entrance and another downstairs at the ticket booths. There is another entrance at the Porte de Lions, on the Seine side of the museum's wing that reaches into the Jardin des Tuileries, but this door is often closed. The third, and often quickest, entrance is in the underground mall, Carrousel du Louvre, where you can buy passes at automatic ticket machines. **Be sure to hold onto your ticket**; it will get you into any and all wings as many times as you like during one day.

Once inside, you should stop by the information desk to pick up a free color-coded map and check which rooms are closed for the day. (Closures rotate through the week.) Beyond this, you'll have all you need—shops, a post office, and places to eat. Café Marly may have an enviable location facing into the Cour Napoléon, but its food is decidedly lackluster. For a more soigné lunch, keep your appetite in check until you get to the museum's stylish Café Richelieu, or head outside the palace walls. (Remember, your entry ticket is valid all day and once you have your ticket you can skip the entry line.)

The awesome collections are divided into seven areas: Asian antiquities, Egyptian antiquities, Greek and Roman antiquities, sculpture, objets d'art, paintings, and prints and drawings. The Louvre also has temporary exhibitions, some held in the Napoléon Hall behind the entry staircase.

In the following pages we've outlined a simple guide that's arranged by location (wing, floor, collection, and room number). This is a selection of favorites, chosen to act as key points for your exploration. The museum bookstore sells plenty of English-language books and catalogs that delve into the collections. There's also a full calendar of lectures, films, concerts, and special exhibits; some are part of the excellent lunch-hour series called Les Midis du Louvre. Most are not included in the basic ticket price—pick up a three-month schedule at the information desk or check online for information. ⊠ *Palais du Louvre, Louvre/Tuileries* ☎ *01–40–20–53–17 information* ⊕ *www.louvre.fr* ⬚ *€8.50, €6 after 6 PM Wed. and Fri. and all day Sun. Free 1st Sun. of month, €8.50 for Napoléon Hall exhibitions* ☉ *Mon., Thurs., and weekends, 9–6, Wed. and Fri. 9 AM–9:45 PM* Ⓜ *Palais-Royal.*

Timing

Consider splitting your visit into more than one day or following an afternoon trip with an evening stint when you've got a second wind. The shortest entry lines tend to be at around 1. Prices drop after 6 for the late-night Monday and Wednesday openings, and the crowds thin out in the evening. Remember that the Louvre is closed on Tuesday.

Richelieu Wing

Below Ground & Ground Floor

As you enter the Richelieu Wing from the Pyramide, on the left and up a flight of stairs is a gallery that displays temporary exhibits composed of the Louvre's most recent acquisitions. Straight ahead is Salle 20 (*salle* is French for "room"), filled with French sculpture, including frilly busts of members of the court of Louis XIV, but most people pass through this room to get to the dramatic **sculpture courtyards** to your right (Cour Puget) and left (Cour Marly). The Cour Marly is filled with classical sculptures, many from the park at Marly commissioned by Louis XIV. In the upper left corner of Cour Marly, you'll find Salle 2, with fragments from Cluny, the powerful Romanesque abbey in Burgundy that dominated 11th-century French Catholicism. In Salles 4–6, follow the evolution of French sculpture as you look at the work of different centuries, especially when you continue forward to the funerary art in Salles 7–10. The late-15th-century tomb of Philippe Pot, in Salle 10, is especially eerie: you see Philippe stretched out in eternal prayer, held aloft by eight black-robed pallbearers. Walking through Salles 11–19, you can see how the hieratic style of medieval French sculpture began to give way to the naturalism of the Renaissance.

To the left of the Cour Puget are Salles 25–33, filled with the products of the Académie Royale, the art school of 18th-century France. To the right, behind the Cour Puget, is the start of the Louvre's **Oriental antiquities** collection. Within the glass cases of Salle 1 are ancient Mesopotamian carvings. Facing the case are the pieced-together fragments of the 3rd-millennium BC Sumerian Stela of the Vultures, containing the oldest-known written history, including images of King Eannatum catching his enemies in a net. Farther along, serene, wide-eyed alabaster statues fill Salle 1b, a troupe of Sumerian figures from the 3rd millennium BC. The centerpiece of Salle 3 is the Codex of Hammurabi, an 18th-century BC black-diorite stela containing the world's oldest written code of laws. Near the top of the text you can see Hammurabi, king of the first Babylonian dynasty, meeting a seated Shamash, the god of justice. On the east side of Salle 3 is a bas-relief lion in glazed terra-cotta tiles, one of numerous such beasts from the 6th-century BC Gates of Babylon.

Salle 4 is the Cour Khorsabad, a re-creation of the temple erected by Assyrian king Sargon II in the 8th century BC at the palace of Dur-Sharrukin. Walking among the temple's five **massive winged bulls,** known as *lamassu*, or benign demigods, is one of the most spectacular experiences in the Louvre. It's hard not to catch your breath, even though the display is incomplete; the frigate transporting the rest of the collection sank en route.

First Floor

Head straight through the objets d'art section to see the magnificently restored **royal apartments of Napoléon III.** (If you can't make it to Versailles, see these for a dose of over-the-top grandeur instead.) En route, you'll pass decorative items such as the solid-crystal Restoration dressing table (Salle 77) that prepare you for the eye-popping luxury of the Second Empire in Salle 87. If the sight of Napoléon III's extravagant

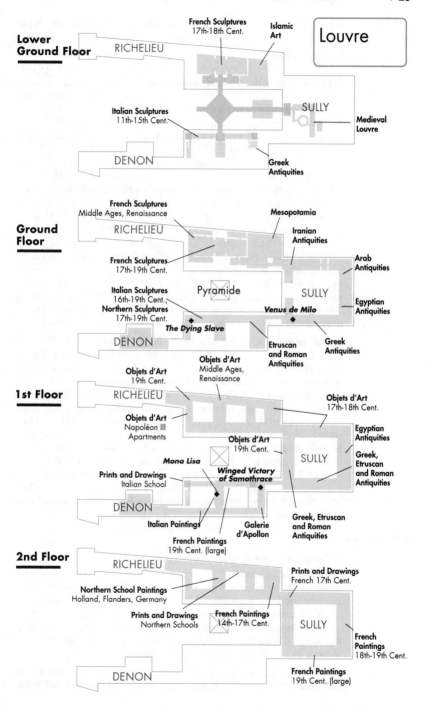

Louvre

dining room makes you hungry, an elegant museum lunch spot is just around the corner, with a pretty view and a limited but tasty menu.

Second Floor

Just behind the escalators is Salle 1, which begins the section devoted to **French and Northern School paintings.** At the entrance to this room is a 14th-century gold-backed painting of John the Good—the oldest-known individual portrait from the north of Italy. In Salle 3 is the remarkable stop-action *Retable of Saint Denis,* by Henri Bellchose, painted for Jean Sans Peur of Burgundy (you can visit Jean's tower near Les Halles). In Salle 4 hangs *The Madonna of Chancellor Rolin,* by the 15th-century Early Netherlandish master Jan van Eyck (late 14th century–1441). This wildly detailed painting exemplifies the breakthrough work of the Flemish painters. The so-called **Flemish Primitives** devised new binding agents for oil paint and then pioneered a technique of layering translucent colors. As the new oils were easier to handle than the previously used tempera, van Eyck and his contemporaries could bring modeling and detail to new heights. In Salle 10 keep an eye out for the bizarre, titillating École de Fontainebleau portrait of Gabrielle d'Estrées and her sister. Also worth noting are three private collections given to the Louvre in the 1970s, which are displayed in Salles 20–23, as you walk from the Richelieu Wing to the Sully Wing on the second floor. The terms of the legacies prevent these collections from being broken up, and they cover a stunning range of work, from Canaletto to Degas.

A cycle of giant matching canvases by Peter Paul Rubens (1577–1640) fills Salle 18, depicting Maria de' Medici's journey from Florence to Paris—an overbearing take on a relatively cushy trip. The swirling baroque paintings were commissioned by Maria herself and originally hung in the nearby Palais du Luxembourg. The *Disembarkation of Maria de' Medici at the Port of Marseille* memorably portrays an artificially slimmed-down Maria about to skip over the roly-poly daughters of Poseidon as a personified France beckons her to shore. In Salle 31 are several **paintings by Rembrandt** van Rijn (1606–69). In his 1648 *Supper at Emmaus,* he daringly centers his subject, attacking the canvas with bold brushstrokes. The masterpiece of the **Dutch collection** is *The Lacemaker,* by Jan Vermeer (1632–75), in Salle 38. Obsessed with optical accuracy, Vermeer painted the red thread in the foreground as a slightly blurred jumble, just as one would actually see it if focusing on the girl.

Sully Wing

Below Ground & Ground Floor

The entrance into the Sully Wing is more impressive than the entrances to the others—you get to walk around and through the foundations and moat of the castle built by Philippe-Auguste in the 13th century. This is the place to start your Louvre experience if you're with kids—the medieval walls lead enticingly to the sphinx-guarded entrance of the **Egyptian wing.** Salles 14 and 15 will delight mummy enthusiasts, and there are rare examples of Egyptian funerary art.

Upstairs, the northern galleries of the Sully continue the ancient **Iranian collection** begun in the Richelieu Wing. To the right is the **Greek collec-**

tion, home to the famous 2nd-century BC *Venus de Milo* (Salle 12). The armless statue, one of the most reproduced and recognizable works of art in the world, is actually as beautiful as they say—it is worth your trouble to push past the lecturing curators and tourist groups to get a closer look at the incredible skill with which the Greeks turned cold marble into something vibrant and graceful. The *Venus* was dug up on the Greek island of Milos in the 19th century and sold for 6,000 francs to the French ambassador in Constantinople, who presented her to King Louis XVIII. The original form of her missing arms remains a mystery.

First Floor

The northern galleries of the first floor continue with the **objets d'art collection,** including works from all over Europe, and connect with the Richelieu wing's Napoléon III apartments.

Second Floor

Sully picks up **French painting in the 17th century** where the Richelieu Wing leaves off. Two directions appear during the time of Louis XIV: the official Academic style, heavily influenced by classic Renaissance art, and the more emotive Northern style, inspired by Flemish artists. The Académiciens are best exemplified by Nicolas Poussin (1594–1665, Salle 19), who spent much of his life in Rome and was the first international painting star to come from France. (Interestingly, Poussin's coldly unemotional paintings were studied intensely by Postimpressionist painter Cézanne.) The antithesis of this style was the candlelighted modest work by outsiders Georges de La Tour (Salle 28) and the more impassive Le Nain brothers. The Académie essentially ignored these upstarts; its head, Charles Lebrun (1619–90), was Louis XIV's principal designer at Versailles. Lebrun created jam-packed historical paintings that combine the cinematic scope of Rubens with the classicism of Poussin. You'll notice some rather flattering references to Louis XIV in Lebrun's *Story of Alexander* in Salle 32.

Fresh energy crackled into **French painting in the 18th century,** after the death of Louis XIV. Antoine Watteau (1684–1721) has long been considered the greatest painter of his era, known for his theatrical scenes and *fêtes galantes,* portrayals of well-dressed figures in bucolic settings. In scenes such as his 1717 *Pilgrimage to the Island of Cythera* (Salle 36), he used delicate brushstrokes and soft tones to convey the court set, here depicted arriving on (or departing from) Cythera, the mythical isle of love. Despite the sensuous trappings, there's a disturbing undercurrent; the island's greenery is fading into autumnal gold, and the revelers seem both drugged by Cythera's pleasures and aware of the fleeting nature of bliss. Maurice-Quentin Delatour (1704–88) was another court favorite; his large pastel work *La Marquise de Pompadour* (Salle 45) shows Louis XV's mistress as a patroness of the arts, with everything a good courtesan should have: books, music manuscripts, engravings, and, of course, a smashing outfit.

The Académie Royale defined the standards of painting through revolution, republic, and empire. Exoticism wafted in during the Napoleonic Empire, as seen in the **Turkish bath paintings of Jean-Auguste-Dominique Ingres** (1780–1867). Though Ingres's long-limbed women hardly look

Turkish, they are singularly elegant and his supersmooth style was extremely influential. In Salle 60 you'll see the same figures reappearing throughout his career; compare the woman from *La Baigneuse* with the one in the *Turkish Bath* or with the slinky figure in his masterpiece, *La Grande Odalisque,* which you can visit in the Denon Wing.

Denon Wing

Below Ground

To the south and east of the Pyramide entrance are galleries displaying **early Renaissance Italian sculpture,** including a 15th-century *Madonna and Child* by the Florentine Donatello (1386–1466). Before going upstairs, it's worth walking through the galleries of **Etruscan and Roman works.** These stretch up to the ground floor and include beautiful mosaics from Antioche, Turkey. In Salle 18 you'll find the 6th-century BC *Etruscan Sarcophagus* from Cerveteri, showing a married couple pieced together from thousands of clay fragments.

Walk up the marble Escalier Daru to discover the sublime **Winged Victory of Samothrace,** who seems poised for flight at the top of the stairs— an exhilarating, breathtaking sight. The 3rd-century BC statue was found on a tiny Greek island in the northern Aegean. Depicted in the act of descending from Olympus, the *Winged Victory,* or *Nike,* to use the ancient Greek name, originally came from the isle of Samothrace and was carved by an unknown master in 305 BC to commemorate the naval victory of Demetrius Poliorcetes over the Turks.

First Floor

From the Escalier Daru, go to the left of the *Winged Victory* to the **Gallerie d'Apollon,** reopened in 2004 after a stunning renovation. Built in 1661 but not finished until 1851, the hall was a model for Versaille's Hall of Mirrors. Its dozens of paintings, sculptures, and tapestries seem to cover almost every square inch of wall space. The gallery also showcases Louis XV's weighty coronation crown, the French crown jewels, and the gift from Napoléon to Marie-Louise for their 1810 wedding: a necklace with no fewer than 38 emeralds and 1,246 diamonds.

Walk back past the *Winged Victory* to find the magnificent **Italian painting** collection. Note that some rooms here are slowly being remodeled. To build up to Leonardo's mysteriously smiling masterpiece, walk through the Italian galleries to see how medieval painters gradually evolved a sense of perspective and personal portraiture. Salle 5 is the beginning of the aptly named **Grande Galerie,** a long, thin gallery where you'll spot Mantegna's powerful *St-Sebastian,* stuck with arrows. Andrea Mantegna (1431–1506) was a follower of the Florentine architect Brunelleschi, who wrote a comprehensive treatise on perspective. As a result, Mantegna's works are some of the first to have a clear vanishing point.

Next you'll find four paintings by the original Renaissance man, painter-engineer-inventor-anatomist Leonardo da Vinci (1452–1519). His enigmatic, androgynous *St-John the Baptist* hangs here, along with more overtly religious works such as the 1483 *Virgin of the Rocks,* with the harmonious pyramidal arrangement of its figures. Take a close look at the pretty portrait of *La Belle Ferronnière,* which Leonardo painted a decade before the *Mona Lisa*; it will give you something to compare with Mona when you finally get to meet her. Continue down the corridor, past masterworks by Raphael and Giuseppe Arcimboldo, whose curious allegories show faces made of fruits and flowers.

And then you'll be in the midst of a crowd, approaching the Most Famous Painting in the World, the **Mona Lisa** (properly, *La Gioconda,* known as *La Joconde* in French). With the guards, barriers, and no-picture policy (to keep the lines moving), it feels as if you're visiting a holy relic. And in some ways you are: this small painting was Leonardo's favorite. It has belonged to innumerable French rulers since its acquisition by François I, including Napoléon, who kept it on his bedroom wall. The canvas has had its brushes with disaster—it was stolen from the Louvre by an Italian nationalist in 1911 (recovered from a Florentine hotel two years later), and it was attacked by acid in 1956, which fortunately only damaged the lower part of the painting. The wife of one Francesco del Giocondo, a Florentine millionaire, was 24 when she sat for this painting in 1503; some historians believe the portrait was actually painted after her death. Either way, she has become immortal through da Vinci's ingenious "sfumato" technique, which combines glowing detail with soft, depth-filled brushwork. Even in a room packed with fellow worshippers, it's hard not to feel that she is looking straight through you. As of 2005, she has a sleek new setting in the Salle des États, near Salles 5 and 6.

The Salle des États also contains the massive *Feast at Cana,* by Pablo Veronese (1528–88), a sumptuous painting reminiscent of the Venetian painter's *Christ in the House of Levi* (which is in Venice). These paintings, filled with partygoers, prompted a formal summons from the pope, asking Veronese to explain in person why he had included the chaos of drunken revelers, dwarves, and animals in what was purportedly a holy scene.

You can now go on to Spanish painting, or double back to find the Italian drawing section. This leads to a small café in the stairwell, and to three huge rooms devoted to **French large-scale 19th-century paintings.** These include some of the most famous and controversial works in the history of French painting. In Salle 77 is the gruesome 1819 painting **The Raft of the Medusa,** by Théodore Géricault (1791–1824). The work is radical because it marks the first time a large-scale historical-treatment painting tackled a current event. Géricault was inspired by a grim news report: survivors of a wrecked French merchant ship were left adrift on a raft without supplies. Stories of cannibalism and murder flared up. Géricault interviewed survivors, visited the morgue to draw corpses, and turned his painting of the disaster into a strong indictment of authority. Literally, the painting shows the ship of state foundering. The Romantic work was intentionally unheroic, the shipwrecked men devolving into a jumbled mass of greenish shadow.

Similarly, when Eugène Delacroix (1798–1863) decided to paint **Liberty Leading the People,** he flew in the face of artistic standards by lionizing street urchins and proletariat rebels. Though he wasn't directly involved in the Trois Glorieuses—a three-day revolution in 1830 that ousted Charles X's autocracy and brought in a parliamentary monarchy—Delacroix felt compelled to commemorate the event. His painting shows the allegorical figure of Liberty, bare-breasted, gripping a rifle, and waving a flag while leading Republicans over barricades and the fallen bodies of other Frenchmen. The faces are neither beautiful nor lighted religiously from within, but rather desperate and dirty. His depiction of Liberty hit such a chord with the public that variations of the figure have appeared on everything from stamps to money.

Head to Salle 75 for an artistic 180°: the gleaming pomp and circumstance of a new empire. French classicist Jacques-Louis David (1748–1825) produced the **Coronation of Napoléon** to commemorate that politically fraught event of December 2, 1804. In a sensible career move, David did not capture the moment when Napoléon snatched the crown from the hands of Pope Pius VII to place it upon his own head, but instead chose the more romantic moment of the new emperor turning to crown his wife, Joséphine. David was the ultimate painter-survivor: he was official designer of the Revolutionary government, endured two rounds of exile, and became one of the greatest of Napoléon's painters. His students included Jean-Auguste-Dominique Ingres (1780–1867), who has several wonderful portraits in this room.

Ground Floor

Drift downstairs to the **Italian sculpture** on the ground level, concluding with Salle 4, where you'll find the 1513–15 **Slaves of Michelangelo**. After carefully selecting his slab of marble, Michelangelo (1475–1564) would spend days envisioning the form of the sculpture within the uncut stone. The sculptures that finally emerged openly eroticized the male body. Parts of the stone were left rough, so that the figures look as though they're trying to free themselves from the stone blocks—a controversial design, but one that was to inspire Rodin and other modern artists.

The above highlights of the Louvre collection are the merest tip of the iceberg. You'll also find walls virtually wallpapered with masterpieces by Fra Angelico, Botticelli, Holbein, Hals, Brueghel, El Greco, Murillo, Boucher, Goya, and Caravaggio—whose *Death of the Virgin* towers over the Grande Galerie—just to mention a few of the famous names, along with one-hit wonders like Enguerrand Quarton's magnificent 15th-century *Pietà*. Other collections here will delight connoisseurs, such as the examples of French furniture. The grandiose 17th- and 18th-century productions of Boulle and Riesener, marvels of intricate craftsmanship, are prized by those with a fondness for opulent decoration.

Carrousel du Louvre

Part of the early 1990s' Louvre renovation program, this subterranean shopping complex is centered on an inverted glass pyramid (overlooked by the regional Île-de-France tourist office) and contains shops, spaces for fashion shows (this is Paris, after all), an auditorium, and a huge parking garage. At lunchtime museum-goers rush to the mall-style food

ON THE TRAIL OF *THE DA VINCI CODE*

HE DA VINCI CODE, Dan Brown's best-selling suspense novel, kicks off with a murder at one of Paris's greatest sights, the Louvre museum. Much of the ensuing action unfolds at real-life Parisian landmarks, so we've whipped up a tour to guide you to the highlights. Fair warning: the end of this tour includes a plot spoiler.

The book opens at that pinnacle of poshness, the **Ritz Paris** (✉ 15 place Vendôme, Louvre/Tuileries Ⓜ Opéra). Professor Robert Langdon is awoken by a late-night surprise visit. Lieutenant police inspector Bezu Fache, from the French equivalent of the FBI, tells him that the man with whom Langdon was supposed to meet earlier that day, Jacques Saunière, has been murdered.

From the Ritz, take rue de Castiglione out of the place Vendôme and hang a left on rue Saint Honoré to reach the **Palais-Royal** (✉ pl. du Palais-Royal, Louvre/Tuileries Ⓜ Palais-Royal). Under the arcades, keep your eyes on the ground to spot the bronze medallions marking the trail of the Rose Line. This line stands for the original zero-longitude line, which passed through Paris before being moved to Greenwich, England. You'll cross its path again.

Next cross the rue de Rivoli to reach the **Louvre** (✉ Palais du Louvre, Louvre/Tuileries Ⓜ Palais-Royal). Jacques Saunière's body is discovered in the Denon wing, not far from two of Leonardo da Vinci's greatest works. Near the body, the police have found an enigmatic message. With the help of Saunière's granddaughter, cryptologist Sophie Neveu, Langdon unravels the message: a series of clues that will lead the two on a quest for the Holy Grail.

The Denon wing houses the museum's Italian painting collection—including the works of the original Renaissance man,

painter-engineer-inventor-anatomist Leonardo da Vinci. The Mona Lisa was Leonardo's own favorite creation. Langdon subscribes to some interesting theories about the painting's meaning; Saunière used the painting to leave behind a crucial clue before he died. La Joconde, as she's called in French, is in a new space as of 2005: the Salle des États. Leonardo's enigmatic, androgynous St-John the Baptist hangs nearby in Salle 5, along with the 1483 Virgin of the Rocks, the hiding place of another clue from Saunière.

Neveu and Langdon flee the Louvre, heading first to the rue de Rivoli and then down the Champs-Élysées to the Arc de Triomphe. On a clear day you can see the Arc de Triomphe from the Arc du Carrousel, the arch standing between the Louvre and the Tuileries gardens. Langdon and Neveu zigzag through the city to throw the police off their trail and eventually make their way to the fictional Depository Bank of Zurich. So instead of tracing their route, cross instead to the Rive Gauche via the Pont du Carrousel, to the left of the Arc du Carrousel if you're facing the Tuileries.

Head south on rue Bonaparte to **Saint-Sulpice** (✉ pl. Saint-Sulpice, Saint-Germain-des-Prés Ⓜ Saint-Sulpice). Silas, an albino monk-assassin, visits this church believing he'll find a keystone to unlock the secret of the Grail. Near the middle of the nave on the right side, next to a stone statue, you can locate one end of the narrow brass strip marking the Rose Line. You can retrace the monk's path north across the nave and transept to an obelisk next to the statue of St. Peter.

Ready for a break? Nab a table at one of the cafés on the square in front of Saint-Sulpice. Or, if you can't rest before the end of your Grail quest, turn back to the Rive Droite. Good thing your Louvre entry ticket is valid all day.

court where fast food goes international. Unlike many stores, Carrousel shops are open every day, making them a good bet for last-minute gifts.

FROM THE TOUR EIFFEL
TO THE ARC DE TRIOMPHE

The Tour Eiffel lords over southwest Paris, and from almost any point on this walk you can see its jutting needle. For years many Parisians felt it was an iron eyesore and called it the Giant Asparagus, a 1,000-foot-tall vegetable that weighed 15 million pounds. But gradually the tower became part of the Parisian landscape, entering the hearts and souls of Parisians and visitors alike. Now it's beloved for its stunning nighttime illumination, topped by a sweeping lighthouse-like beacon that's visible for 80 km (50 mi) around.

Water is the second theme of this walk: fountains playing beneath place du Trocadéro; boat tours along the Seine; and an underground prowl through the city's sewers, if you can stand it. After sinking to the city's depths, you can play to more elevated sensibilities in one of the many museums in the area around Trocadéro. This is Paris at its most monumental, from the Champs de Mars near the start of this walk, where Napoléon once surveyed his troops, to the enormous Arc de Triomphe, standing foursquare at the top of the city's most famous avenue, the Champs-Élysées. This grand boulevard is the last leg of the Tour de France bicycle race, on the third or fourth Sunday in July, and the site of major ceremonies on Bastille Day (July 14) and Armistice Day (November 11). Its trees are often decked with the French *tricolore* and foreign flags to mark visits from heads of state.

There are some excellent megastores, including Virgin (music and video) and Sephora (makeup and perfume), along with a few chic restaurants, plus an opulent branch of the pâtissier Ladurée. Though the avenue has been polished up (wider sidewalks, fresh plantings, etc.), the presence of car showrooms and fast-food outlets dilutes the atmosphere. For a concentrated dose of high style, turn to nearby avenue Montaigne instead, which is edged with luxe boutiques.

Numbers in the text correspond to numbers in the margin and on the Tour Eiffel to Arc de Triomphe map.

a good walk

As you emerge from the métro at **École Militaire** ❶, you'll see the stately military academy ahead of you. Walk to the corner, cross both boulevards, and pass through a less-than-attractive parking lot, and you'll find yourself at the beginning of the **Champ de Mars** ❷. Once used as a parade ground and then as a site of the world exhibitions, this somewhat dusty formal park is a great place for kids to let off steam; it also provides an unbeatable approach to the Iron Lady of Paris, the **Tour Eiffel** ❸. As you get nearer, the tower's colossal bulk (it's far bigger and sturdier than pictures suggest) becomes spectacularly evident. If you want to skip this walk through the parade grounds, just take the RER directly to Champ de Mars for the Tour Eiffel.

Cross the Pont d'Iéna, peeking at the houseboats below and the merry-go-rounds on either side of the bridge. Above the gardens and fountains of the Trocadéro stands the Art Deco **Palais de Chaillot,** a cultural center containing three museums. (Many of its collections are under renovation at this writing.) Pause on the piazza, lined by gold statues, to admire the view of the Tour Eiffel. The south wing of the Palais, to your left as you arrive from the Seine, houses the **Musée de l'Homme** ❹, an anthropology museum, and the **Musée de la Marine** ❺, a maritime museum. The right wing was badly damaged by fire in 1997, and its **Musée des Monuments Français** ❻, with copies of statues, columns, and archways from throughout France, is being reorganized.

From the Palais head right down avenue du Président-Wilson with its street lamps designed by Frank Lloyd Wright. On the next block down on your right is another art deco building fronted by a rotunda lined with mosaics and alternating pinkish beige and pebble-dash concrete: the Conseil Économique et Social (Economic and Social Council). Echoing it across place d'Iéna is another older rotunda, topped by a Thai-inspired pineapple—the **Musée Guimet** ❼, with its extensive collection of Indo-Chinese and Far Eastern art. If you're interested in glittering crystal, make a detour up avenue d'Iéna to the **Maison de Baccarat** ❽, a small, Philippe Starck–designed funhouse museum. Otherwise, continue down avenue du Président-Wilson, where a former private palace (now the **Palais Galliera** ❾, an exhibition hall for displays of clothing design and fashion) squares up to the cool gray outlines of the 1930s of the **Musée d'Art Moderne de la Ville de Paris** ❿ and the **Palais de Tokyo** ⓫. The whole complex is a vestige of the 1930 Universal Exposition. After being derelict for more than a decade, the Palais de Tokyo reopened in 2002 as an ultrahip contemporary arts center. The city's high-powered collection of modern art, meanwhile, reopened in 2005 after its own makeover.

Continue down to place de l'Alma, where a giant golden torch appears to be saluting the memory of Diana, Princess of Wales, who died in a car crash in the tunnel below in 1997. In fact, this replica of the Statue of Liberty's flame was donated by Paris-based U.S. companies in 1989 in honor of the bicentennial of the French Revolution. For several years it served as the princess's unofficial shrine, receiving bouquets and messages from her grieving admirers. These days city workers regularly clean up the flowers, graffiti, and photographs that Diana and Dodi fans still leave here. Across the **Pont de l'Alma** ⓬ (to the left) is the entrance to **Les Égouts** ⓭, Paris's sewers. If you prefer a less malodorous tour of the city, stay on the Rive Droite and head down the sloping side road to the left of the bridge to the embarkation point of the **Bateaux Mouches** ⓮, the motorboat tours.

Across the Seine you'll see the long, low outline of the new **Musée du Quai Branly** ⓯, meant by architect Jean Nouvel to suggest the Tour Eiffel's shadow. Set to open in early 2006, the museum will offer a rich cross-section of state-owned anthropological collections.

From place de l'Alma head up the grand thoroughfare of avenue Montaigne, one of the leading showcases for the great haute-couture houses

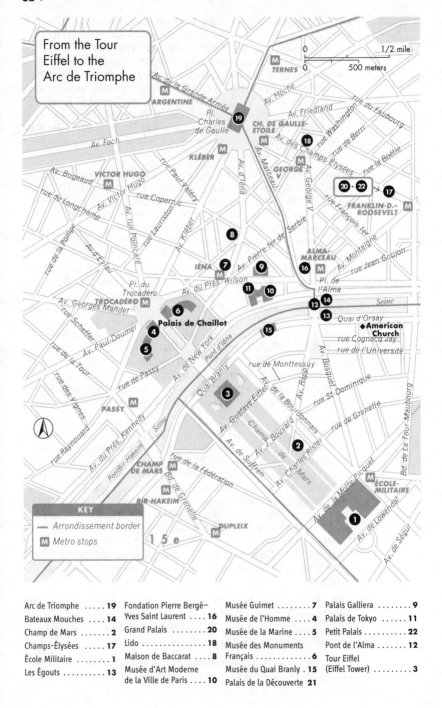

From the Tour
Eiffel to the
Arc de Triomphe

such as Dior, Chanel, Christian Lacroix, Prada, and Louis Vuitton. You'll also pass the Théâtre des Champs-Élysées, where Josephine Baker made her wildly acclaimed debut in 1925. Get a different take on fashion by going over a block to avenue Marceau, where you'll find the **Fondation Pierre Bergé–Yves Saint Laurent** ⑯. The gallery fills what was once the designer Yves Saint Laurent's atelier; now it shows clothes for admiring and studying, not buying. After some dazzling window-shopping, continue on to the Rond-Point des Champs-Élysées, the main traffic nexus of Paris's most famous avenue and turn left up the **Champs-Élysées** ⑰. At No. 116 is the famous **Lido** ⑱ nightclub, opposite the venerable Le Fouquet's restaurant-café, once frequented by Orson Welles.

Continue up to the top of the avenue and place Charles-de-Gaulle, known to Parisians as L'Étoile, or the Star—a reference to the streets that fan out from it—and site of the colossal, 164-foot **Arc de Triomphe** ⑲. L'Étoile is Europe's most chaotic traffic circle: your only way of getting to the Arc de Triomphe in the middle is to take an underground passage from the top right of avenue des Champs-Élysées. From the top of the Arc de Triomphe you can see the star effect of the 12 radiating avenues and the vista down the Champs-Élysées toward place de la Concorde and the distant Louvre. To the west are the verdant Bois de Boulogne, the posh suburb of Neuilly, and the towering office buildings and ultramodern arch of La Défense.

If the glimmer of a glass roof down at the other end of the Champs-Élysées beckons you, wander back down the tree-lined street and turn right onto avenue Winston-Churchill. Looming over the street corner are Jean Cardot's giant bronze statue of General de Gaulle and Cogne's statue of President Clémenceau. On the left is the **Grand Palais** ⑳, the back of which houses the **Palais de la Découverte** ㉑, a science museum with a planetarium. The Grand Palais faces the smaller **Petit Palais** ㉒; both museums were built for the Exposition Universelle of 1900 and at this writing both were undergoing renovation. A 10-foot statue of Churchill gazes toward the Seine and the Pont Alexandre-III. From here it's not much farther to reach the Tuileries gardens (*see* Notre-Dame to Place de la Concorde, *above*), where you can rest with a snack or a drink at a café table under the trees.

TIMING   You can probably cover this 5½-km (3½-mi) walk in about three hours, but if you wish to ascend the Tour Eiffel, take a trip along the Seine, or visit any of the plethora of museums along the way, you should allow most of a day. Going all the way down the Champs adds about half an hour to your walk.

What to See

★ ⑲ **Arc de Triomphe.** Inspired by Rome's Arch of Titus, this colossal, 164-foot triumphal arch was planned by Napoléon—who liked to consider himself the heir to the Roman emperors—to celebrate his military successes. Unfortunately, Napoléon's strategic and architectural visions were not entirely on the same plane, and the Arc de Triomphe proved something of an embarrassment. Although the emperor wanted the monument completed in time for an 1810 parade in honor of his new bride, Marie-Louise, the arch was still only a few feet high, and a dummy arch of painted canvas was strung up to save face.

Empires come and go, and Napoléon's had been gone for more than 20 years before the Arc de Triomphe was finally finished, in 1836. It has some magnificent sculpture by François Rude, such as *The Departure of the Volunteers,* better known as *La Marseillaise,* to the right of the arch when viewed from the Champs-Élysées. Names of Napoléon's generals are inscribed on the stone facades—those underlined are the hallowed figures who fell on the fields of battle. After showing alarming signs of decay, the structure received a thorough overhaul in 1989 and is once again neo-Napoleonic in its splendor. There is a small museum halfway up the arch devoted to its history. France's Unknown Soldier is buried beneath the archway; the flame is rekindled every evening at 6:30, which is the most atmospheric time to visit. To beat the crowds, come early in the morning. ⊠ *Pl. Charles-de-Gaulle, Champs-Élysées* ☎ *01–55–37–73–77* ⊕ *www.monum.fr* ⊠ *€7* ☉ *Apr.–Sept., daily 10 AM–11 PM; Oct.–Mar., daily 10 AM–10:30 PM* Ⓜ *Métro or RER: Étoile.*

☕ ⑭ **Bateaux Mouches.** If you want to view Paris in slow motion, hop on one of these famous motorboats, which set off on their hour-long tours of the city waters regularly (every half hour in summer) from place de l'Alma. Their route heads east to the Île St-Louis and then back west, past the Tour Eiffel, as far as the Allée des Cygnes and its miniature version of the Statue of Liberty. These were used as regular ferries on a daily basis by Parisians until the 1930s. As they bounced from bank to bank on the river, they gave rise, some say, to the name *Bateaux Mouches* (which translates as "fly boats"); more sober historians say the name *mouche* actually refers to a district of Lyon, where the boats were originally manufactured. But you might prefer to take this Seine cruise on the smaller Vedettes du Pont Neuf, which depart from square du Vert-Galant on the Île de la Cité, as the Vedettes have a guide giving commentary in French and English, while the Bateaux Mouches have a loud recorded spiel in several languages. ⊠ *Pl. de l'Alma, Trocadéro/Tour Eiffel* ☎ *01–40–76–99–99* ⊕ *www.bateaux-mouches.fr* ⊠ *€7* Ⓜ *Alma-Marceau.*

❷ **Champ de Mars.** This long, formal garden, landscaped at the start of the 20th century, lies between the Tour Eiffel and École Militaire. It was previously used as a parade ground and was the site of the world exhibitions of 1867, 1889 (date of the construction of the tower), and 1900. Today the park is a bit dusty and has a parade-ground feel, but it's a great spot for pickup soccer, outdoor concerts, or just some time on a bench to admire the view of Lady Eiffel. There's also a playground where kids can let off steam. Ⓜ *École Militaire; RER: Champ de Mars.*

⑰ **Champs-Élysées.** Marcel Proust lovingly described the elegance of the world's most famous avenue, the Champs-Élysées, during its Belle Époque heyday, when its cobblestones resounded to the clatter of horses and carriages. Today, despite the constant surge of cars up and down the avenue and the influx of chain shops, there's still a certain je ne sais quoi about strolling up Les Champs, especially at dusk as the refurbished

CHEAP (SIGHTSEEING) THRILLS

CULTURE ON THE CHEAP—*it can be done. There are several ways to sightsee on a shoestring, starting with a public bus ride through some of the most scenic parts of town (see the "Best Bus Rides" CloseUp box).*

Museums for Free. *Some art collections are free all the time. One of the best is the outstanding permanent collection of Parisian artifacts in the Musée Carnavalet. There's also free entry to the permanent collections of the Musée Cognacq-Jay, a trove of 18th-century decorative art, and the Musée de la Vie Romantique, which focuses on the life of author George Sand. The Centre Georges Pompidou always has free exhibits on the ground floor and in the basement. A gratis welcome mat is out at two writers' homes: the Maison de Victor Hugo and the Maison de Balzac. The Maison Européenne de la Photographie is free on Wednesday after 5 PM, giving you three hours to absorb some great*

photography exhibits. And on the first Sunday of every month almost every museum, including the Louvre, is open for free. Arrive early; the French love a bargain too.

Festival Openings. *Over the Journées du Patrimoine (patrimony) weekend in September, you can get free access to many buildings that are otherwise closed to the public, such as the Hôtel de Ville. In early October, as part of the Nuit Blanche "white night" festival, museums and some government buildings are open for free until the wee hours.*

Churches & Cemeteries. *The old standbys are stellar here. From the soaring cathedral of Notre-Dame to the sprawling cemetery of Père-Lachaise, some of the city's best sights don't cost a cent.*

---

streetlamps are just coming on. The bustle means the café tables are always good for people-watching, while the cinemas, nightclubs, and late-hour shopping ensure the parade continues well into the night—perhaps ending at the futuristic-looking Drugstore Publicis, up near the Arc de Triomphe. The 2-km (1¼-mi) Champs-Élysées, originally cattle-grazing land, was laid out in the 1660s by the landscape gardener André Le Nôtre as a park. Traces of its green origins remain in the lower section of the avenue, where elegant 19th-century park pavilions house the historic restaurants Ledoyen, Laurent, and Le Pavillon Élysées. Ⓜ *Champs-Élysées–Clemenceau, Franklin-D.-Roosevelt, George V, Étoile.*

❶ **École Militaire** (Military Academy). Napoléon was one of the more famous graduates of this military academy, whose harmonious 18th-century building facing the Tour Eiffel across the Champ de Mars is still in use for army training and consequently is not open to the public. ⊠ *Pl. du Maréchal-Joffre, Trocadéro/Tour Eiffel* Ⓜ *École Militaire.*

⑬ **Les Égouts** (The Sewers). Everyone visits the Louvre, so surprise your friends back home by telling them you toured the infamous 19th-century sewers of Paris. Brave their unpleasant—though tolerable—smell to follow an underground display describing the passages and footbridges famously immortalized as the escape routes of Jean Valjean in *Les Misérables* and the Phantom of the Opera. Signs indicate the streets above you, and detailed panels illuminate the history of waste disposal in Paris, whose sewer system is the second largest in the world, after Chicago's. ⊠ *Opposite 93 quai d'Orsay, Trocadéro/Tour Eiffel* ☎ *01–53–68–27–81* ⌨ *€3.80* ◷ *May–Sept., Sat.–Wed. 11–5; Oct.–Apr., Sat.–Wed. 11–4* Ⓜ *Alma-Marceau; RER: Pont de l'Alma.*

off the
beaten
path

AMERICAN CHURCH – The staff of this Rive Gauche neo-Gothic church, built in 1927–31, welcomes English-speaking foreigners. The church hosts free classical music concerts on Sunday from September to June at 6 PM. ⊠ *65 quai d'Orsay, Trocadéro/Tour Eiffel* ☎ *01–40–62–05–00* ⊕ *www.acparis.org* ◷ *Mon.–Sat. 9–noon and 1–10* Ⓜ *Alma-Marceau; RER: Pont de l'Alma.*

🔟 **Fondation Pierre Bergé–Yves Saint Laurent.** With his business partner, Pierre Bergé, iconic fashion designer Yves Saint Laurent reopened his former atelier in 2004—this time as a gallery and archive of his work. Temporary exhibits, some fashion-related, rotate roughly every six months. The first, a show of Saint Laurent's art-inspired clothing, including his Mondrian dress, was a knockout; a more recent exhibit was devoted to avant garde artist Robert Wilson. ⊠ *1 rue Léonce Reynaud, Trocadéro/Tour Eiffel* ☎ *01–44–31–64–00* ⊕ *www.fondation-pb-ysl. net* ⌨ *€5* ◷ *Tues.–Sun. 11–6* Ⓜ *Alma-Marceau.*

🔟 **Grand Palais.** With its curved-glass roof and florid Belle Époque ornament, the Grand Palais is unmistakable when approached from either the Seine or the Champs-Élysées and forms a voluptuous duo with the Petit Palais, on the other side of avenue Winston-Churchill. Both these stone buildings, adorned with mosaics and sculpted friezes, were built for the world's fair of 1900, and, as with the Tour Eiffel, were not intended to remain as permanent additions to the city. But once they were up, no one seemed inclined to take them down. Today the adjoining galleries play host to major exhibitions, but the giant iron-and-glass interior of the Grand Palais itself is closed for renovation until 2007, when it will reopen as a exhibition space for contemporary art. Adjoining galleries are used for special exhibitions; for visits before 1 PM you'll need a reserved ticket, which is a bit more expensive. Regardless, expect long lines. ⊠ *Av. Winston-Churchill, Champs-Élysées* ☎ *01–44–13–17–30* ⊕ *www.rmn.fr/galeriesnationalesdugrandpalais* ⌨ *€11.10 until 1 PM with reservation; €10 after 1, no reservation* ◷ *Thurs.–Mon. 10–8, Wed. 10–10* Ⓜ *Champs-Élysées–Clemenceau.*

🔟 **Lido.** Free-flowing champagne, songs in French and English, and topless razzmatazz pack in the crowds (mostly tourists) every night for the show at this famous nightclub, which has been around since 1946. Thanks to its return as a fashion show and party venue, the cabaret is recapturing a more polished crowd, but your chances of sitting next to a busload of Belgian tourists are still pretty high. Shows start at €80 (not including dinner). ⊠ *116 av. des Champs-Élysées, Champs-Élysées* ☎ *01–40–76–56–10* ⊕ *www.lido.fr* Ⓜ *George V.*

⑧ Maison de Baccarat. Designer Philippe Starck brought an irreverent, *Alice in Wonderland* approach to the HQ of the venerable Baccarat crystal firm. Opened in 2003, the Baccarat museum plays on its building's Surrealist legacy; Cocteau, Dalí, Buñuel, and Man Ray were all frequent guests of the mansion's onetime owner, Countess Marie-Laure de Noailles. At the entrance, talking heads are projected onto giant crystal urns, and a lighted chandelier is submerged in an aquarium. Other fairy-tale touches include a 46-foot-long crystal-legged dinner table and an 8-foot-high chair, perfect for seating a giant princess. Not all the marvels come from Starck though; Baccarat has created exquisite crystal pieces since Louis XV conferred his seal on the glassworks in 1764. Many of the company's masterworks are on display, from the soaring candlesticks made for Czar Nicholas II to the perfume flacon Dalí designed for Schiaparelli. The museum's Cristal Room café restaurant attracts an appropriately glittering crowd, so book well in advance for lunch or dinner. ☒ *11 pl. des Etats-Unis, Trocadéro/Tour Eiffel* ☎ *01–40–22–11–00* ⊕ *www.baccarat.fr* ▦ *€7* ☉ *Mon.–Sat. 10–7* Ⓜ *Trocadéro.*

★ ⑩ Musée d'Art Moderne de la Ville de Paris (Paris Museum of Modern Art). While the city's modern art museum hasn't generated a buzz comparable to that of its main Paris competitor, the Centre Georges Pompidou, it can provide a more pleasant museum-going experience. Like the Pompidou, it shows temporary exhibits of painting, sculpture, and installation and video art, plus it has a permanent collection of top-tier 20th-century works from around the world—but it happily escapes the Pompidou's overcrowding. At this writing, the Art Nouveau leftover from the Exhibition of 1897 was closed for renovation, due to finish in mid-2005. Once its vast, white-walled galleries are open, they'll again be an ideal backdrop for the bold statements of 20th-century art. The museum takes over, chronologically speaking, where the Musée d'Orsay leaves off; among the earliest works are Fauvist paintings by Maurice Vlaminck and André Derain, followed by Pablo Picasso's early experiments in Cubism. Other highlights include works by Georges Braque, Georges Rouault, Robert and Sonia Delaunay, and Amedeo Modigliani. There is also a large room devoted to Art Deco furniture and screens, where Jean Dunand's gilt and lacquered panels consume oceans of wall space. There are no audioguides in English, but the excellent bookshop, which specializes in 19th- and 20th-century art and architecture, has many books in English. A retrospective of French modernist painter Pierre Bonnard (1867–1947) is slated for the fall of 2005. ☒ *11 av. du Président-Wilson, Trocadéro/Tour Eiffel* ☎ *01–53–67–40–00* ⊕ *www.paris.org* ▦ *Permanent collection free, temporary exhibitions €7* ☉ *Tues.–Fri. 10–5:30, weekends 10–6:45* Ⓜ *Iéna.*

⑦ Musée Guimet. This seemingly small building is the surprise treasure of the museum neighborhood; here you'll find an Asian art collection founded by Lyonnais industrialist Émile Guimet, who traveled around the world in the late 19th century amassing priceless Indo-Chinese and Far Eastern objets d'art. In the entrance area you'll see the largest collection of Khmer art outside Cambodia, including astonishingly lifelike yet serene 12th-century portrait heads. Each floor has something fasci-

Fodor'sChoice
★

nating; be sure to peer into the delicate round library (where you'd swear Guimet has just stepped out for tea) and toil up to the top floor's 18th-century ivory replica of a Chinese pavilion. A separate building up the street (included in the entry ticket) displays a vast collection of Buddhas and occasionally holds traditional Japanese tea ceremonies. You can pick up an English-language brochure and free audioguide at the entrance. ✉ *6 pl. d'Iéna, Trocadéro/Tour Eiffel* ☎ *01–56–52–53–00* ⊕ *www. museeguimet.fr* ✉ *€7* ⊗ *Wed.–Mon. 10–6* Ⓜ *Iéna or Boissiére.*

❹ **Musée de l'Homme** (Museum of Mankind). Picasso, it is said, discovered the bold lines of African masks and sculpture here and promptly went off to paint his *Desmoiselles d'Avignon* and create Cubism. Unfortunately, these days you're more likely to be underwhelmed by the confusing displays at this underfunded anthropology museum, currently undergoing renovation as some of its holdings move to the Musée du Quai Branly. The occasional special exhibitions are worth investigating, but overall expect limited information in English. ✉ *17 pl. du Trocadéro, Trocadéro/Tour Eiffel* ☎ *01–44–05–72–72* ⊕ *www.mnhn.fr* ✉ *€7* ⊗ *Wed.–Fri. and Mon., 9:45–5:15, weekends 10–6:30* Ⓜ *Trocadéro.*

🕐 ❺ **Musée de la Marine** (Maritime Museum). After an intensive and ambitious renovation, France's most important maritime history museum is fully rigged and readied—a must-see for fans of Patrick O'Brian's nautical *Master and Commander* books, or anyone who has dreamed of running away to sea. One of the best parts of this little-known collection is the boat models, from 17th-century flagships up through 20th-century naval war machines. Contemporary artists' video works are shown alongside the early navigational equipment and original restored boats that form the bedrock of the collection. There are excellent explanatory panels in English throughout, and a changing roster of special exhibits; for instance, a show on Jules Verne will be up in late 2005. ✉ *17 pl. du Trocadéro, Trocadéro/Tour Eiffel* ☎ *01–53–65–69–69* ⊕ *www. musee-marine.fr* ✉ *€6.50* ⊗ *Wed.–Mon. 10–6* Ⓜ *Trocadéro.*

❻ **Musée des Monuments Français** (French Monuments Museum). One of the most fascinating museums in Paris, with a rich collection of medieval architectural elements, closed after a fire in 1997 and has been struggling to reopen. At this writing it was threatened by a loss of funding, but it hoped to come back by early 2006 as the Cité de l'Architecture et du Patrimoine. If the project gets back on track, it will include the cutting-edge Institut Français d'Architecture along with the Chaillot School, which trains architects in restoration. Founded in 1879 by architect-restorer Viollet-le-Duc (the man mainly responsible for the extensive renovation of Notre-Dame and countless other Gothic cathedrals), the monuments collection is a vast repository of copies of statues, columns, archways, and frescoes from the Romanesque and Gothic periods (roughly 1000–1500). For more information about Cité de l'Architecture et du Patrimoine, visit its Web site, www.archi.fr/IFA-CHAILLOT. ✉ *1 pl. du Trocadéro, Trocadéro/Tour Eiffel* ☎ *01–44–05–39–10* Ⓜ *Trocadéro.*

⓯ **Musée du Quai Branly.** Architect Jean Nouvel is making another mark on the city's culturescape with this new museum, its long, flat shape stretching out next to the Seine. The museum, also known as the Musée des Arts Premiers, is scheduled to open in early 2006. (At this writing, the museum hadn't confirmed its opening date so it's best to check ahead via the Web site.) It will gather together various state-held troves of African, Asian, and Oceanic art, including anthropological collections previously shown in the Louvre. The museum is the legacy of President Jacques Chirac; some observers think it will ultimately bear his name. You can watch the project's progress via a live webcam on the museum's Web site. ✉ *Quai Branly, Trocadéro/Tour Eiffel* ☎ *Not available at press time* ⊕ *www.quaibranly.fr* Ⓜ *Alma-Marceau.*

Palais de Chaillot (Chaillot Palace). This honey-color Art Deco cultural center was built in the 1930s to replace a Moorish-style building constructed for the World Exhibition of 1878. It contains the Institut Français d'Architecture, the Chaillot school, which trains architects as restorers, and three large museums: the **Musée de l'Homme,** the **Musée de la Marine,** and the **Musée des Monuments Français.** The garden leading to the Seine has sculptures and dramatic fountains and is the focus for fireworks demonstrations on Bastille Day. The palace terrace, flanked by gilded statuettes (and often invaded by roller skaters and skateboarders), offers a wonderful picture-postcard view of the Tour Eiffel. ✉ *Pl. du Trocadéro, Trocadéro/Tour Eiffel* Ⓜ *Trocadéro.*

㉑ Palais de la Découverte (Palace of Discovery). A planetarium, working models, and scientific and technological exhibits on such topics as optics, biology, nuclear physics, and electricity make up this science museum behind the Grand Palais. There are some hands-on exhibits, but most of the explanations are in French only; how much you get out of this museum will likely depend on your fluency. ✉ *Av. Franklin-D.-Roosevelt, Champs-Élysées* ☎ *01–56–43–20–21* ⊕ *www.palais-decouverte. fr* 🎫 *€6.50, planetarium additional €3.50* ⊙ *Tues.–Sat. 9:30–6, Sun. 10–7* Ⓜ *Champs-Élysées–Clemenceau.*

❾ Palais Galliera. This luxurious mansion, built in 1888 for the Duchesse de Galliera, opens only for special exhibitions on costume and clothing design. Although the generous Duchesse, who donated her mansion to the city, might not recognize the exhibition rooms, the mansion's garden was restored to its 19th-century style in 2005. Thanks to its aggressive curatorial team, this museum has quickly won attention; its Marlene Dietrich show, for instance, influenced many fashion designer collections. ✉ *10 av. Pierre-1ᵉʳ-de-Serbie, Trocadéro/Tour Eiffel* ☎ *01–56–52–86–00* ⊕ *www.paris.fr/musees/* 🎫 *€8* ⊙ *Tues.–Sun. 10–6* Ⓜ *Iéna.*

★ ⓫ Palais de Tokyo. Derelict for more than a decade, the Art Nouveau twin of the Musée d'Art Moderne reemerged in 2002 as a trendy stripped-down space for contemporary arts with unorthodox, ambitious programming. There is no permanent collection; instead, dynamic temporary exhibits spread over a large, open space that's reminiscent of a construction site, with a trailer for a ticket booth. (In fact, at this writing some sections were under construction, but the shows stayed open throughout.) Rather than traditional museum guards, young art students—most of whom are at least semifluent in English—are on hand to help explain the installations. As if the art exhibits weren't adventurous enough, the cultural programming extends to debates, DJ-driven concerts, readings, and fashion shows; there are also a cafeteria, a funky restaurant, and a bookstore. ⊠ *13 av. du Président-Wilson, Trocadéro/Tour Eiffel* ☏ *01–47–23–54–01* ⊕ *www.palaisdetokyo.com* ✄ *€6* ☉ *Tues.–Sun. noon–midnight* Ⓜ *Iéna.*

need a break?

For an inexpensive bite, check out the Palais de Tokyo restaurant, **Tokyo Eat** (⊠ 13 av. du Président-Wilson, Trocadéro/Tour Eiffel ☏ 01–47–20–00–29), the only museum café in town whose tables are filled with hip locals, especially at lunch.

㉒ Petit Palais. The smaller counterpart to the Grand Palais, just off the Champs-Élysées, usually presents a permanent collection of French painting and furniture, with splendid canvases by Courbet and Bouguereau, but is closed for restoration until at least autumn 2005. You can, however, still admire the two fine statues that flank the building: French World War I hero Georges Clemenceau, facing the Champs-Élysées; and Jean Cardot's resolute image of Winston Churchill, facing the Seine. ⊠ *Av. Winston-Churchill, Champs-Élysées* ☏ *01–42–65–12–73* ⊕ *www.paris.fr/musees/* Ⓜ *Champs-Élysées–Clemenceau.*

⑫ Pont de l'Alma. This bridge is best known for the chunky stone Zouave statue carved into one of the pillars. Zouaves were Algerian infantrymen recruited into the French army and famous for their bravura and colorful uniforms. There is nothing quite so glamorous about the Alma Zouave, however, whose hour of glory comes in times of watery distress: Parisians use him to judge the level of the Seine during heavy rains. The current high-water mark—up to the statue's neck from a 1910 flood—thankfully stands unchallenged. Ⓜ *Alma-Marceau.*

☾ **❸ Tour Eiffel** (Eiffel Tower). If the Statue of Liberty is New York, if Big Ben **Fodor's Choice** is London, if the Kremlin is Moscow, then the Eiffel Tower is Paris. For ★ two years French engineer Gustave Eiffel—already famous for building viaducts and bridges—worked to erect this monument, which was designed to exalt the technical era that had begun to shine in the lamp of Edison and to stammer in the first telephone of Bell. It was created for the World Exhibition of 1889, inaugurated by Edward VII, then Prince of Wales, and was still in good shape to celebrate its 100th birthday in 1989. Such was Eiffel's engineering wizardry that even in the strongest winds his tower never sways more than 4½ inches.

Because its colossal bulk exudes a feeling of mighty permanence, you may have trouble believing that it nearly became 7,000 tons of scrap iron when its concession expired in 1909. At first many Parisians hated the structure, agreeing with designer William Morris, who said, "Why on earth have I come here? Because it's the only place I can't see it from." Only its potential use as a radio antenna saved the day (it still bristles with a forest of radio and television transmitters). By the time of the German occupation, however, Paris trembled when it was suggested that the 12,000 pieces of metal and its 2,500,000 rivets should be "requisitioned." Today the Tour is most breathtaking at night, when every girder is highlighted in a sparkling display originally conceived to celebrate the turn of the millennium. The glittering light show was so popular that the 20,000 lights were reinstalled for permanent use in 2003; the Tour does its electric shimmy for 10 minutes every hour on the hour until 1 AM in winter and 2 AM in summer. You can stride up the stairs as far as the third floor, but if you want to go to the top you'll have to take the elevator. (Be sure to take a close look at the fantastic ironwork.) The view of the flat sweep of Paris at 1,000 feet may not beat that from the Tour Montparnasse skyscraper, but the setting makes it considerably more romantic, especially if you come in the late evening, after the crowds have dispersed. ⊠ *Quai Branly, Trocadéro/Tour Eiffel* ☎ *01–44–11–23–23* ⊕ *www.tour-eiffel.fr* ⌂ *By elevator: 2nd fl. €4.10, 3rd fl. €7.50, 4th fl. €10.70. Climbing: 2nd and 3rd fl. only, €3.80* ☉ *June–late Aug., daily 9 AM–midnight; late Aug.–May, daily 9 AM–11 PM, stairs close at dusk in winter* Ⓜ *Bir-Hakeim; RER: Champ de Mars.*

need a break? Schlepping up and down the tower can bring on an appetite. If you don't want to break the bank at the excellent Jules Verne restaurant, on the second level of the tower, or if you're stuck in the dead zone between lunchtime and dinner, head to the **Café du Marché** (⊠ 38 rue Cler, Trocadéro/Tour Eiffel ☎ 01–47–05–51–27), a relaxed, all-day restaurant where the drinks are cheap, the salads gigantic, and the daily specials truly special.

THE FAUBOURG ST-HONORÉ

Fashions change, but the Faubourg St-Honoré, just north of the Champs-Élysées and the Tuileries, has been unfailingly chic since the early 1700s. The streets of this walk include some of the oldest in Paris. As you stroll from the President's Palace through arcaded streets and 19th-century passageways to the much-renovated market zone of Les Halles, you'll see all that is elegant in Paris, from architecture to fashion to food, all presented with typical Parisian insouciance.

Famous boutiques and 17th-century mansions sit side by side with famous banks—after all, elegance and finance have never been far apart. And politics are generally not far behind. One of the main arteries of the area, rue de Castiglione, was named after a former resident, the glamorous Italian Countess de Castiglione. The countess came to Paris to plead the cause of Italian unity with Napoléon III—instead, she became his mistress. This has long been the neighborhood for ambitious beauties: Coco Chanel made her name and fashion house here on rue Cambon. Today, famous dressmakers, renowned jewelers, exclusive perfume shops, and the chicest hotel in Paris, the Ritz, continue to make this *faubourg* (district) a symbol of luxury throughout the world.

The neighborhood also has a special gastronomic affiliation. The city's very first restaurants came into being here, and some of the finest food shops still call the area home. The massive food market of Les Halles (pronounced "lay-*ahl*") fed the city until 1969. The famed 19th-century building, once called "the Louvre of the people," was torn down to make way for a shopping mall and garden, and Parisians have bemoaned its loss ever since. The current mayor has big plans to redevelop the site.

Numbers in the text correspond to numbers in the margin and on the Faubourg St-Honoré map.

a good
walk

Start your walk in front of the most important home in France: the **Palais de l'Élysée ❶**, the Presidential Palace; barriers and guards keep the public at bay. With the palace and other embassies on your right, strut down the ever-fashionable rue du Faubourg St-Honoré. At Hermès (where you can still order a hand-stitched saddle, along with silk scarves and Kelly bags), turn left onto rue Boissy-d'Anglas and cut right into Cité Berryer; this archway leads to "Village Royal," a shopping passage connecting to rue Royale. To your left is the substantial **Église de La Madeleine ❷**; the surrounding streets offer temptations such as the original branch of Laudrée pâtisserie (No.16 rue Royale) and Hédiard, a foodie's dream emporium (21 place de la Madeleine).

Cross rue Royale, pausing for an unbeatable view of the place de la Concorde, the Assemblé Nationale, and the dome of Invalides. Just down the street at No. 3 is the famed Art Nouveau restaurant Chez Maxim's—owner Pierre Cardin has installed his stunning collection of period furniture in a museum upstairs. Take rue Duphot down to rue St-Honoré, where you'll find **Notre-Dame de l'Assomption,** noted for its huge dome. Just up from here is rue Cambon, where Chanel built her empire from one simple hat shop. Continue along St-Honoré to No. 362; cross through this courtyard to emerge in one of the world's most opulent squares, the **place Vendôme ❸**. That's Napoléon standing at the top of the square's bronze central column—and just to your left is the Ritz. Go back to rue St-Honoré via rue de Castiglione and continue past the sober Italianate church of **St-Roch.**

Take the next right onto rue des Pyramides and cross place des Pyramides, with its gilded statue of Joan of Arc on horseback, to the northwest wing of the Louvre, home to the **Union Centrale des Arts Décoratifs ❹**, with three separate museums dedicated to fashion, publicity, and the decorative arts. Walk along arcaded rue de Rivoli (beware of pickpockets) and go left onto rue Rohan, which leads you to place du Palais-Royal. If you look to your left, you'll see the boulevard leading to the Opéra. Just beyond Jean-Michel Othaniel's psychedelic métro entrance is the **Comédie Française ❺**, the time-honored setting for performances of classical French drama. On the far side of the square is the **Louvre des Antiquaires ❻**, devoted to high-end antiques shops—a fun browse especially if you're a connoisseur. Tucked behind the Comédie is the unobtrusive entrance to the **Palais-Royal ❼**. Walk through this series of classical courtyards, with its hidden peaceful garden. At the far end you can peek through the windows of one of the oldest restaurants in Paris, Le Grand Véfour, to admire its Directoire interior.

Just to the north of the top exit of Palais-Royal, on the corner of rue de Richelieu and rue des Petits-Champs, stands what used to be France's main national library, the **Bibliothèque Nationale Richelieu ❽**, now home to one of the world's largest photography archives. A block east are the passages of **Galerie Colbert** and **Galerie Vivienne** ⑨, two exquisite shopping arcades built in the mid-19th century, now filled with restaurants, boutiques, and antiquarian booksellers. Turn left into Galerie Vivienne and walk down the refined marble corridor to your first right. Once outside, walk past the 17th-century church **Notre-Dame des Victoires,** then veer right onto rue Vide Gousset to reach **place des Victoires** ⑩. That's Louis XIV astride the plunging steed in the center of the square. Head south down rue Croix-des-Petits-Champs, past the Banque de France on your right, and take the second street on the left to the circular **Bourse du Commerce** ⑪, the Commercial Exchange. Behind it to the right is a 100-foot-tall fluted column, the **Colonne de Ruggieri.**

On the far side of the Bourse du Commerce you can stroll in the **Jardin des Halles** ⑫, where greenery has replaced the city's old market halls. Go left at the aisle of fountains to reach the church of **St-Eustache** ⑬, a curious architectural hybrid of Gothic and classical styles. Take bustling rue de Montorgueil beyond the church, and then turn right on rue Étienne Marcel to admire the **Tour Jean Sans Peur** ⑭, a tower built into the old city walls in 1409. Backtrack a few yards and turn right onto rue Française, right again along quaint rue Tiquetonne, and then take your first left into rue Dussoubs. Just to your right is the entrance to one of the city's most elegant covered galleries, the **Passage du Grand-Cerf** ⑮. Turn right at the end of the gallery and go down rue St-Denis past the medieval church of **St-Leu–St-Gilles.**

Stay on rue St-Denis and take a third right, along rue des Prêcheurs, to reach the **Forum des Halles** ⑯, a modern, multilevel shopping mall and train station. Turn left on rue Pierre-Lescot to reach square des Innocents, with its handsome 16th-century Renaissance fountain. Farther east you can see the futuristic funnels of the Centre Pompidou jutting above the surrounding buildings.

Walk past the fountain, under the arches. This is rue de la Ferronerie, where in 1610, after more than two dozen assassination attempts, King Henri IV was fatally stabbed by a religious fanatic. At rue St-Denis, head right toward the river to reach place du Châtelet, with its theaters, fountain, and the **Tour St-Jacques** ⑰ looming up to your left— all that remains of a church that once stood here. Turning right on quai de la Mégisserie, the sidewalk is suddenly taken over by an exotic array of caged birds and all kinds of plants for sale. Continue to the Art Deco Samaritaine department store with its panoramic rooftop café. Turn right on rue de l'Arbre-Sec, and then take the first left onto rue des Prêtres to reach **St-Germain l'Auxerrois** ⑱, once the French royal family's parish church. Opposite is the colonnaded east facade of the Louvre.

TIMING   With brief visits to churches and monuments, this 5½-km (3½-mi) walk should take about 3–4 hours. If it's a nice day, linger in the gardens of the Palais-Royal; on a cold day indulge in hot chocolate at Angélina, a tearoom on rue de Rivoli (writer Gertrude Stein's favorite place for cake). Note: many stores are closed on Sunday and some on Monday as well (though Fauchon, the famed specialty-food haven, stays open).

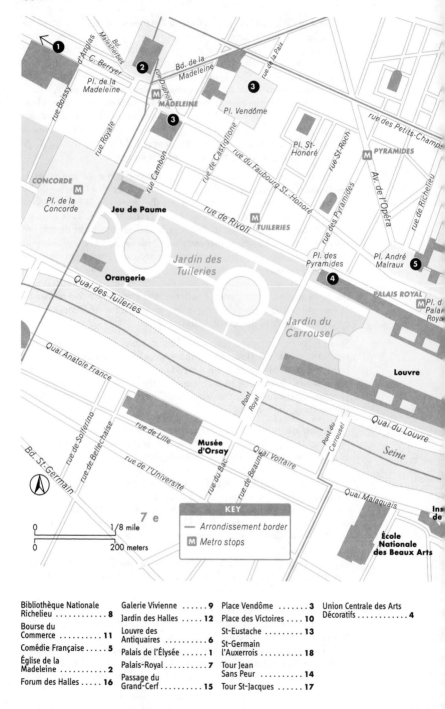

7 e

KEY
— *Arrondissement border*
Ⓜ *Metro stops*

0 _____ 1/8 mile
0 _____ 200 meters

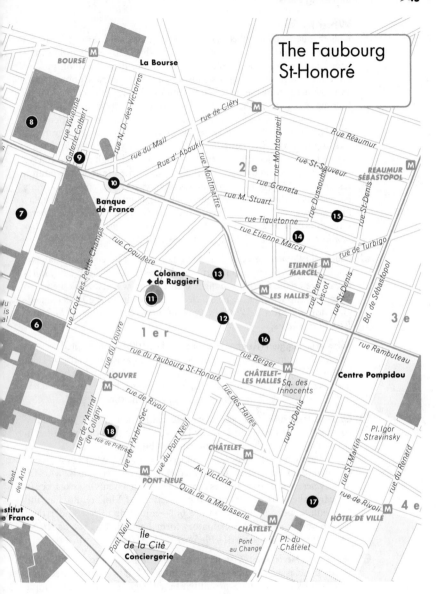

The Faubourg
St-Honoré

What to See

8 Bibliothèque Nationale Richelieu (Richelieu National Library). France's longtime national library, named for formidable 17th-century prime minister Cardinal Richelieu, used to contain more than 7 million printed volumes, but now it hosts a steady stream of temporary photography shows culled from the library's enormous photography collection. Its holdings range from the work of early daguerreotypists, to that of legendary practitioners of the *sixième art* like Nadar, Atget, Cartier-Bresson, Doisneau, and Man Ray, to contemporary French photographers like Sophie Calle. By visiting the photo galleries you'll be able to walk through a magnificent 18th-century courtyard. Though the books have mostly been moved to the Bibliothèque Nationale François-Mitterand, researchers still consult original manuscripts, engravings, coins, and prints here; parts of these collections go on display from time to time. Display information is available in French only. ⊠ *58 rue de Richelieu, Opéra/ Grands Boulevards* ☎ *01–53–79–59–59* ⊕ *www.bnf.fr* ☜ *€4–€8, depending on show* ☉ *Tues.–Sun. 9–8* Ⓜ *Bourse.*

11 Bourse du Commerce (Commercial Exchange). The circular, shallow-domed 18th-century commercial exchange building near Les Halles began life as the Corn Exchange; Victor Hugo waggishly likened it to a jockey's cap without the peak. Step inside to admire the 1889 stained-glass dome. ⊠ *Rue de Viarmes, Opéra/Grands Boulevards* Ⓜ *Métro or RER: Les Halles.*

Colonne de Ruggieri (Ruggieri's Column). The 100-foot-tall fluted column behind the Bourse du Commerce is all that remains of a mansion built here in 1572 for Catherine de' Medici. The column is said to have been used as a platform for stargazing by her astrologer, Ruggieri. Legend has it that his shade still haunts the metal cage at the top. Ⓜ *Les Halles.*

5 Comédie Française. Famous for its classical French drama, this theater company was founded in 1680 by Louis XIV, a king more interested in controlling theater than promoting it. This building opened in 1799 but burned almost to the ground a hundred years later; what you're looking at dates from 1900. The *comedienne* Sarah Bernhardt, who famously performed from palaces in St. Petersbourg to tents in Texas, began her career here. Today, mannered productions of Molierè, Racine, and Corneille appear regularly on the bill—enjoyable if you understand French and don't mind declamatory formal acting. ⊠ *2 rue de Richelieu, Louvre/Tuileries* ☎ *01–44–58–15–15* Ⓜ *Palais-Royal.*

2 Église de la Madeleine. With its rows of uncompromising columns, this sturdy neoclassical edifice—designed in 1814 but not consecrated until 1842—looks more like a proudly inflated version of a Greek temple than a Christian church. The resemblance is no fluke; changing political winds during the construction meant that the building was literally a Greek basilica one day, a temple to Napoléon's glory another, a National Assembly hall the next. At one point, in fact, La Madeleine, as it is known, was nearly selected as Paris's first train station. Inside, the only natural light comes from three shallow domes, but gilded ornaments glint through the murk. The huge fresco of the Last Judgment above should be enough to make you reflect upon your faults. A simpler crypt offers intimate weekday masses; classical music and organ recitals are held throughout the week, though acoustics can be muddy. ⊠ *Pl. de la Madeleine, Opéra/Grands Boulevards* ⊙ *Mon.–Sat. 7:30–7, Sun. 8–7* Ⓜ *Madeleine.*

🔟 **Forum des Halles.** Les Halles, conveniently near the main port of Châtelet yet out of reach of Seine flooding, was the central food market of Paris from 1168 until 1969. The amazing range of food for sale here helped French cuisine to develop as it did. Over the centuries, different buildings evolved to house the food stalls. The best known, the stunning iron-and-glass halls built during the Second Empire, were tragically destroyed in the 1970s, when the wholesale market was moved out to the suburbs. Today, there are few traces of the market's rambunctious 24-hour community, though rue de Montorgueil retains something of its original bustle. The multilevel shopping mall that rose in the halls' place is showing signs of wear and tear, a state of affairs not much helped by the hordes of teenagers and down-and-outs who invade it after dusk. Plans are now underway to remodel Les Halles yet again, using a new design by French architect David Mangin. Until construction gets going in 2007, there are two reasons to visit. First, the up-and-coming young designer section is worth a look. Second, the Forum des Images offers inexpensive screenings of rare, foreign, and historic films, often accompanied by excellent lectures (in French). ⊠ *Main entrance: rue Pierre-Lescot, Beaubourg/Les Halles* ⊕ *www.forum-des-halles.com* ⊙ *Mon.–Sat. 10–7:30* Ⓜ *Les Halles; RER: Châtelet Les Halles.*

⑨ **Galerie Vivienne.** Before department stores came on the scene, Paris shoppers flocked to covered arcades to sate their consumer lust. Of the city's remaining *galeries,* Vivienne has best survived the fickle winds of fashion. Admire the elegant, well-worn marble mosaics and neoclassic bas-reliefs, and consider that even today, the largest French department store has kept an arcade-shopping reference in its name: Galeries Lafayette. ⊠ *6 rue Vivienne (enter on rue des Petits Champs), Louvre/Tuileries* Ⓜ *Palais-Royal/Bourse.*

need a break?

A Priori Thé (⊠ 35 galerie Vivienne, Louvre/Tuileries 🕾 01–42–97–48–75) has been comforting travelers for more than 20 years with its teas and sweets. The reassuringly familiar menu includes brownies and crumbles, a smooth combination of French and Anglo traditions concocted by American owner Peggy Ancock. Another option is the family-run *épicerie* (grocery store) and wine shop **Legrand Filles et Fils** (⊠ 1 rue Banque, Louvre/Tuileries 🕾 01–42–60–07–12), in business since 1880. A wine bar in the back serves simple, delicious fare and a superb selection of wines. (Wine tastings are held most Thursday nights.) For a €15 corking fee, they'll open any bottle in the cellar. Château Pétrus 1961, anyone?

⟳ ⑫ **Jardin des Halles** (Les Halles Garden). This garden, crisscrossed with paths and alleyways flanked by trim lawns, takes up much of the site formerly occupied by Les Halles, the city's central market, remembered as *le ven-*

tre de Paris (the belly of Paris) after Émile Zola's novel by that name. Ⓜ *Les Halles; RER: Châtelet Les Halles.*

❻ **Louvre des Antiquaires.** This "shopping mall" of superelegant antiques dealers, opposite the Louvre, is a minimuseum in itself. Louis XVI *boiseries* (wainscoting) and the pretty sort of bibelots that would have gladdened the heart of Marie-Antoinette vie for shelf space alongside vases by Art Deco master Lalique and the actual shoes worn by dancer Josephine Baker. These stylish glass-walled corridors deserve a browse whether you intend to buy or not. ✉ *Main entrance: pl. du Palais-Royal, Louvre/Tuileries* ☉ *Tues.–Sun. 11–7* Ⓜ *Palais-Royal.*

> **need a break?**
>
> Founded in 1903 and patronized by literary lights like Marcel Proust and Gertrude Stein, **Angélina** (✉ 226 rue de Rivoli, Louvre/Tuileries ☎ 01–42–60–82–00) is beloved for its irresistible (€6.50) *chocolat africain,* a cup of hot chocolate topped with whipped cream. The darkened frescoes and mirrors are showing the tearoom's age, so although this is still among the city's best chocolate hits, finicky Proust might now reserve his affections for *macaron* pastries served at historic **Ladurée,** a short walk east at 16 rue Royale.

❶ **Palais de l'Élysée.** Madame de Pompadour, Napoléon, Joséphine, the Duke of Wellington, and Queen Victoria all stayed at this palace, today the official home of the French president. Originally constructed as a private mansion in 1718, the Élysée—incidentally, when Parisians talk about "L'Élysée," they mean the president's palace, whereas the Champs-Élysées is known simply as "Les Champs"—has housed presidents only since 1873. President Félix Faure died here in 1899 in the arms, so it is said, of his mistress. Although you can peer at the palace forecourt and facade through the rue du Faubourg St-Honoré gateway, it is difficult to get much of an idea of the building's size, or of the extensive gardens that stretch back to the Champs-Élysées, because it is closed to the public. ✉ *55 rue du Faubourg St-Honoré, Champs-Élysées* Ⓜ *Miromesnil.*

★ ❼ **Palais-Royal** (Royal Palace). One of the most quintessentially Parisian sights, the Palais-Royal is an irresistible bundle of contrasts. The sober stone columns of its historic arcades are echoed in the modern, black-and-white-stripe truncated columns in the courtyard, a favorite scrambling spot for children. Large silver spheres revolve slowly in two fountains, while in the formal gardens beyond, lovers whisper and senior citizens crumble croissants for the sparrows beneath regimented trees.

The *palais* dates from the 1630s (parts of the original building still remain) and is *royal* because all-powerful Cardinal Richelieu (1585–1642) magnanimously bequeathed it to Louis XIII. In his early days as king, Louis XIV preferred the relative intimacy of this place to the intimidating splendor of the nearby Louvre (of course, he soon decided that his own intimidating splendor warranted a more majestic home—hence, Versailles). During the French Revolution it became Le Palais Égalité (the Palace of Equality), because its owner, Louis-Philippe d'Orléans, the king's cousin, professed revolutionary ideas, one of which was to convert the arcades of the palace into boutiques and cafés. (Louis XVI reputedly quipped,

"My cousin, now that you are going to keep shop, I suppose we shall see you only on Sundays.") Before one of these shops Camille Desmoulins gave the first speech calling for the French Revolution in 1789.

Today the Palais-Royal contains the French Ministry of Culture, which is closed to the public, and a block of apartments. Former residents include Jean Cocteau and Colette, who wrote while looking out over her *"province à Paris."* Back in the early 19th century the arcades were the haunt of prostitutes and gamblers, a veritable sink of vice. Now it's hard to imagine anything more sinful than a splurge in the boutiques or at the restaurant Le Grand Véfour. You can wander into Didier Ludot's vintage couture boutiques, size up displays of old military medals, or sniff perfumes at the Shiseido fragrance boutique. ⊠ *Pl. du Palais-Royal, Louvre/Tuileries* Ⓜ *Palais-Royal.*

⓯ Passage du Grand-Cerf. Built around 1835, this pretty glass-roof *passage* (gallery) was renovated in 1990, emerging as a nexus for design. A ramble through its dozen or so shops turns up everything from a Mies van der Rohe chair to a miniskirt and bustier made of distressed safety pins. The passage also hosts the twice-yearly Les Puces du Design, which spills out onto surrounding sidewalks as vintage furniture dealers and up-and-coming designers show off their wares. ⊠ *Entrances on rue Dussoubs, rue St-Denis, Beaubourg/Les Halles* Ⓜ *Étienne Marcel.*

❸ Place Vendôme. Snobbish and self-important, this famous square is also gorgeous. Property laws have kept away cafés and other such banal establishments, leaving the plaza stately and refined, the perfect home for the rich and famous. Chopin lived and died at No. 12; today's celebs camp out at the Hotel Ritz at No. 15, while a lucky few, including the family of the sultan of Brunei, actually own houses here. With its granite pavement and Second Empire street lamps, Jules-Hardouin Mansart's rhythmic, perfectly proportioned example of 17th-century urban architecture shines in all its golden-stone splendor. To maintain a uniform appearance, Mansart first built only the facades of the *hôtels particuliers* (mansions)—the lots behind the facades were then sold to buyers who custom-tailored their palaces. Now the square is a fitting showcase for nearby jeweler's display windows. A statue of Napoléon tops the massive column in the square's center; the column itself is made from the melted bronze of 1,200 cannons captured at the Battle of Austerlitz in 1805. Painter Gustave Courbet headed the revolutionary hooligans who, in 1871, toppled the column (into a pile of manure, no less) and shattered it. The Third Republic stuck the pieces together again and sent him the bill. To raise a glass of champagne in honor of the place's famous ghosts, repair to Hemingway's Bar at the Ritz (⇨ Close-Up Box, Hemingway's Paris, *below*). Ⓜ *Opéra.*

❿ Place des Victoires. This circular square, now home to many of the city's top fashion boutiques, was laid out in 1685 by Jules Hardouin-Mansart in honor of the military victories of Louis XIV, that indefatigable warrior whose nearly continuous battles may have brought much prestige to his country but came perilously close to bringing it to bankruptcy, too. Here, Louis is shown galloping along on a bronze horse (the statue

HEMINGWAY'S PARIS

THERE IS AN OLD FAMILIAR SAYING: *"Everyone has two countries, his or her own—and France."* For the Lost Generation after World War I, these words rang particularly true. Lured by favorable exchange rates, free-flowing alcohol, and a booming artistic scene, many American writers, composers, and painters moved to Paris in the 1920s and 1930s, Ernest Hemingway among them. Hemingway arrived in Paris with his first wife, Hadley, in December 1921 and made for the Rive Gauche—the Hôtel Jacob et d'Angleterre, to be exact (still operating at 44 rue Jacob). To celebrate their arrival the couple went to the Café de la Paix for a meal they nearly couldn't afford.

Hemingway worked as a journalist and quickly made friends with other expat writers such as Gertrude Stein and Ezra Pound. In 1922 the Hemingways moved to 74 rue du Cardinal Lemoine, a bare-bones apartment with no running water (his writing studio was around the corner, on the top floor of 39 rue Descartes). Then in early 1924 the couple and their baby son settled at 113 rue Notre-Dame des Champs. Much of The Sun Also Rises, Hemingway's first serious novel, was written at nearby café, La Closerie des Lilas. These were the years in which he forged his writing style, paring his sentences down to the pith. As he noted in A Moveable Feast, *"hunger was good discipline."* There were some particularly hungry months when Hemingway gave up journalism and tried to publish short stories, and the family was *"very poor and very happy."*

They weren't happy for long. In 1926, just when The Sun Also Rises made him famous, Hemingway left Hadley and the next year wedded his mistress, Pauline Pfeiffer, across town at St Honoré-d'Eylau, then moved to 6 rue Férou, near the Musée du Luxembourg, whose collection of Cézanne landscapes (now in the Musée d'Orsay) he revered. You can follow the steps of Jake and Bill in The Sun Also Rises as they *"circle"* the Île St-Louis before the *"steep walking . . . all the way up to the place de la Contrescarpe,"* then right along rue du Pot-de-Fer to the *"rigid north and south"* of rue St-Jacques and on to boulevard du Montparnasse.

For gossip and books, and to pick up his mail, Papa would visit Shakespeare & Co., at 12 rue de l'Odéon, owned by Sylvia Beach, who became a trusted friend. For cash and cocktails Hemingway usually headed to the upscale Rive Droite. He collected the former at the Guaranty Trust Company, at 1 rue des Italiens. He found the latter, when he was flush, at the bar of the Hôtel Crillon, or, when poor, at the Caves Mura, at 19 rue d'Antin, or Harry's Bar, still in brisk business at 5 rue Daunou, with photos of Papa gazing down from the walls. Hemingway's legendary association with the Hotel Ritz, where there is now a bar named for him, was sealed during the Liberation in 1944, when he strode in at the head of his platoon and *"liberated"* the joint by ordering martinis all around. Here Hemingway asked Mary Welsh to become his fourth wife, and here also, the story goes, a trunk full of notes on his first years in Paris turned up in the 1950s, giving him the raw material to write A Moveable Feast. Paris loves naming streets after adopted sons, and it is only fitting that Hemingway has a plaque of his own, heralding short rue Ernest-Hemingway in the 15e arrondissement. This, after all, was the man who wrote: *"There is never any ending to Paris."*

dates from 1822, replacing one destroyed during the Revolution). Louis was so taken with this plaza that he commissioned the architect, who also designed much of Versailles, to build another, place Vendôme, on the other side of avenue de l'Opéra. Ⓜ *Sentier.*

⑬ St-Eustache. Built as the market neighborhood's answer to Notre-Dame on Île de la Cité, this vast, cathedral-like space is acoustically outstanding. Composers such as Berlioz and Liszt liked to premiere works here; organ recitals continue to be popular. The church was built from 1532 to 1637 and includes both late Gothic and early Renaissance elements. Each niche, dedicated to a specific saint, was once sponsored by a different market guild. In the late 1700s, just before the Revolution, a then-fashionable front was stuck onto the entry to the church. Ignore this and focus on the interior's grimy but classical column orders, rounded arches, and thick, comparatively simple window tracery. Outside, check out the impressive Gothic flying buttresses and the bell tower, which once tolled the hours of sale for the nearby market. In the plaza outside the church lies a massive stone head with a hand cupped to its ear: *L'Ecoute* by Henri de Miller. ⊠ *2 rue du Jour, Beaubourg/ Les Halles* ☎ *01–46–27–89–21 concert information* ⊙ *Daily 8–7* Ⓜ *Les Halles; RER: Châtelet Les Halles.*

⑱ St-Germain l'Auxerrois. Until 1789 this church was used by the French royal family as its Paris parish church, conveniently located across the street from their Louvre palace. On August 24, 1572, Catherine de' Medici ordered these bells rung to launch the Massacre of St. Bartholomew, during which at least 30,000 Huguenots were murdered. The church's fluid stonework reveals the influence of 15th-century Flamboyant Gothic style—notice the unusually wide windows in the nave and the equally unusual double aisles. Classical fluted columns around the choir were added in the 18th century, as clerics tried to make their medieval church more fashionable. ⊠ *Pl. du Louvre, Louvre/Tuileries* Ⓜ *Louvre-Rivoli.*

⑭ Tour Jean Sans Peur. Jean San Peur (John the Fearless), duke of Burgundy, built this defensive turret in 1409—and he wasn't simply being paranoid. He'd recently arranged the assassination of the king's brother and was an ambitious player during the ongoing chaos of the Hundred Years' War. The turret was once attached to an elegant house and to the city walls, now gone. But the turret alone is a fun visit, especially for kids, offering a window into a murky time. Toil up the seven flights of stairs, admiring the carved vaulting of sculpted vines, hops, and hawthorn, but first pick up the English pamphlet from the front desk. ⊠ *20 rue Étienne Marcel, Beaubourg/Les Halles* ☎ *01–40–26–20–28* ⊠ *€5* ⊙ *Sept.–June, Wed. and weekends 1:30–6; July–Aug., Tues.–Sun. 1:30–6* Ⓜ *Étienne Marcel.*

⑰ Tour St-Jacques. An ornate 170-foot bell tower that belonged to St-Jacques-de-la-Boucherie, a 16th-century church destroyed in 1797, sits forlornly, swallowed up by traffic and swathed in scaffolding. Once a meeting point for Santiago de Compostela pilgrims and the site of Pascal's gravity experiments in the mid-17th century, it was until recently used as a meteorological station for pollution measurements. ⊠ *Pl. du Châtelet, Beaubourg/Les Halles* Ⓜ *Châtelet.*

need a break? Nab a table at **Le Zimmer** (⊠ 1 pl. du Châtelet, Beaubourg/Les Halles ☎ 01–42–33–08–50), a café overlooking a sphinx-decorated fountain. It serves drinks, ice cream sundaes, and Alsatian-inspired food until after midnight. Well-padded chairs, a selection of newspapers free for perusing, and a friendly staff encourage you to linger. Across the way is one of Sarah Bernhardt's old theaters; now called the Théâtre de la Ville, the space was rented by the actress at the height of her fame and was named after her. When the Nazis arrived they changed the name because Bernhardt was Jewish—but you'll still see the original over the entrance.

★ ❹ **Union Centrale des Arts Décoratifs** (Decorative Arts Center). A must for those with an eye for design, the decorative arts center in the northwestern wing of the Louvre building houses three famously chic museums. The **Musée de la Mode,** with its archives of clothing and accessories dating back to the 18th century, has rotating special exhibits plus a glittering permanent jewelry display. Some descriptive info is available in English. The rotating exhibits of advertising and posters in the **Musée de la Pub-licité** compete for attention with Jean Nouvel's brash decor, combining metal-plaqued walls with exposed brickwork, black-lacquered parquet floors, leopard-skin pillars, and a battery of TV monitors over the bar. In the same building, the **Musée des Arts Décoratifs** holds furniture, tapestries, glassware, paintings, and other necessities of life from the Middle Ages through Napoléon's time and beyond. These period rooms of the Arts Décoratifs, however, are closed for renovation until mid-2006. ⊠ *107 rue de Rivoli, Louvre/Tuileries* ☎ *01–44–55–57–50* ⊕ *www.ucad. fr* 🎫 *€6* ☉ *Tues.–Sun. 11–6* Ⓜ *Palais-Royal.*

THE GRANDS BOULEVARDS

Famously immortalized in the canvases of Monet, Renoir, and Camille Pissarro, the Grands Boulevards are the long chain of avenues that join the Madeleine to the Opéra, continue via the ancient gates of St-Denis and St-Martin to place de la République, and then go on to the Bastille. Together they constitute the longest, most commercial, and most diverse artery of Paris. Parisians have always loved to promenade down their great avenues to feel the city's pulse. The focal point of this walk is the avenue that runs west to east from St-Augustin, the city's grandest Second Empire church, to place de la République, whose very name symbolizes the ultimate downfall of the imperial regime. The avenue's name changes six times along the way, which is why Parisians refer to it, in the plural, as "Les Grands Boulevards."

This walk starts at Parc Monceau, heart of one of the most exclusive residential neighborhoods, but the makeup of the neighborhoods along the Grands Boulevards changes steadily as you head from the posh 8ᵉ *arrondissement* toward traditionally working-class east Paris. The *grands magasins* (department stores) near the start of the walk epitomize upscale Paris shopping. They stand on boulevard Haussmann, named in honor of the regional prefect who oversaw the reconstruction of the city in the 1850s and 1860s. The opulent Opéra Garnier, just past the grands magasins, is the architectural showpiece of the period (often termed Second Empire, corresponding to the rule of Napoléon III).

This area is Haussmann's greatest accomplishment: elegant boulevards lined with seven-story apartment blocks which, when they were built, offered the very latest conveniences. But in fact Paris was famous for boulevards long before the Second Empire. In the 1670s the city's medieval fortifications were razed when Louis XIV's military triumphs appeared to render their raison d'être obsolete. The old defensive walls were replaced by leafy promenades known from the outset as "boulevards" (the word has the same origin as "bulwark").

From the mid-18th century through the Belle Époque, these Grands Boulevards hummed with activity, as theaters, cafés, music halls, and *passages* (glass-roofed, gaslit shopping arcades) kept the crowds coming. At the turn of the 19th century, the boulevard du Temple, near its intersection with the place de la République, was crammed with raffish entertainment, wonderfully depicted in the classic film *Les Enfants du Paradis*. The dodgy aspects attendant on so many easily distracted marks helped to earn the street its nickname, the boulevard du Crime. (In 1862 the fed-up Napoléon III ordered the street razed.) The great portrait photographer Nadar captured Victor Hugo, Baudelaire, and the cream of society in his studio on the boulevard des Capucines; the space was later used to show the first Impressionist exhibits. Though big banks moved into the area between the world wars, the Olympia concert hall has survived on the boulevard des Capucines, helping to keep alive *l'esprit boulevardier.* And recently, trendy cafés have sprouted up, attracting a fresh crop of fashionable wanderers to this perennially interesting strip.

Numbers in the text correspond to numbers in the margin and on The Grand Boulevards map.

a good walk

Take the métro to Monceau in the tony 8ᵉ arrondissement and step through gold-topped iron gates to enter the **Parc Monceau** ❶—the heart of a posh residential neighborhood once called home by the likes of Ignacy Paderewski, Edmond Rostand, and Sarah Bernhardt. Stroll gradually to the left, navigating past preening dogs and well-behaved children, towards avenue Velasquez, which is ornamented with spectacular gates and mansions. One such mansion is the **Musée Cernuschi** ❷, an Asian art museum that's closed for renovation until late 2005. Continue on to boulevard Malesherbes and turn right, then right again onto rue de Monceau, to reach the **Musée Nissim de Camondo** ❸, whose aristocratic interiors bring to life the days of the ancien régime.

More splendor awaits at the **Musée Jacquemart-André** ❹. Continue down rue de Monceau and turn left onto rue de Courcelles (Marcel Proust's family apartment was at No. 45), then left again onto boulevard Haussmann to find this imposing 19th-century marble mansion filled with lacquered antiques and old-master paintings. Continue eastward along the boulevard and cross the square in front of the church of **St-Augustin** ❺. Stay on boulevard Haussmann, then turn right down rue d'Anjou to enter the leafy, intimate square Louis XVI with its **Chapelle Expiatoire** ❻, dedicated to Louis XVI and Marie-Antoinette. Be sure to take a look at the funny stone carvings on the gleaming 1930s-style facade of the bank at the corner of rue Pasquier and rue Mathurins. Some 300 yards farther down boulevard Haussmann are the grands magasins, Paris's most renowned department stores. First comes **Au Printemps** ➐, then **Galeries Lafayette** ➑. Just past Galeries Lafayette is the gilded bulk of the **Opéra Garnier** ➒. Before venturing around to inspect its extravagant facade, you might like to take in a multiscreen overview of Paris and its history at the **Paris Story** ➓ movie venue.

Boulevard des Capucines, lined with cinemas and chain restaurants, heads left from in front of the Opéra, becoming boulevard des Italiens. Look left up rue Laffitte for a neat view of Sacré-Coeur, looming above the porticoed church of Notre-Dame-de-Lorette. After the intersection of boulevard Haussmann with boulevard des Italiens, turn left down rue Drouot to the large 1970s building, **Hôtel Drouot** ⑪, Paris's central auction house. Rue Rossini leads from Drouot, as it is known, to rue de la Grange-Batelière. Halfway along on the right is the **Passage Jouffroy** ⑫, one of the many covered galleries that honeycomb the center of Paris. At the far end of the passage is the **Musée Grévin** ⑬, a waxworks museum. Cross boulevard Montmartre to passage des Panoramas, one of the city's oldest arcades; it was named for its decorative panoramic scenes (now gone) and it was the first arcade to have gas lighting, in 1817. For a bit of time-warp shopping, stop at Stern engravers, which has been here since the passage opened. You'll come out on rue St-Marc. Turn right, then left down rue Vivienne, to find the foursquare, colonnaded **Bourse** ⑭, the Paris stock exchange.

Now turn east (left around the Bourse) and stroll along rue Réaumur, whose huge-windowed buildings once formed the heart of the French newspaper industry. As you cross rue Montmartre, you'll catch sight of St-Eustache church to your right. Take the third left up rue de Cléry, a narrow street that is the exclusive domain of fabric wholesalers and often crammed with vans, pallets, and delivery people creating colorful chaos. You're now in the **Sentier,** Paris's sprawling garment district, which spreads eastward in a narrow corridor all the way to République. The lopsided building at the corner of rue Poissonnière looks as if it is struggling to stay upright on the district's slopes. Continue up rue de Cléry as far as rue des Degrés—the shortest street in Paris, actually a 14-step stairway—then look for the clock and crooked turnip tower of **Notre-Dame de Bonne-Nouvelle** ⑮, hemmed in by rickety housing that looks straight out of Balzac. You can enter via No. 19 bis (meaning the next door down from No. 19) and cross through the church to emerge beneath the front portico on rue de la Lune. Head left as far as rue Poissonnière, and then turn right to return to the Grands Boulevards, by now going under the name of boulevard de Bonne-Nouvelle.

On the near corner of the boulevard stands the flamboyant Art Deco **Cinema Rex** ⑯, which offers a backstage tour (its "Arabian Nights" interior is a first-rate venue for French action movies). Cross the boulevard for a view of its wedding-cake tower, then glance inside Café de la Ville at No. 30, which was once a high-end brothel. Continue east along the boulevard to the butter-color **Porte St-Denis** ⑰, a triumphal arch

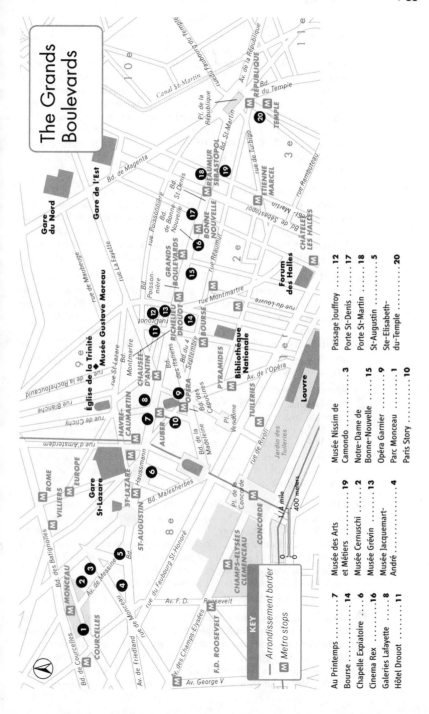

The Grands Boulevards

KEY

— Arrondissement border

Ⓜ Metro stops

Au Printemps **7**
Bourse **14**
Chapelle Expiatoire ... **6**
Cinema Rex **16**
Galeries Lafayette **8**
Hôtel Drouot **11**

Musée des Arts
et Métiers **19**
Musée Cernuschi **2**
Musée Grévin **13**
Musée Jacquemart-
André **4**

Musée Nissim de
Camondo **3**
Notre-Dame de
Bonne-Nouvelle **15**
Opéra Garnier **9**
Parc Monceau **1**
Paris Story **10**

Passage Jouffroy **12**
Porte St-Denis **17**
Porte St-Martin **18**
St-Augustin **5**
Ste-Elisabeth-
du-Temple **20**

dating from the reign of Louis XIV. Continue along to the smaller but similar **Porte St-Martin** ⑱ and turn right on rue St-Martin. Just around the corner at 32 rue Blondel are the red tiles of another former brothel, once patronized by literary voyeurs Henry Miller and Anaïs Nin. (Blondel continues to attract ladies of the night of varying genders and their clientele.) South on rue St-Martin, the leafy square Émile-Chautemps gives you a pleasant view of the red-marble pillared facade of the derelict 19th-century music hall Théâtre de la Gaîté Lyrique; Offenbach conducted here from 1873 to 1875, and Diaghilev's Ballets Russes set the stage alight from 1911 to 1913. Then turn left on rue Réaumur to the **Musée des Arts et Métiers** ⑲, an industrial museum, housed partly in the former church of St-Martin.

Across rue Réaumur is the high, narrow, late-Gothic church of **St-Nicolas-des-Champs.** Continue past the cloister ruins and Renaissance gateway that embellish the far side of St-Nicolas, and head left on rue Turbigo for 500 yards until you meet Passage Ste-Elizabeth on your right; this will bring you around to **Ste-Elisabeth-du-Temple** ⑳. From here, a short walk north brings you to place de la République.

TIMING The distance between Parc Monceau and place de la République is about 7 km (4½ mi), which will probably require at least four hours to walk, including coffee breaks and window-shopping. With museum visits and a good lunch, this could be stretched to an enjoyable day; keep in mind that the Musée Nissim de Camondo is closed on both Monday and Tuesday, though the Musée Jacquemart-André is open daily. The Sentier is busiest on weekdays, when delivery trucks and carts jam the streets and sidewalks.

What to See

❼ **Au Printemps.** The Belle Époque green-and-gold domes of this vast department store have been luring shoppers for over a century. Founded in 1865 by Jules Jaluzot, a former employee of Au Bon Marché (nothing like giving one's old boss some new competition), this company was the inspiration for Emile Zola's novel *Au Bonheur des Dames*. The top floor café has a splendid view of the Paris skyline. ⊠ *64 bd. Haussmann, Opéra/ Grands Boulevards* Ⓜ *Havre Caumartin.*

⑭ **Bourse** (Stock Exchange). Napoléon ordered the construction of this solemn, colonnaded stock exchange; after numerous delays, the doors opened in 1826. The atmosphere is completely different from that of Wall Street; it's quite calm, without people rushing or hollering. Call to reserve a 90-minute guided tour (available in English) of the building's history; you'll need to bring your passport with you. ⊠ *Rue Vivienne, Opéra/Grands Boulevards* ☎ *01–49–27–55–52* 🎟 *€8* ⊘ *Weekdays by reservation only* Ⓜ *Bourse.*

❻ **Chapelle Expiatoire.** Built in 1815, this expiatory chapel marks the original burial site of Louis XVI and Marie-Antoinette. After the deposed monarchs took their turns at the guillotine on place de la Concorde, their bodies were brought to a nearby mass grave. A loyalist marked their place, and their remains were eventually retrieved by Louis XVI's brother, Louis XVIII, who then ordered the monument. The neoclassical mausoleum now emerges defiantly from the lush undergrowth of square Louis-XVI off boulevard Haussmann. Two stone tablets are inscribed with the last missives of the doomed royals, including touching pleas to God to forgive their Revolutionary enemies. This surprisingly subtle and moving tribute to royalty is in sharp contrast to Napoléon's splashy memorial at the Invalides. ⊠ *29 rue Pasquier, Opéra/Grands Boulevards* ☎ *01–44–32–18–00* ⊠ *€2.50* ☉ *Thurs.–Sat. 1–5* Ⓜ *St-Augustin.*

🐾 ⑯ **Cinema Rex.** The cutaway ziggurat of the Rex dominates this corner of the Boulevards. Usually showing first-run action movies in French, this classy Art Deco cinema is resolutely *moderne*. The original "Arabian Nights" auditorium, with its fake constellations and fountains, is meticulously maintained. In the basement, where there was once a kennel and nursery, there are now smaller projection rooms. If you're traveling with kids, you might want to take the 50-minutes behind-the-scenes tour (English is available). ⊠ *1 bd. Poissonnière, Opéra/Grands Boulevards* ☎ *08–36–68–70–23* ⊕ *www.legrandrex.com* ⊠ *€7.50* ☉ *Wed.–Sun. 10–7* Ⓜ *Bonne Nouvelle.*

❽ **Galeries Lafayette.** This turn-of-the-20th-century department store has a vast, shimmering Belle Époque glass dome that can be seen only if you venture inside to the perfume counters. The impressive food hall next door (upstairs from menswear) is guaranteed to make even the fussiest eaters drool. ⊠ *40 bd. Haussmann, Opéra/Grands Boulevards* ☎ *01–42–82–30–25* Ⓜ *Chaussée d'Antin; RER: Auber.*

off the beaten path

MUSÉE GUSTAVE MOREAU – A visit to this town house and studio of painter Gustave Moreau (1826–98), high priest of the symbolist movement, is one of the most distinctive artistic experiences in Paris. The symbolists strove to convey ideas through images, but many of the ideas Moreau was trying to express were so obscure that the artist had to provide explanatory texts, which rather confuses the point. But it's easy to admire his extravagant colors and flights of fantasy, influenced by Persian and Indian miniatures. The museum tour (in French only) includes the artist's studio, some personal ephemera, and a significant collection of his drawings, paintings, watercolors, and sculptures. From Galeries Lafayette (or the Chausséee D'Antin métro stop), follow rue de la Chaussée d'Antin up to Trinité church, turn right on rue St-Lazare and left on rue de la Rochefoucauld. The museum is a block up on the right. ⊠ *14 rue de la Rochefoucauld, Opéra/Grands Boulevards* ☎ *01–48–74–38–50* ⊕ *www.musee-moreau.fr* ⊠ *€4* ☉ *Wed.–Mon. 10–12:45 and 2–5:15* Ⓜ *Trinité.*

⓫ **Hôtel Drouot.** Hidden away in a grid of narrow streets not far from the Opéra is Paris's central auction house, where everything from stamps and toy soldiers to Renoirs and Art Nouveau commodes is sold. Walk in off the street and browse through the open salesrooms—there's no obligation to bid. The mix of ladies in fur coats with money to burn, penniless art lovers desperate to unearth an unidentified masterpiece, and scruffy dealers trying to look anonymous makes up Drouot's unusually rich social fabric. Anyone can attend the sales and viewings. For centuries the French government refused to allow foreign firms to stage auctions, but that changed in 2001, and Drouot faces very stiff competition from Sotheby's and Christie's, who are now established in Paris. ⊠ *9 rue Drouot, Opéra/Grands Boulevards* ☎ *01–48–00–20–00* ⊕ *www.gazette-drouot.com* ☉ *Viewings mid-Sept.–mid-July, Mon.–Sat. 11–noon and 2–6, with auctions starting at 2* Ⓜ *Richelieu Drouot.*

⑲ Musée des Arts et Métiers (National Technical Museum). Prepare to be astounded. This museum of scientific instruments and inventions is a treasure trove, where 16th century astrolabes share shelf space with jeweled celestial spheres, and models of locomotives give way to Edison's early phonographs and early film camera prototypes from the Frères Lumière. The building was originally the medieval church and priory of St-Martin des Champs, built between the 11th and 13th centuries. Confiscated during the Revolution, it was used first as an educational institution, then as an arms factory, before becoming, in 1799, home to its blossoming collection. All displays have information in English. ⊠ *60 rue Réaumur, Opéra/Grands Boulevards* ☎ *01–53–01–82–00* ⊕ *www.arts-et-metiers.net* ☒ *€6.50* ☉ *Tues., Wed., and Fri.–Sun. 10–6, Thurs. 10–9:30* Ⓜ *Arts et Métiers.*

need a break? A tiny Chinatown has popped up near the Arts et Métiers, especially around rue au Maire. Chinese and Vietnamese restaurants are dotted everywhere; most are unremarkable, but you can try delicious *phô* (beef noodle soup) at tiny **Shun Da** (⊠ 16 rue Volta Grands Boulevards ☎ 01–42–72–71–11), a five-table Vietnamese restaurant in a 14th-century timbered building on rue Volta. Stroll through this tiny *quartier* for its lively vibe and crooked medieval buildings.

❷ Musée Cernuschi. Despite extensive renovation delays, at this writing this Asian art museum is expected to reopen by late 2005. A connoisseur's favorite, the collection includes Chinese art from Neolithic pottery (3rd millennium BC) to funeral statuary, painted 8th-century silks, and contemporary paintings, as well as ancient Persian bronze objects. ⊠ *7 av. Velasquez, Parc Monceau* ☎ *01–55–74–61–30* ⊕ *www.paris.fr/musees/* ☒ *Free* ☉ *Tues.–Sun. 10–5:40* Ⓜ *Monceau.*

☾ ⑬ Musée Grévin. Founded in 1882, this waxworks museum in the passage Jouffroy ranks in scope and ingenuity with Madame Tussaud's in London. The grotto-like entrance leads up an Opéra-inspired staircase into the Palais des Mirages, a small mirrored *salon* from the 1900 Paris Exposition. After this classy beginning, wax takes center stage with renderings of 250 historical and contemporary celebrities, from Charlemagne and Jean-Paul Marat to Ernest Hemingway. ⊠ *10 bd. Montmartre, Opéra/ Grands Boulevards* ☎ *01–47–70–85–05* ⊕ *www.grevin.com* ☒ *€16* ☉ *Daily 10–7* Ⓜ *Grands Boulevards.*

★ ❹ Musée Jacquemart-André. Often compared to New York City's Frick Collection, this was one of the grandest private residences of 19th-century Paris. Built between 1869 and 1875, it became a showcase for the art collections of its owners, Edouard André and his wife, Nélie Jacquemart. The couple felt little connection to their contemporary art scene and instead sought out Italian Renaissance masterpieces. During repeated trips to Italy they amassed outstanding Venetian and Florentine paintings; these were supplemented by choice 18th-century French portraits and a few Rembrandts. The Jacquemart-Andrés always intended to make their home a museum, and one of the distinctive pleasures of a visit here is the balance between great art and intimate settings. While walking through the home (free English-language audioguides available), you'll be able to see the private rooms as well as the grand formal spaces. Tiepolo frescoes waft up a stunning double staircase and across the dining-room ceiling. In the salons, done in the fashionable Louis XVI–Empress style (favored by Empress Eugénie), you'll find Uccello's *Saint George Slaying the Dragon,* Rembrandt's *Pilgrims of Emmaus,* and Jacques-Louis David's *Comte Antoine-Français de Nantes.* The Tiepolo dining room now contains a café, where you can lunch on salads named after some of the painters you've seen upstairs. ⊠ *158 bd. Haussmann, Parc Monceau* ☎ *01–45–62–11–59* ⊕ *www.musee-jacquemart-andre.com/jandre/* 🎫 *€8* ⊗ *Daily 10–6* Ⓜ *St-Philippe-du-Roule or Miromesnil.*

need a break? Opened by superchef Alain Ducasse and renowned baker Eric Kayser, **Be** (⊠ 73 bd. de Courcelles, Parc Monceau ☎ 01–46–22–20–20), a *boulangerie-épicerie,* is a hybrid bakery and corner store stocked with gastronomic grocery items like candied tomatoes and walnut oil from the Dordogne. Pick up a superlative sandwich to eat in the nearby Parc Monceau or, if the weather's not cooperating, grab a seat in the back and order soup.

❸ **Musée Nissim de Camondo.** Molière made fun of the *bourgeois gentilhomme,* **Fodor'sChoice** the middle-class man who aspired to the class of his royal betters, but ★ the playwright would have been in awe of Comte Moïse de Camondo, whose sense of style, grace, and refinement could have taught the courtiers at Versailles a thing or two. After making a fortune in the late 19th century, the businessman built this grand *hôtel particulier* (mansion) in the style of the Petit Trianon and proceeded to furnish it with some of the most exquisite furniture, boiseries, and bibelots of the mid- to late 18th century. But this promising family tragically unraveled: the wife ran off and the son, Nissim, was killed in World War I. Upon Moïse's death in 1935, the house and its contents were left to the state as a museum named for the lost son. A few years later the daughter and her family were deported and murdered in Auschwitz. Today the house remains as an impeccable tribute to its founder's life, from the gleaming salons to the refined private rooms, including the 1912 state-of-the-art kitchen. You can even see the condolence letter written by Marcel Proust, a family friend, after the death of Nissim. There are background materials available in English—and if you understand French, don't miss the fascinating video on the second floor. ⊠ *63 rue de Monceau, Parc Monceau* ☎ *01–53–89–06–50* ⊕ *www.ucad.fr* 🎫 *€6* ⊗ *Wed.–Sun. 10–5:30* Ⓜ *Villiers.*

⓯ **Notre-Dame de Bonne-Nouvelle.** This wide, soberly neoclassical church is tucked away off the Grands Boulevards. The previous church (the second) on the spot was ransacked during the Revolution, and the current one, built in 1823–29 after the restoration of the French monarchy, was ransacked by Communard hooligans in May 1871. The highlight is the semicircular apse behind the altar, featuring some fine 17th-century paintings beneath a three-dimensional 19th-century grisaille composition by Abel de Pujol. ⊠ *Rue de la Lune, Opéra/Grands Boulevards* Ⓜ *Bonne Nouvelle.*

★ ❾ **Opéra Garnier.** Haunt of the Phantom of the Opera, the real-life setting for some of Edgar Degas's famous ballet paintings, and still the most opulent theater in the world, the Paris Opéra was begun in 1862 by Charles Garnier at the behest of Napoléon III. Expenses slowed the work down, and it was not completed until 1875, five years after the emperor's abdication. Awash with Algerian colored marbles and gilded putti, it is said to typify Second Empire architecture: a pompous hodgepodge of styles with about as much subtlety as a Wagnerian cymbal crash. The composer Debussy famously compared it to a Turkish bathhouse.

To see the theater and lobby, you don't actually have to attend a performance: after paying an entry fee, you can stroll around at leisure and view the foyer and have a peek into the auditorium. The monumental Grand Foyer is nearly as big as the auditorium (together they fill 3 acres). After all, this was a theater for Parisians who came to the opera primarily to be seen; on opening nights you can still see Rothschilds and rock stars preen on the grand staircase. If the crimson-and-gilt auditorium seems small, it is only because the stage is the largest in the world—more than 11,000 square yards, with room for up to 450 performers. Illuminated by a giant chandelier, the fluid pastel figures of Marc Chagall's 1964 ceiling painting might seem incongruous. This addition was part of a scheme to mesh contemporary art with French tradition. Today, the Opéra is the home of the Paris Ballet. (One or two operas per season are presented here; the rest are performed at the Opéra de la Bastille.) A small, nondescript on-site museum contains a few paintings and theatrical mementos. The guided tours focus on the building's history and architecture, but don't offer much of a glimpse into the current backstage world. ⊠ *Pl. de l'Opéra, Opéra/Grands Boulevards* ☎ *01–40–01–22–63* ⊕ *www.opera-de-paris.fr* ☒ *€6* ⊙ *Daily 10–4:30. Guided tours in English at 3* Ⓜ *Opéra.*

┌─────────┐
│ need a │ Few cafés are as grand as the **Café de la Paix** (⊠ 5 pl. de l'Opéra,
│ break? │ Opéra/Grands Boulevards ☎ 01–40–07–30–10). Once described as
└─────────┘ the "center of the civilized world," it was a regular meeting place for
the glitterati of the Belle Époque, and even well into the 20th century, this was the place to see and be seen. When Charles de Gaulle returned to Paris after the Occupation and famously walked from the Champs-Élysées to Opéra, this is where he chose to lunch. These days, though the clientele is largely just visiting and the prices are steep, the view is still beyond compare.

★ ♻ ❶ **Parc Monceau.** This exquisitely landscaped park began in 1778 as the Duc de Chartres' private garden; though some of the parkland was sold off under the Second Empire (creating the exclusive real estate that now borders the park), the refined atmosphere and some of the fanciful faux-ruins have survived. Immaculately dressed children play, watched by their nannies, while lovers picnic on the grassy lawns. In 1797 André Garnerin, the world's first-recorded parachutist, staged a landing in the park. The rotunda—known as the Chartres Pavilion—is surely the city's grandest public restroom; it started life as a tollhouse. ⊠ *Entrances on bd. de Courcelles, av. Velasquez, av. Ruysdaël, av. van Dyck, Parc Monceau* Ⓜ *Monceau.*

❿ Paris Story. Victor Hugo is your "guide" on this 45-minute split-screen presentation of Paris and its history, with spectacular photography and tasteful musical accompaniment, with St-Saëns's Organ Symphony employed to majestic effect. It's a fun introduction to the city. Be sure to get headphones to hear the English translation. ⊠ *11 bis, rue Scribe, Opéra/Grands Boulevards* ☎ *01–42–66–62–06* ⊕ *www.paris-story. com* ✉ *€8* ◷ *Apr.–Oct., daily 9–8; Nov.–Mar., daily 9–7; screenings on the hr* Ⓜ *Opéra.*

⑫ Passage Jouffroy. Built in 1846, as its giant clock will tell you, this shops-filled passage was one of the favorite haunts of 19th-century dandies and flaneurs like the bohemian poet Gérard de Nerval, who often strolled here in top hat and tails with a large lobster on a pink-ribbon leash. ⊠ *Entrances on bd. Montmartre, rue de la Grange-Batelière, Opéra/ Grands Boulevards* Ⓜ *Richelieu Drouot.*

⑰ Porte St-Denis. Not as grandiose as the Arc de Triomphe, but triumphant nonetheless, Paris's second-largest arch (76 feet) was erected by François Blondel in 1672 to celebrate the victories of Ludovico Magno (as Louis XIV is here styled) on the Rhine. The bas-reliefs by François Girardon include campaign scenes and trophies stacked on shallow, slender pyramids. The arch faces rue St-Denis, formerly the royal processional route into Paris from the north. Last used as such a route by Queen Victoria in 1855, it's now known primarily for its sidewalk queens of the night. ⊠ *Bd. St-Denis, Opéra/Grands Boulevards* Ⓜ *Strasbourg St-Denis.*

⑱ Porte St-Martin. This 56-foot triumphal arch, slightly smaller and younger than the neighboring Porte St-Denis, was designed in 1674. Louis XIV's victories at Limburg (in Flanders) and Besançon in Franche-Comté get bas-relief coverage from Martin Desjardins. ⊠ *Bd. St-Denis, Opéra/ Grands Boulevards* Ⓜ *Strasbourg St-Denis.*

❺ St-Augustin. Victor Baltard, the architect of Les Halles, wedged an innovative church onto this triangle of land. It's the first church in Paris with a metal skeleton (though you can't see the framework for the stone cladding). In another first, the 1868 organ was the earliest to use electricity instead of mechanical pneumatic action. The resulting church feels surprisingly traditional despite its riotous kitchen-sink architecture of Renaissance, Byzantine, and other styles. Stand beside the statue of Joan of Arc to size up this impressive Second Empire aesthetic. ⊠ *Rue de Messine at bd. Haussmann Monceau/Opéra* Ⓜ *St-Augustin.*

⑳ Ste-Elisabeth-du-Temple. This studied essay in baroque (built 1628–46) is pleasantly unpretentious; there's no soaring bombast here. The church has brightly restored wall paintings and a wide, semicircular apse around the choir, where biblical scenes are carved into 17th-century wood paneling transferred from an abbey in Arras in northern France. The massive 1853 organ, refurbished in 1999, accompanies Sunday mass. ⊠ *Rue du Temple, République* Ⓜ *Temple.*

MONTMARTRE

Topped by its "sculpted cloud," the Sacré-Coeur basilica, and set on a dramatic rise above the city, Montmartre resolutely retains an independent spirit. It may be *in* the city, but it's not entirely *of* it, and its sometimes-scruffy streets have an intriguing, timeless quality—once you get away from the swarms of tourists, that is. Long a draw because of its bohemian/artistic history, Montmartre became even more popular after its starring role in the smash-hit films *Amélie* and *Moulin Rouge.* Yet you can still give the hordes the slip and discover some of Paris's most romantic and picturesque corners.

In fact, Montmartre was annexed to Paris relatively recently, in 1860. The village originally bristled with dozens of windmills, which were set up here not just because the hill was a good place to catch the wind—at more than 300 feet, it's the highest point in Paris—but because Montmartre was covered with wheat fields right up to the end of the 19th century. The mills sold cheap pancakes and drinks to the locals; these days, the remaining windmills are just decorative. The hill (often referred to by Parisians as *La Butte,* meaning "the mound") was also a gypsum quarry site and became so honeycombed with tunnels that when the métro arrived, workers had to burrow deep to avoid unstable areas. The local stations, such as Abbesses, are far underground; you may want to take the elevator instead of the stairs to get up to ground level.

By the mid-19th century Montmartre had become a favorite artists' haunt, attracting painters such as Théodore Géricault and, years later, Henri Toulouse-Lautrec, Vincent van Gogh, and Renoir with its light (another advantage of the hilltop perch), its cheap rents, and its nightlife. The bars, *guinguettes,* and, by the turn of the 20th century, cabarets like the Moulin Rouge ensured that the bohemian crowd would never lack for distraction or inspiration. For years, the local nightlife ran mostly on the fumes of its past reputation, and the only artists to be found—other than those fortunate enough to have landed a state-subsidized studio on avenue Junot or rich enough to afford a multimillion-dollar villa—were the portrait sketchers that hustle tourists on the place du Tertre. But today, the less-travelled streets behind Montmartre are making a comeback with artists and actors.

In 1870 Montmartre became the flash point of the Commune. As the city reeled from the extended siege of the Franco-Prussian War, National Guard soldiers seized guns being held on the hill and turned on the standard French troops, sparking months of brutal, street-by-street fighting throughout Paris. It's no accident that Sacré-Coeur was built over the site of the gun cache; part of its purpose was to reunite the populace after the Communard rebellion. The basilica has been called everything from grotesque to sublime; its silhouette, viewed from afar at dusk or at sunrise, looks more like that of a mosque than a cathedral.

No one is quite sure how Montmartre got its name. Some say the name comes from the Roman temple to Mercury that was once here, called the Mound of Mercury, or Mons Mercurii. Others contend that it was an adaptation of Mons Martyrum, a name inspired by the burial here of Paris's first bishop, St. Denis. The popular version of his martyrdom is that he was beheaded by the Romans in AD 250 but arose to carry his severed head from rue Yvonne-Le-Tac to a place 6½ km (4 mi) to the north, an area now known as St-Denis. A final twist on the name controversy is that Montmartre briefly came to be known as Mont-Marat during the French Revolution. Marat was a leading Revolutionary figure who was stabbed to death in his bath.

Numbers in the text correspond to numbers in the margin and on the Montmartre map.

a good walk

If you'd like to start with a visit to one of Paris's least-known but most atmospheric cemeteries, the **Cimetière de Montmartre** ❶, take the métro to place Clichy, walk north to boulevard de Clichy, and turn right. The cemetery gates are on your left. The boulevard de Clichy itself has had its share of celebrities; in 1925, Josephine Baker stayed in a hotel here while she took Paris by storm with her Charleston. Though she received literally hundreds of wedding proposals in her first year in Paris, she chose to live with French poster artist Paul Colin and her pet pig.

If you prefer to skip the cemetery, take the métro to Blanche, where you'll easily spot the luminous namesake of the **Moulin Rouge** ❷, the windmill turned dance hall immortalized by Toulouse-Lautrec and, more recently, by the Baz Luhrmann/Nicole Kidman film. The Café Cyrano, next door to the Moulin Rouge, was once the haunt of Salvador Dalí and his fellow Surrealists. Walk up lively shop-filled rue Lepic, taking a look at the tiny Lux Bar at No. 12 with its colorful 1910 tiles and passing the Café des Deux Moulins (a popular destination since its role in the film *Amélie*). Vincent van Gogh lived with his brother Theo at 54 rue Lepic in the late 1880s; across the street, Degas kept a studio.

Continue up winding Lepic to **Moulin de la Galette** ❸, on your left, famously painted by Renoir opposite rue Tholozé, once a path over the hill. Then turn right down rue Tholozé, past **Studio 28** ❹, the first cinema built expressly for experimental films. When Luis Buñuel and Salvador Dalí premiered their anticlerical film *L'Age D'Or* here in 1930, the incensed crowd trashed the lobby and tore down the screen.

Continue down rue Tholozé to rue des Abbesses. Go left along rue des Abbesses to the triangular **place des Abbesses** ❺ with the redbrick facade of **St-Jean l'Evangéliste** ❻. Tiny rue André-Antoine, to the right of the popular Café St-Jean, leads to what was originally the **Théâtre Libre,** at No. 37. This theater, founded in 1887, popularized the work of then-iconoclastic playwrights such as Henrik Ibsen and August Strindberg. From place des Abbesses, take rue Yvonne-Le-Tac off to the right. Paris's first bishop, St. Denis, is commemorated by the 19th-century

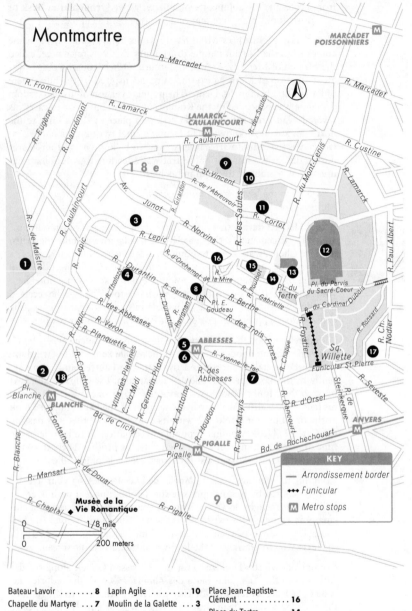

Montmartre

Chapelle du Martyre ❼, at No. 9, built on the spot where he is said to have been beheaded.

Return to the square and follow rue Ravignan as it climbs, via place Émile-Goudeau, a cobbled square with a Wallace fountain, to the **Bateau-Lavoir** ❽, the cradle of Cubism, at its northern edge. Painters Picasso and Braque had studios in this old piano factory. Unfortunately the building burned in 1970 and is now rebuilt rather blandly; check out the historic photographs in the window of No. 11 bis for an idea of how it used to look, then go around the corner up rue d'Orchampt. Follow this narrowing street to emerge near another old windmill.

Cross the street; in half a block, you'll reach the intersection of rue Norvins. Pop across the square to see the sculpture of a man emerging from the wall, a nod to a story by Marcel Aymé about a fellow with this supernatural power. Then go left down avenue Junot (illogically, it's labelled Impasses Girardon at this point). This is part of the Cité Internationale des Arts, where the city authorities rent out studios to artists from all over the world. On avenue Junot two narrow passages delimit what remains of Montmartre's forest, now the world's smallest bird sanctuary. Step up through No. 23 to the *boulodrome* (bowling ground), a setting right out of a Marcel Pagnol novel, complete with pastis-drinking old men. The next passage along avenue Junot is the Villa Léandre cul-de-sac. At different times home to artist Max Ernst, actor Jean Marais, and actress Anouk Aimée, the street's Anglo-Norman villas are among the most coveted bits of real estate in Paris.

Backtrack to rue Girardon and follow it downhill past a small park, with a headless stone sculpture of St-Denis, to Place Dalida, named for the late, dramatic French songstress of the 1960s. (She lived on rue d'Orchampt.) The benches here are an excellent spot to pause for a break. Below you, down the stairs and to the right at rue Gaulard is the tiny **Cimetière St-Vincent** ❾. But directly ahead of you is the winding rue Abreuvoir, which leads you past the Maison Rose (famously painted by Utrillo). Turn left to find 22 rue des Saules, the bar-cabaret **Lapin Agile** ❿, originally one of the raunchiest haunts in Montmartre. Across the way is a pocket-size, carefully tended vineyard.

Head back up rue Abreuvoir. Turn left at rue Cortot, where you'll come the **Musée de Montmartre** ⓫, once home to an illustrious group of artists including Renoir. Composer Eric Satie (who played piano at the Chat Noir) lived a few doors down at No. 6 in a closet-apartment only 6 feet by 4½ feet (with a 9 foot ceiling). Follow the curving street right, then go left onto rue Chevalier de la Barre. Ahead you'll see the scaly white domes of **Sacré-Coeur** ⓬. Visit the interior for its golden mosaics (it's especially atmospheric at Christmastime) and admire the Cinerama-scale city vista from its steps.

Go down the first flight of steps and turn right to pass the tiny church of **St-Pierre de Montmartre** ⓭ and reach the crowded **place du Tertre** ⓮. Restaurant **La Mère Catherine** at No. 6 was a popular hangout of the Russian Cossacks when they occupied Paris in 1814; their shouts of "*bistro*" (Russian for "quickly") inspired the French to call faster-service restaurants "bistros". Fight your way through to the southern end of the square for a breathtaking view of the city. If you're hungry, pop into the piano bar/creperie Tire Bouchon (9 rue Norvins) which appears in Jake Lamar's crime novel *Rendezvous Eighteenth*. Around the corner on rue Poulbot, the **Espace Salvador-Dalí** ⓵ is devoted to works by the namesake Surrealist.

Past Espace Dalí, follow the stairs down to rue Gabrielle. Turn right to reach **place Jean-Baptiste-Clément** ⓰, where Modigliani had a studio. Go downhill two blocks to rue des Trois Frères (Amélie Poulain's greengrocer, still sporting the MAISON COLIGNON sign from the film, is at No. 56). Zigzag along Trois Frères, then go left on rue Tardieu to place St-Pierre. Just past the merry-go-round and garden is the **Halle St-Pierre** ⓱ with its naive-art collection. The neighboring streets teem with fabric shops. Downhill is place Pigalle, once famous for its cafés, notable nowadays for its strippers. Just west of Pigalle on the boulevard is the **Musée de l'Érotisme** ⓲, whose collection of erotic artifacts from around the world pays fulsome tribute to Montmartre's debauched past. Rather than face any jiggly bits, though, you can veer from the Halle St-Pierre down to rue des Martyrs; as this street runs south it gets increasingly busy, with stylish cafés and food shops where you can wind down with a snack.

TIMING Reserve 4–5 hours for this 4.5-km (2¾-mi) walk: many of the streets are steep and slow going. Include half an hour each at Sacré-Coeur and the museums (the Dalí museum is open daily, but the Montmartre museum is closed Monday). From Easter through September Montmartre is besieged by tourists. If you can, aim for late afternoon, when the tour buses have moved on, and stay into the night to admire the twinkling lights from the steps of Sacré Coeur. If you're visiting in October, check the date of the harvest parade, which celebrates the tiny vineyard on rue des Saules.

What to See

❽ **Bateau-Lavoir** (Boat Wash House). Montmartre poet Max Jacob coined the name for the original building here, which reminded him of the laundry boats that used to float in the Seine. He joked that the warren of paint-splattered artists' studios needed a good hosing down. (Wishful thinking, since the building only had one water tap.) It was in the original Bateau-Lavoir that, early in the 20th century, Pablo Picasso and Georges Braque made their first bold stabs at Cubism; Picasso painted the groundbreaking *Les Demoiselles d'Avignon* here in 1906–07. Their experimental work didn't meet with complete acceptance, even in liberal Montmartre. Writer Roland Dorgèles, in teasing protest against the Bateau-Lavoir team, once tied a loaded paintbrush to the tail of a donkey belonging to the Lapin Agile cabaret and sold the resulting oeuvre for 400 francs. But poet Guillaume Apollinaire, also on board the Bateau, set the seal on the movement's historical importance by writing *The Painters of Cubism* in 1913. The replacement building also contains art studios and is quite modest; a sign on the front details the site's history. ⊠ *13 pl. Émile-Goudeau, Montmartre* Ⓜ *Abbesses.*

7 **Chapelle du Martyre** (Martyr's Chapel). It was in the crypt of the original chapel—built over the spot where St. Denis is said to have been martyred around AD 250—that Ignatius of Loyola, Francis Xavier, and five other companions swore an oath of poverty, chastity, and service to the Church in 1534. This led to the founding of the Society of Jesus (the Jesuits) in Rome six years later—a decisive step in the efforts of the Catholic Church to reassert its authority in the face of the Protestant Reformation. ⊠ *9 rue Yvonne-Le-Tac, Montmartre* Ⓜ *Abbesses.*

1 **Cimetière de Montmartre** (Montmartre Cemetery). Although not as large as the better-known Père-Lachaise, this leafy split-level cemetery is just as moving and evocative. Incumbents include painters Jean-Honoré Fragonard, and Degas; Adolphe Sax, inventor of the saxophone; dancer Vaslav Nijinsky; composers Hector Berlioz and Jacques Offenbach; and La Goulue, the Belle Époque cabaret dancer. The florid Art Nouveau tomb of novelist Émile Zola (1840–1902), who died in nearby rue de Clichy, lords over a lawn near the entrance—though Zola's mortal remains were removed to the Panthéon in 1908. ⊠ *Av. Rachel, Montmartre* ⊗ *Mar. 15–Nov. 6, Mon.–Sat. 8–6, Sun. 9–6; Nov. 7–Mar. 14, Mon.–Sat. 8–5:30, Sun. 9–5:30* Ⓜ *Blanche.*

9 **Cimetière St-Vincent** (St. Vincent Cemetery). It's a small graveyard, but if you're a serious student of Montmartre, you have to visit painter Maurice Utrillo's grave. Utrillo (1883–1955) was truly "un enfant de la Butte" (a child of the hill). His mother Suzanne Valadon was a painter and a model for Toulouse-Lautrec and Renoir. Her son inherited her natural talent, though by his late teens he was an alcoholic and went on periodic cures throughout his life. The streets of his native Montmartre are his major subject. His best paintings are generally considered those of his "white period" (1910–1914), when he would mix plaster and sand with thick white paint to best capture the decaying buildings of his neighborhood. ⊠ *Entrance on rue Lucien-Gaulard (via rue St-Vincent), behind Lapin Agile, Montmartre* ⊗ *Mar. 15–Nov. 6, Mon.–Sat. 8–6, Sun. 9–6; Nov. 7–Mar. 14, Mon.–Sat. 8–5:30, Sun. 9–5:30* Ⓜ *Lamarck Caulaincourt.*

15 **Espace Salvador-Dalí** (Dalí Center). Some of the mustached man's less familiar works are among the 25 sculptures and 300 signed etchings and lithographs housed here in the Dalí museum. The "ambience" is meant to approximate the surreal experience, with black walls, low lighting, and a new age–y musical score—punctuated by recordings of Dalí's own voice. There's plenty of information in English, including an audioguide. ⊠ *11 rue Poulbot, Montmartre* ☎ *01–42–64–40–10* 🎫 *€7* ⊕ *www. dali-espacemontmartre.com* ⊗ *Daily 10–6:30* Ⓜ *Abbesses.*

17 **Halle St-Pierre.** This elegant iron-and-glass 19th-century market hall at the foot of Sacré-Coeur houses a children's play area, a café, a children's and outsider-art bookstore, and the **Musée de l'Art Naïf Max-Fourny** (Max Fourny Museum of Naive Art), with its psychedelic collection of outsider, folk, and *brut* (raw) art. The exhibits focus on mainly contemporary artists who for various reasons work outside the fine-art tradition. ⊠ *2 rue Ronsard, Montmartre* ☎ *01–42–58–72–89* ⊕ *www. hallesaintpierre.org* 🎫 *Museum €6* ⊗ *Daily 10–6* Ⓜ *Anvers.*

★ ⑩ **Lapin Agile.** This bar-cabaret is still one of the most picturesque spots in Montmartre. It got its curious name—the Nimble Rabbit—when humorist André Gill created its sign (now in the Musée du Vieux Montmartre). The sign showed a laughing rabbit jumping out of a saucepan clutching a bottle of wine. Once the sign went up, locals rechristened it the *Lapin à Gill*, or Gill's Rabbit, a pun on the agility of the rabbit (*Lapin Agile* has the same pronunciation in French as *Lapin à Gill*). In 1902 the premises were bought by the most celebrated cabaret entrepreneur of them all, Aristide Bruand, portrayed by Toulouse-Lautrec in a series of famous posters, and soon thereafter Picasso painted his famous *Au Lapin Agile* (sold at auction in the 1980s for nearly $50 million and on view at New York City's Metropolitan Museum). Today the Lapin Agile manages to preserve at least something of its earlier flavor. ⊠ *22 rue des Saules, Montmartre* ☎ *01–46–06–85–87* 🎫 *€20* ☉ *Tues.–Sun. 9 PM–2 AM* Ⓜ *Lamarck Caulaincourt.*

❸ **Moulin de la Galette.** This windmill, on a hillock shrouded by shrubbery, is one of the remaining two in Montmartre. Its name comes from the inexpensive *galettes* made from leftover flour ground at the mill. It was once the focal point of an open-air cabaret (made famous in a painting by Renoir, now part of the collection of the Musée d'Orsay), and rumor has it that the miller, Debray, was strung up on its sails and spun to death after striving vainly to defend it against invading Cossacks in 1814. Unfortunately, it can only be admired from the street below. ⊠ *Rue Tholozé, Montmartre* Ⓜ *Abbesses.*

❷ **Moulin Rouge.** Built originally as a windmill, this world-famous cabaret was transformed into a dance hall in 1889. Aristocrats, professionals, and the working class all came to watch the scandalous performers, such as the dancer La Goulue (the Glutton, so called for her habit of draining leftover glasses). There was even a giant elephant in the courtyard, as reimagined in the Baz Luhrmann film. Those wild early days were immortalized by Toulouse-Lautrec in his posters and paintings. If you fancy a Vegas-style night out, with troupes of bare-breasted Doriss Girls sporting feather headdresses, this is the place to go. The cancan, by the way—still a regular sight here—was considerably raunchier when Toulouse-Lautrec was around (girls used to kick off their knickers while dancing). ⊠ *82 bd. de Clichy, Montmartre* ☎ *01–53–09–82–82* ⊕ *www. moulin-rouge.com* Ⓜ *Blanche.*

⑱ **Musée de l'Érotisme** (Museum of Eroticism). The seven-story Museum of Eroticism, at the foot of Montmartre, claims to provide "a prestigious showcase for every kind of erotic fantasy." Its 2,000 works of art—you may find that this term is used rather loosely—include Peruvian potteries, African carvings, Indian miniatures, Nepalese bronzes, Chinese ivories, Japanese prints, and racy Robert Crumb cartoons. Three floors are devoted to temporary exhibitions of painting and photography. ⊠ *72 bd. de Clichy, Montmartre* ☎ *01–42–58–28–73* 🎫 *€7* ☉ *Daily 10 AM–2 AM* Ⓜ *Blanche.*

⑪ **Musée de Montmartre** (Montmartre Museum). In its turn-of-the-20th-century heyday, the building now used for Montmartre's historical museum was a studio block for painters, writers, and assorted cabaret artists. Foremost among them were Renoir—he painted the *Moulin de la Galette,* an archetypal scene of sun-drenched revelers, while he lived here— and Utrillo, Montmartre painter par excellence. The museum recaps the area's history; the collection's strong points are its many Toulouse-Lautrec posters, original Eric Satie scores, and its view of the tiny **vine-yard**—the only one in Paris—on neighboring rue des Saules. A token 125 gallons of wine are still produced every year. It's hardly *grand cru* stuff, but there are predictably bacchanalian celebrations during the harvest on the first weekend of October. There's some basic info available in English. ⊠ *12 rue Cortot, Montmartre* ☎ *01–46–06–61–11* ⊕ *www. museedemontmartre.com* ⊠ *€5.50* ⊙ *Tues.–Sun. 10–12:30 and 1:30–6* Ⓜ *Lamarck Caulaincourt.*

❺ **Place des Abbesses.** This triangular square is typical of the picturesque, slightly countrified style that has made Montmartre famous. Now the hub of the local arts and fashion scene, the place is surrounded by trendy shops, sidewalk cafés, and shabby-chic restaurants, a prime habitat for the young, neo-bohemian crowd and a sprinkling of expats. The entrance to the Abbesses métro station, designed by the great Hector Guimard as a curving, sensuous mass of delicate iron, is one of the two original Art Nouveau entrance canopies left in Paris. (This is also the deepest station, so take the elevator.) Ⓜ *Abbesses.*

Place Blanche. The name—White Square—comes from the clouds of chalky dust that used to be churned up by carts carrying plaster of Paris down from quarries. Carts filled with crushed wheat and flour from the nearby windmills added to the powdery atmosphere. The boulevard de Clichy, which intersects the square, was virtually an artists' highway at the turn of the 20th century; Degas lived and died at No. 6, Picasso lived at No. 11, and art supply stores and dealers lined the street. Today the boulevard is crammed with tourist buses and sex shops, but the side streets are worth exploring for their cafés, nightclubs, edgy boutiques, and tiny, treasure-packed antiques shops. Ⓜ *Blanche.*

off the beaten path

MUSÉE DE LA VIE ROMANTIQUE – This tranquil, countrified town house, set in a little park at the foot of Montmartre (head down rue Blanche from place Blanche; the third left is rue Chaptal), was for years the site of Friday-evening salons hosted by the Dutch-born painter Ary Scheffer. Guests included Ingres, Delacroix, Ivan Turgenev, Chopin, and George Sand. The memory of author Sand (1804–76)—real name Aurore Dudevant—haunts the museum. Portraits, furniture, and household possessions, right down to her cigarette box, have been moved here from her house in Nohant, in the Loire Valley. There's also a selection of Scheffer's competent artistic output on the first floor. Take a moment to enjoy a cup of tea in the garden café. ⊠ *16 rue Chaptal, Montmartre* ☎ *01–48–74–95–38* ⊕ *www.paris.fr/musees/* ⊠ *Free for permanent collection, exhibitions €4.50* ⊙ *Tues.–Sun. 10–5:40* Ⓜ *St-Georges.*

16 Place Jean-Baptiste-Clément. Clément, a singer, was "Mayor of Montmartre" during the heady 70 days of the 1871 Commune, when this area actually seceded from Paris. Painter Amedeo Modigliani (1884–1920) had a studio here at No. 7. Some say he was the greatest Italian artist of the 20th century, fusing the genius of the Renaissance with the modernity of Cézanne and Picasso (who initially lived around the corner at 49 rue Gabrielle). He claimed that he would drink himself to death—and he eventually did, and chose the right part of town to do it in. Look for the octagonal tower at the north end of the square; it's all that's left of Montmartre's first water tower, built around 1840 to boost the area's feeble water supply. ⊠ *Pl. Jean-Baptiste-Clément, Montmartre* Ⓜ *Abbesses.*

14 Place du Tertre. This tumbling square (*tertre* means hillock) regains its village atmosphere only late at night or in deepest winter, when the branches of plane trees sketch traceries against the sky. At any other time of year you'll be confronted by crowds of tourists and a swarm of artists clamoring to do your portrait. If one of them produces a picture of you without your permission, you're under no obligation to buy. Ⓜ *Abbesses.*

| need a break? | There are few attractive food options around Place du Tertre; locals know to slip away to **La Divette du Moulin** (⊠ 98 rue Lepic at rue Orchampt, Montmartre ☎ 01–46–06–34–84) to regain a sense of comraderie and rest their weary feet—there's tasty food or simply a decent cup of coffee, every day of the week. |

★ **12 Sacré-Coeur.** The white domes of the Sacred Heart basilica patrol the Paris skyline from the top of Montmartre. The French government decided to erect Sacré-Coeur in 1873 as a sort of national guilt offering in expiation for the blood shed during the Commune and the Franco-Prussian War in 1870–71. It was meant to symbolize the return of self-confidence to late-19th-century Paris. Even so, the building reflected political divisions within the country: it was largely financed by French Catholics fearful of an anticlerical backlash and determined to make a grandiloquent statement on behalf of the Church. Construction lasted until World War I; the basilica was not consecrated until 1919. In style the Sacré-Coeur borrows elements from Romanesque and Byzantine architecture. Built on a grand scale, the church is strangely disjointed and unsettling; architect Paul Abadie (who died in 1884, long before the church was finished) had made his name by sticking similar scaly, pointed domes onto the medieval cathedrals of Angoulême and Périgueux in southwest France. Golden mosaics glow in the dim, echoing interior; climb to the top of the dome for the view of Paris. On clear days you can also catch grand vistas of the city from the entrance terrace and steps. Try to visit at sunrise or long after sunset, as otherwise this area is crammed with bus groups, young lovers, postcard sellers, guitar-wielding Christians, and sticky-finger types; be extra cautious with your valuables. ⊠ *Pl. du Parvis-du-Sacré-Coeur, Montmartre* ☎ 01–53–41–89–00 🕾 *Free; dome €4.50* ⊘ *Basilica daily 6:45 AM–11 PM; dome and crypt Oct.–Mar., daily 9–6; Apr.–Sept., daily 10–5* Ⓜ *Anvers plus funicular.*

6 St-Jean l'Evangéliste. This redbrick church built in 1904 was one of the first concrete buildings in France; despite its sinuous Art Nouveau curves, the bricks had to be added later to soothe offended locals. The overall effect, with ceramic tile accents and glittering mosaics, is quite lovely. ⊠ *Pl. des Abbesses, Montmartre* Ⓜ *Abbesses.*

---

need a break?

Le Sancerre (⊠ 35 rue des Abbesses, Montmartre ☎ 01–42–58–08–20) is a raucous café/restaurant with large windows, loud music, and loads of true *montmartrois* charm. The tables outside offer quieter seating and a good place to take in the bustling Abbesses street scene.

---

⑬ St-Pierre de Montmartre. Sitting beneath the brooding silhouette of Sacré-Coeur is one of the oldest churches in Paris. Built in the 12th century as the abbey church of a substantial Benedictine monastery, it has been remodeled on a number of occasions through the years; thus the 18th-century facade built under Louis XIV clashes with the mostly medieval interior. Check out the excellent 20th-century stained glass windows. ⊠ *Off pl. du Tertre, Montmartre* Ⓜ *Anvers.*

4 Studio 28. What looks like no more than a generic little movie theater has a distinguished dramatic history: when it opened in 1928 it was the first theater in the world purposely built for *art et essai,* or experimental theater. Over the years the movies of directors like Jean Cocteau, François Truffaut, and Orson Welles have been shown here before their official premieres. Today it is a repertory cinema, showing first-runs, just-runs, and previews, usually in their original language. ⊠ *10 rue Tholozé, Montmartre* ☎ 01–46–06–36–07 Ⓜ *Abbesses.*

THE MARAIS

The Marais is one of Paris's oldest, most picturesque, and now most sought-after residential districts. Its dramatic comeback after 200 years of neglect was sparked in the 1970s by the building of the Centre Pompidou (known to Parisians as Beaubourg, for the neighborhood). The Pompidou ranks alongside Frank Gehry's Guggenheim Museum in Bilbao, Spain, as one of Europe's most architecturally whimsical museums. The gracious 17th- and early-18th century buildings of the area, which had been subdivided as squalid tenements and wholesale warehouses, suddenly came into view when the spotlight swung to the new museum. Today most of the Marais's hôtels particuliers—loosely, private family mansions—have been restored, and many of the buildings have become museums as well, including the history-laden Musée Carnavalet and the popular Musée Picasso. The picturesque, narrow streets are also crammed with trendy cafés, fascinating shops, and cool nightspots.

The Marais, which means "marsh" or "swamp" (so don't be surprised by the sulferous smell after heavy rainfall, even today), first became a fashionable address back when King Charles V moved his court here from the Île de la Cité in the 14th century. However, it wasn't until Henri IV laid out place Royale, today place des Vosges, in the early 17th century, that the Marais became *the* place to live. Aristocratic dwellings began to dot the neighborhood, and their salons filled with the beau monde. By the mid-1700s the area began to fall out of fashion, and the French Revolution wiped out the remaining aristocrats, as residents fled or were executed and their homes ransacked. The magnificent mansions of the Marais gradually fell into disrepair, and as the population of Paris grew, the great houses were subdivided into ever-smaller apartments.

During the 1800s the Marais stayed below the radar. Baron Haussmann's enormous overhaul of Paris ignored this area, allowing the winding medieval streets to survive even as other parts of the city were dismantled and reorganized. In 1962 Culture Minister André Malraux decreed the area an official historic district, launching the restoration. Strolling through the bustling Marais streets today, it's easy to appreciate the fabulous gold-hued facades of these buildings. Also keep your eyes peeled for open passages (*portes cochères*), leading to elegant courtyards.

Jewish communities are an important part of the Marais's history. Jewish immigrants began settling in this area in the 13th century, though the main wave of immigrants (from Russia and central Europe) came in the 19th century. Another wave—of Sephardic Jews from North Africa—arrived here in the 1960s following Algerian independence, bolstering the postwar Jewish presence. Today there are many kosher shops, Orthodox synagogues, and restaurants, particularly around rue des Rosiers, and there's a Jewish museum, the Musée d'Art et d'Histoire du Judaïsme. Longtime residents of the "Pletzl" (the area's Yiddish name) are currently opposing the city government's plan to turn it into a pedestrian-only zone on Sunday; they feel such a step smacks of a theme park. For now, the squeak-through streets, noisy traffic jams, and half-pint sidewalks are part of the game.

Numbers in the text correspond to numbers in the margin and on the Marais map.

a good walk

Begin this walk in front of the **Hôtel de Ville** ❶, facing this wedding cake of a city hall. Depending on the season, you might find a volleyball court or skating rink in this square. You can't go inside city hall, though its chandeliers glint enticingly; instead, head to your right to walk behind the building. This block along the Seine is particularly lovely, with sunlight filtering through the trees, glimpses of Notre-Dame, and *bouquinistes* arranging their bookstalls. To your left, you'll find rue Lobau and a square (filled with parked cars) leading to the church of **St-Gervais–St-Protais** ❷. In front of the impressive classical facade of the church, you'll notice a solitary tree: this is the most recent planting of the famous elm of St-Gervais, which has been a meeting place since the Middle Ages. Elms are carved into benches in the church and appear as a motif on neighboring buildings' window grills. Continue up rue Lobau to rue de Rivoli, where you'll see the popular department store, the Bazar de l'Hôtel de Ville (known as BHV). Cross Rivoli and keep walking uphill to go left onto the first street, rue de la Verrerie. Jog left a bit to rue du Renard and pause to take in an impressive clash of architectural styles: to your left is the medieval silhouette of Notre-Dame; to your right, the gaudy colored pipes of the Centre Pompidou.

Cross rue du Renard, staying on rue de la Verrerie until you get to rue St-Martin. and its ornate 16th-century church of **St-Merri** ❸. Walk around the church, turning right down the narrow rue du Cloître St-Martin to reach **place Igor-Stravinsky** ❹ with its unusual fountain. On one side of the square is IRCAM, where you can hear performances of contemporary classical music. Up ahead looms the **Centre Georges Pompidou** ❺, overlooking a sloping piazza that is often aswarm with musicians, mimes, dancers, and fire-eaters. On the far side you can visit the **Atelier Brancusi** ❻ before crossing rue Rambuteau to the Quartier de l'Horloge; take pedestrian rue de Brantôme and turn left onto rue Bernard-de-Clairvaux to admire Le Défenseur du Temps, a modern mechanical clock that whirs into action on the hour as St. George defends Time against a dragon, an eagle, or a crab (symbols of fire, air, and water). At noon, 6 PM, and 10 PM he takes on all three at once.

Return to rue Rambuteau, turn left, and cross rue Beaubourg. If you're interested in dolls or are travelling with children, you may want to duck into impasse Berthaud to visit the quirky collection in the **Musée de la Poupée** ❼. Otherwise, stay on rue Rambuteau and turn left onto rue du Temple, where the **Musée d'Art et d'Histoire du Judaïsme** ❽ is in the stately Hôtel de St-Aignan at No. 71. Just up the street at No. 79 is another splendid mansion, the **Hôtel de Montmor** ❾. Here, take a right onto rue des Haudriettes; at the next corner on rue des Archives is the **Musée de la Chasse et de la Nature** ❿, a tribute to hunting, housed in yet another fabulous Baroque mansion. Turn right onto rue des Archives and walk down, passing the medieval gateway with two fairy-tale towers, now part of the **Archives Nationales** ⓫, the National Archives. Turn left onto rue des Francs-Bourgeois, past the elegant Archives entrance.

Continue past the Crédit Municipal (the city's grandiose pawnbroking concern, nicknamed "Auntie"), the Dôme du Marais restaurant (housed in a circular 18th-century chamber originally used for auctions), and the church of **Notre-Dame des Blancs-Manteaux** ⓬. A corner turret signals rue Vieille-du-Temple; turn left and walk up past the sedate Hôtel de Rohan (now part of the Archives Nationales), then right onto rue de la Perle and walk up rue de Thorigny to the 17th-century Hôtel Salé, now the **Musée Picasso** ⓭.

Backtrack down rue de Thorigny. At the corner, you have a choice: go straight on to rue Elzévir, where you'll find the **Musée Cognacq-Jay** ⓮ (a must if you are interested in 18th-century decorative arts) or, if you need a break from museum-hopping, go left along rue du Parc Royal to rue Payenne's small sunken garden, Square Georges-Cain. Sitting here, you can admire the 16th-century Hôtel de Marle, now used as a Swedish culture center. Walking down rue Payenne (which becomes rue Pavée as you pass beneath the crooked medieval turret) look into the courtyard to see the cheerfully askew Bibliothèque Historique de la Ville de Paris. Continuing on rue Pavée takes you to **rue des Rosiers,** with its Orthodox Jewish bookshops, synagogues, delis, and falafel shops. Rosiers is the central artery of the Pletzl, a small section of the Marais that has been a Jewish district on and off since Philip Augustus first expelled the Jews from Île de la Cité in the 12th century.

The Marais

rue Rambuteau

Impasse
Berthaud

RAMBUTEAU

rue de Braque

Plateau
Beaubourg

1 e r

rue Simon-LeFranc

rue des Blancs

rue du Temple

rue du Plâtre

Bd. de Sébastopol

rue St-Martin

rue du Renard

rue St-Merri

rue de la Verrerie

rue Ste-Croix de la Bretonnerie

rue des

Archives

Manteaux

rue Aubriot

rue de Moussy

Square de la
Tour Jaques

Av. Victoria

HÔTEL DE VILLE

rue de Bourg-Tibourg

BHV

Pl. de
l'Hôtel
de Ville

rue de Rivoli

rue du Roi de S

Pont
Notre
Dame

rue Lobau

rue François Miron

Pont
d'Arcole

Quai de l'Hôtel de Ville

rue des Barres

rue du Pt. Louis Philippe

rue Geoffrey-l'Asnier

rue de l'Hôtel de Ville

0   1/8 mile

0   200 meters

Seine

Île de la Cité

Pont
Louis Philippe

PONT MARIE

KEY

— Arrondissement border

Ⓜ Metro stops

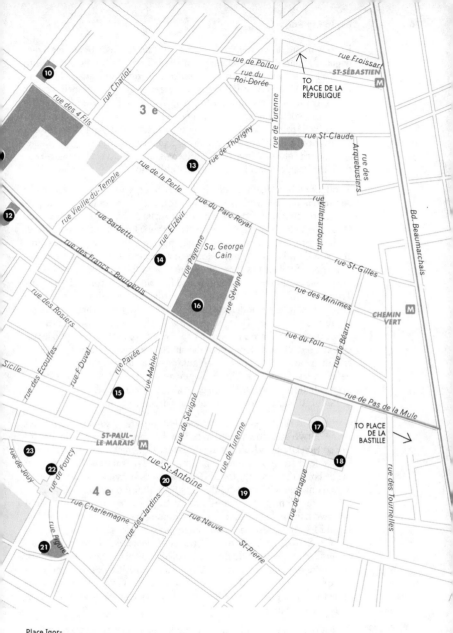

rue Froissart

rue de Poitou

ST-SÉBASTIEN Ⓜ

rue du
Roi-Dorée

TO
PLACE DE LA
RÉPUBLIQUE

Ⓜ **10**

rue des 4 Fils

rue Charlot

rue de Turenne

3 e

rue de Thorigny

rue St-Claude

rue des Arquebusiers

rue de la Perle

13

rue du Parc Royal

Bd. Beaumarchais

Ⓜ **12**

rue Vieille-du-Temple

rue Barbette

rue des Francs - Bourgeois

rue Elzévir

rue Payenne

Sq. George
Cain

rue de Villehardouin

rue St-Gilles

14

rue Sévigné

rue des Minimes

16

rue des Rosiers

rue du Foin

rue de Béarn

CHEMIN
VERT
Ⓜ

Sicile

rue des Écouffes

rue F. Duval

rue Pavée

rue Mahler

rue de Pas de la Mule

15

rue de Sévigné

17

TO PLACE
DE LA
BASTILLE

ST-PAUL–
LE-MARAIS Ⓜ

rue de Turenne

18

23

rue de Fourcy

rue St-Antoine

19

rue des Tournelles

22

20

rue de Jouy

4 e

rue Charlemagne

rue des Jardins

rue Neuve

rue de Birague

21

rue Figuier

St-Pierre

Keep walking down rue Pavée to No. 10, the **Agoudas Hakehilos Synagogue** ⑮, built by Hector Guimard in 1914. Turn right at the corner onto rue du Roi de Sicile and right again onto rue Ferdinand Duval. This street is a classic Marais mixture of gay bars, trendy shops, and, believe it or not, Orthodox Jewish establishments. You'll find yourself on rue des Rosiers (if you're hungry, pick up a falafel at L'As du Falafel). Turn right to get back to rue Pavée, retrace your route up and right onto rue des Francs-Bourgeois. Here, you'll notice the gated garden and guarding angel statue of the **Musée Carnavalet** ⑯, a Renaissance mansion famous nowadays for its period rooms and history collections.

Stroll a few blocks along rue des Francs-Bourgeois to find lovely **place des Vosges** ⑰, lined with covered arcades, and the most beautiful legacy of the French Renaissance still intact in Paris. At No. 6 you can visit the **Maison de Victor Hugo** ⑱, where the workaholic French author once lived. In the southwest corner of the arched passages that line place des Vosges, you'll find a small door leading to a garden: this is the **Hôtel de Sully** ⑲, one of the earliest Baroque mansions in Paris, which now houses the Caisse Nationale des Monuments Historiques (Historic Monuments Trust), at No. 62. Walk through the garden and building to reach rue St-Antoine. (If the wooden corner door is closed, take nearby rue de Birague to St-Antoine.) Cross St-Antoine and go two blocks right to step inside the mighty baroque church of **St-Paul–St-Louis** ⑳. When you leave, take the red left-side door out of the church into narrow passage St-Paul and then turn right onto rue St-Paul. Take the next right down the little alley, rue Eginhard. This passageway will bring you to rue Charlemagne. In front of you, built into the wall and playing field, are the remains of Philip Augustus' defensive wall for Paris, begun in 1189.

Continue to rue Fauconnier and turn left into the garden that stretches between two apartment buildings. You'll come to the painstakingly restored **Hôtel de Sens** ㉑, a strange mixture of defensive stronghold and fairy-tale château. If you are a photography fan, take rue Figuier up to rue de Fourcy to reach the **Maison Européenne de la Photographie** ㉒. Otherwise, continue with the Middle Ages by walking over to rue François-Miron: turn left, past the late-Baroque **Hôtel de Beauvais** ㉓, and you'll find two half-timber medieval houses, among the oldest in Paris, at Nos. 11 and 13. At No. 30, check out the renowned spice shop Izrael. Nearby rue Geoffroy-l'Asnier leads past the stark **Mémorial du Martyr Juif Inconnu** ㉔, commemorating those who died in Nazi concentration camps. Turn here onto rue Grenier sur l'eau, renamed Allée des Justes in honour of those who helped Jews escape during the Occupation, and continue two short blocks to finish the walk on a scenic medieval pedestrian mall, rue des Barres.

TIMING   At just over 5 km (3 mi) long, this walk will comfortably take a whole morning or afternoon. If you choose to spend an hour or two in any of the museums along the way, allow a full day. Be prepared to wait in line at the Musée Picasso. Note that some of the museums don't open until the afternoon and that a few, including the Pompidou and the Picasso museums, are open on Monday but closed Tuesday. Many shops in the Marais don't open until late morning. If you're interested in Judaica, don't plan this tour for a Saturday, when almost all Jewish-owned and -related stores, museums, and restaurants are closed.

What to See

⑮ Agoudas Hakehilos Synagogue. Art Nouveau genius Hector Guimard built this unique synagogue in 1913 for a Polish-Russian Orthodox association. The facade resembles an open book; Guimard consciously used the motif of the Ten Commandments to inspire the building's shape and its interior (which unfortunately can't be visited). Like other Parisian synagogues, this address was dynamited by the Nazis on Yom Kippur 1940. The Star of David over the door was added after the building was restored, symbolizing the renaissance of the Jewish community here. ⊠ *10 rue Pavé, Le Marais* ☎ *No phone* Ⓜ *St-Paul.*

need a break? Detour off rue Sévigné to place Marché Ste-Catherine to order up a Jewish feast appropriate to the Marais' layered history at **Pitchi Poï** (⊠ 7 rue Caron, Le Marais ☎ 01–42–77–46–15). Drift over the square for a vodka-fueled supper, or turn up punctually at noon on Sunday for a superb brunch complete with smoked salmon.

★ ⑪ Archives Nationales (National Archives). The National Archives are a history buff's fantasy; they hold thousands of historical documents dating from the Merovingian period to the 20th century. The highlights are the Edict of Nantes (1598), the Treaty of Westphalia (1648), the wills of Louis XIV and Napoléon, and the Declaration of Human Rights (1789). Louis XVI's diary is also here, containing his sadly ignorant entry for July 14, 1789, the day the Bastille was stormed and when, for all intents and purposes, the French Revolution began: "*Rien*" ("Nothing").

Even if you're not into history, the buildings themselves are worth seeing. The Archives are housed in two elegant mansions built in 1705 by trendsetting architect Alexandre Delamair: **Hôtel de Soubise,** once the grandest house in all of Paris, and the **Hôtel de Rohan,** built for Soubise's son, the Cardinal Rohan. As you enter the main courtyard, check out the medieval turrets to the left: this is the Porte de Clisson, all that remains of a 15th-century mansion. Decorative arts mavens flock to this museum for special exhibits and to see the apartments of the prince and princess de Soubise. Their rooms were among the first examples of the rococo, the light-filled, curving style that followed the heavier baroque opulence of Louis XIV. ⊠ *60 rue des Francs-Bourgeois, Le Marais* ☎ *01–40–27–60–96* ⊕ *www.archivesnationales.culture. gouv.fr* 🎟 *€3* ☉ *Mon. and Wed.–Fri. 10–5:30, weekends 2–5:30* Ⓜ *Rambuteau.*

❻ Atelier Brancusi (Brancusi Studio). Romanian-born sculptor Constantin Brancusi settled in Paris in 1898 at age 22. This small airy museum in front of the Centre Pompidou, designed by Renzo Piano, contains four glass-fronted rooms that reconstitute Brancusi's working studios, crammed with smooth, stylized works from all periods of his career. ⊠ *Pl. Georges-Pompidou, Beaubourg/Les Halles* ☎ *01–44–78–12–33* 🎟 *€7, €10 including Centre Pompidou* ☉ *Wed.–Mon. 2–6* Ⓜ *Rambuteau.*

⑤ Centre Georges Pompidou. Known as Beaubourg (for the neighborhood), this modern art museum and performance center is named for French president Georges Pompidou (1911–74), although the project was actually initiated by his art-loving wife. Designed by then-unknowns Renzo Piano and Richard Rogers, the Centre was unveiled in 1977, three years after Pompidou's death. Its radical purpose-coded colors and spaceship appearance scandalized Parisians, but they've learned to love the futuristic apparition.

On a sunny day, **Place Georges-Pompidou**'s gently sloping piazza (anchored in opposite corners by a giant gold flowerpot and the Atelier Brancusi) is packed with street performers and portrait artists. The piazza leads to the center's sprawling, stationlike lobby, with ticket counters on the back left, and an extensive bookshop topped by a café to the right. After buying a ticket, head left for the escalator that climbs the length of the building; on your way up you'll have spectacular views of Paris, ranging from the Tour Montparnasse, to the left, around to the hilltop Sacré-Coeur to the right. The **Musée National d'Art Moderne** (Modern Art Museum, entrance on Level 4) occupies most of the center's top two stories. One level is devoted to modern art, including major works by Matisse, Modigliani, Marcel Duchamp, and Picasso, the other to contemporary art since the '60s, including video installations. The museum's temporary exhibitions are fantastic; recent shows have included retrospectives on Jean Cocteau, Jean Nouvel, and Sophie Calle. In addition, there are a public reference library, a language laboratory, an industrial design center, two cinemas, a theater, dance space, and a rooftop restaurant, Georges, which is noted for its great view of the skyline. Audioguides with English commentary are available for most exhibits. ✉ *Pl. Georges-Pompidou, Beaubourg/Les Halles* ☎ *01–44–78–12–33* ⊕ *www. cnac-gp.fr* 🎫 *€10, including Atelier Brancusi; €7 for permanent collection only; €7–€9 for temporary exhibits; free 1st Sun. of month* ⊗ *Wed.–Mon. 11–9* Ⓜ *Rambuteau.*

> **need a break?**
> Cross the plaza in front of the Pompidou and grab a table at **Café Beaubourg** (✉ 100 rue St-Martin, Beaubourg/Les Halles ☎ 01–48–87–63–96), an early brainchild of French architecture star Christian de Portzamparc. Flawed service is redeemed by great people-watching and the large nonsmoking section on the ground floor, not to mention the well-designed bathrooms in the basement.

㉓ Hôtel de Beauvais. Newly restored, this mansion from 1655 has an unusually shaped courtyard, built for Pierre de Beauvais with surprisingly generous funding from the normally parsimonious Louis XIV. The reason for the Sun King's unwonted largesse: a reward for de Beauvais's willingness to turn a blind eye to the activities of his wife, Catherine-Henriette Bellier, in educating the young monarch in matters sexual. Louis, who came to the throne in 1643 at the age of 4, was 14 when de Beauvais's 40-year-old wife first gave him the benefit of her expertise. Later, Mozart supposedly stayed here. The hôtel now belongs to the city and is closed to the public apart from tantalizing courtyard glimpses. ✉ *68 rue François-Miron, Le Marais* Ⓜ *St-Paul.*

⑨ Hôtel de Montmor. This 17th-century mansion originally belonged to Louis XIII's financial advisor Jean-Baptiste Colbert. His son ran a salon here frequented by luminaries like playwright Molière, philosopher and mathematician Pierre Gassendi, physicist Gilles de Roberval, and Dutch astronomer Christian Huygens. These gatherings inspired Colbert to create the Académie des Sciences in 1666. The building is private but if you press the main button on the code panel during the week, the door usually opens, so you can admire the curvaceous Louis XV-era courtyard. ✉ *79 rue de Temple, Le Marais* Ⓜ *Rambuteau.*

㉑ Hôtel de Sens. Though much restored, this medieval mansion still shows its rich Gothic lines. Built for the Archbishop of Sens in 1474, the building developed a decidedly more secular side while Henri IV's first wife lived here after her marriage was annulled. Marguerite was renowned for her lovers (she supposedly collected locks of their hair to make wigs for herself) and launched the style for heavy powdering because her face bore terrible smallpox scars. She named this street after the fig tree she had cut down, as it was inconveniencing her carriages. (Notice the fig tree defiantly planted in the back garden.) Today the building houses occasional exhibits and a fine-arts library, the **Bibliothèque Forney.** ✉ *1 rue du Figuier, Le Marais* ☎ *01–42–78–14–60* 🖾 *Exhibitions €3* ☉ *Tues.–Sat. 1:30–8* Ⓜ *Pont Marie.*

⑲ Hôtel de Sully. The best surviving example of early Baroque in Paris, this mansion was built in 1624 with Flemish-inspired carving and a stately secret garden. Like much of the area, the hôtel particulier fell into ruin until the 1950s, when it was rescued by the administration of French historic monuments, **Caisse Nationale des Monuments Historiques.** This is now the administration's head office, complete with an excellent bookshop featuring innumerable publications in French and English about Paris (be sure to look up at the shop's original Louis XIII ceiling). Guided visits to Paris sites and buildings begin here, though all are conducted in French. There are also photography exhibitions here. ✉ *62 rue St-Antoine, Le Marais* ☎ *01–44–61–20–00* ☉ *Tues.–Sun. 10–6:30* Ⓜ *St-Paul.*

❶ Hôtel de Ville (City Hall). Overlooking the Seine, city hall is the residence of the mayor of Paris. Until 1977, Paris was the only city in France without a mayor; with the creation of the post and the election of Jacques Chirac (elected president of France in 1995), leader of the right-of-center Gaullist party, the position became pivotal in both Parisian and French politics. The latest elaborate lighting scheme has turned the building into a nighttime knockout.

The elegant square in front of the Hôtel de Ville is often rather incongruously taken up with tents for temporary public exhibits. In August, there's a beach volleyball court set up here, while in winter an open-air ice rink appears with inexpensive skate rental, making this a particularly romantic spot at night. Parisians feel almost fond of city hall these days with popular Mayor Bertrand Delanoë at the helm. But back in the Middle Ages this was the site of public executions. Most victims were hanged, drawn, and quartered; the lucky ones were burned at the stake.

CloseUp

BEST BUS RIDES

*Imagine passing the Louvre as part of your daily commute. Some of the city's public bus routes are fantastically scenic; hop on the right one and you can get a great tour for just €1.40—sans squawking commentary. The **No. 29** route reaches from the Gare St-Lazare, past the Opéra Garnier, to the heart of the Marais, crossing the place des Vosges before ending up at the Bastille. This is one of the few lines that runs primarily on small streets, not major arteries. Hop the **No. 69***

*bus at the Champ de Mars (by the Tour Eiffel) and ride through parts of the Quartier Latin, across the bridge to the Rive Droite near the Louvre, and on to the Bastille. The **No. 72** bus follows the Seine from the Hôtel de Ville west past the Louvre and most of the big-name Rive Droite sights, also giving you views of the Rive Gauche, including the Tour Eiffel.*

Following the short-lived restoration of the Bourbon monarchy in 1830, the building became the seat of the French government, a role that came to a sudden end with the uprisings in 1848. During the Commune of 1871 the Hôtel de Ville was burned to the ground. Today's building, based on the 16th-century Renaissance original, went up between 1874 and 1884. In 1944, following the liberation of Paris from Nazi rule, General de Gaulle took over the leadership of France from here. ⊠ *Pl. de l'Hôtel-de-Ville, Le Marais* ⊙ *For special exhibitions* Ⓜ *Hôtel de Ville.*

★ ㉒ **Maison Européenne de la Photographie** (MEP; European Photography Center). Much of the credit for photography's current perch in the city's cultural scene can be given to MEP's director. Jean-Luc Monterosso, who also founded Paris's hugely successful Mois de la Photographie festival (held in November in even-numbered years), has made this a terrifically dynamic institution. It stages as many as four exhibitions every three months, lining the walls of its 18th-century hôtel particulier with an impressive range of work. A show on a Magnum photographer could overlap with an Irving Penn display or a collection of 19th-century pieces. Although the MEP specializes in European photography, it also looks farther afield, with shows on American and Asian artists. Programs and guided tours are available in English. ⊠ *5 rue de Fourcy, Le Marais* ☎ *01–44–78–75–00* ⊕ *www.mep-fr.org* ✉ *€5, free Wed. after 5 PM* ⊙ *Wed.–Sun. 11–8* Ⓜ *St-Paul.*

⓲ **Maison de Victor Hugo.** The workaholic French author famed for *Les Misérables* and the *Hunchback of Notre-Dame* lived in a corner of beautiful place des Vosges between 1832 and 1848. The memorabilia here include several of his atmospheric, Gothic-horror-movie-like ink sketches, tribute to Hugo's unsuspected talent as an artist, along with illustrations for his writings by other artists, including Bayard's rendition of Cosette (which has graced countless *Les Miz* T-shirts). Upstairs, in Hugo's original apartment, you can see the tall desk where he stood to write, along with furniture from several of his homes—including the Chinese-theme panels and woodwork he created for his mistress. ⊠ *6 pl. des Vosges, Le Marais* ☎ *01–42–72–10–16* 🎫 *Free* 🕓 *Tues.–Sun. 10–5:45* Ⓜ *St-Paul.*

㉔ **Mémorial du Martyr Juif Inconnu** (Memorial of the Unknown Jewish Martyr). This memorial honors the memory of the 6 million Jews who died "without graves" at the hands of the Nazis. The basement crypt in the **Centre de Documentation Juive Contemporaine** (Center for Contemporary Jewish Documentation) has a dramatic black-marble Star of David containing the ashes of victims from Nazi death camps in Poland and Austria. The center has archives, a library, and a gallery that hosts temporary exhibitions. ⊠ *17 rue Geoffroy-l'Asnier, Le Marais* ☎ *01–42–77–44–72* ⊕ *www.memorial-cdjc.org* 🎫 *€2.30* 🕓 *Sun.–Fri. 10–1 and 2–5:30* Ⓜ *Pont Marie.*

⑧ **Musée d'Art et d'Histoire du Judaïsme** (Museum of Jewish Art and History). With its clifflike courtyard ringed by giant pilasters, the Hôtel St-Aignan, completed in 1650 to the design of Pierre le Muet, is one of the most awesome sights in the Marais. It opened as the city's Jewish museum in 1998 after a 20-year restoration. The interior has been renovated to the point of blandness, but the exhibits have good explanatory English texts on Jewish history and practice, and you can ask for a free audioguide in English. Highlights include 13th-century tombstones excavated in Paris; wooden models of destroyed Eastern European synagogues; a roomful of early paintings by Marc Chagall; and Christian Boltanski's stark, two-part tribute to Shoah (Holocaust) victims, in the form of plaques on an outer wall naming the (mainly Jewish) inhabitants of the Hôtel St-Aignan in 1939, and canvas hangings with the personal data of the 13 residents who were deported and died in concentration camps. Jewish people settled in France in the Rhône Valley as early as the 1st century BC; there was a synagogue in Paris by 582; and until Philip Augustus temporarily expelled the Jews in the 12th century, the main street of Île de la Cité was a Jewish enclave. Further expulsions occurred throughout the centuries, though they were only fitfully enforced, and 40,000 French Jews were granted full citizenship in 1791. France's Jewish population sank from 300,000 to 180,000 during World War II but has since grown to around 700,000, the largest in Europe. ⊠ *71 rue du Temple, Le Marais* ☎ *01–53–01–86–60* ⊕ *www.mahj.org* 🎫 *€6.10* 🕓 *Sun.–Fri. 11–6* Ⓜ *Rambuteau or Hôtel de Ville.*

⑯ **Musée Carnavalet.** If it has to do with Paris, it's here. This collection is a fascinating hodgepodge of Parisian artifacts, from the prehistoric canoes used by Parisii tribes to the furniture of the bedroom where Marcel Proust wrote his evocative, legendarily long novel. The museum fills two adjacent mansions, the Hôtel Le Peletier de St-Fargeau and the Hôtel Carnavalet. This latter building is a Renaissance jewel that in the mid-1600s became the home of writer Madame de Sévigné. The long-lived Sévigné wrote hundreds of letters to her daughter, giving an incomparable view of both public and private life during the time of Louis XIV. The museum offers a glimpse into her world, but the collection covers far more than just the 17th century. The exhibits on the Revolution are especially interesting, with scale models of guillotines and a downright weird cast-

FodorsChoice
★

iron stove in the shape of the Bastille. You can also walk through an amazing assortment of reconstructed interiors from the Middle Ages through rococo and into Art Nouveau—showstoppers include the Fouquet jewelry shop and the Café de Paris's original furinishings. Information in English is on hand. ⊠ *23 rue de Sévigné, Le Marais* ☎ *01–44–59–58–58* ⊕ *www.paris.fr/musees/musee_carnavalet/* ⊠ *Free for permanent collection, €6 for exhibits* ☉ *Tues.–Sun. 10–5:40* Ⓜ *St-Paul.*

> **need a break?**
>
> **Le Loir dans la Théière** (⊠ 3 rue des Rosiers, Le Marais ☎ 01–42–72–90–61) is aptly named for the dormouse who fell asleep at Alice in Wonderland's tea party. This is the perfect place to recover from museum overload—cozy into a leather chair, order a silver pot of tea, and choose a homemade cake.

🄽 Musée de la Chasse et de la Nature (Museum of Hunting and Nature). This collection of weaponry and hunting-inspired art fills part of the Hôtel de Guénégaud, designed around 1650 by François Mansart. There's little descriptive information, and none in English, so the visit is only worthwhile if you're especially keen on the subject. (For taxidermy and animal exhibits, you're better off at the Jardin des Plantes in the Grande Galerie de l'Évolution.) ⊠ *60 rue des Archives, Le Marais* ☎ *01–42–72–86–42* ⊠ *€4.62* ☉ *Wed.–Mon. 11–6* Ⓜ *Rambuteau.*

🄼 Musée Cognacq-Jay. Another rare opportunity to see how cultured rich Parisians once lived, this 16th-century rococo-style mansion contains an outstanding collection of 18th-century artwork in its in boiseried rooms. Ernest Cognacq, founder of the department store La Samaritaine, and his wife, Louise Jay, amassed furniture, porcelain, and paintings—notably by Fragonard, Watteau, François Boucher, and Tiepolo—to create one of the world's finest private collections of this period. Some of the best displays are also the smallest, like the tiny enamel portraits showcased on the third floor, or, up in the attic, the glass vitrines filled with exquisite inlaid snuff boxes, sewing cases, pocket watches, perfume bottles, and cigar cutters. There are English-language guides available. ⊠ *8 rue Elzévir, Le Marais* ☎ *01–40–27–07–21* ⊕ *www.paris.fr/musees/ cognacq_jay/* ⊠ *Free for permanent collection, €4.60 for exhibits* ☉ *Tues.–Sun. 10–5:40* Ⓜ *St-Paul.*

★ **🄱 Musée Picasso.** The Picasso museum certainly has staying power; it opened in 1985 and shows no signs of losing its immense popularity. The building itself, put up between 1656 and 1660 for financier Aubert de Fontenay, quickly became known as the Hôtel Salé—*salé* meaning, literally, "salted"—referring to the enormous profits made by de Fontenay as the sole appointed collector of the salt tax. The mansion was restored by the French government as a permanent home for the pictures, sculptures, drawings, prints, ceramics, and assorted works of art given to the government by Picasso's heirs after the painter's death in 1973 in lieu of death duties. This is the largest collection of Picasso in the world—and these are "Picasso's Picassos," not necessarily his most famous works but rather the paintings and sculptures the artist valued most. Arranged chronologically, the museum gives you a great snapshot (with descriptions in

English) of the painter's life. It also covers Picasso's personal collection of work by friends and influences such as Matisse, Braque, Cézanne, and Rousseau. The hôtel particulier is showing some wear and tear from being one of the city's most popular museums; on peak summer afternoons this place is more congested than the Gare du Lyon. ⊠ *5 rue de Thorigny, Le Marais* ☎ *01–42–71–25–21* ⊕ *www.musee-picasso.fr* ⊠ *€5.50, €6.70 for temporary exhibits plus permanent collection, Sun. €4, free 1st Sun. of month* ☾ *Wed.–Mon. 9:30–5:30* Ⓜ *St-Sébastien.*

☾ ❼ **Musée de la Poupée** (Doll Museum). If you love dolls, make a detour to this quaint, low-ceiling house in a cul-de-sac near the Centre Pompidou to admire the rarefied collection, spanning the 1800s through the Mattel era. Bisque-head dolls with enamel eyes were a Paris specialty; here, the well-labeled (in French only) displays show dolls in original costumes, complete with accessories. Don't miss the miniature greyhound made of rabbit fur, growling at an appropriately alarmed cat figure. Two rooms are devoted to temporary exhibits and there's a well-stocked gift shop. ⊠ *Impasse Berthaud, Beaubourg/Les Halles* ☎ *01–42–72–73–11* ⊠ *€6* ☾ *Tues.–Sun. 10–6* Ⓜ *Arts et Métiers or Hôtel de Ville.*

off the beaten path

NICOLAS FLAMEL'S HOME – Harry Potter fans, take note: Nicolas Flamel, the alchemist whose sorcerer's stone is the source of immortality in the popular book series, really existed. He was a wealthy merchant and left his home at 51 rue Montmorency to the city as a dormitory for the poor, on the condition that the boarders pray daily for his soul. He may not have been immortal, but the building is one of the oldest in Paris, built in 1407. The interesting carvings on the front were added at least a century after Flamel's death, but they add appropriate atmosphere.

⓬ **Notre-Dame des Blancs-Manteaux.** The Blancs Manteaux were white-robed 13th-century mendicant monks whose monastery once stood on this spot. For more than 100 years this late-17th-century church has had an imposing 18th-century facade that belonged to a now-destroyed church on the Île de la Cité. Unfortunately, the narrow streets of the Marais leave little room to step back and admire it. The inside has fine woodwork and a Flemish-style rococo pulpit whose marquetry panels are inlaid with pewter and ivory. ⊠ *Rue des Blancs-Manteaux, Le Marais* ⊕ *notre-dame-des-blancs-manteaux.org* Ⓜ *Rambuteau.*

☾ ❹ **Place Igor-Stravinsky.** The café-lined square next to the Centre Pompidou and backed by the church of St-Merri has a fountain that's a long-time kid magnet. It's animated by the colorful and imaginative sculptures of French artist Niki de St-Phalle, together with the aquatic mechanisms of her Swiss partner, Jean Tinguely. A bright blue hat twirls manically while an elephant spits water; the figure with the golden corona was inspired by Stravinsky's *Firebird*. The fountain is technically not part of the Centre Pompidou, but it fits right in. Ⓜ *Rambuteau.*

★ ⓱ **Place des Vosges.** The oldest monumental square in Paris—and one of hypnotic beauty—place des Vosges was laid out by Henri IV at the start of the 17th century. Originally known as place Royale, it has kept its

Renaissance character nearly intact, Henri IV's precise proportions giving it a placid regularity, although its buildings have been softened by time, their pale pink brick crumbling slightly and the darker stone facings pitting with age. It stands on the site of a former royal palace, the Palais des Tournelles, which was abandoned by the Italian-born queen of France, Catherine de' Medici, when her husband, Henri II, was fatally lanced in the eye during a tournament here in 1559. It was always a highly desirable address, reaching a peak of glamour in the early years of Louis XIV's reign, when nobles were falling over themselves for the privilege of living here. The two larger buildings on either side of the square were originally the king's and queen's pavilions. The statue in the center is of Louis XIII, a 19th-century remake of the 17th-century original, which was melted down in the Revolution. In 1800, under Napoléon, the square's name was changed to honor the French *département* Vosges, the first in the country to cough up taxes to the Revolutionary government. With its arcades, symmetrical brick facades, and trim green garden, there is no better location for a picnic—and you can even sit on the grass. To get inside one of the imposing town houses, visit the **Maison de Victor Hugo,** at No. 6. Ⓜ *Chemin Vert or St-Paul.*

❷ **St-Gervais–St-Protais.** The facade of this Gothic church is its most interesting quality; it's a fantastic early example of the classical orders of decoration. The bottom columns are plain, sturdy Doric, the middle columns are the more elaborate Ionic, and the topmost columns are outrageously ornate Corinthian. There has been a church here since the 7th century. Named for two Roman soldiers martyred by Emperor Nero in the 1st century AD, the present building went up between 1494 and 1598, making it one of the last Gothic constructions in the country. ⊠ *Pl. St-Gervais, Le Marais* ☎ *01–47–26–78–38 concert information* ☺ *Tues.–Sun. 6:30 AM–8 PM* Ⓜ *Hôtel de Ville.*

❸ **St-Merri.** This church near the Centre Pompidou, completed in 1552, has a turret containing the oldest bell in Paris (cast in 1331) and an 18th-century pulpit supported on carved palm trees. Parisians whisper that this was once a center of black witchcraft; nowadays, you can drop by on the weekend for rather magical free concerts. ⊠ *Rue de la Verrerie, Beaubourg/Les Halles* Ⓜ *Hôtel de Ville.*

❷⓪ **St-Paul–St-Louis.** The leading baroque church in the Marais, its elegant dome rising 180 feet above the crossing, was begun in 1627 by the Jesuits and partly modeled on their Gesù church in Rome. Look for Delacroix's dramatic *Christ on the Mount of Olives* high up in the transept, and the two huge shells, used as fonts, presented by Victor Hugo when he lived on nearby place des Vosges. ⊠ *Rue St-Antoine, Le Marais* Ⓜ *St-Paul.*

FROM RÉPUBLIQUE TO LA VILLETTE

Place de la République is the gateway to northeast Paris, a largely residential area that is often underestimated by tourists, but not by the natives. Paris nighthawks will now tell you that the Bastille bubble has burst, and the eventide pulse has beaten a retreat northeast into the heartland of the 11ᵉ arrondissement. For stylemeisters, rue Oberkampf, rue St-Maur, and rue Jean-Pierre-Timbaud are where it's all happening. Another trendy epicenter is the newly cool area around the Canal St-Martin, which has drawn a new, young crowd and forms the focal point of this walk. Today its barges transport mainly visitors and pleasure boats, but it was once a busy thoroughfare linking the Seine to the city's central slaughterhouse at La Villette. The Mitterrand era saw La Villette landscaped beyond recognition, with science and music museums and a concert hall in a wittily designed postmodern park. Nearby, 19th-century city planner Baron Haussmann created yet another fabulous green space with the tumbling Buttes-Chaumont, complete with waterfalls, grottoes, a suspension bridge, and even a lagoon.

Numbers in the text correspond to numbers in the margin and on the Place de la République to La Villette map.

a good walk

Begin your walk at **place de la République** ❶. Cross the square to rue du Faubourg-du-Temple and walk two blocks to **Canal St-Martin** ❷, whose locks and pale-green footbridges conjure up an unexpected flavor of Amsterdam. The canal emerges here after a 2½-km (1½-mi) tunnel that starts at the Seine. Go left along the far side of the canal, with its peaceful bridges and overhanging trees. Make a right turn onto rue Alibert and a left one block later onto rue Bichat to visit the Renaissance courtyard and chapel of the **Hôpital St-Louis** ❸.

Continue down rue Bichat to rejoin the canal, then cross the pedestrian bridge to explore the shops and restaurants clustered around rue des Recollets. Detour through the small park square Villemin to see the yellow day care center created by Frédéric Borel (a rising star in the "architectural hedonism" movement in Paris) and continue through the park to visit the former Couvent des Recollets, now the **Maison de l'Architecture Les Recollets** ❹. Back on the canal, you'll notice an unassuming white facade of the **Hôtel du Nord,** made famous by the film of the same name. A bit further up at 132 quai de Jemmapes is the Clairefontaine building, built in 1896. Its blue-gray iron beam exoskeleton heralds the modern era and is a good reminder of the canal's industrial history. Just before another set of canal locks, at 200 quai de Valmy, you'll find Point Éphémère, a performance space with unpredictable hours that's worth visiting if the doors are open.

The canal continues north to the circular building **Rotonde de la Villette** ❺ and the unruffled sheen of the Bassin de La Villette. Just past the Rotonde is the MK2 cinema and restaurant, in a 19th-century waterside building. Two barges moored nearby are actually theaters, offering comedy and operettas. Continue up the canal—be sure to pause to ask the fishermen if they're catching anything and to cheer on the serious *boules* players—until you reach the Pont de Crimée, near the church of St-Jacques–St-Christophe. The huge pulleys of the 1855 bridge were built by the Fives-Lille company, which designed the slanting elevators for Gustav Eiffel's tower. If you're lucky, a passing boat will trigger the mechanism so you can see it in action. From here, you could continue straight up the canal to **Parc de la Villette** ❻, but if the weather's good, detour to the picturesque **Parc des Buttes-Chaumont** ❼. Cross the pont de Crimée, go one block back down quai de la Loire and head along rue Euryale Dehaynin; pass the metro station Laumière and walk up the broad avenue of the same name, which takes you to the gates of the Buttes-Chaumont. Wend your way left around this park—once a quarry—and skirt the lake before climbing to the top of the old quarry cliff for a panoramic view of the city.

Leave the park from its southeast corner at rue de Crimée and mosey straight down to No. 93. If the door is open, walk in to discover a tiny orthodox Russian church, surrounded by an overgrown garden. The next few blocks may seem run down, but they are home to a vibrant, surprisingly amiable mix of Muslim and Jewish Orthodox immigrants. Continuing on rue Crimée will lead you to the pulley bridge of the canal. Now stroll right up the canal to La Villette, where you can visit the impressive music and science museums and take in a show. When you've exhausted La Villette, hop the metro back down to République. From here, you can dip into the hopping **Oberkampf** district: walk along rue du Faubourg-du-Temple until you hit rue St-Maur, turn right and head to the action on rue Jean-Pierre-Timbaud and rue Oberkampf.

TIMING If you're planning to take in Parc de la Villette, allot a whole morning or afternoon. The stretch along the Canal St-Martin from place de la République to the Bassin de la Villette via the Hôpital St-Louis and the square Villemin is approximately 3 km (1½ mi) and will take at least two hours, more if you window-shop or visit a museum. As for Oberkampf, you could plan on having a late-afternoon or early-evening glass of wine at one of the bars, or come back later to plug into its nightlife (*see* "The Oberkampf Scene" *in* Nightlife & the Arts).

What to See

2 **Canal St-Martin.** The canal was built, at the behest of Napoléon, from FodorśChoice 1802 to 1825, to provide the city with drinking water. But when the Industrial Revolution kicked in, the canal suddenly became a crucial navigational resource, and all kinds of industry set up shop on its banks. (The new apartment blocks you see were built when factories were demolished in the 1970s.) In 1862 Haussmann paved over the canal between Bastille and République, in an attempt to better control the working-class neighborhoods on the far side of the waterway. More recently, President Pompidou attempted to drain the canal for a superhighway, but residents protested. The scenic quays, locks, and footbridges make a lovely promenade, much beloved by filmmakers and novelists (including Georges Simenon), and these days barge traffic is rising again. There are €1.50 **barge rides** (⊠ embarkation at 13 quai de la Loire, La Villette) through the canal's nine locks along the once-industrial Bassin de la Villette to the nearby Parc de la Villette. Ⓜ *Jacques Bonsergent (southern end) or Porte de Pantin (northern end).*

need a break?
Despite its unassuming white facade, the **Hôtel du Nord** (⊠ 102 quai de Jemmappes, République ☎ 01–40–40–78–78 Ⓜ Jacques Bonsergent) is a local star. Now revamped as a café-restaurant serving basic French fare, the hotel is famous for its role in Marcel Carné's 1938 namesake movie. The film's star, actress-icon Arletty, claimed to be unmoved by the romantic canal-side setting in her

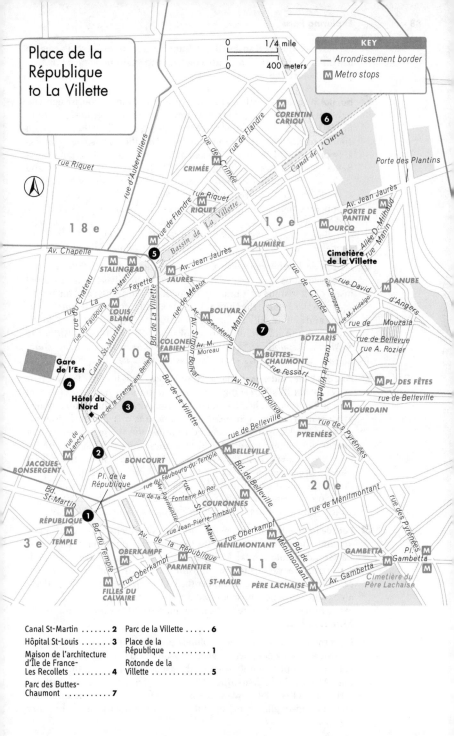

Place de la République to La Villette

KEY
— Arrondissement border
Ⓜ Metro stops

0 — 1/4 mile
0 — 400 meters

18 e

19 e

20 e

11 e

10 e

3 e

rue Riquet

rue d'Aubervilliers

rue de Flandre

rue de Flandre

rue de Flandre

rue de Crimée

CRIMÉE

rue Riquet

RIQUET

rue de La Villette

Canal de L'Ourcq

CORENTIN CARIOU

Porte des Plantins

Av. Jean Jaurès

PORTE DE PANTIN

OURCQ

Allée D. Milhaud

rue Manin

Cimetière de la Villette

Av. Chapelle

Bassin de La Villette

Av. Jean Jaurès

LAUMIÈRE

rue de Crimée

STALINGRAD

St-Martin

Fayette

JAURÈS

rue de Meaux

BOLIVAR

Av. Secrétan

rue David

DANUBE

rue Compans

d'Angers

rue M. Hidalgo

rue de Mouzaïa

rue de Bellevue

rue A. Rozier

rue O. Chateau

La

LOUIS BLANC

Bd. de La Villette

COLONEL FABIEN

Av. Simon Bolivar

Av. M. Moreau

Manin

BOTZARIS

rue de la Villette

PL. DES FÊTES

Gare de l'Est

Canal St-Martin

Bd. de La Villette

BUTTES-CHAUMONT

rue Fessart

Av. Simon Bolivar

rue de Belleville

JOURDAIN

Hôtel du Nord

rue de la Grange aux Belles

rue de Lancry

JACQUES-BONSERGENT

BONCOURT

Pl. de la République

rue du Faubourg-du-Temple

Bd. de Belleville

BELLEVILLE

rue de Belleville

PYRÉNÉES

rue des Pyrénées

Bd. St-Martin

RÉPUBLIQUE

Bd. du Temple

TEMPLE

rue de la Fontaine Au Roi

rue Parmentier

rue Jean-Pierre-Timbaud

COURONNES

rue Oberkampf

MÉNILMONTANT

Bd. de Ménilmontant

rue de Ménilmontant

rue des Pyrénées

OBERKAMPF

rue Oberkampf

PARMENTIER

ST-MAUR

PÈRE LACHAISE

Av. de la République

Mauf

GAMBETTA

Pl. Gambetta

Av. Gambetta

Cimetière du Père Lachaise

FILLES DU CALVAIRE

classic line, loosely translated as "Atmosphere, atmosphere, I've had it with atmosphere!" There are concerts and stand-up comedy (in English) most nights.

❸ Hôpital St-Louis. Though it's not, technically speaking, a tourist sight, no one will begrudge you a discreet visit to this Renaissance hospital. Built in 1607, at the same time as place des Vosges, it's still in use. The main courtyard, with its steep roofs and corner pavilions, has been remarkably preserved. The chapel, tucked away along rue de la Grange-aux-Belles, was the first building in Paris to be lighted by gaslight and shelters *Suffer Little Children to Come unto Me,* a painting by Charles de La Fosse (1636–1716), and a handsome wood balcony carved with trumpeting angels and the monograms of hospital founders Henri IV and Maria de' Medici. ✉ *Entrances on av. Richerand, rue de la Grange-aux-Belles, av. Claude-Vellefaux, République* ⊙ *Daily 5 AM–9 PM; chapel weekday afternoons* Ⓜ *Goncourt or Colonel Fabien.*

❹ Maison de l'architecture d'Île de France–Les Recollets. This elegant Renaissance monastery, created by Marie de' Medici, has had a checkered history. After stints as a military hospital (in the 1800s) and an artists' squat (in the 1980s), the site has become a center for architecture workshops and is gradually becoming an artists' residence. There's a courtyard café and an architecture bookshop. ✉ *148 rue du Faubourg St-Martin, République* ☎ *01–53–26–10–70* ⊕ *www.maisonarchitecture-idf.org* 💲 *Free* ⊙ *Tues.–Sun. 10–5:40* Ⓜ *Gare de l'Est.*

☾ ❼ Parc des Buttes-Chaumont. Inaugurated in 1867, this lush garden was part of Napoléon III's "greening" of Paris (the emperor had spent years in exile in London and loved that city's public parks). Built on abandoned gypsum quarries and a former gallows, the area was insalubrious in the extreme but Haussmann managed to transform the mess into elegant apartments ringing a steep-sloped romantic escape; there are waterfalls, grottoes, mysterious pathways, a lake filled with swans and even a pseudo-Greek temple. There's a Guignol de Paris (an open-air puppet theater) on the northern side of the park; shows start (weather permitting, closed in winter) at 3:30 PM Wednesday and weekends (€2.50 charge). ✉ *Rue Botzaris, Buttes-Chaumont* Ⓜ *Buttes-Chaumont, Botzaris.*

☾ ❻ Parc de la Villette. The 130 acres known as La Villette was a cattle market and abattoir until the 1970s. Only the slaughterhouse, known as **La Grande Halle** (Great Hall), remains. This magnificent iron-and-glass structure was ingeniously transformed into an exhibition-cum-concert center. Today, you can wander through the park's futuristic gardens, an excellent science museum and a music academy, concert hall, and exhibition space. It's one of the most impressive transformations of the Mitterrand era.

Near the Grande Hall is the resolutely postmodern **Cité de la Musique,** a music academy designed by geometry-obsessed Christian de Portzamparc. It's complete with a state-of-the-art concert hall and the spectacular **Musée de la Musique** (✉ 221 av. Jean-Jaurès, La Villette ☎ 01–44–84–44–84 ⊕ www.cite-musique.fr). The music museum contains a mind-tingling array of 900 instruments; their sounds and story are evoked with wireless headphones (ask for English commentary). It's open Tuesday through Saturday noon–6; entry costs €6.10.

The **park** itself was designed in the 1980s by postmodern architecture star Bernard Tschumi, who successfully incorporated industrial elements, children's games (don't miss the dragon slide), lots of green space, and dreamlike light sculptures along the canal into one vast yet unified playground. A great place for a picnic, the lawns of La Villette attract rehearsing samba bands and pick-up soccer games. In August there's a free outdoor cinema festival—people gather at dusk to picnic and watch movies on a huge inflatable screen. In cold weather, visit the museums, the submarine, the circus tent (which features superb contemporary acrobatic theater performances) and **La Géode**. This looks like a huge silver golf ball but is actually a Omnimax cinema made of polished steel, with an enormous hemispherical screen.

The ambitious **Cité des Sciences et de l'Industrie** (⊠ 30 av. Corentin-Cariou, La Villette ☎ 01–40–05–80–00 ⊕ www.cite-sciences.fr Ⓜ Porte de la Villette, Porte de Pantin) tries to do for science and industry what the Centre Pompidou does for modern art. The building was intended to be a new meat-auction building, but when the site was half-built, the slaughterhouse was closed down. Adrien Fainsilber gave it an inspired revamp: a multipurpose center with bright and thought-provoking displays, though many are in French only. The brave attempt to render technology fun and easy involves 60 do-it-yourself contraptions that make you feel more participant than onlooker. Lines (especially during school holidays) can be intimidating. The multilingual children's workshops are perfect spots to while away rainy afternoons. The museum is open Tuesday through Sunday 10–6; standard admission costs €7.50, the planetarium €3, and children's workshops are €5.

❶ Place de la République. This large oblong square laid out by Haussmann in 1856–65 is dominated by a matronly statue symbolizing *The Republic* (1883). The square was one of the principal sites of the Resistance uprising in 1944; now it's often used as a rallying point for protest demonstrations. Ⓜ *République.*

| off the beaten path | **PINACOTHÈQUE DE PARIS** – Borrowing its name from the Greek term for art gallery (*pinakotheke*), the Pinacothèque is a private museum near the Gare de l'Est run by Marc Restellini, an unconventional curator and self-professed megalomaniac who dreams of one day owning 20 museums around the world. Set in the former headquarters of the crystal firm Baccarat, his first effort has a splendid gilded-Regency setting at its disposal. In it, Restellini intends to show an eclectic series of exhibits on international artists, luring crowds with rarely seen or privately held works by art-world stars or edgy newcomers. At this writing, the museum planned to mount its permanent collection in mid-2005. English-language audioguides are available for €4.50. To get here from rue des Recollets, walk past Gare de l'Est and turn left onto rue du Faubourg St-Denis, then make a right at rue de Paradis. ⊠ *30 bis, rue de Paradis, Gare du Nord* ☎ *01–53–34–06–70* ⊕ *www.pinacotheque.com* ⊠ *€12* ⊙ *Subject to change; call to confirm* Ⓜ *Gare de l'Est.* |

⑤ Rotonde de la Villette. This strange circular building was one of the tollhouses built around the edge of Paris by Nicolas Ledoux in the 1780s. Most of these austere, daunting buildings, symbols to the populace of taxes and oppression, were promptly dismantled during the Revolution. Luckily, the rotunda survived as a relic of Ledoux's thrilling architecture. Like Mitterrand, Ledoux was fascinated by Masonic symbols such as spheres and pyramids. The rotunda is partly obscured by the aboveground métro as you approach from the south but its clean-cut outlines and honey-color stonework can be admired from the far side, where you can admire the Bassin de la Villette and the barges lining up at the lock. ✉ Pl. de Stalingrad, La Villette Ⓜ Stalingrad.

EAST OF BASTILLE

Bastille is a concept as much as a place. The neighborhood is named for place de la Bastille, the site of the infamous castle-prison attacked by the populace on July 14, 1789, an event which symbolically launched the French Revolution. These days, Bastille is known more for its nightlife and its many hidden passageways, atmospheric remnants from its Revolutionary days, than for political unrest. As the nearby Marais was restored to glory in the early 1980s, artists—those harbingers of gentrification—moved east of Bastille, finding studio space in former ateliers and derelict 18th-century buildings. In 1989 the bicentennial of the Revolution, these streets became the focus of a tug-of-war between the city, which aimed to rebuild, and the residents, who resented having their run-down but historical buildings obliterated. The resulting compromise brought the modern Opéra Bastille and a number of new apartment complexes to the area, but most old buildings survived, allowing the neighborhood's funky blend of hipster bars, galleries, and experimental theaters to flourish. The trendiness now stretches north to Ménilmontant and Belleville, and south towards Gare de Lyon, where urban renewal projects like the Viaduc des Arts have proved a resounding success. Highlights of this tour include the verdant Bois de Vincennes, the spectacular Bibliothèque Nationale François-Mitterrand, and Père-Lachaise Cemetery, final resting place of Proust, Oscar Wilde, Colette, and many other famous figures.

Numbers in the text correspond to numbers in the margin and on the East of Bastille map.

a good walk

Start your walk at **place de la Bastille** ❶, easily accessible by métro. Stand on the wide sidewalk between rue de la Roquette and boulevard Richard Lenoir (a wonderful market street on Sunday and Thursday mornings) to get a great view of the curving modern **Opéra de la Bastille** ❷ and the Colonne de Juillet, commemorating the revolts of 1830, with the Spirit of Liberty glinting at the top. You're actually standing on top of a canal, which runs underground and emerges on the far side of place de la Bastille. Cross the place and walk along the landscaped east quay of this canal to reach the contemporary arts center **La Maison Rouge** ❸. Once you're aesthetically saturated, retrace your path up to Bastille, cross past the opera, and go through the metal gates to Cour Damoye. Walk down this 18th-century *passage* to emerge on rue Daval. Go right to rue de la Roquette and cross to rue de Lappe, Parisians' answer to Bourbon Street. With bars for every taste, Lappe has long been a favorite for artists and writers, including Henry Miller, for its louche bars and dance halls. Its musical history stretches back to the early 1900s, when Auvergne immigrants introduced *bal musette,* accordion-driven popular music, whose players later collaborated with gypsy jazzman Django Reinhardt. One of its anchors is the Balajo dance club, established in 1930 and still going strong. Post-gentrification, these tangling streets have added unusual shops, theaters, and galleries to their constantly evolving bar lineup.

At the end of rue de Lappe go right onto rue de Charonne, taking it to rue du Faubourg-St-Antoine, famous for its cabinetmakers and for civil unrest. Since the 15th century the Faubourg has been the center for peerless furniture workshops, gilders, woodworkers, and the like. The tight community of artisans was a driving force behind the storming of the Bastille prison, and raised barricades during the uprisings of 1830, 1848, and the Commune battles of 1871. These days demonstrators march down this street when protests are staged between the place de la Nation and the place de la Bastille. Cross rue du Faubourg-St-Antoine and directly in front of you take the unevenly cobbled passage du Chantier, lined with both tatty and swank furniture and decor shops.

Passage du Chantier leads to rue Charenton; turn left, pass the trendy China Club, cross Ledru-Rollin and in the next block veer slightly left onto rue Emilio Castelar. This brings you to bustling **Marché Aligre**, a well-priced covered market. (The building is labelled Beauvau but is known as Aligre.) After a quick appetite-inducing browse, double back to rue Charles Baudelaire and walk down to the old elevated railway, now called the **Viaduc des Arts** ❹. This former industrial zone along avenue Daumesnil has been transformed with artisan boutiques at street level and a wonderful landscaped walkway running up along the former tracks.

Saunter along the viaduct to avenue Ledru-Rollin, turn left and take the first left onto rue de Lyon, which will lead you to the **Gare de Lyon,** a train station built in 1901 for travelers flocking to the newly trendy south of France. Inside, walk up the grand staircase to gape at Le Train Bleu, a hallucinatory Belle Époque restaurant and bar that was once Salvador Dalí's favorite Paris hangout. From Gare de Lyon, return to the Viaduc des Arts via rue Abel. Walk along the Viaduc to No. 73 and take the narrow staircase up to the garden walkway. Continue east and keep your eye out for a line-up of giant swooning sculptures, huge copies of Michelangelo's *Slave,* that crown the local police station.

Continue on through a pretty rose garden and into the Jardin de Reuilly. Here you have a choice: if you're interested in visiting General Lafayette's grave, stay on the walkway for about 1 km (½ mi) before going down the stairs and turning left on rue de Picpus. Some 350 yards up on the right is the entry to the **Cimetière de Picpus** (open only in mid-afternoon) ❺. Continue on rue de Picpus for about 250 yards, and then cross rue Fabre-d'Eglantine to eventually reach **place de la Nation** ❻, flanked to the right by two towering columns that once marked the eastern entry to

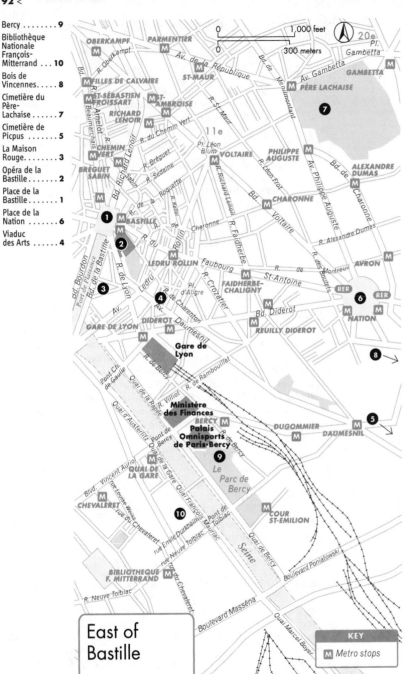

East of Bastille

Paris. From here it's a short métro ride on Line 2 to the city's most famous cemetery, the **Cimetière du Père-Lachaise** ❼, or on Line 1 to the **Bois de Vincennes** ❽, a large wooded park with lakes, a castle, and a zoo.

If you'd like to explore the up-and-coming neighborhood of **Bercy** ❾ instead, leave the Viaduc at Jardin de Reuilly, cross avenue Daumesnil and walk down pedestrian street Descros to rejoin rue de Charenton. Turn left down Charenton (note the unusual caryatids on No. 201), cross a wide intersection, and take your first right onto rue Proudhon. A short underpass brings you to the simple church of Notre-Dame de Bercy, with its charming fire station next door. Continue straight until rue Paul Belmondo. To your left is **Bercy Village**, also known as Cour St-Emilion, a cluster of former wine warehouses that have morphed into restaurants, shops, and a large cinema. To your right is a contemporary garden named for Nobel peace prizewinner Yitzhak Rabin; in the distance, you can see the four L-shape towers of the national library, across the Seine. Keeping them on your left, head to the grass-covered walls of the **Palais Omnisports** stadium, then finish the walk in front of the elephantine Ministère des Finances, designed to echo the old city gates where taxes were paid. You can hop on the métro at the Bercy stop here, heading either back to the center of town or to the national library, the **Bibliothèque Nationale François-Mitterrand** ❿, just two stops away on Line 14. The streets around the library are gradually emerging as a new hot spot, with edgy contemporary art galleries cropping up on rue Louise Weiss.

TIMING   The walk from place de la Bastille to Bercy is about 7 km (4½ mi) long and takes about four leisurely hours to complete. The area is at its best Tuesday through Saturday; the Marché Aligre is closed Monday. On Sundays many shops and passageways are locked up. If you take a side trip to Père Lachaise cemetery or to Bois de Vincennes, count on adding a couple more hours to your day.

What to See

❾ **Bercy.** Bercy is a testament to the French genius for urban renewal. Tucked away south of the Gare de Lyon in the 12ᵉ arrondissement, this colorful district was originally filled with warehouses for storing wine from the provinces. Today, two rows of these stone buildings have been turned into shops and restaurants, complete with cheerful outdoor tables. The far side leads to an immense cineplex; heading back towards the city is the artistic new park, with pleasant wandering paths, climbing vines, and trellised roses. Further on, you'll find the ingeniously sloping, grass-walled **Palais Omnisports,** a weird-looking stadium that hosts sports and music events and seats 17,000, approached on all sides by gleaming white steps. A hundred yards from the Palais Omnisports is a quirky Cubist building designed by Frank Gehry, who described it as "a dancing figure in the park." It opened as the American Center in 1994 but closed in 1996 for lack of funds; at this writing it was slated to reopen as the **Cinémathèque Française** in 2005, but progress has been rocky. Ⓜ *Bercy or Cour St-Emilion.*

❿ **Bibliothèque Nationale François-Mitterrand** (National Library). As the last of former president François Mitterrand's *grands travaux* (grand building projects) before he left office, the TGB or *très grande bibliothèque* (very big library, as some call it, playing off the TGV train acronym) opened in 1997. The library subsumes most of the state's book collections and, with some 11 million volumes between its walls, surpasses the Library of Congress as the largest library in the world. Architect Dominique Perrault's controversial design comprises four soaring towers, imitating open volumes, framing an elevated plaza and a sunken garden. Criticism was heaped on the project because books are housed in the towers, whose windows need to be covered to protect the stacks, while library users are relegated to underground reading rooms. The interior garden—sunk so that from the plaza you see the tops of full-size trees—provides visual relief from the stark space. (Unfortunately, the garden is sealed off, so readers can only gaze at the trees through the windows.) You can visit part of the library for free, but you'll have to pay to inspect one of the temporary exhibits or to consult some of the books. The library is fronted by a giant flight of wooden steps overlooking the Seine (note the red Batofar lightship, a popular nightclub). There are two entrances, each tucked away almost secretively at either end of the plaza. If you're visiting in bad weather, be careful when crossing the plaza; wind whips through here, and the boards are very slippery when wet. ☒ *11 quai François-Mauriac, Bercy/Tolbiac* ☏ *01–53–79–59–59* ⊕ *www.bnf.fr* ✉ *Library €3, exhibitions €5* ☉ *Mid-Sept.–Aug., Tues.–Sat. 10–7, Sun. noon–6* Ⓜ *Métro or RER: Bibliothèque.*

🐾 ❽ **Bois de Vincennes.** Sandwiched between the unexciting suburb of Charenton and the working-class district of Fontenay-sous-Bois, to the southeast of Paris, the Vincennes Woods are often considered a poor man's Bois de Boulogne. But the comparison is unfair: the Bois de Vincennes is no more difficult to get to and has equally illustrious origins. It, too, was landscaped under Napoléon III, although a park had already been created here by Louis XV in 1731. The park has several lakes, notably **Lac Daumesnil**, with two islands, and **Lac des Minimes**, with three; rowboats can be hired at both. In addition, the park contains a zoo, the **Hippodrome de Vincennes** (a cinder-track racecourse), a castle, a flower garden, and several cafés. In spring there's an amusement park, the **Foire du Trône**. Bikes can be rented from the Château de Vincennes métro station for €4 an hour or €15 a day. To reach the park, take the métro to Porte Dorée or Château de Vincennes.

Some 1,200 mammals and birds can be seen at the 33-acre **Parc Zoologique**, the largest zoo in France. The most striking element is the 210-foot steel-and-concrete Grand Rocher, an artificial rock built in 1934, inhabited by wild mountain sheep and penguins. You can take an elevator (€3) to the top. ☒ *53 av. de St-Maurice, Bois de Vincennes* ☏ *01–44–75–20–10* ✉ *€8* ☉ *Apr.–Oct., daily 9–6; Nov.–Mar., daily 9–5* Ⓜ *Porte Dorée.*

An exceptional Art Deco building that once held an African art museum 🐾 now teems with fish instead of artifacts. The **Palais de la Porte Dorée Tropical Aquarium** fills the basement with tanks of colorful tropical fish, crocodiles, and turtles. But the building itself is even more captivating; built for the Colonial Exhibition in 1931, it has an ornately sculpted facade depicting France's erstwhile overseas empire. A small collection of headdresses, masks, and other artifacts from former French colonies is displayed on the main floor (the African art, meanwhile, has been transplanted to the new Quai du Branly complex). ⊠ *293 av. Daumesnil, Bois de Vincennes* ☎ *01–44–74–84–80* ⛬ *€5.50* ☉ *Wed.–Mon. 10–5:30* Ⓜ *Porte Dorée.*

The historic **Château de Vincennes** is on the northern edge of the Bois de Vincennes. Built in the 15th century by various French kings, the castle is France's medieval Versailles, an imposing, high-walled castle surrounded by a dry moat and dominated by a 170-foot keep. The sprawling castle grounds also contain a modest replica (built 1379–1552) of the Sainte-Chapelle on the Île de la Cité and two elegant, classical wings designed by Louis Le Vau in the mid-17th century that house the archives of the French armed forces and are closed to the public. ⊠ *Av. de Paris, Bois de Vincennes* ☎ *01–48–08–31–20* ⊕ *www.boisdevincennes.com* ⛬ *€5.50* ☉ *Apr.–Sept., daily 10–noon and 1:15–6:30; Oct.–Mar., daily 10–noon and 1:15–5* Ⓜ *Château de Vincennes.*

The **Parc Floral de Paris** is the Bois de Vincennes's 70-acre flower garden. It includes a lake and water garden and is renowned for its seasonal displays of blooms. It also contains a miniature train, a game area, and an "exotarium" with tropical fish and reptiles. ⊠ *Rte. de la Pyramide, Bois de Vincennes* ☎ *01–55–94–20–20* ⛬ *€3* ☉ *Apr.–Sept., daily 9:30–8; Oct.–Mar., daily 9:30–5* Ⓜ *Château de Vincennes.*

★ ❼ **Cimetière du Père-Lachaise** (Père-Lachaise Cemetery). The world's most illustrious necropolis, the 118-acre Père-Lachaise cemetery is the final stop for more famous names than you could ever meet in a lifetime. The plots are prime real estate, so now only the outrageously wealthy can afford to be laid to rest with the famous. The steep cobbled avenues exude a serene Gothic aura as you walk past grandiose and sometimes dilapidated tombs; the immense trees make this a welcome stop on a warm day. Named after the Jesuit father—Louis XIV's confessor—who led the reconstruction of the Jesuit Rest House in 1682, the cemetery houses the tombs of the famed medieval lovers Héloïse and Abelard (moved here from separate graves in the romance-oriented 19th century); composer Chopin; artists Ingres and Georges Seurat; playwright Molière; writers Balzac, Proust, Paul Eluard, Colette, La Fontaine (of the fables), Wilde (usually covered in lipstick kisses), and (buried in the same grave) Gertrude Stein and Alice B. Toklas; popular French actress Simone Signoret and her husband, singer-actor Yves Montand; and singer Edith Piaf. One of the most popular shrines is that of rock star Jim Morrison. (Now, along with the Doors fans at the grave, there's a guard who makes sure you don't stay too long.) Another draw is the life-size bronze figure of Victor Noir, whose alleged fertility-enhancing power accounts for the patches rubbed smooth by hopeful hands. Less ostentatiously virile is the sculpted tomb of Romantic artist Théodore Géricault, shown brush in hand above a bronze relief plaque replicating his *Raft of the Medusa.* The cemetery was the site of the Paris Commune's final battle, on May 28, 1871, when the rebel troops were rounded up, lined against the Mur des Fédérés (Federalists' Wall), in the southeast corner, and shot. Buy a map at the entrance on boulevard de Ménilmontant—Père-Lachaise has a confusing layout. But getting lost is part of the pleasure. ⊠ *Entrances on rue des Rondeaux, bd. de Ménilmontant, and rue de la Réunion, Père Lachaise* ⊕ *www.pere-lachaise.com* ⊙ *Easter–Sept., daily 8–6; Oct.–Easter, daily 8–dusk* Ⓜ *Gambetta, Philippe-Auguste, Père-Lachaise.*

❺ Cimetière de Picpus. Most of the 1,300 people executed at the guillotine on place de la Nation in 1794 were buried in a mass grave at the nearby Picpus cemetery. Also buried here is General Lafayette, whose grave site can be identified by its U.S. flag. ⊠ *Entrance at 35 rue Picpus (once inside, ring bell of caretaker's home for access to cemetery), Bastille/ Nation* ☎ *01–43–44–18–54* ◰ *€2.50* ⊙ *Oct.–Easter, Tues.–Sat. 2–4; Easter–Sept., Tues.–Sat. 2–6. Guided visits Tues.–Sun. at 2:30 and 4* Ⓜ *Métro or RER: Nation.*

❸ La Maison Rouge. Former gallery owner Antoine de Galbert opened this exciting contemporary art foundation in summer 2004. Three shows a year bring private collections to the public eye. The building itself is a treat, an industrial space cleverly redone and anchored by the original courtyard building, now painted bright red (hence the foundation's name). So far the only flaw is a comparative lack of information about the art being displayed—a problem you can partly remedy by browsing in the gallery's excellent bookshop. There are free guided tours on Saturday at 4 (in French only). ⊠ *8 bd. de la Bastille, Bastille* ☎ *01–40–01–08–81* ⊕ *www.maisonrouge.org* ◰ *€4.50–€6.50* ⊙ *Wed.–Sun. 11–7, Thurs. 11–9* Ⓜ *Quai de la Rapée/Bastille.*

❷ Opéra de la Bastille. Designed by Uruguay-born architect Carlos Ott, the state-of-the-art Bastille Opera on the south side of place de la Bastille opened on July 14, 1989, in commemoration of the bicentennial of the French Revolution. The steeply sloping auditorium seats more than 3,000 and has earned more plaudits than the curving facade, which is currently plagued with falling marble panels. The guided tour includes part of backstage, but you'll have more fun simply buying a ticket to whatever's on. Shows are consistently spectacular, and inexpensive same-day tickets are often available. ⊠ *Pl. de la Bastille, Bastille/Nation* ☎ *01–40–01–19–70* ⊕ *www.opera-de-paris.fr* ◰ *Guided tours €10* Ⓜ *Bastille.*

> **need a break?** If you work up an appetite looking at the food stalls in Marché Aligre, duck around the corner to the friendly, bustling **Petit Porcheron** (⊠ 3 rue de Prague, Bastille/Nation ☎ 01–43–47–39–47). This spot is both hip and committed to the neighborhood; join the locals for a bite and more than a few glasses of first-class wine.

❶ Place de la Bastille. Nothing remains of the infamous Bastille prison destroyed at the beginning of the French Revolution. Until 1988 there was little more to see here than a huge traffic circle and the **Colonne de Juillet** (July Column), a memorial to the victims of the uprisings in 1830 and 1848. (Imagine what this place would look like if Napoléon's plan for a gigantic statue of an elephant had gone through.) As part of the countrywide celebrations for July 1989, the bicentennial of the French

Revolution, the Opéra de la Bastille was erected, inspiring substantial redevelopment on the surrounding streets, especially along rue de Lappe—once a haunt of Edith Piaf—and rue de la Roquette. What was formerly a humdrum neighborhood has been reenergized with art galleries, funky clubs, and Spanish-style tapas bars.

The ominous Château de la Bastille, or, more properly, the Bastille St-Antoine, was a massive building protected by eight immense towers and a wide moat. (Its ground plan is marked by hard-to-find paving stones set into the modern square.) It was built by Charles V in the late 14th century. He intended the fortress to guard the eastern entrance to the city. By the reign of Louis XIII (1610–43), however, the Bastille was used almost exclusively to house political prisoners, and it became a symbol of the king's ultimate power. A simple *lettre de cachet,* a document bearing the royal seal, would be enough to lock someone up indefinitely. Voltaire, the Marquis de Sade, and the mysterious Man in the Iron Mask were all incarcerated here, along with many other unfortunates. The Bastille's political symbolism and its location between the city center and an impoverished working-class neighborhood made it an obvious target for the largely unarmed local mob that broke into the prison on July 14, 1789. They killed the governor, stole what firearms they could find, and freed the seven remaining prisoners.

Later in 1789 the prison was knocked down. A number of the original stones were carved into facsimiles of the Bastille and sent to each of the provinces as a memento of royal oppression. The key to the prison was given to George Washington by Lafayette, and it has remained at Mount Vernon ever since. The power of legend being what it is, what soon became known as the Storming of the Bastille was elevated to the status of a pivotal event in the course of the French Revolution, demonstrating the newfound power of a long-suffering population. Thus it was that July 14 became the French national day, an event now celebrated with patriotic fervor throughout the country. Ⓜ *Bastille.*

❻ **Place de la Nation.** The towering early-19th-century, statue-topped columns on majestic place de la Nation stand sentinel at the Gates of Paris—the eastern sector's less famous equivalent of the Arc de Triomphe. Place de la Nation (known as place du Trône—Throne Square—until the Revolution) was the scene of 1,300 executions at the guillotine in 1794. Most were buried in a mass grave at the nearby Cimetière de Picpus. Ⓜ *Métro or RER: Nation.*

❹ **Viaduc des Arts.** This redbrick viaduct once brought trains to the edge of the canal at Bastille; now it has brought a swath of greenery and a jolt of energy to this neighborhood. In the past decade the elevated tracks were transformed into a stylish promenade with upscale boutiques and artisans' workshops sheltered in its arches. The beautifully landscaped walkway extends all the way to the Bois de Vincennes and is a great choice for walkers seeking to escape polluted Paris streets. The only hardship is deciding whether to stay up on the garden path or to browse shops down at street level. (Stairways regularly connect the two levels.) ✉ *Av. Daumesnil, Bastille* Ⓜ *Gare de Lyon, Daumesnil, Bel-Air.*

THE QUARTIER LATIN

The neighborhood south of Île de la Cité on the left bank of the Seine has buzzed with rebellious students and intellectual discourse for more than 800 years, since academics first moved out from under the skirts of the bishop of Paris. Early in the 12th century, groups of students broke from Notre-Dame's school and headed over to the Rive Gauche. By the mid-13th century the newly gelled colleges were under papal authority; the earliest degrees were in canonical law, the arts, and theology. The theology college, founded in the 1250s by Robert de Sorbon, became one of the most influential; the university was named the Sorbonne in de Sorbon's honor. The bohemian Quartier Latin (Latin Quarter) was born, so named because Latin was the common language of study and philosophizing for students coming from all over Europe. These are the streets immortalized by the hard-hitting verse of the first great Parisian poet, François Villon (1431–1460s). The student, thief, and condemned murderer wrote, "I know everything except myself." Villon was far from the only rowdy student in the 'hood; throughout the Middle Ages, student elections triggered bursts of violence.

The Sorbonne closed during the Revolution; its buildings were then used for artist studios until 1821, when the university reopened. Later in the 19th century the state rebuilt the university, enhancing the Sorbonne's prestige and its alliance with the French establishment. But these links to the government broke down in the 1960s, when the radical spirit of the Rive Gauche flared again. Student-sparked protests had an explosive impact on French politics and the education system. Frustrated by the university's hidebound policies and practices, leftist students began agitating. Clashes between student-led protest groups and the state riot police peaked in May 1968, when barricades were thrown up in the Quartier Latin, the *pavés* (paving stones) were pried up, and the Sorbonne and other major buildings were occupied by protestors. Later that year the students allied themselves with the trade union movement, and strikes shut down factories throughout the country. De Gaulle's government weathered the storm, but the uprising succeeded in another way; the social reverberations essentially created the cultural and intellectual basis of today's France. The *soixante-huitards*, now middle-aged, continue to influence French politics, as shown by the election of openly gay, Green Party Bertrand Delanoë to the mayoralty of Paris.

After 1968 several crushingly ugly buildings appeared in the neighborhood; a bunkerlike police station and the looming Jussieu campus are the most obvious blights. Still, this quarter of steep sloping streets has preserved its invigorating intellectual atmosphere even as it has become more upscale. Elegant boutiques rub elbows with bookstores, Roman ruins offer quiet nooks for lovers, and endless cafés give students a chance to fill the air with discussions and cigarette smoke.

Numbers in the text correspond to numbers in the margin and on the Quartier Latin map.

a good walk

Start at the Seine along the Pont au Double and head to square René-Viviani, where you'll find a battered acacia—which vies with a specimen in the Jardin des Plantes for the title of oldest tree in Paris—and a spectacular view of Notre-Dame. At the back of this park is the church of **St-Julien-le-Pauvre** ❶, built before Notre-Dame. If you're here in the afternoon or evening, go around the corner to rue de la Bucherie, where George Whitman and his daughter Sylvia run Shakespeare & Company, part bookshop, part myth, and an excellent place to browse. Next, cross rue St-Jacques and walk away from the river to the squat back of **St-Séverin** ❷. The surrounding pedestrian streets are lined with questionable restaurants fronted by waiters cajoling customers to try their towers of seafood or smash-your-plate Greek taverns. To explore, take rue St-Séverin, a right on rue Xavier-Privas, and a left on rue de la Huchette, where at No. 23 you'll find Paris's smallest theater and oldest jazz club. You'll pass a couple of branches of the major student bookstore, Gibert Jeune, just as rue de la Huchette opens onto the **place St-Michel** ❸. The 19th-century fountain depicting St. Michael slaying the dragon was a symbolic warning to rebellious locals from Napoléon III and his prefect Haussmann; St. Michael represents the state crushing the dragon of public dissent. Today the fountain is a somewhat grimy but popular meeting spot.

After checking out the surging chaos around the fountain, turn up boulevard St-Michel to boulevard St-Germain, where you'll see a small park with elaborate ruins. These are what's left of the great Roman baths of Lutetia. Roman building techniques were so stable that many of their walls were incorporated into new buildings as the centuries wore on. Here the Flamboyant Gothic mansion Hôtel de Cluny is attached to and built over the Roman baths. This *hôtel* appropriately has become the **Musée National du Moyen-Age** ❹, devoted to medieval art. The entrance is down rue Sommerard, the next street on the left. Cross place Paul-Painlevé, in front of the museum, up toward the **Sorbonne** ❺ university; the Rive Gauche's student population hangs out in the plaza here after classes. Continue uphill along rue de la Sorbonne until you hit rue Soufflot, where you'll see the imposing dome of the **Panthéon** ❻, originally built as a church but now a monument to France's top historical figures. On the far left corner of place du Panthéon stands **St-Étienne-du-Mont** ❼, a church whose facade is a poetic mishmash of architectural periods. Explore the top of quaint rue de la Montagne-Ste-Geneviève alongside; then turn right onto rue Descartes to reach **place de la Contrescarpe** ❽. En route you'll pass No. 39, where Ernest Hemingway kept a writing studio. (Despite what the plaque says, he did not live in this building but used the attic studio as an office; he actually lived around the corner at 74 rue du Cardinal Lemoine with his first wife, Hadley.) The place de la Contrescarpe looks almost provincial during the day as Parisians flock to the daily market on rue Mouffetard.

At the foot of the market street Mouffetard, head left for 250 yards along rue Censier and turn left again into rue du Gril to discover the beautiful white **Mosquée** ❾, complete with minaret. If you step inside the mosque's pretty tearoom for a mint-tea break, you'll be surrounded by

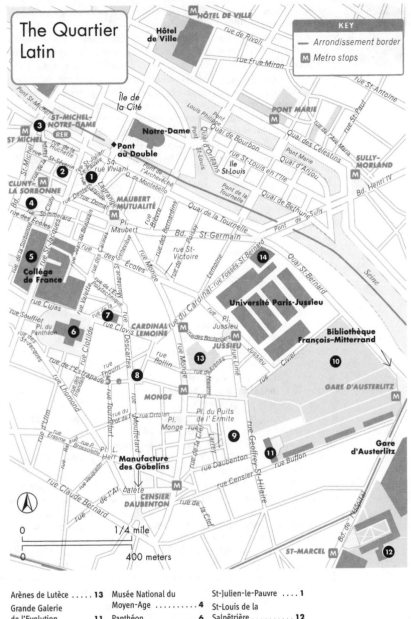

The Quartier Latin

animated students deep in discussion about the meaning of life, along with older Muslim men pausing on their way to pray. Just beyond the mosque is the **Jardin des Plantes** ⑩, a spacious botanical garden begun in the 17th century. The first hall you'll see is the **Grande Galerie de l'Évolution** ⑪, a brilliantly updated exhibition hall from the 1800s. Kids can marvel at enormous whale skeletons, along with all sorts of taxidermy. The garden also has separate museums of paleontology (for young dinosaur enthusiasts) and mineralogy, along with giant greenhouses and an old-fashioned zoo.

Although it's a bit out of the way, **St-Louis de la Salpêtrière** ⑫, the church of the Salpêtrière hospital, is within walking distance of the Jardin des Plantes. Take boulevard de l'Hôpital, at the far end of the park; the church is in the grounds of the hospital beyond Gare d'Austerlitz. Farther up-river, via quai d'Austerlitz and quai de la Gare, is the Bibliothèque Nationale François-Mitterrand, the national library, with its four towers meant to evoke open books (*see* East of Bastille, *above*).

From the northwest exit from the Jardin des Plantes you can follow rue Lacépède and then rue de Navarre to the **Arènes de Lutèce** ⑬, the remains of a Roman amphitheater. Rue des Arènes and rue Limé lead to place Jussieu and its hideous concrete campus. Around the corner, however, there's proof that 20th-century buildings can be gorgeous: the innovative **Institut du Monde Arabe** ⑭. Star French architect Jean Nouvel designed this Arab culture center in the late 1980s; be sure to spend a few minutes watching the facade, as its apertures expand and contract according to the amount of sunlight. The center has terrific temporary shows, so it's worth dropping in to see what's on. Take the elevator upstairs to the café for a restorative snack and more phenomenal views.

TIMING At just under 5 km (about 3 mi), this walk can be done in a morning or afternoon, or serve as the basis for a leisurely day's exploring—given that several sites, notably the Musée National du Moyen-Age, deserve a lengthy visit. Keep in mind that the Institut du Monde Arabe is closed Monday and both the Grande Galerie d'Évolution and the Musée National du Moyen-Age are closed Tuesday. Try to walk through rue Mouffetard on weekend mornings or late-afternoon weekdays (except Monday) so you can see the market in full swing.

What to See

⑬ **Arènes de Lutèce** (Lutetia Amphitheater). This Roman arena was discovered only in 1869 and has since been excavated and landscaped to reveal parts of the original amphitheater. Designed as a theater and circus, the arena was almost totally destroyed by barbarians in AD 280, though you can still see part of the stage and tiered seating. Along with the remains of the baths at the Cluny, this constitutes rare evidence of the powerful Roman city of Lutetia that flourished on the Rive Gauche in the 3rd century. Today it's a favorite spot for picnicking and *boule* playing. ⊠ *Entrance at rue Monge or rue de Navarre, Quartier Latin* ☎ *Free* ☉ *Daily 8–sunset* Ⓜ *Place Monge.*

⑪ **Grande Galerie de l'Évolution** (Great Hall of Evolution). This vast, handsome glass-and-iron structure in the Jardin des Plantes was built, like the Tour Eiffel, in 1889; inside, a parade of taxidermied animals demonstrates the development of species. With installations of gigantic whale skeletons and carefully arranged displays ranging from the tiniest dung beetle to the tallest giraffe, this museum is especially worthwhile for children. Head into the side wing to see the expert display of extinct creatures with detailed explanations as to why they disappeared. There's a reconstituted dodo and a miniature South African zebra, the quagga, which disappeared early in the 20th century. Cool lighting effects include a ceiling that changes color to suggest storms, twilight, or a hot savanna sun. There are some English-language information boards available. ⊠ *36 rue Geoffroy-St-Hilaire, Quartier Latin* ☎ *01–40–79–30–00* ⊕ *www.mnhn.fr* ⊠ *€7* ⊙ *Wed.–Mon. 10–6* Ⓜ *Place Monge or Jussieu.*

★ ⑭ **Institut du Monde Arabe** (IMA; Institute of the Arab World). French architect Jean Nouvel is currently hot news for the upcoming Quai Branly museum, but in 1987 he was already wowing Parisians with this intriguing fusion of Arabian and French building traditions. Nouvel is a master of glass construction; here he tempers transparency with a beautiful facade of variable, iris-like apertures that control the light entering the building and evoke a Moorish-style screen. The IMA's layout reinterprets the traditional enclosed Arabic courtyard. Inside, items largely on loan from Syria and Tunisia help detail Arab culture from prehistory up to the present day, especially focusing on painting and medicine. The museum also runs high-caliber performances, a sound-and-image center, a vast library, and a permanent collection of Arab-Islamic art, textiles, and ceramics. Information in English is limited, but temporary shows usually have English audioguides. Glass elevators whisk you to the ninth floor, where you can sip mint tea in the rooftop café and appreciate Nouvel's subtle bridging of the massive Jussieu complex with the medieval wonder of Notre-Dame. ⊠ *1 rue des Fossés-St-Bernard, Quartier Latin* ☎ *01–40–51–38–38* ⊕ *www.imarabe.org* ⊠ *Exhibitions €7, museum €3* ⊙ *Tues.–Sun. 10–6* Ⓜ *Cardinal Lemoine.*

☾ ⑩ **Jardin des Plantes** (Botanical Gardens). Bordered by the Seine, the Gare d'Austerlitz, and the utilitarian Jussieu campus (a branch of the Paris university system), this swath of greenery contains botanical gardens, the Grande Galerie de l'Évolution, and three other natural history museums, all opened in 1898. A fabulous menagerie of taxidermied animals fills the **Grande Galerie de l'Évolution** (⇨ *above*). Next door are several greenhouses from the 1930s filled with tropical and desert plants, complete with an Indiana Jones–inspired cavelike staircase. Farther inside the park is the dusty but enjoyable **Musée Paléontologique** (with fossils dating from prehistoric times) and the **Musée Minéralogique** (rocks and minerals). These museums have limited information in English. The stock of plants in the botanical gardens, dating from the first collections from the 17th century, has been enhanced by subsequent generations of devoted French botanists. The garden shelters what is claimed to be Paris's oldest tree, an *acacia robinia,* planted in 1636. There are also an alpine garden, an aquarium, a maze, several hothouses, and one of the world's oldest zoos, the Ménagerie, started by Napoléon. The zoo has a few locally famous inhabitants, including Kiki, an ancient Seychelles tortoise, and an alligator who was abandoned in a Parisian hotel. (Remember that this is not a modernized zoo, so the animals are kept in very close quarters.) ⊠ *Entrances on rue Geoffroy-St-Hilaire, rue Civier, and rue Buffon, Quartier Latin* ☎ *01–40–79–30–00* ⊕ *www.mnhn.fr* ▨ *Museums and zoo €7, hothouses €2.50* ☉ *Museums Wed.–Mon. 10–5. Zoo June–Aug., daily 9–6; Sept.–May, daily 9–5. Hothouses Wed.–Mon. 1–5. Garden daily 7:30 AM–sunset* Ⓜ *Place Monge.*

❾ Mosquée (Mosque). This beautiful white mosque was built between 1922 and 1925, complete with arcades and a minaret decorated in the style of Moorish Spain. Students from nearby Jussieu and Censier universities pack themselves into the tea salon for cups of sweet mint tea at the café and for copious quantities of couscous at the restaurant. The sunken garden and tile patios are also open to the public (the prayer rooms are not), as are the *hammams,* or Turkish baths. ⊠ *2 pl. du Puits-de-l'Ermite, Quartier Latin* ☎ *01–43–31–18–14 for the baths* ▨ *Guided tour €3, Turkish baths €15* ☉ *Guided tours, daily 9–noon and 2–8; baths for women only Mon. and Wed. 10–9 and Fri. 2–7; baths for men only Tues. 2–9; baths for men and women Sat. 10–9* Ⓜ *Place Monge.*

> **off the beaten path**
>
> **CHINATOWN –** If China, rather than Arabia, is your cup of tea, take the métro from the Censier Daubenton station, near the mosque, to the Tolbiac station for a walk through Chinatown. Although not as ornamental as San Francisco's or New York's, Paris's Chinatown nevertheless has plenty of intriguing shops and its restaurants often stay open when others in the city are shuttered (Sunday, some religious holidays). **Tang-Frères Chinese supermarket** (⊠ 48 av. d'Ivry, Chinatown) packs in a serious crowd of shoppers for all kinds of Asian specialties, from fish sauce to spices. The **Temple de l'Association des Résidents d'Origine Chinoise** (⊠ 37 rue du Disque, Chinatown) is a small Buddhist temple that looks like a cross between a school cafeteria and an exotic Asian enclave filled with Buddha figures, fruit, and incense.

❹ Musée National du Moyen-Age (National Museum of the Middle Ages).

Fodor'sChoice The **Hôtel de Cluny** has been a museum since medievalist Alexandre Du
★ Sommerard established his collection here in 1844. The over-the-top mansion was a choice location for such a collection; the 15th-century building was created for the abbot of Cluny, leader of the most powerful monastery in France. Symbols of the abbot's power literally surround the building, from the crenellated walls that proclaimed his independence from the king to the carved Burgundian grapes (symbolizing his valuable vineyards) twining up the entrance to the scallop-shell decorations covering the facade. *Coquilles-Saint-Jacques* (scallops) symbolize pilgrimage and the great pilgrimage route to Spain, rue St-Jacques, once lay just around the corner. (The pilgrimage activity was a steady source of income for the abbot.) Now the hôtel holds a stunning array of tapestries, including the world-famous *Dame à la Licorne* (*Lady and the Unicorn*) series, woven in the 15th or 16th century, probably in Belgium. These tapestries represent the senses with allegorical tableaux; in

each, a unicorn and a lion surround an elegant lady against an elaborate millefleur background. The enigmatic tapestry for the "sixth sense," called *Mon seul désir,* is thought to symbolize love or understanding. There are also stellar examples of Byzantine crosses, architectural fragments and medieval paintings. The collection includes the original sculpted heads of the *Kings of Israel and Judah* from Notre-Dame, discovered in 1977; these had been decapitated from the cathedral during the Revolution and hidden by a nobleman near today's Galeries Lafayette. At the Cluny you can also visit the remnants of the city's Roman baths— both hot (*caldarium*) and cold (*frigidarium*), the latter containing the *Boatmen's Pillar,* Paris's oldest sculpture. The park includes a medieval garden filled with flora depicted in the unicorn tapestries. ⊠ *6 pl. Paul-Painlevé, Quartier Latin* ☎ *01–53–73–78–00* ⊕ *www.musee-moyenage.fr* ⊡ *€5.50, free 1st Sun. of month, otherwise €4 on Sun.* ⊙ *Wed.–Mon. 9:15–5:45* Ⓜ *Cluny–La Sorbonne.*

❻ Panthéon. In 1744 a sick Louis XV swore he would build a new church here if he recovered; he survived but left the church building to his unlucky son, who commissioned Germain Soufflot to undertake a mighty domed design. Begun in 1764, the building was almost complete when the French Revolution erupted; meanwhile, Soufflot, the architect, had died, supposedly from worrying that the dome would collapse. Revolutionaries blocked in the stained-glass windows and turned the church into a shrine to heroes of the French nation. After a brief return to Christendom, the Panthéon has come down to us as a monument to France's most glorious historical and cultural figures. The crypt holds the remains of Voltaire, Zola, Dumas, Henri Rousseau, and dozens of other luminaries. In 1995 Nobel Prize–winning scientist Marie Curie became the first woman to join their ranks. Soufflot needn't have worried so much about the building's structural stability—the dome is so perfect that Foucault used this space to test his famous pendulum. ⊠ *Pl. du Panthéon, Quartier Latin* ☎ *01–44–32–18–00* ⊕ *www.monum.fr* ⊡ *€7* ⊙ *Apr.–Sept., daily 10–6:30; Oct.–Mar., daily 10–6* Ⓜ *Cardinal Lemoine; RER: Luxembourg.*

❽ Place de la Contrescarpe. This intimate square behind the Panthéon doesn't start to swing until dusk, when its cafés and bars fill up. During the day the square has something of a small-town feel to it, as people size up and haggle over the produce at the daily market at the bottom of rue Mouffetard, a steeply sloping, colorful street. ⊠ *Quartier Latin* Ⓜ *Monge.*

> off the beaten path

MANUFACTURE DES GOBELINS – Tapestries have been woven on this spot in southeastern Paris, on the banks of the long-covered Bièvre River, since 1662. Guided tours combine historical explanation with the chance to admire both old tapestries and today's weavers at work in their airy workshops. To get here from the place de la Contrescarpe, go south on rue Mouffetard and continue down rue de Bazeilles, which becomes avenue des Gobelins (about a 15-minute walk). Call ahead to check that the guide on duty speaks English. ⊠ *42 av. des Gobelins, Les Gobelins* ☎ *01–44–54–19–33* ⊡ *€8* ⊙ *Tues.–Thurs., guided tours only at 2 and 2:45* Ⓜ *Les Gobelins.*

LA BUTTE AUX CAILLES – Need a break from big-city sights? Head to this village-like neighborhood in the 13ᵉ arrondissement, south of the place d'Italie. It centers on rue Butte aux Cailles, which runs up the prominent local feature: a hill over 100 feet tall. A hip crowd fuels the small scene, keeping the neighborhood's bars and cafés buzzing until well after the last métro stops running. You can settle in for bistro fare at the fun, cooperatively run **Les Temps des Cerises** (⊠ 18–20 rue de la Butte aux Cailles, La Butte aux Cailles ☎ 01–45–89–69–48), whose name recalls a song made famous by the Paris Commune. The worker-led Commune made its only successful stand here at Butte aux Cailles in 1871, when government troops violently put down uprisings all over the city. These days there's another battle building, as longtime residents fight to keep their neighborhood from changing into a noisy *bobo* (bourgeois bohemian) corridor.

❸ Place St-Michel. This square was named for Gabriel Davioud's grandiose 1860 fountain sculpture of St. Michael slaying the dragon—a loaded political gesture from Baron Haussmann, who hoped St. Michael would quell the Revolutionary fervor of this neighborhood. Today the fountain is a meeting spot for those perennial international students of life who are attracted by the bookshops, repertory cinemas, and seething bars in the surrounding streets. ⊠ *Quartier Latin* Ⓜ *Métro or RER: St-Michel.*

❼ St-Étienne-du-Mont. The ornate facade of this mainly 16th-century church lures visitors past the Panthéon and into a magnificent interior with the only rood screen in Paris. This curving masterpiece of carved knot work is from 1525; the organ buffet is also the oldest remaining in the city, from 1631. The church has been visited by several popes because the patron saint of Paris, Ste-Geneviève, lies here in a gilded tomb. The chaotic combination of Gothic, Renaissance, and early baroque styles you'll see here makes an interesting contrast with the cold and pure classicism of the Panthéon. ⊠ *Pl. de l'Abbé-Basset, Quartier Latin* Ⓜ *Cardinal Lemoine.*

❶ St-Julien-le-Pauvre. Founded in 1045, this small church became a crucial meeting place for university students in the 12th century; the students' riotous behavior eventually led to their expulsion. Ruins in the nearby park attest to the original size of the church and its cloisters; this was Dante's church when he was in Paris writing the beginning of his *Divine Comedy* in 1300. Today's structure dates mostly from the 1600s, but keep an eye out for the older pillars, which crawl with disturbing carvings of harpies and demons. The congregation is now Greek Orthodox. ⊠ *Rue St-Julien-le-Pauvre, Quartier Latin* Ⓜ *St-Michel.*

off the beaten path

MUSÉE DES COLLECTIONS HISTORIQUES DE LA PRÉFECTURE DE POLICE DE PARIS – Climb to the third floor of the 5ᵉ arrondissement's police station to see its police museum. While the exhibit is only in French, photographs, letters, memorabilia, and drawings help evoke life as a city *flic* (cop). Relics include a guillotine, examples of uniforms, and remnants the World War II occupation, including what's left of a firing post, German machine guns, and the star insignias worn by Jews. The museum is open weekdays 10–5 and

Saturday 10–5; admission is free. To get here from St-Julien-le-Pauvre, go down rue Lagrange and jog across place Maubert to the head of rue des Carmes. ✉ *1 bis, rue des Carmes, Quartier Latin* ☎ *01–44–41–52–50.*

⑫ **St-Louis de la Salpêtrière.** The church of the Salpêtrière hospital stands next to the Gare d'Austerlitz, which it dominates with its unmistakable lantern-topped, octagonal dome. The church was built (1670–77) in the shape of a Greek cross from the designs of Libéral Bruant. ✉ *Bd. de l'Hôpital, Quartier Latin* Ⓜ *Gare d'Austerlitz.*

❷ **St-Séverin.** The Romanesque tower of this unusually shaped Gothic church overshadows the neighborhood's narrow streets. The dusty churchyard covers the only remaining boneyard in the city, used as a burial place for the impoverished or the unclaimed during plague years. Ruined cloisters cling to the edge of rue St-Jacques, on the far side of the churchyard. In the 11th century the church that stood here was the parish church for the entire Rive Gauche. Louis XIV's cousin, a capricious woman known simply as the Grande Mademoiselle, adopted St-Séverin when she tired of St-Sulpice; she then spent vast sums getting court decorator Le Brun to modernize the chancel in the 17th century. Note the splendidly deviant spiraling column in the forest of pillars behind the altar. ✉ *Rue des Prêtres-St-Séverin, Quartier Latin* ☾ *Mon.–Sat. 11–7:30, Sun. 9–8:30* Ⓜ *St-Michel.*

❺ **Sorbonne.** Named after Robert de Sorbon, a medieval canon who founded a theological college here in the 1250s for 16 students, the Sorbonne is one of the oldest universities in Europe. For centuries it has been one of France's principal institutions of higher learning, as well as the hub of the Quartier Latin and nerve center of Paris's student population. The church and university buildings were restored by Cardinal Richelieu in the 17th century, and the maze of amphitheaters, lecture rooms and laboratories, surrounding courtyards, and narrow streets retains a hallowed air. You can occasionally get into the main courtyard, on rue de la Sorbonne, and peek into the main lecture hall, a major meeting point during the tumultuous student upheavals of 1968 and also of interest for a giant mural by Puvis de Chavannes, the *Sacred Wood* (1880–89). The square is dominated by the university church, the noble, Corinthian-columned **Église de la Sorbonne.** Inside is the white-marble tomb of that ultimate crafty cleric, Cardinal Richelieu himself. ✉ *Rue de la Sorbonne, Quartier Latin* Ⓜ *Cluny–La Sorbonne.*

off the
beaten
path

CENTRE DE LA MER ET DES EAUX (Center for Sea and Waters) – From the Sorbonne you can seek out schools of another sort: schools of fish. Settle in for a spell of mesmerizing fish-gazing at this aquarium. To get here, go up rue de la Sorbonne, and then take the first left on rue Cujas and a right on rue St-Jacques. ✉ *195 rue St-Jacques, Quartier Latin* ☎ *01–44–32–10–70* ⊕ *www.oceano.org* ▱ *€4.60* ☾ *Tues.–Fri. 10–12:30 and 1:30–5:30, weekends 10–5:30* Ⓜ *RER: Luxembourg.*

FROM ORSAY TO ST-GERMAIN

This walk winds through some of the most exclusive streets of the Rive Gauche, taking in the Musée d'Orsay in the stately 7ᵉ arrondissement and the Faubourg St-Germain, the lively and colorful heart of the 6ᵉ arrondissement. You'll end up in the glorious Luxembourg gardens, a lush park whose tree-lined promenades and playing children have won it a soft spot in the public's heart.

The northern reaches of this area are named for the oldest church in Paris, St-Germain-des-Prés, and the quartier has become a prized address for the rich and stylish. In the late 19th century, however, this wasn't silver-spoon territory. Émile Zola depicted these streets as the backdrop for his sordid tale *Thérèse Raquin,* in which the title character and her lover kill her husband; Claude Monet and Auguste Renoir shared a studio at 20 rue Visconti; and the young Picasso barely eked out an existence in a room on rue de Seine. By the 1950s the St-Germain bars bopped with jazz and the sidewalk terraces were crammed with students hoping to catch sight of existentialist heroes Albert Camus, Jean-Paul Sartre, and Simone de Beauvoir, who played out their lives at the café tables here. Today, even though most of the philosophizing is now done by tourists, a slew of bookshops, art stores, and luscious antiques shops ensure that St-Germain retains its artistic–intellectual appeal. The neighborhood is a treat for the wandering flaneur; with numerous hotels, it is also (surprise) one of the most tourist-friendly.

The headliner on this tour is the Musée d'Orsay, which houses a superb collection of Impressionist paintings in a knockout converted Belle Époque rail station on the Seine. Farther along the river, the 18th-century Palais Bourbon, where the National Assembly convenes, sets the tone. This is Edith Wharton territory—select, discreet *vieille France,* where aristocrats lived in sprawling apartments or *maisons particuliers* (town houses). Luxurious ministries and embassies—including the Hôtel Matignon, residence of the French prime minister—line the streets, their majestic scale completely in keeping with the Hôtel des Invalides, whose gold-leaf dome rises above Napoléon's tomb. The splendid Musée Rodin—one of the few houses here where you can explore the grand interior—is only a short walk away.

Numbers in the text correspond to numbers in the margin and on the Orsay to St-Germain map.

a good walk

Arrive at the **Musée d'Orsay** ❶ early (and consider making reservations) to avoid the crowds that pile in to see the museum's outstanding collections, including dozens of the world's most beloved Impressionist paintings. Many late-19th-century artists, including Manet and Monet, painted the train stations that were reshaping their city, so it's fitting that the museum occupies a revamped train station. Beyond the Orsay, facing the Seine, stands the **Musée de la Légion d'Honneur** ❷, where you can find an array of French and foreign decorations. A stylish two-tiered footbridge, opened in 2000, crosses the Seine to the Tuileries, but for now, stay on this side of the river. Head straight along the Seine to the

Palais Bourbon ❸, home of the Assemblée Nationale (the French Parliament). There are sometimes outdoor photo exhibitions here on the Assemblée's railings, and there's a fine view across the Seine to place de la Concorde and the church of the Madeleine. If you want to save the Invalides for another day, cut down rue de Bellechasse (first left after the Orsay) to rue de Varenne.

Just past the Assemblée Nationale is the absurdly ornate Alexandre III Bridge. To your left are the broad, grassy Esplanade des Invalides and the **Hôtel des Invalides** ❹, founded by Louis XIV to house wounded (*invalide*) veterans. The most impressive dome in Paris towers over the church at the back of the Invalides—the Église du Dôme. From the church turn left, then left again onto boulevard des Invalides, then right on rue de Varenne to reach the beautifully landscaped Hôtel Biron, today known as the **Musée Rodin** ❺. Here you can see a fine collection of Auguste Rodin's emotionally charged statues. The quiet, distinguished 18th-century streets in this neck of the woods are filled with embassies and ministries. The most famous, farther along rue de Varenne, is the **Hôtel Matignon** ❻, residence of the French prime minister. Nearby, at No. 53, you can pay your respects to American novelist Edith Wharton, who lived and worked here from 1910 to 1920. Take a glance at the next building as well, which leads to one of the city's sought-after private culs-de-sac. Now turn left onto rue du Bac, then right onto rue de Grenelle, past the **Musée Maillol** ❼, dedicated to the work of sculptor Aristide Maillol, and Bouchardon's monumental **Fontaine des Quatre Saisons** ❽, which seems to be guarding the museum.

Turn left down boulevard Raspail and cross to rue de Luynes, zipping across boulevard St-Germain to inspect the stately 17th-century church of **St-Thomas d'Aquin** ❾. Then double back and head left along boulevard St-Germain until you reach rue des Sts-Pères. Make another left, walking three blocks past the somber medical school of the Université de Paris, then make one more left on rue de Verneuil to find No. 5 bis, the graffiti-covered former home of French chansonnier Serge Gainsbourg (1928–1991), which he bought with longtime lover Jane Birkin (his partner in the heavy-breathing song "Je T'Aime . . ."). Gainsbourg continues to inspire a cult something like Jim Morrison's, and his fans keep hoping the building will be made into a museum. Double back to rue des Sts-Pères and turn left onto rue Jacob.

The *lèche-vitrine* (window-shopping) opportunities on this stretch are terrific; soon you'll turn right onto rue St-Benoit. Walk up to boulevard St-Germain, where you'll find **Café de Flore** ❿, one of the haunts of the intelligentsia after World War II. Turn left, passing the marvelous bookshop La Hune, to find **Les Deux Magots** ⓫, another famed meeting spot for existentialists and artists. Soaring above the intersection is the square steeple of **St-Germain-des-Prés** ⓬, Paris's oldest church.

Follow rue de l'Abbaye, along the far side of the church, to rue de Furstenberg. The street opens out into place Furstenberg, an adorable square with white globe lamps and catalpa trees, where you'll find Eugène Delacroix's atelier, the **Musée Delacroix** ⓭. Leaving the square, take a left

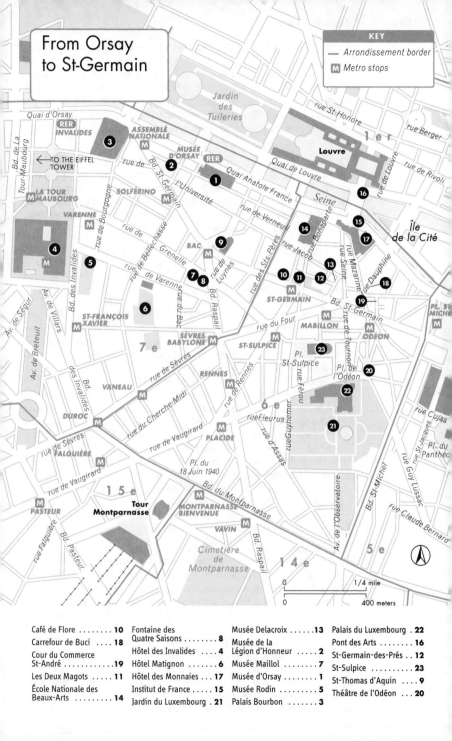

From Orsay to St-Germain

on rue Jacob to rue Bonaparte. To your left, at No. 36, is the hotel where *New Yorker* columnist Janet Flanner lived throughout the 1920s and '30s; writer Henry Miller also stayed here briefly. Walk down toward the river on rue Bonaparte to the **École Nationale des Beaux-Arts** 🆚, whose students can often be seen painting and sketching on the nearby quays and bridges. Wander into the courtyard and galleries of the school to see the casts and copies of the statues stored here for safekeeping during the Revolution.

Continue down to the Seine and turn right along the quai, past the **Institut de France** 🆚. With its distinctive dome and commanding position overlooking the **Pont des Arts** 🆚—a footbridge where you'll have great views of the Louvre and the Île de la Cité—the institute is one of the city's most impressive waterside sights. Farther along, on quai de Conti, you pass the **Hôtel des Monnaies** 🆚, the old national mint.

Head up rue Dauphine, the street that singer Juliette Greco put on the map when she opened the Tabou jazz club here in the '50s. It's linked 150 yards up by the open-air passage Dauphine to rue Mazarine. For a step down into the Middle Ages, take the stairs of the Mazarine parking lot here to lower level 2, where you'll find part of the 12th-century surrounding wall of Paris, built by Philippe Augustus. As the street level rose over the centuries, the wall became hidden down here. Back aboveground, rue Mazarine leads left to the **Carrefour de Buci** 🆚, a busy crossroad. Fanning out from the Carrefour are lively rue de Buci, with one of the most scenic food markets in Paris; rue de l'Ancienne-Comédie, so named because it was the first home of the legendary Comédie Française, cutting through to busy place de l'Odéon; and rue St-André des Arts. Head left along the latter to find the historic **Cour du Commerce St-André** 🆚 (opposite No. 66), a magnificently cobbled pedestrian street where the 18th century seems preserved in amber. It's lined with cafés, including, halfway down on the left, Paris's oldest, Le Procope. Opposite this landmark is the entry to the **Cour de Rohan,** a series of three lovely cloistered courtyards. The Cour is private and fenced off, but if the door happens to be open, peek through to see the apartment-ateliers, some now occupied by the Fondation Giacometti. Cecil Beaton picked one in the first courtyard as the locale of Gigi's home in the famed Lerner and Loewe 1958 musical film *Gigi.*

Head to the end of cour du Commerce St-André, cross boulevard St-Germain, and climb rue de l'Odéon. Notice the small plaque at No. 12 commemorating Sylvia Beach's original Shakespeare & Co. bookstore. A friend and tireless supporter of writers like Ernest Hemingway and Gertrude Stein, Beach was also the first publisher of James Joyce's *Ulysses.* Continue up to the colonnaded **Théâtre de l'Odéon** 🆚; no one's treading the boards these days, as the theater's closed for renovation, but it's still a handsome sight. Behind the theater, across rue de Vaugirard, lies the **Jardin du Luxembourg** 🆚, one of the most stylish parks in the city. The large pond, usually animated by an armada of toy boats that can be hired alongside, has a scenic backdrop in the 17th-century **Palais du Luxembourg** 🆚. Today the palace houses the French Senate and is not open to the public, but its adjacent art museum is.

After strolling in the park, return to rue de Vaugirard and head left under the arches. Near No. 36 look for the **Metre Étalon,** set in the wall. This was part of the Revolution's new system of measurement; 16 of these metersticks were installed in public places throughout Paris so people could learn to use the new system. This is the only meter that remains in its original location. Now turn right onto rue Férou, where Hemingway lived at sphinx-guarded No. 6 just after his groundbreaking novel *The Sun Also Rises* made him famous. Continue to place St-Sulpice, a spacious square that sometimes hosts book and antiques fairs; Yves Saint Laurent's first Rive Gauche store is at No. 6. Anchoring the square is the church of **St-Sulpice** ㉓. If you've still got some energy, this is a good jumping-off point for Montparnasse; walk west down rue du Vieux-Colombier and take the métro three stops to Vavin.

TIMING   Depending on how long you spend in the museums and shops along the way, this 6½-km (4-mi) walk could take anywhere from four hours to several days. Aim for an early start—that way you can hit the Musée d'Orsay early, when crowds are smaller (to avoid the worst of the entry wait, book admission tickets in advance via the Internet). Then go to the rue de Buci street market in the late afternoon, when it's in full swing. Note that the Hôtel des Invalides is open daily, but the Musée Rodin and the Orsay are closed Monday. The Delacroix and Maillol museums, meanwhile, are closed Tuesday. You might consider returning to one or more museums on another day or night—the Orsay, along with its stylish restaurant, is open late on Thursday evening.

What to See

⑩ **Café de Flore.** Through the Occupation, Jean-Paul Sartre and Simone de
Fodor'sChoice   Beauvoir would meet friends and keep warm at this popular café. These
★   days this quintessential slice of Paris is a popular tourist stop, with play readings in English upstairs some evenings. Stick with coffee and croissants and enjoy the view; meals are overpriced and subpar. ✉ *172 bd. St-Germain, St-Germain-des-Prés* Ⓜ *St-Germain-des-Prés.*

⑱ **Carrefour de Buci.** This crossroads was once a notorious Rive Gauche landmark: during the 18th century it contained a gallows, an execution stake, and an iron collar used for punishing troublemakers. In September 1792 the Revolutionary army used this daunting site to enroll its first volunteers, and many royalists and priests lost their heads here during the bloody course of the Revolution. There's nothing sinister, however, about the carrefour today, as brightly colored flowers spill onto the sidewalk at the flower shop and devotees line up for pastries at Carton. **Rue de Buci** has a good outdoor food market, open Tuesday–Saturday 8–1 and 4–7, Sunday 9–1. Ⓜ *Mabillon.*

need a
break?   If you happen to arrive when the market on rue de Buci is closed, the patisserie **La Vieille France** (✉ 14 rue de Buci, St-Germain-des-Prés ☎ 01–43–26–55–13) is the perfect place to help fill your hunger gap.

⑲ **Cour du Commerce St-André.** Like an 18th-century engraving come to life,
Fodor'sChoice   this exquisite, cobblestone street arcade is one of Paris's loveliest sights.
★   But before you give yourself over to the romantic mood of this passageway, remember that Dr. Guillotin conceived the idea for a new "humane"

method of execution, testing the machine on sheep, at No. 9. Among the guillotine's many later victims was Charlotte Corday, who stabbed famous journalist Jean-Paul Marat (who ran the Revolutionary newspaper *L'Ami du Peuple,* at No. 8) in his bath, in his house just across boulevard St-Germain. That other great agitator of the French Revolution, Danton, lived at No. 20. Most famed for its Revolutionary inhabitants, this poetic passageway also contains a turret from the 12th-century wall of Philippe-Auguste (visible through the windows of the Catalogne tourism office).

Marat's ashes were kept in a memorial at Paris's oldest café, **Le Procope** (☎ 01–40–46–79–00), opened in 1686 by an Italian named Francesco Procopio. Many of Paris's most famous literary sons and daughters have imbibed here through the centuries, ranging from erudite academics like Denis Diderot to debauchees like Oscar Wilde, as well as Voltaire, Balzac, George Sand, Victor Hugo, and even Benjamin Franklin, who popped in whenever business brought him to Paris. The café started out as the Sardi's of its day, because the Comédie-Française was nearby. Jean Racine and Molière were regulars. The place is still going strong, so you, too, can enjoy its period (though now gussied-up) trimmings and traditional menu. ⊠ *Linking bd. St-Germain and rue St-André-des-Arts, St-Germain-des-Prés* Ⓜ *Odéon.*

⑪ Les Deux Magots. This old-fashioned St-Germain café named after the two Chinese figurines, or *magots,* inside has seen everyone from Oscar Wilde drinking his evening absinthe at a sidewalk table, to Hemingway drinking with James Joyce, to those 1950s coffee enthusiasts Jean-Paul Sartre and Richard Wright. It remains packed, though these days you're more likely to rub shoulders with tourists than with philosophers and writers. Still, if you are in search of the mysterious glamour of the Rive Gauche, you can do no better than to station yourself at one of the sidewalk tables—or at a window table on a wintry day—to watch the passing parade. ⊠ *6 pl. St-Germain-des-Prés, St-Germain-des-Prés* ☎ *01–45–48–55–25* Ⓜ *St-Germain-des-Prés.*

⑭ École Nationale des Beaux-Arts (National Fine Arts College). Occupying three large mansions near the Seine, the national fine-arts school—today the breeding ground for painters, sculptors, and architects—was once the site of a convent founded in 1608 by Marguerite de Valois, the first wife of Henri IV. After the Revolution the convent was turned into a museum for works of art salvaged from buildings attacked by the rampaging French mobs. In 1816 the museum was turned into a school. Today its peaceful courtyards harbor some contemporary installations and exhibits, and the school staff includes international art stars like Christian Boltanski and Annette Messager. ⊠ *14 rue Bonaparte, St-Germain-des-Prés* ☉ *Daily 1–7* Ⓜ *St-Germain-des-Prés.*

need a break?

The popular café **La Palette** (⊠ 43 rue de Seine, St-Germain-des-Prés ☎ 01–43–26–68–15), on the corner of rue de Seine and rue Callot, brings out lilac pots in the spring and has long been a favorite haunt of Beaux-Arts students. One of them painted the ungainly portrait of their patron, François, that presides with mock authority.

⑧ **Fontaine des Quatre Saisons** (Four Seasons Fountain). This allegorical fountain of the four seasons, designed by Edme Bouchardon in 1739 to help boost the district's water supply, has a wealth of sculpted detail. Flanked by a majestic curved screen, the seated figure of Paris, framed by Ionic columns, surveys the rivers Seine and Marne, while bas-reliefs peopled by industrious cupids represent the seasons. ⊠ *57–59 rue de Grenelle, St-Germain-des-Prés* Ⓜ *Rue du Bac.*

④ **Hôtel des Invalides.** Les Invalides, as it is widely known, is an outstanding monumental baroque ensemble designed by architect Libéral Bruant in the 1670s at the behest of Louis XIV's minister of finance, the incorruptible Colbert, to house wounded soldiers. Along the facade are eerie dormer windows shaped like 17th-century armor. Although no more than a handful of old soldiers live at the Invalides today, the military link remains in the form of the **Musée de l'Armée**, one of the world's foremost military museums, with a vast collection of arms, armor, uniforms, banners, and military pictures down through the ages. At press time, the west wing was undergoing renovation and scheduled to finish sometime in 2006, at which point it will be the east wing's turn to be renovated. But there's plenty to look at while the museum is undergoing its face-lift.

FodorśChoice
★

The 17th-century **Église St-Louis des Invalides**, the Invalides' original church, was the site of the first performance of Berlioz's *Requiem,* in 1837. The most impressive dome in Paris, based on that of St. Peter's Basilica in Rome, towers over Jules Hardouin-Mansart's church, the **Église du Dôme**, built onto the end of Église St-Louis but blocked off from it in 1793—no great pity, perhaps, as the two buildings are vastly different in style and scale. Fittingly, for this military complex, **Napoléon's Tomb** is found here—his remains are kept in a series of no fewer than six coffins, one inside the next, within a bombastic memorial of red porphyry, ringed by low reliefs and a dozen statues symbolizing his campaigns. Among others commemorated in the church are French World War I hero Marshal Foch; Napoléon's brother Joseph, an erstwhile king of Spain; and military architect Sébastien de Vauban. ⊠ *Pl. des Invalides, Trocadéro/Tour Eiffel* ☎ *01–44–42–37–72 Army and Model museums* ⊕ *www.invalides.org* ⊠ *€7* ⊙ *Église du Dôme and museums Apr.–Sept., daily 10–6; Oct.–Mar., daily 10–5. Closed 1st Mon. of every month* Ⓜ *La Tour–Maubourg.*

⑥ **Hôtel Matignon.** This subdued rococo residence of the French prime minister, built in 1722, is the Rive Gauche counterpart to the president's Palais de l'Élysée. From 1888 to 1914 it was the embassy of the Austro-Hungarian Empire; only since 1958 has it housed heads of government. ⊠ *57 rue de Varenne, Invalides* ⊙ *Not open to public* Ⓜ *Varenne.*

⑰ **Hôtel des Monnaies** (Royal Mint). Louis XVI transferred the royal mint to this imposing mansion in the late 18th century. Although the mint was moved again, to Pessac, near Bordeaux, in 1973, weights and measures, medals, and limited-edition coins are still made here. The **Musée de la Monnaie** has an extensive collection of coins, documents, engravings, and paintings. On Tuesday and Friday at 2 you can catch the coin-metal craftsmen at work in their ateliers overlooking the Seine. ⊠ *11* *quai de Conti, St-Germain-des-Prés* ☎ *01–40–46–56–66* 🌐 *€8 (includes audioguide in English)* ⊘ *Tues.–Fri. 11–5:30, weekends noon–5:30* Ⓜ *Pont Neuf or Odéon.*

⑮ Institut de France (French Institute). The *institut* is one of France's most revered cultural institutions, and its curved, dome-topped facade is one of the Rive Gauche's most impressive waterside sights. The Tour de Nesle, which formed part of Philippe-Auguste's wall fortifications along the Seine, used to stand here. The tower had many royal occupants, including Henry V of England, but it was mostly remembered because the lovers of a number of French queens were tossed from its windows. French novelist Alexandre Dumas (1824–95) even used this stormy history for one of his melodramas. In 1661 the wealthy Cardinal Mazarin willed 2 million French *livres* (pounds) for construction of a college that would be dedicated to educating students from Piedmont, Alsace, Artois, and Roussillon, provinces that had been annexed to France during the years of his ministry. Mazarin's coat of arms is sculpted on the dome, and the 350,000-volume library in the east wing still bears his name.

At the beginning of the 19th century Napoléon transferred the Institut here from the Louvre; of the five academies that compose the institute, the oldest is the **Académie Française,** created by Cardinal Richelieu in 1635. Its first major task was to edit the definitive French dictionary (still unfinished). It is also charged with safeguarding the purity of the French language, making it a hive of serious debate about the ruinous impact of *franglais* terms like *le weekend* and *email* on the mother tongue. Election to its ranks, subject to approval by the French head of state, is the highest literary honor in the land; there can only be 40 "immortal" lifelong members at any one time. Appointments are usually reserved for literary types, a practice breached by the controversial recent arrival of Valéry Giscard d'Estaing, a former president. ✉ *Pl. de l'Institut, St-Germain-des-Prés* ⊘ *Guided visits reserved for cultural associations only* Ⓜ *Pont Neuf.*

☺ ㉑ Jardin du Luxembourg. Immortalized in countless paintings, the Luxembourg Gardens present all that is unique and befuddling about Parisian parks: swarms of pigeons, cookie-cutter trees, ironed-and-pressed dirt walkways, and immaculate lawns meant for admiring, not touching. The tree- and bench-lined paths offer a reprieve from the incessant bustle of the Quartier Latin, as well as an opportunity to discover the dotty old women and smooching university students who once found their way into Doisneau photographs. Somewhat austere during the colder months, the garden becomes intoxicating as spring fills the flower beds with daffodils, tulips, and hyacinths; the pools teem with boats nudged along by children, and the paths with Parisians thrusting their noses toward the sun. The park's northern boundary is dominated by the Palais du Luxembourg, surrounded by a handful of well-armed guards; they are protecting the senators who have been deliberating in the palace since 1958. Feel free to move the green chairs around to create your own picnic area or people-watching site.

Although the garden may seem purely French, the original 17th-century planning took its inspiration from Italy. When Maria de' Medici acquired

FodorsChoice ★

FINDING THE BEST POSTCARDS

You've got to scribble something at those café tables—and what other souvenir retails for €.10 each? For the best prices, check out the news kiosks along rue de Rivoli and the Grands Boulevards, or visit the bookstore **Mona Lisait** (⊠ 9 rue St-Martin Beaubourg/Les Halles ☎ 01–42–74–03–02 Ⓜ Châtelet). For more unusual cards, pop into **Images de Demain** (⊠ 141 rue St-Martin, Beaubourg/Les Halles ☎ 01–44–54–99–99 Ⓜ Rambuteau), opposite the Pompidou, and say hello to the tabby cat who lives in the framing department. **Mondial Art** (⊠ 10 rue St-André des Arts, St-Germain-des-Prés ☎ 01–55–42–19–00 Ⓜ St-Michel) has racks of stylish choices including cards quoting famous French authors. Keep an eye out for vintage postcards, too, sold by the bouquinistes along the Seine and by collectors inside Passage des Panoramas. You can buy stamps at any tabac as well as at post offices.

the estate of the deceased duke of Luxembourg in 1612, she decided to turn his mansion into a version of the Florentine Medici home, the Palazzo Pitti. She ended up with something more Franco-Italian than strictly Florentine. The land behind the palace was loosely modeled on the Boboli Gardens, though the result turned out to be a combination of romantic English-style lawns and formal French flower gardens. The landscapers, like the architects, didn't design a true version of the Florentine garden, opting instead for the emerging style of heavy-handed human manipulation of nature—linear vistas, box-trimmed trees, and color-coordinated flower beds—which further defined the "French" garden. A tiny corner of the park still has that nature-on-the-brink-of-overwhelming-civilization look that was the trademark of the Renaissance Italian garden—namely, the intentionally overgrown cluster of trees and bushes lining the 1624 **Fontaine de Médicis.** A sculpture with figures from Greek mythology and the Medici coat of arms stands at the head of a rectangular basin, where fish wink through the shadowy water. The park captured the hearts of Parisians when it became public after the Revolution. Dozens of statues now stand along the terraces and walks, including a light-footed dancing faun and a memorial to painter Delacroix.

One of the great attractions of the park is the **Théâtre des Marionnettes,** where on Saturday and Sunday at 11 and 3:15 and on Wednesday at 3:15 you can catch one of the classic *guignols* (marionette shows) for a small admission charge. The wide-mouthed kids are the real attraction; their expressions of utter surprise, despair, or glee have fascinated the likes of Henri Cartier-Bresson and François Truffaut. The park also offers a merry-go-round, swing sets, and pony rides; older visitors should look for the music pergola, which has live performers on summer weekends, the apiary, and an area devoted to trellised fruit trees. Finally, for those eager to burn off their pastry breakfasts, the Jardin du Luxembourg has a well-maintained trail around the perimeter, one of the few public places the French will be seen in athletic clothes. It takes an average jogger 20 minutes to get all the way around; water fountains are strategically placed along the way. Men of all ages are also strategically placed around the garden, and their comments can be aggravating for women in the park alone. Otherwise this is a great escape. ⊠ *Bordered by bd. St-Michel and rues de Vaugirard, de Médicis, Guynemer, and Auguste-Comte, St-Germain-des-Prés* Ⓜ *Odéon; RER: Luxembourg.*

⓭ **Musée Delacroix.** The final apartment of artist Eugène Delacroix (1798–1863) contains only a small collection of his sketches and drawings, but it offers access to the studio he had specially built in the large garden at the back. From here you can pay homage to the foremost Romantic painter of France, who had the good luck to live on place Furstenberg, one of the tiniest, most romantic squares in Paris. ⊠ *6 rue Furstenberg, St-Germain-des-Prés* ☎ *01–44–41–86–50* ⊕ *www.museedelacroix.fr* ⊠ *€5* ⊘ *Wed.–Mon. 9:30–5* Ⓜ *St-Germain-des-Prés.*

❷ **Musée de la Légion d'Honneur** (Legion of Honor Museum). French and foreign decorations are displayed in the Seine-side Legion of Honor Museum, which is linked to the Tuileries by the elegant, two-tier Solférino footbridge. The original building, the Hôtel de Salm, was constructed in 1786 as one of the largest and grandest mansions in town; unsurprisingly, it was burned during the Commune in 1871. Rebuilt in 1878 in glittering neoclassical style, the building was renovated in 2005. ⊠ *2 rue de Bellechasse, St-Germain-des-Prés* ☎*01–40–62–84–25* Ⓜ *Solférino; RER: Musée d'Orsay.*

❼ **Musée Maillol.** Bronzes by Art Deco sculptor Aristide Maillol (1861–1944), whose sleek, stylized nudes adorn the Tuileries gardens, can be admired at this handsome town house lovingly restored by his former muse, Dina Vierny. Maillol's drawings, paintings, and tapestries are also on show. Works by other artists include a roomful of Poliakoff abstractions and two sensuous Zitman nudes in the barrel-vaulted cellar café. Popular temporary exhibits of painters such as Jean-Michel Basquiat and Francis Bacon often trigger long lines. ⊠ *61 rue de Grenelle, St-Germain-des-Prés* ☎ *01–42–22–59–58* ⊕ *www.museemaillol.com* ⊠ *€8* ⊘ *Wed.–Mon. 11–6* Ⓜ *Rue du Bac.*

❶ **Musée d'Orsay.** It may seem strange that some of the most famous Impressionist and Postimpressionist paintings are housed in a Belle Époque train station, but once you're inside, you'll more than likely be impressed by the exhilarating use of space. The Orsay contains the Louvre's collection of art from 1848 through 1914, creating a bridge between the Louvre's displays and the modern art collections shown in the Pompidou and the Musée Moderne. And a fabulous collection it is, with paintings from Delacroix to van Gogh and decorative objects from Second Empire eclecticism to Hector Guimard's Art Nouveau mastery.

Fodor'sChoice
★

Before heading inside, admire the building itself. Beginning in 1900, this station was a depot for routes between Paris and southwestern France. By 1939 the Gare d'Orsay had become too small for anything except suburban trains. Closed in the '60s, the dusty station was used as a theater, an auction house, and the dilapidated setting for Orson Welles's 1962 movie

The Trial before it was finally slated for demolition. However, the destruction of the 19th-century Les Halles (market halls) across the Seine provoked a furor among conservationists, and in the late 1970s former president Giscard d'Estaing ordered that the Orsay be transformed into a museum. Architects Pierre Colboc, Renaud Bardou, and Jean-Paul Philippon were commissioned to remodel the building; Gae Aulenti, known for her renovation of the Palazzo Grassi in Venice, was hired to reshape the interior. Aulenti's modern design provoked much controversy, but the museum's attributes soon outweighed any criticism when it opened in December 1986.

The museum is arranged on three floors. Once past the ticket booths (get your tickets in advance through the Web site to avoid the lines), you can pick up an English-language audioguide along with a free color-coded map of the museum. Then step down the stairs into the sculpture hall. Here the vastness of the space compliments a ravishing collection of French sculpture from 1840 to 1875. Paintings are hung in wings accessible from this main gallery. Don't miss the large **Salle 7,** which contains Courbet's difficult masterpieces *L'Enterrement à Ornans* and *L'Atelier du Peintre.* Courbet's realist painting influenced the Impressionists, whose work is upstairs. Also on the ground floor are little-known academic painters who demonstrate the prevailing artistic atmosphere of the period. There are also more experimental visions, from Gustave Moreau's myth-laden decadence to Puvis de Chavanne's surprisingly modern line. This makes the leap into Impressionism much easier to understand; by **Salle 14** the radical movement has been launched with Edouard Manet's revolutionary reworking of a classical motif in his reclining nude *Olympia.* When it was first shown, in 1865, Olympia's frank, cooly direct gaze was more than Parisian proprieties could stand; her unfinished hands were derided as monkey paws and the black cat (a symbol of female sexuality) was considered outrageous. Across from Olympia's I-dare-you-to-look smile, you'll find two pieces from Claude Monet's great unfinished *Déjeuner sur l'Herbe,* painted in response to his friend Manet's painting of the same name (now upstairs).

The great hall also contains two separate temporary exhibition spaces—painting to the left, photography to the right. And at the rear of the great hall is a wonderful display about the Opéra neighborhood, complete with a to-scale model under the glass floor. From here take the long escalators to the top floor, where Impressionism really gets going. Up here you'll find Manet's *Déjeuner sur l'Herbe (Lunch on the Grass),* the painting that scandalized Paris in 1863 at the Salon des Refusés, an exhibit organized by artists refused permission to show their work at the academy's official annual salon. The painting shows a nude woman and two clothed men picnicking in a park, with a woman in a shift bathing in the background. Manet took the subject, poses and all, from a little-known Renaissance print in the Louvre but updated the clothing to mid-19th-century France. What would otherwise have been thought a respectable "academic" painting thus became deeply shocking: two clothed men with a stark naked woman in a contemporary scene! The loose, bold brushwork, a far cry from the polished styles of the Renaissance, added insult to artistic injury.

This top-floor collection allows Impressionism to break free of its clichés: here Monet's *Les Coquelicots* (*Poppy Fields*) appears perfectly fresh in the sparkling company of small works by Alfred Sisley, Pissarro, and Degas. Daring curator choices also allow for interesting juxtapositions and thoughtful comparisons, such as the positioning of Gustave Caillebotte's floor scrapers, or James Whistler's portrait of his mother, alongside Impressionist contemporaries. It's also a pleasure to see work by one of the few successful female Impressionists, Berthe Morisot, displayed among her contemporaries. Worn wicker chairs invite you to sit and contemplate paintings such as Renoir's *Le Moulin de la Galette* (the name of a popular dancehall in Montmartre), which differs from many other Impressionist paintings in that Renoir worked from numerous studies and completed it in his studio rather than painting it in the open air. Its focus on the activities of a group of ordinary Parisians amusing themselves in the sun on a Montmartre afternoon is typical of the essential spontaneity of Impressionism.

In **Salle 36** modernism begins breaking into the Impressionist idyll. Cézanne's darker palette, blocky brushstrokes, and shifting perspectives set the stage for a postwar revolution. The Postimpressionist galleries include world-famous works by van Gogh, Paul Gauguin, and Toulouse-Lautrec, along with the delicate pastels of Odilon Redon. The collection then moves downstairs to the middle floor.

The middle floor offers two serious treats: a charming restaurant and an exquisite collection of Art Nouveau furniture and decorative objects. Here you can see rare surviving works by Hector Guimard (designer of the swooping green Paris métro entrances) and Barcelona maestro Antoni Gaudí, along with glassware by Lalique and Tiffany, furniture by Carlo Bugatti, and arts and crafts masterpieces. Keep an eye out for the useful explanatory boards available at the entrance to **Salle 65**, among other locations; these English-language texts give helpful pointers about what you're looking at. ⊠ *1 rue de la Légion d'Honneur, St-Germain-des-Prés* ☎ *01–40–49–48–14* ⊕ *www.musee-orsay.fr* ⊠ *€7.50, €5.50 on Sun. Free 1st Sun. of month* ☉ *Tues.–Wed. and Fri.–Sat. 10–6, Thurs. 10–9:45, Sun. 9–6* Ⓜ *Solférino; RER: Musée d'Orsay.*

need a break? If those *Déjeuner sur l'Herbe* paintings make you think about lunch, stop at the middle floor's **Musée d'Orsay Restaurant** (☎ 1–45–49–47–03), in the former train station's sumptuous dining room. Train food, however, this is not: An elegant lunch is available 11:30–2:30, high tea from 3:30 to 5:40 (except Thursday, when dinner is served instead, from 7 to 9:30). For an anytime simple snack, salad, or coffee, visit the top-floor **Café des Hauteurs** and drink in its panoramic view across the Seine toward Montmartre.

❺ **Musée Rodin.** The splendid Hôtel Biron, with its spacious vestibule, broad staircase, and patrician salons lined with boiseries, retains much of its 18th-century ambience and makes a brilliant frame for the sculptures of Auguste Rodin (1840–1917). Rodin took rooms in the building in 1908, when it was a temporary crash pad for artists such as Jean

Fodor'sChoice ★

Cocteau and Isadora Duncan. When the state claimed the hôtel a few years later, Rodin offered his collections to the government if they would turn the house into a museum of his work. The state was initially wary, as Rodin's work was a hot button at the time, but the museum opened in 1919.

Rodin's funeral, at the height of World War I, drew the largest nonmilitary crowd of the time (26,000); while alive, however, he was stalked by controversy. His career took off in 1876 with *L'Age d'Airain* (*The Bronze Age*), inspired by a pilgrimage to Italy and the sculptures of Michelangelo. Because the work was so realistic, some critics accused Rodin of having stuck a live boy in plaster, while others blasted him for what was seen as a sloppy sculpting and casting technique. His seeming messiness, though, was intentional; Rodin refused to smooth out his work, leaving fingerprints along with marks from tools and rags (used to keep the clay moist), because he wanted his sculptures to reflect the artistic process of creation.

Rodin's most celebrated work is *Le Penseur* (*The Thinker*, circa 1880), the muscular man caught in a moment of deep thought and flex. The version here in the garden is the original—the city of Paris, its intended owner, refused to accept it. Before installing the bronze statue on the steps of the Panthéon, Rodin set up a full-scale plaster cast. Its physicality horrified the public; crowds gathered around the statue, debates ensued, and Rodin was ridiculed in the press. Around the same time, Rodin was commissioned to create the doors for the newly proposed Musée des Arts Décoratifs (Museum of Decorative Arts). He set out to sculpt a pair of monumental bronze doors in the tradition of Italian Renaissance churches, calling his proposal *La Porte de l'Enfer* (*The Gate of Hell*). The *Gate*, a visual representation of stories from Dante's *Divine Comedy*, became his obsession: he spent the last 37 years of his life working on it and it now stands in the garden opposite *The Thinker*. The absorbed lovers of *The Kiss* were originally designed for these doors, but they became an independent sculpture (shown indoors).

A troubled episode in Rodin's life is evidenced by works by his student and mistress Camille Claudel (1864–1943), a remarkable sculptor in her own right. Her torturous relationship with Rodin drove her out of his studio—and out of her mind. In 1913 she was packed off to an asylum, where she remained, barred from any artistic activities, until her death.

The gardens of the Musée Rodin are nearly as much a work of art as the sculptures. The powerful *Balzac,* portrayed in his dressing gown and subject of yet another scandal, and figures from the mythic *Burghers of Calais* take their places among evergreens, ferns, allées of trees, and, most notably, rosebushes (more than 2,000 of them, representing 100 varieties). The museum has some information in English. ⊠ *75 rue de Varenne, Trocadéro/Tour Eiffel* ☎ *01–44–18–61–10* ⊕ *www.musee-rodin.fr* ▨ *€5; Sun. €3; gardens only, €1* ☉ *Apr.–Oct., Tues.–Sun. 9:30–5:45; Nov.–Mar., Tues.–Sun. 9:30–4:45* Ⓜ *Varenne.*

need a break?

They call it the **Cafétéria du Musée Rodin** (✉ 75 rue de Varenne, Trocadéro/Tour Eiffel ☎ 01–44–18–61–10), but the pretty tables under the linden trees are a far cry from a school lunchroom. It's especially welcoming in summer, when the leafy old trees shield you from the sun. And while you munch on delicious *tartines*, salads, or the *plat du jour*, the kids can run around on the wide stretch of lush grass. Admission to the garden is €1, and it's closed Monday.

③ Palais Bourbon. The most prominent feature of the Palais Bourbon—home of the **Assemblée Nationale,** the French Parliament since 1798—is its colonnaded facade, commissioned by Napoléon to match that of the Madeleine, across the Seine. Cortot's sculpted pediment portrays France holding the tablets of Law, flanked by Force and Justice. ✉ *Pl. du Palais-Bourbon, St-Germain-des-Prés* ☉ *During temporary exhibits only* Ⓜ *Assemblée Nationale.*

off the beaten path

BASILIQUE STE-CLOTILDE – Once the most fashionable church in 19th-century Paris, this neo-Gothic church (built 1846–58) is notable for its imposing twin spires and excellent organ concerts. The garden in front of the basilica is often filled with parents and their children. From the Palais Bourbon take rue Bourgogne south; then take a left on rue Las-Cases. ✉ *Rue Las-Cases, St-Germain-des-Prés* ⊕ *www. sainte-clotilde.com* Ⓜ *Solférino.*

㉒ Palais du Luxembourg (Luxembourg Palace). The gray, imposing Luxembourg Palace was built, like the surrounding Jardin du Luxembourg, for Maria de' Medici, widow of Henri IV, at the beginning of the 17th century. Maria was born and raised in Florence's Pitti Palace, and having languished in the Louvre after the death of her husband, she was eager to build herself a new palace where she could recapture something of the lively, carefree atmosphere of her childhood. In 1612 she bought the Paris mansion of the duke of Luxembourg, tore it down, and built her palace. It was not completed until 1627, and Maria was to live there for just five years (the grand series of canvases Rubens painted to decorate the palace are now in the Louvre). In 1632 Cardinal Richelieu had her expelled from France, and she saw out her declining years in Cologne, Germany, dying there almost penniless in 1642. The palace remained royal property until the Revolution, when the state took it over and used it as a prison. Danton, the painter David, and Thomas Paine were all detained here. Today the French Senate meets here, so the building is not open to the public. However, next to the palace is the **Musée de Luxembourg** (☎ 01–42–34–25–95 ⊕ www.museeduluxembourg.fr). Once home to many of the masterpieces now on view at the Musée d'Orsay, it is open occasionally for temporary exhibitions. Its shows have proved very popular, so you should anticipate a line. Recent exhibits have included work from Paolo Caliari and Matisse. A Titian show will be in residence from autumn 2005 through winter 2006. *Musée* ✉ *17 rue de Vaugirard, St-Germain-des-Prés* Ⓜ *Odéon; RER: Luxembourg.*

⑯ Pont des Arts. Immortalized in paintings by Renoir and Pissarro, this iron-and-wood footbridge linking the Louvre to the Institut de France is a favorite of painters, art students, and misty-eyed romantics moved by the views of the Île de la Cité. The bridge got its name because the Louvre was once called the Palais des Arts (Palace of Art). Ⓜ *Pont Neuf.*

⓬ **St-Germain-des-Prés.** Paris's oldest church was first built to shelter a relic of the true cross brought back from Spain in AD 542. The Romanesque square tower dates from the early 11th century, while the chancel was enlarged and the church then reconsecrated by Pope Alexander III in 1163, after no less than four sackings by the Vikings. The colorful 19th-century frescoes in the nave are by Hippolyte Flandrin, a pupil of the classical master Ingres. The church stages superb organ concerts and recitals. ✉ *Pl. St-Germain-des-Prés, St-Germain-des-Prés* ⊙ *Weekdays 8–7:30, weekends 8 AM–9 PM* Ⓜ *St-Germain-des-Prés.*

㉓ **St-Sulpice.** Dubbed the Cathedral of the Rive Gauche, this enormous 17th-century church has entertained some unlikely christenings—those of the Marquis de Sade and Charles Baudelaire, for instance—and the nuptials of irreverent wordsmith Victor Hugo. The 18th-century facade was never finished, and its unequal towers add a playful touch to an otherwise sober design. The interior is oddly impersonal, despite the two magnificent Delacroix frescoes. The congregation, though, makes for good people-watching on days of confirmation and wedding parties. And Catherine Deneuve and other St-Germain celebrities are occasionally spotted in the square's Café de la Mairie, once the existential haunt of Albert Camus. ✉ *Pl. St-Sulpice, St-Germain-des-Prés* Ⓜ *St-Sulpice.*

⓿ **St-Thomas d'Aquin.** This elegant, domed church designed by Pierre Bulet in 1683 was originally dedicated to St. Dominique and flanked by a convent—whose buildings now belong to the army. The east-end chapel was added in 1722 and the two-tier facade in 1768. Pope Pius VII popped in during his trip to Paris for Napoléon's coronation in December 1804. ✉ *Pl. St-Thomas-d'Aquin, St-Germain-des-Prés* Ⓜ *Rue du Bac.*

⓴ **Théâtre de l'Odéon.** At the north end of the Jardin du Luxembourg sits the colonnaded Odéon Theater—a masterpiece of the neoclassical style. It was established in 1792 to house the Comédie Française troupe; the original building was destroyed by fire in 1807. Since World War II it has specialized in 20th-century productions and was the base for Jean-Louis Barrault and Madeleine Renaud's theater company, the Théâtre de France, until they fell out of favor with the authorities for their alleged role in spurring on student revolutionaries in May 1968. Today the theater is the French home of the Theater of Europe and stages excellent productions by major foreign companies, sometimes in English. At press time, the building was due to reopen in late 2005 after a renovation. ✉ *1 pl. de l'Odéon, St-Germain-des-Prés* ☎ *01–44–85–40–00* ⊕ *www.theatre-odeon.fr* Ⓜ *Odéon.*

MONTPARNASSE

Montparnasse has no actual connection to Greece; the neighborhood's name, referring to the Greek mountain dedicated to Apollo and the Muses, is an ancient student in-joke. There was a hill here in the 17th century, and as the area was outside the city walls it attracted students with out-of-bounds distractions. The students' artistic pretentions led to the sardonic Parnassus nickname. The hill was flattened just before the Revolution; by 1860, when Montparnasse was incorporated into Paris, the quartier was full of dance halls and cabarets.

A legitimate artistic connection developed in the early 20th century when artists, writers, and their muses discovered the inexpensive charms of the streets near the Montparnasse train station. Pablo Picasso, Amedeo Modigliani, Ernest Hemingway, Man Ray and his model Kiki, Lee Miller, and Leon Trotsky were among those who spawned an intellectual café society in this southern sphere of the Rive Gauche. Their creative energy attracted the party people of the Roaring Twenties, whose prodigious drinking habits launched a string of brasseries along the district's main thoroughfare, the broad boulevard du Montparnasse.

The boulevard maintained its aura into the early 1960s—think of Godard's *nouvelle vague* films, which often showed the pulsing street life—but today the area feels more sedate than scintillating. If you spend an afternoon walking among modern developments or on the quiet paths of Montparnasse cemetery, passing the graves of Baudelaire, Sartre, and actress Jean Seberg (who snared Belmondo in Godard's film *Breathless*), the neighborhood's artistic fireworks may seem to be extinguished. But at night there's still a crackling energy beneath the bourgeois veneer, as bars, clubs, restaurants, and movie houses come to life in the shadow of continental Europe's tallest high-rise, the 59-story Tour Montparnasse. This tower was so hated during its construction that it spurred the government to pass laws controlling building height within Paris city limits. Fortunately, there's more successful contemporary architecture nearby; don't miss Ricardo Bofill's semicircular Amphithéâtre housing complex, with its whimsical postmodernist details, and Jean Nouvel's marvelous Fondation Cartier, essentially a house of glass cards. Another Cartier adds further artistic luster to the quartier: the Fondation Henri Cartier-Bresson, a photo gallery created by the eponymous photographer shorly before his death in 2004.

Where there was once a warren of artist studios, today there's the massive glass-fronted Montparnasse train station and shopping complex. But several small museums in the area commemorate both the artistic flowering and the darker history of the area. The Paris Resistance had its headquarters nearby, in the Roman catacombs, during the Nazi occupation. Appropriately enough, after ignoring Hitler's orders to blow up the city, Governor von Choltitz signed the German surrender in Montparnasse in August 1944.

Numbers in the text correspond to numbers in the margin and on the Montparnasse map.

a good
walk

Take the métro or walk to the Vavin station, where Rodin's controversial statue of Balzac oversees boulevard Raspail. In front of you, strung along boulevard Montparnasse, are the cafés that made the street famous; you'll be right beside Picasso's favorite, La Rotonde. A block farther on is Le Sélect, at No. 99, which opened in 1925 and was the first all-night joint in the area. Across the street is the Café du Dôme (No.

108), which was an unfashionable dive until the early 1920s, when the manager of La Rotonde refused to serve a young American woman. The lady in question wasn't wearing a hat, and even more shocking, she was smoking a cigarette. When La Rotonde refused to serve her a drink, she marched across the street, taking all her friends and acquaintances with her. The Dôme instantly became a trendy address, making its fortune serving people regardless of their accessories. Walk a little farther, to No. 102, **La Coupole ❶**, with its painted columns and restored Art Deco interior, then keep on in this direction along boulevard du Montparnasse to **place du 18-Juin-1940 ❷**. Towering above the square is the **Tour Montparnasse ❸**. Behind the building is the huge, gleaming glass facade of Gare Montparnasse, the train station that is the terminus for the 200-mph TGV Atlantique, serving western France.

Cross place Bienvenüe, to the right of Tour Montparnasse, take rue de l'Arrivée, walk up the stairs, and take avenue Maine to rue Antoine-Bourdelle. Turn left toward the sharp brick outlines of the **Musée Bourdelle ❹**, devoted to the powerful sculpture of Antoine Bourdelle. Continue to the end of the street and turn left onto rue Armand-Moissant; note the elegant beige-and-green facade of the École Commerciale on your left before turning right onto boulevard de Vaugirard. A short way along the boulevard is the **Musée de la Poste ❺**, a must if you're a stamp collector. Otherwise, simply cross the boulevard and take the elevator near No. 25 to reach the **Jardin Atlantique ❻**, a modern park laid over the rail tracks of Montparnasse station. Memories of World War II—notably the French Resistance and the Liberation of Paris—are evoked in the Musée Jean Moulin to the left.

Cross to the far-diagonal end of the Jardin Atlantique and glance to your right: there's a splendid vista of that other Tour, Eiffel. One block to your left is **place de Catalogne ❼**. Wander down rue Vercingetorix, admiring the curves of Richard Bofill's 1985 housing complex. Tucked back here is the small church of Notre-Dame du Travail, its turn-of-the-20th-century internal metal structure recalling train stations of the same era. Back in place de Catalogne, go toward the left, past the hospital to rue Jean-Zay. Make a sharp right onto rue de l'Ouest (a reference to the trains going west from Gare Montparnasse), then turn left onto pretty rue Lebouis. A few doors down you'll see impasse Lebouis, a cul-de-sac that's now the site of the **Fondation Henri Cartier-Bresson ❽** photography collection. The buildings in this area are an engaging assortment of styles from the 1890s through 1930, their large windows and high ceilings designed with the needs of working artists and photographers in mind. Farther down rue Lebouis, go through the gate that leads to a small bamboo park. The path leads to rue Ray-Losserand, which connects to the high-walled **Cimetière du Montparnasse ❾**, to your left at the corner of avenue du Maine and rue Froidevaux. You can walk through the cemetery to place Denfert-Rochereau, or else continue along Froidevaux to Denfert-Rochereau, guarded by the *Lion of Belfort,* a huge bronze sculpture by Frédéric-Auguste Bartholdi, of Statue of Liberty fame. Just beyond the lion lies the entrance to the underground labyrinth of the **catacombs ❿**, which tunnel under much of the Rive Gauche and the suburbs.

Walk up boulevard Raspail, past architect Jean Nouvel's transparent **Fondation Cartier pour l'art contemporain** ⑪, a contemporary art showcase. At 247 boulevard Raspail, step into the movie-set-ish cobblestone Passage d'Enfer (Hell's Passageway), which leads to the handsome rue Campagne-Première. Photographer Man Ray called No. 29 home, while down at No. 17, Stanley Hayter ran his Atelier 17 print shop, working for Picasso, Alberto Giacometti, Chagall, and Miró. (Hayter also hid Spanish refugees here in the late 1930s.) Turn right at the bottom of the street onto boulevard du Montparnasse. At avenue de l'Observatoire stands the great bastion of Rive Gauche café culture, the **Closerie des Lilas** ⑫. Up avenue de l'Observatoire is the **Observatoire de Paris** ⑬, Louis XIV's astronomical observatory. In the other direction, the tree-lined avenue sweeps past the **Fontaine de l'Observatoire**, a 19th-century fountain topped by four bronze female nudes holding a globe. Straight ahead is the Jardin du Luxembourg. To the right of the fountain, if you go up to the corner of rue du Val-de-Grâce, you'll see the imposing baroque dome of **Val de Grâce** ⑭.

TIMING This walk around Montparnasse is just under 5 km (3 mi) long and should comfortably take a morning or an afternoon if you choose to check out one of the historic cafés and the catacombs along the way. Note that the catacombs and most of the museums in this area are closed Monday.

What to See

⑩ **Catacombs.** *"Arrête! C'est ici l'Empire de la Mort"* ("Halt! This is the Empire of Death"). This message scrawled at the entrance was enough to convince German troops in World War II to turn tail before they guessed that Resistance fighters used the catacomb tunnels as a base. This dire warning now welcomes you after a winding descent through dark, clammy passages to Paris's principal ossuary. Bones from the notorious Cimetière des Innocents were the first to be transplanted here in 1786, when decomposing bodies started seeping into Les Halles cellars, bringing swarms of ravenous rats with them. The legions of bones dumped here are arranged not by owner but by type—witness the rows of skulls, stacks of tibias, and piles of spinal disks. There are also some bizarre attempts at bone art, like skulls arranged in the shape of hearts. It's macabre and makes you feel very . . . mortal. Among the bones in here are those of the Comte de Mirabeau (1749–91), the Revolutionary leader; 16th-century satirist and writer François Rabelais (1490–1553), transplanted from the former cemetery at the Église St-Paul–St-Louis; and famous courtesan Madame de Pompadour (1721–64), mixed in with the rabble after a lifetime spent as the mistress to Louis XV. Be prepared for stairs and a long underground walk; the floor can be damp, so wear appropriate shoes. You won't be shrouded in tomblike darkness, though; the tunnels are well lighted. There are no tours in English. At this writing, the catacombs were closed for refurbishment, due to reopen in spring 2005. ⊠ *1 pl. Denfert-Rochereau, Montparnasse* ☎ *01–43–22–47–63* ⊕ *www.paris.fr/musees* ⊠ *€5, guided tours in French €3 extra* ☼ *Tues.–Sat. 10–5* Ⓜ *Métro or RER: Denfert-Rochereau.*

⑨ **Cimetière du Montparnasse** (Montparnasse Cemetery). Behind these high walls lies a peaceful cemetery, perhaps with fewer picturesque old trees

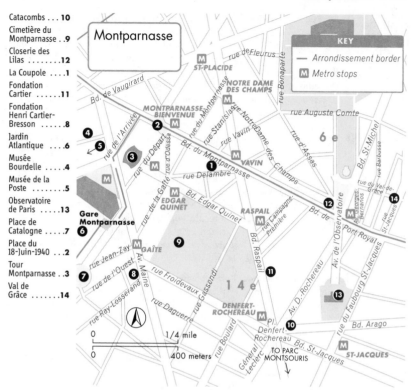

than Père Lachaise but with an appeal of its own (for starters, it has the ruins of an old stone windmill, once a student hangout). Many of the neighborhood's most illustrious residents are buried here, only a stone's throw from where they lived and loved: Baudelaire, Bartholdi (who designed the Statue of Liberty), Alfred Dreyfus, Guy de Maupassant, and, more recently, photographer Man Ray, playwright Samuel Beckett, writers Marguerite Duras, Sartre, and de Beauvoir, actress Jean Seberg, and singer-songwriter Serge Gainsbourg. ⊠ *Entrances on rue Froidevaux, bd. Edgar-Quinet, Montparnasse* ⊙ *Mid-Mar.–mid-Nov., weekdays 8–6, Sat. 8:30–6, Sun. 9–6; mid-Nov.–mid-Mar., weekdays 8–5:30, Sat. 8:30–5:30, Sun. 9–5:30* Ⓜ *Raspail, Gaîté.*

⓬ **Closerie des Lilas.** Now a pricey bar-restaurant, the Closerie remains a staple of all literary tours of Paris. Commemorative plaques fastened to the bar honor literati such as Baudelaire, Verlaine, and Hemingway. (Hemingway wrote pages of *The Sun Also Rises* here; he lived around the corner at 115 rue Notre-Dame-des-Champs.) Although the lilacs that graced the garden are gone—they once shaded such habitués as Ingres, Whistler, and Balzac—the terrace still opens onto a garden wall of luxuriant evergreen foliage and is as crowded in summer as it ever was. ⊠ *171 bd. du Montparnasse, Montparnasse* ☎ *01–40–51–34–50* Ⓜ *Vavin; RER: Port Royal.*

off the beaten path

MUSÉE ZADKINE – Russian-born sculptor Ossip Zadkine (1890–1967) trained in London before setting up in Paris in 1909. The works on exhibit at this museum, in Zadkine's former house and studio, reveal the influences of Rodin, African art, and Cubism. From the Closerie des Lilas, take rue d'Assas off to your left to get to the museum. ✉ *100 bis, rue d'Assas, Montparnasse* ☎ *01–55–42–77–20* ⊕ *www.paris.fr/musees* ✉ *Permanent collection free, exhibitions €4* ⊙ *Tues.–Sun. 10–6* Ⓜ *Vavin.*

❶ La Coupole. One of Montparnasse's most famous brasseries, La Coupole opened in 1927 as a bar-restaurant and dance hall and soon became a home-away-from-home for Apollinaire, Max Jacob, Cocteau, Satie, Stravinsky, and Hemingway. In the 1980s the brasserie was bought by the Flo chain, which preserved the interior fittings, tore down the building, rebuilt what you see today, and put the restaurant back together inside its new home. As a result, you can still dine beneath the columns painted by a host of Parisian artists, including Chagall and Brancusi. ✉ *102 bd. du Montparnasse, Montparnasse* ☎ *01–43–20–14–20* ⊙ *Daily 8:30 AM–2 AM* Ⓜ *Vavin.*

★ ⓫ Fondation Cartier pour l'art contemporain (Cartier Foundation). This eye-catching contemporary art gallery (funded by jewelry giant Cartier) is a perfect example of the architect Jean Nouvel's interest in new kinds of glass. Launched in 1993, the exhibition space seems to be a series of glass cards, layered between the boulevard and the garden. The nearly self-effacing building highlights a cedar of Lebanon planted 180 years ago by French writer Chateaubriand, who once lived at this address. Along with thought-provoking art shows, the foundation hosts performance nights on Thursday evening, some in English. These "Nuits Nomades" start at 8:30; call for the program. ✉ *261 bd. Raspail, Montparnasse* ☎ *01–42–18–56–50* ⊕ *www.fondation.cartier.fr* ✉ *€6.50* ⊙ *Tues.–Sun. noon–8* Ⓜ *Raspail.*

★ ❽ Fondation Henri Cartier-Bresson. An exciting addition to the city's photography scene, this 1913 artists' atelier was restored and opened in 2003 by the nonpareil French photographer Cartier-Bresson as a showcase for young contemporary photographers. The foundation grants the HCB award every two years to an up-and-coming photographer; the 2005 winner will have a solo exhibition here in fall 2006. Be sure to go up to the top floor to see a small gallery of Cartier-Bresson's own work. There, too, you can consider the deep roots photography has in Montparnasse; it was in these small streets that great experimenters like Louis Daguerre and Man Ray lived and worked. ✉ *2 impasse Lebouis, Montparnasse* ☎ *01–56–80–27–00* ⊕ *www.henricartierbresson.org* ✉ *€4* ⊙ *Wed. 1–8:30, Thurs.–Fri. 1–6:30, Sat. 11–6:45.*

❻ Jardin Atlantique (Atlantic Garden). Built over the tracks of Gare Montparnasse, this smart designer park opened in 1994 is noted for its assortment of trees and plants found in coastal regions near the Atlantic Ocean—hence the name. A museum building at the station end of the garden houses souvenirs and video coverage of World War II inside the **Mémorial du Maréchal-Leclerc,** commemorating the liberator of Paris,

ARTISTS, WRITERS & EXILES

PARIS FIRST BECAME A MAGNET *for the international avant-garde in the mid-1800s, and the city remained Europe's most creative and bohemian capital until the 1950s. It all began just south of **Montmartre,** when Romantics including writers Charles Baudelaire and George Sand, with her lover, Polish composer Chopin, moved into the streets below boulevard de Clichy. Impressionist painters Claude Monet, Edouard Manet, and Mary Cassatt kept studios here, near Gare St-Lazare, so they could conveniently commute to the countryside or simply paint the bustle of the train station itself. By the 1880s the neighborhood dance halls had a new attraction: the cancan, a dance that flashed Basic Instinct-esque skin. By 1889 the Zidler brothers opened the Moulin Rouge cabaret. Toulouse-Lautrec designed posters advertising the stars of the neighborhood and sketched prostitutes in his spare time.*

Montmartre's influence had legs; the artistic maelstrom continued through the Belle Époque and beyond. In the early 1900s Picasso and Braque launched Cubism from a ramshackle hillside studio, the Bateau-Lavoir. Meanwhile a similar beehive of activity was established at the south end of the city in a curious studio building called La Ruche (the beehive; at the Convention métro stop). Artists from different disciplines worked together on experimental productions. For instance, in 1917 the modernist ballet Parade hit the stage, danced by impresario Sergei Diaghilev's Ballet Russes, with music by Erik Satie and costumes designed by Picasso—and everyone involved was hauled off to court, accused of being cultural anarchists.

World War I shattered this creative frenzy, and when peace returned, the artists had moved. The narrow streets of

Montparnasse offered old buildings suitable for studios, and the area hummed with a wide, new, café-filled boulevard. At nearby No. 27 rue Fleurus, the American literary innovator Gertrude Stein held weekly court with her partner, Alice B. Toklas. Picasso drew admirers to La Rotonde, while F. Scott Fitzgerald drank at the now-defunct Dingo. In the '30s La Coupole became a favorite brasserie of the writers Henry Miller, Anaïs Nin, and Lawrence Durrell.

*The Spanish Civil War, followed by World War II, brought an end to carefree Montparnasse. But the literati soon reconvened not far away, in **St-Germain-des-Prés.** The cafés Flore and Deux Magots had long been popular with an alternative artsy crowd, from Oscar Wilde (who died at nearby 13 rue des Beaux-Arts) to surrealist writer Louis Aragon. Expat writers like Samuel Beckett and Richard Wright joined existentialists Jean-Paul Sartre, Simone de Beauvoir, and Albert Camus in the neighborhood, drawn into the orbit of literary magazines and publishing houses. Man-about-town, writer, and musician Boris Vian played trumpet in local underground jazz clubs. In the tiny Théâtre de la Huchette Ionesco's bald soprano still sings nightly for her supper.*

*Although Paris can no longer claim to be the epicenter of Western artistic innovation, pockets of outrageous creativity still bubble up. The galleries on rue Louise Weiss in **Tolbiac** and the open-studio weekends in **Belleville** and **Oberkampf** reveal the city's continuing artistic spirit.*

— Lisa Pasold

and the **Musée Jean-Moulin,** devoted to the leader of the French Resistance. In the center of the park, what looks like a quirky piece of metallic sculpture is actually a meteorological center, with a battery of flickering lights reflecting temperature, wind speed, and monthly rainfall. ✉ *Pont des Cinq-Martyrs-du-Lycée-Buffon, Montparnasse* ☎*01-40-64-39-44* ⊕*www.paris.fr/musees* ▣*Free* ☉ *Musée Tues.–Sun. 10–5:40* Ⓜ *Montparnasse Bienvenüe.*

❹ **Musée Bourdelle** (Bourdelle Museum). Opened in 1949 in the studios and gardens where Rodin's pupil Antoine Bourdelle (1861–1929) lived and worked, this spacious museum was extended by Christian de Portzamparc in 1992. The collection includes 500 works in plaster, marble, and bronze, including castings of Bourdelle's landmark works, the bombastic *Heracles the Archer* and the *Dying Centaur.* Recent exhibits have brought in contemporary work by artists like Luciano Fabro to juxtapose with those of Bourdelle's era. ✉ *18 rue Antoine-Bourdelle, Montparnasse* ☎ *01-49-54-73-73* ⊕ *www.paris.fr/musees* ▣ *Permanent collections free, exhibitions €4.50* ☉ *Tues.–Sun. 10–6* Ⓜ *Falguière.*

❺ **Musée de la Poste** (Postal Museum). Go postal in a good way. On display at this five-story museum of postal history are international and French stamps (dating as far back as 1849), postal carriers' uniforms and mailboxes, sorting and stamp-printing machines, and one of the balloons used to send mail out of Paris during the Prussian siege of 1870. Look for an exhibit on France's new stamp of Marianne—the symbol of the Republic—released in January 2005 after a high-profile national competition. ✉ *34 bd. de Vaugirard, Montparnasse* ☎ *01-42-79-24-24* ⊕ *www.laposte.fr/musee* ▣ *€4.50* ☉ *Mon.–Sat. 10–6* Ⓜ *Montparnasse Bienvenüe.*

⓭ **Observatoire de Paris** (Paris Observatory). The observatory was constructed in 1667 for Louis XIV by architect Claude Perrault. Its four facades are aligned with the four cardinal points—north, south, east, and west—and its southern wall is the determining point for Paris's official latitude, 48° 50′11″N. French time was based on this Paris meridian until 1911, when the country decided to adopt the international Greenwich Meridian. The interior is not open to the general public. ✉ *Av. de l'Observatoire, Montparnasse* Ⓜ *RER: Port Royal.*

❼ **Place de Catalogne** (Catalonia Square). This circular square is the best example of contemporary architect Ricardo Bofill's work. His 1985 **Amphithéâtre** housing complex is a tip of the hat to French classicism. Here his trademark contemporary riff on the baroque gives inhabitants huge, round bay windows discreetly hidden in the vast courtyards of the building. Beyond is the turn-of-the-20th-century **Notre-Dame du Travail** church; this neighborhood was once home to many builders, who worked on the Tour Eiffel and other exposition constructions. The church's riveted iron-and-steel framework was meant to symbolize their exciting new techniques, along with the work ethos evoked in the church's name. The Sebastopol Bell above the facade is a trophy from the Crimean War. ✉ *Pl. de Catalogne, Montparnasse* Ⓜ *Gaîté.*

② **Place du 18-Juin-1940.** Next to Tour Montparnasse, this square memorializes the date Charles de Gaulle broadcast a radio speech from London urging the French to resist the Germans after the Nazi invasion of May 1940. German military governor Dietrich von Choltitz surrendered to the Allies here in August 1944, ignoring Hitler's orders to destroy the city as he withdrew. A plaque on the wall of what is now a shopping center—originally the Montparnasse train station extended this far—commemorates the event. Ⓜ *Montparnasse Bienvenüe.*

③ **Tour Montparnasse** (Montparnasse Tower). Continental Europe's tallest skyscraper, completed in 1973, the 680-foot Montparnasse Tower offers a stupendous view of Paris from its open-air roof terrace, renovated in 2005. It attracts 800,000 gawkers each year; on a clear day you can see for 40 km (25 mi). A glossy brochure, "Paris Vu d'en Haut" ("Paris from on High"), explains just what to look for. It also claims to have the fastest elevator in Europe. Most of the 59 stories are taken up by offices, and a vast commercial complex, including a Galeries Lafayette department store, spreads over the ground floors. Banal by day, the tower becomes Montparnasse's neon-lighted beacon at night. ⊠ *Rue de l'Arrivée, Montparnasse* ☎ *01–45–38–52–56* ⊕ *www.tourmontparnasse56. com* ⊠ *€8.20* ☉ *Apr.–Sept., daily 9:30 AM–11:30 PM; Oct.–Mar., daily 9:30 AM–10:30 PM (last elevator 30 mins before closing)* Ⓜ *Montparnasse Bienvenüe.*

⑭ **Val de Grâce.** This imposing 17th-century church was commissioned by Anne of Austria and designed by François Mansart. Its rhythmic two-story facade rivals the Dôme church at the Invalides as the city's most striking example of Italianate baroque. Pierre Mignard's 1663 cupola fresco bursts with more than 200 sky-climbing figures. The church's original abbey buildings are now a military army hospital, with a small museum of army medical history. ⊠ *1 pl. Alphonse-Laveran, Quartier Latin* ☎ *01–40–51–51–94* ⊠ *€4.60* ☉ *Museum Tues.–Wed. noon–6, weekends 1:30–5* Ⓜ *RER: Port Royal.*

PASSY, AUTEUIL & THE BOIS DE BOULOGNE

Passy and Auteuil were independent villages until Baron Haussmann soldered them together in 1860 and annexed them to Paris under the mundane title of the 16ᵉ arrondissement. Tumbling alleys and countrified culs-de-sac recall those bygone days; they're now mixed with early-20th-century streets that showcase some of the city's finest buildings by Guimard, Perret, Le Corbusier, and Mallet-Stevens. If that weren't enough to spur you on, one of the city's most overlooked museums is here—the Musée Marmottan, with its enormous Monet collection.

Not far from those sun-dappled Monets is the sprawling Bois de Boulogne, an aristocratic holdover that became an enormous park under Napoléon III, who commanded Haussmann to create a new version of London's Hyde Park. The 16ᵉ is the largest arrondissement in Paris, and Le Bois, as it is known, is of almost equal size. Public transportation to the Bois is poor, and few Parisians ever get to know all its glades and pathways—but all know and love the Bois's Pré Catalan and Bagatelle gardens, landscaped enclaves surrounded by wilder parkland. The photogenic Lac Inférieur is easily reached on foot from the métro.

Numbers in the text correspond to numbers in the margin and on the Passy, Auteuil, and Bois de Boulogne map.

a good walk

Start at the small **Cimetière de Passy** ❶, above place du Trocadéro. Check the map to the left of the entrance to locate tombs such as that of the painter Manet. As you leave, cross avenue Paul-Doumer, and veer toward a small garden (Square Yorktown) where there is a statue of Benjamin Franklin. Turn right down rue Benjamin-Franklin. Gardens flank the curved wing of the Palais de Chaillot, to your left. Hunt down No. 25 bis, built in 1903 by Modernist Auguste Perret, who was only 29 when he created this apartment, the first ever made with reinforced concrete posts. Perret went on to great things, several of them in the neighborhood. Be sure to take a close look at the floral-patterned ceramic facade, a beautiful crossover detail between Art Nouveau and Art Deco styles.

Continue through place Costa-Rica, with its plummeting view of the aboveground métro as it shoots across the Seine, and take rue Raynouard. Just past No. 9, turn left down rue des Eaux, a sinister-looking staircase flanked by barbed wire: these plunging narrow stairs feel like the maid's entrance, but they're a great shortcut to the high-class rue Charles-Dickens. When you reemerge into daylight, to the left there's a templelike town house with huge Greek columns (actually the Algerian embassy) and, beyond the gate, the strange **Musée du Vin** ❷, with waxwork exhibits in its medieval cellars. After an excursion through bacchanalian pastures, big-city reality hits again as you continue down rue des Eaux to reach avenue du Président Kennedy. As you walk along the river you'll see the Allée des Cygnes, a strip of artificial island; beyond, on the far side of the river, is the 1970s Front de Seine complex (which replaced bombed-out parts of the city destroyed by Allies targeting occupied auto factories). If you'd like to see a mini version of the **Statue of Liberty** ❸, cross to the skinny island and walk to the far end. Otherwise continue ahead along President Kennedy until rue Ankara, where you'll turn right.

A policeman generally lurks a hundred yards on, barring the leafy driveway to the Turkish embassy. You might have to consult him for advice as you search for rue Berton, a cobbled, ivy-clad alley that sneaks off to the left. This remnant of the village of Passy gave writer Balzac a secret getaway from his creditors—notice the small doors leading into the buildings above. A flight of stairs leads back to rue Raynouard and overlooks the gardens of Balzac's former home. The **Maison de Balzac** ❹ is a deceptively large bungalow with well-manicured lawns. Rue Benjamin-Franklin returns at the corner of rues Raynouard and Singer where—says a tall, tapering plaque—the great man invented the lightning conductor between 1777 and 1785. Rue Raynouard tumbles down past the circular bulk of **Maison de Radio France** ❺, the headquarters of state radio and television.

Continue on rue Raynouard, which becomes rue La Fontaine, to inspect Hector Guimard's masterful **Castel-Béranger** ❻, at No. 14, one of the

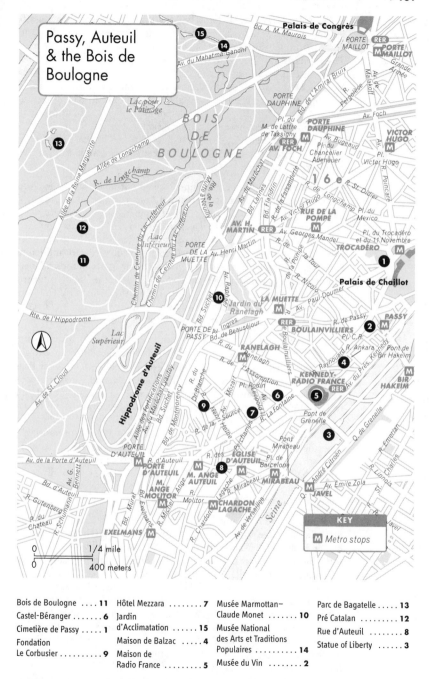

Passy, Auteuil
& the Bois de
Boulogne

city's earliest Art Nouveau buildings. If you're a fan of sculptor Auguste Rodin, you may want to make a detour next right up avenue du Recteur-Poincaré to **place Rodin** to see a small bronze casting of his male nude *The Bronze Age*. Otherwise stay on rue La Fontaine, past the Orphelins d'Auteuil, a still-functioning orphanage. Pause at No. 60, the **Hôtel Mezzara** ❼, another fine Guimard mansion. Some 150 yards along turn left onto rue des Perchamps. Note the bay-windowed, striped-tile Studio Building at No. 20—it looks contemporary but was built by Henri Sauvage in 1927. Also note the white mansion at the corner of rue Leconte-de-l'Isle, with its heavy outsize triglyphs. Some beefy baroque caryatids are visible across the street at No. 33, incongruously supporting a row of wafer-thin balconies.

Continue along rue des Perchamps to **rue d'Auteuil** ❽. To the left you can just glimpse the spire of the Église d'Auteuil, modeled on the papal tiara. Head right along this old, crooked shopping street to sloping place Jean-Lorrain, where you'll find a crowded market Wednesday and Saturday mornings; then turn right down rue La Fontaine toward the chunky Crédit Lyonnais bank. Veer left up avenue Mozart and pause at No. 122; this is the Art Nouveau mansion Guimard built for his American artist wife, who tried unsuccessfully to have the building turned into a museum after Guimard's death. Around the corner in Villa Flore, a tiny cul-de-sac, you can see the oddly shaped site Guimard had to contend with; notice also the large painting studio on the top floor.

Take the next left up rue Henri-Heine, with its row of elegant town houses; then turn at the second left onto rue du Dr-Blanche and left again to get to square du Dr-Blanche, a leafy cul-de-sac. At the far end is the **Fondation Le Corbusier** ❾. After visiting this stellar example of spartan design, retrace your path along rue du Dr-Blanche, continuing until you reach rue Mallet-Stevens, a calm impasse entirely built by modernist master Robert Mallet-Stevens in the late 1920s. Back on Dr-Blanche, turn right at rue de l'Assomption, then, opposite the end of rue du Ranelagh, cross the disused Petite Ceinture rail line. Veer right on avenue Raphaël, which overlooks the elegant Jardin du Ranelagh—site of the world's first hot-air balloon launch, in 1783. At the corner of rue Louis-Boilly is the **Musée Marmottan–Claude Monet** ❿, famed for its collection of Impressionist pictures and illuminated manuscripts.

Continue on avenue Raphaël and cross boulevard Suchet to sprawling place de Colombie. Turn left down avenue de St-Cloud to reach the large **Bois de Boulogne** ⑪. Walk along rue de la Muette á Neuilly; straight ahead is the bigger of the park's two lakes, the Lac Inférieur; you can cross to the island in the middle on a little ferry for a picnic, or you can eat at the lovely Chalet des Îles. The smaller Lac Supérieur is less picturesque, so follow the scenic footpath around to chemin de Ceinture, then turn left onto route de la Grande-Cascade, pass the fenced Racing Club, to reach the pretty **Pré Catalan** ⑫ with its Shakespeare Garden (closed in winter months). Cross the Pré Catalan and exit to the left of the Relais du Bois de Boulogne. If you're short on time, go right onto the bike path, following the narrow canal, which will lead you back to Porte de la Muette via the Carrefour. But if you have the energy it's well worth continuing straight to the **Parc de Bagatelle** ⑯ with its magnificent flower garden, 18th-century château, and pricey but delightful Restaurant Bagatelle. The Parc de Bagatelle's exit is behind the restaurant; by going right from here you'll end up on avenue du Mahatma-Gandhi, where there is the **Musée National des Arts et Traditions Populaires** ⑭ and a children's amusement park (the **Jardin d'Acclimatation** ⑲), to Porte Maillot, where you can get a métro back to central Paris.

TIMING This walk, which divides neatly into two—town (Passy and Auteuil) and country (Bois de Boulogne)—will probably take you a full day. As it's a good idea to be out of the Bois de Boulogne by dusk, you may want to save it for another day. The Lac Inférieur is a good midway spot to stop for lunch. By then you'll have covered 5–6 km (3–3½ mi), depending on whether you detour to the Statue of Liberty. The second half of the tour covers just under 4 km (2½ mi) if you return from the Pré Catalan to Porte de la Muette or just under 6 km (3½ mi) if you take in the Parc de Bagatelle and return to Porte Maillot. Sturdy, comfortable footwear is a must to negotiate the slopes and steps of the city sector and the sometimes muddy pathways of the Bois de Boulogne. Remember that most museums, including the Marmottan, are closed Monday and that the morning market on place Jean-Lorrain is open only on Wednesday and Saturday.

What to See

⑪ **Bois de Boulogne.** Until Napoléon III's time, this 2,200-acre park was truly a wild woods. But Baron Haussmann's brilliant landscaper Alphand (who also created the Buttes-Chaumont and Parc de Montsouris) redesigned the land along the lines of a London park, making the Bois's elegant promenades, romantic lakes, and formal playgrounds an immediate hit with Parisians. Emphasizing that onetime glamour is Haussmann's approach road from the Arc de Triomphe: avenue Foch, Paris's widest boulevard (120 yards across). The Porte Dauphine métro station, at the bottom of avenue Foch, retains its original Art Nouveau iron-and-glass entrance canopy designed by Hector Guimard.

The wood is crisscrossed by broad, leafy roads leading from one lake to the next, with architectural follies and restaurants scattered throughout. On fine days the Bois is filled with rowers, joggers, strollers, riders, *pétanque* players (*see* "Eyes on the Boule" *in* Chapter 5), and picnickers. Meetings at the **Longchamp** and **Auteuil** racetracks are high up the social calendar and re-create something of its Belle Époque heyday. The French Open tennis tournament, at the beautiful **Roland Garros** stadium in late May, is another sporting occasion.

Rowboats can be rented at both **Lac Inférieur** and **Lac Supérieur.** A cheap and frequent ferry crosses to the idyllic island in the middle of Lac Inférieur. The **Fête à Neu-Neu,** a giant carnival, takes place every September and October around the two lakes. Buses traverse the Bois de Boulogne during the day (take Bus 244 from Porte Maillot), but the Bois becomes a distinctly adult playground after dark, when male, female, and everything-in-between prostitutes come prowling for clients. Even in daylight, the Bois's most heavily wooded paths are best avoided by women walking solo. Use your spider senses. ⊠ *Main entrance at bot-*

tom of av. Foch, Bois de Boulogne Ⓜ *Porte Maillot, Porte Dauphine, Porte d'Auteuil; Bus 244.*

❻ Castel-Béranger. Dreamed up in 1898 by Hector Guimard, this building is considered the city's first Art Nouveau structure. The apartments attracted creative tenants including Postimpressionist Paul Signac, who encouraged friends to visit his "amusing" new home with the very latest accoutrement—the telephone. Guimard, only 28 at the time of construction, kept his office on the ground floor at the corner facing into the alley (some wall details are still visible). The wild combination of materials and the grimacing grillwork led neighbors to call this the Castle Dérangé (Deranged). But this private commission catapulted Guimard into the public eye, leading to his famous métro commission. After admiring the sea-inspired front entrance, go partway down the alley to admire the inventive treatment of the traditional Parisian courtyard, complete with a melting water fountain. You can see Guimard's evolution by walking to the subtler Agar complex at the end of the block (at the corner of rue Lafontaine and rue Gros). Tucked beside the stone entrance at the corner of rue Gros is a tiny café-bar with an Art Nouveau glass front and furnishings. ⊠ *14 rue la Fontaine, Passy-Auteuil* Ⓜ *Ranelagh; RER: Maison de Radio France.*

need a break? It seats just 15, but the **Café-Bar Antoine** (⊠ 17 rue la Fontaine, Passy-Auteuil ☎ 01–40–50–14–30) warrants a visit for its Art Nouveau facade, floor tiles, and carved wooden bar. Count on €32 for a meal or stick to a snack and coffee.

❶ Cimetière de Passy (Passy Cemetery). Perched on a spur above place du Trocadéro in the shadow of the Tour Eiffel, this cemetery was opened in 1820 when Passy was a country village. Its handsome entrance—two sturdy pavilions linked by a colonnade—is a 1930s Art Deco cousin to the nearby Palais de Chaillot. Precocious painter-poetess Marie Baskirtseff's tomb, with its pinnacles and stone Byzantine dome, dominates the cemetery. Just left of the main crossroads is a weathered bust of Impressionist Manet, buried with other members of his family, including his brother's wife, painter Berthe Morisot. Notice the poignant figure of a girl in a hat—calling to mind Zola's novel *Une Page d'Amour* (*Love Episode*), which ends with the burial of the young heroine Jeanne in Passy's cemetery, "alone, facing Paris, forever." Claude Debussy is also among the incumbents. ⊠ *Rue du Commandant-Schloesing, Trocadéro/Tour Eiffel* ☉ *Daily 9–8 or dusk* Ⓜ *Trocadéro.*

❾ Fondation Le Corbusier (Le Corbusier Foundation). The Villa Laroche is less of a museum in honor of Swiss architect Charles-Edouard Jeanneret, better known as Le Corbusier (1887–1965), than a well-preserved 1923 example of his innovative construction techniques, based on geometric forms, recherché color schemes, and unblushing recourse to iron and concrete. The sloping ramp that replaces the traditional staircase is one of the most eye-catching features. ⊠ *10 sq. du Dr-Blanche, Passy-Auteuil* ☎ 01–42–88–41–53 ⊕ *www.fondationlecorbusier.asso.fr* 🗃 €1.50 ☉ *Tues.–Fri. 10–12:30 and 1:30–6, Mon. 1:30–6* Ⓜ *Jasmin.*

❼ Hôtel Mezzara. With its sumptuous wrought-iron staircase, Art Nouveau windows, and plaster molding, this Hector Guimard mansion built in 1911 as a workshop for textile designer Paul Mezzara has one of the finest 20th-century interiors in Paris. Unfortunately, it is only open during rare exhibitions. ⊠ *60 rue la Fontaine, Passy-Auteuil* ☎ *01-45-27-02-29* Ⓜ *Jasmin.*

❂ ❶ Jardin d'Acclimatation. At this children's amusement park on the northern edge of the Bois de Boulogne you can see a mix of exotic and familiar animals, take a boat trip along an "enchanted river," ride a miniature railway, and enjoy various fairground booths that keep young and old entertained. The zoo and amusement park can be reached via the miniature railway that runs from Porte Maillot on Wednesday and weekends beginning at 1:30; tickets cost €1. Many of the attractions have separate entry fees (except the zoo, which is spread throughout the park), notably the child-oriented art museum and workshop center, the **Musée en Herbe** (literally, Museum in the Grass); admission is €3. ⊠ *Bd. des Sablons, Bois de Boulogne* ☎ *01-40-67-90-82* 🎟 *€2.50, workshops €4.50* ☉ *July–Aug. daily 10–7; Sept.–June daily 10–6* Ⓜ *Les Sablons.*

❹ Maison de Balzac (Balzac's House). The Paris home of the great French 19th-century novelist Honoré de Balzac (1799–1850) contains exhibits charting his tempestuous yet prolific life (he was the author of nearly 100 novels and stories known collectively as *The Human Comedy*, many of them set in Paris). You can still feel his larger-than-life presence in his writing study and pay homage to his favorite coffeepot—his weird working hours may have had more than a little to do with his tremendous consumption of the "black ink." There's some English-language information available. ⊠ *47 rue Raynouard, Passy-Auteuil* ☎ *01-55-74-41-80* ⊕ *www.paris.fr/musees/* 🎟 *Free* ☉ *Tues.–Sun. 10–5:40* Ⓜ *Passy.*

❺ Maison de Radio France. Headquarters to France's state radio, this monstrous circular building was completed in 1962. More than 500 yards in circumference, it's said to have more floor space than any other building in France. Its 200-foot tower overlooks the Seine. You can explore the foyer, obtain tickets to attend recordings, or join a guided tour (in French) of the studios and the museum, with its notable collection of old radios. ⊠ *116 av. du Président-Kennedy, Passy-Auteuil* ☎ *01-56-40-15-16* ⊕ *www.radiofrance.fr* 🎟 *Guided tours (at half past the hr) €5* ☉ *Tours weekdays 10:30–11:30 and 2:30–4:30* Ⓜ *Ranelagh; RER: Maison de Radio France.*

★ ❿ Musée Marmottan–Claude Monet. One of the most underestimated museums in town, the Marmottan is Paris's "other" Impressionist museum (after the Musée d'Orsay). A few years ago this elegant 19th-century mansion tacked CLAUDE MONET onto its official name—and justly so, as this may be the best collection of the artist's works anywhere. Monet occupies a specially built basement gallery, where you'll find such captivating works as the *Cathédrale de Rouen* series (1892–96) and *Impression: Soleil Levant* (*Impression–Sunrise,* 1872), the work that helped give the Impressionist movement its name. Other exhibits include letters exchanged by Impressionist painters Berthe Morisot and Mary Cassatt. There's a roomful of priceless illuminated medieval manuscripts on the ground floor. Empire furniture makes you feel as if you're at an actual Napoleonic salon, with comfortable couches and windows overlooking the Jardin de Ranelagh on one side and the hotel's private yard on the other. To best understand the work's context, buy an English-language catalog in the museum shop on your way in. ⊠ *2 rue Louis-Boilly, Passy-Auteuil* ☎ *01–44–96–50–33* ⊕ *www.marmottan.com* ⊠ *€6.50* ⊙ *Tues.–Sun. 10–6* Ⓜ *La Muette.*

🐣 ⑭ **Musée National des Arts et Traditions Populaires** (National Museum of Folk Arts and Traditions). In a nondescript modern building next to the Jardin d'Acclimatation, this museum of folk arts and traditions displays an impressive variety of artifacts, from beautifully carved marionettes to 18th-century waffle irons. Many exhibits have buttons to press and knobs to twirl; however, there are no descriptions in English. The museum is a favorite destination for school field trips, so avoid weekday afternoons. ⊠ *6 av. du Mahatma-Gandhi, Bois de Boulogne* ☎ *01–44–17–60–00* ⊕ *www.culture.gouv.fr/culture/atp/mnatp* ⊠ *€2.60* ⊙ *Wed.–Mon. 9:45–5:15* Ⓜ *Les Sablons.*

❷ **Musée du Vin** (Wine Museum). In the vaulted 15th-century cellars of a former abbey, this small museum is devoted to traditional wine-making artifacts. Wax figures depict historical scenes and there's an authentically musty underground smell. The visit includes a wine tasting (often the musée's own rough Gaillac) at the museum's restaurant. There's an English brochure available. ⊠ *5 sq. Charles-Dickens, Passy-Auteuil* ☎ *01–45–25–63–26* ⊠ *€6* ⊙ *Tues.–Sun. 10–6* Ⓜ *Passy.*

⑬ **Parc de Bagatelle.** This beautiful floral garden counts irises, roses, tulips, and water lilies among its showstoppers; it is at its most colorful between April and June. Peacocks pick their way across velvety green lawns, while the bijou château (only open when hosting exhibitions) is fronted by a terrace with attractive views of the Seine. The white-wall château was built by the Comte d'Artois in 1777 on a bet with Marie-Antoinette that it could be finished within two months; 900 construction workers toiled day and night (by torchlight) to make it happen. ⊠ *Rte. de Sèvres-à-Neuilly or rte. des Lacs-à-Bagatelle, Bois de Boulogne* ☎ *01–40–67–97–00* ⊠ *Gardens €1.50, château entrance according to exhibition* ⊙ *Daily 9–dusk* Ⓜ *Pont de Neuilly.*

⑫ **Pré Catalan.** This garden in the Bois de Boulogne contains one of Paris's largest trees: a copper beech more than 200 years old. The **Jardin Shakespeare** on the west side has a sampling of the flowers, herbs, and trees mentioned in Shakespeare's plays. The master gardeners here are only too happy to share rare cuttings and planting secrets. The nearby restaurant Le Pré Catalan, where *le tout Paris* of the Belle Époque used to dine on its elegant terrace, still lures fashionable diners, especially on weekends. ⊠ *Rte. de la Grande-Cascade, Bois de Boulogne* ⊠ *Pré Catalan free, Shakespeare Garden €1* ⊙ *Pré Catalan daily 8–dusk. Shakespeare Garden spring–fall* Ⓜ *Porte Dauphine.*

8 **Rue d'Auteuil.** This narrow, crooked shopping street escaped Hauss-mann's urban renovations; it retains the country feel of Auteuil. Molière once lived on the site of No. 2; Racine was on nearby rue du Buis; the pair met up to clink glasses and exchange drama notes at the Mouton Blanc Inn, now a brasserie, at No. 40. Nos. 19–25 and 29 are an in-teresting combination of 17th- and 18th-century buildings, which have evolved into a mixture of private housing and shop fronts. At the foot of the street, the scaly dome of the **Église d'Auteuil** (built in the 1880s) is an unmistakable small-time cousin of the Sacré-Coeur. Rue d'Auteuil is at its liveliest on Wednesday and Saturday mornings, when a much-loved street market crams onto place Jean-Barraud. Ⓜ *Michel-Ange Auteuil, Église d'Auteuil.*

off the beaten path

MUSÉE NATIONAL DE LA CÉRAMIQUE – Hundreds of the finest creations of the world-famous Sèvres porcelain works are displayed at the National Ceramics Museum, at the southern end of the wooded Parc de St-Cloud. You can get here by taking the métro from the Michel-Ange Auteuil station on the rue d'Auteuil. Labels are only in French. ✉ *Pl. de la Manufacture, Sèvres* ☎ *01–41–14–04–20* ⊕ *www.museums-of-paris.com* ✉ *€5* ⊗ *Wed.–Mon. 10–5* Ⓜ *Pont de Sèvres.*

SERRES D'AUTEUIL – Tropical and exotic plants sweat it out in mighty hothouses just off place de la Porte-d'Auteuil, on the southern fringe of the Bois de Boulogne. A bewildering efflorescence of plants and flowers is grown here for use in Paris's municipal parks and for displays on official occasions. The surrounding gardens' leafy paths and well-tended lawns offer cooler places to admire floral virtuosity. ✉ *3 av. de la Porte-d'Auteuil, Bois de Boulogne* ☎ *01–40–71–74–00* ✉ *€1* ⊗ *Daily 9–dusk* Ⓜ *Porte d'Auteuil.*

9 **Statue of Liberty.** Just in case you'd forgotten that the enduring symbol of the American dream is actually French, a reduced version of Frédéric-Auguste Bartholdi's figure brandishes her torch at the southern tip of the Allée des Cygnes. To Bartholdi's dismay, she originally faced the city and was only turned around to gaze across the waters of the Seine in 1937. To see her best, take a boat tour, which makes an obliging U-turn right in front. The original statue—the one that lifts her lamp in New York City's harbor—is known in French as *La Liberté Éclairant le Monde* (*Liberty Lighting Up the World*). It was made in Paris in 1886 with the help of a giant steel framework designed by Gustave Eiffel. ✉ *Allée des Cygnes, Passy-Auteuil* Ⓜ *Javel; RER: Maison de Radio France.*

OFF THE BEATEN TRACK

If you're in search of wide-open green spaces, skyscrapers, the church where Gothic architecture made its first appearance, or great art deco architecture, make brief excursions to the city's peripheries.

What to See

★ **Basilique de St-Denis.** Built between 1136 and 1286, the St. Denis basilica is in some ways the most important Gothic church in the Paris region. It was here, under dynamic prelate Abbé Suger, that Gothic architecture (typified by pointed arches and rib vaults) arguably made its first appearance. The kings of France soon chose St-Denis as their final resting place, and their richly sculpted tombs—along with what remains of Suger's church—can be seen in the choir area at the east end of the church. The basilica was battered during the Revolution; afterward, Louis XVIII reestablished it as the royal burial site by moving the remains of Louis XVI and Marie-Antoinette here to join centuries' worth of monarchial bones. The vast 13th-century nave is a brilliant example of structural logic; its columns, capitals, and vault are a model of architectural harmony. The facade, retaining the rounded arches of the Romanesque that preceded the Gothic style, is set off by a small rose window, reputedly the earliest in France. You can also check out the extensive archaeological finds, such as a Merovingian queen's grave goods; there's information in English. ⊠ *1 rue de la Légion d'Honneur, St-Denis* ☎ *01–48–09–83–54* ⊠ *Choir and tombs €6.10* ⊙ *Easter–Sept., Mon.–Sat. 10–6:30, Sun. noon–6; Oct.–Easter, Mon.–Sat. 10–4:30, Sun. noon–4:30. Guided tours daily at 11:15 and 3* Ⓜ *St-Denis Basilique.*

La Défense. First conceived in 1958, this modernist suburb just west of Paris was inspired by Le Corbusier's dream of high-rise buildings, pedestrian walkways, and sunken vehicle circulation. An experiment to keep high-rises out of the historic downtown, this Parisian business hub has survived economic uncertainty to become a surprising success. Visiting La Défense gives you a crash course in contemporary skyscraper evolution, from solid blocks of the 1960s and '70s to the curvy fins of the '90s and beyond. (Office architecture shifted to the thin tower partly because of employees' dislike of the open plan block: the newer slim towers mean more people have their own window.) Today, 20,000 people live in this suburb but 150,000 people work here. While riding the métro Line 1 here, you'll get a view of the Seine, then emerge at a pedestrian plaza studded with some great public art, including César's giant thumb and one of Calder's great red "Stabile"s. The **Grande Arche de La Défense** dominates the area; it was designed as a controversial closure to the historic axis of Paris (an imaginary line that runs through the Arc de Triomphe, the Arc du Carrousel, and the Louvre glass pyramid). Glass bubble elevators whisk you 360 feet to the viewing platform; if you prefer to stay on the ground, you can catch a half-hour (€5.50) minitrain tour of La Défense (March–November, daily 11–5, departure in front of the Arche). ⊠ *Parvis de La Défense, La Défense* ☎ *01–49–07–27–57* ⊕ *www.grandearche.com* ⊠ *Grande Arche: €7.50* ⊙ *Daily 10–7* Ⓜ *Métro or RER: Grande Arche de La Défense.*

Ⓒ **Parc André-Citroën** (Andre-Citroën Park). This innovative and lovely park in southwest Paris was built on the site of the former Citroën automobile factory. Now it has lawns, Japanese rock gardens, rambling wildflowers, and elegant greenhouses full of exotic plants and flowers, not to mention a delightful computer-programmed "dancing fountain."

There's also **Le Ballon Eutelsat** (☎ 01–44–26–20–00), the largest outdoor balloon in the world. The balloon's attached to the ground by sturdy cables and climbs up to 450 feet high to give you one of the most spectacular (and perfectly silent) views of the city; the ride costs €10. Be sure to call to check the weather in advance; the balloon usually goes up from 1 to 5 but if it's too windy, it's grounded. ⊠ *Entrances on rue St-Charles and rue de la Montagne de l'Esperou, Passy-Auteuil* ⊙ *Weekdays 8–dusk, weekends 9–dusk* Ⓜ *Métro or RER: Javel.*

Parc Montsouris and Cité Universitaire (Montsouris Park and University City). This picturesque park, the last of Haussmann's green spaces, and the university "city," or campus, are in the residential 14e arrondissement, south of Montparnasse. Parc Montsouris has cascades, a lake, and a meteorological observatory disguised as a Tunisian palace. The Cité Universitaire, opposite Parc Montsouris and next to the futuristic Stade Charléty athletics stadium, houses 5,000 international students in buildings that date mainly from the 1930s and reflect the architecture of different countries. Le Corbusier designed the Swiss and Brazilian houses; John D. Rockefeller funded the Maison Internationale; and the Sacré-Coeur church recalls the simple, muscular confidence of buildings erected in Mussolini's Italy. ⊠ *Parc Montsouris: entrances on av. Reille, bd. Jourdan, and rue Gazan; Cité Universitaire: entrance at 19 bd. Jourdan, Montparnasse* ☎ *01–44–16–64–00 Cité Universitaire information* Ⓜ *RER: Cité Universitaire.*

Parcours des Années Trente and Musée des Années 30 (1930s Trail and 1930s Museum). For a look at outstanding Art Deco buildings by such architects as Le Corbusier, Auguste Perret, Raymond Fisher, and Robert Mallet-Stevens, follow this 1930s trail in the suburb of **Boulogne-Billancourt.** The route is outlined in an illustrated booklet (in French only) available at the magnificent Hôtel de Ville (av. André-Morizet), built by Tony Garnier in 1934. It's worth talking to the helpful staff inside the impressive lobby, towards the back of the main floor. More Art Deco is to be found at the Musée des Années 30, near the Hôtel de Ville. This museum has a wealth of beautifully presented paintings and sculpture produced in France during the interwar period. There's also an intriguing section on "colonial art," which teeters between the naive and the patronizing. ⊠ *28 av. André-Morizet, Boulogne-Billancourt* ☎ *01–55–18–46–42* ⊠ *€4.10* ⊙ *Tues.–Sun. 11–6* Ⓜ *Marcel-Sembat.*

Where to Eat

WORD OF MOUTH

"On our day of arrival, it was raining and cold. While getting our bearings we stopped at that crepe stand. Stood under our umbrellas, lapping up every dripping, hot morsel. It still ranks up there with other 'best meals.' "

—JeanneB

"[She] strolled around St-Germain-des-Prés, returning with a treasure trove of goodies. *Food!* Lovely French food. She had purchased a cheese tray. . . . We had Fourme d'Ambert, a blue, Livarot, a firm cheese with a creamy yellow color . . . and Comté, which was hard and nutty. All were delicious. We sipped a glass of wine and rounded off our cocktail hour with delicate, delectable *macarons* from Ladurée."

—din

Revised and
updated by
Rosa Jackson

PARIS HAS WORKS OF ART OF VARIED KINDS. Some hang on the walls of the Louvre. Some smile up at you from a plate. Anyone who has ordered a dessert at Le Cinq and received a concoction that looks like a hat styled by Christian Lacroix knows that in Paris food is far more than fuel. The French regard gastronomy as essential to the art of living, the art of transforming the gross and humdrum aspects of existence into something witty, charming, gracious, and satisfying. Above all, Parisians believe that every meal is, if not a complete way of life, certainly an event that demands undivided attention. Happily, the city's chefs exist principally to please its citizens on that score, so it is no surprise that Paris is also a place where you come to experience full gastronomic rapture.

Even though a widely heralded improvement in the restaurants of cities from Boston to Brisbane has narrowed the gap that once made Paris nonpareil, no other metropolis in the world has yet developed a food sensibility as refined, reasoned, and deeply rooted as that clinging to the French capital. The edible genius of haute-cuisine wizards Eric Frechon, Alain Ducasse, and Pierre Gagnaire can easily reduce you to a pleasurable stupor. For a change of pace you can always slip away to a casual little place for an earthy, bubbling cassoulet; make a midnight feast of the world's silkiest oysters; or even opt out of Gaul altogether for superb paella, couscous, or an herb-bright Vietnamese stir-fry. Once you know where to go (and this is crucial), Paris is a city where perfection awaits at all stations of the food chain.

The biggest recent development is a recognition that not everyone wants a three-course blowout every time they go to a restaurant. Meals have long followed a predictable entrée-*plat*-dessert pattern. This is changing, however, thanks to pioneering chefs such as Joël Robuchon. In his Atelier, the man once voted "chef of the 20th century" encourages dining on small or larger portions, according to your appetite. His opening hours even suggest that it's OK to graze outside traditional mealtimes—*une révolution*. (His latest restaurant, La Table de Joël Robuchon, retains the "small plates" concept but accepts reservations.) Taking a similar approach are Hélène Darroze, whose modern bistro annex serves tapas-style portions, and Alain Dutournier of Pinxo, who has actually persuaded Parisians to eat with their fingers and steal food off their companions' plates.

Chefs are also developing a freer hand with spices, thanks to their experiences abroad and the changing tastes of their followers. One of the first to successfully incorporate spices into French cuisine without falling into fusion follies was Pascal Barbot at L'Astrance. During a stint in Australia, Barbot learned to juggle Asian flavors; then he honed his French technique at L'Arpège and the result is some of the most elegant and original food in Paris. Working in a more casual register, Philippe Delacourcelle has made Le Pré Verre one of the city's most fascinating bistros, thanks to his adventurous use of spices (inspired by his years in Asia) and a lively setting that feeds on the many affordable wines. At Ze Kitchen Galerie, chef William Ledeuil puts the emphasis on presentation, drawing on ingredients from Chinatown and Middle Eastern grocery stores. Equally creative is Flora Mikula, who at her classy restaurant,

Flora, serves Mediterranean cooking with the occasional Asian twist. More recently, chef Michel Troisgros—of the famed eponymous Roanne restaurant—has created an innovative new menu for the bijou Hotel Lancaster, introducing such bold fare as frogs' legs with tamarind.

Even as their palates grow more adventurous, however, the French are re-embracing *terroir*. Nothing illustrates this better than the purchase of the turn-of-the-century bistro Aux Lyonnais by Alain Ducasse, founder of the Spoon, Food & Wine fusion chain. Never one to miss a trend, Ducasse knows that Parisians will always love regional food when it is prepared with care and served in a gorgeous setting. Another success has been the takeover of the long-established Basque restaurant L'Ami Jean by Stephane Jégo, who kept the Basque classics on the menu but also brought a southwestern France–inspired touch to his own inventions—sprinkling scallops in their shells, for instance, with sharp ewe's-milk cheese. Taking this trend to its extreme is a new breed of restaurant specializing in a single ingredient: the tomato (at Rouge Tomate) or the apple (at Pomze), to name just two.

The bistro boom is so big, in fact, that it has now invaded the haunts of haute cuisine. Even the most luxurious kitchens are getting back to the bedrock of French culinary traditions—a.k.a. The Patrimony. Don't, therefore, be surprised to find *grandmère*'s lamb with white beans on the *carte* at the superexpensive Le Bristol. Yet something else is going on: chefs, even at the highest level, no longer fear playfulness. Jean-François Piège, chef at Le Crillon, says he is proud to belong to "the first generation that grew up with the Carambar (a chewy caramel candy) and the Tagada (a pink sugar-coated marshmallow)." His wild strawberry-and-rose ice cream comes topped with a whimsical hat of cotton candy.

The French press often bandies about the term *le fooding*, a contraction of "food" and "feeling." Its meaning remains vague but connotes such unusual restaurant trends and culinary events as top chefs serving soups to the masses at open-air markets, a picnic at the Palais de Tokyo, and annual *fooding* awards. They promote the idea that it's time for the French to relax their occasionally rigid dining mores—by eating outside traditional mealtimes, for instance, or grazing through tapas-style menus.

If what interests you is not le fooding but rather a good feed amid entertaining surroundings, visit at least one traditional, established brasserie. Though the Flo group, run by brasserie maestro Jean-Paul Bucher, and the similarly ambitious Frères Blanc have been criticized for their sometimes heavy-handed restorations, their big, buzzy dining rooms still provide exceptional people-watching—a mix of multigenerational French families, jet-lagged tourists, moon-eyed couples and, yes, even occasional intellectuals. Though the food in these standbys makes no bold gastronomic claims, there is usually plenty on the menu to please everyone (kids included), from gargantuan seafood platters to a simple steak-frites.

One trend not worth celebrating is higher prices. Since the French bade farewell to the franc in 2002 the bargain meal has become increasingly elusive. Restaurateurs seized the opportunity to bump up their prices, and today a puny bottle of mineral water can easily set you back five

2

Mealtimes

Generally Paris restaurants are open from noon to about 2 and from 7:30 or 8 to about 11. Brasseries have longer hours and often serve all day and late into the evening; some are open 24 hours. The iconoclastic wine bars pretty much do as they wish, frequently serving hot food only through lunch, then cold assortments of charcuterie and cheese until a late-afternoon or early-evening close.

Cafés are the best breakfast option—most Parisians content themselves with a tartine (baguette slathered with butter), but a basket of croissants and pains au chocolat usually sits invitingly on the counter, and you pay for what you eat (they can also be served at the table, often as part of a *formule* that includes orange juice and coffee). Brasseries generally serve breakfast, though usually nothing elaborate. The hip Belgian chain Le Pain Quotidien (*see* Refueling) is more imaginative, serving a variety of breads with mouthwatering spreads such as praline, plus egg dishes or yogurt if you want something more filling. If you have the means, you can always take the plunge on two soft-boiled eggs with caviar (€48) at Alain Ducasse au Plaza Athénée—luxury hotels are *the* places to indulge your breakfast fantasies.

Assume a restaurant is open every day unless otherwise indicated. Surprisingly, many restaurants close on Saturday as well as Sunday, and Monday closings are also frequent. July and August are the most common months for annual closings, but Paris in August is no longer the total culinary wasteland it used to be.

Menus

All establishments must post menus outside, so they're available for a look-over before you enter. Most restaurants have two basic types of menu: à la carte and fixed price (prix-fixe, *un menu,* or *la formule*). The prix-fixe menu is usually the best value, though choices are more limited. Most menus begin with a first course (*une entrée*), often subdivided into cold and hot starters, followed by fish and poultry, then meat; it's rare today that anyone orders something from all three. However, except for brasseries, wine bars, and other casual places it's usually inappropriate to order a single dish, as you'll understand when you see the waiter's expression. If you feel like indulging more than usual, the *menu dégustation* (tasting menu), consisting of numerous small courses, allows for a wide sampling of a chef's offerings. In general, consider the season when ordering; daily specials are usually based on what's freshest in the market that day.

See the Menu Guide at the back of the book for guidance with menu items that appear frequently on French menus and throughout the reviews that follow.

Prices

Since the advent of the euro, Paris restaurant prices have gone up to match those of other European capitals—only London and certain Italian cities remain consistently more expensive. You will be lucky to find a good bistro meal for €25 or less, even at lunch, so consider economizing on one meal to have more to spend on the other. You might try slurping inexpensive Japanese noodles on rue Ste-Anne or having a picnic in a park with fresh market ingredients. Many visitors rent apartments with kitchens, which allows them to eat in at least once a day and sample the city's wonderful groceries.

By French law prices must include tax and tip (*service compris* or *prix nets*), but pocket change left on the table in basic places, or an additional 5% in better restaurants, is always appreciated. Beware of bills stamped SERVICE NOT INCLUDED in English or restaurants slyly using American-style credit-card slips, hoping that you'll be confused and add the habitual 15% tip. In neither case should you tip beyond the guidelines suggested above.

WHAT IT COSTS IN EUROS					
	$$$$	**$$$**	**$$**	**$**	**¢**
AT DINNER	over €30	€23–€30	€17–€22	€11–€16	under €11

per person for a main course at dinner, including tax (19.6%) and service; note that if a restaurant offers only prix-fixe (set-price) meals, it has been given the price category that reflects the full prix-fixe price.

Reservations
In the restaurant reviews, reservations are mentioned only when they are essential (and when booking weeks or months in advance is necessary) or when they are not accepted. However, because restaurants are open for only a few hours for lunch and dinner and because meals are long affairs here, it's always wisest to make reservations. Here are a few key sentences, if needed, for booking: "*Bonjour madame/monsieur* (hello, ma'am/sir; say *bonsoir* after 6 PM). *Je voudrais faire une reservation pour* (I would like a reservation for) *un/une* (1)/*deux* (2)/*quatre* (4)/*six* (6) *personnes pour le diner* (persons for dinner)/*le déjeuner* (lunch) *aujourd'hui à X heures* (today at X o'clock)/*demain à X heures* (tomorrow at X o'clock)/*lundi* (Monday)/*mardi* (Tuesday)/*mercredi* (Wednesday)/*jeudi* (Thursday)/*vendredi* (Friday)/*samedi* (Saturday)/*dimanche* (Sunday) *à X heures* (at X time). *Le nom est* (your own name). *Merci bien.*" Note that most wine bars do not take reservations; reservations are also unnecessary for brasserie and café meals at odd hours.

Smoking
You can count on it: Parisians smoke before, during, and after meals. Restaurants are supposed to have no-smoking sections—if you want to sit in one, make this clear at the outset—though these areas are often limited to a very few tables where the no-smoking policy is not strictly monitored. A few places, most notably L'Atelier de Joël Robuchon, have forbidden smoking in the interests of their guests' palates.

What to Wear
Casual dress is acceptable at all but the fanciest restaurants. Be aware that in Paris, however, casual usually means stylish sportswear, which is often more dressed up than you may be used to. When in doubt, leave the blue jeans and sneakers behind and go for a sweater or button-down rather than a T-shirt. If an establishment requires jacket and tie, it is noted in the reviews.

Wine No matter what restaurant you're heading to, try to enjoy a taste of the grape along the way, whether *vin ordinaire* (table wine) or a Romanée-Conti. As the French say, a day without wine is like a day without sunshine. The wine that suits your meal is the wine you like. The traditional rule of white with fish and red with meat no longer applies. If the restaurant has a sommelier, let him (yes, it's usually a man) help you. *Pourriez-vous nous conseiller un vin?* (could you suggest a wine?) and *je vous fais confiance* (I put myself in your competent hands) are two polite ways to ask for advice. Most sommeliers are knowledgeable about their lists and will suggest what is appropriate after you've made your tastes and budget known. In addition to the wine list, informal restaurants will have a *vin maison* (house wine) that is less expensive. Simpler spots will have wines *en carafe* (in a carafe) or *en pichet* (in a pitcher). Many restaurants now sell wine by the glass, but beware the price—you might save money by ordering a bottle or half-bottle. If you'd like something before the meal, consider ordering your wine for the meal ahead of time, or sample a typical French aperitif, such as a *kir*, which is chilled white wine with black-currant liqueur.

---

euros, and finding a bottle of wine for under 15 euros can prove extremely challenging. With few exceptions, 30 euros is the minimum price for a three-course dinner, and with side dishes and drinks the bill often climbs over 100 euros for two people. This gives you all the more reason to plan carefully, so as to make the most of your budget. You might consider resisting aperitifs, which are often shockingly priced, and drink humble tap water instead. Increasingly, restaurants are offering wine by the glass, which can prove a better value than ordering an entire bottle. In another civilized development, many establishments will slip an unfinished bottle into a bag for you to take home. (Ask for a "wine bag" rather than a "doggy bag, " a term that makes the French cringe.)

If money is no object—or if you've saved your centimes for a once-in-a-lifetime meal—it's hard to go wrong at Taillevent, Lucas Carton, or Guy Savoy. If you relish the avant-garde don't miss the far-flung culinary acrobatics of Pierre Gagnaire, who is half mad scientist, half inspired artist. Budget-wise gourmands know that many of Paris's best restaurants have prix-fixe lunch menus that are dramatically more affordable (but much more limited) than ordering from their regular à la carte menus. You'll probably have to ask for the lunch menu for obvious reasons—most restaurants would prefer that you order à la carte. So watch out for that chilly look if you do pipe up and ask to see the prix-fixe lunch menu.

If you've come to Paris looking for a dose of elegance in an increasingly Gap-clad world, the revival of the dining rooms in the city's grande-dame hotels provides an ideal opportunity to show off new Diors and Chanels in truly gilded surroundings. Decor, of course, is not always the key to great food: some of the best bistros in Paris look downright simple, a kind of reverse *snobbisme*. For regal ambience but no demand to wear jacket and tie, don't forget the restaurants in some of the city museums, notably the Restaurant Musée d'Orsay (a gigantic Second Empire salon swimming in gilt, frescoes, chandeliers, and marble), the café at the Musée

Jacquemart-André (where else can you munch on salads beneath a Tiepolo ceiling?), and the Café Marly, set in the main courtyard of the Louvre (go for afternoon tea).

Included in this chapter are a wide range of restaurants and prices. More than half are in the 1ᵉʳ–8ᵉ arrondissements, within easy reach of hotels and sights; many others are in the 14ᵉ and 16ᵉ, also popular visitor areas; and some are in the 11ᵉ–20ᵉ, outlying, often residential neighborhoods where cheaper rents allow young chefs to strike out on their own. Recognizing that even in Paris you may not want to eat French food at every meal, other cuisines are also included. (One area worth exploring—especially at lunchtime—is Paris's Chinatown, in the 13ᵉ arrondissement; the main streets are avenue d'Ivry and avenue du Choisy.)

Restaurants by Arrondissement

1ᵉʳ Arrondissement (Louvre/Tuileries & Beaubourg/ Les Halles)

See Where to Eat on the Rive Droite: Île de la Cité to Montmartre map.

CONTEMPORARY ✕ **Pinxo.** The word *pinxo* means "to pinch, " which is how the food in
$–$$$ this fashionable hotel restaurant is designed to be eaten—often with your fingers and off your dining companion's plate. (Each dish is served in three portions to allow for sharing.) Alain Dutournier, who also runs the more formal Le Carré des Feuillants nearby, drew on his southwestern roots to create this welcoming modern spot in black, plum, and dark wood. Freed from the tyranny of the entrée-*plat*-dessert cycle, you can nibble your way through such mini-dishes as marinated herring with Granny Smith apple and horseradish, and squid cooked *à la plancha* (on a griddle) with ginger and chile peppers, then end, perhaps, with fresh pineapple and a piña colada sorbet. ⊠ *Hôtel Plaza Paris Vendôme, 9 rue d'Alger, Louvre/ Tuileries* ☎ *01–40–20–72–00* ▤ *AE, DC, MC, V* Ⓜ *Tuileries.*

FRENCH ✕ **Le Grand Véfour.** Victor Hugo could stride in and still recognize this
★ $$$$ place—in his day, as now, a contender for the title of most beautiful restaurant in Paris. Originally built in 1784, set in the arcades of the Palais-Royal, it has welcomed everyone from Napoléon to Colette to Jean Cocteau—nearly every seat bears a plaque commemorating a famous patron. The mirrored ceiling and early-19th-century glass paintings of goddesses and muses create an air of restrained seduction. Foodies as well as the fashionable gather here to enjoy chef Guy Martin's unique blend of sophistication and rusticity. He hails from Savoie, so you'll find lake fish and mountain cheeses on the menu alongside such luxurious dishes as foie gras–stuffed ravioli in a truffle-cream emulsion. For dessert try the house specialty, *palet aux noisettes* (meringue cake with milk-chocolate mousse, hazelnuts, and caramel ice cream). ⊠ *17 rue Beaujolais, Louvre/Tuileries* ☎ *01–42–96–56–27* ⌔ *Reservations essential* 🏛 *Jacket and tie* ▤ *AE, DC, MC, V* ☺ *Closed weekends and Aug. No dinner Fri.* Ⓜ *Palais-Royal.*

★ $$–$$$$ ✕ **Restaurant du Palais-Royal.** This stylish modern bistro decorated in jewel tones serves food to match its stunning location under the arcades of the Palais-Royal, looking onto the magnificent symmetrical gardens. Sole,

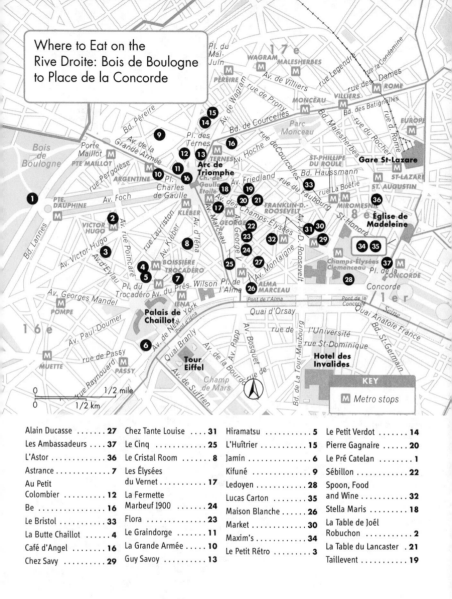

Where to Eat on the
Rive Droite: Bois de Boulogne
to Place de la Concorde

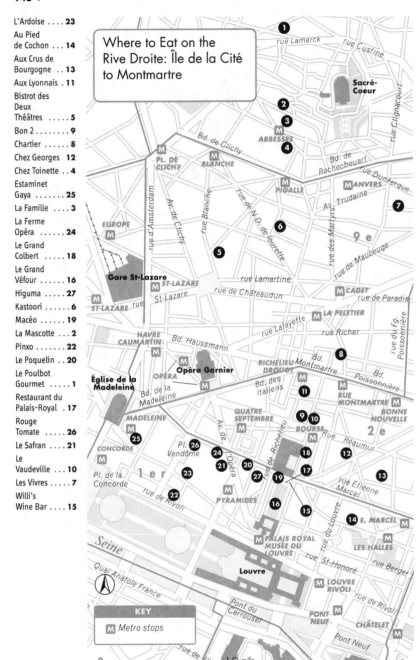

Where to Eat on the
Rive Droite: Île de la Cité
to Montmartre

KEY

Ⓜ *Metro stops*

scallops, and risotto—including a dramatic squid-ink and lobster version—are beautifully prepared, but juicy steak with *pommes Pont Neuf* (thick-cut frites) is also a favorite of the expense-account lunchers who love this place. Finish up with an airy mille-feuille that changes with the seasons—berries in summer, chestnuts in winter. Be sure to book in advance, especially in summer, when the terrace tables are hotly sought after. ⊠ *Jardins du Palais-Royal, 110 Galerie Valois, Louvre/Tuileries* ☎ *01–40–20–00–27* ⊟ *AE, DC, MC, V* ⊗ *Closed weekends Oct.–Apr., Sun. in summer, 4 wks between Dec. and Jan.* Ⓜ *Palais-Royal.*

$$$ ✕ **Macéo.** Natural light streams through both sides of this restaurant, while a broad, curved staircase leads to a spacious upstairs salon. With its reasonably priced set menus ranging from €29 to €38, this is an ideal spot for a relaxed meal after a day at the Louvre. It's also a hit with vegetarians, as chef Jean Paul Deyries whips up a meatless set menu with two starter and three main course options—perhaps a Moroccan-style vegetable *pastilla* (phyllo-dough pie) to start, followed by a crêpe filled with wild mushrooms and served with roasted endive (though his efforts can be a little hit-or-miss). Meat lovers might sink their teeth into Lozère lamb with herb tabbouleh and mango. The wine list spotlights little-known producers alongside the big names—as befits this sister restaurant to Willi's Wine Bar. ⊠ *15 rue des Petits-Champs, Louvre/Tuileries* ☎ *01–42–97–53–85* ⊟ *MC, V* ⊗ *Closed Sun. No lunch Sat.* Ⓜ *Palais-Royal.*

$$–$$$ ✕ **Le Poquelin.** The theaterlike setting—burgundy velvet curtains, framed photos of Molière plays—gives this little restaurant a look that's both elegant and low-key. Owners Maggie and Michel Guillaumin, whose son Benoît now runs the kitchen, serve classic French cooking with a daring twist; look for braised pork cheek on a Szechuan pepper *sablé* (shortcrust pastry) with apple sauce and pickled onions, or sea bream with vanilla-flavored honey sauce and fennel with mint and olive oil. The popular, regularly changing *menu Molière* is excellent value at €35, offering a choice of six starters, six mains (three meat and three fish), and six desserts. Wines are well chosen and fairly priced, and the house foie gras is available in jars to take home. ⊠ *17 rue Molière, Louvre/Tuileries* ☎ *01–42–96–22–19* ⊟ *AE, DC, MC, V* ⊗ *Closed Sun. No lunch Mon. and Sat.* Ⓜ *Palais-Royal.*

$–$$$ ✕ **Au Pied de Cochon.** One of the few remnants of this neighborhood's raucous all-night past—Les Halles was the city's wholesale market until the late 1960s—this brasserie still draws both a French and foreign crowd with its round-the-clock hours and trademark traditional fare, such as breaded pigs' trotters and cheese-crusted onion soup. Neither of these choices makes for a light meal, but it's perfect rib-sticking fare for a winter's day or to finish off a bar crawl. The dining room, with its white tablecloths and little piggy details, feels resolutely cheerful. ⊠ *6 rue Coquillière, Beaubourg/Les Halles* ☎ *01–40–13–77–00* ⊟ *AE, DC, MC, V* Ⓜ *Les Halles.*

$$ ✕ **L'Ardoise.** This minuscule storefront painted white and decorated
Fodor$Choice with enlargements of old sepia postcards of Paris is the very model of
★ the contemporary bistros making waves in Paris. Chef Pierre Jay's first-rate three-course menu for €31 tempts with such original dishes as scallops panfried with oyster mushrooms and a langoustine risotto (you can

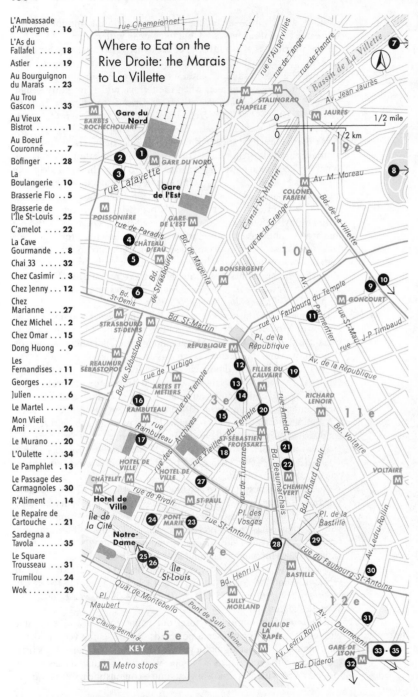

Where to Eat on the
Rive Droite: the Marais
to La Villette

1/2 mile

1/2 km

KEY

Ⓜ *Metro stops*

also order à la carte, but it's less of a bargain). Just as enticing are the desserts, such as a superb *feuillantine au citron*—caramelized pastry leaves filled with lemon cream and lemon slices—and a boozy baba au rhum. With friendly waiters, service all weekend, and a small but well-chosen wine list, L'Ardoise would be perfect if it weren't often crowded and noisy. ⊠ *28 rue du Mont Thabor, Beaubourg/Les Halles* ☎ *01–42–96–28–18* ▭ *MC, V* ⊗ *Closed Mon., Aug., 1 wk at Christmas, 1 wk in May* Ⓜ *Concorde.*

$ ✕ **Rouge Tomate.** The name of this epicerie-restaurant is misleading, since not all the tomatoes served here are red—the shop specializes in little-known varieties sourced mostly in France, with green, yellow, and striped varieties on display in summer. Off-season, rather than rely on pallid imports, the cook uses homemade preserves (jars of tomato sauces and jams are sold in the shop). The airy space feels like a coffee shop and adjoins a quiet terrace. Enjoy such reasonably priced dishes as goat cheese-and-tomato terrine with tomato confit, tagliatelle with yellow-tomato sauce, chicken and cumin, and chocolate fondant with tomato-orange confit. ⊠ *34 place du Marché St-Honoré, Louvre/Tuileries* ☎ *01–42–61–16–09* ▭ *AE, MC, V* Ⓜ *Tuileries, Pyramides.*

$ ✕ **Le Safran.** Passionate chef Caroll Sinclair works almost exclusively with organic produce, and her small menu changes according to what she finds in the market—a tomato-and-feta mille-feuille, lamb cooked for seven hours, and meaty tuna cooked rare and topped with melting foie gras are some signature dishes. Put yourself in her capable hands by asking for a *menu surprise* (€39), or opt for the vegetarian prix-fixe (€24). On a busy night the small kitchen can get overwhelmed, so be prepared for a slow-food experience. And be sure to clean your plate, or you will have to answer to the attentive chef (and her enormous but very gentle black dog). ⊠ *29 rue d'Argenteuil, Louvre/Tuileries* ☎ *01–42–61–25–30* ▭ *MC, V* ⊗ *Closed Sun. No lunch Sat.* Ⓜ *Tuileries, Pyramides.*

$ ✕ **Willi's Wine Bar.** Don't be fooled by the name—this British-owned spot is no modest watering hole but rather a stylish haunt for Parisian and visiting gourmands, who might stop in for a glass of wine at the polished oak bar or settle into the beamed dining room. The selection of reinvented classic dishes changes daily to reflect the market's offerings, and might include panfried scallops with mushrooms, venison in wine sauce with roast pears and celery-root chips, and mango candied with orange and served with a vanilla cream. The extensive list of about 250 wines reflects co-owner Mark Williamson's passion for the Rhône Valley and Spanish sherries. ⊠ *13 rue des Petits-Champs, Louvre/Tuileries* ☎ *01–42–61–05–09* ▭ *MC, V* ⊗ *Closed Sun. and 2 wks in Aug.* Ⓜ *Bourse.*

JAPANESE ✕ **Higuma.** When it comes to steaming bowls of noodles, this no-frills ☺ ¢ dining room, divided into three sections, beats its many neighboring competitors. Behind the counter—an entertaining spot for solo diners, if you don't mind the fumes—cooks toil over giant flames, tossing strips of meat and quick-fried vegetables, then ladling noodles and broth into giant bowls. A choice of *formules* allows you to pair various soups with six delicious *gyoza* (pork-and-vegetable dumplings), and the stir-fried dishes are excellent, too. ⊠ *32 rue Ste-Anne, Pyramides* ☎ *01–47–03–38–59* ▭ *MC, V* Ⓜ *Pyramides.*

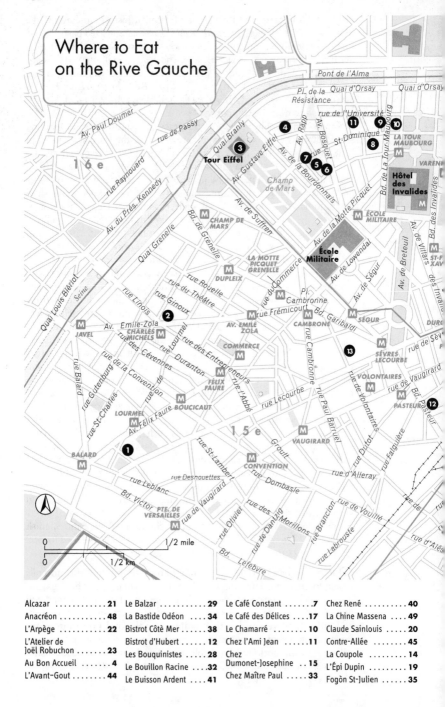

Where to Eat on the Rive Gauche

RESTAURANT TYPES

WHAT'S THE DIFFERENCE between a bistro and a brasserie? Can you order food at a café? Can you go to a restaurant just for a snack? The following definitions should help.

A **restaurant** traditionally serves a three-course meal (first, main, and dessert) at lunch and dinner. Although this category includes the most formal three-star establishments, it also applies to more casual neighborhood spots—the line can be fuzzy between bistros and restaurants. In general, restaurants are for when you want a complete meal and have the time to linger over it; don't expect to grab a quick snack. Hours are fairly consistent. This is the most expensive category and prices usually start at €30 per person without drinks—the sky's the limit at haute cuisine establishments.

It has been said that **bistros** served the world's first fast food. After the fall of Napoléon, the Russian soldiers who occupied Paris were known to bang on zinc-topped café bars, crying, bistro—Russian for "quickly." In the past bistros were simple places with minimal fixings and service. Although many nowadays are quite upscale, with beautiful interiors and chic clientele, most remain cozy establishments serving straightforward, frequently gutsy cooking, a wide variety of meats, and long-simmered dishes such as pot-au-feu and blanquette de veau (veal stew in white sauce). A bistro meal starts at €10 per person for a great-value lunch and can climb to €50 or more, depending on the setting and the quality of the food.

Brasseries—ideal places for quick meals—originated when Alsatians fleeing German occupiers after the Franco-Prussian War came to Paris and opened restaurants serving specialties from home. Pork-based dishes, choucroute (sauerkraut), and beer (brasserie also means brewery) were—and still are—mainstays here. The typical brasserie is convivial and keeps late hours. Some are open 24 hours a day—a good thing to know, since many restaurants stop serving at 10:30 PM. A main dish usually runs about €15–€18, or you can have a full meal for upwards of €35 per person, without drinks.

Like bistros and brasseries, **cafés** come in a confusing variety. Often informal neighborhood hangouts, cafés may also be veritable showplaces attracting well-heeled crowds. At most cafés regulars congregate at the bar, where coffee and drinks are cheaper than at tables. At lunch, tables are set, and a limited menu is served. Sandwiches, usually with jambon (ham), fromage (cheese, often Gruyère or Camembert), or mixte (ham and cheese), are served through the day, but beware—food and drinks can be surprisingly expensive (about €12 for a plat du jour, €4 for a half-bottle of mineral water). Cafés are for lingering, for people-watching, and for daydreaming; they are listed separately at the end of the chapter.

Wine bars, or bars à vins, are a newer phenomenon. These informal places often serve limited menus, perhaps no more than open-face sandwiches (tartines) and selections of cheeses and cold cuts (charcuterie). Owners concentrate on their wine lists, which often include less well-known regional selections, many available by the glass. Some wine bars are very upscale indeed, with full menus and costly wine lists. Still, most remain friendly and unassuming places for sampling wines you might otherwise never have a chance to try. They're listed separately at the end of this chapter. Expect to spend €15 to €40 per person for a meal, including drinks, at a wine bar.

2° Arrondissement (Opéra/Grands Boulevards)

See Where to Eat on the Rive Droite: Île de la Cité to Montmartre map.

CONTEMPORARY
$–$$$

✕ **Bon 2.** Designer Philippe Starck's second restaurant in the moneyed Bourse district proves that fashion restaurants can indeed be *très bon.* Here you'll find dressed-up bistro food with southern French touches, such as sea bream roasted with fennel and served with purple rice, and lamb with new potatoes and green olives. Even very simple dishes like roast chicken with frites are just as they should be. Only desserts from Ladurée, which taste of the fridge, disappoint. Bon 2 is less outlandish than Bon the first, but giant chandeliers and mismatched chairs set a distinctive tone. ✉ *2 rue du Quatre Septembre, Opéra/Grands Boulevards* ☎ *01–44–55–51–55* ▤ *AE, MC, V* ✆ *Closed Sun. No lunch Sat.* Ⓜ *Bourse.*

FRENCH
$$$

✕ **Chez Georges.** If you were to ask Parisian bankers, aristocrats, or antiques dealers to name their favorite bistro, many would choose Georges. The traditional fare, written in authentically hard-to-decipher handwriting, is good—chicken liver terrine, curly endive salad with bacon and a poached egg, steak with béarnaise—and the atmosphere is better. In the dining room a white-clothed stretch of tables lines the mirrored walls; attentive waiters sweep efficiently up and down its length. Order one of the wines indicated in colored ink on the menu and you can drink as much or as little of it as you want (and be charged accordingly); there's also a separate wine list that has grander bottles. ✉ *1 rue du Mail, Louvre/Tuileries* ☎ *01–42–60–07–11* ▤ *AE, DC, MC, V* ✆ *Closed Sun. and 3 wks in Aug.* Ⓜ *Sentier.*

$$–$$$
Fodor'sChoice
★

✕ **Aux Lyonnais.** For Alain Ducasse it's not enough to run some of the world's most expensive restaurants (in Paris, Monte Carlo, New York, and Las Vegas) and an ever-expanding string of Spoon, Food & Wine fusion bistros. He also has a passion for the old-fashioned bistro, so he has resurrected this 1890s gem by appointing a terrific young chef to oversee the short, frequently changing and reliably delicious menu of Lyonnais specialties. Dandelion salad with crisp potatoes, bacon, and silky poached egg, watercress soup poured over parsleyed frogs' legs, and a sophisticated rendition of coq au vin show he is no bistro dilettante. The decor hews to tradition too; there's a zinc bar, an antique coffee machine, and original turn-of-the-20th-century woodwork. ✉ *32 rue St-Marc, Opéra/Grands Boulevards* ☎ *01–42–96–65–04* ▤ *AE, MC, V* ✆ *Closed Sat.–Mon.* Ⓜ *Bourse.*

$–$$$

✕ **Aux Crus de Bourgogne.** This delightfully old-fashioned bistro with its bright lights and red-check tablecloths attracts a lively crowd. Open since 1905, it has been run by the same family since 1932. They made it popular by serving two luxury items—foie gras and cold lobster with homemade mayonnaise—at surprisingly accessible prices, a tradition that happily continues. Among the bistro classics on the seasonal menu are soul-warming dishes such as salmon fillet cooked with *fleur de sel* (the finest sea salt, unprocessed), and *coq au Brouilly,* rooster simmered in fruity wine. ✉ *3 rue Bachaumont, Beaubourg/Les Halles* ☎ *01–42–33–48–24* ▤ *AE, MC, V* ✆ *Closed weekends* Ⓜ *Sentier.*

$–$$$

✕ **Le Grand Colbert.** One of the few independently owned brasseries remaining in Paris, Le Grand Colbert, with its globe lamps and ceiling moldings, feels grand yet not overpolished—old theater posters still line the walls. It attracts a wonderfully Parisian mix of elderly lone diners, business lunchers, tourists, and couples who come for enormous seafood platters, duck foie gras with Sauternes jelly, and steak tartare. Whet your appetite with one of the "unjustly forgotten" aperitifs, such as bitter Salers or sweet Lillet Blanc. It's best to stick to classics, as these are what the kitchen does best. Finish with profiteroles (choux pastry filled with ice cream and smothered in hot chocolate sauce). ⊠ *2–4 rue Vivienne, Louvre/Tuileries* ☎ *01–42–86–87–88* ▭ *AE, DC, MC, V* Ⓜ *Bourse.*

\$–\$\$\$ ✕ **Le Vaudeville.** One of Jean-Paul Bucher's seven Flo brasseries, Le Vaudeville is filled with journalists, bankers, and locals *d'un certain âge* who come for its good-value assortment of prix-fixe menus and highly professional service. Shellfish, house-smoked salmon, and desserts such as profiteroles are particularly enticing. Enjoy the graceful 1920s decor—almost the entire interior of this intimate dining room is done in real or faux marble—and lively dining until 1 AM daily. ⊠ *29 rue Vivienne, Opéra/Grands Boulevards* ☎ *01–40–20–04–62* ▭ *AE, DC, MC, V* Ⓜ *Bourse.*

☾ ¢ ✕ **La Ferme Opéra.** If your arm is aching from trying to flag down café waiters, take a break in this bright, superfriendly self-service restaurant not far from the Louvre, specializing in produce from the Île-de-France region (around Paris). Inventive salads and sandwiches, quiches such as the three-cheese with pecan, hot dishes like chicken with dates and prunes served with polenta, and fruit crumbles, tarts, and cheesecakes taste impeccably fresh and delicious. There is an interesting selection of juices, and the barnlike dining room with its benches and square stools feels airy and relaxing (though one room is quite smoky). ⊠ *55–57 rue St-Roch, Opéra/Grands Boulevards* ☎ *01–46–33–35–36* ▭ *MC, V* Ⓜ *Pyramides.*

3ᵉ Arrondissement (Le Marais)

See Where to Eat on the Rive Droite: the Marais to La Villette map.

CONTEMPORARY ✕ **Le Murano.** If you love Baccarat's Cristal Room, you'll simply adore
\$\$\$–\$\$\$\$ the restaurant in the swank, new Murano Urban Resort in the achingly chic northern Marais. There is nothing subtle about the ostentation in this hip hotel's dining room, whose ceiling drips with white tubes of various lengths. Dress to the nines and arrive with plenty of attitude (or brace yourself with three test tubes of alcohol at the bar). The light, modern, Mediterranean-inspired food neither distracts nor offends—smoked salmon with too-pink *tarama* (cod roe), sautéed squid, waffle-style potato chips. If you can survive the sneering once-over at the door, surprisingly good-humored dining room staff add to the experience. ⊠ *13 bd. du Temple Le Marais* ☎ *01–42–71–20–00* ⌂ *Reservations essential* ▭ *AE, DC, MC, V* Ⓜ *Filles du Calvaire.*

FRENCH ✕ **Le Pamphlet.** Chef Alain Carrère's affordable and modern take on south-
★ **\$\$\$** western French cooking—which is somewhat at odds with the rather sedate, dressed-up dining room—has made this Marais bistro popular with gourmets, tourists, and arty types from the neighborhood's galleries. The market-driven prix-fixe daily menu runs from first courses such as a carpaccio of duck breast or cream of lentil soup to entrées such

as a juicy pork chop with béarnaise sauce and hand-cut frites. Finish up with a slice of tangy sheep's cheese or one of the comforting, calorific desserts. ✉ *38 rue Debelleyme, Le Marais* ☎ *01–42–72–39–24* ⚑ *Reservations essential* ▤ *MC, V* ☉ *Closed Sun. and 2 wks in Aug. No lunch Mon. or Sat.* Ⓜ *St-Sébastien Froissart.*

$–$$$ ✕ **Chez Jenny.** Part of the Frères Blanc group, this classic two-story brasserie is famed for its infectious buzz and outstanding choucroute, delivered weekly by a private supplier in Alsace and served with a panoply of charcuterie and an oversize grilled ham knuckle. If this sounds like too much meat, the seafood platters are reliably good, too. To finish, the perfectly aged Muenster cheese and homemade blueberry tart are fine choices. Staff in regional dress and woodwork by Charles Spindler add a charming Alsatian touch. Although reservations aren't required, prepare to stand in line without one. ✉ *39 bd. du Temple, République* ☎ *01–44–54–39–00* ▤ *AE, DC, MC, V* Ⓜ *République.*

★ $–$$ ✕ **L'Ambassade d'Auvergne.** A rare Parisian bistro that refuses to change (or raise its prices, thankfully), the Ambassade claims one of the city's great restaurant characters: the maître d', with his handlebar mustache and gravelly voice. Settle into the cast-in-amber dining room in this ancient Marais house to try dishes from the Auvergne, a region in central France. Lighter dishes are available, such as turbot with fennel, but it would be missing the point not to indulge in a heaping serving of lentils in goose fat with bacon or in Salers beef in red wine sauce with *aligot* (mashed potatoes with cheese). The Auvergnat wines come with appetizing descriptions, but don't expect anything remarkable from this (justifiably) little-known wine region. ✉ *22 rue du Grenier St-Lazare, Le Marais* ☎ *01–42–72–31–22* ▤ *AE, MC, V* ☉ *Closed Sun. mid-Jul–mid-Aug* Ⓜ *Rambuteau.*

$ ✕ **R'Aliment.** Combining fashion and virtue on a hip northern Marais street, R'Aliment is a modern, health-conscious alternative to more traditional cafés. Perch at one of the stools around the cramped central counter or grab one of the sleek white chairs to sample tasty dishes (vegetable soups, quiches served with colorful salads, gratins, and a hot dish such as fresh grouper) made with organic ingredients in the open kitchen. Service is friendly but not particularly speedy despite the sandwich-bar setting. Run by a nearby graphic-design agency, it attracts hip commercial artists and dedicated foodies. ✉ *57 rue Charlot, République* ☎ *01–48–04–88–28* ▤ *MC, V* Ⓜ *Temple.*

NORTH AFRICAN ✕ **Chez Omar.** The fashion pack has largely moved on (to places such
$–$$ as Le Martel, run by a former Chez Omar waiter), but the quality of the couscous has never dropped at this popular, no-reservations address (arrive early to avoid an agonizing wait). Order your couscous with grilled skewered lamb, spicy *merguez* sausage, lamb shank, or chicken—portions are generous—and sip a glass of robust, fruity Algerian or Moroccan wine. Proprietor Omar Guerida speaks English and is famously friendly to all. The setting is that of a beautifully faded French bistro, complete with elbow-to-elbow seating, so be prepared to partake of your neighbors' conversations. ✉ *47 rue de Bretagne, République* ☎ *01–42–72–36–26* ⚑ *Reservations not accepted* ▤ *No credit cards* ☉ *No lunch Sun.* Ⓜ *Temple, République.*

4° Arrondissement (Le Marais & Île St-Louis)

See Where to Eat on the Rive Droite: the Marais to La Villette map.

CONTEMPORARY ✕ **Georges.** One of those rooftop showstopping venues so popular in
$–$$$ Paris, Georges preens atop the Centre Georges Pompidou. The staff is
as streamlined and angular as the furniture, and at night the terrace has
distinct snob appeal: come snappily dressed or suffer the consequences
(you may be relegated to something resembling a dentist's waiting
room). Part of the Costes brothers' empire, the establishment trots out
predictable fare such as penne with morel mushrooms and raw tuna with
a sesame crust. It's all considerably less dazzling than the view, except
for desserts by star pâtissier Stéphane Secco, whose YSL (as in Yves Saint
Laurent, darling) bitter-chocolate cake is an event. ⊠ *Centre Pompidou,
6th fl., rue Rambuteau, Beaubourg/Les Halles* ☎ *01-44-78-47-99*
▤ *AE, DC, MC, V* ⊙ *Closed Tues.* Ⓜ *Rambuteau.*

FRENCH ✕ **Bofinger.** One of the oldest, loveliest, and most popular brasseries in
♨ **$–$$$** Paris has generally improved since it joined the Flo group, known for
its restorations of historic brasseries. Stake out one of the tables dressed
in crisp white linen under the glowing Art Nouveau glass cupola—this
part of the dining room is no-smoking—and enjoy classic brasserie fare
such as oysters, seafood-topped choucroute, or lamb fillet (stick to simple fare as some of the more ambitious dishes can be simply odd). The
prix-fixe includes a decent half bottle of red or white wine, and there is
an especially generous children's menu. ⊠ *5–7 rue de la Bastille, Bastille/
Nation* ☎ *01-42-72-87-82* ▤ *AE, DC, MC, V* Ⓜ *Bastille.*

$–$$$ ✕ **Au Bourguignon du Marais.** The handsome, contemporary look of this
Marais bistro and wine bar is the perfect backdrop for the good tradi-
tional fare and excellent Burgundies served by the glass and bottle. Al-
ways on the menu are Burgundian classics such as *jambon persillé* (ham
in parsleyed aspic jelly), escargots, and *oeufs en meurette* (eggs poached
in a red-wine sauce); more up-to-date picks include a cèpe-mushroom
velouté with poached oysters (though the fancier dishes are generally
less successful). The terrace is hotly sought after in warm weather. ⊠ *19
rue de Jouy, Beaubourg/Les Halles* ☎ *01-48-87-15-40* ▤ *AE, DC, MC,
V* ⊙ *Closed weekends* Ⓜ *St-Paul.*

$–$$$ ✕ **Brasserie de l'Île St-Louis.** Opened in 1870—when Alsace-Lorraine was
taken over by Germany and its chefs decamped to the capital—this out-
post of Alsatian cuisine remains a cozy cocoon filled with stuffed animal heads, antique fixtures fashioned from barrels, and folk-art paintings.
The food is *gemütlich,* too: coq au Riesling, omelets with Muenster cheese,
onion tarts, and choucroute garnie (sauerkraut studded with ham,
bacon, and pork loin—one variant is made with smoked haddock). In
warm weather the crowds move out to the terrace overlooking the Seine
and Notre-Dame. With the famed *glacier* Berthillon so close by, it's best
not to bother with the pricey desserts here. ⊠ *55 quai de Bourbon, Île
St-Louis* ☎ *01-43-54-02-59* ▤ *DC, MC, V* ⊙ *Closed Wed. and Aug.
No lunch Thurs.* Ⓜ *Pont Marie.*

$–$$ ✕ **Mon Vieil Ami.** "Modern Alsatian" might sound like an oxymoron,
Fodor'sChoice but once you've tasted the cooking of Antony Clémot—a young pro-
★ tégé of the celebrated Strasbourg chef Antoine Westermann—you'll un-

derstand. The updated medieval dining room—stone walls, wooden beams, dark-wood tables, and small glass panes—provides a stylish milieu for his inventive cooking, which showcases perfect produce. Pâté *en croûte* (wrapped in pastry) with a knob of foie gras is hard to resist among the starters. Long-cooked, wine-marinated venison comes with succulent accompaniments of quince, prune, celery root, and chestnuts. Panfried skate paired with sautéed potatoes and lemon confit also earns kudos. If you don't want to go the whole hog, order the €15 *plat du jour* with a glass of wine (about €4–€5). ⊠ *69 St-Louis-en-l'Isle, Île St-Louis* ☎ *01–40–46–01–35* ▭ *AE, DC, MC, V* ☉ *Closed Sun. No lunch Mon.* Ⓜ *Pont Marie.*

$–$$ ✕ **Trumilou.** Crowds of students, artists, and others on a budget come here for bistro cuisine such as duck with prunes, veal sweetbreads *grand-mère* (cooked with mushrooms and bacon and flambéed in cognac), and apple tarts. It's no longer the bargain it once was, however, with the cheapest set menu at €17.50 for extremely simple, if generously served, food in boisterous, smoky surroundings. The nondecor is somehow homey, the staff is friendly, and the location facing the Seine and the Île St-Louis is especially pleasant in nice weather, when you can sit on the narrow though noisy terrace under the trees. ⊠ *84 quai de l'Hôtel de Ville, Le Marais* ☎ *01–42–77–63–98* ▭ *MC, V* ☉ *Closed 2 wks in Aug., 1 wk at Christmas* Ⓜ *Pont Marie.*

MIDDLE EASTERN ✕ **Chez Marianne.** You'll know you've found Marianne's place when you
★ $–$$ see the line of people reading the bits of wisdom and poetry painted across her windows. The restaurant-deli, with a second cloistered room in the back, serves excellent Middle Eastern and Jewish specialties such as hummus, fried eggplant, and soul-warming chopped liver, which you can accompany with one of the very affordable wines. The sampler platter lets you try four, five, or six items—even the smallest plate makes a filling feast. Falafel sandwiches are served in the restaurant only on weekdays at lunch, though you can get them anytime at the takeout window. ⊠ *2 rue des Hospitalières-St-Gervais, Le Marais* ☎ *01–42–72–18–86* ▭ *MC, V* Ⓜ *St-Paul.*

☺ **¢–$** ✕ **L'As du Fallafel.** Look no farther than the fantastic falafel stands on rue de Rosiers for some of the cheapest and tastiest meals in Paris: L'As (the Ace) is widely considered the best of the bunch. A falafel costs €5, but shell out a little extra money for the *spécial* with grilled eggplant, cabbage, hummus, tahini, and hot sauce. Though takeout is popular, it can be more fun (and not as messy) to eat off a plastic plate in the frenetic but fascinating fast-food style dining room. The fresh lemonade is the falafel's best match. ⊠ *34 rue des Rosiers, Le Marais* ☎ *01–48–87–63–60* ▭ *MC, V* ☉ *Closed dusk Fri.–dusk Sat. and Jewish holidays* Ⓜ *St-Paul.*

5ᵉ Arrondissement (Quartier Latin)

See Where to Eat on the Rive Gauche map.

CHINESE ✕ **Mirama.** Regulars at this popular and rather chaotic no-frills Chinese
☺ **¢–$$** restaurant order the soup, a rich broth with a nest of thick noodles garnished with dumplings, barbecued pork, or smoked duck. Main courses are generous—the best are made with shellfish, and the Peking duck is

CloseUp

REFUELING

L E FAST FOOD" is not what Paris does best; you can easily spend two hours, albeit pleasantly, having lunch in a café. There's no point trying to make a Parisian waiter move faster than he wants to; instead, head to a new breed of snack shop that puts speed first without sacrificing quality. Prices are a bit high for what you get (expect to spend €10–€15 for a meal), but it's still a lot cheaper than eating in most bistros.

Le Pain Quotidien: Part bakery, part café, this Belgian chain with locations throughout the city serves fresh salads and sandwiches at lunch and is one of the best places for breakfast. Avoid peak times, when it can be overrun with office workers.

Cosi (⌧ 54 rue de Seinem, 6ᵉ ☎ 01–46–33–36–36): Miles from the cardboard panini served at so many crepe stands, this Italian sandwich shop in St-Germain piles fillings onto crusty bread. Order at the counter and carry your

sandwich upstairs, where there is (oh, miracle) a no-smoking area.

Nils (⌧ 36 rue Montorgueil, 2ᵉ ☎ 01–55–34–39–49 ⌧ 10 rue de Buci, 6ᵉ ☎ 01–46–34–82–82): The Danes eat lunch in 15 minutes and live to be over 80, which is reason enough to eat at these Scandinavian delis. Try a rolled Swedish sandwich or a smoked fish plate, and save room for a blueberry tart.

Be (⌧ 73 bd. de Courcelles, 17ᵉ ☎ 01–46–22–20–20): Star chef Alain Ducasse and wizard baker Eric Kayser make sandwiches a luxury item; snag one of the handful of tables amid the heavenly bakery aromas and choose from condiments hand-selected by the great chef.

Oh Poivrier! (⌧ 2 bd. Haussmann, 9ᵉ ☎ 01–42–46–22–24 ⌧ 25 quai Grands Augustins, 6ᵉ ☎ 01–43–29–41–77): Specializing in quirkily named open-faced sandwiches, this chain makes a good alternative to slower-paced cafés, with terraces in some scenic spots.

also excellent. Service is brisk, so plan on coffee in a nearby café. It's quick, easy, and a far more reliable bet than the countless Asian *traiteurs* selling microwave-reheated food of suspect origins. ⌧ 17 rue St-Jacques, Quartier Latin ☎ 01–43–29–66–58 ▭ MC, V Ⓜ St-Michel.

CONTEMPORARY ★ $–$$$ ✕ **Le Pré Verre.** Chef Philippe Delacourcelle knows his cassia bark from his cinnamon, thanks to a long stint in Asia. He opened this sharp bistro (with purple-gray walls and photos of jazz musicians) to showcase his unique culinary style, rejuvenating archetypal French dishes with Asian and Mediterranean spices. His bargain prix-fixe-only menu changes constantly, but crisp salt cod with cassia bark and supersmooth smoked potato purée is a winner, as is an unlikely dessert of roasted figs with olives. Ask for advice in selecting one of the wines from small producers. The dining room can get smoky and noisy, so be prepared to leave hoarse but happy. ⌧ 8 rue Thénard, Quartier Latin ☎ 01–43–54–59–47 ▭ MC, V ⊘ Closed Sun. and 2 wks in Aug. No lunch Mon. Ⓜ Maubert-Mutualité.

FRENCH ★ $$$$ ✕ **La Tour d'Argent.** Beyond the wonderful if resolutely classic food, many factors conspire to make a meal at this venerable landmark memorable: the extraordinary wine cellar, considerate service, the grandeur of the dining room, and, of course, that privileged vista across the Seine to Notre-Dame. You'll even be entitled to succulent slices of one of the restaurant's numbered ducks (the great duck slaughter began in 1919 and is now well past the millionth mallard, as your numbered certificate will attest). The most celebrated dish, *canard au sang* (duck in a blood-based sauce), is available à la carte or for a €22 supplement. Don't get too daunted by the wine list—more of a bible, really—for with the help of one of the sommeliers you can splurge a little (about €80) and perhaps taste a rare vintage Burgundy. ⊠ *15 quai de la Tournelle, Quartier Latin* ☎ *01–43–54–23–31* ⚐ *Reservations essential* 🏛 *Jacket and tie* ⊟ *AE, DC, MC, V* ⊗ *Closed Mon. No lunch Tues.* Ⓜ *Cardinal Lemoine.*

$$–$$$ ✕ **Bistrot Côte Mer.** If proximity to the water makes you crave a fish feast, head to this inviting bistro a few steps from the Seine. The blue facade, stone walls and marble-topped tables combine Parisian and seaside style, and the menu is equally eclectic, hopping from classic (oyster plates) to more inventive dishes such as *croustillant de langouste* (rock lobster in a crispy crust). Crêpes flambéed in Grand Marnier are a house classic that is rarely seen in Paris these days. The dining room can get a bit noisy when full; the summertime terrace is more peaceful, albeit on a busy boulevard. ⊠ *16 bd. St-Germain, Quartier Latin* ☎ *01–43–54–59–10* ⊟ *AE, MC, V* ⊗ *Closed 3 wks in Aug.* Ⓜ *Maubert-Mutualité.*

$–$$$ ✕ **Le Buisson Ardent.** Just across the street from the university's hideous Jussieu campus, this cozy spot is a good example of how the modern bistro genre is thriving in Paris. The airy front room—often filled with bon vivant academics while students line up for sandwiches nearby—is a pleasant place for a meal, with a solicitous proprietor, good waiters, and scrumptious food from chef Philippe Duclos. His style shows in such dishes as panfried scallops with vegetable strips, roasted duck breast with tandoori spices, and a pork chop with lentils and foie gras. ⊠ *25 rue Jussieu, Quartier Latin* ☎ *01–43–54–93–02* ⊟ *AE, MC, V* ⊗ *Closed weekends and Aug.* Ⓜ *Jussieu.*

★ **$–$$$** ✕ **Chez René.** Think there's nowhere left in Paris that serves *boeuf bourguignon*, coq au vin, and frogs' legs in a timeworn bistro setting—crisp tablecloths, burgundy woodwork, waiters in black aprons? Then you haven't been to Chez René, whose specialty—aside from robust Burgundian classics—is reassuring continuity, as illustrated by the photos of the staff, taken every decade, that adorn the walls. Be sure to enjoy some of the Mâconnais and Beaujolais wines with your meal. ⊠ *14 bd. St-Germain, Quartier Latin* ☎ *01–43–54–30–23* ⊟ *MC, V* ⊗ *Closed Sun., Mon., Christmas wk, and Aug. No lunch Sat.* Ⓜ *Maubert-Mutualité.*

⟲ **$–$$** ✕ **Le Balzar.** Regulars grumble about the uneven cooking at Le Balzar, but they continue to be regulars because they can't resist the waiters' wry humor and the dining room's amazing people-watching possibilities. It attracts politicians, writers, tourists, and local eccentrics. Despite being purchased by the Flo group several years ago, causing great uproar among Rive Gauche intellectuals, this remains one of the city's classic brasseries, the perfect stop before or after a Woody Allen film in a local art-house cinema. Don't expect miracles from the kitchen, but stick to evergreens such as snails in garlic butter, French onion soup, and panfried veal liver with sautéed potatoes. ☒ *49 rue des Écoles, Quartier Latin* ☎ *01–43–54–13–67* ▣ *AE, MC, V* Ⓜ *Cluny–La Sorbonne.*

★ **$-$$** ✕ **Le Reminet.** Chandeliers and mirrors add an unexpected grace note to this mellow bistro set in a narrow salon with stone walls (there is a second room upstairs) and run by a friendly couple. The menu changes regularly and showcases the young chef's talent with dishes like shrimp ravioli with coconut milk and grilled lamb with a cumin-and-red-pepper crust. Desserts are equally inventive: don't even try to resist the mini baba au rhum with panfried winter fruits. You can score a deal with the weekday €13 prix-fixe lunch or the €17 dinner menu on Monday and Thursday. ☒ *3 rue des Grands-Degrés, Quartier Latin* ☎ *01–44–07–04–24* ▣ *MC, V* ☉ *Closed Tues., Wed., 2 wks in Feb., and 2 wks in Aug.* Ⓜ *Maubert-Mutualité.*

¢–$ ✕ **Les Pipos.** The tourist traps along romantic rue de la Montagne Ste-Genevieve are enough to make you despair—and then you stumble across this bistro, bursting with chatter and laughter. Les Pipos is everything you could ask of a Quartier Latin bistro: the space is cramped, the food (such as Charolais steak and duck confit) is substantial (the cheese comes from the Lyon market, though the Poilâne bread could be fresher), and conversation flows as freely as the wine. It gets crowded, so arrive early to snag a table. You can also stop in for a glass of wine and a plate of *saucisson* (French sausage) in the late afternoon and watch the sun set behind the Panthéon. ☒ *2 rue de L'École Polytechnique, Quartier Latin* ☎ *01–43–54–11–40* ▣ *No credit cards* ☉ *Closed Sun. and 2 wks in Aug.* Ⓜ *Maubert-Mutualité.*

SPANISH ✕ **Fogòn St-Julien.** On one of Paris's oldest streets, across from the ancient St-Julien-le-Pauvre church, this sunny yellow, rather formal restaurant is a source for outstanding Spanish food and unusual wines to match. The seasonal all-tapas menu is tempting at €36 per person, but that would mean missing out on what must be the city's finest paella (€18 per person, but at least two people must order the same version): saffron with seafood, inky squid, or Valencia-style with rabbit, chicken, and vegetables. Finish up with the custardy crème Catalan accompanied by a glass of muscatel. ☒ *10 rue St-Julien-le-Pauvre, Quartier Latin* ☎ *01–43–54–31–33* ⚐ *Reservations essential* ▣ *MC, V* ☉ *Closed Mon., 2 wks in Jan., 2 wks in late Aug.–early Sept. No lunch Tues.–Fri.* Ⓜ *St-Michel.*
★ **$-$$**

6e Arrondissement (St-Germain-des-Prés)
See Where to Eat on the Rive Gauche map.

CONTEMPORARY ✕ **Alcazar.** To take in the scene at Sir Terence Conran's brasserie—and quite a scene it is, as this place seats 300 under a skylight roof—opt for a table on the mezzanine, where a long brushed-steel bar gives you a bird's-eye view and you can choose from a number of set menus that include a drink. Chef Guillaume Lutard trained at Taillevent and Prunier, and his background informs the seasonal contemporary menu, which changes every two months. However, the open kitchen has always turned out inconsistent food, although the fish-and-chips served with British malt vinegar are fantastic. The DJs and the tasty, €28 Sunday brunch—served up with a soothing Shiatsu massage—both have their
$-$$$

loyal followers. ✉ *62 rue Mazarine, St-Germain-des-Prés* ☎ *01–53–10–19–99* ▭ *AE, DC, MC, V* Ⓜ *Odéon.*

$–$$$ ✕ **Ze Kitchen Galerie.** William Ledeuil made his name at the popular Les Bouquinistes (a Guy Savoy baby bistro) before opening this pared-down contemporary bistro in a loftlike space nearby. If the name isn't exactly inspired, the cooking shows unbridled creativity and a sense of fun: from a deliberately deconstructed menu featuring raw fish, soups, pastas, and *à la plancha* (grilled) plates, consider chicken wing, broccoli, and artichoke soup with lemongrass, or pork ribs with curry jus and white beans. Worldly eaters might find the flavors rather subtle, but the food here is adventurous for Paris. The menu changes monthly, and art exhibits rotate every three months; Ledeuil also gives cooking classes. The only thing missing is a no-smoking section. ✉ *4 rue des Grands-Augustins, Quartier Latin* ☎ *01–44–32–00–32* ▭ *AE, DC, MC, V* ⊙ *Closed Sun. No lunch Sat.* Ⓜ *St-Michel.*

★ $$ ✕ **Le Café des Délices.** There is a lot to like about this bistro, from the Art Nouveau facade and the warm and spacious Asia-meets-Africa decor (lots of dark wood and little pots of spices on each table) to the polished service and mouthwatering food. Drop in for the bargain €15 lunch (the plat du jour with a glass of wine and coffee), or go for à la carte dishes such as scallops with balsamic vinegar or blood pudding flavored with cocoa. Tongue-in-cheek comfort-food desserts tout such ingredients as Chupa Chups lollipops and sugary cereal. Not everything works, but the chef deserves credit for his gutsy approach. ✉*87 rue d'Assas, Montparnasse* ☎ *01–43–54–70–00* ▭ *AE, MC, V* ⊙ *Closed weekends* Ⓜ *Vavin.*

FRENCH
★ $$$$ ✕ **Hélène Darroze.** The eponymous chef here has won a lot of followers with her refined take on southwestern French cooking from the lands around Albi and Toulouse. You know it's not going to be *la même chanson*—the same old song—as soon as you see the contemporary Tse & Tse tableware, and her intriguingly modern touch comes through in such dishes as a sublime duck foie gras confit served with an exotic-fruit chutney or a blowout of roast wild duck stuffed with foie gras and truffles. Expect to spend a hefty €350 for two à la carte (with drinks) upstairs, but there's a more reasonable lunch menu at €68. The livelier downstairs bistro, which has an open kitchen, a long central table, and banquettes strewn with puffy velvet cushions, offers similar food in (even) smaller tapas-style portions—however, inconsistent food and inexpert service mar what should be a more relaxed experience. ✉ *4 rue d'Assas, St-Germain-des-Prés* ☎ *01–42–22–00–11* ▭ *AE, DC, MC, V* ⊙ *Closed Sun. and Mon. No lunch Tues.* Ⓜ *Sèvres Babylone.*

$$$–$$$$ ✕ **Chez Dumonet–Josephine.** Theater types, politicos, and well-padded locals fill the moleskin banquettes of this venerable bistro; the frosted-glass lamps and amber walls put everyone in a good light. Unlike most bistros, Josephine caters to the indecisive, since half-portions allow you to graze your way through the tempting menu. Try the very good boeuf bourguignon, roasted saddle of lamb with artichokes, anything with truffles in season, or the mille-feuille or *tarte fine* (a crisp-crust fruit tart) for dessert. The wine list, like the food, is excellent but expensive. ✉ *117 rue du Cherche-Midi, St-Germain-des-Prés* ☎ *01–45–48–52–40* ▭ *AE, MC, V* ⊙ *Closed weekends* Ⓜ *Duroc.*

$$$ ✕ **Les Bouquinistes.** Run by chef William Cosimo, this is the most popular of Guy Savoy's "baby bistros." You can expect to hear more English than French in the cheery, contemporary dining room looking out onto the Seine, but the seasonal, haute cuisine–inspired food—such as crab rémoulade with lemongrass shrimp and a beet *raviole,* perhaps followed by British Hereford beef with carrots and fava beans and a rhubarb crème brûlée—is as authentic as you could hope for. The €26.50 *retour du marché* menu pales and seems less imaginative than the pricier à la carte options—though it does include three courses, a glass of wine, and coffee. Service is friendly but erratic and occasionally overfamiliar. ⊠ *53 quai des Grands-Augustins, St-Germain-des-Prés* ☎ *01–43–25–45–94* ▤ *AE, DC, MC, V* ⊘ *Closed Sun. No lunch Sat.* Ⓜ *St-Michel.*

★ **$$$**   ✕ **Lapérouse.** Émile Zola, George Sand, and Victor Hugo were regulars, and the restaurant's mirrors still bear diamond scratches from the days when mistresses didn't take jewels at face value. It's hard not to fall in love with this 17th-century Seine-side town house whose warren of intimate, boiserie-graced salons breathes history. The latest chef, Alain Hacquard, has found the right track with a daring (for Paris) spice-infused menu: his lobster, Dublin Bay prawn, and crayfish bisque is flavored with Szechuan pepper and lemon. Game is prominent in the fall, with a selection of southwestern wines to accompany dishes like Scottish grouse. For a truly intimate meal, reserve one of the legendary private salons where anything can happen (and probably will). ⊠ *51 quai des Grands Augustins, Quartier Latin* ☎ *01–43–26–68–04* ⌦ *Reservations essential* ▤ *AE, DC, MC, V* ⊘ *Closed Sun., 1 wk in July, and 3 wks in Aug. No lunch Sat.* Ⓜ *St-Michel.*

$$–$$$ ✕ **L'Épi Dupin.** Other bistros might be more welcoming, but L'Épi Dupin's cramped, beamed dining room continues to attract an eager crowd of tourists and Gaultier-clad locals who don't seem to mind waiting in the rain for their reserved tables—don't expect to linger over coffee if you book an early sitting. The prix-fixe-only menu of updated French standards is revised regularly and might include an upside-down tart of caramelized Belgian endive and goat cheese, curried saddle of rabbit with sweet-potato chutney, and crisp, pyramid-shape pastry filled with apples and candied fennel for dessert. Many of chef Francois Pasteau's dishes have unusual sweet notes. He will whip up a vegetarian dish on request. ⊠ *11 rue Dupin, St-Germain-des-Prés* ☎ *01–42–22–64–56* ⌦ *Reservations essential* ▤ *AE, MC, V* ⊘ *Closed weekends, Aug., and 1 wk in Feb. No lunch Mon.* Ⓜ *Sèvres Babylone.*

$–$$$ ✕ **Chez Maître Paul.** This calm, comfortable spot is a great place to discover the little-known cooking of the Jura and Franche-Comté regions of eastern France. Though sturdy, this cuisine appeals to modern palates, too, as you'll discover with the *montbéliard,* a smoked sausage served with potato salad, or the veal sweetbreads with morel mushrooms. Also try one of the free-range chicken dishes, either in a sauce of *vin jaune*—a dry wine from the region that resembles sherry—or baked in cream and cheese. The walnut meringue is sinfully wonderful, and there's a regional selection of Arbois wines. ⊠ *12 rue Monsieur-le-Prince, St-Germain-des-Prés* ☎ *01–43–54–74–59* ▤ *AE, DC, MC, V* ⊘ *Closed Sun. and Mon. in July and Aug.* Ⓜ *Odéon.*

$$ ✕ **La Bastide Odéon.** The kitchen of this popular Provençal bistro near the Jardin du Luxembourg with terra-cotta floors and upholstered chairs has been opened up so you can watch the cooks at work. Chef Gilles Ajuelos demonstrates an expert, loving, and creative hand with Mediterranean cuisine—expect unusual dishes, such as aged Spanish ham with a grilled pepper pipérade and artichoke; mushroom and pea risotto with arugula; duck breast with orange sauce, date puree, polenta, and wild asparagus; and, to finish things off, pear poached with lemon and saffron and served with a *fromage blanc* sorbet. An entire section of the menu is devoted to vegetarian dishes. ⊠ *7 rue Corneille, St-Germain-des-Prés* ☎ *01–43–26–03–65* ▭ *AE, MC, V* ⊘ *Closed Sun., Mon., and Aug.* Ⓜ *Odéon; RER: Luxembourg.*

$$ ✕ **Claude Sainlouis.** A favorite with politicians, this discreetly lighted, red-hued bistro serves the type of hearty, no-compromise food cherished by French heads of state: veal kidney brochette served with fluffy mousseline potatoes; one of the city's most authentic renditions of *tête de veau*; and *quenelles* (pike-perch dumplings) and sausages from the famed Lyon charcutier Bobosse. The prix-fixe menus are democratic, starting at €18 for lunch, €28 for dinner. ⊠ *27 rue du Dragon, St-Germain-des-Prés* ☎ *01–45–48–29–68* ▭ *MC, V* ⊘ *Closed Sun., Mon., Aug., and 1 wk in late Dec.* Ⓜ *St-Germain-des-Prés.*

★ $$ ✕ **La Table d'Aude.** Rive Gauche students, senators, and book editors who dine here are on to a good thing, since this jolly restaurant serves some of the best cassoulet in Paris. Owner Bernard Patou and his wife Véronique take a contagious pleasure in serving up dishes from their home turf—the Aude, a long, narrow region in the Languedoc-Roussillon. Almost everyone orders the cassoulet, bubbling hot in a small, high-sided ceramic dish and filled to the brim with white beans, sausage, and preserved duck. What makes it special here is that the meats are grilled separately before being added to the pot, reducing the fat in the finished dish. Of the house wines, go with the rich, cherry-color Corbières. ⊠ *8 rue de Vaugirard, St-Germain-des-Prés* ☎ *01–43–26–36–36* ▭ *MC, V* ⊘ *Closed Sun. No lunch Sat., no dinner Mon.* Ⓜ *Odéon.*

$–$$ ✕ **Le Timbre.** Working in a tiny open kitchen, Manchester native Chris Wright could teach many a French chef a thing or two about *la cuisine française.* He works with only the finest suppliers to produce a constantly changing seasonal menu that keeps the locals coming back. A spring meal might begin with lightly cooked vegetables atop tapenade on toast, and fat, halved asparagus spears dabbed with an anise-spiked sauce, balsamic vinegar, and Parmesan. The mille-feuille is spectacular, but try not to miss *le vrai et le faux fromage,* a two-year-old British cheddar juxtaposed with a farmer's goat cheese from the Ardèche. Black-and-white photos of Paris add real charm to the narrow dining room. ⊠ *3 rue Ste-Beuve Montparnasse* ☎ *01–45–49–10–40* ▭ *MC, V* ⊘ *Sun. and 3 wks in Aug. No lunch Sat.* Ⓜ *Vavin.*

$ ✕ **Le Bouillon Racine.** Originally a *bouillon*—one of the Parisian soup kitchens popular at the turn of the 20th century—this two-story restaurant is now a lushly renovated Belle Époque haven with a casual setting downstairs and a lavish upstairs room. The menu now changes seasonally. Lamb knuckle with licorice, wild boar *parmentier* (like a shepherd's pie, with a layer of mashed potatoes on top and meat underneath), and roast suckling pig are a few of the warming winter dishes. For dessert, dig a spoon into chestnut cream spiked with Jack Daniels. ✉ *3 rue Racine, St-Germain-des-Prés* ☎ *01–44–32–15–60* ✍ *Reservations essential* ▤ *AE, MC, V* Ⓜ *Odéon.*

JAPANESE ✕ **Yen.** If you're having what is known in French as a *crise de foie* (liver
★ **$–$$$** crisis), the result of overindulging in rich food, this Japanese noodle house offers the perfect antidote. The blond-wood walls soothe the senses, the staff is happy to explain the proper slurping technique, and the soba (buckwheat noodles), served in soup or with a restorative broth for dipping, will give you the courage to face another round of caramelized foie gras. At lunch you might opt for one of the bento boxes, with rice, fish, and vegetables arranged like jewels in a lacquered box. Desserts come from Sadaharu Aoko, who is famous for his green-tea éclairs. ✉ *22 rue St-Benoît, St-Germain-des-Prés* ☎*01–45–44–11–18* ▤ *AE, DC, MC, V* ✆ *Closed 2 wks in Aug. and 2 wks at Christmas and 1 wk at Easter. No lunch Sun.* Ⓜ *St-Germain-des-Prés.*

7ᵉ Arrondissement (Invalides, Tocadéro/Tour Eiffel & St-Germain-des-Prés)
See Where to Eat on the Rive Gauche map.

CONTEMPORARY ✕ **Petrossian.** Although young chef Sebastien Faré now mans the stoves,
★ **$$$$** Petrossian still jangles with the wildly imaginative style of his predecessor, Philippe Conticini. Conticini keeps his hand in as a consultant, which is good news for the restaurant's *gauche caviar* (luxe-loving Rive Gauche socialist) clientele. Smoked fish and caviar star in such house classics as breaded soft-boiled egg topped with caviar (and resembling a Fabergè egg); other winning concoctions include risotto with squid ink and porcini, and a Moroccan-inspired salad with crisp Dublin Bay shrimp. Don't miss the "drinkable perfumes," an alluring series of vividly colored infusions of flowers, barks, and roots; served cold in shot glasses, they cleanse the palate in preparation for the tongue-tickling desserts. Feeling indecisive? For each course you can succumb to *tentation*, a selection of four miniportions. ✉ *18 bd. de La Tour–Maubourg, Invalides* ☎ *01–44–11–32–32* ▤ *AE, DC, MC, V* ✆ *Closed Sun., Mon., and 3 wks in Aug.* Ⓜ *La Tour–Maubourg, Invalides.*

★ **$$$–$$$$** ✕ **Le Chamarré.** Chamarré means "richly colored," and that perfectly describes the cooking at this classy, if slightly too formal, ocher-walled restaurant. Antoine Heerah is Mauritian and Jérôme Bodereau is French—the result is artfully presented food that draws on exotic ingredients such as *combawa* (a type of lime) and green mango. Each plate looks like an edible painting, with dabs of chutney, drizzles of foamy sauces, and sprinklings of spice, and the quality of the cooking is beautifully consistent. Lunch prix-fixes run from €28 to €45; they're a good chance to sample the likes of Jerusalem artichoke velouté with curry-infused cream or Atlantic octopus with a tropical mango sauce, though you might find yourself tempted by the pricey *carte.* ✉ *13 bd. de La Tour–Maubourg, Invalides* ☎*01–47–05–50–18* ▤ *AE, MC, V* ✆ *Closed Sun. No lunch Sat.* Ⓜ *La Tour–Maubourg, Invalides.*

WITH CHILDREN?

Although luxuries like high chairs and coloring books aren't standard except in overtly child-friendly chains such as **Hippopotamus**, which serves good steak-frites, some French restaurants can be warmly welcoming to budding gastronomes. You can help the experience by preparing the ground: Pack a folding booster seat for a toddler, since in the rare cases where high chairs are provided, they are usually missing pieces. Cigarette smoke is likely to be a problem, so ask for the no-smoking area.

Brasseries are one of the best choices for kids; they're lively and noisy and provide familiar options, such as pommes frites (french fries), croque monsieurs (toasted ham-and-cheese sandwiches), and roast chicken. Creperies are also fun, fast, and quintessentially French: what child can resist a crepe filled with warm banana and smothered in chocolate sauce? Or you could try one of the big Chinese restaurants: **Dragons Elysées** (⊠ 11 rue de Berri ☎ 01–42–89–85–10) has aquariums underfoot.

FRENCH ✕ **L'Arpège.** Breton-born Alain Passard, one of the most respected chefs
$$$$ in Paris, famously shocked the French culinary world by declaring that he was bored with meat and fish. Though his vegetarianism is more theoretical than practical—L'Arpège still caters to fish and poultry eaters—he does cultivate his own vegetables outside Paris, which are zipped into the city by high-speed train. His dishes elevate the humblest vegetables to sublime heights: roasted beets with aged balsamic vinegar, leeks with black truffles, black radishes, and cardoon with Parmigiano Reggiano. Fish dishes such as turbot cooked at a very low temperature for three hours are also extraordinary. The understated decor places the emphasis firmly on the food, but try to avoid the gloomy cellar room. ⊠ 84 *rue de Varenne, Invalides* ☎ 01–45–51–47–33 ▤ AE, DC, MC, V ⊙ *Closed weekends* Ⓜ *Varenne.*

$$$$ ✕ **Jules Verne.** A table at this all-black restaurant on the second level of the Tour Eiffel, 400 feet removed from the gritty reality of Parisian life, is one of the hardest to snag in Paris. At its best, Alain Reix's cooking justifies a wait of two months or more for dinner (you can usually book a lunch reservation with a few days' notice), but lately his food has been a deflating experience. The wisest approach, then, is to go for the €53 lunch menu (weekdays only) and to expect good but not exquisite food, such as pigeon fricassee or squid with duck liver, an intriguing meeting of land and sea. There's always the exceptional view—the highlight of any meal here has to be the ride up the restaurant's private elevator. If you dine early you have a much better chance of snagging a window seat. ⊠ *Tour Eiffel, Trocadéro/Tour Eiffel* ☎ 01–45–55–61–44 ⟁ *Reservations essential* ⓜ *Jacket and tie* ▤ AE, DC, MC, V Ⓜ *Bir-Hakeim.*

$$$$ ✕ **Le Violon d'Ingres.** Christian Constant, former head of the Hôtel Crillon's kitchens and mentor to many a successful bistro chef, runs his own dressed-up restaurant in a hushed, posh corner of the city (though his two newer ventures on the same street—Le Café Constant and the tiny, affordable fish restaurant Les Fables de la Fontaine—show his affinity for

more casual settings). The menu changes often, though to please his suit-clad regulars Constant almost always offers his signature pig's trotter tatin, crispy sea bass with almonds, and souffléed potatoes with licorice mousselin. The food is generally rich, with few modern compromises. If you let them know when you make your reservation, the kitchen will also cater to vegetarians. ☒ *135 rue St-Dominique, Invalides* ☎ *01–45–55–15–05* ☖ *Reservations essential* ⊟ *AE, DC, MC, V* ☉ *Closed Sun. and 3 wks in Aug. No lunch Sat. and Mon.* Ⓜ *École Militaire.*

$$$–$$$$ ✕ **L'Atelier de Joël Robuchon.** Famed chef Joël Robuchon had retired from
FodorśChoice the restaurant business for several years before opening this red-and-
★ black-lacquered space with a bento-box-meets-tapas aesthetic (and branches in Tokyo and Las Vegas). Seats line up around U-shape bars; this novel plan encourages neighbors to share recommendations and opinions. Robuchon and his devoted kitchen staff whip up "small plates" for grazing (€10–€25) as well as full portions. Highlights from the oft-changing menu have included an intense tomato jelly topped with avocado puree, thin-crusted mackerel tart, and his inauthentic (but who's complaining?) take on carbonara with cream and bacon from Alsace. L'Atelier takes reservations only for 11:30 AM and 6:30 PM seatings. As if the reservations policy weren't shocking enough to the French, the entire restaurant is smoke-free. ☒ *5 rue Montalembert, St-Germain-des-Prés* ☎ *01–42–22–56–56* ⊟ *MC, V* Ⓜ *Rue du Bac.*

$$–$$$$ ✕ **Thoumieux.** Here you'll find all the ingredients of a quintessential Parisian bistro: red-velour banquettes, yellow walls, bustling waiters in white aprons, and locals with their poodles. Little has changed here since 1923 except the prices. Thoumieux has been owned by the same family for three generations, and their roots in the Corrèze region of southwest France show in the number of duck-based dishes, including rib-sticking rillettes, duck confit, and cassoulet. Thoumieux has also resurrected such neglected dishes as tripes à la mode de Caen (slow-cooked with onions, leeks, and calvados) and fricassee *de crêtes et de couilles de coq* (two extremes of the rooster). ☒ *79 rue St-Dominique, Invalides* ☎ *01–47–05–49–75* ⊟ *AE, MC, V* Ⓜ *Invalides.*

★ **$$–$$$** ✕ **Au Bon Accueil.** To see what well-heeled Parisians like to eat these days, book a table at this extremely popular bistro as soon as you get to town. The dining room is open and airy, and the sidewalk tables have a Tour Eiffel view. The excellent, reasonably priced *cuisine du marché* has made it a hit: typical of the winter fare is shoulder of lamb confit with lemon. Homemade desserts could include fruit tarts or the superb *pistache*, a pastry curl filled with homemade pistachio ice cream. ☒ *14 rue de Monttessuy, Trocadéro/Tour Eiffel* ☎ *01–47–05–46–11* ☖ *Reservations essential* ⊟ *MC, V* ☉ *Closed weekends* Ⓜ *Métro or RER: Pont de l'Alma.*

★ **$–$$** ✕ **Chez l'Ami Jean.** If you loved Yves Cambdeborde's southwestern France-inflected cooking at La Régalade, head to this tavernlike Basque restaurant run by Cambdeborde's longtime second-in-command, Stéphane Jego. If his style is even more regional than Camdeborde's, he uses the same suppliers and has a similar knack for injecting basic ingredients with sophistication. You can go hearty with *piquillo* peppers stuffed with salt cod paste and poulet basquaise (chicken stewed with peppers), or go lighter with inventive fish and seafood dishes. The restaurant is popular with rugby fans (it's a sport beloved of Basques), who create a festive prematch mood. ✉ *27 rue Malar, Invalides* ☎ *01–47–05–86–89* 🖃 *MC, V* ☉ *Closed Sun., Mon., and Aug.* Ⓜ *Métro or RER: Invalides.*

★ $ ✕ **Le Café Constant.** Parisian thirty- and fortysomethings are a nostalgic bunch, which explains the popularity of this down-to-earth new venue from esteemed chef Christian Constant. This is a relatively humble bistro (cream-color walls, red banquettes, wooden tables), and seeing Constant relax in the dining room after the lunch rush, you get the feeling that this is where he feels most at home. The menu reads like a French cookbook from the 1970s—who cooks veal cordon bleu these days?—and, with Constant overseeing the kitchen, the dishes taste even better than you remember. There's a delicious creamy lentil soup with morsels of foie gras, and the artichoke salad comes with fresh, not bottled or frozen, hearts. A towering *vacherin* (meringue pastry) might bring this delightfully retro meal to a close. ✉ *139 rue St-Dominique, Invalides* ☎ *01–48–04–88–28* 🍴 *Reservations not accepted* 🖃 *MC, V* ☉ *Closed Sun. and Mon.* Ⓜ *Métro École Militaire, Métro or RER: Pont de l'Alma.*

$ ✕ **Le Petit Troquet.** Atmospheric bric-a-brac like old tin signs for clocks and soda siphons warms up this tiny, pleasant bistro in the shadow of the Tour Eiffel. The prix-fixe-only menu for €28 changes daily but may include such dishes as goat-cheese mousse with smoked salmon, cassoulet with duck confit (made on the premises), and fruit crumble for dessert. Everything is homemade here, even (very unusual for Paris) the bread. It may not have a high profile but it's popular with locals, so book ahead. ✉ *28 rue de l'Exposition, Trocadéro/Tour Eiffel* ☎ *01–47–05–80–39* 🖃 *MC, V* ☉ *Closed Sun. and 3 wks in Aug. No lunch Mon. and Sat.* Ⓜ *École Militaire.*

8ᵉ Arrondissement (Champs-Élysées)

See Where to Eat on the Rive Droite: Bois du Boulogne to Place de la Concorde map.

CONTEMPORARY ✕ **Maison Blanche.** The celebrated Pourcel twin brothers preside over this
$$$$ edgy "White House," which basks in its show-off view across Paris from the top floor of the Théâtre du Champs-Élysées. Typical of the globe-trotting, southern French–inspired (and not always successful) fare are the vegetable pot-au-feu with white Alba truffle (a section of the menu is dedicated to vegetarian dishes), crisp-crusted scallop tart with crab and baby leeks, and French beef with an herb crust, mushrooms, and shallots slow-cooked in Fitou wine. A side order of mashed potatoes, green beans, or salad will set you back a sobering €10—this is a place for the fat of wallet and trim of figure. Desserts are divided into chocolate and fruit sections, the fruit options being the most playful. In keeping with the snow-white setting, staff can be rather frosty. ✉ *15 av. Montaigne, Champs-Élysées* ☎ *01–47–23–55–99* 🖃 *AE, MC, V* ☉ *No lunch weekends* Ⓜ *Franklin-D.-Roosevelt.*

★ $$$–$$$$ ✕ **Flora.** Alain Passard–trained Flora Mikula made her name at Les Olivades, a Provençal bistro in the 7ᵉ, before joining a gaggle of ambitious restaurateurs in this platinum-card neck of the woods. Moving away from the bistro register, she's turning out refined food with southern twists in a dressed-up setting with plaster moldings and mirrors of various sizes that feels much like a bourgeois apartment. Standout dishes on the frequently changing seasonal menu are a scallop *tarte fine* with truffle vinaigrette, roast sea bass with a potato-olive purée, roasted-apple mille-feuille with salted-caramel ice cream and a spectacular Grand Marnier soufflé. Service, like the food, is impeccable with the occasional minor slip-up. ⊠ *36 av. George V, Champs-Élysées* ☎ *01–40–70–10–49* ▭ *AE, MC, V* ⊘ *Closed Sun. No lunch Sat.* Ⓜ *Franklin-D.-Roosevelt.*

$$$–$$$$ ✕ **Spoon, Food and Wine.** Star chef Alain Ducasse's bistro may be the granddaddy of style-conscious restaurants around the Champs-Élysées, but its popularity shows no signs of waning. What draws the black-clad crowd are the playful, Asian- and American-inspired menu; the hypercool interior (white by day, plum by night); and the fact that it's so hard to get a dinner reservation. Fashion folk love this place for its many vegetable and pasta dishes and its irresistible desserts, particularly the TobleSpoon, a takeoff on Toblerone. If you've sampled the Spoon concept elsewhere in the world, don't expect the same here; each branch is tailored to a particular city's tastes, and what looks exotic in Paris (bagels and bubble-gum ice cream) might seem humdrum in New York. ⊠ *14 rue de Marignan, Champs-Élysées* ☎ *01–40–76–34–44* ⚇ *Reservations essential* ▭ *AE, MC, V* ⊘ *Closed weekends, 4 wks in July and Aug., and 2 wks in late Dec.* Ⓜ *Franklin-D.-Roosevelt.*

$$$–$$$$ ✕ **La Table du Lancaster.** Operated by one of the most enduring families
Fodor'sChoice in French gastronomy—the Troisgros clan has run a world-famous
★ restaurant in Roanne for three generations—this stylish boutique-hotel restaurant is the perfect setting for tasting the stellar cosmopolitan cuisine. Try to sit in the stunning Asian-inspired courtyard with its red walls and bamboo trees. Often drawing on humble ingredients, such as eel or even pigs' ears, the food reveals fascinating flavor and texture contrasts, as in silky sardines on crunchy melba toast, or tangy frogs' legs in tamarind. A classic borrowed from the menu in Roanne is cod in a seaweed bouillon over short-grain white rice, a subtle and sensual dish. Don't miss the desserts, such as not one but two slices of sugar tart with grapefruit slices for contrast. ⊠ *Hotel Lancaster, 7 rue de Berri Champs-Élysées* ☎ *01–40–76–40–18* ⚇ *Reservations essential* ▭ *AE, DC, MC, V* ⊘ *Closed mid-July–mid-Aug. No lunch weekends* Ⓜ *George V.*

$$–$$$$ ✕ **Market.** Celebrated New York–based Alsatian chef Jean-Georges Vongerichten (think Vong, Mercer Kitchen, and Jean-Georges) set up shop in this strategic neighborhood to much fanfare, as this is his first restaurant in France. Put together with deceptively simple raw materials—burnt pine and stone offset with African masks—the dining room makes a soigné if sometimes noisy arena for well-traveled dishes such as truffled pizza, spiced sea bream, and sweet chestnut soufflé. The sometimes lackluster food, however, suggests that the worldly Vongerichten might be spreading himself too thin. This is a fine place for a breakfast meeting, however, over a plate of buttery pastries by star pâtissier Pierre Hermé (available 9–11 AM daily). ⊠ *15 av. Matignon, Champs-Élysées* ☎*01–56–43–40–90* ⚇ *Reservations essential* ▭*AE, MC, V* Ⓜ*Franklin-D.-Roosevelt.*

FRENCH ✕ **Alain Ducasse au Plaza Athénée.** This previously sober dining room
★ **$$$$** now glimmers with 10,000 crystals, following a whirlwind revamp by
decorator Patrick Jouin. Clementine-color tablecloths and space-age
cream-and-orange chairs with pull-out plastic trays (a bit airplanelike)
provide a more cheerful setting for the cooking of young chef Christophe
Moret, who still seems to be finding his footing in a dining room heavy
with gastronomic expectations. Some dishes taste too subtle, while in
others strong flavors overwhelm more delicate ingredients. Even so, a
meal here is delightfully luxe, starting with a heavenly amuse-bouche
of Dublin Bay shrimp with caviar and a tangy lemon cream. You can
continue with a full truffle- and caviar-fest, or opt for slightly more down-
to-earth dishes such as lobster in spiced wine with quince or saddle of
lamb with small sautéed artichokes. If you find yourself hesitating over
dessert, opt for the baba au rhum, which comes with a trolley of fine
rums. ⊠ *Hôtel Plaza Athenée, 27 av. Montaigne, Champs-Élysées*
☏ *01–53–67–66–65* ⌕ *Reservations essential* ⌂ *Jacket required* ⊟ *AE,
DC, MC, V* ☉ *Closed weekends, 2 wks in late Dec., and mid-July–mid-
Aug. No lunch Mon.–Wed.* Ⓜ *Alma-Marceau.*

★ **$$$$** ✕ **Les Ambassadeurs.** A former star—more of a comet, really—in the Alain
Ducasse galaxy, Jean-Francois Piége is now establishing his own identity in Hôtel Le Crillon's hallowed 18th-century dining room, recently
updated in muted tones that offset the glistening marble and dripping
chandeliers. Born in 1970, he is young enough to play with food—de-
constructing and reconstructing an egg to look like a square marshmallow,
its yolk studded with white truffle—and grown-up enough to serve unabashedly rich classics of French cooking, such as deboned squab stuffed
with foie gras. An expert at pairing langoustines and caviar, he has come
up with a new version for Le Crillon, wrapping the ingredients in a delicate crêpe. ⊠ *Hôtel de Crillon, 10 pl. de la Concorde, Champs-Élysées*
☏ *01–44–71–16–17* ⌕ *Reservations essential* Ⓜ *Concorde.*

$$$$ ✕ **L'Astor.** Chef Christophe Dié stepped into the clogs of Eric Lecerf, a
Joël Robuchon lieutenant, and quickly hit his stride with offerings such
as spider crab served in its shell with anise jelly and fennel cream and
a refined *steak au poivre* (steak with pepper sauce) flambéed in cognac.
The service and wine list are superb; the dining room takes a cue from
the '30s with star appliqués on the walls and a checkerboard carpet. The
€45 prix-fixe lunch menu, including mineral water, wine, and coffee,
is a notably good value—it has even gone down in price by €10 since
2004. ⊠ *Hôtel Astor, 11 rue d'Astorg, Opéra/Grands Boulevards*
☏ *01–53–05–05–20* ⊟ *AE, DC, MC, V* ☉ *Closed weekends and Aug.*
Ⓜ *Madeleine.*

$$$$ ✕ **Le Bristol.** After a rapid ascent at his own nouvelle-wave bistro that
led to his renown as one of the more inventive young chefs in Paris, Eric
Frechon became head chef at the Bristol, that home-away-from-home
of billionaires and power brokers. Frechon uses one of the grandest
pantries in Paris to create masterworks—say, Breton lobster with an intense tomato jus and fork-crushed avocado—that never stray too far from
the comfort-food tastes found in bistro cooking. The €70 lunch menu
makes his cooking accessible not just to the palate but to many pock-
etbooks. No wonder his tables are so coveted. Though the two dining

rooms are impeccable—an oval oak-paneled one for fall and winter and a marble-floor pavilion overlooking the courtyard garden for spring and summer—they provide few clues to help the world-weary traveler determine which city this might be. ✉ *Hôtel Bristol, 112 rue du Faubourg St-Honoré, Champs-Élysées* ☎ *01–53–43–43–00* ✍ *Reservations essential* 👔 *Jacket and tie* 💳 *AE, DC, MC, V* Ⓜ *Miromesnil.*

★ $$$$ ✕ **Le Cinq.** The massive flower arrangement at the entrance proclaims the no-holds-barred luxury that is on offer here. Painted powder blue, with stucco medallions worked into the ceiling trim, this beautiful though staid room makes a fitting stage set for chef Philippe Legendre. Formerly a legend at Taillevent, he is clearly thriving in these kitchens. Occasionally, the luxe menu (line-caught turbot with pumpkin-and-grapefruit marmalade, a licorice-infused pear cube with Szechuan pepper ice cream) is brought back down to earth by such selections as grouse and haggis in an aged Scotch whiskey sauce. And there's a €75 lunch menu. ✉ *Hôtel Four Seasons George V, 31 av. George V, Champs-Élysées* ☎ *01–49–52–70–00* ✍ *Reservations essential* 👔 *Jacket and tie* 💳 *AE, DC, MC, V* Ⓜ *George V.*

$$$$ Fodor'sChoice ★ ✕ **Les Élysées du Vernet.** Eric Briffard landed on his feet when he took over this intimate dining room, whose gorgeous *verrière* (glass ceiling) was designed by none other than Gustave Eiffel. Bringing together prosaic and luxury ingredients, Briffard makes his mark with dishes such as truffled pig's trotter, monkfish with ginger and lime, and potato salad with truffles—though sometimes his cooking seems overly fussy. This restaurant remains relatively affordable at lunch (€60 or €68 for a set menu), and the wine service is outstanding. ✉ *Hôtel Vernet, 25 rue Vernet, Champs-Élysées* ☎ *01–44–31–98–98* ✍ *Reservations essential* 💳 *AE, DC, MC, V* ⏲ *Closed weekends, Aug., and 1 wk at Christmas. No lunch Mon.* Ⓜ *George V.*

$$$$ ✕ **Ledoyen.** Tucked away in the quiet gardens flanking the Champs-Élysées, Ledoyen was once a study in the grandiose style of Napoléon III (you'll find most of the historic rooms upstairs; avoid downstairs). Unfortunately, this aging beauty needs a face-lift, at least from the look of the upholstery. Still, young Breton chef Christian Le Squer's menu is a treat. He uses flawless produce, as seen in *les coquillages* (shellfish), a delicious dish of herb risotto topped with lobster, langoustine, scallops, and grilled ham. The turbot with truffled mashed potatoes is excellent, too, and don't skip the superlative cheese trolley. ✉ *1 av. Dutuit, on the Carré des Champs-Élysées, Champs-Élysées* ☎ *01–53–05–10–01* ✍ *Reservations essential* 💳 *AE, DC, MC, V* ⏲ *Closed weekends and Aug. No lunch Mon.* Ⓜ *Concorde, Champs-Élysées–Clemenceau.*

$$$$ ✕ **Lucas Carton.** At the time of this writing, Alain Senderens was closing his Michelin 3-star restaurant in order to renovate and reopen in fall 2005 with a new menu, more affordable prices, and possibly a new name. The location is expected to remain the same. ✉ *9 pl. de la Madeleine Opéra/Grands Boulevards* ☎ *01–42–65–22–90* 💳 *AE, DC, MC, V* Ⓜ *Madeleine.*

$$$$ ✕ **Maxim's.** Count Danilo sang "I'm going to Maxim's" in Lehar's *The Merry Widow,* Leslie Caron was klieg-lighted here by Cecil Beaton for *Gigi,* and Audrey Hepburn adorned a banquette with Peter O'Toole in *How to Steal a Million.* In reality, Maxim's has lost some of its luster—the restaurant had its heyday 100 years ago during the Belle Époque, when *le tout Paris* swarmed here—but this exuberant Art Nouveau sanctuary still offers a taste of the good life under its breathtaking painted ceiling. It's just a shame that Maxim's is so jaw-droppingly expensive for food—like the Billy-bi mussel consommé with cream or braised sole in vermouth—that would feel at home in a brasserie. A set menu would attract a bigger crowd and make the room feel more festive. ⊠ *3 rue Royale, Louvre/ Tuileries* ☎ *01–42–65–27–94* ⌾ *Reservations essential* ☐ *AE, DC, MC, V* ⊘ *Closed Sun. and Mon. No lunch Sat.* Ⓜ *Concorde.*

$$$$ ✕ **Pierre Gagnaire.** If you want to venture to the frontier of luxe cooking today—and if money is truly no object—a dinner here is a must. Chef Pierre Gagnaire's work is at once intellectual and poetic, often blending three or four unexpected tastes and textures in a single dish. Just taking in the menu requires concentration, so complex are descriptions such as "suckling lamb from Aveyron: sweetbreads, saddle, and rack; green papaya and turnip velouté thickened with Tarbais beans." The Grand Dessert, a seven-dessert marathon, will leave you breathless. The businesslike gray-and-wood dining room feels refreshingly informal, especially at lunch, but it also lacks the grandeur expected at this level. The uninspiring prix-fixe lunch, uneven service, and occasional ill-judged dishes linger as drawbacks, and prices keep shooting skywards, making Pierre Gagnaire an experience only for the financial elite. ⊠ *6 rue de Balzac, Champs-Élysées* ☎ *01–58–36–12–50* ⌾ *Reservations essential* ☐ *AE, DC, MC, V* ⊘ *Closed Sat. and 2 wks in July. No lunch Sun. and Aug.* Ⓜ *Charles-de-Gaulle–Étoile.*

$$$$
Fodor'sChoice
★

✕ **Taillevent.** Perhaps the most traditional—for many diners this is only high praise—of all Paris luxury restaurants, this grande dame basks in newfound freshness under brilliant chef Alain Solivérès, who draws inspiration from the Basque country, Bordeaux, and Languedoc for his daily-changing menu. Signatures such as the *boudin de homard* (an airy sausage-shape lobster soufflé) are now matched with choices such as a splendid spelt risotto with truffles and frogs' legs or panfried duck liver with caramelized fruits and vegetables. One of the 19th-century paneled salons has been turned into a winter garden, and contemporary paintings adorn the walls. The service is flawless and the exceptional wine list is well priced. All in all, a meal here comes as close to the classic haute-cuisine experience as you can find in Paris. Not surprisingly, you must reserve your table for dinner a month in advance. ⊠ *15 rue Lamennais, Champs-Élysées* ☎ *01–44–95–15–01* ⌾ *Reservations essential* 🎩 *Jacket and tie* ☐ *AE, DC, MC, V* ⊘ *Closed weekends and Aug.* Ⓜ *Charles-de-Gaulle–Étoile.*

$$$–$$$$ ✕ **Stella Maris.** A pretty Art Deco front window is the calling card for this pristine spot near the Arc de Triomphe, whose dining room was recently spruced up with a gleaming black floor and hanging lights. An expense-account crowd mixes with serious French gourmands to dine on the subtle cuisine of likable Japanese chef Taderu Yoshino, who trained with Joël Robuchon and rewrites his menu four times a year. You'll find hints of Japan in dishes—made with organic ingredients—such as eel blanquette with grilled cucumber, salmon prepared four ways (in salt, marinated with dill, smoked, and panfried), and a unique take on the French classic *tête de veau,* with a spice and turtle jus. Put your trust in Yoshino by opting for the tasting menu or the chef's menu, which change daily. ✉ *4 rue Arsène-Houssaye, Champs-Élysées* ☎ *01–42–89–16–22* ⌕ *Reservations essential* 🖃 *AE, DC, MC, V* ☉ *Closed Sun. and 2 wks in Aug. No lunch Sat.* Ⓜ *Étoile.*

$$–$$$ ✕ **La Fermette Marbeuf 1900.** Graced with one of the most mesmerizing Belle Époque rooms in town—accidentally rediscovered during renovations in the 1970s—this is a favorite haunt of French celebrities, who adore the sunflowers, peacocks, and dragonflies of the Art Nouveau mosaic and stained-glass mise-en-scène. The menu rolls out a solid, updated classic cuisine. Try the snails in puff pastry, saddle of lamb with *choron* (a tomato-spiked béarnaise sauce), and bitter-chocolate fondant—but ignore the rather depressing €30 prix-fixe unless you're on a budget. Popular with tourists and businesspeople at lunch, La Fermette becomes truly animated around 9 PM. ✉ *5 rue Marbeuf, Champs-Élysées* ☎ *01–53–23–08–00* 🖃 *AE, DC, MC, V* Ⓜ *Franklin-D.-Roosevelt.*

$–$$$
Fodor'sChoice
★
✕ **Chez Savy.** Just off the glitzy avenue Montaigne, Chez Savy exists in its own circa-1930s dimension, oblivious to the area's galloping fashionization. The Art Deco cream-and-burgundy interior looks blissfully intact (avoid the back room unless you're in a large group), and the waiters show not a trace of attitude. Fill up on rib-sticking specialties from the Auvergne in central France—lentil salad with bacon, foie gras (prepared on the premises), perfectly charred lamb with featherlight shoestring frites—order a celebratory bottle of Mercurey and feel smug that you've found this place. ✉ *23 rue Bayard, Champs-Élysées* ☎ *01–47–23–46–98* 🖃 *AE, MC, V* ☉ *Closed weekends and Aug.* Ⓜ *Franklin-D.-Roosevelt.*

$–$$$ ✕ **Sébillon.** The original Sébillon has nurtured chic residents of the fashionable suburb of Neuilly for generations; this graceful branch off the Champs-Élysées continues the tradition in a setting reminiscent of a gentleman's club. The house specialty is roast leg of lamb sliced table-side, served until you beg the waiter to stop. Save room, however, for a chocolate or coffee éclair big enough to give the standard éclair a serious complex. Service is notably friendly. ✉ *66 rue Pierre Charron, Champs-Élysées* ☎ *01–43–59–28–15* 🖃 *AE, DC, MC, V* Ⓜ *Franklin-D.-Roosevelt.*

$$ ✕ **Chez Tante Louise.** In this bastion of Burgundian cooking, the vintage '30s decor is almost completely intact. The food is pleasantly old-fashioned and substantial, like *oeufs en meurette à la bourguignonne* (poached eggs in red-wine sauce with bacon); sole Tante Louise, in which a steamed fillet comes with a mussel-based sauce; and melting chocolate cake with a fromage blanc sorbet. Of course, there's a nice selection of Burgundies, and service is prompt and professional for the well-dressed crowd. ✉ *41 rue Boissy d'Anglas, Opéra/Grands Boulevards* ☎ *01–42–65–06–85* ▭ *AE, DC, MC, V* ⊘ *Closed weekends and Aug.* Ⓜ *Madeleine.*

9ᵉ Arrondissement (Opéra/Grands Boulevards)

See Where to Eat on the Rive Droite: Île de la Cité to Montmartre map.

FRENCH ✕ **Bistrot des Deux Théâtres.** This theater-lover's bistro with red-velour
$$$$ banquettes, black-and-white photos of actors, and a giant oil painting depicting dozens of personalities is always packed, and with good reason: the prix-fixe-only menu for €32, including a *kir royale* (sparkling white wine with cassis), three courses, half a bottle of wine, and coffee, is a fantastic value. This isn't a place for modest eaters, so have foie gras or escargots to start, then a meaty main such as the crackly crusted rack of lamb, and a potent baba au rhum or a rustic lemon meringue tart for dessert. Waiters are jokey, English-speaking, and efficient. ✉ *18 rue Blanche, Montmartre* ☎ *01–45–26–41–43* ▭ *AE, MC, V* Ⓜ *Trinité.*

$ ✕ **Les Vivres.** The brainchild of Jean-Luc André, chef at the elegant Pétrelle next door, Les Vivres translates as "survival supplies," and many devotees now feel they couldn't live without it. Down the hill from Montmartre on a quiet residential street, this stylish dining room—like the French country home you wish you had—serves lunch nonstop from 11-7 and dinner on Friday nights. You'll always find seasonal vegetables, which are grilled, marinated, or slow-roasted; a savory tart; and such hearty dishes as farmer's rabbit with Nyons olives, *hachis parmentier* (shepherd's pie), and squid fricassee. Jars of jams and preserves are available to take home for future emergencies. ✉ *28 rue Pétrelle, Montmartre* ☎ *01–42–80–26–10* ▭ *MC, V* ⊘ *Closed Sun., Mon., July 25–Aug. 25 and Dec. 25–Jan. 3. No dinner Sat.–Thurs.* Ⓜ *Anvers.*

☺ ¢–$ ✕ **Chartier.** People come here more for the bonhomie and the stunning 1896 interior than the cooking, which could be politely described as unambitious. This cavernous restaurant—the only original turn-of-the-century *bouillon* to remain true to its mission of serving cheap, sustaining food to the masses—enjoys a huge following. You may find yourself sharing a table with strangers as you study the long, old-fashioned menu of such standards as hard-boiled eggs with mayonnaise, pot-au-feu, and blanquette de veau. The simplest dishes bring the most satisfaction. ✉ *7 rue du Faubourg-Montmartre, Opéra/Grands Boulevards* ☎*01–47–70–86–29* ⌾ *Reservations not accepted* ▭ *MC, V* Ⓜ *Montmartre.*

INDIAN ✕ **Kastoori.** On a pretty little restaurant-strewn square down the hill
¢ from Montmartre, Kastoori is something of a miracle. Not only is its terrace one of the most agreeable in Paris, but the modest dining room draped with Indian fabrics feels equally relaxing on a rainy day, and the reliably good food offers a tremendous value. The best bets at lunch are the €8 or €10 daily-changing *thali* platters, silver trays bearing curried meat (usually chicken or lamb), vegetables, and saffron rice. Work it all off with a hike up the hill to Sacré-Coeur. ✉ *4 place Gustave Toudouze, Montmartre* ☎ *01–44–53–06–10* ▭ *MC, V* ⊘ *Closed Mon.* Ⓜ *St-Georges.*

SEAFOOD   ✕ **Estaminet Gaya.** Come here for seafood in all its guises, from mari-
$$$–$$$$ nated anchovies to Basque tuna to bouillabaisse. The colorful Por-
tuguese tiles on the ground floor are delightful; the upstairs dining room
decorated with photos seems plain by comparison. Given the often-ex-
orbitant prices at fish restaurants in Paris, the €32 prix-fixe menu
(lunch and dinner) is an excellent value. Other prices vary with the day's
catch. ✉ *17 rue Duphot, Opéra/Grands Boulevards* ☎ *01–42–60–43–03*
🖃 *AE, MC, V* ☽ *Closed weekends and 3 wks in Aug.* Ⓜ *Madeleine.*

10ᵉ Arrondissement (République)

See Where to Eat on the Rive Droite: the Marais to La Villette map.

FRENCH   ✕ **Chez Michel.** Effusive chef Thierry Breton has become a magnet with
★ **$$$**   his wonderful market-inspired cooking, despite the out-of-the-way lo-
cation near Gare du Nord. The prix-fixe-only menu changes constantly,
but you'll almost invariably find the Breton specialties *kig ha farz* (a robust pork stew with a bread stuffing) and *kouing aman* (the butteriest
cake imaginable). In winter don't miss the game dishes (for a supplement) such as the surprisingly mild-tasting boar chops, served in a cast-
iron pot with tiny potatoes and roasted garlic. The cheese course, served
on a slate, is outstanding. There is a long, sociable table in the vaulted
cellar, while the beamed main room feels like a country inn. ✉ *10 rue
Belzunce, Opéra/Grands Boulevards* ☎ *01–44–53–06–20* ✑ *Reservations essential* 🖃 *MC, V* ☽ *Closed weekends and 2 wks in Aug. No
lunch Mon.* ✑ *Reservations essential* Ⓜ *Gare du Nord.*

$$–$$$ ✕ **Julien.** Famed for its 1879 decor—think Art Nouveau stained glass,
La Bohème–ish street lamps hung with vintage hats—this Belle Époque
dazzler certainly lives up to its oft-quoted moniker, "the poor man's
Maxim's." Look for smoked salmon, stuffed roast lamb, cassoulet, and,
to finish, profiteroles or the *coupe Julien* (ice cream with cherries). The
crowd here is lots of fun; this place has a strong following with the fashion crowd, so it's mobbed during the biannual fashion and fabric shows.
The downside? Readers have complained about some lackluster dishes
and even worse service (and the area is frankly not the safest in Paris).
There's service until midnight, with a late-night menu for €23.50 from
10 PM. ✉ *16 rue du Faubourg St-Denis, Opéra/Grands Boulevards*
☎ *01–47–70–12–06* 🖃 *AE, DC, MC, V* Ⓜ *Strasbourg St-Denis.*

$–$$$ ✕ **Brasserie Flo.** The first of brasserie king Jean-Paul Bucher's many
Paris addresses is hard to find down its passageway near the Gare de
l'Est, but it's worth the effort, as much for its Alsatian rich woods and
stained glass as for its brasserie standards (such as sole meunière, steak
tartare, and choucroute). Order a carafe of Alsatian wine to go with your
meal. It's open until 1:30 AM, with a special late-night menu for €23.50
from 10 PM. ✉ *7 cour des Petites-Écuries, Opéra/Grands Boulevards*
☎ *01–47–70–13–59* 🖃 *AE, DC, MC, V* Ⓜ *Château d'Eau.*

$ ✕ **Chez Casimir.** Another project of chef Thierry Breton of Chez Michel,
this (too) brightly lit, easygoing bistro next door is popular with pol-
ished Parisian professionals for whom it serves as a sort of canteen—
why cook when you can eat this well for so little money? The menu covers
lentil soup with fresh croutons, braised endive and andouille (tripe
sausage) salad, and roast lamb on a bed of Paimpol beans. Good, if not

exceptional, desserts include *pain perdu*, a dessert version of French toast—here it's topped with a roasted pear or whole cherries. ⊠ *6 rue de Belzunce, Opéra/Grands Boulevards* ☎ *01–48–78–28–80* ▤ *MC, V* ◷ *Closed Sun., Mon., and 3 wks in Aug.* Ⓜ *Gare du Nord.*

¢–$ ✕**Au Vieux Bistrot.** If you're staying near the Gare du Nord or looking for a meal in the area before taking the train, this pleasant old-school neighborhood bistro is a good bet. From the big zinc bar to the steak with mushroom sauce, duck confit, and veal in cream, this place delivers a traditional bistro experience at prices that seem to belong to another era. (There are prix-fixe menus at €10 and €12.) ⊠ *30 rue Dunkerque, Opéra/Grands Boulevards* ☎ *01–48–78–48–01* ▤ *MC, V* ◷ *Closed Sun. No dinner Sat.* Ⓜ *Gare du Nord.*

NORTH AFRICAN ✕**Le Martel.** Of the scads of neighborhood couscous joints in Paris, a
★ $–$$ few have become fashionable thanks to the host's magnetic personality and the quality of the food. This converted bistro ranks among the more recent of that set. It's crowded and smoky, but the clientele of fashion designers, photographers, models, and media folk is as cool as it gets. Everyone digs into a mix of French standbys (such as artichokes with vinaigrette) and more exotic fare like lamb tagine with almonds, prunes, and dried apricots. ⊠ *3 rue Martel, République* ☎ *01–47–70–67–56* ▤ *DC, MC, V* ◷ *No lunch weekends* Ⓜ *Château d'Eau.*

11ᵉ Arrondissement (Bastille/Nation & République)
See Where to Eat on the Rive Droite: the Marais to La Villette map.

CHINESE ✕**Wok.** Design-it-yourself Asian stir-fry in a slick, minimalist room has
$$ made this spot a hit with the penny-wise hipsters around party-hearty Bastille. You select the type of noodle you want and load up at a buffet with meats, seafood, and vegetables; then join the line to negotiate your preferred seasoning with the chefs who man the woks in the open kitchen. (A couple of gestures should be all the communication you need.) The all-you-can-eat single-price tariff (€20) lets you walk the wok as many times as you want. Otherwise, there are deep-fried spring rolls as starters and a signature dessert of caramelized fruit salad. It's mobbed on Friday and Saturday but unfortunately doesn't serve lunch. ⊠ *23 rue des Taillandiers, Bastille/Nation* ☎ *01–55–28–88–77* ▤ *MC, V* ◷ *Closed Sun. No lunch* Ⓜ *Bréguet Sabin, Bastille, Ledru-Rollin.*

FRENCH ✕**C'amelot.** This minuscule bistro brings in the crowds with its excel-
★ $$–$$$$ lent home-style cooking, consistently some of the best bistro food in Paris. Chef Didier Varnier trained with guru Christian Constant at the Crillon, and it shows in such choices as pumpkin soup with goat-cheese ravioli, sweet-and-sour duck with dried-fruit tabbouleh, and spice-bread pudding with lemon cream—the selection changes daily. Service is friendly, and the house wines are a treat. ⊠ *50 rue Amelot, Bastille/Nation* ☎ *01–43–55–54–04* ⌕ *Reservations essential* ▤ *AE, MC, V* ◷ *Closed Sun. and Mon. No lunch Sat.* Ⓜ *République.*

★ $$$ ✕**Astier.** The prix-fixe menu (there's no à la carte) at this tried-and-true restaurant must be one of the best values in town, with a lunch menu for €22.50 and a second lunch menu and dinner menu for €27. Among the deftly prepared seasonal dishes are tomato-and-goat cheese tart on

A CHEESE PRIMER

THE COOKING MIGHT BE GETTING LIGHTER in Paris restaurants, but the French aren't ready to relinquish their cheese. Nearly every restaurant, no matter how humble or haute, takes pride in its odorous offerings. Some present just a single, lovingly selected slice, while others wheel in an entire trolley of specimens aged on the premises. These may be labeled, but most often the cheese waiter will name and describe them. Always, though, cheese comes after the main course and before—or instead of—dessert.

Among the best restaurants for cheese are Astier, where a giant wicker basket of oozy wonders lands on the table; Chez Michel, where perfectly aged specimens arrive on a slab of slate; and Les Fernandises, which specializes in Camembert. A few bars à fromages are springing up, establishments devoted to cheese the way bars à vins are dedicated to wine. **La Fromagerie 31** (✉ 64 rue de Seine, St-Germain-des-Prés ☎ 01–43–26–50–31) is one terrific example. Armed with the following phrases, you can wow the waiter and happily work your way through the most generous platter.

Avez-vous le Beaufort d'été? (Do you have the summer Beaufort?) Beaufort is similar to Gruyère, and the best Beaufort is made with milk produced during the summer, when the cows munch on fresh grass and alpine flowers. Beaufort that has aged for more than a year is even more reminiscent of a mountain hike.

Je voudrais un chèvre bien frais/bien sec. (I'd like a goat cheese that's nice and fresh/nice and dry.) France produces many dozens of goat cheeses, some so fresh they can be scooped up with a spoon and some tough enough to use as doorstops. It's a matter of taste, but hard-core cheese

eaters favor the drier specimens, which stick to the roof of the mouth and have a frankly goaty aroma.

C'est un St-Marcellin de vache ou de chèvre? (Is this St-Marcellin made with cow's or goat's milk?) St-Marcellin makes a more original choice than the ubiquitous crottin de chèvre (poetically named after goats' turds). It was originally a goat cheese but today is more often made with cow's milk. The best have a delightfully oozy center, though some people like it dry as a hockey puck.

C'est un Brie de Meaux ou de Melun? (Is this Brie from Meaux or Melun?) There are many kinds of Brie; Brie de Meaux is the best known, with a smooth flavor and runny center, while the much rarer Brie de Melun is more pungent and saltier.

Je n'aime pas le Camembert industriel! (I don't like industrial Camembert!) Camembert might be a national treasure, but most of it is industrial. Real Camembert has a white rind with rust-color streaks and a yellow center.

Avez-vous de la confiture pour accompagner ce brebis? (Do you have any jam to go with this sheep's cheese?) In France's Basque region berry jam is the traditional accompaniment for sharp sheep's-milk cheeses, such as Ossau-Iraty.

C'est la saison du Mont d'Or. (It's Mont d'Or season.) This potent mountain cheese, also known as Vacherin, is produced only from September to March. So runny is the texture that it's traditionally eaten with a spoon.

Avez-vous du cheddar? (Do you have any cheddar?) Ask this, and you're asking for trouble—unless you happen to be at Willi's Wine Bar, Macéo, or Le Timbre, where the owners are British.

— Rosa Jackson

curly endive, rabbit in mustard sauce with fresh tagliatelle, and an old-fashioned blanquette de veau and *marquise au chocolat* (chocolate mousse cake). This is a great place to come if you're feeling cheesy, since it's locally famous for having one of the best *plateaux de fromages* (cheese plates) in Paris—a giant wicker tray lands on the table and you help yourself. The lengthy, well-priced wine list is a connoisseur's dream. ✉ *44 rue Jean-Pierre Timbaud, République* ☎ *01–43–57–16–35* ⩜ *Reservations essential* 🖃 *MC, V* ⊗ *Closed weekends, Aug., Christmas wk, and Easter wk* Ⓜ *Parmentier.*

$–$$ ✕ **Les Fernandises.** The chef-owner of this neighborhood spot near place de la République, the self-declared "king of Camembert, " is more concerned with his Normandy-inspired cuisine than with his restaurant's inconsequential decor. Fresh foie gras sautéed in cider, skate wing with Camembert, and crêpes flambéed in calvados show off the star ingredients of a regional cuisine that has few representatives in Paris. Choose from at least six Camemberts at any given time, including one doused in calvados and another coated in hay. ✉ *17 rue Fontaine-au-Roi, République* ☎ *01–43–57–46–25* 🖃 *MC, V* ⊗ *Closed Sun., Mon., 1 wk in May, and Aug.* Ⓜ *République.*

$–$$ ✕ **Le Passage des Carmagnoles.** Feeling carnivorous? Search out this friendly spot not far from place de la Bastille in an obscure passage. Though it bills itself as a wine bar, it has a full menu, including the celebrated andouillette sausage of Mr. Artois in the town of Vouvray. The initials AAAAA, by the way, mean the sausage has the stamp of approval from the French andouillette aficionados' association. As the andouillette's pungent tripey aroma makes it an acquired taste, other, less fragrant dishes are available, such as rabbit with mustard, steak tartare flavored with mint, game in season, and even ostrich. The wine bar claim is far from unfounded, though; Le Passage has many unusual bottles. ✉ *18 passage de la Bonne Graine (enter by 108 av. Ledru-Rollin), Bastille/Nation* ☎ *01–47–00–73–30* 🖃 *AE, DC, MC, V* ⊗ *Closed Sun.* Ⓜ *Ledru-Rollin.*

$–$$ ✕ **Le Repaire de Cartouche.** In this split-level, dark-wood bistro between Bastille and République, young chef Rodolphe Paquin applies a disciplined creativity to earthy French regional dishes. The menu changes regularly, but typical are a salad of *haricots verts* (string beans) topped with tender slices of squid, scallops on a bed of diced pumpkin, juicy lamb with white beans, and old-fashioned desserts like custard with tiny madeleine cakes. The wine list is very good, too, with bargains like a Cheverny from the Loire Valley for €17. ✉ *99 rue Amelot, Bastille/Nation* ☎ *01–47–00–25–86* ⩜ *Reservations essential* 🖃 *MC, V* ⊗ *Closed Sun., Mon., and Aug.* Ⓜ *Filles du Calvaire.*

VIETNAMESE ✕ **Dong Huong.** Dong Huong isn't a secret, but you wouldn't find it by
¢ accident: these two undecorated dining rooms on a Belleville side street are where the local Chinese and Vietnamese come for a reassuring bowl of *pho* (soup) or a big plate of grilled lemongrass-scented meat with rice. Non-Asians will be instantly directed to the smoking room (on the assumption that they are French), so make it clear if you prefer a no-smoking area. Spicy, peanutty *saté* soup is a favorite, and at this price (€6.50)

you can also spring for a plate of crunchy imperial rolls, to be wrapped in lettuce and mint. Try one of the lurid nonalcoholic drinks, too. ⊠ *14 rue Louis-Bonnet, Père Lachaise* ☎ *01–43–57–18–88* ▭ *MC, V* ⊘ *Closed Tues. and 2 wks in Aug.* Ⓜ *Belleville.*

12ᵉ Arrondissement (Bastille/Nation)
See Where to Eat on the Rive Droite: the Marais to La Villette map.

CONTEMPORARY ✕ **Chai 33.** Thierry Begué, one of the names behind the trendsetting
$–$$$ nightspots Buddha Bar and Barrio Latino, created something more personal with this forward-looking spot. Appropriately set in a neighborhood once dedicated to the wine trade, it's a restaurant, bar, and wine shop rolled into one. It aims to make wine unintimidating—instead of the usual regional listings, wines are classified by style, and you can go into the cellar to choose a bottle with the help of an expert sommelier. Go for the funky wine cocktails or the perfectly fine food, such as white-bean salad with andouille or seared tuna with pistachio and cumin, served on a terrace in summer. Good-value prix-fixes range from € 15 to € 21. ⊠ *33 Cour St-Emilion, Bercy/Tolbiac* ☎ *01–53–44–01–01* ▭ *AE, MC, V* Ⓜ *Cour St-Emilion.*

FRENCH ✕ **Au Trou Gascon.** This classy establishment off place Daumesnil—well
★ $$$–$$$$ off the beaten tourist track but worth the trip—is overseen by celebrated chef Alain Dutournier, whose wife runs the dining room. He does a refined take on the cuisine of Gascony—a region renowned for its ham, foie gras, lamb, and duck. Most popular with the regulars are the surprisingly light cassoulet (all the meats are grilled before going into the pot) and a superb duck confit. You'll also find an ethereal dessert of raspberries, ice cream, and meringue. With some 875 wines and 100 Armagnacs to choose from, this is the place to splurge on vintage. ⊠ *40 rue Taine, Bastille/Nation* ☎ *01–43–44–34–26* ▭ *AE, MC, V* ⊘ *Closed weekends, Aug., and 2 wks in Dec.–Jan.* Ⓜ *Daumesnil.*

$$–$$$$ ✕ **L'Oulette.** Chef-owner Marcel Baudis's take on the cuisine of his native southwestern France is original and delicious, and service here is effusive—qualities that will help you overlook the out-of-the-way location and out-of-date design. The menu changes with the seasons: you might come across a scallop brochette with vegetable rémoulade in a truffle vinaigrette or the chef's own take on aïoli, with all kinds of fish and vegetables. Nearly everyone wisely opts for the €46 prix-fixe menu, which includes wine and coffee. The restaurant, in the rebuilt Bercy district, is a bit hard to find, so head out with your map. ⊠ *15 pl. Lachambeaudie, Bastille/Nation* ☎ *01–40–02–02–12* ▭ *AE, DC, MC, V* ⊘ *Closed weekends* Ⓜ *Dugommier.*

★ $–$$$ ✕ **Le Square Trousseau.** This beautiful Belle Époque bistro is a favorite of the fashion set. Even models can't resist the peppered country pâté, slow-cooked lamb, or tender baby chicken with mustard and bread-crumb crust. Wines might seem a little pricey but are lovingly selected from small producers—you can also buy them, along with superb Spanish ham, at the restaurant's small boutique/wine bar next door. If you're on a budget, try the lunch menu at €20 or €25. ⊠ *1 rue Antoine Vollon, Bastille/Nation* ☎ *01–43–43–06–00* ▭ *AE, MC, V* ⊘ *Closed Sun. and Mon., 3 wks in Aug., 1 wk at Christmas, and 2 wks in Feb.* Ⓜ *Ledru-Rollin.*

ITALIAN ✕ **Sardegna a Tavola.** Paris might have more Italian restaurants than you
★ **$–$$** can shake a noodle at, but few smack of authenticity like this out-of-
the-way Sardinian spot with peppers, braids of garlic, and cured hams
hanging from the ceiling. Dishes are listed in Sardinian with French translations—*malloredus* is a small, gnocchilike pasta, while Sardinian ravioli are stuffed with cheese and mint. Perhaps best of all are the clams
in a spicy broth with tiny pasta and the orange-scented Dublin Bay prawns
with tagliatelle. If charcuterie *artisanale* sounds too tame, try the horse
carpaccio. ⊠ *1 rue de Cotte, Bastille/Nation* ☏ *01–44–75–03–28*
🗏 *MC, V* ☺ *Closed Sun., and Aug. No lunch Mon.* Ⓜ *Ledru-Rollin.*

13e Arrondissement (Bercy/Tolbiac)
See Where to Eat on the Rive Gauche map.

FRENCH ✕ **Le Petit Marguery.** As the diorama of a stuffed ferret amid a fairy-tale
★ **$$$–$$$$** mushroom forest announces, this charming ruby-color bistro offers
some of the earthiest dishes in the French canon. With its historic fin-
de-siècle charm, this is the place to head for if you're hunting for game—
catch it here in late fall, in such dishes as the deeply flavored *lièvre à la
royale* (hare in a wine-and-blood sauce) or the *noisette de biche* (doe).
Some dishes are so *authentique* they are even topped with pine needles.
Watch out, however, for the hefty price supplements on many seasonal
dishes. ⊠ *9 bd. de Port Royal, St-Germain-des-Prés* ☏ *01–43–31–58–59*
🗏 *AE, MC, V* ☺ *Closed Sun., Mon., and Aug.* Ⓜ *Les Gobelins.*

$$–$$$$ ✕ **Anacréon.** André le Letty, who polished his cooking technique at La
Tour d'Argent, may dream up dishes such as pressed duck with red pep-
percorns and fresh cod with spices for his regularly changing menu, but
he also has a fondness for old-faithfuls such as veal kidney with mustard sauce and prune clafoutis. The St-Joseph is a perfect choice from
the interesting wine list. The menu is prix-fixe: €20 at lunch and €32
at dinner. Overlooking a busy boulevard, the dining room feels a bit soul-
less after a recent renovation. ⊠ *53 bd. St-Marcel, St-Germain-des-Prés*
☏ *01–43–31–71–18* ⌦ *Reservations essential* 🗏 *AE, DC, MC, V*
☺ *Closed Sun., Mon., and Aug. No lunch Wed.* Ⓜ *Les Gobelins.*

★ ☖ **$** ✕ **L'Avant-Goût.** Christophe Beaufront belongs to a generation of gifted
bistro chefs who have rejected the pressure-cooker world of haute cuisine for something more personal and democratic. The result: a lot of
delighted customers, even if the restaurant is closed three days a week.
The three-course prix-fixe costs €28; there's also a more elaborate tasting menu for €40. Typical of his market-inspired cooking is his signature pot-au-feu *de cochon aux épices,* with spiced pork standing in for
the usual beef. Homemade desserts and a good-value wine list round
off a truly satisfying experience; children get an especially good welcome
here. ⊠ *26 rue Bobillot, Bercy/Tolbiac* ☏ *01–53–80–24–00* ⌦ *Reservations essential* 🗏 *MC, V* ☺ *Closed Sat.–Mon., 1st wk in Jan., 1st wk
in May, 3 wks in Aug., and 1 wk in Sept.* Ⓜ *Place d'Italie.*

$ ✕ **L'Ourcine.** La Régalade-trained chef Sylvain Danière knows just what
it takes to open a cult bistro: choose an obscure location, decorate it
simply but cheerfully, work extremely hard, set competitive prices, and
constantly reinvent your menu. The real key ingredient is talent, though,
and Danière has plenty of it, as demonstrated with such singular cre-

ations as *gougonettes* (strips) of John Dory with white beans and red onion, and pork cheeks with lentils and foie gras, a winning trio. For dessert, the puckery-tart lime cream scores points, while a layered chocolate mousse with strong coffee syrup proves less successful. Locals mingle with well-informed tourists in the red-and-cream dining room, and you can watch the chef hard at work in his small kitchen. ✉ *92 rue Broca, Les Gobelins* ☎ *01–47–07–13–65* 🖃 *MC, V* ☉ *Closed weekends, 3 wks in Aug., and Christmas wk* Ⓜ *Les Gobelins.*

PAN ASIAN ✕ **La Chine Massena.** With wonderfully overwrought rooms that seem
☾ ¢–$$ draped in what looks like a whole restaurant-supply catalog's worth of Asiana (plus four monitors showing the very latest in Hong Kong music videos), this is a fun place to come with friends. Not only is the Chinese-Vietnamese-Thai food good and moderately priced, but the place itself has a lot of entertainment value—wedding parties often provide a free floor show, and on weekends Asian disco follows variety shows. Steamed dumplings, lacquered duck, and the fish you'll see swimming in the tanks are specialties. For the best value come at noon on weekdays for the bargain lunch menus, starting at €8. ✉ *Centre Commercial Massena, 13 pl. de Venetie, Chinatown* ☎ *01–45–83–98–88* 🖃 *AE, MC, V* Ⓜ *Porte de Choisy.*

14ᵉ Arrondissement (Montparnasse)

See Where to Eat on the Rive Gauche map.

FRENCH ✕ **La Régalade.** Bruno Doucet was a brave man to take over what must
$$$ have been the most celebrated bistro in Paris when it was helmed by chef Yves Camdeborde, this despite a grim location near the Périphérique. After a strong start that impressed the French critics, he seems to be struggling slightly—some dishes, such as snails *en cassolette* (in a small dish), are lip-smackingly good, while others, namely the foie gras *royale* that skimps on the foie gras, fail to live up to the bistro's reputation. Doucet has a solid background and overall a meal here still represents a good value, but La Régalade no longer merits a trip across town when there are many other just-as-worthy bistros. The strict reservations policy remains, however. ✉ *49 av. Jean-Moulin, Montparnasse* ☎ *01–45–45–68–58* ⌚ *Reservations essential* 🖃 *MC, V* ☉ *Closed weekends and Aug. No lunch Mon.* Ⓜ *Alésia.*

$–$$$ ✕ **La Coupole.** This world-renowned cavernous spot with Art Deco murals practically defines the term *brasserie*. La Coupole might have lost its intellectual aura since the Flo group's restoration, but it has been popular since the days when Jean-Paul Sartre and Simone de Beauvoir were regulars and is still great fun. Today it attracts a mix of bourgeois families, tourists, and elderly lone diners treating themselves to a dozen oysters. Expect the usual brasserie menu—including perhaps the largest shellfish platter in Paris—choucroute, a very un-Indian but tasty lamb curry, and some great over-the-top desserts. They don't take reservations after 8:30 PM Monday–Thursday and after 8 PM Friday–Sunday, so be prepared for a wait at the bar. ✉ *102 bd. du Montparnasse, Montparnasse* ☎ *01–43–20–14–20* 🖃 *AE, DC, MC, V* Ⓜ *Vavin.*

$$ ✕ **Contre-Allée.** Rive Gauche students (the well-off ones, at least) and professors pile into this large restaurant for simple seasonal selections

ranging from squid salad with mussels to roast cod with Parmesan; home-made fresh pasta accompanies many dishes and plate rims come sprin-kled with spices. If the bullfighting posters in the stylish dining room dampen your appetite, you can try for a table on the sidewalk terrace in warm weather. ⊠ *83 av. Denfert-Rochereau, Montparnasse* ☎ *01–43–54–99–86* ▭ *AE, DC, MC, V* ☉ *Closed Sun., Mon., 3 wks in Aug., and 1 wk at Christmas.* Ⓜ *Denfert-Rochereau.*

15e Arrondissement (Trocadéro/Tour Eiffel)

See Where to Eat on the Rive Gauche map.

FRENCH ✕ **L'Os à Moelle.** Designed for serious eaters, this small, buzzing bistro
★ **$$$$** serves a six-course dinner menu for €38 (there's no à la carte) that changes daily (a less elaborate lunch menu costs €32). You might find white-bean soup, *rouget* (red mullet) fillets with red peppers, or a roasted pear with cinnamon ice cream—don't expect miniportions. With a strong list of fairly priced wines, your bill can stay comfortably low, but if you're feeling broke, the restaurant's casual wine bar across the street, with its country buffet for €20 and farmhouse-style seat-ing, makes an ideal runner-up. ⊠ *3 rue Vasco-de-Gama, Trocadéro/Tour Eiffel* ☎ *01–45–57–27–27* ⌁ *Reservations essential* ▭ *MC, V* ☉ *Closed Sun., Mon., 3 wks in Aug., and 1 wk at Christmas.* Ⓜ *Balard.*

$$–$$$$ ✕ **Bistrot d'Hubert.** In a studied environment that might have sprung from the pages of *Elle Decor,* this bistro entices with an unusual menu that changes often. Once split into two sections—"tradition" and "discovery"—the menu now focuses chiefly on discovery, with complex dishes such as chicken strips tandoori-style served with coriander-braised green cabbage and caraway-flavored rutabaga, followed by just-as-elaborate desserts. Culi-nary experimentation happily works here, and service is friendly. Best value is the €35 prix-fixe at lunch or dinner. ⊠ *41 bd. Pasteur, Montparnasse* ☎ *01–47–34–15–50* ⌁ *Reservations essential* ▭ *AE, DC, MC, V* ☉ *Closed Sun. No lunch Sat. and Mon.* Ⓜ *Pasteur.*

★ **$$–$$$$** ✕ **Le Troquet.** A quiet residential street shelters one of the best-value bistros around. Prix-fixe menus start at €22 at lunch and rise to €38 for a six-course tasting menu at dinner, but it's the quality, not quantity, that counts. Chef Christian Etchebest sends out a changing roster of dishes from the Basque and Béarn regions of southwestern France. A typical meal might include vegetable soup with foie gras and cream, panfried scallops in crab sauce or *axoa de veau* (a Basque veal sauté), and a vanilla soufflé with cherry jam. ⊠ *21 rue François-Bonvin, Trocadéro/Tour Eiffel* ☎ *01–45–66–89–00* ▭ *MC, V* ☉ *Closed Sun., Mon., 3 wks in Aug., and Christmas wk.* Ⓜ *Ségur.*

THAI ✕ **Sawadee.** Once you've tried the Thai food here you'll understand why
$ this off-the-beaten-path spot is full every night. Statues and wood carv-ings dress up the warm dining room, while a casual atmosphere and friendly service add to the appeal. A dizzying array of prix-fixe menus is available: start with Thai stuffed mussels or the fish cooked in a ba-nana leaf, a house specialty, then try the shrimp sautéed with salt and pepper or the chopped beef with basil and green peppercorns. ⊠ *53 av. Émile-Zola, Trocadéro/Tour Eiffel* ☎ *01–45–77–68–90* ▭ *AE, MC, V* ☉ *Closed Sun. and 10 days in Aug.* Ⓜ *Charles Michel.*

HITTING THE SWEET SPOT

HIGH PRICES ARE MAKING *luxury all the more elusive in Paris, yet there is still one indulgence that most people can afford, at least occasionally—fine breads and pastries, produced by some of the world's most skilled bakers. The city bursts with extraordinary pâtisseries (pastry shops) and boulangeries (bakeries specializing in bread) where for €.80 and up you can treat yourself to a slice of the good life. Parisians say that you should not buy your pastries where you buy your bread— bakers either specialize in one or the other, though there are some talented exceptions. If you love croissants, pains au chocolat, and pains aux raisins (sweet dough rolled with raisins and custard), skip the hotel breakfast and search out the best.*

Parisians not only seek out the best overall pâtisseries and boulangeries but also hold passionate opinions on the specialties of each establishment. Ask for a tip and you could be sent to one boulangerie for a baguette and another, on the other side of town, for a croissant.

Some stores follow the traditional three-step customer service protocol. First you place your order at the counter and receive a receipt. You pay at the caisse and get your receipt stamped. Finally, you return to the first counter to exchange the stamped receipt for your package of edible art. Many of the sweet spots below have multiple locations; only the original store is listed.

No bread in Paris is more celebrated than the artisanal sourdough loaves from **Poilâne** *(⊠ 8 rue du Cherche-Midi, 6ᵉ ☎ 01-45-48-42-59 Ⓜ Saint-Sulpice), the surprisingly modest boulangerie of the late master Lionel Poilâne. Try the delicate finger sandwiches at* **Ladurée** *(⊠ 16 rue Royale, 8ᵉ ☎ 01-42-60-21-79 Ⓜ Madeleine) for a savory bite. This*

19th-century tearoom also offers coffee-, caramel-, and rose-flavor religieuses (cream-filled pastries vaguely resembling nuns in full habit) and a dozen kinds of macarons, the airy, ganache-filled cookies Ladurée claims as its invention.

A masterful rendition of the classic opéra (almond cake layered with chocolate and coffee cream) beckons from the cases of **Lenôtre** *(⊠ 61 rue Lecourbe, 15ᵉ ☎ 01-42-73-20-97 Ⓜ Sèvres-Lecourbe). Opéra lovers flock to* **Fauchon** *(⊠ 26 pl. de la Madeleine, 8ᵉ ☎ 01-47-42-60-11 Ⓜ Madeleine), the fine-food emporium. Another traditional pastry is the mont-blanc, a miniature mountain of chestnut purée capped with whipped cream, best rendered by* **Jean-Paul Hévin** *(⊠ 3 rue Vavin, 6ᵉ ☎ 01-43-54-09-85 Ⓜ Vavin).* **Christian Constant** *(⊠ 37 rue d'Assas, 6ᵉ ☎ 01-53-63-15-15 Ⓜ Rennes) uses chocolate with a high percentage of cocoa butter in his pastries, resulting in an incredibly intense chocolate fix.* **La Maison du Chocolat** *(⊠ 225 rue du Faubourg St-Honoré, 8ᵉ ☎ 01-42-27-39-44 Ⓜ Ternes), the cocoa-color boutique of preeminent chocolatier Robert Linxe, sells exquisite pastries, cocoa, and truffles.*

Two Rive Gauche pâtissiers have particularly devoted fans of their macarons. The flavors at **Gérard Mulot** *(⊠ 76 rue de Seine, 6ᵉ ☎ 01-43-26-85-77 Ⓜ Mabillon) include pistachio, caramel, and a terrific orange-cinnamon.* **Pierre Hermé** *(⊠ 72 rue Bonaparte, 6ᵉ ☎ 01-43-54-47-77 Ⓜ Saint-Sulpice) challenges the classics with exotic flavors like peach-saffron, olive oil, and white truffle. An up-and-coming force in the avant-garde pâtisserie world is Tokyo-born* **Sadaharu Aoki** *(⊠ 35 rue Vaugirard, 6ᵉ ☎ 01-45-44-48-90 Ⓜ Rennes); look for his green-tea madeleines and black-sesame éclairs.*

16ᵉ Arrondissement (Trocadéro/Tour Eiffel & Bois de Boulogne)

See Where to Eat on the Rive Droite: Bois de Boulogne to Place de la Concorde map.

CONTEMPORARY

$$$$

Fodor'sChoice

★

✕ **Astrance.** Pascal Barbot may have risen to fame thanks to his restaurant's amazing-value food and casual atmosphere, but a few years later Astrance has become resolutely haute with prices to match. Most diners put their faith in the chef by ordering his €150 tasting menu, which unfolds over two to three hours in a series of surprisingly light courses. Even à la carte meals here cost at least €100, but Barbot's cooking has such an ethereal quality that it's worth even the monthlong wait for a table at dinner. Barbot's dishes often draw on Asian ingredients, as in grilled lamb with miso-laquered eggplant and a palate-cleansing white sorbet spiked with chile pepper and lemongrass. Wines by the glass offer great value but don't always match the quality of the food. If you're looking for an affordable lunch menu, you sadly must look elsewhere. ⊠ *4 rue Beethoven, Trocadéro/Tour Eiffel* ☎ *01–40–50–84–40* ⌂ *Reservations essential* ▤ *AE, DC, MC, V* ⊗ *Closed Sat.–Mon. and Aug.* Ⓜ *Passy.*

$$$$

✕ **Hiramatsu.** In fall 2004 Hiramatsu left its Seine-side perch on Île St-Louis for this spacious Art Deco dining room with just 40 seats, 32 of them for nonsmokers (an audacious move in Paris, but there's a bar-salon reserved for *fumeurs*). Chef Hajime Nakagawa continues his variations on the nuanced Japanese-inspired cuisine of restaurant namesake Hiroyuki Hiramatsu, who still sometimes works the kitchen. Luxury ingredients feature prominently in dishes such as a duck foie-gras medallion in a truffle emulsion on a truffle shaving, all wrapped in a curly cabbage leaf, or Breton lobster with a caramelized hazelnut cream. For dessert, classic tarte Tatin (a caramelized apple tart) comes with a dill-scented exotic fruit coulis and Earl Grey sorbet. There is no way to get out of this restaurant cheaply, so save it for a special occasion, when you might be tempted to order a tasting menu for €130 or €180 (there is a simpler €70 menu at lunch). ⊠ *52 rue de Longchamp, Trocadéro/ Tour Eiffel* ☎ *01–56–81–08–80* ⌂ *Reservations essential* ▤ *AE, DC, MC, V* ⊗ *Closed weekends, 3 wks in Aug., and 3 wks in Feb. and Mar.* Ⓜ *Trocadéro.*

$$–$$$$

Fodor'sChoice

★

✕ **La Table de Joël Robuchon.** Despite La Table's striking gilt decor, it occupies an unlucky address—it's the third restaurant to open here in as many years. Under Robuchon's expert leadership, however, success appears almost certain. Chef Frédéric Simonin, who formerly worked with Ghislaine Arabian, lends northern and southern French touches to Robuchon's style in veal rib chops with olives, fava beans, and tiny artichokes or, for dessert, the "total rhubarbe," which raises this humble cold-weather stalk to sublime heights. As at Robuchon's L'Atelier you'll find a selection of small plates alongside more substantial dishes, but the seating arrangement is more conventional (no bar, just tables and chairs) and La Table accepts reservations—in fact, you should book weeks in advance. ⊠ *16 av. Bugeaud, Trocadéro/Tour Eiffel* ☎ *01–56–28–16–16* ⌂ *Reservations essential* ▤ *MC, V* ⊗ *Closed Sun. and 2 wks in Aug. No lunch Mon. and Sat.* Ⓜ *Victor-Hugo.*

$$$ ✕ **Le Cristal Room.** Can't get a reservation at the spectacular restaurant in the Maison Baccarat? You're not alone; a table here is so in demand that you should reserve at least one month in advance. Its success stems not only from the stunning decor by Philippe Starck—mirrors, patches of exposed-brick wall, and a black chandelier—but from the work of chef Thierry Burlot, who often plays with textures, as in a dish of hot bouillon poured over jellied oysters. Want to avoid the wait list? Make a reservation for breakfast (weekdays 8:30–10 and Saturdays at 10), which is far easier than getting a table for lunch or dinner, or come for tea (Sat. 3–5), when reservations aren't taken. ✉ *11 pl. des Etats-Unis, Trocadéro/ Tour Eiffel* ☎ *01–40–22–11–10* ⌣ *Reservations essential* 🖃 *AE, MC, V* ⊗ *Closed Sun.*

FRENCH ✕ **Jamin.** This intimate if rather frilly restaurant where Joël Robuchon
★ **$$$$** made his name serves brilliant food well away from the media spotlight. The best value is the lunch prix-fixe at €50, which entitles you to a generous meal with extras such as the sorbet trolley. The dinner prix-fixes at €95 and €130 also compare favorably with the offerings at other restaurants of Jamin's caliber. Benoît Guichard, Robuchon's second for many years, is a particularly marvelous *saucier* (sauce maker). The menu changes regularly, but Guichard favors dishes with a Mediterranean touch, such as sea bass with pistachios in fennel sauce and braised beef with cumin-scented carrots. The seasonal gratin of rhubarb with a berry sauce makes an excellent dessert. ✉ *32 rue de Longchamp, Trocadéro/ Tour Eiffel* ☎ *01–45–53–00–07* ⌣ *Reservations essential* 🖃 *AE, DC, MC, V* ⊗ *Closed weekends, Aug., and 1 wk in Feb.* Ⓜ *Iéna.*

$$$$ ✕ **Le Pré Catelan.** Live a Belle Époque fantasy by dining beneath the chestnut trees on the terrace of this fanciful landmark *pavillon* in the Bois de Boulogne. Among the winning dishes that have appeared on chef Frédéric Anton's menu are spit-roasted squab in a caramelized sauce, sweetbreads with morels and asparagus tips, and roasted pear on a caramelized waffle with bergamot ice cream. For a taste of the good life at a (relatively) gentle price, order the €60 lunch menu and soak up the opulent surroundings along with service that's as polished as the silverware. ✉ *Rue de Surèsnes, Bois de Boulogne* ☎ *01–44–14–41–14* ⌣ *Reservations essential* 🍽 *Jacket and tie* 🖃 *AE, DC, MC, V* ⊗ *Closed Sun. and Mon. Nov.–Apr., Mon. May–Oct. No dinner Sun. May–Oct.* Ⓜ *Porte Dauphine.*

$$–$$$$ ✕ **La Grande Armée.** The Costes brothers, of the too-cool Costes hotel, are perpetually in the forefront of whatever's trendy in town. Their brasserie near the Arc de Triomphe is a handy way to sample their cheeky flair, since it's open daily, serves nonstop, and has knockout over-the-top Napoléon III decor dreamed up by superstar designer Jacques Garcia—black-lacquered tables, leopard upholstery, Bordeaux velvet, and a carefully tousled clientele picking at sea bass carpaccio, club sandwiches, tandoori chicken skewers, or waffles. ✉ *3 av. de la Grande Armée, Champs-Élysées* ☎ *01–45–00–24–77* 🖃 *AE, DC, MC, V* Ⓜ *Charles-de-Gaulle–Étoile.*

$$ ✕ **La Butte Chaillot.** A dramatic iron staircase connects two levels in turquoise and earth tones at one of the most popular of chef Guy Savoy's fashionable bistros. Dining here is part theater, as the à la mode clientele demonstrates, but it's not all show: the generally good food includes roasted free-range chicken with mashed potatoes and stuffed veal breast with rosemary. A wide sidewalk terrace fronts tree-shaded avenue Kléber. ☒ *112 av. Kléber, Trocadéro/Tour Eiffel* ☎ *01–47–27–88–88* ▤ *AE, DC, MC, V* ⊘ *Closed 3 wks in Aug. No lunch Sat.* Ⓜ *Trocadéro.*

$$ ✕ **Le Petit Rétro.** Two clienteles—men in expensive suits at noon and well-dressed locals in the evening—frequent this little bistro with Art Nouveau tiles and bentwood furniture. You can't go wrong with the daily special, which is written on a chalkboard presented by one of the friendly waitresses. You might spot crisp-skinned blood sausage with apple and honey sauce, blanquette de veau, and a crêpe mille-feuille with orange and Grand Marnier. Arrive with an appetite, as the food is particularly hearty. ☒ *5 rue Mesnil, Trocadéro/Tour Eiffel* ☎ *01–44–05–06–05* ▤ *AE, MC, V* ⊘ *Closed Sun. and 3 wks in Aug. No lunch Sat.* Ⓜ *Victor-Hugo.*

17ᵉ Arrondissement (Parc Monceau & Champs-Élysées)

See Where to Eat on the Rive Droite: Bois du Boulogne to Place de la Concorde map.

FRENCH ✕ **Guy Savoy.** Revamped with dark African wood, rich leather, and ★ **$$$$** cream-color marble, Guy Savoy's luxury restaurant has stepped gracefully into the 21st century. Come here for a perfectly measured contemporary haute-cuisine experience, since Savoy's several bistros have not lured him away from his kitchen. The artichoke soup with black truffles, sea bass with spices, and veal kidneys in mustard-spiked jus reveal the magnitude of his talent, and his mille-feuille is an instant classic. Half portions allow you to graze your way through the menu—unless you choose a blowout feast for €210 or €285—and reasonably priced wines are available (though beware the cost of wines by the glass). Best of all, the atmosphere is joyful—Savoy senses that having fun is just as important as eating well. ☒ *18 rue Troyon, Champs-Élysées* ☎ *01–43–80–40–61* ⌕ *Reservations essential* ⌂ *Jacket and tie at dinner* ▤ *AE, MC, V* ⊘ *Closed Sun., Mon., and mid-July–mid-Aug. No lunch Sat.* Ⓜ *Charles-de-Gaulle–Étoile.*

$$$–$$$$ ✕ **Au Petit Colombier.** This is a perennial favorite among Parisians, who come to eat comforting *cuisine bourgeoise* (traditional cuisine) in the warm dining rooms accented with wood and bright copper. Seasonal specialties include milk-fed lamb chop *en cocotte* (in a small enameled casserole), game in all its guises, and truffles. There's a good-value menu for €35. A seafood annex, Au Petit Colombier Côté Mer, opened next door in late 2003. Service is friendly and unpretentious. ☒ *42 rue des Acacias, Champs-Élysées* ☎ *01–43–80–28–54* ▤ *AE, MC, V* ⊘ *Closed Sun. and Aug. No lunch Sat.* Ⓜ *Charles-de-Gaulle–Étoile.*

$$–$$$ ✕ **Le Graindorge.** Steeped in vintage 1930s character, this restaurant thrives under chef-owner Bernard Broux, who blends the cuisines of southwestern France and his native Flanders. Try the succulent eel terrine in herb aspic (seasonal) or rouget with endive in beer sauce, followed by a small but judicious selection of potent northern cheeses. If you're counting your pennies, go for the €32 set menu at dinner or the €28 menu at lunch. Madame Broux can help you select one of the many fine beers. ☒ *15* *rue de l'Arc-de-Triomphe, Champs-Élysées* ☎ *01–47–54–00–28* ▱ *AE, MC, V* ⊘ *Closed Sun. and 2 wks in Aug. No lunch Sat.* Ⓜ *Charles-de-Gaulle–Étoile.*

$$ ✕ **Café d'Angel.** A trend-conscious yuppie crowd frequents this relaxed little bistro near the Arc de Triomphe, whose name is echoed in its angel-print tablecloths—the "clouds" you see in the dining room are not the heavens, however, but cigarette smoke. The menu changes regularly but offers interesting modern bistro dishes and good value for the money. Try the seasonal fish dishes, rabbit compote with lentils, and intriguing upside-down mille-feuille with apple, quince, and spice bread. ⊠ *16 rue Brey, Champs-Élysées* ☎ *01–47–54–03–33* ▱ *MC, V* ⊘ *Closed weekends and 3 wks in Aug.* Ⓜ *Charles-de-Gaulle–Étoile.*

$–$$ ✕ **Le Petit Verdot.** Sandwich bars might be threatening the traditional two-hour lunch, but that doesn't stop this old-fashioned neighborhood bistro from flourishing—even though it's open at lunch only, except Thursday and Friday. Businessmen loosen their neckties to feast on homemade pâté, plate-engulfing steak for two, or guinea hen with cabbage, with one of 40 or so small producers' wines, which are delivered directly to the restaurant. The dining room was redone in July 2004 with a wine theme—vines and a chateau are painted on the faux stone walls. ⊠ *9 rue Fourcroy, Champs-Élysées* ☎ *01–42–27–47–42* ▱ *MC, V* ⊘ *Closed weekends. No dinner Mon.–Wed.* Ⓜ *Charles-de-Gaulle–Étoile.*

JAPANESE ✕ **Kifuné.** Removed from the Japanese hub of rue Ste-Anne near the Opéra,
$$–$$$ Kifuné attracts those with a yen for the real thing. It's rare to see a non-Japanese face in the modest dining room, where you can sit at the bar and admire the sushi chef's lightning-quick skills or opt for a more intimate table. Crab-and-shrimp salad makes a sublime starter, and the miso soup with clams is deeply flavored; you can't go wrong with the sashimi. A meal here will leave a dent in your wallet—consider it a mini-trip to Japan. ⊠ *44 rue St-Ferdinand, Champs-Élysées* ☎ *01–45–72–11–19* ⟋ *Reservations essential* ▱ *MC, V* ⊘ *Closed Sun., 2 wks in Aug., and 2 wks in winter. No lunch Mon.* Ⓜ *Argentine.*

SEAFOOD ✕ **L'Huîtrier.** If you have a single-minded craving for oysters, this is the
$$–$$$ place for you. The friendly owner will describe the different kinds available; you can follow these with any of several daily fish specials. The excellent cheeses are from the legendary shop of Roger Alléosse. Blond wood and cream tones prevail. Should you have trouble getting a table, L'Huîtrier also runs the Presqu'île next door. ⊠ *16 rue Saussier-Leroy, Parc Monceau* ☎ *01–40–54–83–44* ▱ *AE, DC, MC, V* ⊘ *Closed Mon.; Sun. in May, June, and Sept.; July; Aug. No lunch Mon.* Ⓜ *Ternes.*

18ᵉ Arrondissement (Montmartre)

See Where to Eat on the Rive Droite: Île de la Cité to Montmartre map.

FRENCH ✕ **Le Poulbot Gourmet.** Engravings of Old Montmartre and discreet light-
$$–$$$ ing put diners in an affable mood in this tiny and rather formal restaurant named after the chef-owner's favorite painter, Francisque Poulbot. Jean-Paul Langevin puts nearby tourist traps to shame with seasonal, straight-ahead dishes such as poached egg in puff pastry, veal kidney with morels (the menu is offally rich), and hot apple charlotte with a

calvados-spiked caramel. There's a well-chosen wine list and prix-fixe menus for € 18 and € 35. ☒ *39 rue Lamarck, Montmartre* ☎ *01–46–06–86–00* ▤ *MC, V* ☉ *Closed Sun. June–Sept. and 2 wks in Aug. No dinner Sun. Oct.–May.* Ⓜ *Lamarck Caulaincourt.*

$–$$$ ✕ **La Mascotte.** Though everyone talks about the "new Montmartre," exemplified by a wave of chic residents and throbbingly cool cafés and bars, it's good to know that the old Montmartre is alive and well at the untrendy-and-proud-of-it La Mascotte. This old-fashioned café-brasserie is where you'll find neighborhood fixtures such as the drag queen Michou (of the nearby club Chez Michou), who always wears blue. Loyalists come for the seafood platters, the excellent steak tartare, and the gossip around the *comptoir* up front. ☒ *52 rue des Abbesses Montmartre* ☎ *01–46–06–28–15* ▤ *MC, V* Ⓜ *Abbesses.*

★ **$–$$** ✕ **Chez Toinette.** Between the red lights of Pigalle and the Butte Montmartre, this cozy bistro with red walls and candlelight hits the romance nail on the head. In autumn and winter game comes into play in long-simmered French dishes—choose from *marcassin* (young wild boar), venison, and pheasant. Regulars can't resist the crème brûlée and the raspberry tart. Prices have crept up, but Chez Toinette is still a rare find for this neighborhood. ☒ *20 rue Germaine Pilon, Montmartre* ☎ *01–42–54–44–36* ▤ *MC, V* ☉ *Closed Sun., Mon., Aug., and 2 wks at Christmas. No lunch* Ⓜ *Pigalle.*

$–$$ ✕ **La Famille.** Inaki Aizpitarte, originally from the Basque region, opened this hip restaurant on a street known for its role in the film *Amélie*. Happily, La Famille is worth visiting for what it brings to the plate, not the screen. The spare space attracts the *bobo* (bohemian bourgeois) neighbors who are bringing a new energy to Montmatre. Aizpitarte's globetrotting menu might include pan-fried foie gras with miso sauce or chocolate custard with fiery Basque peppers. On the last Sunday of every month a tasting menu is served (the restaurant is otherwise closed Sunday). ☒ *41 rue des Trois-Frères, Montmartre* ☎ *01–42–52–11–12* ▤ *MC, V* ☉ *Closed Sun. and Mon. No lunch* Ⓜ *Abbesses.*

19ᵉ Arrondissement (Buttes-Chaumont)

See Where to Eat on the Rive Droite: the Marais to La Villette map.

FRENCH ✕ **La Cave Gourmande.** In the space that once housed Eric Frechon, who
$$$$ now cooks at Le Bristol, American chef Mark Singer continues to draw crowds to this out-of-the-way neighborhood with inventive bistro cooking. Wine racks and wooden tables give the room a local bistro feel belied by dishes such as a leek and shellfish terrine in a light curry sauce, or pike perch with chorizo. Singer makes astute use of spices and exotic ingredients, and his prix-fixe menu (€28 at lunch and €32 at dinner) changes every few weeks. ☒ *10 rue du General-Brunet, La Villette* ☎ *01–40–40–03–30* ▤ *MC, V* ☉ *Closed weekends, 1 wk in Feb., and 3 wks in Aug.* Ⓜ *Botzaris.*

$–$$ ✕ **Au Boeuf Couronné.** La Villette once housed the city's meat market, and this independent brasserie devoted to fine beef (whether French or Irish) soldiers on as if nothing has changed. if you're beginning to tire of the Flo brasserie formula, it's worth the trek out to this far-flung neighborhood to sample the 11 takes on the beef theme (plus gargantuan marrow bone), or some very good fish and seafood dishes, such as scallops in season. You'll find bon vivants from all over Paris in the buzzy dining room, and there is a separate salon for cigar-smokers. ☒ *188 av. Jean-Jaures, La Villette* ☎ *01–42–39–54–54* ☰ *AE, DC, MC, V* Ⓜ *Porte de Pantin.*

20ᵉ Arrondissement (Père Lachaise)

See Where to Eat on the Rive Droite: the Marais to La Villette map.

FRENCH ✕ **La Boulangerie.** This friendly, incredibly good-value bistro—three
$ courses cost €18.50—is a great bet if you're planning on a night out in the increasingly trendy Ménilmontant neighborhood or maybe hoping to bring yourself back to life after a visit to Père-Lachaise Cemetery. Occupying a former bakery, this place attracts a young local crowd along with some adventurous tourists who come for the sincere and satisfying seasonal dishes. The menu changes every two-and-a-half months but runs to dishes like wild mushrooms in pastry; monkfish, salmon and scallop stew; and crêpes filled with chestnut cream and pear. ☒ *15 rue des Panoyaux, Père Lachaise* ☎ *01–43–58–45–45* ☰ *MC, V* ☉ *Closed 2 wks in Aug. No lunch Sat.* Ⓜ *Père-Lachaise.*

Cafés & Salons de Thé

Along with air, water, and wine, the café remains one of the basic necessities of life in Paris. Though they continue to close in the face of changing work and eating habits, cafés still occupy nearly every prominent street corner. Until recently, the overall style of neighborhood cafés and PMUs (where you can bet on horses) dated from the '60s and '70s—but now, especially around the Bastille, many have shrewdly updated their light fixtures and banquettes, turned up the music a notch or two, and hiked up their prices. The more modest establishments (look for nonchalant locals) will give you a cheaper cup of coffee and a feeling of what real French café life is like. Cafés are required to post a *tarif des consommations,* a list that includes prices for the basics ranging from *café* (espresso) to *vin rouge* (red wine) and list two prices, *au comptoir* (at the counter) and *à terrasse* or *à salle* (seated at a table).

If you just need a quick cup of coffee, have it at the counter and save yourself money—a café crème now costs a shocking €4 or more in most central neighborhoods (often complete with surly service), which helps explain the growing popularity of the Starbucks outposts that seem to be popping up everywhere. If you have a rendezvous, take a table: remember that you're paying considerable rent on that little piece of wood, and hang out as long as you care to. Though most cafés serve lunch and some are open for dinner, don't expect a bargain meal—the average price of a main course is about €12, and it can be wiser to visit a good bistro if you want to eat something memorable, often at comparable prices. Service is not necessarily speedier in cafés either, even for a simple croque monsieur. Some cafés do serve excellent food, though—some better ones are included here.

If you're looking for a slice of intellectual café life, head to the Café de Flore on Monday night for play readings and the first Wednesday of each month for philosophy debates, both held in English.

1ᵉʳ & 2ᵉ Arrondissements (Les Halles & Louvre/Tuileries)

A Priori Thé. Stop in for a comforting tea and a crunchy fruit crumble at this cozy American-run spot—perfect for a rainy day—after browsing through the lovely Galerie Vivienne shopping arcade. The giant salads served at lunch are delicious and original. ⊠ *35–37 Galerie Vivienne, at 66 rue Vivienne, Louvre/Tuileries* ☎ *01–42–97–48–75* Ⓜ *Bourse.*

Au Père Tranquille. In a neighborhood swarming with all sorts—tourists, Parisian teens, street musicians—this café's popular terrace is a particularly prime spot for people-watching. ⊠ *16 rue Pierre Lescot, Beaubourg/ Les Halles* ☎ *01–45–08–00–34* Ⓜ *Les Halles.*

★ **Café Marly.** Run by the Costes brothers, this café overlooking the main courtyard of the Louvre and I. M. Pei's glass pyramid is one of the most stylish places in Paris to meet for a drink or a coffee, whether in the stunning dining rooms with their molded ceilings or on the long terrace. The regular café service shuts down during meal hours, when fashion-conscious folks dig into Asian-inspired salads and pseudo-Italian pasta dishes. ⊠ *Cour Napoléon du Louvre (enter from Louvre courtyard), 93 rue de Rivoli, Louvre/Tuileries* ☎ *01–49–26–06–60* Ⓜ *Palais-Royal.*

Café Verlet. Many Parisians think this compact coffee roaster crowded with wooden tables and fashionable shoppers serves the best coffee in town—you might find unusual beans from Rwanda or India. You can also get sandwiches and lustrous tarts. ⊠ *256 rue St-Honoré, Louvre/ Tuileries* ☎ *01–42–60–67–39* Ⓜ *Tuileries.*

★ **Le Fumoir.** This café-restaurant has passed from red-hot chic to favored mainstay. Its location just across from the Louvre helps, but ultimately what makes it work is the high quality of its food, not to mention the notably good brunches. Its salons seem variously inspired by Vienna, Edward Hopper, and Scandinavia. ⊠ *Pl. du Louvre, 6 rue de l'Amiral-Coligny, Louvre/Tuileries* ☎ *01–42–92–00–24* Ⓜ *Louvre.*

Le Ruc Univers. Actors from the Comédie Française and attitudinous hipsters hang out at this sleekly modern café near the Louvre. ⊠ *1 pl. André-Malraux, Louvre/Tuileries* ☎ *01–42–60–31–57* Ⓜ *Palais-Royal.*

4ᵉ Arrondissement (Le Marais & Île St-Louis)

Café Beaubourg. Near the Centre Pompidou, this slick (though slightly worn) modern café designed by architect Christian de Portzamparc is one of the trendiest rendezvous spots for fashion and art types, drawing a strong gay contingent from the neighborhood. Omelets and decent salads are served if you've missed lunch or want a light dinner. ⊠ *43 rue St-Merri, Beaubourg/Les Halles* ☎ *01–48–87–63–96* Ⓜ *Hôtel de Ville.*

La Charlotte en l'Ile. The witch who baked gingerbread children in *Hansel and Gretel* might take a fancy to this place—set with fairy lights, carnival masks, and decoupaged detritus, it's a tiny storybook spot that offers more than 30 varieties of tea along with hot chocolate so thick it's almost solid and wickedly good cakes. It's the perfect spot for sugar overkill. ⊠ *24 rue St-Louis-en-l'Île, Île St-Louis* ☎ *01–43–54–25–83* Ⓜ *Pont Marie.*

L'Etoile Manquante. Owned by Xavier Denamur, who runs several stylish cafés on this très gay street, the Missing Star is a great spot for people-watching, but the real attraction in each of his cafés is the restrooms: here, an electric train zooming through the loo is just one of the surprises in store. ✉ *34 rue Vieille-du-Temple, Le Marais* ☎ *01–42–72–48–34* Ⓜ *Hôtel de Ville, St-Paul.*

Le Flore en l'Île. At this café on the Île St-Louis you can find renowned Berthillon ice cream and a magnificent view of the Seine. The terrace looking onto the back of Notre-Dame is the place to be. ✉ *42 quai d'Orléans, Île St-Louis* ☎ *01–43–29–88–27* Ⓜ *Pont Marie.*

★ **Le Loir dans la Théière.** Sink into one of the comfortably shabby armchairs of this wonderful tearoom in the heart of the Marais and indulge in fabulous patisseries, most memorably a sky-high lemon-meringue tart. ✉ *3 rue des Rosiers, Le Marais* ☎ *01–42–72–90–61* Ⓜ *St-Paul.*

Ma Bourgogne. On the exquisite place des Vosges, this is a calm oasis for a coffee or a light lunch away from the noisy streets. In summer, aim for a terrace seat under the arcades fringing this ancient square. The specialty is steak tartare. ✉ *19 pl. des Vosges, Le Marais* ☎ *01–42–78–44–64* Ⓜ *St-Paul.*

Mariage Frères. This 19th-century tea purveyor runs its own salons, each stocked with hundreds of kinds of tea. Peruse the menu for all kinds of brews—black tea, green tea, white tea, smoked, iced, herbal, and evocatively named (Marco Polo, Casablanca). Tea finds its way into the pastries too. ✉ *30 rue du Bourg-Tibourg, Le Marais* ☎ *01–42–72–28–11* Ⓜ *Hôtel de Ville* ✉ *13 rue des Grands Augustins, St-Germain-des-Prés* ☎ *01–40–51–82–50* Ⓜ *Odéon.*

Petit Fer à Cheval. Great coffee is served in the perfect setting for watching the fashionable Marais locals saunter by; food such as a leathery *bavette* (beef skirt steak), however, leaves something to be desired. You can't go wrong with a coffee at the horseshoe-shape bar. ✉ *30 rue Vieille-du-Temple, Le Marais* ☎ *01–42–72–47–47* Ⓜ *St-Paul.*

6ᵉ Arrondissement (St-Germain-des-Prés & Montparnasse)

★ **Brasserie Lipp.** This brasserie, with its turn-of-the-20th-century decor, was a favorite spot of Hemingway's; today television celebrities, journalists, and politicians come here for coffee on the small glassed-in terrace off the main restaurant. ✉ *151 bd. St-Germain, St-Germain-des-Prés* ☎ *01–45–48–53–91* Ⓜ *St-Germain-des-Prés.*

Café de Flore. Picasso, Chagall, Sartre, and de Beauvoir, attracted by the luxury of a heated café, worked and wrote here in the early 20th century. Today you'll find more tourists than intellectuals, and prices are hardly aimed at struggling artists, but the outdoor terrace is still popular. ✉ *172 bd. St-Germain, St-Germain-des-Prés* ☎ *01–45–48–55–26* Ⓜ *St-Germain-des-Prés.*

Café de la Mairie. Preferred by Henry Miller and Saul Bellow to those on noisy boulevard St-Germain, this place still retains the quiet and unpretentious air of a local café—although Catherine Deneuve could easily be a passerby here. ✉ *8 pl. St-Sulpice, St-Germain-des-Prés* ☎ *01–43–26–67–82* Ⓜ *St-Sulpice.*

Les Deux Magots. Dubbed the second home of the *élite intellectuelle,* this café counted Arthur Rimbaud, Paul Verlaine, Stéphane Mallarmé, Oscar

Wilde, and the Surrealists among its regulars. These days it's overpriced and mostly filled with tourists, but the hot chocolate served in a porcelain jug is still exceptionally good. ✉ *170 bd. St-Germain, St-Germain-des-Prés* ☎ *01–45–48–55–25* Ⓜ *St-Germain-des-Prés.*

★ **Les Editeurs.** Strategically placed near prestigious Rive Gauche publishing houses, this café attracts passersby with red-velour seats and glossy books on display. The terrace just off the boulevard St-Germain is great for people-watching but not ideal for catching a waiter's eye. ✉ *4 carrefour de l'Odéon, St-Germain-des-Prés* ☎ *01–43–26–67–76* Ⓜ *St-Germain-des-Prés.*

La Palette. In good weather the terrace is as popular with local art students and gallery owners as it is with tourists. On a rainy afternoon the interior, too, is cozy—it's decorated with works of art by its habitués. ✉ *43 rue de Seine, St-Germain-des-Prés* ☎ *01–43–26–68–15* Ⓜ *Odéon.*

La Rotonde. The café, a second home to foreign artists and political exiles in the 1920s and '30s, has a less exotic clientele today. But it's still a pleasant place to have a coffee on the sunny terrace. ✉ *105 bd. Montparnasse, Montparnasse* ☎ *01–43–26–68–84* Ⓜ *Montparnasse.*

Le Sélect. Isadora Duncan and Hart Crane used to hang out here; now it's a popular spot for a post-cinema beer or a well-made cocktail. ✉ *99 bd. Montparnasse, Montparnasse* ☎ *01–45–48–38–24* Ⓜ *Vavin.*

Le Vieux Colombier. Squeeze into a seat on the lovely wicker furniture in front of one of the big windows in this Art Nouveau gem just around the corner from St-Sulpice and the Vieux Colombier theater. ✉ *65 rue de Rennes, St-Germain-des-Prés* ☎ *01–45–48–53–81* Ⓜ *St-Sulpice.*

8ᵉ Arrondissement (Champs-Élysées)

★ **Ladurée.** Pretty enough to bring a tear to Proust's eye, this ravishing salon de thé looks barely changed from 1862. Grandmother's grandmother, antiques dealers, and lovers of beauty make up the clientele, which dotes on the signature lemon and caramel macaroons and a slew of teas that will make you want to stick out your pinky. A more recent branch, heavy on the Belle Époque ornateness, is at 75 avenue des Champs-Élysées, and there's a Rive Gauche location, too, at 21 rue Bonaparte. ✉ *16 rue Royale, Opéra/Grands Boulevards* ☎ *01–42–60–21–79* Ⓜ *Madeleine.*

Le Paris. This buzzy little café with a cool crowd and decor is a sign that this famous avenue is coming back into fashion. Service can be chilly, but it's worth putting up with for the interesting crowd and good light food. ✉ *93 av. des Champs-Élysées, Champs-Élysées* ☎ *01–47–23–54–37* Ⓜ *George V.*

11ᵉ Arrondissement (Bastille/Nation)

Café de l'Industrie. Have a late-afternoon coffee or beer in the warm yellow rooms of this Bastille hangout where the walls are covered with photos of movie stars. ✉ *16 rue St-Sabin, Bastille/Nation* ☎ *01–47–00–13–53* Ⓜ *Bastille.*

Pause Cafe. This Bastille corner attracts a chic, artsy crowd for coffee, cheap beer, and—above all—the much-sought-after terrace seats. Avoid the food, though, which now seems an afterthought. ✉ *41 rue de Charonne, Bastille/Nation* ☎ *01–48–06–80–33* Ⓜ *Ledru-Rollin.*

14ᵉ Arrondissement (Montparnasse)

Café du Dôme. Now a fancy fish brasserie—though you can still just have a cup of coffee or a drink here—this place began as a dingy meeting place for exiled artists and intellectuals such as Lenin, Picasso, and Chaim Soutine. ☒ *108 bd. Montparnasse, Montparnasse* ☎ *01–43–35–25–81* Ⓜ *Vavin.*

Café de la Place. This café is a charming wood-paneled spot that is perfect for watching the activity inside and out. ☒ *23 rue d'Odessa, Montparnasse* ☎ *01–42–18–01–55* Ⓜ *Montparnasse.*

18ᵉ Arrondissement (Montmartre)

La Crémaillère. Alphonse Mucha frescoes decorate the walls at this veritable monument to 19th-century fin-de-siècle art. ☒ *15 pl. du Tertre, Montmartre* ☎ *01–46–06–58–59* Ⓜ *Anvers.*

Le Sancerre. Sit on the terrace sipping a coffee or a beer and watch the ebb and flow of artists, hipsters, and tourists and guess how many people are on an *Amélie* quest. ☒ *35 rue des Abbesses, Montmartre* ☎ *01–45–58–08–20* Ⓜ *Abbesses.*

19ᵉ Arrondissement (Buttes-Chaumont)

Café de la Musique. This vast postmodern café is next to the Cité de la Musique in the Parc de La Villette. In the evening it's primarily filled with people attending concerts, but the free jazz on Wednesday night and the interesting crowd make it worth the trip. ☒ *214 av. Jean-Jaurès, La Villette* ☎ *01–48–03–15–91* Ⓜ *Porte de Pantin.*

Wine Bars

Bars à vins (wine bars), are the perfect place to enjoy a glass (or bottle) of wine with a plate of cheese, charcuterie, or a tasty hot meal—the food in many wine bars rivals that in very good bistros. Bar owners are often true wine enthusiasts ready to dispense expert advice—it's unfortunate, though, that only rarely do they provide the appropriate glassware for the wines they serve. With few exceptions, the focus is squarely on French wines, but there is plenty of terroir to explore. Hours vary widely, so it's best to check ahead if your heart is set on a particular place; many, however, close around 10 PM.

Au Sauvignon. Edge your way in among the lively tipplers in this homey spot with an ideally placed terrace. Pair your *verre* with a *tartine* (open-face sandwich). ☒ *80 rue des Sts-Pères, 7ᵉ, St-Germain-des-Prés* ☎ *01–45–48–49–02* Ⓜ *Sèvres Babylone.*

Le Baron Bouge. Formerly known as Le Baron Rouge, this wine bar near the place d'Aligre market has changed in name only. In winter months you'll often find an oyster feast in midswing outside its door; inside, expect the regulars to welcome you with the same frosty suspicion as cowboys would at their local saloon. ☒ *1 rue Théophile Roussel, 12ᵉ, Bastille/Nation* ☎ *01–43–43–14–32* Ⓜ *Ledru-Rollin.*

Bu Bar. In summertime look for the hip professional crowd spilling out the front of this signless, red-wallpapered wine bar in a formerly dead corner of the Marais. It's named for Jean-Paul, the bartender (*bubar* or *barbu* is French slang for "bearded"). The ever-changing wine menu—with many selections available by the glass—features not only French wines, but also (quel surprise) small-batch vintages from South Africa, Chile, and Argentina as well as lesser-known parts of France. ✉ *3 rue des Tournelles, 4ᵉ, Le Marais* ☎ *01–40–29–97–72* Ⓜ *Bastille.*

★ **Jacques Mélac.** This wine bar is named after the jolly owner who harvests grapes from the vine outside and bottles several of his own wines—he even hosts a harvest festival every September. Nonsmokers, make your way through the tiny kitchen to the fume-free back room. Cheese is hacked off a giant hunk of Cantal and the hot dish of the day is always tasty. ✉ *42 rue Léon-Frot, 11ᵉ, Bastille/Nation* ☎ *01–43–70–59–27* Ⓜ *Charonne.*

★ **Les Papilles.** Part wine shop and epicerie, part restaurant, Les Papilles has a winning formula—you can pick any bottle off the shelf and pay a €6 corkage fee to drink it with your meal. Look for discoveries from little-known regions such as the Ardèche. The southwestern inspired bistro fare is delicious, though the choices are limited. ✉ *30 rue Gay-Lussac, 5ᵉ, Quartier Latin* ☎ *01–43–25–20–79* Ⓜ *Cluny–La Sorbonne.*

La Robe et le Palais. Come here for the more than 120 wines from all over France, served *au compteur* (according to the amount consumed), as well as a daily selection of good bistro-style dishes for lunch and dinner. ✉ *13 rue des Lavandières-Ste-Opportune, 1ᵉʳ, Beaubourg/Les Halles* ☎ *01–45–08–07–41* Ⓜ *Châtelet Les Halles.*

★ **Le Rouge Gorge.** This sophisticated Marais wine bar attracts discriminating locals who come for unusual wines by the glass, often from the more obscure regions, and the hearty food, which has a Moroccan touch. ✉ *8 rue St-Paul, 4ᵉ, Le Marais* ☎ *01–48–04–75–89* Ⓜ *Bourse.*

Le Rubis. This resolutely old-time bar specializes in Burgundies. It's most crowded during the day; if you're there from 7 PM to 9:30 PM it's best if you're smoke resistant. ✉ *10 rue du Marché St-Honoré, 1ᵉʳ, Louvre/Tuileries* ☎ *01–42–61–03–34* Ⓜ *Tuileries.*

La Tartine. Inexpensive wine and tartines in a tatty, almost seedy late-19th-century bar have given this place antihero status among the cognoscenti. ✉ *24 rue de Rivoli, 4ᵉ, Le Marais* ☎ *01–42–72–76–85* Ⓜ *St-Paul.*

Where to Stay

3

Revised and
updated by
Heather
Stimmler-Hall

YOUR EYES CRACK OPEN, slowly adjusting to the spatter of sunlight. Above you, rough-hewn wooden beams span the ceiling. Sitting up in bed, you glance out the windows and take in the view over the zinc roofs and chimney pots, the clouds giving way to a patchwork of blue. The smell of croissants and *café crème* teases you further awake.

If this is some version of your Parisian fantasy, good news: you need not be Ritz-rich to realize it. That beamed ceiling could be in a palatial, antiques-filled suite or in a simple room under the eaves. The smell of croissants could be wafting from room service or from the corner *boulangerie*. The city has more than 1,450 hotels, giving millions of expectant visitors stylish options in all price ranges.

Generally, there are more hotels on the Rive Droite offering luxury—at any rate, formality—than on the Rive Gauche, where the hotels are frequently smaller and richer in old-fashioned charm. The Rive Droite's 1er and 8e arrondissements are still the most exclusive, and prices here reflect this. The most palatial hotels can charge more than €500 a night without batting an eye. Less expensive alternatives on the Rive Droite can be found in the fashionable Marais quarter (3e and 4e arrondissements) and the 11e and 12e arrondissements, near the Opéra Bastille. The hotbed of chic hotels on the Rive Gauche is the 6e arrondissement; choices get cheaper as you leave Montparnasse and head deeper into the 13e, 14e, and 15e arrondissements. Of course, this chapter highlights many exceptions to these rules, with a handful of budget-priced sleeps in the shadow of Notre Dame, St-Germain-des-Prés, and the Louvre.

Recognizing the recently painful dollar–euro exchange rate for Americans, many establishments have held their prices to 2004 levels, and guaranteed U.S. dollar rates are increasingly promoted in all hotel classes. Heightened competition also means the bar for service and amenities has been raised everywhere. Virtually every hotel is now equipped with cable TV to meet the needs of international guests, and it's not uncommon for midrange hotels to have a smoke-free floor and air-conditioning. Hotels in all price ranges are jumping onto the wireless Internet bandwagon, particularly since it's so much easier to install in old, historic buildings than high-speed cables. Usually you'll have to buy an access card from the front desk; Wi-Fi is rarely included in room rates, except at some smaller, informal properties.

Despite widespread improvement, many Paris hotels (especially budget-level accommodations) still have idiosyncrasies—some endearing, others less so. Paris hotel rooms are generally smaller than their American counterparts, as are French double beds. Air-conditioning is not always available, nor is it a prerequisite for comfort in Paris, even in summer (although several hotels now have oscillating fans on request). Elevators can be suitcase width. Cigarettes may be banned from common areas like lobbies, but so-called no-smoking rooms may mean the housekeeper has simply spritzed the room with perfume. Light sleepers may want to pack earplugs, since double-glazed windows won't necessarily keep out the sounds from hallways or neighboring rooms.

Reviews indicate the number of rooms with private bathroom (which mean they have a shower or a tub, but not necessarily both). Tubs don't always have fixed showerheads or curtains; how the French rinse themselves with the handheld nozzle without flooding the entire bathroom remains a cultural mystery. It's rare to find moderately priced places that expect guests to share toilets or bathrooms, but be sure you know what facilities you are getting when you book a budget hotel.

Almost all Parisian hotels charge extra for breakfast, with per-person prices ranging from €5 to more than €30 at luxury establishments. Occasionally Continental breakfast is included in the hotel rate. We denote this with a CP, for Continental Plan. But you may find the standard Continental breakfast of coffee, baguette, croissant, jam, and butter neither a good value nor sufficiently robust. If you decide to eat elsewhere, inform the desk staff and make sure breakfast hasn't been charged to your bill. That said, many hotels now offer pricier buffet breakfasts with more substantial fare—cheese, cereal, fruit, meat, and eggs made to order—in pleasant breakfast areas or a stone basement *cave* (listed as "dining rooms" in this guide). Full-fledged hotel restaurants serving lunch and dinner are common only at luxury establishments.

Typical check-in and check-out times are 2 PM and noon, respectively, although some properties allow check-in as early as noon and require check-out as early as 11 AM. Many flights from North America arrive early in the morning, and having to wait six hours for a room after arriving jet-lagged at 8 AM isn't the ideal way to start a vacation. Alert the hotel of your early arrival; larger establishments can often make special early-check-in arrangements, but don't expect more than baggage storage and use of a public bathroom to freshen up at budget hotels.

Unless otherwise stated, hotels have elevators, and all guest rooms have air-conditioning, TV, telephone, and private bathroom. Remember that in France the first floor is the floor above the ground floor, or *rez-de-chaussée*. Note that we use "in-room data ports" to designate the presence of genuine high-speed lines and mention wireless access where available (otherwise, expect escargot-paced Web surfing).

1er Arrondissement (Louvre/Tuileries)

See Where to Stay on the Rive Droite: Île de la Cité to Montmartre map.

$$$$ ▦ **Hôtel Costes.** Since 1995 many have considered Jean-Louis and Gilbert Costes's eponymous party spot the top Paris boutique hotel. It's been a magnet for off-duty celebs like Catherine Deneuve, John Malkovich, and Johnny Depp. Nearly every room remains swathed in enough pomegranate-red fabrics, swagging, and braided trim to choke a runway of supermodels. The army of perfectly coiffed hosts and hostesses has a knack for making you feel underdressed and unimportant. Sister hotel Costes K on rue Kléber in the 16e arrondissement feels even more exclusionary. ⊠ *239 rue St-Honoré, Louvre/Tuileries, 75001* ☎ *01-42-44-50-00* 📠 *01-42-44-50-01* ⊕ *www.hotelcostes.com* ⬎ *77 rooms, 5 suites* ⚏ *Restaurant, room service, in-room data ports,*

Hotel Reservations

It's always a good idea to make hotel reservations in Paris as far in advance as possible, especially for late spring, summer, and fall. Calling works, but nowadays e-mailing is the easiest way to make contact. Faxing is also convenient (plus, the staff is probably more likely to read English than to understand it over the phone long-distance). Specify your arrival and departure dates; the size (single or double) and type (standard, deluxe, or suite) of the room you want; how many people in your party; what size bed you want (twin beds or double or larger); and whether you want a bathroom with a shower or bathtub (or both). You might also ask if a deposit (or your credit card number) is required, and if so what happens if you cancel. Cross-cultural transactions inevitably attract snafus, so be sure to confirm the details of your reservation and request that the hotel fax or e-mail you back. This way you'll have a written confirmation in hand when you arrive at the hotel. If you arrive in Paris without a reservation, the tourist offices can always help at the last minute, but they charge a small fee.

3

Keep in mind that some smaller hotels may only have one person on staff who speaks any English, and he or she may not be available at all times. Here are some French words that can come in handy when booking a room: air-conditioning (*climatisation*); private bath (*salle de bain privée*); bathtub (*baignoire*); shower (*douche*).

Note that the quality of accommodations (room and bath size, noise level, natural light), particularly in older properties and even in luxury hotels, can vary from room to room. If you don't like the room you're given, ask to see another. You'll often see a sign outside a hotel with a painted shield bearing from one to four stars; these are based on a government rating system. At the bottom end are one-star hotels, where you might have to share a bathroom and do without an elevator. Two- and three-star hotels generally have private bathrooms, elevators, double-paned windows to block sound, laundry service, and in-room televisions. While you shouldn't expect a four-star experience from the little guys, the star ratings can be misleading. Official stars are granted for specific amenities and services rather than for ambience, style, or overall comfort, so you may find that a two-star hotel eclipses a three-star establishment. Besides, many hotels prefer to remain "understarred" for tax reasons.

Prices

Hotels are listed by arrondissement and then by price. Often a hotel in a certain price category will have a few less-expensive rooms; it's worth asking about this possibility. In the off-season—mid-July, August, November, early December, and late January—tariffs can be considerably lower. You should also inquire about promotional specials and weekend deals, and you may be able to get a better rate per night if you are staying a week or longer. Rates must be posted in all rooms (usually on the back of the door), with all extra charges clearly shown (typically, breakfast is *not* included in the *tarif*). There is a nominal city *taxe de séjour* ranging between €.20 and €1.20 per person, per night, based on the hotel's star rating. Sometimes this tax is included in the room price, sometimes not. (This issue is confused by the fact that many rate cards state that other taxes and services are *compris* [included], but then city tax is added to your bill. Ask beforehand.)

	WHAT IT COSTS IN EUROS				
	$$$$	$$$	$$	$	¢
FOR 2 PEOPLE	over €225	€151–€225	€101–€150	€75–€100	under €75

Prices are for two people in a standard double room in high season, including tax (19.6%) and service charge.

in-room safes, minibars, cable TV, in-room VCRs, indoor pool, gym, sauna, bar, babysitting, laundry service, meeting rooms, parking (fee), some pets allowed ⊟ AE, DC, MC, V Ⓜ Tuileries.

★ $$$$ ⊞ **Hôtel Meurice.** The Meurice has welcomed royalty and celebrity since 1835, from the Duchess of Windsor to sumo champions. No client request seems too outrageous: Salvador Dalí once demanded a herd of sheep be brought to his suite, whereupon he took out his pistol (filled with blanks) and shot at them. Rooms have a gilded Louis XVI or Napoleonic Empire style, with antique furnishings covered in sumptuous French and Italian brocades. Most rooms have a Tuileries/Louvre or Sacré-Coeur view, but the massive Royal Suite takes in a 360° panorama (reportedly Paris's only). Baths are marble, with two sinks and deep, spacious tubs. Goodies are extraordinary: the honey in the minibars is gathered from bees buzzing on the roof of the Opéra, while the health club includes grape seed–based Caudalíe treatments, such as "cabernet sauvignon" massages. Complimentary in-room high-speed Internet is available. ✉ 228 rue de Rivoli, Louvre/Tuileries, 75001 ☎ 01–44–58–10–10 🖷 01–44–58–10–15 ⊕ www.meuricehotel.com ➴ 160 rooms, 36 suites ♨ 2 restaurants, room service, in-room safes, minibars, cable TV with movies, in-room data ports, health club, bar, laundry service, concierge, Internet, business services, meeting rooms, some pets allowed, no-smoking floors ⊟ AE, DC, MC, V Ⓜ Tuileries, Concorde.

$$$$ ⊞ **Hôtel de Vendôme.** With a discreet entrance on the posh place Vendôme and a tiny jewel box of a lobby with inlaid marble and carved mahogany paneling, the Vendôme has all the comfort and luxury of neighboring palace hotels without the ostentatious size. Rooms are done handsomely in French period styles from Louis XIV to Art Deco, with marble baths, antique furniture, and hand-carved wood detailing. Technical touches include wireless Internet, flat-screen TVs, and a bedside console that controls the lights, curtains, music, and electronic do-not-disturb sign. The British-style restaurant and bar, decorated with leather chesterfields and wood paneling, hosts a live pianist Thursday through Saturday and presents contemporary French-fusion fare. ✉ 1 pl. Vendôme, Louvre/Tuileries, 75001 ☎ 01–55–04–55–00 🖷 01–49–27–97–89 ⊕ www.hoteldevendome.com ➴ 18 rooms, 11 suites ♨ Restaurant, room service, in-room data ports, in-room fax, in-room

safes, minibars, cable TV with movies, some in-room VCRs, piano bar, babysitting, laundry service, concierge, meeting room, parking (fee), some pets allowed (fee) ▤ *AE, DC, MC, V* Ⓜ *Concorde, Opéra.*

$$$$ 🏨 **Plaza Paris Vendôme.** Hiding behind a classic 19th-century facade is a fresh, contemporary hostelry with subtle 1930s influences. Under a huge atrium skylight, the lobby's polished black marble floors, lacquered hardwood furnishings, neutral fabrics, and decadent antiques set the mood. The small library has free wireless Internet and a wood-burning fireplace, while the intimate Bar Chinois is decorated with elaborate Chinese wallpaper. Imported woods and black slate accent the hotel's sauna, steam room, and countercurrent swimming pool. Rooms have flannel fabrics and fluffy white comforters, with such modern amenities as flat-screen TVs, CD and DVD players, and complimentary high-speed Internet. The marble bathrooms contain Bulgari toiletries and heated towel racks. Contemporary French and Basque-style cuisine are served in the hotel's Pinxo Restaurant, frequented at lunch by Parisians working nearby. ⊠ *4 rue du Mont Thabor, Louvre/Tuileries, 75001* ☎ *01–40–20–20–00* 🖷 *01–40–20–20–01* ⊕ *www.plazaparisvendome.com* ⤴ *84 rooms, 13 suites* � *Restaurant, room service, in-room data ports, in-room safes, minibars, cable TV with movies, in-room VCRs, indoor pool, gym, massage, sauna, steam room, bar, library, babysitting, dry cleaning, concierge, Internet, parking (fee), some pets allowed (fee), no-smoking rooms* ▤ *AE, DC, MC, V* Ⓜ *Tuileries.*

☾ $$$$ 🏨 **Ritz.** Ever since César Ritz opened the doors of his hotel in 1898, the mere name of this venerable institution has become synonymous with luxury. You could easily spend days here without even venturing onto the magnificent place Vendôme; the shops, gardens, bars, clubs, and restaurants could monopolize you. There's the famed Ritz Escoffier cooking school, where you can learn the finer points of *gateaux*; the Hemingway Bar; and the Greek-temple-ish subterranean spa and swimming pool. Guest rooms match this level of luxe; even the "humbler" spaces have every modern doodad cleverly camouflaged with the decor of gleaming mirrors, chandeliers, and antiques. (Think marble baths with gold pull chains that summon the valet or maid.) The most palatial suites bear names of famous Ritz residents: the Coco Chanel, the Prince of Wales, and the Elton John. ⊠ *15 pl. Vendôme, Louvre/Tuileries, 75001* ☎ *01–43–16–30–30* 🖷 *01–43–16–36–68* ⊕ *www.ritz.com* ⤴ *106 rooms, 56 suites* � *3 restaurants, room service, in-room safes, minibars, cable TV with movies, in-room data ports, indoor pool, health club, hair salon, spa, squash, 2 bars, dance club, shops, children's programs (ages 6–12), laundry service, concierge, Internet, business services, meeting rooms, parking (fee)* ▤ *AE, DC, MC, V* Ⓜ *Opéra.*

$$$ 🏨 **Hôtel Brighton.** Many of Paris's most prestigious palace hotels face the Tuileries or the place de la Concorde. The Brighton breathes the same rarified air under the arcades for a fraction of the price. Smaller rooms with showers look onto a courtyard; street-facing chambers have balconies and a royal view onto the gardens and the Rive Gauche in the distance. Extensive renovations throughout 2004 updated many of the older rooms, but the hotel's still not wired for Internet. ⊠ *218 rue de Rivoli, Louvre/Tuileries, 75001* ☎ *01–47–03–61–61* 🖷 *01–42–60–41–78*

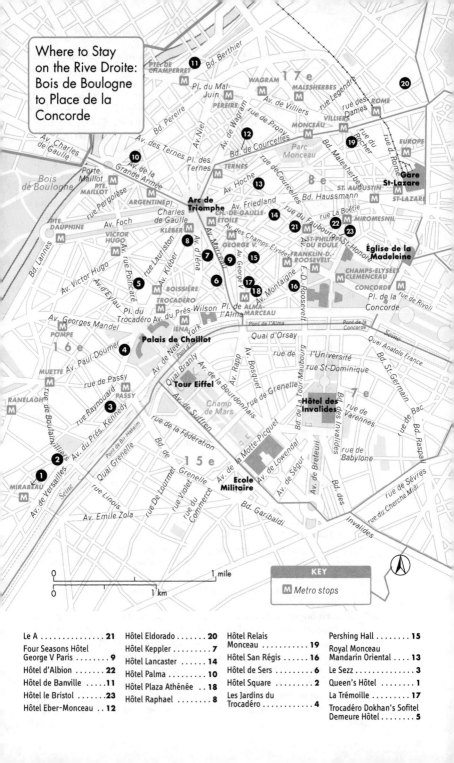

Where to Stay on the Rive Droite: Bois de Boulogne to Place de la Concorde

KEY

Ⓜ *Metro stops*

⊕ *www.esprit-de-france.com* 🗊 *65 rooms* ⟠ *Dining room, in-room data ports, in-room safes, minibars, cable TV, laundry service, some pets allowed; no a/c in some rooms* ⊟ *AE, DC, MC, V* Ⓜ *Tuileries.*

$$$ 🔲 **Hôtel Britannique.** Open since 1861 and just a stone's throw from the Louvre behind the Place du Châtelet, the Britannique blends courteous English service with old-fashioned French elegance. Take the winding staircase up to rooms done in a mix of Pottery Barn–esque repro furniture and antiques in beige, scarlet, and gold tones. Wireless Internet access and in-room flat-screen TVs lend an air of modernity. During World War I the hotel served as headquarters for a Quaker mission. ✉ *20 av. Victoria, Beaubourg/Les Halles, 75001* ☎ *01–42–33–74–59* 🖷 *01–42–33–82–65* ⊕ *www.hotel-britannic.com* 🗊 *38 rooms, 1 suite* ⟠ *Dining room, in-room safes, minibars, cable TV, in-room data ports, bar, laundry service* ⊟ *AE, DC, MC, V* Ⓜ *Châtelet.*

$$–$$$ 🔲 **Hôtel Louvre Sainte Anne.** This small but modern hotel between the Opéra and the Louvre has bright rooms decorated in a peach-and-ivy country theme, with little extras like wireless Internet and heated towel racks. The two spacious triples on the top floor cost a bit extra but have little terraces with views of Sacré Coeur. Breakfast is served in a stone vaulted cellar, and the exceptionally friendly staff can recommend plenty of noteworthy nearby restaurants. ✉ *32 rue Ste-Anne, Louvre/Tuileries, 75001* ☎ *01–40–20–02–35* 🖷 *01–40–15–91–13* ⊕ *www.louvre-ste-anne.fr* 🗊 *20 rooms* ⟠ *Dining room, room service, in-room data ports, in-room safes, minibars, cable TV, Internet, some pets allowed, no-smoking rooms* ⊟ *AE, MC, V* Ⓜ *Pyramides.*

$$ 🔲 **Hôtel du Cygne.** Passed down from mother to daughter, the Swan Hotel is decorated with such feminine touches as hand-sewn curtains, country quilts, and white wooden furniture. Renovated bathrooms are in marble, while older ones have mosaic tiling. Book early for the larger rooms, which include Nos. 16, 26, 35, and 41. Ancient wooden beams run the length of the two stairwells, which make for uneven stepping that challenge even the most agile guests, but the hotel opens onto a central pedestrian street of Les Halles, within walking distance of the Louvre, Notre Dame, and the Marais. ✉ *3 rue du Cygne, Beaubourg/Les Halles, 75001* ☎ *01–42–60–14–16* 🖷 *01–42–21–37–02* ⊕ *www.hotelducygne.fr* 🗊 *18 rooms* ⟠ *Dining room, in-room safes, cable TV; no a/c* ⊟ *MC, V* Ⓜ *Étienne Marcel, Les Halles.*

$–$$ 🔲 **Hôtel Londres St-Honoré.** An appealing combination of character and comfort distinguishes this small, inexpensive hotel a five-minute walk from the Louvre. Exposed oak beams, statues in niches, and rustic stone walls give this place an old-fashioned air. Though rooms have floral bedspreads and standard hotel furniture, they are pleasant, and the price is right. Note that elevator service begins on the second floor. ✉ *13 rue St-Roch, Louvre/Tuileries, 75001* ☎ *01–42–60–15–62* 🖷 *01–42–60–16–00* 🗊 *21 rooms, 4 suites* ⟠ *Dining room, minibars, cable TV, Internet, some pets allowed, no-smoking rooms; no a/c in some rooms* ⊟ *AE, DC, MC, V* Ⓜ *Pyramides.*

$ 🔲 **Hôtel Louvre Forum.** This hotel is a find: settled between the Louvre, Les Halles, and Palais-Royal, it has modern, spotless rooms that are quite well equipped for the price. Furniture is of the Ikea genre, and the baths

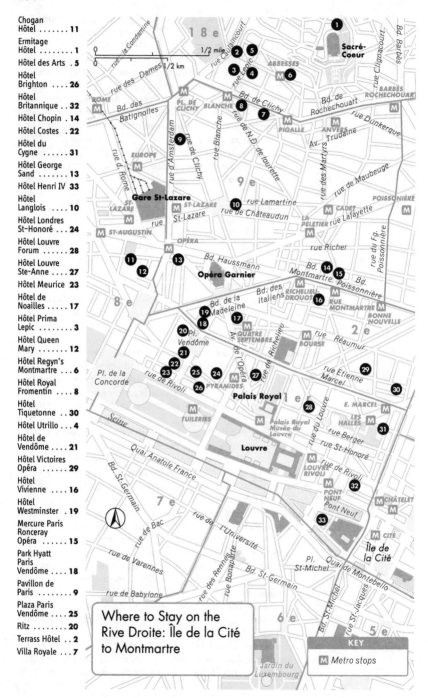

Where to Stay on the
Rive Droite: Île de la Cité
to Montmartre

KEY

Ⓜ Metro stops

are simple white tile, but a few old beams do poke through. Bonuses include a bright sitting area and stone cellar breakfast room, both with murals. ☒ *25 rue du Bouloi, Louvre/Tuileries, 75001* ☏*01–42–36–54–19* 🖶 *01–42–33–66–31* ⊕ *www.paris-hotel-louvre-forum.com* ⟿ *27 rooms* ⟐ *Dining room, in-room safes, minibars, cable TV, bar* ☐ *AE, DC, MC, V* Ⓜ *Louvre.*

¢ 🖭 **Hôtel Henri IV.** When tourists think of staying on one of the islands, it's Île St-Louis, not Île de la Cité, they consider. But the overlooked isle shelters one of the city's most beloved rock-bottom sleeps. This 17th-century building that once housed King Henri IV's printing presses offers few comforts. The narrow staircase (five flights, no elevator) creaks, and the ragged rooms show their age. Most bathrooms are in the hallway, and they may not be up to your standard of hygiene; pay a little extra and get a room with private shower, or reserve room No. 16, the only one with a tub. The payoff is a location overlooking the oasislike place Dauphine, just a few steps from the Pont Neuf and Sainte-Chapelle. ☒ *25 pl. Dauphine, Île de la Cité, 75001* ☏ *01–43–54–44–53* ⟿ *20 rooms, 7 with bath* ⟐ *Dining room; no a/c, no room phones, no room TVs* ☐ *MC, V* ⑩ *CP* Ⓜ *Cité, St-Michel, Pont Neuf.*

2ᵉ Arrondissement (Opéra/Grands Boulevards)

See Where to Stay on the Rive Droite: Île de la Cité to Montmartre map.

$$$$ 🖭 **Hôtel Westminster.** This former inn and coach stop on an elegant street between the Opéra and place Vendôme was built in the mid-19th century. Even now that wireless Internet has arrived (on the ground floor), the public areas and rooms happily retain their period furniture, marble fireplaces, crystal chandeliers, and piped-in classical music. The pleasant Duke's piano bar is a popular rendezvous spot, and the hotel's Michelin one-star restaurant, Le Céladon, serves outstanding French cuisine. The fitness center has views over Paris's rooftops and a Moorish-inspired steam room. The hotel often offers excellent promotional rates on its Web site. ☒ *13 rue de la Paix, Opéra/Grands Boulevards, 75002* ☏ *01–42–61–57–46* 🖶 *01–42–60–30–66* ⊕ *www.hotelwestminster. com* ⟿ *80 rooms, 21 suites* ⟐ *Restaurant, room service, in-room safes, minibars, cable TV with movies, in-room data ports, health club, spa, piano bar, babysitting, laundry service, concierge, Internet, business services, meeting rooms, parking (fee), some pets allowed, no-smoking floor* ☐ *AE, DC, MC, V* Ⓜ *Opéra.*

★ $$$$ 🖭 **Park Hyatt Paris Vendôme.** Understated luxury with a contemporary Zen vibe differentiates this Hyatt from its more classic neighbors between the place Vendôme and Opéra Garnier. Architect Ed Tuttle converted five Haussmann-era office buildings into a showcase for polished beige limestone, mahogany veneer surfaces, and bronze Roseline Granet sculptures. The minimalist coolness in the rooms extends to the Bang & Olufsen entertainment systems and the Japanese-inspired brass-and-stone spalike baths, under-floor heating, and spacious dressing area. Chef Christophe David conjures up bold signature dishes in the unusual restaurant-in-the-round, Le Park, and in summer you can dine in the Mediterranean-style courtyard. Spa treatments feature French Carita products, and the entire hotel is Wi-Fi accessible. ✉ *3–5 rue de la Paix, Opéra/ Grands Boulevards, 75002* ☎ *01–58–71–12–34* 📠 *01–58–71–12–35* ⊕ *www.paris.vendome.hyatt.com* ⇒ *142 rooms, 35 suites* ⚶ *2 restaurants, room service, in-room safes, minibars, cable TV, some in-room VCRs, in-room data ports, gym, massage, sauna, spa, steam room, bar, laundry service, concierge, Internet, business services, meeting rooms, free parking, some pets allowed, no-smoking floors* ▤ *AE, DC, MC, V* Ⓜ *Concorde, Opéra.*

$$$–$$$$ ▦ **Hôtel de Noailles.** With a nod to the work of postmodern designers like Putman and Starck, this nouveau-wave inn (part of the Tulip Inn group) is near the top of Paris's short list of well-priced, style-driven boutique hotels. Connectable into suites, the imaginative rooms have sleek, Japan-meets-Scandinavia furnishings and contemporary decolike details such as frosted glass, veneer paneling, and skinny, antenna-like lamps. There's also wireless Internet access. A spacious outdoor terrace is off the breakfast lounge. ✉ *9 rue de Michodière, Opéra/Grands Boulevards, 75002* ☎ *01–47–42–92–90* 📠 *01–49–24–92–71* ⊕ *www.paris-hotel-noailles.com* ⇒ *61 rooms* ⚶ *Dining room, room service, in-room safes, minibars, cable TV, massage, sauna, bar, laundry service, Internet, meeting rooms, some pets allowed, no-smoking floors* ▤ *AE, DC, MC, V* Ⓜ *Opéra.*

$$$ ▦ **Hôtel Victoires Opéra.** This hotel is an oasis of calm amid the colorful bustle of Montorgueil, a very popular pedestrian-only market street near Les Halles and the fashion boutiques of Rue Étienne Marcel. Few modern hotels capture any sense of character, but the streamlined lobby, corridors, and rooms here exude a regal aesthetic, with plenty of plum-, mustard-, and burgundy-color fabrics and highly polished surfaces. ✉ *56 rue Montorgueil, Beaubourg/Les Halles, 75002* ☎ *01–42–36–41–08* 📠 *01–45–08–08–79* ⊕ *www.paris-hotel-opera.com* ⇒ *20 rooms, 4 suites* ⚶ *Dining room, in-room safes, minibars, cable TV, in-room data ports, laundry service, no-smoking rooms* ▤ *AE, DC, MC, V* Ⓜ *Étienne Marcel, Les Halles.*

¢–$ ▦ **Hotel Vivienne.** The decor is a bit schizoid; some guest rooms have chandeliers, others have fuzzy brown rugs and busy bedspreads, yet another is fashionably minimalist, and rooms 39, 40, and 41 are blessed with large rooftop balconies. But the overall spruceness and the location near the Opéra Garnier and Grands Boulevards department stores make this a strong bet in this price range. Higher-price rooms have private shower and toilet facilities. ✉ *40 rue Vivienne, Opéra/Grands Boulevards 75002* ☎ *01–42–33–13–26* 📠 *01–40–41–98–19* ⇒ *45 rooms, 35 with bath* ⚶ *Dining room, cable TV, Internet, some pets allowed, no-smoking rooms; no a/c* ▤ *MC, V* Ⓜ *Bourse, Richelieu-Drouot.*

¢ ▦ **Hôtel Tiquetonne.** Just off the Montorgueil market and a short hoof from Les Halles (and the slightly seedy rue St-Denis), this is one of the least expensive hotels in the city center. The so-old-fashioned-they're-vintage-cool rooms aren't much to look at, nor do they offer amenities, but they're always clean and some are downright spacious. Book one of the top two floors facing the quiet, pedestrian rue Tiquetonne, not the loud, car-strangled rue Turbigo. ✉ *6 rue Tiquetonne, Beaubourg/ Les Halles, 75002* ☎ *01–42–36–94–58* 📠 *01–42–36–02–94* ⇒ *45* *rooms, 33 with bath ⟨⟩ Some pets allowed; no a/c, no room TVs ⊟ AE, MC, V ⊘ Closed Aug. and last wk of Dec. Ⓜ Étienne Marcel.*

3e Arrondissement (Le Marais)

See Where to Stay on the Rive Droite: The Marais to La Villette map.

$$$$ 🖼 **Murano Urban Resort.** As the epicenter of Parisian cool migrates east-

Fodor'sChoice ward, it's no surprise that a design-conscious hotel has followed. Opened
★ in summer 2004 on the trendy northern edge of the Marais (known for its contemporary art galleries and gay-friendly tearooms), this cheeky hotel that dares to call itself a resort combines Austin Powers playfulness with serious 007-inspired gadgetry. A psychedelic elevator zooms guests to ultraviolet-lit hallways, where they enter pristine white rooms via fingerprint sensor locks. White shag carpeting, black slate bathrooms, pop-art furniture, and bedside control panels that change the color of the lighting keep guests amused until it's time for aperitifs. Available in-room goodies include stress-relieving squeeze toys, scented candles, lollipops, and heavy Murano glass ashtrays. Two suites have private terraces with heated, countercurrent pools. Stylish Parisians pack the hotel's vodka bar and sleek restaurant, where a live DJ holds court in the elevated booth and staff seem genuinely happy to help. As of this writing, a fab spa with an indoor heated pool and Anne Sémonin beauty treatments was in the works for late summer 2005. ⊠ *13 bd. du Temple, République, 75003* 🕾 *01–42–71–20–00* 🖨 *01–42–71–21–01* ⊕ *www.muranoresort.com* ⟲ *43 rooms, 9 suites ⟨⟩ Restaurant, room service, in-room data ports, in-room safes, minibars, cable TV, in-room VCRs, indoor pool, gym, health club, spa, bar, lounge, dry cleaning, concierge, Internet, business services, car rental, parking (fee), some pets allowed, no-smoking floors* ⊟ *AE, DC, MC, V* Ⓜ *Filles du Calvaire.*

★ **$$$$** 🖼 **Pavillon de la Reine.** This enchanting countrylike château hides off the regal place des Vosges behind a buffer of sorts, a stunning cobblestone courtyard. Gigantic beams, chunky stone pillars, original oils, and a weathered fireplace speak to the building's 1612 origins. The hotel has large doubles, duplexes, and genuine suites decorated in either contemporary or 18th-century-style wall fabrics. Many rooms look out on the entry court or an interior Japanese-inspired garden. A spiral-posted wooden canopy bed is the centerpiece of Suite 58. There's wireless Internet. ⊠ *28 pl. des Vosges, Le Marais, 75003* 🕾 *01–40–29–19–19, 800/447–7462 in the U.S.* 🖨 *01–40–29–19–20* ⊕ *www.pavillon-de-la-reine.com* ⟲ *30 rooms, 26 suites ⟨⟩ Dining room, room service, in-room safes, minibars, cable TV, bar, laundry service, concierge, Internet, meeting room, free parking, some pets allowed* ⊟ *AE, DC, MC, V* Ⓜ *Bastille, St-Paul.*

¢ 🖼 **Hôtel Bellevue et du Chariot d'Or.** Here you have an old Belle Époque time traveler, proud to keep its dingy chandeliers and faded gold trimming as is. Budget groups from France and the Netherlands come for the clean, sans-frills rooms; some units sleep four. Halls are lined with stamped felt that helps muffle sound trickling up from the spacious marble-floor lobby and bar. There may be some quirks, like the hefty old-fashioned room keys and the bathtub/showers without curtains, but you're just a few blocks from hipper addresses in the heart of the Marais. Get here before the fashionista crowd turns it into a shabby-chic hangout. ✉ *39 rue de Turbigo, Beaubourg/Les Halles, 75003* ☎ *01–48–87–45–60* 🖨 *01–48–87–95–04* ⊕ *www.hotelbellevue75.com* ↻ *59 rooms* ⚭ *Dining room, cable TV, bar; no a/c* ⊟ *AE, DC, MC, V* ⊙ *CP* Ⓜ *Réaumur-Sébastopol, Arts et Métiers.*

¢ ⛨ **Hôtel de Roubaix.** Although this faded ghost hasn't updated its grandmotherly decor or creaky elevator in recent decades, it conveys an amiable, family-run coziness and charges unbeatable prices, especially given the location just five minutes from the Marais and the Pompidou Center. Rooms are bright if basic, with large beds and tiled walk-in showers. Vending machines in the hall supply munchies round the clock. ✉ *6 rue Greneta, Beaubourg/Les Halles, 75003* ☎ *01–42–72–89–91* 🖨 *01–42–72–58–79* ✐ *hotel.de.roubaix@wanadoo.fr* ↻ *53 rooms* ⚭ *Dining room, cable TV; no a/c* ⊟ *MC, V* ⊙ *CP* Ⓜ *Réaumur-Sébastopol, Arts et Métiers.*

4ᵉ Arrondissement (Le Marais & Île St-Louis)

See Where to Stay on the Rive Droite: The Marais to La Villette map.

$$$$ ⛨ **Hôtel du Jeu de Paume.** Set off the street by heavy doors and a small courtyard, the showpiece of this lovely 17th-century hotel on Île St-Louis is the stone-walled, vaulted lobby–cum–breakfast room. It stands on an erstwhile court where French aristocrats once played *jeu de paume,* an early version of tennis using the palms of their hands. The bright rooms are nicely done up in butter yellow or blue, with beamed ceilings and damask upholstery; however, the starker modern decor in the smaller rooms doesn't quite jibe with the style of the rest of the hotel. Superior rooms and suites open onto a sunny garden patio. ✉ *54 rue St-Louis-en-l'Île, Île-St-Louis, 75004* ☎ *01–43–26–14–18* 🖨 *01–40–46–02–76* ⊕ *www.jeudepaumehotel.com* ↻ *23 rooms, 5 suites* ⚭ *Dining room, in-room safes, minibars, cable TV, exercise equipment, sauna, billiards, bar, laundry service, Internet, meeting rooms, some pets allowed; no a/c* ⊟ *AE, DC, MC, V* Ⓜ *Pont Marie.*

★ $$$–$$$$ ⛨ **Hôtel Bourg Tibourg.** Scented candles and subdued lighting announce the designer-du-jour Jacques Garcia's theatrical mix of haremlike romance and Gothic contemplation. Royal blue paint and red velvet line the claustrophobic halls. The rooms are barely bigger than the beds, and every inch has been upholstered, tasseled, and draped in a cacophony of stripes, florals, and medieval motifs; Byzantine alcoves hold mosaic-tile tubs. A stone staircase winds down to the intimate lounge where you can order drinks and plan your next tryst. A pocket garden has room for three tables, leafy plants, and a swath of stars above. ✉ *19 rue Bourg Tibourg, Le Marais, 75004* ☎ *01–42–78–47–39* 🖨 *01–40–29–07–00* ⊕ *www.hoteldubourgtibourg.com* ↻ *29 rooms, 1 suite* ⚭ *Dining room, in-room safes, minibars, cable TV, laundry service* ⊟ *AE, DC, MC, V* Ⓜ *Hôtel de Ville.*

$$$–$$$$ ⛨ **Hôtel Saint Merry.** Due south of the Pompidou Center is this small and FodorśChoice stunning Gothic hideaway, once the presbytery of the adjacent St-Merry ★ church. In its 17th-century stone interior you can gaze through stained glass, relax on a church pew, or lean back on a headboard recycled from

an old Catholic confessional. With a massive hardwood table, fireplace, and high ceiling, the suite is fit for a royal council. Room 9 is bisected by stone buttresses still supporting the church. The Saint Merry's lack of an elevator and 21st-century temptations like TV are also in keeping with its ascetic past (and keeps the place monkishly quiet). ☒ *78 rue de la Verrerie, Beaubourg/Les Halles, 75004* ☎ *01–42–78–14–15* 🖷 *01–40–29–06–82* ⊕ *www.france-hotel-guide.com/h75004stmerry. htm* ➘ *11 rooms, 1 suite* ⚙ *Room service, in-room safes, some minibars, laundry service, some pets allowed; no a/c, no TV in some rooms* ▤ *AE, MC, V* Ⓜ *Châtelet, Hôtel de Ville.*

★ **$$$** 🏨 **Hôtel Axial Beaubourg.** This stylish but cozy family-owned hotel is a rare find. Modernized in 2001, the 16th-century building retains its beamed ceilings and stone basement (now a breakfast lounge with a rattan floor). Offering a pleasing contrast is the stylish, earthy palette of ocher, violet, and eggplant and the sleek, formless furniture. Wireless Internet is available in the lobby and on the first floor, and guest rooms have dial-up Internet connections. The bright lounge done in burgundy and chestnut has big picture windows overlooking the lively streets of the hip Marais district. ☒ *11 rue du Temple, Le Marais, 75004* ☎ *01–42–72–72–22* 🖷 *01–42–72–03–53* ⊕ *www.axialbeaubourg.com* ➘ *39 rooms* ⚙ *Dining room, in-room safes, minibars, cable TV, laundry service, Internet* ▤ *AE, DC, MC, V* Ⓜ *Hôtel de Ville.*

★ **$$–$$$** 🏨 **Hôtel Caron de Beaumarchais.** The theme of this intimate hotel is the work of former next-door neighbor Pierre-Augustin Caron de Beaumarchais, supplier of military aid to American revolutionaries and author of *The Marriage of Figaro.* First-edition copies of his books adorn the public spaces, and the salons faithfully reflect the taste of 18th-century French nobility, right down to the wallpaper and 1792 piano-forte. Richly decorated with floral fabrics and white wooden period furnishings, the rooms have original beams, hand-painted bathroom tiles, and gilt mirrors. Street-side rooms on the second through fifth floors are the largest, while smaller sixth-floor garrets under the mansard roof have beguiling views across Rive Droite rooftops. Each room is equipped with flat-screen TVs and wireless Internet. ☒ *12 rue Vieille-du-Temple, Le Marais, 75004* ☎ *01–42–72–34–12* 🖷 *01–42–72–34–63* ⊕ *www. carondebeaumarchais.com* ➘ *19 rooms* ⚙ *Dining room, in-room safes, minibars, cable TV with movies, in-room data ports, laundry service, Internet* ▤ *AE, DC, MC, V* Ⓜ *Hôtel de Ville.*

$$ 🏨 **Hôtel de la Bretonnerie.** This small hotel is in a 17th-century *hôtel particulier* (town house) on a tiny street in the Marais, a few minutes' walk from the Centre Pompidou and the bars and cafés of rue Vieille du Temple. Rooms are classified as either *chambres classiques* or *chambres de charme,* the latter being more spacious, and naturally pricier, but with more elaborate furnishings, like Louis XIII–style four-poster canopy beds and marble-clad bathtubs. Overall, the establishment is spotless, and the staff is welcoming. Breakfast is served in the vaulted cellar. ☒ *22 rue Ste-Croix-de-la-Bretonnerie, Le Marais, 75004* ☎ *01–48–87–77–63* 🖷 *01–42–77–26–78* ⊕ *www.bretonnerie.com* ➘ *22 rooms, 7 suites* ⚙ *Dining room, in-room safes, minibars, cable TV, some in-room data ports, laundry service; no a/c* ▤ *MC, V* Ⓜ *Hôtel de Ville.*

$$ ⊞ **Hôtel de la Place des Vosges.** Despite a lack of some expected comforts and an elevator that doesn't serve all floors, a loyal clientele swears by this small, historic hotel on a street leading directly into place des Vosges. The Louis XIII–style reception area and rooms with oak-beam ceilings, rough-hewn stone, and a mix of rustic finds from secondhand shops evoke the Old Marais. The lone top-floor room, the hotel's largest, has a Jacuzzi and a view over the Rive Droite rooftops. Other, considerably smaller rooms are less expensive, but five have showers with multijet heads to invigorate you after a shopping or museum marathon. ✉ *12 rue de Birague, Le Marais, 75004* ☎ *01–42–72–60–46* 🖷 *01–42–72–02–64* ⊕ *www.hotelplacedesvosges.com* 🛏 *16 rooms* ♿ *Dining room, cable TV; no a/c* ⊟ *AE, DC, MC, V* Ⓜ *Bastille.*

$$ ⊞ **Hôtel Saint Louis.** The coveted location on the Île St-Louis is the real draw of this modest hotel, which retains many of its original 17th-century stone walls and wooden beams. Request one of the remodeled rooms on the fourth and fifth floors, as some of the older rooms can be a bit tattered. Minibalconies on the upper levels also have Seine views. Number 51 has a tear-shape tub and a peek at the Panthéon. Breakfast is served in the vaulted stone cellar. ✉ *75 rue St-Louis-en-l'Île, Île St-Louis, 75004* ☎ *01–46–34–04–80* 🖷 *01–46–34–02–13* ⊕ *www.hotelsaintlouis. com* 🛏 *19 rooms* ♿ *Dining room, in-room safes, cable TV, some pets allowed* ⊟ *MC, V* Ⓜ *Pont Marie.*

$$ ⊞ **Hôtel Saint-Louis Marais.** Once an annex to a local convent, this 18th-century hôtel particulier has retained its stone walls and beams while adding red-clay tile floors and antiques. A wooden-banistered stair leads to the small but proper rooms, decorated with basic red carpet and green bedspreads. (Those with heavy luggage, beware: no elevator.) The hotel's in Village St-Paul, a little tangle of medieval lanes just south of the well-traveled Marais that has an excellent English-language bookstore and is not yet overrun by tourists. ✉ *1 rue Charles V, Le Marais, 75004* ☎ *01–48–87–87–04* 🖷 *01–48–87–33–26* ⊕ *www.saintlouismarais.com* 🛏 *20 rooms* ♿ *Dining room, in-room safes, cable TV, laundry service, Internet, some pets allowed; no a/c* ⊟ *DC, MC, V* Ⓜ *Sully Morland, Bastille.*

$$ ⊞ **Hôtel du Vieux Marais.** This pleasingly minimalist hotel with a turn-of-the-20th-century facade is on a quiet street in the heart of the Marais. Rooms are bright and impeccably clean, with contemporary oak furnishings, burgundy-leather seating, and velour curtains. Bathrooms are immaculately tiled in Italian marble, with walk-in showers or combination shower/tubs. Visitors who prefer a bit of extra space should ask about special rates on the triple rooms. The staff is exceptionally friendly. ✉ *8 rue du Plâtre, Le Marais, 75004* ☎ *01–42–78–47–22* 🖷 *01–42–78–34–32* ⊕ *www.vieuxmarais.com* 🛏 *30 rooms* ♿ *Dining room, in-room safes, cable TV, Internet* ⊟ *MC, V* Ⓜ *Hôtel de Ville.*

★ $ ⊞ **Grand Hôtel Jeanne-d'Arc.** You'll get your money's worth at this hotel in an unbeatable location off the tranquil place du Marché Ste-Catherine, one of the city's lesser-known pedestrian squares. The 17th-century building has been a hotel for more than a century, and while rooms are on the spartan side they are well maintained, fairly spacious, and done in cheery Provençal colors (some rooms facing the back are dimmer). The welcoming staff is informal and happy to recount the history of this former market

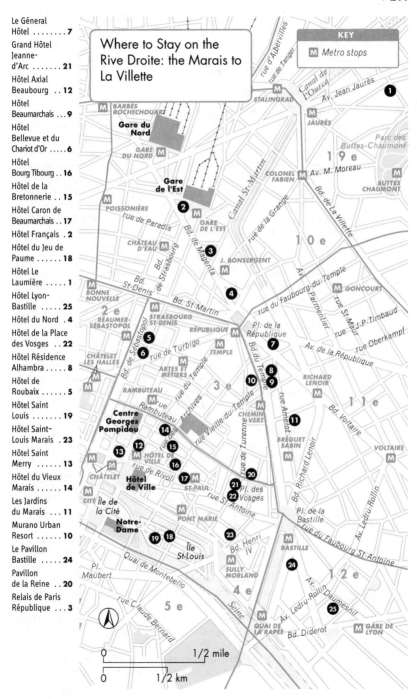

Where to Stay on the
Rive Droite: the Marais to
La Villette

KEY

Ⓜ *Metro stops*

quartier. ⊠ *3 rue de Jarente, Le Marais, 75004* ☎ *01–48–87–62–11* 🖨 *01–48–87–37–31* ⊕ *www.hoteljeannedarc.com* 📠 *36 rooms* ♻ *Dining room, cable TV, some pets allowed; no a/c* ➭ *MC, V* Ⓜ *St-Paul.*

5° Arrondissement (Quartier Latin)

See Where to Stay on the Rive Gauche map.

★ $$$–$$$$ 🏨 **Hôtel des Grands Hommes.** The great men this hotel honors with its name rest in peace within the towering Panthéon monument across the street. The hotel's Empire look combines urns and laurel-wreath motifs with plush beige, aubergine, and burgundy fabrics and plaster busts of writers and statesmen (surrealist André Breton invented "automatic writing" here in 1919). Top-floor rooms have balconies with tables and chairs and fantastic north-facing views of the cityscape. All rooms have period furnishings and interesting architectural details. There's free wireless Internet in the lobby. ⊠ *17 pl. du Panthéon, Quartier Latin, 75005* ☎*01–46–34–19–60* 🖨*01–43–26–67–32* ⊕*www.hoteldesgrandshommes.com* 📠 *31 rooms* ♻ *Dining room, in-room data ports, in-room safes, minibars, cable TV, laundry service, Internet, meeting room, some pets allowed* ➭ *AE, DC, MC, V* Ⓜ *RER: Luxembourg.*

♻ $$$–$$$$ 🏨 **Hôtel Résidence Henri IV.** Sometimes travelers, especially those with children, need a home base where they can kick back and make their own meals. The lemon-yellow-and-peach rooms and apartments here don't offer any particular charms, but each does come equipped with a basic kitchenette: two-burner stove, dorm-size fridge, sink, and basic dishware. The location on a quiet cul-de-sac by the École Polytechnique is steps from the Panthéon and the Sorbonne. Ask about the special weekend rates. ⊠ *50 rue des Bernadins, Quartier Latin, 75005* ☎*01–44–41–31–81* 🖨*01–46–33–93–22* ⊕ *www.residencehenri4.com* 📠 *8 rooms, 5 apartments* ♻ *Dining room, in-room safes, kitchenettes, cable TV, laundry service, Internet, some pets allowed; no a/c* ➭ *AE, DC, MC, V* Ⓜ *Maubert-Mutualité.*

$$$ 🏨 **Hôtel Henri IV.** From the ashes of the legendary dive bar Polly Magoo, this smart new hotel rose in 2003; it's just 50 paces from Notre-Dame and the Seine. The identical, impeccable rooms have beige and rose blossom–print linens and framed prints of architectural drawings. Street-side rooms get a bit of traffic noise, but views of the 15th-century Église St-Severin make up for it. The lobby has pleasing terra-cotta floor tiles, pale green walls, and a stone fireplace. (Note: don't confuse this with other Henri IV hotels in the area.) ⊠*9–11 rue St-Jacques, Quartier Latin, 75005* ☎ *01–46–33–20–20* 🖨 *01–46–33–90–90* ⊕ *www.hotel-henri4.com* 📠 *23 rooms* ♻ *Dining room, in-room safes, minibars, cable TV with movies, Internet, some pets allowed* ➭*AE, DC, MC, V* Ⓜ *St-Michel.*

$–$$$ 🏨 **Les Degrés de Notre Dame.** On a quiet lane a few yards from the
FodorsChoice Seine, this diminutive budget hotel is lovingly decorated with the
★ owner's flea-market finds. No. 23 is the largest of the lower-priced rooms, while the slightly more costly No. 24 has even more space, wooden floors, and particularly appealing antique furnishings. The most expensive room, No. 501, occupies the entire top floor, with views of Notre Dame and space for four guests. There's no elevator, but colorful murals of Parisian scenes decorate the winding stairwell. The

restaurant/bar (closed Sunday), frequented by locals, serves French and North African specialities and has a large sidewalk terrace. ✉ *10 rue des Grands Degrés, Quartier Latin, 75005* ☎ *01–55–24–88–88* 🖷 *01–40–46–95–34* ⊕ *www.lesdegreshotel.com* ↵ *10 rooms* ⚏ *Restaurant, in-room safes, bar; no a/c, no kids under 12* ▤ *MC, V* ⫶◐⫶ *CP* Ⓜ *Maubert-Mutualité.*

$$ ▦ **Hôtel Grandes Écoles.** Guests enter Madame Lefloch's country-style domain through two massive wooden doors. Distributed among a trio of three-story buildings, her baby-blue-and-white guest rooms and their flowery Louis-Philippe furnishings and lace bedspreads create a grandmotherly vibe, which may not be to everyone's taste. But the Grandes Écoles is legendary for its stunning interior cobbled courtyard and garden, which becomes the second living room and a perfect breakfast spot when *il fait beau.* Rooms 29 and 30 open directly onto the greenery and calm. ✉ *75 rue du Cardinal Lemoine, Quartier Latin, 75005* ☎ *01–43–26–79–23* 🖷 *01–43–25–28–15* ⊕ *www.hotel-grandes-ecoles.com* ↵ *51 rooms* ⚏ *Dining room, room service, parking (fee), some pets allowed; no a/c, no room TVs* ▤ *MC, V* Ⓜ *Cardinal Lemoine.*

★ $$ ▦ **Hôtel des Jardins du Luxembourg.** Blessed with a personable staff and a smart, stylish look, this hotel on a calm cul-de-sac a block from the Luxembourg Gardens is an oasis for contemplation. A cheery hardwood-floor lobby with fireplace leads to smallish rooms furnished with wrought-iron beds with puffy duvets, pastel bathroom tiles, and contemporary Provençal fabrics. Ask for one with a balcony overlooking the street; the best, Room 25, has dormer windows with a peekaboo view of the Tour Eiffel. The entire hotel has wireless Internet access. It's an easy commute to either the airport or the Eurostar via the RER train that stops at the end of the street. ✉ *5 impasse Royer-Collard, Quartier Latin, 75005* ☎*01–40–46–08–88* 🖷*01–40–46–02–28* ⊕*monsite.wanadoo.fr/jardinslux* ↵ *26 rooms* ⚏ *Dining room, in-room safes, minibars, sauna, laundry service, Internet* ▤ *AE, DC, MC, V* Ⓜ *RER: Luxembourg.*

★ $$ ▦ **Hôtel Saint-Jacques.** Nearly every wall in this bargain hotel is bedecked with faux-marble and trompe-d'oeil murals. As in many old and independent Paris hotels, each room has unique features, furnishings, and layout. Generous amenities for the price include an Internet kiosk, in-room safes, and fax service. About half the rooms have tiny step-out balconies that give a glimpse of Notre-Dame and the Panthéon. Room 25 has a long round-the-corner balcony; also popular is the all-yellow room, No. 31, set right under the roof. The Saint-Jacques's chirpy staff rewards repeat guests with souvenir knickknacks, the most loyal with T-shirts. ✉*35 rue des Écoles, Quartier Latin, 75005* ☎*01–44–07–45–45* 🖷 *01–43–25–65–50* ⊕ *www.hotel-saintjacques.com* ↵ *35 rooms* ⚏ *Dining room, in-room safes, cable TV, Internet; no a/c* ▤ *AE, DC, MC, V* Ⓜ *Maubert-Mutualité.*

$–$$ ▦ **Hôtel Collège de France.** Exposed-stone walls, wooden beams, and medieval artworks echo the style of the Cluny Medieval Museum, just two blocks from this small, family-run hotel. Rooms convey a less elaborate, more streamlined aesthetic than the lobby and are relatively quiet owing to the side-street location. Rooms with shower/tubs offer more space than those with showers only. No. 62, on the top floor, costs a

APARTMENT RENTALS

I F YOU WANT A HOME BASE *that's roomy enough for a family and comes with cooking facilities, consider a furnished rental. These can save you money, especially if you're traveling with a group. Home-exchange directories sometimes list rentals as well as exchanges. You might also look in the bimonthly journal France USA Contacts (known as FUSAC, distributed for free in Paris, or see www. fusac.fr), which lists rentals as well as apartment exchanges. Policies differ from company to company, but you can generally expect a minimum required stay of one week; a refundable deposit (expect to pay $200–$500) payable on arrival; sometimes an agency fee; and weekly or biweekly maid service.*

The following is a list of good-value residence hotels and apartment services, each with multiple properties in Paris: **Citadines Résidences Hôtelières** *(☎ 08–25–33–33–32 ⊕ www.citadines.fr).* **Lodgis Paris** *(☎ 01–70–39–11–11 🖷 01–70–39–11–15 ⊕ www.lodgis. com).* **Paris Appartements Services** *(☎ 01–40–28–01–28 🖷 01–40–28–92–01 ⊕ www.paris-apts.com).* **Rothray** *(☎ 01–48–87–13–37 🖷 01–42–78–17–72 ⊕ rothray.free.fr).*

Agencies based in the U.S. can also help you find an apartment in Paris: **Drawbridge to Europe** *(⊠ 102 Granite St., Ashland, OR 97520 ☎ 541/482–7778 or 888/268–1148 🖷 541/482–7779 ⊕ www.drawbridgetoeurope.com).* **Interhome** *(⊠ 1990 N.E. 163rd St., Suite 110, North Miami Beach, FL 33162 ☎ 305/940–2299 or 800/882–6864 🖷 305/940–2911 ⊕ www.interhome. com).* **New York Habitat** *(⊠ 307 7th Ave., Suite 306, New York, NY 10001 ☎ 01–42–36–78–70 in France, 212/255–8018 in the U.S. 🖷 212/627–1416 in the U.S. ⊕ www.nyhabitat.com).* **Rentals in Paris** *(☎ 516/977–3318 🖷 516/977–*

3318 ⊕ www.rentals-in-paris.com). **Villanet** *(⊠ 1251 N.W. 116th St., Seattle, WA 98177 ☎ 206/417–3444 or 800/964–1891 🖷 206/417–1832 ⊕ www. rentavilla.com).* **Villas International** *(⊠ 4340 Redwood Hwy., Suite D309, San Rafael, CA 94903 ☎ 415/499–9490 or 800/221–2260 🖷 415/499–9491 ⊕ www.villasintl.com).*

Hosted Rooms

Literally, "alcove and banquet, " **Alcôve & Agapes** *(☎ 01–44–85–06–05 🖷 01–44–85–06–14 ⊕ www.bed-and-breakfast-in-paris.com) is Paris's answer to the urban B&B. Françoise Fôret acts as a broker for around 100 Parisians who offer up chambre d'hôte–style accommodations in their own Haussmann-era apartments or artist ateliers. The Web site shows photos of each property (including non-B&B private studios with kitchens). Prices range from roughly €70 to €120 per couple (breakfast included), and many hosts (90% of whom speak English) offer extra services like guided tours and dinner. Before booking you'll be sent a questionnaire allowing you to choose a neighborhood and other preferences. Minimum stay is usually two or three nights.*

bit extra but has a small balcony with superb views. ⊠ *7 rue Thénard, Quartier Latin, 75005* ☎ *01–43–26–78–36* 🖷 *01–46–34–58–29* ⊕ *www. hotel-collegedefrance.com* ⇨ *29 rooms* ⌂ *Dining room, room service, in-room data ports, in-room safes, cable TV; no a/c* ⊟ *AE, DC, MC, V* Ⓜ *Maubert-Mutualité, St-Michel–Cluny–La Sorbonne.*

⛄ **$–$$** 🏨 **Hôtel Devillas.** A great value if you don't mind relying upon public transportation, this contemporary, family-run hotel lies a few minutes' walk from the kid-friendly Jardin des Plantes and a quick métro ride to the Bastille district. Completely remodeled in 2004, the hotel has a TV lounge with a bar and small library, a computer station in the lobby, and wireless Internet throughout. Contemporary furnishings and wooden floors fill the warmly painted rooms; those overlooking the busy Parisian boulevard get plenty of sunlight (several of them have wrought-iron balconies), while the quietest rooms face a tranquil inner courtyard. ⊠ *4 bd. St-Marcel, Gobelins, 75005* ☎ *01–43–31–37–50* 🖷 *01–43–31–96–03* ⊕ *www.hoteldevillas.com* ⇨ *40 rooms* ⌂ *Dining room, room service, in-room safes, cable TV, bar, lounge, Internet, parking (fee), some pets allowed (fee), no-smoking floors* ⊟ *AE, DC, MC, V* Ⓜ *St-Marcel.*

⛄ **¢–$** 🏨 **Hôtel Marignan.** Paul Keniger, the energetic third-generation owner, has cultivated a convivial atmosphere here for independent international travelers. The Marignan lies squarely between no-star and youth hostel (no TVs or elevator) and offers lots of communal conveniences—a fully stocked and accessible kitchen, free laundry machines, copious tourist information, and Internet access. Rooms are modest (some sleeping four or five) but have firm mattresses, new bed frames, and clean bathrooms. The least expensive rooms share toilets and/or showers with two other rooms on the same floor. Room phones only take incoming calls. Ask about multinight packages with free *bateau-mouche* tickets. ⊠ *13 rue du Sommerard, Quartier Latin, 75005* ☎ *01–43–54–63–81* 🖷 *01–43–25–16–69* ⊕ *www.hotel-marignan.com* ⇨ *30 rooms, 12 with bath* ⌂ *Dining room, kitchen, laundry facilities, Internet; no a/c, no room TVs* ⊟ *MC, V* ⏻ *CP* Ⓜ *Maubert Mutualité.*

★ **¢–$** 🏨 **Port-Royal Hôtel.** Not many budget hotels offer such a smart-looking, well-decorated lobby and rooms as the Port-Royal. Just below the rue Mouffetard market at the edge of the 13e arrondissement, it may be somewhat removed from the action, but the snug antiques-furnished lounge areas, white-stone courtyard, and rooms with wrought-iron beds, mirrors, and armoires make it worth the trip. Rooms at the lower end of the price range are equipped only with sinks and share showers. ⊠ *8 bd. de Port-Royal, Les Gobelins, 75005* ☎ *01–43–31–70–06* 🖷 *01–43–31–33–67* ⊕ *www. portroyalhotel.fr.st* ⇨ *46 rooms, 20 with bath* ⌂ *Dining room; no a/c, no room TVs* ⊟ *No credit cards* Ⓜ *Les Gobelins.*

6e Arrondissement (St-Germain-des-Près)

See Where to Stay on the Rive Gauche map.

$$$$ 🏨 **L'Hôtel.** Baroque mirrors, gold-leaf peacock murals, and sinfully
Fodor's Choice plush robes are just a few of the highlights at this eccentric and opulent
★ boutique hotel. Once an 18th-century *pavilion d'amour* (inn for trysts), as a hotel it welcomed Oscar Wilde, who in 1900 permanently checked

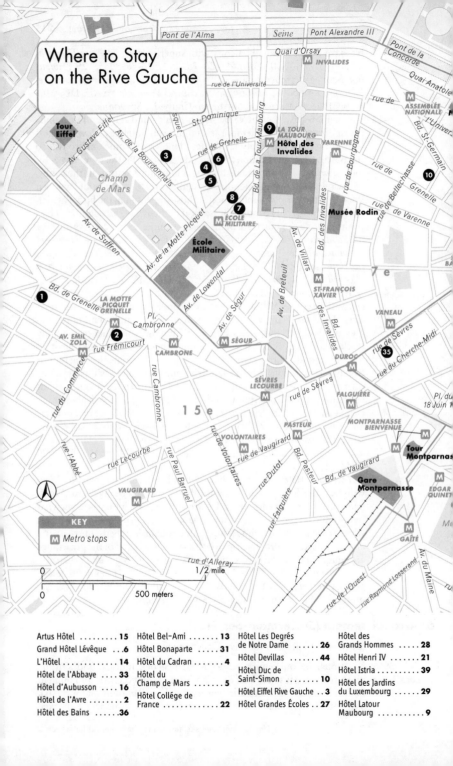

Where to Stay
on the Rive Gauche

Pont de l'Alma · Seine · Pont Alexandre III
Pont de la Concorde
Quai d'Orsay
Quai Anatole
rue de l'Université
Ⓜ INVALIDES
Tour Eiffel
Av. Gustave Eiffel
Av. de la Bourdonnais
rue ...quet
St-Dominique
rue de l'Univer-
ASSEMBLÉE NATIONALE
Bd. St-Germain
rue de Grenelle
❸
❹ ❻
❺
Ⓜ LA TOUR MAUBOURG ❾
VARENNE
Bd. de la Tour-Maubourg
LA TOUR MAUBOURG
Hôtel des Invalides
rue de Bourgogne
rue de
rue de Bellechasse
❿
Champ de Mars
❽
❼
Ⓜ ÉCOLE MILITAIRE
rue de Grenelle
rue de Varenne
Musée Rodin
Av. de Suffren
Av. de la Motte Picquet
École Militaire
Bd. des Invalides
Av. de Villars
7 e
Ba...
Av. de Lowendal
Av. de Ségur
Av. de Breteuil
❶
Bd. de Grenelle
LA MOTTE PICQUET GRENELLE
Pl. Cambronne
ST-FRANÇOIS XAVIER Ⓜ
Bd. des Invalides
VANEAU Ⓜ
AV. EMIL ZOLA
❷ Ⓜ
rue Frémicourt
CAMBRONNE
Ⓜ CAMBRONE
Ⓜ SÉGUR
DUROC Ⓜ
rue de Sèvres
rue du Cherche-Midi
❸❺
rue du Commerce
rue Cambronne
SÈVRES LECOURBE Ⓜ
rue de Sèvres
FALGUIÈRE Ⓜ
Pl. du 18 Juin
rue de l'Abbé
rue Lecourbe
rue Paul Barruel
15 e
rue de Volontaires
PASTEUR Ⓜ
MONTPARNASSE BIENVENUE Ⓜ
Ⓜ VOLONTAIRES
rue de Vaugirard
Bd. Pasteur
Ⓜ Tour Montparnas-
VAUGIRARD Ⓜ
rue Dutot
rue Falguière
Bd. de Vaugirard
Gare Montparnasse
EDGAR QUINET Ⓜ
rue d'Alleray
GAÎTÉ Ⓜ
Me
Av. du Maine
rue de l'Ouest
rue Raymond Losserand
ru...

KEY
Ⓜ Metro stops

0 ———— 1/2 mile
0 ———— 500 meters

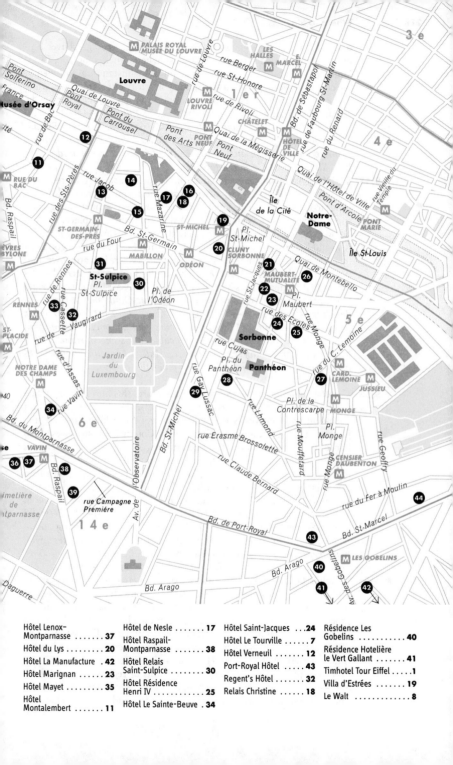

out in Room 16. Designed by Jacques Garcia, the rooms deliver Empire Age pipe dreams, their sole downside being their snug size. Modern assets don't intrude; the fax machines, for instance, are hidden in the closets. A skylight tops a spectacular six-story circular atrium, while a grotto holds a dipping pool, steam room, and round sitting room. ⊠ *13 rue des Beaux-Arts, St-Germain-des-Prés, 75006* ☎ *01–44–41–99–00* 🖷 *01–43–25–64–81* ⊕ *www.l-hotel.com* ⋧ *16 rooms, 4 suites* ♢ *Restaurant, room service, in-room safes, minibars, cable TV, indoor pool, steam room, piano bar, laundry service, Internet, some pets allowed* ⊟ *AE, DC, MC, V* Ⓜ *St-Germain-des-Prés.*

★ **$$$$** 🏨 **Hôtel d'Aubusson.** Dapper in their pin-striped suits, the staff greets you warmly at this 17th-century town house and former literary salon that clings to its "country in the city" past. The showpiece is the stunning salon spanned by massive beams and headed by a gigantic fireplace. Decked out in rich burgundies, greens, or blues, the bedrooms are filled with Louis XV- and Regency-style antiques; even the smallest rooms are a good size by Paris standards. Behind the paved courtyard (where in warmer weather you can have your breakfast or predinner drink) there's a second structure with three apartments handy for families. The Café Laurent café/piano bar hosts jazz three times per week. ⊠ *33 rue Dauphine, St-Germain-des-Prés, 75006* ☎ *01–43–29–43–43* 🖷 *01–43–29–12–62* ⊕ *www. hoteldaubusson.com* ⋧ *49 rooms* ♢ *Dining room, room service, in-room data ports, in-room safes, minibars, cable TV, some in-room VCRs, piano bar, shop, laundry service, concierge, Internet, meeting rooms, parking (fee), some pets allowed, no-smoking floors* ⊟ *AE, DC, MC, V* Ⓜ *Odéon.*

$$$$ 🏨 **Hôtel Bel-Ami.** Just a stroll from Café Flore, this hotel fills up when the fashion circus comes to town. The Bel-Ami hides its past as an 18th-century printworks beneath its veneer furnishings and Nehru-jacketed staff. You're immediately hit by the Conran Shop–meets–espresso bar lobby, with club music and sleek fireplace lounge to match. There's wireless Internet throughout, and a fitness center with sauna and Tibetan massage treatment rooms was added in December 2004. Rooms lean toward minimalist chic in soothing colors but are transformed often to keep up with the hotel's young and trendy clientele. ⊠ *7–11 rue St-Benoît, St-Germain-des-Prés, 75006* ☎ *01–42–61–53–53* 🖷 *01–49–27–09–33* ⊕ *www.hotel-bel-ami.com* ⋧ *113 rooms, 2 suites* ♢ *Dining room, room service, in-room safes, minibars, cable TV with movies, gym, massage, sauna, bar, laundry service, concierge, Internet, meeting rooms, no-smoking rooms* ⊟ *AE, DC, MC, V* Ⓜ *St-Germain-des-Prés.*

★ **$$$$** 🏨 **Relais Christine.** This exquisite property was once a 13th-century abbey, but don't expect monkish quarters. You enter from the impressive stone courtyard into a lobby and fireside honor bar done up in rich fabrics, stone, wood paneling, and antiques. The cavernous breakfast room and adjacent fitness center flaunt their vaulted medieval stonework. The spacious, high-ceilinged rooms (many spanned by massive beams) offer a variety of classical and contemporary styles: Asian-themed wall fabrics or plain stripes, rich aubergine paints or regal scarlet-and-gold. Split-level lofts house up to five people, and several ground-level rooms open onto a lush garden with private patios and heaters. There's a sauna, gym, and Jacuzzi in the vaulted stone cellar. ⊠ *3 rue Christine, St-Germain-des-Prés, 75006* ☎ *01–40–51–60–80, 800/525–4800 in the U.S.* 🖷 *01–40–51–60–81* ⊕ *www.relais-christine.com* ⇨ *33 rooms, 18 suites* ⚘ *Dining room, room service, in-room safes, minibars, cable TV, some in-room VCRs, gym, hot tub, massage, sauna, lounge, laundry service, concierge, Internet, meeting rooms, free parking, some pets allowed, no-smoking rooms* ☰ *AE, DC, MC, V* Ⓜ *Odéon.*

★ **$$$$** 🏨 **Villa d'Estrées.** The Napoleonic era meets North Africa in this moody den. The lobby is bedecked in scarlet drapery, tasseled lamps, vintage photos of 19th-century sheiks, and marble inlaid with a Greek key pattern. With only two rooms per floor, running into your neighbors is unlikely. The spacious rooms have boldly striped or patterned wall fabrics in deep red, sea blue, black, tan, or beige and king-size beds with snow-white duvets. Small but sumptuous baths are completely covered in black Moroccan marble tile. If you plan a longer stay and would be better served by a guest room with kitchenette, check out the sister property across the street, the Hôtel Résidence des Arts. ⊠ *17 rue Gît-le-Coeur, Quartier Latin, 75006* ☎ *01–55–42–71–11* 🖷 *01–55–42–71–00* ⊕ *www.paris-hotel-latin-quarter.com* ⇨ *5 rooms, 5 suites* ⚘ *Room service, in-room safes, minibars, cable TV, laundry service, some pets allowed; no smoking* ☰ *AE, DC, MC, V* Ⓜ *St-Michel.*

$$$–$$$$ 🏨 **Artus Hôtel.** You'll find modern art on the walls, an arty graffiti-flecked stairwell, and zebra-pattern upholstered chairs in the lobby at this petite property formerly known as the Buci Latin. Each room's door is inspired by the work of a famous artist—Magritte, Léger, Monet, Basquiat—but executed by local painters. Rooms are small but clean and neat, with ocher walls, open-weave armoires, and contoured tables. The more spacious duplex suite under the roof, No. 140, has a small bathroom loft with a shower, makeup table, and freestanding bathtub. The hotel has wireless Internet. ⊠ *34 rue de Buci, St-Germain-des-Prés, 75006* ☎ *01–43–29–07–20* 🖷 *01–43–29–67–44* ⊕ *www.artushotel.com* ⇨ *25 rooms, 2 suites* ⚘ *Dining room, room service, minibars, cable TV, in-room data ports, laundry service, Internet, some pets allowed* ☰ *AE, DC, MC, V* ⧖❙ *CP* Ⓜ *Mabillon.*

$$$ 🏨 **Hôtel de l'Abbaye.** This hotel on a tranquil side street near St-Sulpice welcomes you with a cobblestone ante-courtyard and vaulted stone entrance. Paneled in bright wood, the rooms are spotless, if a little impersonal. The collision of modern art and country design—fruit baskets and flat-screen TVs—may not be to everyone's taste, but it's all redeemed by the lobby's salons with vestiges of the original 18th-century convent and the spacious garden with fountain. Some first-floor rooms open onto it. Upper-floor accommodations have oak beams and sitting alcoves, and duplexes have lovely private terraces. The hotel has wireless Internet access. ⊠ *10 rue Cassette, St-Germain-des-Prés, 75006* ☎ *01–45–44–38–11* 🖷 *01–45–48–07–86* ⊕ *www.hotel-abbaye.com* ⇨ *42 rooms, 4 suites* ⚘ *Dining room, room service, in-room safes, cable TV, bar, laundry service, Internet* ☰ *AE, MC, V* ⧖❙ *CP* Ⓜ *St-Sulpice.*

$$$ 🏨 **Hôtel Relais Saint-Sulpice.** A savvy clientele frequents this fashionable
FodorśChoice little hotel sandwiched between place St-Sulpice and the Luxembourg
★ Gardens. Eclectically selected art objects and furnishings, some with an

Asian theme, oddly pull off a unified look. A zebra-print stuffed fauteuil sits beside a deco desk, while an African mud cloth hangs above a neo-Roman pillar. The rooms themselves, set around an ivy-clad courtyard, are understated, with simple colors and comfortable furnishings and sisal floor mats. Wireless Internet makes the hotel high-tech, plus there's a sauna downstairs, right off the atrium breakfast salon, whose glass roof shoots right through the courtyard. Room 11 has a terrific view of St-Sulpice. ⊠ *3 rue Garancière, St-Germain-des-Prés, 75006* ☎ *01–46–33–99–00* 🖷 *01–46–33–00–10* ⊕ *monsite.wanadoo.fr/ relaisstsulpice* ↩ *26 rooms* ⚒ *Dining room, in-room safes, minibars, cable TV, sauna, laundry service, meeting rooms* ▭ *AE, DC, MC, V* Ⓜ *St-Germain-des-Prés, St-Sulpice.*

$$ 🏨 **Hôtel Bonaparte.** The congeniality of the staff makes a stay in this intimate place even more of a treat. Old-fashioned upholsteries, 19th-century furnishings, and paintings make the relatively spacious rooms feel comfortable and unpretentious. Rooms have empty refrigerators; you're invited to stock them with drinks and snacks. Services may be basic, but the location in the heart of St-Germain about 30 steps from place St-Sulpice is nothing short of fabulous. Light sleepers should request rooms overlooking the courtyard. ⊠ *61 rue Bonaparte, St-Germain-des-Prés, 75006* ☎ *01–43–26–97–37* 🖷 *01–46–33–57–67* ↩ *29 rooms* ⚒ *Dining room, in-room safes, refrigerators; no a/c in some rooms* ▭ *MC, V* ⦿ *CP* Ⓜ *St-Germain-des-Prés.*

★ $$ 🏨 **Hôtel du Lys.** To jump into an inexpensive Parisian fantasy, just climb the convoluted stairway to your room (there's no elevator) in this former 17th-century royal residence. Well-maintained by Madame Steffen, the endearingly odd-shape guest rooms have tiny nooks, weathered antiques, and exposed beams throughout. Breakfast is served in the lobby or in your room. It may be modest, but it's extremely atmospheric. ⊠ *23 rue Serpente, Quartier Latin, 75006* ☎ *01–43–26–97–57* 🖷 *01–44–07–34–90* ⊕ *www.hoteldulys.com* ↩ *22 rooms* ⚒ *In-room safes, cable TV, some pets allowed; no a/c* ▭ *MC, V* ⦿ *CP* Ⓜ *St-Michel, Odéon.*

$$ 🏨 **Hôtel Mayet.** This fresh and quirky hotel a few blocks from Bon Marché department store and Montparnasse Tower feels a bit like an art-school dormitory. The identical rooms are decorated in battleship gray and maroon, with big Kriptonite wall clocks, chunky propellerlike ceiling fans, and metal storage containers. The basement breakfast room blasts you with its primary colors, while in the entry hangs a canvas by graffitist André, whose top-hatted character Mr. A is spray-painted all over town. Small fifth-floor balconies overlook the street the Mayet shares with an anglophone tearoom and used-book store. ⊠ *3 rue Mayet, Montparnasse, 75006* ☎ *01–47–83–21–35* 🖷 *01–40–65–95–78* ⊕ *www. mayet.com* ↩ *23 rooms* ⚒ *Dining room, cable TV, Internet, some pets allowed; no a/c* ▭ *AE, DC, MC, V* ☉ *Closed Aug.* ⦿ *CP* Ⓜ *Duroc.*

$$ 🏨 **Hôtel Le Sainte-Beuve.** Smack between the Jardin du Luxembourg and boulevard de Montparnasse's timeless cafés and brasseries, tucked into a tiny tranquil street, you'll find the pleasant Sainte-Beuve. A spacious lobby bathed in light has a wood-fire hearth and is ringed by Greek revival columns. Whites and pastels dominate in the conservatively decorated rooms designed by Brit David Hicks, who prefers antiques and a clean, uncluttered look. Each floor has two rooms that can be booked individually or as adjoining suites. Extras like bathrobes and breakfast pastries delivered to your room from famed pâtissier Mulot are a treat. ⊠ *9 rue Ste-Beuve, Montparnasse, 75006* ☎ *01–45–48–20–07* 🖷 *01–45–48–67–52* ⊕ *www.paris-hotel-charme.com* ⮑ *22 rooms* ⟋ *Room service, in-room safes, minibars, cable TV, bar, laundry service, Internet, some pets allowed* ⊟ *AE, DC, MC, V* Ⓜ *Vavin.*

★ $ 🔟 **Hôtel de Nesle.** This one-of-a-kind budget hotel is like a quirky and enchanting dollhouse. The services are bare-bones—no elevator, phones, or breakfast—but the payoff is in the snug rooms cleverly decorated by theme. Sleep in Notre-Dame de Paris, lounge in an Asian-style boudoir, spend the night with writer Molière, or steam it up in Le Hammam. Decorations include colorful murals, canopy beds, custom lamps, and clay tiles. Most rooms overlook an interior garden, and the dead-end street location keeps the hotel relatively quiet. If you book one of the 11 rooms without a shower, you'll have to share the one bathroom on the second floor. ⊠ *7 rue de Nesle, St-Germain-des-Prés, 75006* ☎ *01–43–54–62–41* 🖷 *01–43–54–31–88* ⊕ *www.hoteldenesleparis.com* ⮑ *20 rooms, 9 with bath* ⟋ *Some pets allowed, no-smoking floors; no a/c, no room phones, no room TVs* ⊟ *MC, V* Ⓜ *Odéon.*

$ 🔟 **Regent's Hôtel.** The cobblestone courtyard and excellent location between the Jardin du Luxembourg and St-Sulpice would be enough to make this low-cost hotel worth reserving. But it also has surprisingly charming, country-style decor and immaculate tile bathrooms. Rooms on the top floor have small terraces, while the family-size room for four (No. 2) opens directly onto the garden courtyard, where breakfast is served in summer. ⊠ *44 rue Madame, St-Germain-des-Prés, 75006* ☎ *01–45–48–02–81* 🖷 *01–45–44–85–73* ✍ *regents.hotel@wanadoo.fr* ⮑ *34 rooms* ⟋ *Dining room, room service, in-room safes, cable TV, some pets allowed; no a/c* ⊟ *MC, V* Ⓜ *St-Sulpice.*

7ᵉ Arrondissement (Trocadéro/Tour Eiffel & St-Germain-des-Prés)

See Where to Stay on the Rive Gauche map.

★ $$$$ 🔟 **Hôtel Duc de Saint-Simon.** If it's good enough for the notoriously choosy Lauren Bacall, you'll probably fall for the Duc's charms, too. Its hidden location between boulevard St-Germain and rue de Bac is one plus; another is the shady courtyard entry. Rooms in shades of yellow, green, pink, and blue teem with antiques and countrified floral and striped fabrics. Four rooms have spacious terraces overlooking the courtyard and the drooping wisteria. The 16th-century basement lounge is a warren of stone alcoves with a zinc bar and plush seating. To keep the peace, parents are discouraged from bringing children along. ⊠ *14 rue St-Simon, St-Germain-des-Prés, 75007* ☎ *01–44–39–20–20* 🖷 *01–45–48–68–25* ⊕ *www.hotelducdesaintsimon.com* ⮑ *29 rooms, 5 suites* ⟋ *Dining room, in-room safes, cable TV, bar, laundry service, parking (fee); no a/c in some rooms, no kids* ⊟ *AE, DC, MC, V* Ⓜ *Rue du Bac.*

★ $$$$ 🔟 **Hôtel Montalembert.** A jewel in Grace Leo-Andrieu's hotel crown, the Montalembert led the Parisian movement toward clean-line design while preserving the architectural frosting of its circa-1926 roots. Choose 19th-century Louis-Philippe-era armoires and beds in the classic rooms or eggplant and lilac hues in the streamlined rooms. Cascais marble baths have custom chrome fixtures; other features include DVD players, flat-screen TVs, and wireless Internet. Top-floor Suite 83 has three terraces (including one off the bathroom) with grand views toward Eiffel's masterpiece in one direction, Église St-Sulpice's towers in the other. Indoors or out, the restaurant serves stellar contemporary fare. Beside the bar are leather armchairs and a hearth that, coupled with the gentle service, adds genuine warmth to your stay. ⊠ *3 rue de Montalembert, St-Germain-des-Prés, 75007* 🕾 *01–45–49–68–68* 🖷 *01–45–49–69–49* ⊕ *www.montalembert.com* 🛏 *48 rooms, 8 suites* ⚴ *Restaurant, room service, in-room safes, minibars, cable TV, in-room VCRs, massage, bar, laundry service, concierge, Internet, business services, meeting room, some pets allowed* ⊟ *AE, DC, MC, V* Ⓜ *Rue du Bac.*

$$$$ 🏨 **Le Walt.** Wood floors and rich fabrics in chocolate and plum tones accent this family-run boutique hotel in the chic district between the Tour Eiffel and Les Invalides. The small lobby opens to a dining room and bar overlooking a private patio, where breakfast is served in summer. Spotlit red carpets lead you to the rooms, decorated with contemporary walnut furnishings and oversize oil-portrait headboards. Bathrooms have heated towel racks; other perks include champagne-stocked minibars and complimentary high-speed Internet. Some rooms on the 6th floor have views of the sparkling *Dame de Fer.* The slightly larger sister hotel, Le Marquis, offers similar services and style just a few blocks down the street. ⊠ *37 av. de la Motte Picquet, Invalides, 75007* 🕾 *01–45–51–55–83* 🖷 *01–47–05–77–59* ⊕ *www.inwoodhotel.com/walt* 🛏 *25 rooms* ⚴ *Dining room, room service, in-room data ports, in-room safes, minibars, cable TV, bar, laundry service, parking (fee), some pets allowed, no-smoking rooms* ⊟ *AE, DC, MC, V* Ⓜ *École Militaire.*

$$$ 🏨 **Hôtel du Cadran.** The charming Madame Chaine and her gracious staff go out of their way to ensure that you enjoy your stay at this comfortable hotel near the Rue Cler market. A fireplace, grandfather clock, and player piano lend warmth to the lobby. Rooms have coordinating drapes and bedspreads in cheery colors, wireless Internet, and Roger & Gallet toiletries. Some rooms have views of the Tour Eiffel, and No. 108 has its own tiny garden patio. Rates are at the lower end of this price category; ask about last-minute deals. ⊠ *10 rue du Champ de Mars, Invalides, 75007* 🕾 *01–40–62–67–00* 🖷 *01–40–62–67–13* ⊕ *www.cadranhotel.com* 🛏 *42 rooms* ⚴ *Dining room, in-room safes, minibars, cable TV, some in-room VCRs, bar, laundry service, Internet, no-smoking floors* ⊟ *AE, DC, MC, V* Ⓜ *École Militaire.*

★ $$$ 🏨 **Hôtel Latour Maubourg.** Part hotel, part private residence, with a city B&B feel, this small converted town house is homey and unpretentious. Its rooms have antique armoires and suitcase stands, marble fireplaces, high ceilings, and high-quality beds with either wool blankets or duvets (plus, hypoallergenic pillows and bathrobes are available). Constantly updating their level of service (they recently added wireless Internet in deluxe rooms and in the lobby), proud owners Victor and Maria Orsenne and their dog, Faust, are enthusiastic and helpful. There's even a fridge at your disposal for storing snacks. There's no elevator, but Latour Maubourg has just three levels. ⊠ *150 rue de Grenelle, Invalides, 75007* ☎ *01–47–05–16–16* 🖷 *01–47–05–16–14* ⊕ *www.latourmaubourg.fr* ➥ *9 rooms, 1 suite* ♺ *Dining room, minibars, cable TV, laundry service, Internet, some pets allowed (fee), no-smoking rooms; no a/c in some rooms* ⊟ *MC, V* ⏐○⏐ *CP* Ⓜ *La Tour-Maubourg.*

$$$ ⊞ **Hôtel Le Tourville.** Here is a rare find: a cozy upscale hotel that doesn't cost a fortune. Each room has crisp, milk-white damask upholstery set against pastel or ocher walls, a smattering of antique bureaus and lamps, original artwork, and fabulous old mirrors. The junior suites have hot tubs, while the superior room has its own private garden terrace. The staff couldn't be more helpful. ⊠ *16 av. de Tourville, Invalides, 75007* ☎ *01–47–05–62–62* 🖷 *01–47–05–43–90* ⊕ *www.hoteltourville.com* ➥ *27 rooms, 3 suites* ♺ *Dining room, room service, some in-room safes, cable TV, in-room data ports, bar, Internet, laundry service, some pets allowed, no-smoking floor* ⊟ *AE, DC, MC, V* Ⓜ *École Militaire.*

$$ ⊞ **Hôtel Verneuil.** The Verneuil's location on a narrow street near the Seine is unbeatable. The rooms may be more petite than you'd hoped for, but each is painstakingly decorated. The white-cotton quilts on the beds, framed pressed flowers on the walls, and faux-marble trompe-l'oeil trim work and stained-glass windows in the hall make you feel you've arrived *chez grandmère.* Fans of Serge Gainsbourg can pilgrimage to his former home directly across the street. ⊠ *8 rue de Verneuil, St-Germain-des-Prés, 75007* ☎ *01–42–60–83–14* 🖷 *01–42–61–40–38* ⊕ *www.hotelverneuil. com* ➥ *26 rooms* ♺ *Dining room, room service, in-room safes, minibars, cable TV, bar, laundry service, Internet, some pets allowed (fee); no a/c in some rooms* Ⓜ *RER: Musée d'Orsay.*

$–$$ ⊞ **Grand Hôtel Lévêque.** The Tour Eiffel is around the corner, but the real draw here is the bustling pedestrian street market, one of the city's finest, just outside the hotel's front door. This immaculate hotel has an eager-to-please staff, comfortable if slightly sterile rooms, and a bistrostyle breakfast room. Make sure to get a room facing the street and reserve early—this is a very popular address among French and American foodies. ⊠ *29 rue Cler, Invalides, 75007* ☎ *01–47–05–49–15* 🖷 *01–45–50–49–36* ⊕ *www.hotel-leveque.com* ➥ *50 rooms, 45 with bath* ♺ *Dining room, in-room data ports, in-room safes, cable TV* ⊟ *AE, MC, V* Ⓜ *École Militaire.*

$ ⊞ **Hôtel du Champ de Mars.** If you'd like an affordable, B&B-ish, but fully modern room near the Tour Eiffel and Les Invalides, this is an excellent choice. Françoise and Stéphane Gourdal's hotel has an appealing downhome feel. Chippie, their faithful old dog, can be found lounging in the vibrant Provençal lobby. Rooms include custom wall stenciling and chair covers, and are named for flowers such as *lilas* and *mimosa*; the two on the ground floor open onto a private leafy courtyard. ⊠ *7 rue du Champ de Mars, Invalides, 75007* ☎ *01–45–51–52–30* 🖷 *01–45–51–64–36* ⊕ *www.hotel-du-champ-de-mars.com* ➥ *25 rooms* ♺ *Dining room, in-room safes, cable TV; no a/c* ⊟ *MC, V* Ⓜ *École Militaire.*

$ ⊞ **Hôtel Eiffel Rive Gauche.** On a quiet side street just a couple of blocks from the Tour Eiffel, this modern hotel with a leafy patio is a great budget find. The look is functional, but rooms are spacious and comfortable; some have red-and-gold wall fabrics and hardwood furniture. The owner, Monsieur Chicheportiche, is a walking multilingual encyclopedia of Paris. Bonuses include rooms with Tour Eiffel views, alarm clocks, and radios, an attractive lobby and breakfast room, and wireless Internet connections. ⊠ *6 rue du Gros Caillou, Trocadéro/Tour Eiffel, 75007* ☎ *01–45–51–24–56* 🖷 *01–45–51–11–77* ⊕ *www.hotel-eiffel.com* 🖚 *30 rooms* ⚲ *Dining room, in-room safes, cable TV, laundry service, Internet, business services; no a/c* ▤ MC, V Ⓜ *École Militaire.*

8° Arrondissement (Champs-Élysées)

See Where to Stay on the Rive Droite: Bois du Boulogne to Place de la Concorde map.

$$$$ 🖼 **Le A.** By wearing its fashion-fixated heart on its sleeve, Le A lured the trendy crowd immediately upon opening in spring 2003. The lounge area's white walls and original drawings and paintings by Fabrice Hybert evoke an art gallery rather than a hotel. Guest rooms may strike you as either cutting-edge or chilly with their pale walls, chocolate or white-and-green-striped carpets, glass tables, white slipcovers and bedding, and black-and-white tile baths. Dimmer switches help soften the mood. And this stylishness comes at less than half the price of fashionista haunts like the Costes. ⊠ *4 rue d'Artois, Champs-Élysées 75008* ☎ *01–42–56–99–99* 🖷 *01–42–56–99–90* ⊕ *www.hotel-le-a.com* 🖚 *25 rooms* ⚲ *Room service, in-room data ports, in-room safes, minibars, cable TV, bar, lounge, laundry service, Internet, no-smoking floors* ▤ AE, DC, MC, V Ⓜ *St-Philippe du Roule.*

$$$$ 🖼 **Chogan Hôtel.** Opened in late 2004 just two blocks from the city's largest department stores and the place de la Madeleine, the stylish Chogan welcomes you into a contemporary but inviting lobby with red marble floors and oil paintings of polo players. Rooms are decorated with fresh flowers, duvet comforters, bold floral prints or neutral striped wall fabrics. They include complimentary bottled water, flat-screen TVs, and wireless Internet. Sunlight from the glass atrium floods into the pale green breakfast room and library lounge with wood-burning fireplace. ⊠ *43 rue des Mathurins, Opéra/Grands Boulevards, 75008* ☎ *01–44–94–20–94* 🖷 *01–44–94–00–44* ⊕ *www.choganhotel.com* 🖚 *29 rooms, 6 suites* ⚲ *Dining room, room service, in-room safes, minibars, cable TV, bar, library, laundry service, Internet, some pets allowed, no-smoking rooms* ▤ AE, DC, MC, V Ⓜ *Havre Caumartin.*

☾ **$$$$**
FodorśChoice
★
🖼 **Four Seasons Hôtel George V Paris.** The George V is as poised and polished as the day it opened in 1928: the original Art Deco detailing and 17th-century tapestries have been restored, the bas-reliefs regilded, the marble-floor mosaics rebuilt tile by tile. Rooms are decked in yards of fabrics and Louis XVI trimmings but also have homey touches like selections of CDs and French books. Le Cinq restaurant is one of Paris's hottest tables, thanks to the legendary Philippe Legendre of Taillevent fame. The low-lit spa and fitness center pampers guests with 11 treatment rooms, walls covered in toile de Jouy fabrics, and an indoor swimming pool surrounded by trompe l'oeil scenes from Marie-Antoinette's Versailles gar-

dens. A relaxation room is available for guests who arrive before their rooms are ready. Even children get the four-star treatment with personalized T-shirts and portable DVD players to distract them at dinnertime. ⌧ *31 av. George V, Champs-Élysées, 75008* ☎ *01–49–52–70–00, 800/ 332–3442 in the U.S.* ⊟ *01–49–52–70–10* ⊕ *www.fourseasons.com/ paris* ⇋ *184 rooms, 61 suites* ⚭ *2 restaurants, room service, in-room safes, some kitchenettes, minibars, cable TV with video games, in-room VCRs, in-room data ports, indoor pool, health club, hair salon, spa, bar, shop, children's programs (ages 1–12), laundry service, concierge, Internet, business services, meeting rooms, airport shuttle, some pets allowed, no-smoking floors* ⊟ *AE, DC, MC, V* Ⓜ *George V.*

$$$$ ▦ **Hôtel Le Bristol.** The understated facade on rue du Faubourg St-Honoré might mislead the unknowing, but the Bristol ranks among Paris's most exclusive hotels and has the prices to prove it. Some of the spaciously elegant rooms have authentic Louis XV and Louis XVI furniture and marble bathrooms in pure 1920s Art Deco; others have a more relaxed 19th-century style. The public salons are palatially stocked with old-master paintings, sculptures, sumptuous carpets, and tapestries. The huge, interior garden restaurant and Saturday fashion shows in the bar draw the posh and wealthy. ⌧ *112 rue du Faubourg St-Honoré, Champs-Élysées, 75008* ☎ *01–53–43–43–00* ⊟ *01–53–43–43–01* ⊕ *www.lebristolparis.com* ⇋ *127 rooms, 48 suites* ⚭ *Restaurant, room service, in-room safes, minibars, cable TV, in-room data ports, indoor pool, gym, hair salon, sauna, spa, bar, laundry service, concierge, Internet, business services, meeting rooms, free parking, some pets allowed* ⊟ *AE, DC, MC, V* Ⓜ *Miromesnil.*

★ **$$$$** ▦ **Hôtel Daniel.** A contemporary antidote to the minimalist trend, the Daniel opened in 2004 with sumptuous fabrics and antique furnishings from France, North Africa, and the Far East. The lobby feels like a living room, with deep sofas covered in colorful satin pillows, dark hardwood floors, and delicate Chinese floral wallpaper. Rooms have toile de Jouy fabrics, wireless Internet, and flat-screen TVs. Little luxuries include lavender sachets and padded hangers in the closets, and glass jars of sea salts in the marble or Moroccan-tile bathrooms. Room 601, under the mansard roof, has a huge claw-foot bathtub. ⌧ *8 rue Frédéric Bastiat, Champs-Élysées, 75008* ☎ *01–42–56–17–00* ⊟ *01–42–56–17–01* ⊕ *www. hoteldanielparis.com* ⇋ *17 rooms, 9 suites* ⚭ *Restaurant, room service, in-room safes, minibars, cable TV, bar, laundry service, Internet, parking (fee), some pets allowed* ⊟ *AE, DC, MC, V* Ⓜ *St-Philippe-du-Roule.*

$$$$ ▦ **Hôtel Lancaster.** Modern flourishes like perfume-bottle lamp bases and a Japanese garden revitalized the public spaces of this former Spanish nobleman's town house in 2004, along with a revamped restaurant by three-star Michelin veteran Michel Troisgros. Not everything is contemporary, though; room keys and doorbells are vintage, and hanging throughout the hotel are 1930s paintings by Boris Pastoukhoff, who donated 80 canvases to pay his bill. He probably rubbed shoulders with Marlene Dietrich, who stayed in her eponymous suite in the late '30s. Rooms can be elegant—the Emile Wolf Suite has a baby grand—but the pinkish-beige combo in some can seem outdated. The minibars have health enthusiasts in mind; they're stocked with cans of oxygen instead of alcohol. The fitness room has a splendid view of Sacré-Coeur. ⊠ *7 rue de Berri, Champs-Élysées, 75008* ☎ *01–40–76–40–76, 877/757–2747 in the U.S.* 🖥 *01–40–76–40–00* ⊕ *www.hotel-lancaster.fr* ⇆ *49 rooms, 11 suites ౨ Restaurant, room service, in-room safes, minibars, cable TV, in-room VCRs, in-room data ports, gym, sauna, bar, laundry service, Internet, meeting rooms, parking (fee), some pets allowed (fee)* ⊟ *AE, DC, MC, V* Ⓜ *George V.*

$$$$
Fodor'sChoice
★

Hôtel Plaza Athénée. Prime-time stardom as Carrie Bradshaw's Parisian pied-à-terre in the final episodes of *Sex & the City* may have boosted the street cred of this 1911 palace hotel, but its revival as the city's last word in luxury owes more to the meticulous attention of the renowned chef Alain Ducasse, who overlooks everything from the hotel's flagship restaurant and restored 1930s Relais Plaza brasserie to the quality of the croissants served at breakfast. You can choose your preferred guest-room look; each accommodation has been redone in either Regency, Louis XVI, or deco style, with remote control air-conditioning, mini hi-fi/CD players, and TVs with Internet. A new line of products is steeped in the hotel's signature deep red. The trendy bar has as its centerpiece an impressive Bombay glass *comptoir* glowing like an iceberg. ⊠ *25 av. Montaigne, Champs-Élysées, 75008* ☎ *01–53–67–66–65, 866/732–1106 in the U.S.* 🖥 *01–53–67–66–66* ⊕ *www.plaza-athenee-paris.com* ⇆ *145 rooms, 43 suites ౨ 3 restaurants, café, room service, in-room safes, minibars, cable TV with movies, some in-room VCRs, in-room data ports, exercise equipment, massage, sauna, steam room, bar, shop, laundry service, concierge, Internet, business services, meeting rooms, some pets allowed, no-smoking floors* ⊟ *AE, DC, MC, V* Ⓜ *Alma-Marceau.*

★ **$$$$**
Hôtel San Régis. On a quiet side street near avenue Montaigne (read: extreme shopping), this discreet hotel walks softly but bears an enviable reputation. All guest rooms and suites have unique mixes of carefully chosen antiques, embroidered silks and brocades, and richly patterned wallpaper; bathrooms are done in Italian marble. Ask for a suite at the top of the 19th-century building for the best views. The elegant wood-paneled Boiseries lounge leads to the tiny English Bar and a dining room that serves traditional Provençal cuisine. ⊠ *12 rue Jean-Goujon, Champs-Élysées, 75008* ☎ *01–44–95–16–16* 🖥 *01–45–61–05–48* ⊕ *www.hotel-sanregis.fr* ⇆ *33 rooms, 11 suites ౨ Restaurant, room service, in-room safes, minibars, cable TV, bar, laundry service, Internet* ⊟ *AE, DC, MC, V* Ⓜ *Franklin-D.-Roosevelt.*

$$$$
Hôtel de Sers. High expectations greeted the anouncement of the complete gutting and rebuilding of the sagging Hotel Queen Elizabeth by a 28-year-old architect and his team of twentysomething designers. Opened with a new name in December 2004, the Sers has maintained the original 19th-century structural and architectural specs, such as the grand staircase and ballroom, and filled the space with minimalist contemporary furnishings. This somewhat uneasy mix—with angular chrome, lacquered wood, and pop-art accessories—may not be to everyone's taste, but there's no doubt about the hotel's dedication to comfort: rooms have king-size beds with fluffy comforters, claw-foot tubs, and B&O flat-screen TVs with DVD players. Two suites afford panoramic views of the city. The curious can sneak a peek from the hotel's courtyard-facing restaurant or the sleek

white marble bar. ✉ *41 av. Pierre 1er de Serbie, Champs-Élysées, 75008* ☎ *01–53–23–75–75* 🖶 *01–53–23–75–76* ⊕ *www.hoteldesers.com/* 🛏 *44 rooms, 7 suites, 1 apartment* ⚒ *Restaurant, room service, in-room data ports, in-room safes, minibars, cable TV with movies, in-room VCRs, gym, massage, sauna, steam room, bar, library, laundry service, concierge, Internet, meeting rooms, parking (fee), some pets allowed, no-smoking rooms* ☰ *AE, DC, MC, V* Ⓜ *George V, Alma-Marceau.*

$$$$ 🏨 **Pershing Hall.** Formerly an American Legion hall, this circa-2001 boutique hotel quickly became a must-stay address for the dressed-in-black pack. Designed by Andrée Putman, Pershing Hall champions masculine minimalism, with muted surfaces of wood and stone and even cooler attitudes to match. Rooms have stark-white linens, triptych dressing mirrors, slender tubelike lamps and tubs perched on round marble bases. The only trace of lightheartedness is the free minibars. All deluxe rooms and suites face the courtyard dining room whose west wall is a six-story hanging garden with 300 varieties of plants. The lounge bar serves drinks, dinner, and DJ-driven music until 2 AM. ✉ *49 rue Pierre-Charron, Champs-Élysées, 75008* ☎ *01–58–36–58–00* 🖶 *01–58–36–58–01* ⊕ *www.pershinghall.com* 🛏 *20 rooms, 6 suites* ⚒ *Restaurant, room service, in-room safes, minibars, cable TV, in-room VCRs, in-room data ports, gym, spa, bar, laundry service, concierge, Internet, meeting rooms, some pets allowed, no-smoking rooms* ☰ *AE, DC, MC, V* Ⓜ *George V, Franklin-D.-Roosevelt.*

$$$$ 🏨 **Royal Monceau Mandarin Oriental.** After enduring a slow slide into the shadows of other palace hotels, the latest member of the exclusive Madarin Oriental group has been given a new lease on life. The Royal Monceau entered 2005 completely remodeled and restyled by in-demand hotel designer Jacques Garcia. The grand lobby feels more intimate now with pale turquoise walls and deep, gold-and-green velour sofas and chairs. Le Jardin has an Empire design in pale green and purple, while the Sicilian Carpaccio Restaurant captures the sexy feel of an Italian palazzo. Mirrored tiles and red burgundy velour dominate the maharaja-style Royal's Bar. Rooms have been greatly enlarged and outfitted with taffeta, velour, and silk fabrics in gold, royal blue, copper, or deep purple. Hi-tech cabinets containing CD/DVD players and fax/printer/scanners are disguised behind discreet screens, while glass-front drawers in the closets help you see if you've left anything behind. The indoor swimming pool is as divine as ever, and new massage treatments have a decidedly Asian influence. ✉ *37 av. Hoche, Champs-Élysées, 75008* ☎ *01–42–99–88–00* 🖶 *01–42–99–89–90* ⊕ *www.royalmonceau.com* 🛏 *124 rooms, 56 suites* ⚒ *2 restaurants, room service, in-room data ports, in-room fax, in-room safes, cable TV with movies, in-room VCRs, indoor pool, health club, hair salon, hot tub, massage, sauna, bar, babysitting, laundry service, concierge, Internet, convention center, parking (fee)* ☰ *AE, DC, MC, V* Ⓜ *Charles-de-Gaulle-Etoile/Ternes.*

$$$$ 🏨 **La Trémoille.** Once in the league of stuffy Golden Triangle hotels, La Trémoille now offers business travelers a trendy home base. The 2002 top-to-bottom overhaul retained the Haussmann-era marble fireplaces and plaster moldings but implemented 31 decorating schemes that include contemporary armoires, furniture upholstered in fake fur and Nobilis silk, and funky mohair curtains. Unique to this hotel is the "hatch," a silent butler closet by each door, where meals and laundry can be delivered without disturbing the guests. Four ways to connect to the Internet (including wireless access) and pants presses in each room are other pluses. Designed in collaboration with Terence Conran, the ultra-sleek Senso restaurant and bar becomes loungish, with a DJ most evenings. ⊠ *14 rue de La Trémoille, Champs-Élysées, 75008* ☎ *01–56–52–14–00* ⊟ *01–40–70–01–08* ⊕ *www.hotel-tremoille.com* ⇆ *88 rooms, 5 suites* ⌂ *Restaurant, room service, in-room safes, cable TV with movies, in-room data ports, gym, sauna, spa, bar, laundry service, concierge, Internet, business services, meeting rooms, parking (fee), some pets allowed (fee)* ⊟ *AE, DC, MC, V* Ⓜ *Alma-Marceau.*

$$$ **Hôtel Queen Mary.** A warm welcome just two blocks from the place de
Fodor'sChoice   la Madeleine and Paris's famous department stores awaits you in this cheer-
★   fully cozy hotel. Sunny yellow walls, plush carpeting, and fabrics in burgundy, gold, and royal blue soften the regal architectural detailing and high ceilings. Rooms are handsomely appointed with large beds and such thoughtful extras as trouser presses, Roger & Gallet toiletries, and decanters of sherry. Guests mingle in the bar during happy hour and in good weather enjoy breakfast in the garden courtyard. ⊠ *9 rue Greffulhe, Opéra/Grands Boulevards, 75008* ☎ *01–42–66–40–50* ⊟ *01–42–66–94–92* ⊕ *www. hotelqueenmary.com* ⇆ *35 rooms, 1 suite* ⌂ *Dining room, room service, in-room data ports, in-room safes, minibars, cable TV with movies, bar, laundry service, Internet, some pets allowed* ⊟ *MC, V* Ⓜ *Madeleine, St-Lazare, Havre Caumartin.*

$$$ **Hôtel Relais Monceau.** Within six blocks of the prim Parc Monceau, one of Paris's most coveted gardens, this friendly and fashionable hotel is an oasis of refined tranquillity. Ivy-covered trellises surround the lovely breakfast garden. Soft tones lend warmth to the rooms; the efficient and professional staff work hard to assist guests. In 2004 the hotel refitted guest rooms and added wireless Internet, air-conditioning, and conference facilities. The management also runs the equally smart and stylish Relais Saint-Sulpice and Jardins du Luxembourg hotels, over on the Rive Gauche. ⊠ *85 rue du Rocher, Parc Monceau, 75008* ☎ *01–45–22–75–11* ⊟ *01–45–22–30–88* ⊕ *www.relais-monceau.com* ⇆ *50 rooms, 1 suite* ⌂ *Dining room, in-room safes, minibars, cable TV, in-room data ports, bar, laundry service, no-smoking rooms* ⊟ *AE, DC, MC, V* Ⓜ *Villiers.*

$$ **Hôtel d'Albion.** The modestly stylish Albion reveals an eclectic taste in art. The halls are hung with children's-book illustrations, while African art decorates guest-room doors. The cheerful lobby meanders around to a small breakfast area and even smaller outdoor garden terrace. Apricot and beige predominate in the snug and simply furnished rooms, whose details hint at particular themes: music (with framed sheet-music collages) or theater (comedy/tragedy mask motifs). The staff may be lackadaisical, but this is a rare cheap sleep with character in an otherwise budget-busting neighborhood. ⊠ *15 rue de Penthièvre, Champs-Élysées, 75008* ☎ *01–42–65–84–15* ⊟ *01–49–24–03–47* ⊕ *www.hotelalbion.net* ⇆ *22 rooms, 4 suites* ⌂ *Dining room, room service, in-room data ports, in-room safes, cable TV, laundry service; no a/c* ⊟ *AE, DC, MC, V* Ⓜ *Miromesnil.*

WITH CHILDREN?

MOST HOTELS IN PARIS *allow children under a certain age to stay in their parents' room at no extra charge. Hotel rooms are often on the small side, so inquire about connecting rooms or suites. The budget-priced* **Hôtel Marignan** *(⊠ 13 rue Sommerand 75005 ☎ 01–43–54–63–81) has rooms that sleep four or five, as well as access to a communal laundry room and kitchen facilities, and the* **Hôtel Résidence Henri IV** *(⊠ 50 rue Bernadins 75005 ☎ 01–44–41–31–81) has rooms with kitchenettes.*

The chain **Novotel** *(☎ 800/221–4542 for reservations, 08–25–88–44–44 in France) is a good bet as it allows two children under 16 to stay free in their parents' room; kids are offered free breakfast and gifts. Many Novotel hotels have playgrounds and children's corners with video games.*

Renting a furnished apartment is a convenient choice for families. Weekly rentals can be just as economical as

an inexpensive hotel (⇨ Apartment Rentals box).

On the other end of the price spectrum, the palace hotels are increasingly attuned to travelers with children. Many have special activities geared to make kids feel welcome in the formal surroundings. The **Four Seasons Hôtel George V Paris** *(⊠ 31 av. George V 75008 ☎ 1–49–52–70–00 ⊕ www.fourseasons.com/paris) has a "George the Frog" program which includes personalized T-shirts, in-room milk and cookies, and hotel-wide scavenger hunts. The* **Hôtel Meridien Montparnasse** *(⊠ 19 rue de Commandant-Mouchotte 75014 ☎ 01–44–36–44–36 ⊕ www.lemeridien.com) offers games, face painting, and a Sunday brunch where kids have their own buffet. The* **Ritz** *(⊠ 15 pl. Vendôme 75001 ☎ 01–43–16–30–30 ⊕ www.ritz.com) treats young guests like kings, with special cooking classes, gifts, and kids' menus.*

9e Arrondissement (Opéra)

See Where to Stay on the Rive Droite: Île de la Cité to Montmartre map.

$$$$ 🏨 **Pavillon de Paris.** If you're allergic to flowered chintz, this might be the place for you. The decor is foursquare and minimalist, with only the occasional striped or plaid fabric breaking the mellow wash of cocoa brown and beige. Guest rooms are small but are well equipped for business travelers, with faxes and complimentary wireless Internet. The traditional large reception area is done away with; instead, the check-in desk, a downlighted cube, is a less obtrusive part of the lounge. This lounge and bar area usually has an art exhibit or black-and-white photos on display. ⊠ *7 rue de Parme, Montmartre 75009* ☎ *01–55–31–60–00* 🖨 *01–55–31–60–01* ⊕ *www.pavillondeparis.com* ⇆ *30 rooms* ⌂ *Café, room service, in-room fax, minibars, cable TV, in-room data ports, bar, lounge* ➟ *AE, DC, MC, V* Ⓜ *Place de Clichy.*

★ **$$$–$$$$** 🏨 **Hôtel George Sand.** Opened in summer 2004, this family-run boutique hotel where the 19th-century writer George Sand once lived is fresh and modern, while preserving some of the original architectural details. Rooms have duvet comforters and coffee/tea-making trays, with hi-tech comforts such as complimentary high-speed Internet and cordless phones. Bathrooms are decked out in yacht-inspired wood flooring, with Etro toiletries. Paris's most famous department stores lie right around the corner. ⊠ *26 rue des Mathurins, Opéra/Grands Boulevards, 75009* ☎ *01–47–42–63–47* 🖷 *01–40–17–04–27* ⊕ *www.hotelgeorgesand. com* ⇆ *20 rooms* ⚇ *Dining room, room service, in-room data ports, in-room safes, minibars, cable TV, library, laundry service* ⊟ *AE, MC, V* Ⓜ *Havre Caumartin.*

$$$–$$$$ 🏨 **Villa Royale.** On place Pigalle, within view of Sacré-Coeur and just a catcall from all the sleazy sex-shop action, the Villa Royale has been designed to evoke the Moulin Rouge's bygone days. Every square foot of lobby, lounge, corridor, and room is draped in blood-red satin, circustent stripes, or deep-blue velvet; bathrooms are brash gold, brass, and marble. Named after the likes of Catherine Deneuve and Claude Debussy, royal suites are equipped with Jacuzzis, flat-screen TVs hidden behind gilt picture frames, and gas fireplaces that light up the gaudy love nests. For theatrical luxury, it's the best show in this part of town. ⊠ *2 rue Duperré, Montmartre, 75009* ☎ *01–55–31–78–78* 🖷 *01–55–31–78–70* ⇆ *27 rooms, 4 suites* ⚇ *Dining room, room service, in-room safes, some in-room hot tubs, minibars, cable TV, laundry service, some pets allowed, no-smoking floors* ⊟ *AE, DC, MC, V* Ⓜ *Pigalle.*

$$$ 🏨 **Mercure Paris Ronceray Opéra.** On one of Haussmann's Grands Boulevards between a historic covered shopping passage and the Grévin Wax Museum, the Ronceray Opéra is convenient for exploring Montmartre, department store browsing, or enjoying the area's revival in local nightlife. The Drouot auction house and Hard Rock Café are also nearby. The hotel's original 19th-century architecture has been preserved in the elegant Rossini bar and ballroom, where breakfast is served under crystal chandeliers. Comfortably modern rooms glow with wood-paneled walls, warm red fabrics, and marble baths. Nos. 319 and 419 have views of Sacré-Coeur. ⊠ *10 bd. Montmartre (Passage Jouffroy), Opéra/Grands Boulevards, 75009* ☎ *01–42–47–13–45* 🖷 *01–42–47–13–63* ⊕ *www. mercure.com* ⇆ *128 rooms, 2 suites* ⚇ *Dining room, room service, in-room safes, minibars, cable TV, bar, laundry service, Internet, convention center, some pets allowed (fee); no a/c in some rooms* ⊟ *AE, DC, MC, V* Ⓜ *Grands Boulevards.*

★ $$ 🏨 **Hôtel Royal Fromentin.** At the border of Montmartre's now tamed redlight district sits this former cabaret with much of its deco wood paneling and theatrical trappings intact. The decor is dark and rich, with green walls, red fauteuils, an antique caged elevator, and vaudeville posters in the stained glass–ceilinged lounge. Reproduction furniture, antique prints and oils, and busy modern fabrics fill out the larger-than-average rooms. Some windows face Sacré-Coeur, and fifth-floor balconies add even more breathing room. Guests receive a complimentary book illustrating the history of the mythical Belle Époque liqueur absinthe, which is once again served in the hotel's historic bar. ⊠ *11 rue Fromentin, Montmartre, 75009* ☎ *01–48–74–85–93* 🖷 *01–42–81–02–33* ⊕ *www. hotelroyalfromentin.com* ⇆ *47 rooms* ⚇ *Dining room, cable TV, bar, laundry service, Internet, meeting room, some pets allowed, no-smoking rooms; no a/c* ⊟ *AE, DC, MC, V* Ⓜ *Blanche.*

$–$$ ⊞ **Hôtel Langlois.** After starring in *The Truth About Charlie* (a remake of
Fodor'sChoice   *Charade*), this darling hotel gained a reputation as one of the most at-
★   mospheric budget sleeps in the city. Rates have crept up, but the former
circa-1870 bank retains its beautiful wood-paneled reception area and
wrought-iron elevator. The individually decorated and spacious rooms are
decked out with original glazed-tile fireplaces and period art. Rooms on
the lower floors have the largest bathrooms, but those on the fifth and
sixth have wonderful views of Paris rooftops. Nos. 63 and 64 look out
on Sacré-Coeur. ⊠ *63 rue St-Lazare, Opéra/Grands Boulevards, 75009*
☎ *01–48–74–78–24* 🖷 *01–49–95–04–43* ⊕ *www.hotel-langlois.com*
⇗ *24 rooms, 3 suites* ♿ *Dining room, minibars, cable TV, Internet,
some pets allowed; no a/c* ⊟ *AE, MC, V* Ⓜ *Trinité.*

$ ⊞ **Hôtel Chopin.** At the end of the passage Jouffroy—one of the many glass-
roof shopping arcades built in Paris in the early 19th century—the Chopin
recalls its 1846 birth date with a creaky-floored lobby and aged woodwork. The basic but comfortable rooms overlook the arcade's quaint toy
shops and bookstores or the rooftops of Paris, but none face the busy nearby
streets. The decoration leans heavily toward oppressive salmon walls, green
carpets, and repro-antique furniture, but rooms on the first and second
floors contain blue toile de Jouy prints. The best rooms end in "7" (No.
407 overlooks the Grévin Wax Museum's ateliers), while those ending in
"2" tend to be darkest and smallest (but also cheapest). ⊠ *10 bd. Montmartre (46 passage Jouffroy), Opéra/Grands Boulevards, 75009*
☎ *01–47–70–58–10* 🖷 *01–42–47–00–70* ⇗ *36 rooms* ♿ *Dining room,
in-room safes, cable TV; no a/c* ⊟ *AE, MC, V* Ⓜ *Grands Boulevards.*

10ᵉ Arrondissement (République)

See Where to Stay on the Rive Droite: The Marais to La Villette map.

$$ ⊞ **Relais de Paris République.** Part of a small chain, this attractive, mini-
malist hotel sits between Gare de l'Est and the up-and-coming Canal St-
Martin quarter, now popular for café life and waterside strolling. The guest
rooms are spotless and earth tones predominate: dark brown veneer fur-
nishings, rust-color bedspreads, orange-and-white-tile baths, and leath-
ery desk chairs. Five of the triples are actually small two-room combos;
top-floor rooms overlook the rooftops. ⊠ *38 bd. de Magenta, République,
75010* ☎ *01–44–52–75–55* 🖷 *01–44–52–75–59* ⊕ *www.lesrelaisdeparis.
fr* ⇗ *65 rooms* ♿ *Dining room, minibars, cable TV, Internet, some pets
allowed (fee)* ⊟ *AE, DC, MC, V* Ⓜ *Jacques Bonsergent.*

$ ⊞ **Hôtel Français.** This Haussmann-era budget hotel faces historic Gare
de l'Est and is just two blocks from Gare du Nord and the popular Canal
St-Martin district. Older rooms are decorated in pastels and light-wood
furnishings, while newer ones have contemporary wood furnishings
and warm-color fabrics. All have irons and trouser presses, and some
overlook the charming "indoor patio" breakfast room. The busy neigh-
borhood isn't very attractive, but the métro station across the street has
direct access to Notre Dame, the Latin Quarter, St-Germain-des-Prés,
and the *Marché aux Puces.* ⊠ *13 rue du 8 Mai 1945, République,
75010* ☎ *01–40–35–94–14* 🖷 *01–40–35–55–40* ⊕ *www.hotelfrancais.
com* ⇗ *71 rooms* ♿ *Dining room, room service, in-room data ports,*

in-room safes, minibars, cable TV, in-room VCRs, bar, meeting rooms, parking (fee), some pets allowed ⊟ *AE, MC, V* Ⓜ *Gare de l'Est.*

¢ ⊞ **Hôtel du Nord.** Behind the rustic facade of this budget hotel around the corner from the place de la République is a charming little lobby with clay-tile floors, exposed stone walls, and wooden beams. Rooms are simply decorated in different colors, with tile floors and en suite bathrooms with shower. There are few perks, but the hotel does have bikes available free to guests, perfect for a ride down to the nearby Marais district or a cruise along the tree-lined Canal St-Martin. ⊠ *47 rue Albert Thomas, République, 75010* ☎ *01–42–01–66–00* 🖨 *01–42–01–92–10* ⊕ *www. hoteldunord-leparivelo.com* ⊅ *24 rooms* ⚙ *Dining room, bicycles; no a/c* ⊟ *MC, V* Ⓜ *République.*

11° Arrondissement (République)

See Where to Stay on the Rive Droite: The Marais to La Villette map.

★ $$$–$$$$ ⊞ **Les Jardins du Marais.** Behind an unassuming facade on a narrow street, this amazing hotel's nine historic buildings (including Gustave Eiffel's old workshop) surround a capacious garden courtyard punctuated by Art Deco sculpture. Complete renovations have transformed this former budget residence hotel, introducing neutral linens and Art Deco furnishings (similar to those in the owner's other property, the Hilton Arc de Triomphe) while keeping some of the wet bars and coffee/tea-making facilities. Every room overlooks the garden, where meals are served in summer. In cooler weather you can still enjoy garden views from the glass conservatory restaurant and bar. ⊠ *74 rue Amelot, Bastille/Nation, 75012* ☎ *01–40–21–20–00* 🖨 *01–47–00–82–40* ⊕ *www.homeplazza. com* ⊅ *201 rooms, 64 suites* ⚙ *Restaurant, room service, in-room data ports, in-room safes, minibars, cable TV with movies, gym, bar, Internet, convention center, parking (fee), no-smoking rooms* ⊟ *AE, DC, MC, V* Ⓜ *St-Sébastien-Froissart.*

★ $$$ ⊞ **Le Général Hôtel.** Designer Jean-Philippe Nuel's sleek hotel opened in 2003, courting a discerning à la mode clientele. The daring interior splashes fuchsia on the walls, lobby armchairs, and custom-print wall fabrics in the breakfast area. Rooms are more subdued in cream, chocolate, and chestnut. Clever elements include clear-plastic desk chairs and silver "three-star general" rubber duckies to float in the tubs. The fifth- and sixth-floor rooms facing the street offer balconies with chimney-pot views to the west; one of the hotel's two seventh-floor suites has a bathtub right in the bedroom. There's free wireless Internet. ⊠ *5–7 rue Rampon, République, 75011* ☎ *01–47–00–41–57* 🖨 *01–47–00–21–56* ⊕ *www.legeneralhotel.com* ⊅ *45 rooms, 2 suites* ⚙ *Dining room, in-room safes, cable TV with movies, exercise equipment, sauna, bar, laundry service, Internet, business services, some pets allowed, no-smoking floors* ⊟ *AE, DC, MC, V.*

$$ ⊞ **Hôtel Beaumarchais.** This bold hotel serves as a gateway to the hip student and artist neighborhood of Oberkampf and the 11° and 20° arrondissements. Brightly colored vinyl armchairs, an industrial metal staircase, and glass tables mark the lobby. Out back a small courtyard is decked in hardwood, a look you'll rarely see in Paris. The rooms hum with pri-

mary reds and yellows, some with Keith Haring prints. Kaleidoscopes of ceramic fragments tile the bathrooms. The Beaumarchais lures in artsy budget travelers; for the price and attention to detail, the popularity is justified. ⊠ *3 rue Oberkampf, République, 75011* ☎ *01–53–36–86–86* 🖷 *01–43–38–32–86* ⊕ *www.hotelbeaumarchais.com* ↝ *31 rooms* ⚐ *Dining room, in-room safes, cable TV, some pets allowed; no a/c in some rooms* ▭ *AE, MC, V* Ⓜ *Filles du Calvaire, Oberkampf.*

¢–$ 🖼 **Hôtel Résidence Alhambra.** The white facade, rear garden, and flower-filled window boxes brighten this lesser-known neighborhood between the Marais and rue Oberkampf. A major face-lift still left the smallish, modern rooms with run-of-the-mill bedspreads and drapes. Some overlook the flowery courtyard. The best reasons to stay here are the rock-bottom price and the proximity to five métro lines at place de la République. ⊠ *13 rue de Malte, République, 75011* ☎ *01–47–00–35–52* 🖷 *01–43–57–98–75* ⊕ *www.hotelalhambra.fr* ↝ *58 rooms* ⚐ *Dining room, cable TV, some pets allowed; no a/c* ▭ *AE, DC, MC, V* Ⓜ *Oberkampf.*

12e Arrondissement (Bastille/Nation)

See Where to Stay on the Rive Droite: The Marais to La Villette map.

$$ 🖼 **Hôtel Lyon-Bastille.** Just a block from the Gare de Lyon is this cozy, congenial, family-run hotel, open since 1903. Its turn-of-the-20th-century pedigree shows up in its curves and alcoves; tall French windows let in plenty of light. Some rooms have been done up in pale blues and lilacs. The Marché Aligre and Viaduc des Arts artisan boutiques are just a few blocks away. ⊠ *3 rue Parrot, Bastille/Nation, 75012* ☎ *01–43–43–41–52* 🖷 *01–43–43–81–16* ⊕ *www.hotellyonbastille.com* ↝ *47 rooms, 1 suite* ⚐ *Dining room, in-room safes, minibars, cable TV, no-smoking rooms* ▭ *AE, DC, MC, V* Ⓜ *Gare de Lyon* ⑂ *CP.*

$$ 🖼 **Le Pavillon Bastille.** Here's an address (across from the Opéra Bastille) for travelers who appreciate getting more perks for less. The transformation of this 19th-century hôtel particulier into a colorful, high-design hotel garnered architectural awards. Some clients take to the hotel's blue-and-gold color scheme—from the bedspreads, curtains, and faux-marble walls to the funky track lighting fixtures hanging above the breakfast room—others find it brash. ⊠ *65 rue de Lyon, Bastille/Nation, 75012* ☎ *01–43–43–65–65, 800/233–2552 in the U.S.* 🖷 *01–43–43–96–52* ⊕ *www.paris-hotel-pavillonbastille.com* ↝ *24 rooms, 1 suite* ⚐ *Dining room, room service, in-room safes, minibars, cable TV, some in-room VCRs, bar, laundry service, Internet, some pets allowed, no-smoking floors* ▭ *AE, DC, MC, V* Ⓜ *Bastille.*

13e Arrondissement (Bercy/Tolbiac)

See Where to Stay on the Rive Gauche map.

$$ 🖼 **Hôtel La Manufacture.** Just behind place d'Italie and a short stroll from

Fodor'sChoice both the Jardins de Plantes and rue Mouffetard, La Manufacture's ★ lesser-known location makes you feel like a *vrai* Parisian. The lobby has oak flooring, subtle lighting, a wooden bar, and a breakfast room with

A ZEN RETREAT

If you're looking to retreat from the city's noise and bustle, look no further than the **Maison Zen** *(✉ 35 rue de Lyon, Bastille/ Nation 75012 ☎ 01–44–87–08–13 🖷 01–44–87–09–07 ⊕ www.maisonzen. com Ⓜ Bastille). Part of the Paris Zen Center (www.pariszencenter.com) opened in 1995 by Polish Zen and dharma masters Jacob and Graznya Perl, it contains a half-dozen studios open to the general public for a minimum stay of one week. Non-Buddhists are welcome, while those*

interested in attending daily meditation sessions can find the complete schedule and rules of etiquette on the Zen Center Web site. Instruction available for beginners is on an individual basis. Weekly rates start at €420 for two people in a minimally furnished, no-smoking studio with fully equipped kitchenette and linens. A lounge contains the only public phone and TV, and it closes after 10 PM so that everyone can enjoy the silence.

patio chairs and gingham-covered benches. Rooms employ clean lines and natural colors, and Arts and Crafts–inspired furnishings. Room options include triples and eight connecting rooms for families. The most expensive top-floor rooms are more spacious and have Tour Eiffel or Panthéon views. ✉ *8 rue Philippe de Champagne, Les Gobelins, 75013* ☎ *01–45–35–45–25* 🖷 *01–45–35–45–40* ⊕ *www.hotel-la-manufacture. com* ⇋ *57 rooms* ♿ *Dining room, cable TV, bar, laundry service, some pets allowed, no-smoking rooms* ▤ *AE, DC, MC, V* Ⓜ *Place d'Italie.*

$ ⊡ **Résidence Hôtelière Le Vert Gallant.** In a little-known neighborhood west of place d'Italie awaits a sincere welcome from proprietor Madame Laborde. More like her own house, this plain but proper hotel encloses a peaceful green space. One fantastic feature of the Vert Gallant: six of the rooms have kitchenettes, allowing you to reduce dining-out costs—unless you patronize L'Auberge Etchegorry (where authors Victor Hugo and Vicomte Chateaubriand used to drink and sing), the outstanding Basque restaurant run by Monsieur Laborde, a veteran chef who will tempt you with foie gras. ✉ *41–43 rue Croulebarbe, Les Gobelins, 75013* ☎ *01–44–08–83–50* 🖷 *01–44–08–83–69* ⇋ *15 rooms* ♿ *Restaurant, dining room, in-room safes, some kitchenettes, minibars, cable TV, laundry service, parking (fee); no a/c* ▤ *AE, DC, MC, V* Ⓜ *Les Gobelins.*

¢–$ ⊡ **Résidence Les Gobelins.** Wicker furniture and sunny colors warm up this small, simple hotel on a quiet side street between place d'Italie and the Quartier Latin, not far from the market street rue Mouffetard. Some rooms overlook a small flower-filled garden, as does the lounge (which doubles as a breakfast room). Jennifer Poirier is the Jamaican half of the couple (her husband Philippe is French) that runs the Résidence, and her wholehearted welcome is a big part of this hotel's draw. ✉ *9 rue des Gobelins, Les Gobelins, 75013* ☎ *01–47–07–26–90* 🖷 *01–43–31–44–05* ⊕ *www.hotelgobelins.com* ⇋ *32 rooms* ♿ *Dining room, cable TV; no a/c* ▤ *AE, MC, V* Ⓜ *Les Gobelins.*

14° Arrondissement (Montparnasse)

See Where to Stay on the Rive Gauche map.

$$ ▦ **Hôtel Istria.** This small family-run hotel on a quiet side street was a Montparnasse artists' hangout in the 1920s and '30s. It has a flower-filled courtyard and simple, clean, comfortable rooms with soft, pastel Japanese wallpaper and light-wood furnishings. Breakfast is served in a pretty vaulted cellar. ⊠ *29 rue Campagne-Première, Montparnasse, 75014* ☎ *01–43–20–91–82* 🖷 *01–43–22–48–45* 🖵 *26 rooms* ⚐ *Dining room, in-room safes, minibars, cable TV, in-room data ports, laundry service* ⊟ *AE, MC, V* Ⓜ *Raspail.*

$$ ▦ **Hôtel Lenox-Montparnasse.** Few budget hotels this close to the famous Dôme and Coupole brasseries and the Jardin du Luxembourg offer this level of service and amenities for the price. A smooth head-to-toe face-lift gave the largest (and best) rooms tile fireplaces, white-painted exposed beams, and violet or beige color schemes. The small standard rooms—there's barely a suitcase-width between the wall and the foot of the bed—follow a more functional contemporary style, with rich colors and print bedspreads. ⊠ *15 rue Delambre, Montparnasse, 75014* ☎ *01–43–35–34–50* 🖷 *01–43–20–46–64* ⊕ *www.hotellenox.com* 🖵 *46 rooms, 6 suites* ⚐ *Dining room, room service, in-room safes, minibars, cable TV, in-room data ports, laundry service, Internet, parking (fee), no-smoking rooms* ⊟ *AE, DC, MC, V* Ⓜ *Vavin.*

$$ ▦ **Hôtel Raspail-Montparnasse.** Guest rooms here are named after the artists who made Montparnasse the art capital of the world in the 1920s and '30s—Picasso, Chagall, and Modigliani. Man Ray and other Surrealists used to hang their hats here, too. Pastels prevail, complemented by contemporary blond-wood furniture and crisp cotton upholstery. Pay a bit extra–and reserve well in advance–for one of the three deluxe corner rooms, which have windows facing the Tour Eiffel. All are sound-proofed. ⊠ *203 bd. Raspail, Montparnasse, 75014* ☎ *01–43–20–62–86* 🖷 *01–43–20–50–79* ⊕ *www.charming-hotel-paris.com* 🖵 *38 rooms* ⚐ *Dining room, in-room safes, minibars, cable TV, bar, laundry service* ⊟ *AE, DC, MC, V* Ⓜ *Vavin.*

¢–$ ▦ **Hôtel des Bains.** A charming neighborhood, tastefully decorated rooms, satellite TV, a friendly staff, even a few private parking spaces: can anyone explain why this hotel has only one government-ranked star? The price can't be beat, especially for the family-friendly two-room suites (€91–€137), one with a terrace, in a separate building off the courtyard garden. Local artisans contributed different artworks to each room. ⊠ *33 rue Delambre, Montparnasse, 75014* ☎ *01–43–20–85–27* 🖷 *01–42–79–82–78* ⊕ *www.hotel-des-bains-montparnasse.com* 🖵 *35 rooms, 8 suites* ⚐ *Dining room, in-room safes, cable TV, parking (fee), some pets allowed; no a/c* ⊟ *MC, V* Ⓜ *Vavin or Edgar Quinet.*

15° Arrondissement (Trocadéro/Tour Eiffel)

See Where to Stay on the Rive Gauche map.

$$ ▦ **Timhotel Tour Eiffel.** Part of a small Parisian chain, this inexpensive '70s-era hotel is within walking distance of the Tour Eiffel. The entire hotel was given a face-lift in 2004 and early 2005. Rooms have light-wood furniture and fresh damask for a clean if simple look, and all have double-glazed windows that keep out street noise. An open-air food market sets up across the street every Wednesday and Sunday. ⊠ *11 rue Juge, Trocadéro/Tour Eiffel, 75015* 🕾 *01–45–78–29–29* 🖨 *01–45–78–60–00* ⊕ *www.timhotel.com* 🛏 *39 rooms* ⌂ *Dining room, cable TV, laundry service, Internet, some pets allowed, no-smoking floors; no a/c in some rooms* ⊟ *AE, DC, MC, V* Ⓜ *Dupleix.*

¢–$ 🖬 **Hôtel de l'Avre.** The unassuming Hôtel de l'Avre is hidden on a secluded lane around the corner from the shopping street rue du Commerce and a twice-weekly outdoor food market. The gracious staff helps to create an at-home feel. No-frills rooms are prim, proper, and clean; above some beds, instead of a standard headboard, cushions hang from the wall. Yellow-and-blue- or white-and-red-floral fabrics match the flowers in the pebbled courtyard, where you can sit for breakfast. ⊠ *21 rue de l'Avre, Trocadéro/Tour Eiffel, 75015* 🕾 *01–45–75–31–03* 🖨 *01–45–75–63–26* ⊕ *www.hoteldelavre.com* 🛏 *26 rooms* ⌂ *Dining room, cable TV, Internet, some pets allowed; no a/c* ⊟ *AE, DC, MC, V* Ⓜ *La Motte–Piquet Grenelle.*

16ᵉ Arrondissement (Trocadéro/Tour Eiffel & Bois de Boulogne)

See Where to Stay on the Rive Droite: Bois du Boulogne to Place de la Concorde map.

$$$$ 🖬 **Hôtel Raphael.** The Raphael was built in 1925 to cater to travelers spending a season in Paris, so every space is generously sized for such long, lavish stays—the closets, for instance, have room for ball gowns and plumed hats. Guest rooms, most with king-size beds, are turned out in 18th- and early-19th-century antiques and have 6-foot windows, Oriental rugs, silk damask wallpaper, chandeliers, and ornately carved wood paneling. Bathrooms are remarkably large; most have claw-foot bathtubs and separate massage-jet showers. The roof terrace, topped in summer with a restaurant, has a panoramic view of the city, the Arc de Triomphe looming in the foreground. ⊠ *17 av. Kléber, Trocadéro/Tour Eiffel, 75116* 🕾 *01–53–64–32–00* 🖨 *01–53–64–32–01* ⊕ *www.raphael-hotel.com* 🛏 *52 rooms, 38 suites* ⌂ *2 restaurants, room service, in-room safes, some in-room hot tubs, minibars, cable TV with movies, some in-room VCRs, in-room data ports, gym, sauna, steam room, bar, babysitting, laundry service, concierge, Internet, meeting rooms, some pets allowed (fee), no-smoking floors* ⊟ *AE, DC, MC, V* Ⓜ *Kléber.*

$$$$ 🖬 **Hôtel Square.** There's little that's "square" about this very hip boutique hotel. Rooms are bright and spacious, decorated in what is best described as extravagant minimalism. Curved doors, walls, and furniture break up a hard-edged design dominated by stripes and squares, while flowers, designer lamps, and enormous beds soften the Zen aesthetic. Baths in Carrara marble include Carita beauty products. Large desks plus three phone lines and a fax-answering machine in each room make it ideal for business travelers. In the evening, mingle with Parisian media types in the art gallery, sleek bar, or trendy Zebra Square restaurant. ⊠ *3 rue de Boulainvilliers, Passy-Auteuil, 75016* 🕾 *01–44–14–91–90* 🖨 *01–44–14–91–99*

⊕ *www.hotelsquare.com* ⟿ *18 rooms, 4 suites* ⌂ *Restaurant, room service, in-room safes, minibars, cable TV, in-room data ports, bar, laundry service, Internet, business services, meeting rooms, parking (fee)* ⊟ *AE, DC, MC, V* Ⓜ *Passy.*

★ **$$$$** ▦ **Le Sezz.** The latest contender in the boutique hotel category, Le Sezz was still shrouded in secrecy at the time of this writing, but here's a sneak preview. As the first hotel by the hot French furniture designer Christophe Pillet, Le Sezz mixes rough, stacked stone walls reminiscent of Frank Lloyd Wright with flashes of bright color and tall glass sculptures. Rooms have black parquet floors and camp-style beds positioned smack in the center. One-way glass walls separate the sleeping areas from the Boffi-designed bathrooms, many which have tubs big enough for two. The owner has pushed the trend of scaled-down reception desks even further by not having one at all. All of the paperwork is done in advance so you can go directly to your room without having to stand around in the lobby. A champagne bar and *Espace Bien-Être,* equipped with a yoga practice room, cater to a hip new generation of international jet-setters. ⊠ *6 av. Frémiet, Passy-Auteuil, 75016* ☏*01–56–75–26–26* 🖷*01–56–75–26–16* ⊕*www.hotelsezz. com* ⟿ *13 rooms, 14 suites* ⌂ *Dining room, room service, in-room safes, minibars, cable TV, hot tub, massage, steam room, bar, laundry service, concierge, Internet, meeting rooms* ⊟ *AE, DC, MC, V* Ⓜ *Passy.*

$$$$ ▦ **Trocadéro Dokhan's Sofitel Demeure Hôtel.** An idiosyncratic style keeps this hotel popular among fashionistas. Its attention to detail is what truly sets it apart from other posh addresses in this very upscale neighborhood: a Louis Vuitton steamer-trunk elevator; an elegant bar stocked with 50 varieties of bubbly (reportedly the largest selection of champagne of any city bar); wireless Internet access; boldly striped chairs and white-and-black star-print curtains in the guest rooms; and marble bathrooms with Roger et Gallet toiletries. The best rooms are the deluxe doubles; only the suites have views of the Tour Eiffel. ⊠ *117 rue Lauriston, Trocadéro/Tour Eiffel, 75016* ☏ *01–53–65–66–99* 🖷 *01–53–65–66–88* ⊕ *www.dokhans. com* ⟿*41 rooms, 4 suites* ⌂ *Dining room, room service, in-room safes, minibars, cable TV with movies, bar, babysitting, laundry service, concierge, Internet, parking (fee), some pets allowed, no-smoking floors* ⊟*AE, DC, MC, V* Ⓜ *Porte Dauphine.*

$$$–$$$$ ▦ **Hôtel Duret.** Only one block from métro line 1 and a five-minute walk from the Élysées, this smart boutique hotel in contemporary plum, lime, and chocolate hues opened in 2004. Bayadère-striped halls lead to rooms decorated in one of the hotel's signature colors, with a mix of wool and satin fabrics and either whitewashed or walnut furnishings. The stone bathrooms have hair dryers and lines to hang laundry, and superior rooms have small walk-in closets. You can connect to the high-speed Internet for free in your room or in the lounge. ⊠ *30 rue Duret, Champs-Élysées, 75116* ☏ *01–45–00–42–60* 🖷 *01–45–00–55–89* ⊕ *www.hotelduret.com* ⟿ *25 rooms, 2 suites* ⌂ *Dining room, room service, in-room data ports, in-room safes, minibars, cable TV, bar, babysitting, laundry service, Internet, meeting rooms, some pets allowed, no-smoking floors* ⊟ *AE, DC, MC, V* Ⓜ *Argentine.*

$$$–$$$$ ▦ **Les Jardins du Trocadéro.** This hotel near the Trocadéro and the Tour Eiffel seamlessly blends old-style French elegance (period antiques,

Napoleonic draperies, classical plaster busts) with modern conveniences (VCRs and wireless Internet). Wall paintings of djinns and dressed-up monkeys add fanciful dash. Beds are huge: either king- or queen-size. Marble bathrooms come complete with terry-cloth robes and whirlpool baths. Bonuses include drinks and fashion show invites. ☒ *35 rue Benjamin-Franklin, Trocadéro/Tour Eiffel, 75116* ☎ *01–53–70–17–70,* *800/246–0041 in the U.S.* 🖷 *01–53–70–17–80* ⊕ *www.jardintroc.com* ⮑ *20 rooms* ⭔ *Restaurant, room service, in-room safes, in-room hot tubs, minibars, cable TV, some in-room VCRs, in-room data ports, massage, bar, laundry service, Internet, meeting room, parking (fee), no-smoking rooms* ▭ *AE, DC, MC, V* Ⓜ *Trocadéro.*

$$–$$$ 🏨 **Queen's Hôtel.** One of only a handful of hotels in the tony residential district near the Bois de Boulogne, Queen's is a small, comfortable, old-fashioned place with a high standard of service. The Queen's calls itself a *hôtel-musée,* for it contains works by contemporary French artists such as René Julian and Maurice Friedman, whose paintings hang in the walls of rooms and public areas. Guest rooms pair contemporary and older furnishings; renovated rooms have hot tubs and new beds. ☒ *4 rue Bastien-Lepage, Passy-Auteuil, 75016* ☎ *01–42–88–89–85* 🖷 *01–40–50–67–52* ⊕ *www.queens-hotel.fr* ⮑ *21 rooms, 1 suite* ⭔ *Dining room, in-room safes, minibars, cable TV, some in-room data ports, some hot tubs, Internet, some pets allowed (fee), no-smoking floors; no a/c in some rooms* ▭ *AE, DC, MC, V* Ⓜ *Michel-Ange Auteuil.*

$$ 🏨 **Hôtel Keppler.** On the border of the 8ᵉ and 16ᵉ arrondissements, near the Champs-Élysées, is this small modern hotel in a 19th-century building. The prices are a bargain for this chic neighborhood. The spacious, airy rooms have simple furnishings and floral upholstery; upper-floor rooms face the Tour Eiffel. A big lounge and dining room provide plenty of hangout space. ☒ *12 rue Keppler, Champs-Élysées, 75016* ☎ *01–47–20–65–05* 🖷 *01–47–23–02–29* ⊕ *www.hotelkeppler.com* ⮑ *49 rooms* ⭔ *Dining room, in-room safes, cable TV, bar; no a/c* ▭ *AE, MC, V* Ⓜ *George V.*

17ᵉ Arrondissement (Parc Monceau/Clichy)

See Where to Stay on the Rive Droite: Bois du Boulogne to Place de la Concorde map.

$$$ 🏨 **Hôtel de Banville.** It's easy to forgive the edge-of-town location of this sexy little boutique hotel considering the same style and comfort in the center of town would cost twice as much. The contemporary and elegant Banville mixes such materials as cut stone, red crocodile skin, and brushed steel with designer lighting features throughout. An open fireplace warms up the lounge bar, where a live pianist plays every Tuesday night. Superior rooms with whimsical names like Prelude and Pastourelle have open bathrooms in Italian marble and claw-foot tubs or romantic bed canopies. Classic rooms are more modern with walk-in showers. All have complimentary high-speed Internet. ☒ *166 bd. Berthier, Parc Monceau, 75017* ☎ *01–42–67–70–16* 🖷 *01–44–40–42–77* ⊕ *www.hotelbanville.fr* ⮑ *37 rooms, 1 suite* ⭔ *Dining room, room service, in-room data ports, in-room safes, cable TV, piano bar, laundry* *service, Internet, parking (fee), some pets allowed (fee), no-smoking rooms* ▤ *AE, DC, MC, V* Ⓜ *Porte de Champerret.*

$$–$$$ 🏨 **Hôtel Eber Monceau.** This small hotel is just one block from Parc Monceau and is one of only two in Paris part of the Relais du Silence group, a membership meant to guarantee tranquillity and comfort. With a mix of antiques, the bright rooms are tastefully done in whites, beiges, and browns with painted overhead beams and joists. Ask for one overlooking the courtyard. The engaging owner, Jean-Marc Eber, delights in welcoming first-time guests. ✉ *18 rue Léon-Jost, Parc Monceau, 75017* ☎ *01–46–22–60–70* 🖷 *01–47–63–01–01* ⊕ *www.hotelseber.com* ⟲ *13 rooms, 5 suites* ⌂ *Dining room, minibars, cable TV, laundry service* ▤ *AE, DC, MC, V* Ⓜ *Courcelles.*

$$ 🏨 **Hôtel Palma.** This modest hotel in a small 19th-century building between the Arc de Triomphe and Porte Maillot is an exceptional deal considering its rather aristocratic neighbors. Cheerful and homey, rooms have hand-painted wood furnishings, floral-motif fabrics, and tile bathrooms renovated in 2004; ask for one on an upper floor with a view across Rive Droite rooftops. There's air-conditioning on the sixth (top) floor only. ✉ *46 rue Brunel, Champs-Élysées, 75017* ☎ *01–45–74–74–51* 🖷 *01–45–74–40–90* ⊕ *www.hotelpalma-paris.com* ⟲ *37 rooms* ⌂ *Dining room, in-room data ports, cable TV, some pets allowed (fee); no a/c in some rooms* ▤ *AE, MC, V* Ⓜ *Argentine.*

¢ 🏨 **Hôtel Eldorado.** The Eldorado is for guests happy lying low without room phones, TVs, or an elevator and who enjoy nesting in the relatively undiscovered Batignolles quartier just west of Montmartre. Each room has its individual distressed-chic charms—leopard spots and zebra stripes, knick-knacks from Africa and the Far East, flea-market antiques, and club chairs. Many rooms face the garden courtyard, decorated with bamboo plants and hanging lamps, where artsy bohemian types from the hotel's wine bistro hang out on summer nights. Rooms 16 and 17 even have their own little balconies. Ask for a room in the back building for a quiet night's sleep. ✉ *18 rue des Dames, Montmartre, 75017* ☎ *01–45–22–35–21* 🖷 *01–43–87–25–97* ⊕ *www.eldoradohotel.fr* ⟲ *33 rooms, 23 with bath* ⌂ *Restaurant, no-smoking rooms; no a/c, no room phones, no room TVs* ▤ *AE, DC, MC, V* Ⓜ *Place de Clichy.*

FodorśChoice
★

18° Arrondissement (Montmartre)

See Where to Stay on the Rive Droite: Île de la Cité to Montmartre map.

$$$$ 🏨 **Terrass Hôtel.** The hulking Terrass, known for its views over Paris, dwarfs its rather humble Montmartre neighbors, including the adjacent cemetery. There's a mix of French-country color schemes in the guest rooms, which have such special touches such as tea kettles and complimentary cosmetics. Superior rooms have two sinks, shower, and standard or whirlpool tub, and six rooms have their own steam rooms. But the most popular accommodations are on the upper floors, such as junior suite No. 802, with its big wood-deck balcony facing the Tour Eiffel. Reserve these well in advance, or prepare to shell out for the views from the rather pricey seventh-floor restaurant with an outdoor panoramic terrace. ✉ *12 rue Joseph de Maistre, Montmartre, 75018* ☎ *01–44–92–34–14*

THE HOSTEL SCENE

NO MATTER WHAT YOUR AGE, you can save on lodging costs by staying at hostels. Most of Paris's hostels and foyers (student hostels) are bargains at €16–€30 a night for a bed in shared rooms (usually three–six beds) or €50–€80 for a private double, with free showers and a baguette-and-coffee wake-up call. In summer you should reserve in writing a month in advance (deposits are often taken via credit card for advance reservations); if you don't have a reservation it's a good idea to check in as early as 8 AM. Some foyers have age restrictions. Be sure to check if there's a night curfew and/or lockouts during the day, and don't forget to pack your earplugs!

Paris's major public hostels are run by the Féderation Unie des Auberges de Jeunesse (FUAJ). For about €20, a bed, sheets, shower, and breakfast are provided, with beds usually three or four to a room. *Maisons Internationales des Jeunes Étudiants* (MIJE) have the plushest hostels for guests ages 18–30. Private hostels have accommodations that run from pleasant, if spartan, double rooms to dormlike arrangements.

The best hostel options in Paris include: **Aloha Hostel** (✉ 1 rue Borromée Trocadéro/Tour Eiffel, 75015 ☎ 01–42–73–03–03 🖷 01–42–73–14–14 ⊕ www.aloha.fr). **Auberge de Jeunesse d'Artagnan FUAJ** (✉ 80 rue Vitruve Père Lachaise, 75020 ☎ 01–40–32–34–56 🖷 01–40–32–34–55 ⊕ www.fuaj. org). In the Marais, three 17th-century properties run by MIJE (✉ Le Fauconnier, 11 rue de Fauconnier; Fourcy, 6 rue Fourcy; Maubuisson, 12 rue des Barres, 75004 ☎ 01–42–74–23–45 🖷 01–42–74–08–93 ⊕ www.mije.com). **Peace & Love Hostel & Bar** (✉ 245 rue de La Fayette Butte-Chaumont, 75010 ☎ 01–46–07–65–91 ⊕ www.paris-hostels.com).

Le Village (✉ 20 rue d'Orsel, Montmartre, 75018 ☎ 01–42–64–22–02 🖷 01–42–64–22–04 ⊕ www.villagehostel.fr). **Young and Happy Youth Hostel** (✉ 80 rue Mouffetard, Quartier Latin, 75005 ☎ 01–45–35–09–53 🖷 01–47–07–22–24 ⊕ www.youngandhappy.fr).

Membership in any Hostelling International (HI) association, open to travelers of all ages, allows you to stay in HI-affiliated hostels at member rates; one-year membership is $28 for adults (C$35 for a two-year minimum membership in Canada, £14 in the United Kingdom, A$52 in Australia, and NZ$40 in New Zealand); hostels run about $10–$30 per night. Members have priority if the hostel is full; they're also eligible for discounts.

For more information about hosteling, contact your local youth hostel office: **Australian YHA** (✉ Level 3, 10 Mallett St., Camperdown, NSW 2050, Australia ☎ 02/9565–1699 🖷 02/9565–1325 ⊕ www.yha.com.au). **Féderation Unie des Auberges de Jeunesse** (FUAJ/Hostelling International; ✉ 9 rue Brantôme, 3ᵉ, Paris ⊕ www.fuaj.org ✉ Centre National ✉ 27 rue Pajol, 18ᵉ, Paris ☎ 01–44–89–87–27). **HI—American Youth Hostels** (✉ 733 15th St. NW, Suite 840, Washington, DC 20005 ☎ 202/783–6161 🖷 202/783–6171 ⊕ www.hiusa. org). **HI—Canada** (✉ 205 Catherine St., Suite 400, Ottawa, Ontario K2P 1C3, Canada ☎ 613/237–7884 🖷 613/237–7868 ⊕ www.hostellingintl.ca). **YHA of England and Wales** (✉ Trevelyan House, Dimple Rd., Matlock, Derbyshire DE4 3YH, U.K. ☎ 0162/959–2600 in the U.K. ⊕ www.yha.org.uk). **YHA of New Zealand** (✉ Level 1, Moorhouse City, 166 Moorhouse Ave., Box 436, Christchurch, New Zealand ☎ 6403/379–9970 🖷 6403/365–4476 ⊕ www.yha. org.nz).

🖨 *01–42–52–29–11* ⊕ *www.terrass-hotel.com* 🗗 *85 rooms, 15 suites* ♨ *Restaurant, room service, some in-room safes, minibars, cable TV with movies, in-room data ports, bar, laundry service, concierge, Internet, meeting rooms, no-smoking floors* ▤ *AE, DC, MC, V* ⅠⓄⅠ*CP* Ⓜ *Place de Clichy.*

$–$$ ▦ **Hôtel Prima Lepic.** An impressive value, the Prima Lepic stands out among dozens of mediocre traps in this tourist zone. Elements from the original 19th-century building remain, such as vintage tiling in the entry and heavy-duty white iron furniture in the breakfast area. The bright rooms are full of spring colors and florals; the so-called Baldaquin rooms have reproduction canopy beds. Modern conveniences include wireless Internet access, in-room teapots and bathrobes, and—in some cases—flat-screen TVs. Larger rooms are suitable for families but have little natural light. Shop for your picnic on the thriving market street rue Lepic. ⊠ *29 rue Lepic, Montmartre, 75018* ☎ *01–46–06–44–64* 🖨 *01–46–06–66–11* ⊕ *www.hotel-paris-lepic.com* 🗗 *38 rooms* ♨ *Dining room, in-room data ports, in-room safes, cable TV, babysitting, laundry service; no a/c* ▤ *AE, DC, MC, V* Ⓜ *Blanche.*

$–$$ ▦ **Hôtel Regyn's Montmartre.** The lobby is cramped, the plain dining room tiny, and the staircase skinny, but folks book the Regyn's for the *Amélie Poulain* place des Abbesses location and the views. Bathrooms are modern with old-style ceramic pedestal sinks. Ask to stay on one of the two top floors for great views of either the Tour Eiffel or Sacré-Coeur; those on the lower floors are darker and less inviting. Overall, courteous service and a relaxed charm make this an attractive low-budget choice. There's also wireless Internet access. ⊠ *18 pl. des Abbesses, Montmartre, 75018* ☎ *01–42–54–45–21* 🖨 *01–42–23–76–69* ⊕ *www.paris-hotels-montmartre.com* 🗗 *22 rooms* ♨ *Dining room, in-room safes, cable TV with movies, some pets allowed; no a/c* ▤ *AE, MC, V* Ⓜ *Abbesses.*

★ $ ▦ **Ermitage Hôtel.** Resembling a squat, modest mansion, the Ermitage is in fact a former residence converted into a hotel in the 1970s by legendary hosts Monsieur and Madame Canipel. Now their daughter Maggie runs the show, and the same tranquillity and one-of-the-family welcome awaits. The building dates from Napoléon III's time and is filled with mirrored armoires, chandeliers, and other antiques. There's a private terrace for the two ground-level rooms; second-floor windows open wide toward north Paris. All rooms have funky flowery decor. The building is only two stories high (no elevator), and the highest-tech item is the fax machine. ⊠ *24 rue Lamarck, Montmartre, 75018* ☎ *01–42–64–79–22* 🖨 *01–42–64–10–33* 🗗 *12 rooms* ♨ *Dining room, some pets allowed; no a/c, no room TVs* ▤ *No credit cards* ⅠⓄⅠ*CP* Ⓜ *Lamarck Caulaincourt.*

$ ▦ **Hôtel des Arts.** The location in the heart of Montmartre's winding streets is reason enough to stay at this affordable hostelry. But the scattering of antiques in the lounge, bookcases in the lobby, and vintage cabaret scenes painted onto each elevator door lend a distinctive feel usually lacking in this price range. Rooms have red or green carpeting, modern wooden furnishings, and floral or plaid linens. No. 42 is a larger double with a balcony overlooking Paris, but the best views are from the sixth floor (these cost an additional €20). There's wireless Internet. ⊠ *5 rue Tholozé, Montmartre, 75018* ☎ *01–46–06–30–52* 🖨 *01–46–06–10–83* ⊕ *www.*

arts-hotel-paris.com ➥ *50 rooms* ⚐ *Dining room, room service, in-room safes, cable TV, Internet; no a/c* ⊟ *AE, DC, MC, V* Ⓜ *Abbesses.*

$ 🏨 **Hôtel Utrillo.** This very likable hotel is on a quiet side street at the foot of Montmartre, near colorful rue Lepic. Reproduction prints and marble-top breakfast tables make every room feel charmingly old-fashioned, while the cheery French country colors make them appear brighter and more spacious than they actually are. The sauna is a luxury for this price. Two rooms (Nos. 61 and 63) have views of the Tour Eiffel. ⊠ *7 rue Aristide-Bruant, Montmartre, 75018* ☎ *01–42–58–13–44* 🖷 *01–42–23–93–88* ⊕ *www.hotel-paris-utrillo.com* ➥ *30 rooms* ⚐ *Dining room, minibars, cable TV, some in-room data ports, sauna, some pets allowed; no a/c* ⊟ *AE, DC, MC, V* Ⓜ *Abbesses, Blanche.*

19ᵉ Arrondissement (Buttes-Chaumont)

See Where to Stay on the Rive Droite: The Marais to La Villette map.

¢ 🏨 **Hôtel Le Laumière.** Though it's some distance from the city center, this family-run hotel near the rambling Buttes-Chaumont park has irresistable rock-bottom rates. The staff, too, is exceptionally helpful. Unfortunately, the modern modular furniture offers little inspirations, though some of the larger rooms overlook a garden and lawn and have balconies. ⊠ *4 rue Petit, Buttes-Chaumont, 75019* ☎ *01–42–06–10–77* 🖷 *01–42–06–72–50* ⊕ *www.hotel-lelaumiere.com* ➥ *54 rooms* ⚐ *Dining room, cable TV, parking (fee), some pets allowed, no-smoking rooms; no a/c* ⊟ *MC, V* Ⓜ *Laumière.*

Nightlife &
the Arts

4

NIGHTLIFE

Revised and
updated by
Heather
Stimmler-Hall

PARIS AT NIGHT is whatever you want it to be. Whether you're a jazz fiend or a dance freak, a patron of the arts or a lounge lizard seeking refuge in a bar where the model count is high, you can sate your cravings here. The hottest nightspots are in the northeastern districts of Paris, particularly around Ménilmontant, Oberkampf, and Belleville, while the Bastille clubs and the Marais bars are still going strong. The Grands Boulevards and Pigalle/Montmartre are also lively places with plenty of theaters, bars, and concert venues. By comparison, the Rive Gauche is a relatively minor player, dominated by student pubs and jazz bars in the Latin Quarter and a sprinkling of chic hangouts toward St-Germain-des-Prés. The Gucci–and–Vuitton-clad jet set can still be found around the Champs-Élysées and Rue St-Honoré, with prices (and some seriously surly bouncers) to match the ritzy surroundings. In warmer months Parisians flock to the floating clubs and bars, moored along the Seine from Bercy to the Eiffel Tower. Midweek, people are usually home after closing hours, around 2 AM, but weekends mean late-night partying. Take note: the last métro runs between 12:30 AM and 1 AM. You can take a cab, but it can be hard to find one between midnight and 2 AM on weekends. You could also try to catch a Noctambus (night bus); these run every hour from 1 to 5:30 AM, with extra service on the weekends, and their stops are marked with a white owl sign(*see* Bus Travel within Paris *in* Smart Travel Tips). Or it may just be worth staying out until the métro starts running again at 5:45 AM.

Bars

The Paris bar scene could best be described as tribal. Parisians tend to stick with the same place once they've found something they like. This gives many a spot—be it a wine bar, corner café, or hip music club—a welcoming the-gang's-all-here atmosphere. If you want to hit bars at a relatively quiet hour, try them during the *apéritif* (around 6 PM), when many also offer happy-hour specials. That's when Parisians congregate to decide where they want to go later. Many bars charge slightly higher rates after 10 PM, and—annoyingly—turn off the espresso machine for the night. Some bars have table service; at others (designated by SERVICE AU BAR signs), you must fetch your own drinks. For reviews of *bars à vins*, see the Wine Bars section at the end of the Where to Eat chapter. These serve simple meals and snacks (charcuterie, cheese) as well as wine; they usually close quite early.

Bastille & Eastward

In the early 1990s the Bastille was the hottest nightlife area in town. Though the scene has migrated north toward the Belleville and Oberkampf districts, the Bastille remains popular. Fun and flashy, the block-long rue de Lappe has the most bars per foot in Paris; nearby rue de la Roquette and rue de Charonne also have many en vogue options. Up north, rue Oberkampf and surrounding streets abound with laid-back theme bars—many playing live music—while bourgeois bohemian types head up to the latest lounges around metro Belleville and the Canal St-Martin.

THE OBERKAMPF SCENE

AN APPETITE for an antidote to the fashionable bar scene paradoxically turned the gritty Oberkampf into a trendy nightlife area. The streets between boulevard Voltaire and boulevard de Ménilmontant, particularly rue Oberkampf, rue St-Maur, and rue Jean-Pierre-Timbaud, crackle with energy, none more than rue Oberkampf between the Ménilmontant and Parmentier métro stations. The bars and restaurants here have taken their cue from **Café Charbon** (⌂ 109 rue Oberkampf ☎ 01–43–57–55–13), a converted turn-of-the-20th-century dance hall ostentatiously proud of its huge mirrors, smoke-stained ceilings, and dance space. **Café Mercerie** (⌂ 98 rue Oberkampf ☎ 01–43–38–81–30), across from Café Charbon, takes its name—and painted sign—from the draper's shop that used to be here. The first wave of bars and boutiques hereabouts looked like they had

been thrown together by impoverished art students during a particularly drunken weekend; many of those, sadly, are long gone, replaced by more conventionally cool joints.

But rue Oberkampf's neighboring streets still have their edges intact and are home to many hot haunts. **Les Couleurs** (⌂ 117 rue St-Maur ☎ 01–43–57–95–61) is a hangout most reminiscent of the original Oberkampf vibe. **Les Trois Tetards** (⌂ 46 rue Jean-Pierre-Timbaud ☎ 01–43–14–27–37) functions as a late-night coffeeshop. The friendly **Café Cannibale** (⌂ 93 rue Jean-Pierre-Timbaud ☎ 01–49–29–95–59) has a mood set by faded antiques and candlelight. A little farther south, near métro Charonne, is **Jacques Mélac** (⌂ 42 rue Léon Frot ☎ 01–43–70–59–27), where genial Jacques sprouts the largest mustache in town and grows his own grapes on a vine along the front of the building.

Café Charbon (⌂ 109 rue Oberkampf, 11ᵉ, République ☎ 01–43–57–55–13 Ⓜ St-Maur, Parmentier) is a beautifully restored 19th-century café whose trendsetting clientele gossips to a jazz background. The vibe gets livelier after 10 PM, when a DJ takes over.

Café Chéri(e) (⌂ 44 bd. de la Villette, 19ᵉ, Père Lachaise ☎ 01–42–02–02–05 Ⓜ Belleville) pulls in more people than its location might suggest. Trendy locals in artfully ripped jeans and thirtysomething Parisians trying to escape the more touristy Oberkampf drink cheap beer on the huge sidewalk terrace and groove to live jazz and eclectic DJ sets.

Chez Prune (⌂ 36 rue Beaurepaire, 10ᵉ, République ☎ 01–42–41–30–47 Ⓜ Jacques Bonsergent) is a lively bar with a terrace overlooking one of the footbridges over Canal St-Martin. The area has become one of the hottest in Paris, yet while you're likely to spot some hip fashion designer, celebrity photographer Mario Testino, and lots of beautiful people, the neighborhood mood feels refreshingly more relaxed than poseurish.

★ **China Club** (⌂ 50 rue de Charenton, 12ᵉ, Bastille/Nation ☎ 01–43–43–82–02 Ⓜ Ledru-Rollin) has a restaurant and bar with lacquered furnishings and a colonial-Asia theme on the ground floor, a low-lit cigar-and-rum bar upstairs, and a swinging live-music dive downstairs.

La Fabrique (✉ 53 rue du Faubourg St-Antoine, 11ᵉ, Bastille/Nation ☎ 01–43–07–67–07 Ⓜ Bastille)—a bar, club, and restaurant—draws a festive, party-minded clientele of all ages. It really gets going every evening after 10 PM, when a DJ hits the turntables.

★ **La Favela Chic** (✉ 18 rue du Faubourg du Temple, 11ᵉ, République ☎ 01–40–21–38–14 Ⓜ République) was one of the bars that made Oberkampf so hip. Now hidden behind gates in a courtyard in the République district, this Latin cocktail bar remains highly popular, offering an organic juice bar, caipirinhas and mojitos, guest DJs, and a nonstop Latino party atmosphere with dancing on the tables into the wee hours.

Le Lèche Vin (✉ 13 rue Daval, 11ᵉ, Bastille/Nation ☎ 01–43–55–98–91 Ⓜ Bastille), which literally means "Lick Wine," is more interested in off- (and on)-the-wall humor than setting trends, with a blasphemous mix of kitsch religious icons and nudie pics. High-quality beers and cheap cocktails keep the crowd well-oiled till the 2 AM closing bell.

Sanz Sans (✉ 49 rue du Faubourg St-Antoine, 11ᵉ, Bastille/Nation ☎ 01–44–75–78–78 Ⓜ Bastille) glows in purple velvet and gilt and has lamp shades fashioned from cymbals, which the staff clang jovially. Arrive early on weekends, when it's heaving with cosmopolitan twentysomethings juicing up for a night of dancing until dawn.

Opéra/Grands Boulevards & Louvre/Tuileries

Nightlife around the Grands Boulevards pulses nonstop, with several all-night brasseries, lively pubs, and an increasing array of chic watering holes. The side streets around the Opéra Garnier and above the Tuileries Gardens hide some good spots, but unlike the nearby Champs Élysées, the nightlife here is spread thinly over a large area. It's thus a good idea to know where you're going ahead of time.

Barramundi (✉ 3 rue Taitbout, 9ᵉ, Opéra/Grands Boulevards ☎ 01–47–70–21–21 Ⓜ Richelieu Drouot) is one of Paris's hubs of nouveau-riche chic. The lighting is dim, the copper bar is long, and the walls are artfully textured. During the week chill-out and world music pipe through the bar. By the weekend, however, things get moving with a program of regular soirees, with names like "Super Nature," "Reelax," and "Corpus Noctem."

FodorśChoice **De la Ville Café** (✉ 34 bd. Bonne Nouvelle, 10ᵉ, Opéra/Grands Boulevards ☎ 01–48–24–48–09 Ⓜ Bonne Nouvelle, Grands Boulevards) ★ conveys a funky, industrial baroque ambience, with its huge, heated sidewalk terrace, mosaic-tile bar, and swish lounge. As the anchor of the slowly reawakening Grands Boulevards scene, it requires that you arrive early on weekends for a seat.

★ **Le Fumoir** (✉ 6 rue Amiral-de-Coligny, 1ᵉʳ, Louvre/Tuileries ☎ 01–42–92–00–24 Ⓜ Louvre) is a fashionable spot where neighboring gallery owners and fashion industry types meet for late-afternoon wine, early evening cocktails, or dinner. There's a bar in front, a library with shelves of books in back, and leather couches throughout.

★ **Harry's New York Bar** (✉ 5 rue Daunou, 2ᵉ, Opéra/Grands Boulevards ☎ 01–42–61–71–14 Ⓜ Opéra), a cozy, wood-paneled hangout decorated with dusty college pennants and popular with expatriates, welcomes the ghosts of Ernest Hemingway and F. Scott Fitzgerald. This place claims to have invented the Bloody Mary, and true or not, the bartenders here do mix a mean one. Don't miss the piano bar downstairs where Gerswhin composed "An American in Paris."

SoMo (⊠ 168 rue Montmartre, 2e, Opéra/Grands Boulevards ☎ 01–40–13–08–80 Ⓜ Grands Boulevards), part of the expat-owned Cheap Blonde bar group that includes the Lizard Lounge, feels hip and contemporary. The low-lit bar and restaurant attract the suit-and-tie crowd during the day and sleek young things who come for the DJ sets at night.

Champs-Élysées

The Champs-Élysées ("Les Champs" to the initiated) and the streets branching off from it have seen many glitzy bars open and quickly gain a reputation by inviting models and stars. After the first few weeks, however, the model count drops and the slicked-back-hair, sharp-suit, mobile-phone crowd moves in.

The namesake of **Buddha Bar** (⊠ 8 rue Boissy d'Anglas, 8e, Champs-Élysées ☎ 01–53–05–90–00 Ⓜ Concorde), towering, a gold-painted Buddha, contemplates enough Dragon Empress screens and colorful chinoiserie for five MGM movies. A spacious mezzanine bar overlooks the dining room, where cuisines East and West meet somewhere between Blandsville and California. Although past its prime as a Parisian hot spot, it manages to fill up nightly with an eclectic bunch.

Man Ray (⊠ 34 rue Marbeuf, 8e, Champs-Élysées ☎ 01–56–88–36–36 Ⓜ Franklin-D.-Roosevelt) keeps its profile high despite the almost nonexistent face time by owners Johnny Depp, Sean Penn, and Simply Red's Mick Hucknall. The ravishing Asian–art deco style recalls a slightly Disneyesque 1930s supper club in Chinatown. Devotees come to flash their bling and don't bat an eye at the extortionate drink prices (€10 for a Coke) and curt service.

Polo Room (⊠ 3 rue Lord Byron, 8e, Champs-Élysées ☎ 01–40–74–07–78 Ⓜ George V), on the first floor of a building on a sleepy street off the Champs-Élysées, was the very first martini bar in Paris. American owners target a business clientele with a New York–ish mood. There are polo photos on the wall, a 36-foot bar, and a selection of 28 different martinis (who can resist the Martini Chocolat?).

Quartier Latin & St-Germain-des-Prés

In the heart of expensive (and touristy) Paris, bars here can't afford to be too cutting edge. (And the price of your beer will probably reflect the pricey neighborhood real estate.) Almost all bars fall into one of two categories: casual student hangouts and lairs for the preening types. Both tend to have a lot of other English-speaking travelers out on the town.

Alcazar (⊠ 62 rue Mazarine, 6e, St-Germain-des-Prés ☎ 01–53–10–19–99 Ⓜ Odéon), Sir Terence Conran's first makeover of a Parisian landmark, has a stylish mezzanine-level bar, where you can sip a glass of wine under the huge glass roof. The theme changes nightly, from Sinatra oldies to digital-video mixes and house music.

Le Bilboquet (⊠ 13 rue St-Benoît, 6e, St-Germain-des-Prés ☎ 01–45–48–81–84 Ⓜ St-Germain-des-Prés) is the place to sip cocktails in a ritzy Belle Époque salon while a jazz combo sets the mood.

Chez Georges (⊠ 11 rue de Canettes, 6ᵉ, St-Germain-des-Prés ☎ 01–43–25–32–79 Ⓜ Mabillon) has been serving glasses of red wine, pastis, and beer for the past 60-odd years. In the basement, students and loyal locals crowd around tiny tables, but don't be intimidated if the place looks packed—there's always room to squeeze in somewhere, and the regulars are more than willing to make new friends.

Les Étages (⊠ 5 rue de Buci, 6ᵉ, St-Germain-des-Prés ☎ 01–46–34–26–26 Ⓜ Odéon) is a laid-back, studenty type of place occupying three floors of a building near St-Germain-des-Prés. The walls are rustic red and ocher, the decor is simple, and the terrace is the perfect place to sit in summer.

The Fifth (⊠ 62 rue Mouffetard, 5ᵉ, Quartier Latin ☎ 01–43–37–09–09 Ⓜ Place Monge) is a popular international bar on student- and tourist-friendly rue Mouffetard with low ceilings and creative "cocktails of the week" served by a friendly staff. There's a pool table and big-screen TV on the lower mezzanine.

Le Piano Vache (⊠ 8 rue La Place, 5ᵉ, Quartier Latin ☎ 01–46–33–75–03 Ⓜ Maubert-Mutualité) has been a popular student haunt since it opened in 1969, playing old pop and rock favorites. It's wallpapered with '70s posters, is supersmoky, and has a Goth party Wednesday evenings.

Le Marais

Le Marais continues to be the place where you can spend a night out in style. It's far from Oberkampf's modish chaos, but not so posh as to turn people away at the door.

Andy Wahloo (⊠ 69 rue des Gravilliers, 3ᵉ, Le Marais ☎ 01–42–71–20–38 Ⓜ Arts et Métiers) draws a refreshingly mixed crowd who come primarily to smoke hookahs beneath silk-screened Moroccan coffee ads and get down to a blend of classic '80s tunes and Raï remixes. More authentic than many of its counterparts, it's not just another Parisian club playing with ethnic chic.

Café Klein Holland (⊠ 36 rue du Roi de Sicile, 11ᵉ, Le Marais ☎ 01–42–71–43–13 Ⓜ St-Paul) is the place to go if you'd prefer a pint of Grolsch to Guinness. Try out the Dutch specialties, such as *bitterballen* (fried meatballs) and *vlammetjes* (spicy egg rolls).

La Chaise au Plafond (⊠ 10 rue du Trésor, 4ᵉ, Le Marais ☎ 01–42–76–03–22 Ⓜ St-Paul) has the feel of a traditional bistro with a few off-beat contemporary touches. Never overcrowded, it's the perfect place for an excellent glass of wine and people-watching.

Jokko (⊠ 5 rue Elzévir, 4ᵉ, Le Marais ☎ 01–42–74–35–96 Ⓜ St-Paul) doubles as a cultural center, introducing modern African art and music. The decor, much of it created from found objects, is a work of art itself, and the cool cocktails and concerts—from *m'balax* (Senegalese music) to the blues—attract a fun-loving crowd.

★ **La Perla** (⊠ 26 rue François Miron, 4ᵉ, Le Marais ☎ 01–42–77–59–40 Ⓜ Hôtel de Ville, St-Paul) is one of the chicest spots in town for Latin lovers. Sit back, sip a margarita, munch on a few Latin tapas, and take in all the lovely people.

Le Trésor (⊠ 7 rue du Trésor, 4ᵉ, Le Marais ☎ 01–42–71–35–17 Ⓜ St-Paul) is a lively, sophisticated spot, where Thursday through Saturday DJs spin a mix of house and funk in a room full of mismatched baroque furnishings.

Montmartre

Montmartre, long equated with "bohemian" places of all stripes, is now getting a new lease on the bar scene. An edgy local clan helped push the quartier's offerings beyond the old cabaret stereotypes; most of the trendy spots are near the place Pigalle, which clings to its red-light past.

Café le Fourmi (⊠ 74 rue des Martyrs, 18ᵉ, Montmartre ☎ 01–42–64–70–35 Ⓜ Pigalle) is Pigalle's trendiest address, a spacious café where all the cool locals hang out, comfortably oblivious to the surrounding seediness.

La Jungle Montmartre (⊠ 32 rue Gabrielle, 18ᵉ, Montmartre ☎ 01–46–06–75–69 Ⓜ Abbesses) is a gem of a place on a very sleepy, off-the-beat street in Montmartre. Upstairs is an African restaurant; downstairs is a small bar with Senegalese sculptures and tiger and leopard designs on the tabletops. DJ-spun tunes range from reggae and funk to techno and drum and bass.

Moloko (⊠ 26 rue Fontaine, 9ᵉ, Montmartre ☎ 01–48–74–50–26 Ⓜ Blanche) is a scruffy, smoky, late-night bar with several rooms, a mezzanine, a jukebox, and a small dance floor. Its 6 AM closing time attracts an energetic crowd.

Le Sancerre (⊠ 35 rue des Abbesses, 18ᵉ, Montmartre ☎ 01–42–58–08–20 Ⓜ Abbesses), a café by day, turns into a lively watering hole for Montmartrois and artist types at night with Belgian beers on tap and an impressive list of cocktails.

Montparnasse

Commuters on their way to and from the Montparnasse train station make up the first wave of evening customers in this neighborhood's brasseries and pubs. Later on a mix of twentysomethings-and-up filters in. It's still a good snapshot of Paris at the end of the day.

American Bar at La Closerie des Lilas (⊠ 171 bd. du Montparnasse, 6ᵉ, Montparnasse ☎ 01–40–51–34–50 Ⓜ Montparnasse) lets you drink in the swirling action of the adjacent restaurant and brasserie and do it at a bar hallowed by plaques honoring such former habitués as Man Ray, Jean-Paul Sartre, and Samuel Beckett. Happily, many Parisians still call this watering hole their home away from home.

Bercy/Tolbiac

Beneath the looming high-rises of Chinatown lie the cobbled lanes of Butte-aux-Cailles. This tiny hilltop, anchored by the rue de la Butte-aux-Cailles, makes a popular escape for Parisian drinkers who prefer its simple, unassuming charm to the clubs fawned over by trendoids. Near the Seine, many new bars have opened around François Mitterrand's looming Bibliothèque Nationale and inside Bercy Village. On the Seine itself you can find some of the most popular floating bar-clubs.

Folie en Tête (⊠ 33 rue de la Butte aux Cailles, 13ᵉ, Bercy/Tolbiac ☎ 01–45–80–65–99 Ⓜ Corvisart, Place d'Italie), decorated with colorful African percussion instruments, is known for its reggae and jazz.

Frog at Bercy Village (⊠ 25 cour St-Emilion, 12ᵉ, Bercy/Tolbiac ☎ 01–43–40–70–71 Ⓜ Cour St-Emilion), one of the four British-style Frog pubs in Paris, brews its beer (such as Dark de Triomphe and Frog

Natural Blonde) on premises. Set within the renovated stone-and-glass warehouses of the historic Bercy wine district, this bright and airy pub shows live sports matches to a mix of expat students and Parisians.

Hotel Bars

Some of Paris's best hotel bars mix historic pedigrees with hushed elegance—and others go for a modern, edgy luxe. High prices and the fickle Parisian fashion pack mean that only the latest, highly hyped bars draw in locals regularly.

L'Hôtel (✉ 13 rue des Beaux-Arts, 6ᵉ, St-Germain-des-Prés ☎ 01–44–41–99–00 Ⓜ St-Germain-des-Prés) has an exquisite, hushed baroque bar called Le Bélier that makes for the perfect Rive Gauche rendezvous. Designed in typically gorgeous Jacques Garcia style, it evokes the decadent spirit of Oscar Wilde, who lived in a somewhat squalid room upstairs.

Hôtel Le Bristol (✉ 112 rue du Faubourg St-Honoré, 8ᵉ, Champs-Élysées ☎ 01–53–43–43–42 Ⓜ Miromesnil) attracts the rich and powerful with a posh setting that includes weekly fashion shows every Saturday at tea time (reservations required), live piano music nightly, and Pascal Havel's famous Crazy Horse cocktail.

Hôtel Costes (✉ 239 rue St-Honoré, 1ᵉʳ, Louvre/Tuileries ☎ 01–42–44–50–25), cradle of the famed Costes lounge compilation albums, draws many, many big names during the couture show weeks. Mere mortal visitors to this red-velvet Jacques Garcia–designed hive should be prepared for a cool welcome and somewhat dismal service, not to mention sky-high prices.

Hôtel de Crillon (✉ 10 pl. de la Concorde, 8ᵉ, Champs-Élysées ☎ 01–44–71–15–39 Ⓜ Concorde) allures with creamy elegance and antique armchairs. This gilded palace bar, designed originally by sculptor Cesar in 1907, has received a major makeover from fashion designer Sonia Rykiel. Dress smartly (no sneakers or T-shirts) and order the signature Duc de Crillon cocktail (Tattinger Champagne with Armagnac).

Hôtel Lutetia (✉ 45 bd. Raspail, 6ᵉ, St-Germain-des-Prés ☎ 01–49–54–46–46 Ⓜ Sèvres Babylone) has two bars, the Lutece and Ernest. The latter is a seductive boîte with red table lamps, seminude bronze statues, and a large selection of cigars. There's live jazz many nights and piano nightly.

Hôtel Meurice (✉ 228 rue de Rivoli, 1ᵉʳ, Louvre/Tuileries ☎ 01–44–58–10–66 Ⓜ Tuileries) converted its ground-floor Fontainebleau library into a small, intimate bar with dark-wood paneling and huge murals depicting the illustrious royal hunting forests of Fontainebleau. Order a Fragolada cocktail, made with fresh raspberry and strawberry coulis. It's a fashion-industry fave.

Hôtel Plaza Athenée (✉ 25 av. Montaigne, 8ᵉ, Champs-Élysées ☎ 01–53–67–66–00 ✉ Champs-Élysées–Clemenceau) is Paris's perfect chill-out spot, with a sexy, glowing bar designed by Philippe Starck protégé Patrick Jouin and offering one of the most inventive cocktail lists in town: try the acclaimed Rose Royale, with champagne and freshly crushed raspberries.

★ **Murano Urban Resort** (✉ 13 bd. du Temple, 3ᵉ, République ☎ 01–42–71–20–00 Ⓜ Filles du Calvaire, République) is the hip lounge *du jour,* with a never-ending black-stone bar, candy-color fabric wall panels, and a genuinely friendly staff. It overflows nightly with beautiful culture-vultures and fashionistas from the Marais.

Pershing Hall (✉ 49 rue Pierre Charron, 8ᵉ, Champs-Élysées ☎ 01–58–36–58–36 Ⓜ George V) has a stylish lounge designed by Andrée Putnam in muted colors and minimalist lines, and an enormous "vertical garden" in the courtyard. A team of innovative DJs provides the aural backdrop.

FodorśChoice ★ Legendary barman Colin Field presides over **Ritz's Hemingway Bar** (✉ 15 pl. Vendôme, 1ᵉʳ, Louvre/Tuileries ☎ 01–43–16–33–65 Ⓜ Opéra). There's plenty of Papa memorabilia (this is where the writer drank to the liberation of Paris), but you have to wonder if he would have conformed to today's "semiformal" dress code. Across the hall the hotel's original Cambon Bar reopened in late 2004 as a champagne lounge; it was here that Cole Porter composed "Begin the Beguine."

Trocadéro Dokhan's Sofitel Demeure Hôtel (✉ 117 rue Lauriston, 16ᵉ, Trocadéro/Tour Eiffel ☎ 01–53–65–66–99 Ⓜ Trocadéro) has a bar decorated by top Parisian designer Frédéric Méchiche (emerald-velvet walls and gilt Empire-style wainscoting make for a soigné setting). It serves nothing but champagne.

Cabarets

Paris's cabarets range from boîtes once haunted by Picasso and Piaf to those sinful showplaces where *tableaux vivants* offer acres of bare female flesh. These extravaganzas—sadly more Las Vegas than the petticoat vision re-created by Hollywood in Baz Luhrmann's *Moulin Rouge*—are often shunned by Parisians but loved by tourists. You can dine at many of them, but the food is akin to mass catering: prices range from €30 (simple admission plus one drink) to more than €130 (dinner plus show).

FodorśChoice ★ **Au Lapin Agile** (✉ 22 rue des Saules, 18ᵉ, Montmartre ☎ 01–46–06–85–87 Ⓜ Lamarck Caulaincourt), a miraculous survivor from the 19th century, considers itself the doyen of cabarets. Founded in 1860, it still inhabits a modest house, once a favorite subject of painter Maurice Utrillo. At one point owned by Aristide Bruant (immortalized in many Toulouse-Lautrec posters), it became the home away from home for Braque, Modigliani, Apollinaire, and Maurice Vlaminck. The most famous habitué, however, was Picasso, who once paid for a meal with one of his paintings, then promptly went out and painted another, which he named after this place. Don't expect topless dancers. This is an authentic French cabaret of songs, poetry, and humor in a publike setting.

Le Canotier du Pied de la Butte (✉ 62 bd. Rochechouart, 18ᵉ, Montmartre ☎ 01–46–06–02–86 Ⓜ Anvers) played host in the past to Edith Piaf, Jacques Brel, and Maurice Chevalier. Today it has three shows nightly with modern-day songsters interpreting the traditional French repertoire and magicians performing tricks.

Le Caveau de la Bolée (✉ 25 rue de l'Hirondelle, 6ᵉ, Quartier Latin 🕾 01–43–54–62–20 Ⓜ St-Michel) was a prison in the 14th century, but these days you'll be captured by magicians, comics, and mind readers, or on Wednesday you can sing along to French classics à la Yves Montand.

★ **Crazy Horse** (✉ 12 av. George V, 8ᵉ, Champs-Élysées 🕾 01–47–23–85–56 Ⓜ Alma-Marceau) honed striptease to an art. Founded by Alain Bernardin in 1951, it is renowned for pretty dancers and raunchy routines characterized by lots of humor and few clothes.

Lido (✉ 116 bis, av. des Champs-Élysées, 8ᵉ, Champs-Élysées 🕾 01–40–76–56–10 Ⓜ George V) stars the famous Bluebell Girls; the owners claim no show this side of Vegas rivals it for special effects.

★ **Le Limonaire** (✉ 21 rue Bergère, 9ᵉ, Opéra/Grands Boulevards 🕾 01–45–23–33–33 Ⓜ Grands Boulevards), a small restaurant, simply oozes Parisian charm. This is the kind of place where you could imagine Edith Piaf belting out "*Je ne regrette rien.*" At 10 PM, Tuesday–Sunday, food service gives way to singing. One of Le Limonaire's finest guest artists is the modern-day Little Sparrow, Kalifa. There's no entrance fee—singers pass a hat around.

Michou (✉ 80 rue des Martyrs, 18ᵉ, Montmartre 🕾 01–46–06–16–04 Ⓜ Pigalle) is owned by the always blue-clad Michou, famous in Paris circles. The men on stage wear extravagant drag—high camp and parody are the order of the day.

Moulin Rouge (✉ 82 bd. de Clichy, 18ᵉ, Montmartre 🕾 01–53–09–82–82 Ⓜ Blanche), when it opened in 1889, captured an extravagant, circus-like atmosphere that lured Parisians of all social stripes with a garden with a real elephant, donkey rides for the ladies, and the incomparable cancan revue, immortalized for posterity in Toulouse-Lautrec paintings. Today, the cancan is still a popular highlight of what has become a more Vegas-y show, starring 100 dancers, acrobats, ventriloquists, and contortionists, and more than a 1,000 costumes. In another nod toward modernity, there's a strict no-smoking policy. Dinner shows start at 7, with standard shows commencing at 9 and 11 (arrive 30 minutes early; men should wear a jacket and tie).

★ **Paradis Latin** (✉ 28 rue du Cardinal Lemoine, 5ᵉ, Quartier Latin 🕾 01–43–25–28–28 Ⓜ Cardinal Lemoine), in a building by Gustav Eiffel, peppers its shows with acrobatics and special lighting effects, making it the liveliest, busiest, and trendiest cabaret on the Rive Gauche.

Clubs

Paris's over-hyped boîtes de nuit (nightclubs) are both expensive and exclusive—if you're friends with a regular or you've modeled in *Vogue,* you'll have an easier time getting through the door. Cover charges at these spots push the €20 range, with drinks at the bar starting at €10 for a beer. If you're with a group, it helps to call ahead and reserve a table, although you'll be required to order an absurdly priced bottle of liquor. Don't worry if you don't measure up to the model-friendly door policy—it's a stretch to call this scene truly "happening." The snootier spots are chiefly the domain of rich, spoiled teens. Locals looking to boogie stick to the smaller clubs, where the cover ranges from free (usually on slower week-days) to €15 and the focus is on the music and an upbeat atmosphere. Door policies at these venues favor those in designer jeans and sneakers rather than Prada-clad poseurs. Club popularity depends on the night or event, as Parisians are more loyal to certain DJs than venues and often hit two or three places before ending up at one of the many after-parties, which can last until noon the next day.

BASTILLE & EAST PARIS

Les Bains (⊠ 7 rue du Bourg-l'Abbé, 3ᵉ, Marais ☎ 01–48–87–01–80 Ⓜ Éti-enne Marcel), opened in 1978, was one of the hottest clubs in Paris until the star promoters Kathy and David Guetta jumped ship in 2002 and opened their own place near the Champs-Élysées. Today you're likely to see other tourists or French suburbanites dancing to mainstream house music.

Le Balajo (⊠ 9 rue de Lappe, 11ᵉ, Bastille/Nation ☎ 01–47–00–07–87 Ⓜ Bastille), a casual dance club in an old Java ballroom, has been around since 1936. Latin groove, funk, and R&B disco are the standards, with salsa on Wednesday nights and tango on the last Sunday of the month. Thursday is ladies' night with free entrance before 1 AM.

★ **Le Batofar** (⊠ 11 quai François Mauriac, 13ᵉ, Bercy/Tolbiac ☎ 01–56–29–10–33 Ⓜ Bibliothèque) is an old lighthouse tugboat re-fitted with a bar and concert venue. Themes at this trendy spot are eclectic, from live world-beat music to the full gamut of electronic and techno. There are popular after-parties, starting at 6 AM, the first Sunday of the month. Entrance fees are usually reasonable. (Stylish) sneakers are recommended on the slippery deck.

Le Gibus (⊠ 18 rue du Faubourg du Temple, 11ᵉ, République ☎ 01–47–00–78–88 Ⓜ République) is one of Paris's most famous music venues. In more than 30 years there have been upwards of 6,500 concerts and more than 3,000 performers (including the Police, Deep Purple, and Billy Idol). Today the Gibus's cellars are *the* place for trance, techno, hip-hop, hard-core, and jungle.

La Java (⊠ 105 rue du Faubourg du Temple, 10ᵉ, République ☎ 01–42–02–20–52 Ⓜ Belleville), where Edith Piaf and Maurice Cheva-lier made their names, has live Latin music and Cuban jam sessions on Thursday–Saturday from dusk to dawn. Before the party proper gets under way, there are also salsa lessons.

Fodor's Choice
★ **Le Nouveau Casino** (⊠ 109 rue Oberkampf, 11ᵉ, République ☎ 01–43–57–57–40 Ⓜ Parmentier) is a concert hall and club tucked behind the illustrious bar, Café Charbon. Pop and rock concerts prevail during the week, with clubbing on Friday and Saturday from midnight until dawn. Electronic, house, disco, and techno DJs are the standard, with occasional themed minimusic festivals.

La Scène Bastille (⊠ 2 bis, rue des Taillandiers, 11ᵉ, Bastille/Nation ☎ 01–48–06–50–70 Ⓜ Bastille) is one of the more refreshing venues in the Bastille club scene, with a laid-back, eclectic crowd and a cozy lounge atmosphere. Gay Fridays (open to "gays and friends") feature electro-pop music, while Saturday focuses on soul and funk. Tuesday and Wednesday target students, and Sunday features fashionable gay "tea dance" parties.

Le Baron (✉ 6 av. Marceau, 8ᵉ, Champs-Élysées ☎ 01–47–20–04–01 Ⓜ Alma-Marceau), formerly a "hostesse" bar, didn't bother to update its decadent cabaret decor when it opened in fall 2004—that's part of the charm. It fills up nightly with pretty young things and their dates in Italian suits. With a capacity of just 150, this is basically a VIP room, and it has one of the toughest door policies in Paris. Arrive before midnight for the best chance of getting in.

Le Cab (✉ 2 pl. du Palais-Royal, 1ᵉ, Louvre/Tuileries ☎ 01–58–62–56–25 Ⓜ Palais-Royal) is one of the more popular fashion-week clubs, when models, photographers, and stylists bypass the lesser beings at the velvet rope. Improve your chances of entry by arriving in a limo wearing your most expensive sunglasses, or reserving a table for dinner in the ground-level restaurant. There's no cover Wednesday or Thursday.

Les Étoiles (✉ 61 rue Château d'Eau, 10ᵉ, Opéra/Grands Boulevards ☎ 01–47–70–60–56 Ⓜ Château d'Eau), open Thursday–Saturday, is the place for salsa (with a live band). Dinner, highlighting South American specialties, is served 9–11.

Nirvana Lounge (✉ 3 av. Matignon, 8ᵉ, Champs-Élysées ☎ 01–53–89–18–91 Ⓜ Champs-Élysées–Clemenceau) is Claude Challe of Buddha Bar fame's Bollywood-esque haven of mauve and sequins. Evening cocktails are innovative if pricey; the dance scene leaves a little to be desired, with mainstream lounge and disco tunes on some nights and house and R&B on others. Dress skews toward trendy street wear.

★ **Le Rex** (✉ 5 blvd. Poissonnière, 2ᵉ, Opéra/Grands Boulevards ☎ 01–42–36–83–98 Ⓜ Grands Boulevards), open Thursday through Saturday, is the Paris temple of techno and house. On Thursday you'll sometimes find France's most famous DJ, Laurent Garnier, at the turntables. The techno "Automatik" soirees on Friday are particularly popular with students.

Bus Palladium (✉ 6 rue Fontaine, 9ᵉ, Montmartre ☎ 01–53–21–07–33 Ⓜ Pigalle) is trying to return to its rock-club roots of the early 1980s, attracting a fashionable thirtysomething, relaxed crowd. There's no techno—just rock, funk, disco, punk, and R&B. Thursday nights are free from 11:30 PM, and on Tuesday, drinks and entrance are free for *les femmes*.

L'Élysée Montmartre (✉ 72 bd. de Rochechouart, 18ᵉ, Montmartre ☎ 01–55–07–06–00 Ⓜ Anvers) holds extremely popular *bals* (balls) every second and fourth Saturday of the month from 11 PM, where the music runs the gamut of hits from the '40s to the '80s and the DJ is backed up by a 10-piece orchestra.

Les Folies Pigalle (✉ 11 pl. Pigalle, 9ᵉ, Montmartre ☎ 01–48–78–55–25 Ⓜ Pigalle) is a former cabaret decorated like a '30s bordello. The ambience is decadent, and the music is house, techno, R&B, and electro. After-parties get going on Sunday morning.

La Locomotive (✉ 90 bd. de Clichy, 18ᵉ, Montmartre ☎ 01–53–41–88–88 Ⓜ Blanche) is a very inclusive club that doesn't strive for originality, but its three floors rotate pop, house, and R&B, assuring a varied crowd. There's free entry for women on Friday and everyone on weekends before midnight.

LEFT BANK **L'Amnesia** (✉ 33 ave. du Maine, 15ᵉ, Montparnasse ☎ 01–56–80–37–37 Ⓜ Montparnasse Bienvenüe), with its whitewashed walls, fake palm trees, and house music, tries to make clubbers feel like they're on the Côte d'Azur. When it opened beneath the Tour Montparnasse in 2003, the large dance floor and the glamour surrounding owner/rock star Johnny Hallyday were the main draws. A new owner took over in 2005, improved the sound system, toned down the tropical decor, and promised to bring in top DJs.

Dancing La Coupole (✉ 100 bd. du Montparnasse, 14ᵉ, Montparnasse ☎ 01–43–20–14–20 Ⓜ Vavin), the gorgeous dance hall beneath the famous brasserie, has "Latin Fever" nights on Friday from 7:45 PM (for beginners) until dawn. Saturday is the popular "Re-Definition" night of hip-hop, R&B, and afro-zouk from 11:30.

Le RedLight (✉ 34 rue du Départ, 15ᵉ, Montparnasse ☎ 01–42–79–94–53 Ⓜ Montparnasse Bienvenüe) has two giant dance floors playing mainly house and electronic music by big-name international DJs every Friday and Saturday from midnight until dawn. The place draws a casual, mixed crowd, and popular after-parties follow.

WAGG (✉ 62 rue Mazarine, 6ᵉ, St-Germain-des-Prés ☎ 01–55–42–22–00 Ⓜ Odéon) in a vaulted stone cellar that was Jim Morrison's hangout back when it was the Whiskey-a-Go-Go, has been turned into a small, sleek club. Run by the übertrendy London club Fabric, Wagg has state-of-the-art sound and lighting, guest DJs, and large helpings of house techno music. It's beneath the popular Alcazar restaurant.

Gay & Lesbian Bars & Clubs

Gay and lesbian bars and clubs are mostly concentrated in the Marais and include some of the hippest addresses in the city. Keep in mind, however, that clubs fall in and out of favor at lightning speed. The best way to find out what's hot is by picking up a copy of the free weekly *e.m@le* in one of the bars listed below.

For Men & Women

Amnésia Café (✉ 42 rue Vieille-du-Temple, 4ᵉ, Le Marais ☎ 01–42–72–16–94 Ⓜ Rambuteau, St-Paul) has an underlighted bar and Art Deco ceiling paintings that attract a young professional gay and lesbian crowd.

Banana Café (✉ 13 rue de la Ferronnerie, 1ᵉʳ, Beaubourg/Les Halles ☎ 01–42–33–35–31 Ⓜ Châtelet Les Halles) has a trendy, energetic, and scantily clad mixed crowd; dancing on the tables is the norm. Monday night is the "soirée sans interdit"—ooh la la!

L'Open Café (✉ 17 rue des Archives, 4ᵉ, Le Marais ☎ 01–42–72–26–18 Ⓜ Hôtel de Ville) is less of a meat market than neighboring Café Cox, with sunny yellow walls. In summer the crowd spills out onto the street.

Queen (✉ 102 av. des Champs-Élysées, 8ᵉ, Champs-Élysées ☎ 08–92–70–73–30 Ⓜ George V), the mythic gay club of the '90s, is not quite as monumental as it once was, but its doors are still some of the hardest to get through. Boasting a fantastic roster of house DJs, it's known for soirees such as "Cream Fresh," "Overkitsch," and "Disco

Inferno." Queen is mostly gay on Wednesday and Friday–Sunday but mixed the rest of the week.

Mostly Men

★ **Bar d'Art/Le Duplex** (⊠ 25 rue Michel-Le-Comte, 3ᵉ, Beaubourg/Les Halles ☎ 01–42–72–80–86 Ⓜ Rambuteau) teems with young tortured-artist types who enjoy the frequent art exhibitions, alternative music, and dim lighting.

Café Cox (⊠ 15 rue des Archives, 4ᵉ, Le Marais ☎ 01–42–72–08–00 Ⓜ Hôtel de Ville) is a prime gay pickup joint. Behind the smoked-glass windows men line the walls and check out the talent.

Le Dépôt (⊠ 10 rue aux Ours, 3ᵉ, Beaubourg/Les Halles ☎ 01–44–54–96–96 Ⓜ Étienne Marcel) is a cruising bar, club, and backroom. The ever-popular Gay Tea Dance on Sunday (from 2 PM) is held here.

Le Vinyl (⊠ 25 bd. Poissonnière, 2ᵉ, Opéra/Grands Boulevards ☎ 01–40–26–28–30 Ⓜ Grands Boulevards) is the latest name for one of Paris's longest-standing gay nightclubs, formerly known as Le Vogue. A new owner took over in spring 2005 with a new look; it remains a popular electro and house scene.

Mostly Women

Bliss Kfé (⊠ 30 rue du Roi de Sicile, 4ᵉ, Le Marais ☎ 01–42–78–49–36 Ⓜ St-Paul) is a buzzing bar in the heart of the Marais. There is happy hour every evening and a DJ in the tiny bar in the basement on Friday and Saturday evenings. Men are allowed in small numbers on weekdays.

Champmeslé (⊠ 4 rue Chabanais, 2ᵉ, Opéra/Grands Boulevards ☎ 01–42–96–85–20 Ⓜ Bourse) is the hub of lesbian nightlife (open until dawn). Every first Wednesday is Fantasmgothic fetish night for men and women. Thursday night is a cabaret of traditional French songs.

Fodor'sChoice ★ **Le Pulp** (⊠ 25 bd. Poissonnière, 2ᵉ, Opéra/Grands Boulevards ☎ 01–40–26–01–93 Ⓜ Grands Boulevards), one of the rare lesbian clubs in Paris, has some of the best DJs in town playing garage, house, rock, and pop for a mixed crowd Wednesday–Friday. Saturday is for women only, with R&B, dance music, and '80s pop. Entrance is free on Wednesday and Thursday.

Jazz Clubs

No other European city caught onto jazz the way Paris did. From the heady days following World War I, when Josephine Baker and Sidney Bechet swept the city off its feet, through the defiant Django Reinhart–inspired licks of the 1940s to the introduction of bop to Rive Gauche cellars by Art Blakey and Miles Davis in the following decade, Paris has continually been one of the world's most receptive audiences to jazz. It's fitting, then, that its performing calendar offers plenty of variety, including some fine, distinctive local talent. For nightly schedules consult the specialty magazines *Jazz Hot, Jazzman,* or *Jazz Magazine.* Note that nothing gets going until 10 or 11 PM and that entry prices vary widely, from about €7 to more than €20. Also look out for the annual **Villette Jazz Festival** (☎ 01–40–03–75–75 ⊕ www.villette.com), held at the Parc de La Villette every fall, and the **Paris Jazz Festival**

(☎ 01–49–57–24–84 ⊕ www.parcfloraldeparis.com) at the Bois de Vincennes' Parc Floral every weekend in summer.

BEAUBOURG/LES HALLES **Au Duc des Lombards** (✉ 42 rue des Lombards, 1er, Beaubourg/Les Halles ☎ 01–42–33–22–88 Ⓜ Châtelet Les Halles) has modern, contemporary jazz in a dim, romantic bebop venue with decor inspired by the Paris métro.

Fodor'sChoice ★ **New Morning** (✉ 7 rue des Petites-Écuries, 10e, Opéra/Grands Boulevards ☎ 01–45–23–51–41 Ⓜ Château d'Eau) is a premier spot for serious fans of avant-garde jazz, folk, and world music; the look is spartan, the mood reverential.

Le Sunset (✉ 60 rue des Lombards, 1er, Beaubourg/Les Halles ☎ 01–40–26–46–60 Ⓜ Châtelet Les Halles) delivers jazz from both French and American musicians, with an accent on jazz fusion and groove. Concerts start at 10 PM.

Le Sunside (✉ 60 rue des Lombards, 1er, Beaubourg/Les Halles ☎ 01–40–26–21–25 Ⓜ Châtelet Les Halles) is at the same address as Le Sunset. It specializes in more classic traditional jazz and swing; a featured vocalist takes the mike on Monday night. Concerts start at 9 PM.

CHAMPS-ÉLYSÉES **Lionel Hampton Jazz Club** (✉ Méridien Hotel, 81 bd. Gouvion–St-Cyr, 17e, Champs-Élysées ☎ 01–40–68–30–42 Ⓜ Porte Maillot), named for the zingy vibraphonist loved by Parisians, hosts a roster of international jazz musicians in a spacious, comfortable set of rooms.

ÎLE ST-LOUIS & THE RIVE GAUCHE **Caveau de la Huchette** (✉ 5 rue de la Huchette, 5e, Quartier Latin ☎ 01–43–26–65–05 Ⓜ St-Michel), one of the only surviving cellar clubs from the 1940s, is a Paris classic, big with swing dancers and Dixieland musicians.

Le Petit Journal (✉ 71 bd. St-Michel, 5e, Quartier Latin ☎ 01–43–26–28–59 Ⓜ Luxembourg ✉ 13 rue du Commandant-Mouchotte, 14e, Montparnasse ☎ 01–43–21–56–70 Ⓜ Montparnasse Bienvenüe), with two locations, has long attracted the greatest names in French and international jazz. It now specializes in big band (Montparnasse) and Dixieland (St-Michel) jazz and also serves dinner 8:30–midnight.

MONTMARTRE **Bar le Houdon** (✉ 5 rue des Abbesses, 18e, Montmartre ☎ 01–42–62–21–34 Ⓜ Abbesses) transforms from humdrum café to makeshift jazz venue Thursday through Saturday. The musicians are top-notch, the audience is intent, and the price is right. Concerts begin at 9:30.

Pubs

Pubs wooing English-speaking clients with a selection of British and Irish beers are becoming increasingly popular with Parisians. They're also good places to find reasonably priced food at off hours.

Auld Alliance (✉ 80 rue François Miron, 4e, Le Marais ☎ 01–48–04–30–40 Ⓜ St-Paul) has walls adorned with Scottish shields and a bar staff dressed in kilts. There are more than 120 malt whiskeys to choose from, Scottish beer, soccer and rugby on TV, and the odd evening of live music.

CloseUp

AFTER-HOURS RESTAURANTS

STARVING AFTER A WEE-HOURS *bull session? Craving steak au poivre after midnight? Most late-night brasseries and round-the-clock restaurants don't need reservations; here are some of the best.*

Au Chien Qui Fume (✉ 33 rue du Pont-Neuf, 1ᵉʳ, Louvre/Tuileries ☎ 01–42–36–07–42 Ⓜ Les Halles), open until 2 AM, is filled with witty paintings (in the style of old masters) of smoking dogs. Traditional French cuisine and seafood platters are served until 1 AM.

Au Pied de Cochon (✉ 6 rue Coquillière, 1ᵉʳ, Beaubourg/Les Halles ☎ 01–40–13–77–00 Ⓜ Les Halles) once catered to the all-night workers at the adjacent Paris food market. Its Second Empire carvings and gilt have been restored, and traditional dishes like pig's trotters and chitterling sausage still grace the menu. Open 24 hours daily.

Le Bienvenu (✉ 42 rue d'Argout, 2ᵉ, Louvre/Tuileries ☎ 01–42–33–31–08 Ⓜ Louvre) certainly doesn't look like much (check out the slightly kitsch mural on the back wall), but it serves up simple French food and a welcome couscous in the early hours of the morning. Open until 6 AM.

La Cloche d'Or (✉ 3 rue Mansart, 9ᵉ, Montmartre ☎ 01–48–74–48–88 Ⓜ Place de Clichy) is a Paris institution where the likes of the late president François Mitterrand and the dancers from the Moulin Rouge have all dined on its traditional French dishes. It's open until 4 AM every day except Sunday, when it closes at 1 AM. Closed in August.

Les Coulisses (✉ 1 rue St-Rustique, 18ᵉ, Montmartre ☎ 01–42–62–89–99 Ⓜ Abbesses), near picturesque place du Tertre, has the most character of all the late-night restaurants: its red banquettes and 18th-century Venetian mirrors make it look like an Italian theater. The food—

traditional French—is served until 2 AM. In the basement is a club, open Thursday–Saturday.

L'Enfance de Lard (✉ 21 rue Guisarde, 6ᵉ, St-Germain-des-Prés ☎ 01–46–33–89–65 Ⓜ Mabillon, St-Sulpice) is a safe bet for late-night munchies on the Left Bank. Traditional French fare is served until 4 AM Tuesday–Saturday, and until 11:30 PM Sunday and Monday.

Grand Café des Capucines (✉ 4 bd. des Capucines, 9ᵉ, Opéra/Grands Boulevards ☎ 01–43–12–19–00 Ⓜ Opéra), whose exuberant pseudo–Belle Époque dining room matches the mood of the neighboring Opéra, serves excellent oysters, fish, and meat dishes at hefty prices. It's open around the clock.

Le Tambour (✉ 41 rue Montmartre, 2ᵉ, Beaubourg/Les Halles ☎ 01–42–33–06–90 Ⓜ Étienne Marcel, Les Halles) is full of old-fashioned flea-market charm. The owner has one of those quintessentially Parisian mustaches, there is an old métro map on the wall, and advertising signs from yesteryear catch the eye. Come for the traditional French fare of onion soup, foie gras, steak tartare, and confit de canard. It's open from 6 PM to 6:30 AM, last dinner service at 3:30 AM.

Connolly's Corner (✉ 12 rue Mirbel, 5ᵉ, Quartier Latin ☎ 01–43–31–94–22 Ⓜ Censier-Daubenton) is Irish all the way, with Guinness on tap and live music many nights. Just make sure you don't wear a tie—it will be snipped off and stuck on the wall (though you'll be compensated with a free pint).

Frog and Rosbif (✉ 116 rue St-Denis, 2ᵉ, Beaubourg/Les Halles ☎ 01–42–36–34–73 Ⓜ Étienne Marcel) has everything you could want from an English "local." Beers are brewed on premises, and rugby and soccer matches are shown on the giant-screen TV.

The Shebeen (✉ 16 rue Pot de Fer, 5ᵉ, Quartier Latin ☎ 01–45–87–34–43 Ⓜ Place Monge) is a stylish but laid-back bar run by a native South African with open mike on Monday, live music on Thursday, and live sporting events on the TV.

Rock, Pop & World-Music Venues

France's contemporary music scene may not have the mainline rock credentials of the United Kingdom, but in the past few years its international profile has been on the rise. Artists such as Manu Chao, Air, Tarmac, and Les Nubians infuse traditional melodies with innovative beats and the lyricism of the French language. Paris is a great place to catch your favorite bands on tour, in addition to a variety of world music that you might not hear at home. Most places charge about €15–€30 and get going around 11 PM. The best way to find out about upcoming concerts is to consult the bulletin boards in FNAC stores or the weekly entertainment guide *Zurban*.

Le Bataclan (✉ 50 bd. Voltaire, 11ᵉ, République ☎ 01–43–14–35–35 Ⓜ Oberkampf) is a legendary venue for live rock, rap, and reggae in an intimate setting.

Canal Opus (✉ 167 quai de Valmy, 10ᵉ, Canal-St-Martin ☎ 01–40–34–70–00 Ⓜ Louis Blanc), on the picturesque Canal St-Martin, has jazz, pop, and soul concerts.

La Cigale (✉ 120 bd. Rochechouart, 18ᵉ, Montmartre ☎ 01–49–25–81–75 Ⓜ Pigalle) is a great spot to check out indie bands—both French and international—as well as the occasional bigger star.

Divan du Monde (✉ 75 rue des Martyrs, 18ᵉ, Montmartre ☎ 01–42–52–02–46 or 01–40–05–06–99 Ⓜ Anvers) collects a varied crowd, depending on the music of the evening: reggae, soul, funk, or punk. Most nights after the concert a DJ takes over.

L'Élysée Montmartre (✉ 72 bd. Rochechouart, 18ᵉ, Montmartre ☎ 08–92–69–23–92 ⊕ www.elyseemontmartre.com Ⓜ Anvers) dates from Gustave Eiffel, its builder, who, it is hoped, liked a good concert. It's one of the prime venues for emerging French and international rock groups.

Olympia (✉ 28 bd. des Capucines, 9ᵉ, Opéra/Grands Boulevards ☎ 08–92–68–33–68 Ⓜ Madeleine), a legendary venue once favored by Jacques Brel, Edith Piaf, and Art Blakey, still hosts leading French singers and jazz icons like Sonny Rollins. Strangely, the original hall was demolished to make way for underground parking and an identical theater constructed in the same building.

Palais Omnisports de Paris-Bercy (⊠ 8 bd. de Bercy, 12ᵉ, Bastille/Nation 🕾 08–92–69–23–00 Ⓜ Bercy) is the largest venue in Paris; English and American pop stars shake their spangles here.

Zénith (⊠ Parc de La Villette, 211 av. Jean-Jaurès, 19ᵉ, La Villette 🕾 01–42–08–60–00 Ⓜ Porte de Pantin), a large concert hall, primarily stages rock shows; here's your chance to see the White Stripes or Limp Bizkit while surrounded by screaming Parisians.

THE ARTS

It's no secret why some of the world's greatest artists and performers have made Paris their home over the centuries: Parisians are a fantastic audience. The city's culture-vultures and experimental artists have created buzzing circuits of energy for decades. In just about every modern art form you'll find a major movement that took shape here. While Ionesco and Beckett were at work changing the world of theater, gypsy guitarist Django Reinhart was making his mark in jazz, and soon after, *nouvelle vague* (new wave) cinema revolutionized film. Nowadays, despite lavish government subsidies, the city's artistic life doesn't have the avant-garde edge it once did, but Parisians are still as passionate about the arts as ever. In addition, the phenomenal number of movie theaters here makes Paris a cinephile's heaven.

The music and theater season runs September–June; in summer most productions are found at festivals elsewhere in France. There is, however, an excellent festival in July and August called Paris–Quartier d'Été, which attracts international stars of dance, classical music, and jazz. Detailed entertainment listings can be found in the weekly magazines **Pariscope, L'Officiel des Spectacles,** and **Zurban.** Also look for **Aden** and **Figaroscope,** Wednesday supplements to the newspapers *Le Monde* and *Le Figaro,* respectively. Tickets can be purchased at the theater itself; try to get them in advance. The 24-hour hotline and the Web site of the **Paris Tourist Office** (🕾 08–92–68–30–00 in English, €.34/minute ⊕ www.parisinfo.com) are also excellent resources.

Your hotel or a travel agency such as **Opéra Théâtre** (⊠ 7 rue de Clichy, 9ᵉ, Opéra/Grands Boulevards 🕾 01–42–81–98–85 Ⓜ Trinité) may be able to help you get tickets—but they take a 20% commission. Tickets can be purchased at **FNAC stores** (Forum des Halles ⊠ 1–5 rue Pierre Lescot, 3rd level down, 1ᵉʳ, Beaubourg/Les Halles 🕾 08–92–68–36–22 Ⓜ Châtelet Les Halles), especially the one in the Forum des Halles. **Virgin Megastore** (⊠ 52 av. des Champs-Élysées, 8ᵉ, Champs-Élysées 🕾 01–49–53–50–00 Ⓜ Franklin-D.-Roosevelt) also sells theater and concert tickets. Half-price tickets for same-day theater performances are available at the **Kiosques Théâtre** (⊠ Across from 15 pl. de la Madeleine, Opéra/Grands Boulevards Ⓜ Madeleine ⊠ Outside Gare Montparnasse, pl. Raoul Dautry, 15ᵉ, Montparnasse Ⓜ Montparnasse Bienvenüe), open Tuesday–Saturday 12:30–8 and Sunday 12:30–4. Half-price tickets are also available at many private theaters during the first week of each new show. Check the weekly guides for details.

Circus

You don't need to know French to enjoy the circus. Venues change frequently, so it is best to check one of the weekly guides; tickets range from €7 to €39. **Cirque Alexis Gruss** (✉ Pelouse de St-Cloud, Bois de Boulogne, Bois de Boulogne ☎ 01–45–01–71–26 ⊕ www.alexis-gruss.com Ⓜ Ranelagh) is in Paris five months of the year and remains an avowedly old-fashioned production with showy horsemen. From tigers to yaks, dogs, and clowns, **Cirque Diana Moreno Bormann** (✉ 112 rue de la Haie Coq, 19ᵉ, Porte de La Chapelle ☎01–64–05–36–25 ⊕www.cirque-diana-moreno.com Ⓜ Porte d'Aubervilliers) is good for all ages; performances are on Saturday, Sunday, and Wednesday at 3. **Cirque d'Hiver Bouglione** (✉ 110 rue Amelot, 11ᵉ, République ☎ 01–47–00–28–81 Ⓜ Filles du Calvaire ⊕ www.cirquedhiver.com), brings together two famous circus institutions. The beautiful Cirque d'Hiver hall, constructed in 1852, is now home to the Bouglione troupe, known for its rousing spectacle of acrobats, jugglers, clowns, contortionists, trapeze artists, snakes, and doves. **Cirque de Paris** (✉ 115 bd. Charles-de-Gaulle, Villeneuve-la-Garenne ☎ 01–47–99–40–40 Ⓜ Porte de Clignancourt, then Bus 137) offers a "Day at the Circus": a peek behind the scenes in the morning, lunch with the artists, and a performance in the afternoon.

Classical Music

Note that the **Salle Pleyel**, a longtime regular venue for the Orchestre de Paris, is undergoing renovations and will be closed until fall 2006. For updates, log on to ⊕ www.pleyel.com.

Cité de la Musique (✉ In Parc de La Villette, 221 av. Jean-Jaurès, 19ᵉ, La Villette ☎ 01–44–84–44–84 Ⓜ Porte de Pantin) presents a varied program of classical, experimental, and world-music concerts in a postmodern setting.

IRCAM (✉ 1 pl. Igor-Stravinsky, 4ᵉ, Beaubourg/Les Halles ☎ 01–44–78–48–43 Ⓜ Châtelet Les Halles, Hôtel de Ville) organizes concerts of contemporary classical music, heavily influenced by the latest technology, in its own theater and at the Centre Pompidou next door.

Maison de Radio France (✉ 116 av. du Président-Kennedy, 16ᵉ, Passy-Auteuil ☎ 01–56–40–15–16 Ⓜ RER: Maison de Radio France) is home to France's many state-owned radio stations as well as the Orchestre National de France and Orchestre Philharmonique de Radio France. In addition to the program of orchestral concerts on-site, the public can also attend live broadcasts and recordings for free, space permitting; show up an hour in advance at the Grand Hall for tickets.

★ **Salle Cortot** (✉ 78 rue Cardinet, 17ᵉ, Parc Monceau ☎ 01–47–63–85–72 Ⓜ Malesherbes) is an acoustic gem, built by Auguste Perret in 1918. At the time he promised to construct "a hall that sounds like a violin." Today jazz and classical concerts are held here. There are also free student recitals at noon and 12:30 on Tuesday and Thursday.

Salle Gaveau (✉ 45 rue de la Boétie, 8ᵉ, Champs-Élysées ☎ 01–49–53–05–07 Ⓜ Miromesnil) is a small gold-and-white hall of only 1,200 seats with a distinctly Parisian allure and fantastic acoustics. It plays host to chamber music, piano, and vocal recitals.

Théâtre des Champs-Élysées (⊠ 15 av. Montaigne, 8ᵉ, Champs-Élysées ☎ 01–49–52–50–50 Ⓜ Alma-Marceau) was the scene of the famous Battle of the Rite of Spring in 1913, when police had to be called in after the audience started ripping up the seats in outrage at Stravinsky's *Le Sacre du Printemps* and Nijinsky's choreography. Today this elegantly restored, plush Art Deco temple is worthy of a visit if only for its architecture. It also hosts top-notch opera, dance performances, jazz, world music, and chamber concerts.

Church & Museum Concerts

Paris has a never-ending stream of free or inexpensive lunchtime and evening church concerts, ranging from organ recitals to choral music and orchestral works, held everywhere from the cathedral of Notre-Dame to modest local spaces. Some are scheduled as part of the **Festival d'Art Sacré** (☎ 01–44–70–64–10 for information), which takes place between mid-November and Christmas. Check weekly listings or flyers posted outside the churches themselves for information; telephone numbers for most church concerts vary with the organizer.

★ Following are the best venues for church concerts. **Sainte-Chapelle** (⊠ 4 bd. du Palais, 1ᵉʳ, Île de la Cité ☎ 01–42–77–65–65 Ⓜ Cité), a Gothic tour-de-force of shimmering stained glass, holds memorable candlelight concerts March through November. Make reservations well in advance. **La Madeleine** (⊠ Pl. de la Madeleine, 8ᵉ, Opéra ☎ 01–44–51–69–00 ⊕ www.eglise-lamadeleine.com Ⓜ Madeleine) has regular choral and orchestral productions, such as Mozart's *Requiem* and Schubert's *Ave Maria*. **St-Ephrem** (⊠ 17 rue des Carmes, 5ᵉ, Quartier Latin Ⓜ Maubert Mutualité) is a popular venue for both soloists and choral groups. **St-Germain-des-Prés** (⊠ Pl. St-Germain-des-Prés, 6ᵉ, St-Germain-des-Prés ☎ 01–43–25–41–71 Ⓜ St-Germain-des-Prés), Paris's oldest church, is known for both organ recitals and larger concerts. **St-Julien-Le-Pauvre** (⊠ 23 quai de Montebello, 5ᵉ, Quartier Latin Ⓜ St-Michel), by far the smallest and most intimate concert space, is a magical place for classical music of all kinds. Tickets for many of these concerts can be purchased through **AMP Concerts** (⊠ 128 rue de l'abbé Groult, 15ᵉ, Montparnasse ☎ 01–42–50–96–18 Ⓜ Félix-Faure). For concerts at **Notre-Dame** (⊠ Pl. du Parvis Notre-Dame, 4ᵉ, Île de la Cité Ⓜ Cité) obtain tickets through **Musique Sacrée à Notre-Dame** (☎ 01–44–41–49–99).

Several museums also host regular classical concerts. Concert tickets are generally sold separately, rather than included in museum admission. Paris weeklies such as *Pariscope* publish performance schedules. Some of the best classical concerts are held in the **Auditorium du Louvre** (⊠ Palais du Louvre, 1ᵉʳ, Louvre/Tuileries ☎ 01–40–20–55–55 Ⓜ Palais-Royal, Louvre), which presents chamber music, string quartets, and a special series of promising new musicians on Thursdays. The **Musée d'Orsay** (⊠ 1 rue de Bellechasse, 7ᵉ, St-Germain-des-Prés ☎ 01–40–49–47–57 Ⓜ RER: Musée d'Orsay) regularly holds small-scale concerts (song cycles, piano recitals, or chamber music) in the lower-level auditorium. The **Musée du Moyen Age** (⊠ 6 pl. Paul Painlevé, 5ᵉ, Quartier Latin ☎ 01–53–73–78–16

Ⓜ Cluny–La Sorbonne) stages medieval music concerts between October and July, including the free *l'Heure Musicale* every Friday at 12:30 and Saturday at 4.

There is a fine Chopin Festival at the delightfully picturesque **Orangerie de Bagatelle** (✉ Parc de Bagatelle, av. de Longchamp, 16ᵉ, Bois de Boulogne ☎ 01–45–00–22–19 Ⓜ Porte Maillot, then bus 244) in late June and early July. In August and September there are also free outdoor classical concerts in the **Parc Floral** (☎ 01–49–57–24–84) of the Bois de Vincennes on weekends at 4 (entrance to the park itself is €3).

Dance

The biggest news on the French dance scene is the spanking new National Dance Center (Centre National de la Danse), opened just outside Paris in late 2004, as a center for teaching, rehearsing, exhibiting, and otherwise supporting the dancing arts. As a rule, more avant-garde or up-and-coming choreographers show their works in the smaller performance spaces in the Bastille and the Marais and in theaters in nearby suburbs. Classical ballet is found in places as varied as the opera house and the sports stadium. Tickets cost from €5 to €160 for the more elaborate National Opera productions, but most venues hover around the €15–€25 range, with discounts for limited-visibilty seats, students, and seniors.

Centre National de la Danse (✉ 1 rue Victor Hugo, Pantin ☎ 01–41–83–27–27 Ⓜ Hoche or RER: Pantin), sidelined by politics and budget problems for a decade, finally opened in a former jail on the canal of the Pantin suburb of Paris. Revived with a contemporary architectural twist, the space is dedicated to supporting professional dancers, with classes, 11 rehearsal studios, and a multimedia dance library. There's also a regular program of performances, expositions, and conferences open to the public.

Maison des Arts de Créteil (✉ 1 pl. Salvador Allende, Creteil ☎ 01–45–13–19–19 Ⓜ Créteil Préfecture), just outside Paris, is a fine venue for dance; it often attracts top-flight international and French companies, such as Blanca Li, Bill T. Jones, and the annual EXIT Festival.

FodorśChoice
★ **Opéra Garnier** (✉ pl. de l'Opéra, 9ᵉ, Opéra/Grands Boulevards ☎ 08–92–89–90–90 Ⓜ Opéra) is the sumptuous Napoléon III home of the well-reputed Ballet de l'Opéra National de Paris, and rarely hosts other dance companies. The venue has presented *Wuthering Heights* and *Orpheus and Eurydice* and hosted the Merce Cunningham Dance Company. Seat prices range from €7–€160. Note that many of the cheaper seats have obstructed views, more of an obstacle than in opera performances.

Théâtre de la Bastille (✉ 76 rue de la Roquette, 11ᵉ, Bastille/Nation ☎ 01–43–57–42–14 Ⓜ Bastille) merits mention as an example of the innovative activity in the Bastille area; it has an enviable record as a launching pad for tomorrow's modern-dance stars.

Théâtre de la Cité Internationale (✉ 17 bd. Jourdan, 14ᵉ, Parc Montsouris ☎ 01–43–13–50–50 Ⓜ RER: Cité Universitaire) is a complex of three theaters in the heart of the international student residence, the Cité Universitaire. It often stages young avant-garde companies and is also the main venue for the Presqu'Îles de Danse festival in February.

Théâtre de la Ville (⊠ 2 pl. du Châtelet, 4ᵉ, Beaubourg/Les Halles Ⓜ Châtelet ⊠ 31 rue des Abbesses, 18ᵉ, Montmartre Ⓜ Abbesses ☎ 01–42–74–22–77 for both) is *the* place for contemporary dance. Troupes like La La La Human Steps and Anne-Teresa de Keersmaeker's Rosas company are presented here. Book early; shows sell out quickly.

Film

The French call movies the *septième art* (seventh art) and discuss the latest releases with the same intensity as they do gallery openings or theatrical debuts. That's not to say they don't like popcorn flicks, but you're as likely to see people standing in line for a Hitchcock retrospective or a hard-hitting documentary as for a Hollywood cream puff. Paris has hundreds of cinemas showing contemporary and classic French and American movies, as well as a tempting menu packed with independent, international, and documentary films. Most theaters are in the principal tourist areas, such as the Champs-Élysées, boulevard des Italiens near the Opéra, Châtelet, and Odéon, and run English-language films undubbed, with subtitles. When checking movie listings, note that *v.o.* means *version originale,*; films that are dubbed are indicated with *v.f.* (*version française*). Admission runs €6–€9.50; many cinemas have reduced rates on certain days (normally Monday, sometimes Wednesday) or for early shows. Some theaters post two showtimes: the *séance,* when the commercials, previews, and, sometimes, short films begin; and the feature presentation, which usually starts 10–25 minutes later. Paris has many theaters in addition to the Cinémathèque Française that show classic and independent films, often found in the Quartier Latin. Showings are often organized around retrospectives. Here are some noteworthy independent cinemas.

First-Run Films

Fodor'sChoice **La Pagode** (⊠ 57 bis, rue de Babylone, 7ᵉ, Trocadéro/Tour Eiffel
★ ☎ 01–45–55–48–48 Ⓜ St-François Xavier)—where else but in Paris would you find movies screened in an antique pagoda? A Far East fantasy, this structure was built in 1896 for the wife of the owner of Le Bon Marché department store. By the 1970s it had been slated for demolition but was then saved by a grass-roots wave of support spearheaded by director Louis Malle. (At this writing, some restoration work was in progress, due to finish in late 2005.) Though the fare is standard, the surroundings are enchanting—who can resist seeing a flick in the silk-and-gilt Salle Japonaise? Come early to have tea in the bamboo-fringed garden (summer only).

Gaumont Grand Écran (⊠ 30 pl. d'Italie, 13ᵉ, Chinatown ☎ 08–92–69–66–96 Ⓜ Place d'Italie) boasts the biggest screen in Paris. **Grand Rex** (⊠ 1 bd. Poissonnière, 2ᵉ, Opéra/Grands Boulevards ☎ 08–92–68–05–96 Ⓜ Bonne Nouvelle) opened in 1932 with a mammoth house of 2,800 seats. **Max Linder Panorama** (⊠ 24 bd. Poissonnière, 9ᵉ, Opéra/Grands Boulevards ☎ 08–92–68–50–52 Ⓜ Grands Boulevards), opened in 1932, is named for French burlesque actor Max Linder; check out the

marble floors and Florentine stucco on the walls. **MK2 Bibliothèque**
(✉ 128–162 av. de France, 13ᵉ, Tolbiac ☎ 08–92–69–84–84 Ⓜ Quai
de la Gare, Bibliothèque) is a slick new cineplex in the shadow of Mitterrand's National Library, with trademark two-person chairs in scarlet red, restaurants, music and DVD shops, and even a DJ bar, the
Limelight. **MK2 Quai de Seine** (✉ 14 quai de Seine, 19ᵉ, Canal-St-Martin ☎ 08–92–68–14–07 Ⓜ Stalingrad), a restaurant–cinema complex
showing major releases, is well worth a visit for its location on the Bassin
de la Villette. **UGC Ciné-Cité Bercy** (✉ 2 cour St-Emilion, 12ᵉ, Bercy
☎ 08–92–70–00–00 Ⓜ Cour St-Emilion) is a huge 18-screen complex
in the outdoor shopping complex called Bercy Village—for sound and
seating, it's one of the best.

Special Screenings

For the cinephile brought up on Federico Fellini, Ingmar Bergman, and
Pierre Resnais, the main mecca is the famed **Cinémathèque Française** (✉ 51
rue de Bercy, 12ᵉ, Bercy ☎ 01–56–26–01–01 Ⓜ Bercy), which pioneered the preservation of early films. Its new home, in the former
American Center designed by Frank Gehry, was set to open in fall 2005
with a grand retrospective of Jean Renoir and will include a museum
and video library, as well as four theaters.

Accatone (✉ 20 rue Cujas, 5ᵉ, Quartier Latin ☎ 01–46–33–86–86
Ⓜ Cluny–La Sorbonne, Luxembourg) shows mainly European art films.
Action Écoles (✉ 23 rue des Écoles, 5ᵉ, Quartier Latin ☎ 01–43–29–79–89
Ⓜ Maubert Mutualité) specializes in American classics and cult films.
Champo (✉ 51 rue des Écoles, 5ᵉ, Quartier Latin ☎ 01–43–54–51–60
Ⓜ Cluny–La Sorbonne) often programs Hitchcock films. **Grande Action**
(✉ 5 rue des Écoles, 5ᵉ, Quartier Latin ☎ 01–43–29–44–40 Ⓜ Cardi-
nal Lemoine, Jussieu) usually runs American classics. **Quartier Latin** (✉ 9
rue Champollion, 5ᵉ, Quartier Latin ☎ 01–43–26–84–65 Ⓜ Cluny–La
Sorbonne) is one of a number of cinemas near the Sorbonne screening
first-runs and foreign films. **St-André-des-Arts** (✉ 30 rue St-André-des-
Arts, 6ᵉ, Quartier Latin ☎ 01–43–26–48–18 Ⓜ St-Michel) is one of the
best cinemas in Paris and generally has an annual festival devoted to a
single director, such as Bergman or Tarkovski.

Le Balzac (✉ 1 rue Balzac, 8ᵉ, Champs-Élysées ☎ 01–45–61–10–60
Ⓜ George V) often holds talks by directors before screenings. **Cinéma
des Cinéastes** (✉ 7 av. de Clichy, 17ᵉ, Montmartre ☎ 01–53–42–40–20
Ⓜ Place de Clichy) shows previews of feature films, as well as documentaries, short subjects, and rarely shown movies; it's in an old cabaret
transformed into a movie theater and wine bar. **L'Entrepôt** (✉ 7 rue
Francis-de-Pressensé, 14ᵉ, Montparnasse ☎ 01–45–40–07–50 Ⓜ Per-
nety) has special screenings, and it has a popular café, bar, restaurant,
and live concerts. **Le Forum des Images** (✉ Forum des Halles, Porte St-
Eustache entrance, 1ᵉʳ, Beaubourg/Les Halles ☎ 01–44–76–63–07 Ⓜ Les
Halles) organizes thematic viewings from its archive of films and videos
on the city of Paris. For €5.50 you can watch four films and two hours
of video and can surf the Web for 30 minutes. **La Géode** (✉ At Cité des
Sciences et de l'Industrie, Parc de La Villette, 26 av. Corentin-Cariou,
19ᵉ, La Villette ☎ 08–92–68–45–40 Ⓜ Porte de La Villette) screens wide-

angle Omnimax films—usually documentaries—on a gigantic spherical surface. In summer at the **Parc de La Villette** (Ⓜ Porte de Pantin, Porte de La Villette) free movies are shown outdoors on a large screen. Most people take along a picnic. You can also rent deck chairs by the entrance.

Galleries

Art galleries are scattered throughout the city, but those focusing on the same aesthetic period are often clustered in one neighborhood. There are many contemporary art galleries, for instance, near the Centre Pompidou, the Musée Picasso, and the Bastille Opéra. The city's hottest avant-garde art scene is on and around the rue Louise Weiss near the Bibliothèque François-Mitterrand in the 13ᵉ, where a handful of young galleries continue to attract crowds and accolades for their internationally minded expositions. Around St-Germain the galleries are generally more traditional, and works by old masters and established modern artists dominate the galleries around rue du Faubourg St-Honoré and avenue Matignon. What's known as the **Carré Rive Gauche,** around rue du Bac in St-Germain, shelters dozens of art and antiques galleries on its narrow streets. Log on to www.carrerivegauche.com for current show schedules.

Note that it's not uncommon for galleries to be hidden away in courtyards, with the only sign of their presence a small plaque on the front of the building; take these as invitations to push through the doors. To help you plot your gallery course, get a free copy of the map published by the **Association des Galeries**; it's available at many of the galleries listed below and on the Web at www.associationdesgaleries.org. For listings of antiques galleries, *see* Chapter 6.

The Parisian art world is abuzz because the main French auctioneers, most based at the **Hôtel Drouot** (⊠ 9 rue Drouot, 9ᵉ, Opéra/Grands Boulevards ☎ 01–48–00–20–20 Ⓜ Richelieu Drouot), have lost their monopoly on art auctions in Paris. **Christie's** (⊠ 9 av. Matignon, 8ᵉ, Champs-Élysées ☎ 01–40–76–85–85 Ⓜ Champs-Élysées Clémenceau) has opened shop with lavish showrooms and a calendar of auctions. **Sotheby's** (⊠ 76 rue du Faubourg St-Honoré, 8ᵉ, Champs-Élysées ☎ 01–53–05–53–05 Ⓜ St-Philippe-du-Roule), Christie's arch rival, has an ambitious calendar of sales scheduled.

Agathe Gaillard (⊠ 3 rue Pont Louis-Philippe, 4ᵉ, Le Marais ☎ 01–42–77–38–24 Ⓜ Hôtel de Ville) was the first person to open a photo gallery in Paris way back in 1975. Since then she has exhibited many of the great names of the genre, from André Kertész and Henri Cartier-Bresson to Edouard Boubat. Today she also represents a stable of up-and-coming stars.

FodorśChoice ★ **Air de Paris** (⊠ 32 rue Louise Weiss, 13ᵉ, Tolbiac ☎ 01–44–23–02–77 Ⓜ Chevaleret), named for Marcel Duchamp's famous bottle of air, is one of the most prominent of the avant-garde galleries, with experimental artists such as Liam Gillick, Paul McCarthy, and Olaf Breuning. Don't miss the Random Gallery, a collaboration between Air de Paris and the neighboring **Gallery Praz-Delavallade,** consisting of visiting artist exhibitions in the storefront windows between the two galleries.

Artcurial (✉ 61 av. Montaigne, 8ᵉ, Champs-Élysées ☎ 01–42–99–16–16 Ⓜ Franklin-D.-Roosevelt) has the feel of a museum shop. It sells artist-designed decorative objects and exhibits works by such artists as Bram van Velde and Zao Wou-Ki.

Enviedart (✉ 24 rue Treilhard, 8ᵉ, Champs-Élysées ☎ 01–53–30–00–10 Ⓜ Miromesnil) incorporates a wide range of contemporary styles in its impressive collection. They pull off an admirable number of intriguing shows from emerging names such as Yanne Kintgen, Hanna Sidorowicz, and Yang Din.

Galerie Arnoux (✉ 27 rue Guénégaud, 6ᵉ, St-Germain-des-Prés ☎ 01–46–33–04–66 Ⓜ Odéon), one of many galleries on this street, specializes in abstract painting of the '50s, as well as in the works of young painters and sculptors.

Galerie Camera Obscura (✉ 268 bd. Raspail, 14ᵉ, Montparnasse ☎ 01–45–45–67–08 Ⓜ Raspail) is a small photography gallery with a very Zen-like atmosphere. Photographers represented include Lucien Hervé, Willy Ronis, and Yasuhiro Ishimoto.

Galerie Claude Bernard (✉ 5 rue des Beaux-Arts, 6ᵉ, St-Germain-des-Prés ☎ 01–43–26–97–07 Ⓜ St-Germain-des-Prés) is very well established in the domain of traditional figurative work.

Galerie Dina Vierny (✉ 36 rue Jacob, 6ᵉ, St-Germain-des-Prés ☎ 01–42–60–23–18 Ⓜ St-Germain-des-Prés) was set up after the war by the former muse of sculptor Aristide Maillol. Since then she has discovered artists such as Serge Poliakoff, Vladimir Yankelevsky, and Ilya Kabakov.

Galerie Lelong (✉ 13 rue de Téhéran, 8ᵉ, Miromesnil ☎ 01–45–63–13–19 Ⓜ Miromesnil), which also has galleries in New York and Zurich, represents a mix of contemporary artists.

Galerie Louis Carré (✉ 10 av. de Messine, 8ᵉ, Miromesnil ☎ 01–45–62–57–07 Ⓜ Miromesnil) has a long history of promoting French artists, including Jean Bazaine, but it is not lost in the past.

Galerie Maeght (✉ 42 rue du Bac, 7ᵉ, St-Germain-des-Prés ☎ 01–45–48–45–15 Ⓜ Rue du Bac) is the Paris branch of the Fondation Maeght in St-Paul-de-Vence. You'll find paintings by contemporary artists such as Paul Rebeyrolle and Marco del Re, as well as books, prints, and reasonably priced posters.

Galerie Templon (✉ In courtyard of 30 rue Beaubourg, 3ᵉ, Beaubourg/Les Halles ☎ 01–42–72–14–10 Ⓜ Rambuteau) was the first to bring American artists to Paris in the '60s; now it represents artists from various countries, including French star Jean-Pierre Raynaud.

★ **Galerie 213** (✉ 58 rue de Charlot, 3ᵉ, Le Marais ☎ 01–43–22–83–23 Ⓜ Filles du Calvaire) is owned by Marion de Beaupré, former agent of top photographers such as Peter Lindbergh and Paolo Roversi. In an 18th-century building in the Marais, the gallery exhibits work by the likes of Elger Esser, Gueorgui Pinkhassov, and Guido Mocafico. Up front is a bookstore.

Galerie Yvon Lambert (✉ 108 rue Vieille-du-Temple, 3ᵉ, Le Marais ☎ 01–42–71–09–33 Ⓜ St-Sébastien Froissart) is run by the man known to the French as the discoverer of minimalism and conceptual art—indeed, one of his more famous exploits was his sale of a painting to a blind man. Over the years he has exhibited everyone from Daniel Buren and Christo to Sol Lewitt and Julian Schnabel. Today he exhibits artists like Jenny Holzer, Douglas Gordon, and Christian Boltanski.

Joyce (✉ Palais-Royal, 9 rue de Valois, 1ᵉʳ, Louvre/Tuileries ☎ 01–40–15–03–06 Ⓜ Palais-Royal) is a gallery and boutique set up by successful Asian retailer Joyce Ma, who regularly invites Asian artists to show their work.

Louvre des Antiquaires (✉ 2 pl. du Palais-Royal, 1ᵉʳ, Louvre/Tuileries ☎ 01–42–97–27–27 Ⓜ Palais-Royal) is an elegant multifloor complex where 250 of Paris's leading dealers showcase their rarest objects, including Louis XV furniture, tapestries, and antique jewelry.

★ **Thaddaeus Ropac** (✉ 7 rue Debelleyme, 3ᵉ, Le Marais ☎ 01–42–72–99–00 Ⓜ St-Sébastien Froissart) is at the cutting-edge crossover between fashion and art. Ropac represents some of the contemporary scene's hippest artists, including Tom Sachs, Sylvie Fleury, and Yasumasa Morimura.

Opera

Paris offers some of the best opera in the world—and thousands know it. Consequently, getting tickets to the two main venues, the **Opéra de la Bastille** and the **Opéra Garnier,** can be difficult on short notice, so it is a good idea to plan ahead. Check performances at www.opera-de-paris.com or in the Paris Tourist Office's *Saison de Paris* booklet. Prices for tickets start at €5 for standing room (at the Opéra Bastille only) to €160. A word of caution: buying from a scalper is risky, as some sell counterfeit tickets.

Opéra de la Bastille (✉ pl. de la Bastille, 12ᵉ, Bastille/Nation ☎ 08–92–89–90–90 ⊕ www.opera-de-paris.fr Ⓜ Bastille), the ultramodern facility built in 1989 and designed by architect Carlos Ott, has taken over the role of Paris's main opera house from the Opéra Garnier. Like the building, performances tend to be on the avant-garde side—you're just as likely to see a contemporary adaptation of *La Bohème* as you are to hear Kafka set to music. Tickets for the Opéra de Paris productions range from €5 to €150 and go on sale at the box office two weeks before any given show or a month ahead by phone. The opera season usually runs September through July, and the box office is open Monday–Saturday 11–6:30.

Opéra Comique (✉ 5 rue Favart, 2ᵉ, Opéra/Grands Boulevards ☎ 08–25–00–00–58 ⊕ www.opera-comique.com Ⓜ Richelieu Drouot) is a jewel of an opera house run by France's enfant terrible theater director Jérôme Savary. As well as staging operettas, the hall also hosts modern dance, classical concerts, and vocal recitals. Tickets cost €7–€60 and can be purchased at the theater, by mail, online, or by phone.

FodorśChoice
★ **Opéra Garnier** (✉ pl. de l'Opéra, 9ᵉ, Opéra/Grands Boulevards ☎ 08–92–89–90–90 ⊕ www.opera-de-paris.fr Ⓜ Opéra), the magnificent and magical former haunt of the Phantom, painter Edgar Degas, and any number of legendary opera stars, still hosts occasional performances of the Opéra de Paris, along with a fuller calendar of dance performances, as the auditorium is the official home of the Ballet de l'Opéra National de Paris. The grandest opera productions are usually mounted at the Opéra de la Bastille, while the Garnier now presents smaller-scale operas such as Mozart's *La Clemenza di Tito* and *Così Fan Tutte.* Gor-

geous though the Garnier is, its tiara-shape theater means that many seats have limited sight lines, so it's best to ask specifically what the sight lines are when booking (partial view in French is *visibilité partielle*). Needless to say, the cheaper seats are often those with partial views—of course, views of Garnier's house could easily wind up being much more spectacular than any sets on stage, so it's not really a loss. Seats go on sale at the box office two weeks before any given show or a month ahead by phone or online; you must go in person to buy the cheapest tickets. Last-minute discount tickets, if available, are offered 15 minutes before a performance for seniors and anyone under 28. The box office is open 11–6:30 daily.

Théâtre Musical de Paris (⊠ Pl. du Châtelet, 1ᵉʳ, Beaubourg/Les Halles ☎ 01–40–28–28–40 ⊕ www.chatelet-theatre.com Ⓜ Châtelet), better known as the Théâtre du Châtelet, puts on some of the finest opera productions in the city and regularly attracts international divas like Cecilia Bartoli and Anne-Sofie von Otter. It also plays host to classical concerts, dance performances, and the occasional play.

Puppet Shows

On most Wednesday, Saturday, and Sunday afternoons, the Guignol—the French equivalent of Punch and Judy—can be seen going through their ritualistic battles in a number of Paris's parks. All but the Jardins du Ranelagh have weatherproof performance spaces called the *Théâtre de Marionnettes*. Entrance costs €2.50–€4. All performances are in French. Another possibility is Le Lucernaire (*see* Theater, *below*).

Guignol du Jardin d'Acclimatation (⊠ 16ᵉ, Bois de Boulogne ☎ 01–45–01–53–52 Ⓜ Sablons) is a popular amusement park for toddlers. The entrance fee (€2.50) to the park includes admission to the puppet show. Other attractions, such as the carousel and circus, require tickets.

Marionnettes du Champ de Mars (⊠ 7ᵉ, Trocadéro/Tour Eiffel ☎ 01–48–56–01–44 Ⓜ École Militaire) is an enclosed theater a stone's throw from the Tour Eiffel that often puts on the stories of Charles Perrault, such as *Puss in Boots*.

Marionnettes du Jardin du Luxembourg (⊠ 6ᵉ, St-Germain-des-Prés ☎ 01–43–26–46–47 Ⓜ Vavin) has been entertaining children since 1933 and stages the most traditional performances, including *Pinocchio* and *The Three Little Pigs*.

Theater

A number of theaters line the Grands Boulevards between the Opéra and République, but there is no Paris equivalent to Broadway or the West End. Shows are mostly in French, with a few notable exceptions listed here and in the free *Paris Voice* magazine (⊕ www.parisvoice.com). English-language theater groups playing in various venues throughout Paris include the **International Players** (⊕ www.internationalplayers.info) and the **Lester McNutt Company** (⊕ www.colestermcnutt.com). Information about performances can be obtained at ⊕www.theatreonline.fr, which lists 170 theaters, offers critiques, and provides an online reservation service (in French). Ticket prices for theater productions in Paris are generally €15–€35. Broadway-scale singing-and-dancing musicals are staged at either the Palais des Sports or the Palais des Congrès.

Bouffes du Nord (✉ 37 bis, bd. de la Chapelle, 10ᵉ, Stalingrad/La Chapelle ☎ 01–46–07–34–50 Ⓜ La Chapelle) is the wonderfully atmospheric, slightly decrepit home of English director Peter Brook, who regularly delights with his wonderful experimental productions in French and, sometimes, English, too.

Café de la Gare (✉ 41 rue du Temple, 4ᵉ, Le Marais ☎ 01–42–78–52–51 Ⓜ Hôtel de Ville) is a fun spot to experience a particularly Parisian form of theater, the *café-théâtre*—part satire, part variety revue, riddled with slapstick humor, and performed in a café salon. You need a good grasp of French slang and current events to keep up with many of the jokes.

La Cartoucherie (✉ In Bois de Vincennes, Bois de Vincennes ☎ 01–43–74–88–50 or 01–43–74–24–08 Ⓜ Château de Vincennes, then shuttle bus or bus 112), a complex of five theaters (Théâtre du Soleil, Théâtre de l'Aquarium, Théâtre de la Tempête, Théâtre de l'Epée de Bois, and the Théâtre du Chaudron) in a former munitions factory, turns cast and spectators into an intimate theatrical world. The resident director is the revered Ariane Mnouchkine. Go early for a simple meal; the cast often helps serve "in character."

Comédie des Champs-Élysées (✉ 15 av. Montaigne, 8ᵉ, Champs-Élysées ☎ 01–53–23–99–19 Ⓜ Alma-Marceau) offers fine productions in a theater neighboring the larger Théâtre des Champs-Élysées. This is where Yasmina Reza's international hit play *Art* first hit the boards.

★ **Comédie Française** (✉ pl. Colette, 1ᵉʳ, Louvre/Tuileries ☎ 01–44–58–15–15 Ⓜ Palais-Royal ✉ **Studio Théâtre** ✉ Galerie du Carrousel du Louvre, 99 rue de Rivoli, 1ᵉ, Louvre/Tuileries ☎ 01–44–58–98–54 Ⓜ Palais-Royal ✉ **Théâtre du Vieux Colombier** ✉ 21 rue Vieux Colombier, 6ᵉ, St-Germain-des-Prés ☎ 01–44–39–87–00 Ⓜ St-Sulpice) dates from 1680 and is the most hallowed institution in French theater. It specializes in classical French plays by the likes of Racine, Molière, and Marivaux. Reserve seats in person about two weeks in advance, or turn up an hour beforehand and wait in line for cancellations.

Le Lucernaire (53 rue Notre-Dame-des-Champs, 6ᵉ, Montparnasse ☎ 01–45–44–57–34 Ⓜ Notre-Dame-des-Champs) bats.1000 as far as cultural centers are concerned. With two theaters (six performances per night), three movie screens, an art gallery, and a bookstore, it caters to young intellectuals—and thanks to the puppet shows (Wednesday and Saturday), their children too.

Odéon–Théâtre de l'Europe (✉ pl. de l'Odéon, 6ᵉ, St-Germain-des-Prés ☎ 01–44–85–40–00 Ⓜ Odéon), once home to the Comédie Française, has today made pan-European theater its primary focus, offering a variety of European-language productions in Paris. After three years of extensive renovations, the theater is scheduled to re-open in fall 2005.

Sudden Theatre (✉ 14 bis, rue Ste-Isaure, 18ᵉ, Montmartre ☎ 01–42–62–35–00 Ⓜ Jules Joffrin) is a tiny, contemporary theater and acting academy with regular English-language productions.

Théâtre Darius Milhaud (✉ 80 allée Darius Milhaud, 19ᵉ, La Villette ☎ 01–42–01–92–26 Ⓜ Porte de Pantin) shows classics by Camus and Beaudelaire, as well as occasional productions in English.

Théâtre de la Huchette (✉ 23 rue de la Huchette, 5ᵉ, Quartier Latin ☎ 01–43–26–38–99 Ⓜ St-Michel) is a highlight for Ionesco admirers; this tiny Rive Gauche theater has been staging *The Bald Soprano* every night since 1950! (Note that the box office is open only Monday–Saturday 5 PM–9 PM.)

Théâtre Marigny (✉ Carré Marigny, 8ᵉ, Champs-Élysées ☎ 01–53–96–70–30 Ⓜ Champs-Élysées–Clemenceau) is a private theater where you're likely to find a big French star topping the bill.

Théâtre Mogador (✉ 25 rue de Mogador, 9ᵉ, Opéra/Grands Boulevards ☎ 08–92–70–01–00 Ⓜ Trinité), one of Paris's most sumptuous theaters, is the place for musicals and other productions with popular appeal.

Théâtre National de Chaillot (✉ 1 pl. du Trocadéro, 16ᵉ, Trocadéro/Tour Eiffel ☎ 01–53–65–30–00 Ⓜ Trocadéro) is a cavernous place with two theaters dedicated to drama and dance. Since 2003 it has hosted the groundbreaking duo of Deborah Warner (director) and Fiona Shaw (actress) for several excellent English-language productions. Top-flight dance companies like the Ballet Royal de Suède and William Forsythe's Ballet Frankfurt are also regular visitors.

Théâtre de la Renaissance (✉ 20 bd. St-Martin, 10ᵉ, Opéra/Grands Boulevards ☎ 01–42–08–18–50 Ⓜ Strasbourg St-Denis) was put on the map by Belle Époque star Sarah Bernhardt (she was the manager from 1893 to 1899). Big French stars often perform in plays here.

Sports &
the Outdoors

5

WORD OF MOUTH

"We did the night tour [of Paris] on Fat Tire Bike Tours. . . . I didn't realize that it would be a tour of the city, with explanations of the sites . . .This would be a great way for a first timer to see the city, day or night."

—susanna

"August is one of our favorite times in Paris. Do visit Paris Plage, just for the sight of a lot of happy people! Stand under a mist machine there if the temperature is high. Very refreshing. Have a wonderful time!"

—Dave_in_Paris

Revised and
updated by
Mathew
Schwartz

PARISIANS HAVE FAMOUSLY CONSIDERED SWEATING something you don't do on purpose, at least in public. That belief is changing, however, as city residents discover the stress-reducing benefits of a good workout—especially when conducted in subdued designer outfits and full, water-proof makeup.

No surprise then that sleek gyms and chic day spas have made their presence known. Better yet, even the most exclusive palace-hotels have made their luxurious facilities and architectural dream pools accessible to the public. The city's green spaces make for strikingly beautiful exercise settings too. A number of these gardens and wooded areas offer a variety of children's activities, such as trampoline jumping and pony rides in the Tuileries or pedal-powered go-carts and a large playground complex in the Jardin du Luxembourg. The Buttes-Chaumont, meanwhile, is a park with enough space for soccer and other games and a rather hilly jog. Paris's two largest parks—the Bois de Boulogne, on the western fringe of the city, and the Bois de Vincennes, on the eastern side—have thousands of acres of space.

While that's impressive, the French passion for spectator sports is yet more amazing. No fewer than 33 stadiums cater to a fan base rabid for soccer, rugby, tennis, and horse racing. The daily sports paper *L'Equipe* is the country's best-selling national newspaper. Paris often hosts major international sporting events; it is the location for the French Open every May. Information on upcoming events can be found on posters around the city or in the weekly guide *Pariscope.* You can also get information about spectator sports from the tourist board; they're an excellent resource for practical info, including opening hours, prices, and exact locations. Their official Web site, www.paris.org, has more limited details.

If you're planning to rent a bike, in-line skates, or other sports equipment, keep in mind that most rental shops require a significant deposit or that you turn over your passport as a security; some establishments take only cash or local check for the deposit. It's best to call ahead to find out particulars.

For the local lowdown on participant sports (in simple French), including sports facilities in each arrondissement, hit the invaluable ⊕ www. sport.paris.fr. *Le Guide du Sport à Paris,* a free book available from the Paris Tourist Office or in the city hall, or *mairie,* of many of the arrondissements, lists much of the same information. It also includes a map of all bike lanes and a calendar of major sporting events.

Bicycling

Founded in 1903 as a way to sell newspapers, the amazingly popular
★ **Tour de France** (⊕ www.letour.fr) is three weeks of grueling racing torture, as the world's best cyclists cover more than 3,500 km (2,175 mi) of French terrain. The competitors face—among other things—high-speed chases, uphill climbing, mountain passes, and the sometimes extreme weather conditions of July. The athletes finish in a blaze of adulation, as tradition requires and the winner no doubt merits, on the Champs-

Élysées with the president of the Republic, the mayor of Paris, live music, and hundreds of thousands of celebrating fans in attendance. The race usually begins the end of June or early July and finishes in Paris sometime in July. Want in on the action? Climb the Eiffel Tower early on the final day of the race to watch the riders depart below, then amble over to the Champs-Élysées to hold a spot for the afternoon's finale. Don't expect to see the finish line, but you can get close.

Maps of Paris's main cycle paths can be found in the free brochure *Paris À Vélo,* available in any city hall or tourist office. Paris's two large parks are the best places for biking. Bike enthusiasts on the western side of Paris tend to flock to the **Bois de Boulogne** (Ⓜ Porte Maillot, Porte Dauphine, Porte d'Auteuil; Bus 244) and its 23 km (14 mi) of trails. On the east side of Paris the largest number of bike trails can be found in the vast **Bois de Vincennes** (Ⓜ Château de Vincennes, Porte Dorée). Roads are closed to motorized traffic in both parks on weekends and holidays.

The city also has 200 km (124 mi) of **bike lanes,** with more added every year. They are marked with a white bicycle silhouette on the pavement. Unfortunately, most bike routes are along the main axes of the city, which means that you may find yourself riding in traffic, sharing a bus lane, and contending with unaware pedestrians. Signs with a white bicycle on a blue background, however, designate dedicated bike lanes, with concrete barriers or parked cars separating cyclists from traffic.

Ⓒ **Cycling on Sunday** is particularly enjoyable thanks to the *Paris Respire* (Paris Breathes) campaign that bans cars from certain scenic routes on Sunday and national holidays year-round. Look for the telltale white UN BON PLAN À PARIS signs with precise details along each route. These routes include the extrawide road on the banks of the Seine, which is cleared of cars from 9 to 5, and the tranquil, picturesque Canal St-Martin, clear from noon to 6.

Fodor's Choice ★

The following places rent bikes, and many of these establishments also organize guided excursions. Unless otherwise noted, prices include helmets and locks. **Bike 'n Roller** (✉ 38 rue Fabert, 7ᵉ, Trocadéro/Tour Eiffel ☎ 01–45–50–38–27 ⊕ www.bikenroller.fr Ⓜ La Tour-Maubourg) hires bikes for €12 for three hours and €17 for the day. Add €3 for a helmet. It's open Monday through Saturday from 10 to 7:30, Sunday from 10 to 7. **Fat Tire Bike Tours** (✉ 24 rue Edgar Faure, 15ᵉ, Trocadéro/Tour Eiffel ☎ 01–56–58–10–54 ⊕ www.fattirebiketoursparis.com Ⓜ Dupleix), formerly Mike's Bike Tours, organizes fun guided trips around Paris daily from March to November and by appointment from December to February. Tours are peppered with historical information and give a great overview of the city; tours of Versailles are available, too. Day tours run €24, night tours €28. Fat Tire also offers small-group day or night Segway tours—the first in Paris—for €70. Reservations are essential. For bike rentals, hybrid road/mountain bikes cost €2 per hour or €15 for the day; child seats are free. The city's public transportation organization, RATP, runs **La Maison Roue Libre** (✉ 1 passage Mondétour, 1ᵉʳ, Beaubourg/Les Halles ☎ 08–10–44–15–34 ⊕ www.rouelibre.fr Ⓜ Châtelet Les Halles). Its sturdy bikes rent for €7 a day on weekdays and €4 per

Fodor's Choice ★

EYES ON THE BOULE

A low crouch, a flick of the wrist, and a grapefruit-size silver boule (ball) arcs through the air, or gets bowled underhand, settling near a small cochonnet ("little piggy" ball). A sharp retort sounds as one boule displaces another; voices call out in excitement or disbelief. This scenario isn't limited to Provence; boules, also known as pétanque, is popular in the French capital too. Two teams battle, and after all boules are thrown, teams get a point for each boule closer to the cochonnet (thrown at the round's start) than the opponent's boule. First team to 13 wins; spectators are welcome to come watch the action for free.

Historically a men's game, the boules field is diversifying; Paris now has a junior league for teenage boys and girls. It may be simple, but it's nail-biting entertainment— players even refrain from smoking. To find a game, check Le Guide du Sport à Paris or try the Jardin du Luxembourg boulodrome.

hour or €15 a day on weekends, including bike baskets, plus a bottle of water, lock, and baby seat (supplies permitting). This is the cheapest place in town for rentals. It's open daily from 9 to 7 but closes December 15–January 15. **Paris à Vélo, C'est Sympa** (✉ 37 bd. Bourdon, 4ᵉ, Bastille/Nation ☎ 01–48–87–60–01 ⊕ www.parisvelosympa.com Ⓜ Bastille) rents bikes for €9.50 for a half day and €12.50 for a full day. It also organizes three-hour excursions of both the heart of Paris and lesser-known sites. Times vary according to season; it's best to call ahead and make a reservation. Tours cost €30. **Pariscyclo** (✉ Rond Point de Jardin d'Acclimatation, in the Bois de Boulogne, 16ᵉ, Bois de Boulogne ☎ 01–47–47–76–50 Ⓜ Les Sablons) is the perfect place for bike rentals if you want to explore the Bois de Boulogne. Rentals are €5 for an hour, €10 for the day. **Paris Vélo Rent a Bike** (✉ 2 rue Fer à Moulin, 5ᵉ, Quartier Latin ☎ 01–43–37–59–22 Ⓜ Censier Daubenton) rents Canondale hybrid bikes for €12 for half-day and €14 for full-day rentals (plus an additional security deposit of €300). Day (€23) and night (€28) tours are also offered.

Climbing

Itching to scale something? Take to the free, 6-meter (20-foot) climbing wall in the basement of **Au Vieux Camper** (✉ 48 rue des Écoles, 5ᵉ, Quartier Latin ☎ 01–53–10–48–48 ⊕ www.au-vieux-campeur.fr Ⓜ Maubert-Mutualité). You can borrow the store's equipment, but bring your own spotter. The staff can suggest other local climbing walls and day climbing expeditions from Paris.

Health Clubs

Short-term passes are available from the following health clubs. Many instructors and personal trainers can accommodate English speakers, but to be sure of working with someone fluent in English, call ahead.

SPA-GOING AS A SPORT

WALK THROUGH PARIS and you'll notice that on almost every street corner stands an institut de beauté, a haven of skin care and beauty treatments. Many Parisians consider a massage or a stint in a sauna to be as healthful as a workout—and French women have ritualized steaming, polishing, and plucking since Marie-Antoinette took lukewarm milk baths. All the posh palace hotels have luxurious, expensive spa treatments on demand. But you don't have to spend all day (and more than your plane ticket) being royally pampered; instead, make like a local and devote an hour or two to your bien-être (well-being). You could even combine this with shopping, as a few spas have opened branches in a couple of major department stores. Reserve at least one month in advance, two months for a weekend appointment. Tax and service charges are generally included in listed prices, but you may tip extra for outstanding service.

Les Bains du Marais (✉ 31-33 rue des Blancs Manteaux, 4ᵉ, Le Marais ☎ 01–44–61–02–02 ⊕ www. lesbainsdumarais.com Ⓜ Rambuteau), on the site of ancient bathing spots, provides facial care, massages, saunas, and traditional steam rooms for both men (Thursday and Friday) and women (Monday–Wednesday). Steam rooms are mixed-gender on Wednesday evenings and weekends; swimsuits are required. Your €30 fee allows you to spend as long as you want in the steam rooms and includes bathrobe, slippers, and a towel. For another €30 you can also get a massage and body scrub.

The Zen **Cinq Mondes** (✉ 6 square Louis Jouvet, 9ᵉ, Opéra/Grands Boulevards ☎ 01–55–37–93–83 ⊕ www. cinqmondes.com Ⓜ Opéra) blends traditional techniques from five ancient schools. Try the "urban ritual," which includes a ceremonial Japanese bath in an oval cedarwood tub afloat with rose petals and essential oils. Treatments start at €45.

The sleek, glass-encased **Daniel Jouvance Espace Mer** (✉ 91 av. des Champs-Élysées, 8ᵉ, Champs-Élysées ☎ 01–47–23–48–00 ⊕ www.danieljouvance.com Ⓜ George V) brings the benefits of thalassothérapie (healing with ocean water) to the city. Try the Aquaprima body treatment, an hour and a half of exfoliation, hydromassage, massage, and a seaweed wrap, for €112, or the 40-minute Aquanova facial with shiatsu massage for €40.

Nickel (✉ 48 rue des Francs-Bourgeois, 4ᵉ, Le Marais ☎ 01–42–77–41–10 ⊕ www.nickel.fr Ⓜ St-Paul), a silver-and-dark-blue spa with no-frills service, specializes in treatments for men. Get the hands of a croupier with a manicure for €14, or a one-hour love-handle liquidation treatment for €60.

32 rue Montorgueil (✉ 32 rue Montorgueil, 1ᵉʳ Beaubourg/Les Halles ☎ 01–55–80–71–40 Ⓜ Les Halles) is the hip spa by the creators of the Nuxe line of skin care products. The ancient cellar with its arched corridors, exposed cream stone, and hush-hush atmosphere is smack in the middle of one of the busiest areas in Paris. Try the rêve de miel (honey dream), a spectacular, nourishing 1½-hour body treatment for €140.

Mediterranean-style **Villa Thalgo** (✉ 218-220 rue du Faubourg St-Honoré, 8ᵉ, Champs-Élysées ☎ 01–45–62–00–20 ⊕ www.thalgo.com Ⓜ Charles-de-Gaulle–Étoile) has a heated saltwater swimming pool and massages to relaunch the lymphatic system, eliminate toxins, and stimulate circulation. Facials and body packs filled with trace sea minerals promote rejuvenation.

Club Jean de Beauvais (⊠ 5 rue Jean-de-Beauvais, 5ᵉ, Quartier Latin ☎ 01–46–33–16–80 ⊕ www.clubjeandebeauvais.com Ⓜ Maubert-Mutualité) has an entire floor of exercise equipment, classes in a comfortable space with exposed timber beams, and a sauna. A one-day pass costs €38; a week costs €95. You can also spring for seawater-based treatments and mud wraps for an additional cost. The club is open weekdays 7 AM–10 PM, Saturday 8:30–7, and Sunday 9–7.

★ **Club Quartier Latin** (⊠ 19 rue de Pontoise, 5ᵉ, Quartier Latin ☎ 01–55–42–77–88 ⊕ www.clubquartierlatin.com Ⓜ Maubert-Mutualité) has a pool with skylights, squash courts, and exercise equipment. For €15 per day you can use the gym and pool (the pool only is €3.80, plus a mandatory €0.45 for a cabin); add another €12 per 40 minutes for squash (€2.50 racket rental). The club's open weekdays 9 AM–midnight, weekends 8–7, but call ahead for precise pool hours.

Espace Vit'Halles (⊠ Pl. Beaubourg, 48 rue Rambuteau, 3ᵉ, Beaubourg/Les Halles ☎ 01–42–77–21–71 Ⓜ Rambuteau), kitty-corner from the Centre Georges Pompidou, has a variety of aerobics and spinning classes, an extensive selection of exercise machines, plus a sauna and steam room (€25 a day). It's open weekdays 8 AM–10:30 PM, Saturday 10–7, and Sunday 10–6.

★ **Pilates Studio** (⊠ 39 rue du Temple, 4ᵉ, Le Marais ☎ 01–42–72–91–74 ⊕ www.studiopilatesdeparis.com Ⓜ Hôtel de Ville) is run by Philippe Taupin, who studied in New York with one of the pupils of the technique's founder, Joseph Pilates. It may be based in just a three-room apartment, but it attracts numerous celebrities, such as actor Robert Downey Jr. and actress Catherine Deneuve. One-hour group classes on mats are €28, and group classes with Pilates machines are €59. Call ahead for a reservation and to make sure there's an English-speaking instructor available.

Hotel Health Clubs

The hotels with the best fitness facilities are generally the newer ones around the perimeter of the city center.

Fodor'sChoice The Paris Ritz is known for opulence—the former haunt of Joyce and Fitzgerald, home of the cigar set's Hemingway Bar—and the **Ritz Health**
★ **Club** (⊠ Pl. Vendôme, 1ᵉʳ, Louvre/Tuileries ☎ 01–43–16–30–60 ⊕ www.ritzparis.com Ⓜ Opéra) lives up to its setting. Have a drink next to the large, Romanesque swimming pool with its mosaic, mermaid-strewn bottom, or sample the sauna, steam room, hot tub, exercise machines, or aerobics classes. It's free for hotel guests, €150 per day for nonguests, and open daily from 9 AM to 10 PM.

Sofitel Paris Club Med Gym (⊠ 8 rue Louis-Armand, 15ᵉ, Montparnasse ☎ 01–45–54–79–00 Ⓜ Balard) offers various classes, has a 15-meter pool, sauna, steam room, and hot tub, plus a stunning 22nd-story view of the Paris skyline. It costs €32 per day for nonguests and is free for hotel guests. It's open weekdays 8 AM–10 PM, Saturday 8–7, and Sunday 9–3.

Horse Racing

When spring came to Paris, wrote Ernest Hemingway, "there were no problems except where to be happiest," and for him that often meant picnicking at the hippodromes (racetracks) such as Auteuil, handicapping horses, and betting for better or worse. To this day, Paris and its suburbs are remarkably well furnished with tracks. Admission is between €2.30 and €7.63. Details of meetings can be found in the daily newspaper *Le Parisien* or the specialist racing paper *Paris Turf.* Tracks offer parking, restaurants, some covered seating—perfect for a day's getaway. The easiest racetrack to get to is the well-manicured **Hippodrome d'Auteuil** (⊠ Bois de Boulogne, 16ᵉ, Bois de Boulogne ☎01–40–71–47–47 Ⓜ Porte d'Auteuil). Also in the Bois de Boulogne is the city's most beautiful track, the **Hippodrome de Longchamp** (⊠Rte. des Tribunes, 16ᵉ, Bois de Boulogne ☎01–44–30–75–00 Ⓜ Porte d'Auteuil, then free shuttle), the stage for the prestigious (and glamorous) Prix de l'Arc de Triomphe on the first weekend in October. Built in 1879, the **Hippodrome de Vincennes** (⊠ Rte. Ferme, Bois de Vincennes ☎01–49–77–17–17 Ⓜ RER: Joinville-Le-Pont) is a cinder track used for trotting races. The French Derby (Prix du Jockey-Club) and the very chic French Oaks (Prix de Diane-Hermès) are held at the beginning of June at **Chantilly,** north of Paris (*see* Chapter 7). Direct trains from the Gare du Nord take about 40 minutes. There are stunning views of the nearby Château de Chantilly, as well as a horse-racing museum.

Ice-Skating

From mid-December through the end of February, weather permitting, discover Paris *sur glace* (on ice) as the city transforms three outdoor sites into spectacular ice-skating rinks with pretty, festive Christmas lights, music, and on-site instructors. The rinks are free to the public; skate rental for adults costs €5 but is free for kids. The **Place de l'Hôtel de Ville** (the square in front of the Hôtel de Ville) is transformed into a 1,200-square-meter (3,960-square-foot) rink, with free antique merry-go-rounds nearby. **Patinoire Montparnasse** (⊠ pl. Raoul Dantry, 15ᵉ, Montparnasse Ⓜ Montparnasse Bienvenüe) has an 800-square-meter (2,624-square-foot) rink next to the Tour Montparnasse skyscraper and in front of the eponymous train station. The **Patinoire Sonja Henie** (⊠ 8 bd. de Bercy, 12ᵉ, Bercy/Tolbiac ☎ 01–40–02–60–60 ⊕ www.bercy.fr Ⓜ Bercy) is a 500-square-meter (1,650-square-foot) indoor rink open year-round to the public from 3 PM to 6 PM on Wednesday, Saturday and Sunday, also 10 AM–noon on Sunday. Admission is €4, plus €5 for skates, helmet, and safety pads. Friday and Saturday nights from 9:20 to 12:30 it turns into an ice-skating nightclub, with pumping music, giant screens, and disco lights. Admission, not including rentals, is €6.

In-Line Skating

Seeing people with skates on their feet used to be rare in Paris. Now it seems like almost every other Parisian practices *le roller*—some successfully. To avoid pedestrians and road crossings, many skaters use the city's cycle paths. You'll also see them doing their tricks on place du Palais-Royal and the esplanade at the Musée d'Art Moderne de la Ville de Paris on avenue du Président-Wilson. On Sunday, when cars are banned on certain major roads, the quai de la Tournelle, along the Seine (9–5), and the Canal St-Martin (noon–6) are also ideal in-line skating spots.

Every Friday night starting at 10, weather permitting, thousands of in-line skaters gather for **Friday Night Fever** (✉ Pl. Raoul Dautry, 14ᵉ, Montparnasse ⊕ www.pari-roller.com Ⓜ Montparnasse Bienvenüe), a three-hour group skate. There's a different route each week, and the roads are blocked to other traffic. The pace is pretty hairy, so novices are discouraged. A more leisurely three-hour route organized by **Rollers & Coquillages** (✉ 23-25 rue Jean-Jacques Rousseau, 1ᵉʳ Beaubourg/Les Halles ☎ 01–44–54–94–42 ⊕ www.rollers-coquillages.org Ⓜ Les Halles) sets off Sunday at 2:30 from the Roller Location Nomades rental shop (*see below*). If you're acrobatically inclined, try the two ramps and 200 square meters (650 square feet) of skating territory at **Stade Boutroux** (✉ 1 av. Boutroux, 13ᵉ, Chinatown ☎ 01–45–84–08–46 Ⓜ Porte d'Ivry).

In-line skates can be rented from **Bike 'n Roller** (✉ 38 rue Fabert, 7ᵉ, Trocadéro/Tour Eiffel ☎ 01–45–50–38–27 ⊕ www.bikenroller.fr Ⓜ La Tour-Maubourg) for €9 for three hours, €12 for the whole day, plus helmet and safety pads for under €2. **Roller Location Nomades** (✉ 37 bd. Bourdon, 4ᵉ, Bastille/Nation ☎ 01–44–54–07–44 ⊕ www.nomadeshop. com Ⓜ Bastille) rents skates for €8 per day (€9 on weekends), plus €1 for helmet and safety pads. It's open 11–1 and 2–7 on weekdays and 10–6 on weekends, and it takes only cash. **Vertical Line** (✉ 4 rue de la Bastille, 4ᵉ, Bastille ☎ 01–42–74–70–70 ⊕ www.vertical-line.com Ⓜ Bastille) rents skates for the day (€10) or half day (€7), with all safety gear included. To rent high-performance brands, add €2. The shop is open 11–8 on Monday, Tuesday, and Thursday, 11–9 on Wednesday and Friday, and 10–8 on weekends.

Rugby

Although soccer holds a preeminent place in French hearts, rugby runs a close second. The good news for spectators is that rugby teams play in smaller stadiums—mostly former *cyclodromes* (bike-racing stadiums)—so you get closer to the action.

The **Paris Université Club** plays home matches on Sunday in winter at 3 in the Bois de Vincennes at **Le Cipale** (✉ av. de Gravelle, 12ᵉ, Bois de Vincennes ☎ 01–44–16–62–69 for the club ⊕ www.puc-rugby.com Ⓜ Château de Vincennes, Porte Dorée); tickets are €5. For information and game dates, call the club. France's national rugby team plays at the **Stade de France** (✉ St-Denis ☎ 01–55–93–00–00 ⊕ www.stadefrance. fr Ⓜ RER: La Plaine–Stade de France). Admission starts at €20; your best bet is to get tickets from FNAC or Virgin Megastore in advance or contact the **Fédération Française de Rugby** (☎ 01–53–21–15–15 ⊕ www. ffr.fr). The **Racing Club de France** has games Saturday or Sunday afternoon at the **Stade Charléty** (✉ 17 av. Pierre de Coubertin, 13ᵉ, Bercy/Tolbiac ☎ 01–45–67–55–86 ⊕ www.metroracing.com.fr Ⓜ Cité Université). Paris's top team, Le Stade Français, usually plays home matches on Saturday or Sunday afternoon at 3 at the **Stade Jean Bouin** (✉ 26 av. du Général Sarrail, 16ᵉ, Trocadéro/Tour Eiffel ☎ 01–46–51–51–11 ⊕ www.stade. fr Ⓜ Porte d'Auteuil).

Running & Jogging

While running through the streets of Paris may sound romantic, go early in the day—otherwise there's just too much traffic on the narrow streets. Exceptions are the quai de la Tournelle along the Seine and the quiet urban scenery of the Canal St-Martin (though solo joggers might not want to venture farther, along Bassin de la Villette, at night). Jogging up boulevard Richard Lenoir from place de la Bastille is a pleasant way to reach the canal. When running on the streets, remember that even after threat of heavy fines (up to €450 per infraction), dog owners don't reliably clean up.

In general, the city's central parks are better places to run during the day, at least for doing circuits, though many Parisians decamp there for lunch. (At night many parks are closed or unlighted.) The **Champ de Mars** (Ⓜ École Militaire), next to the Eiffel Tower, measures 2½ km (1½ mi) around the perimeter. Many jogging fans prefer the pleasant 1½-km (1-mi) loop—though more crowded than the Champ de Mars—that's just inside the fence around the **Jardin du Luxembourg** (Ⓜ Odéon; RER: Luxembourg). The **Jardin des Tuileries** (Ⓜ Concorde, Tuileries) measures about 1½ km (1 mi) around. For hillier terrain try the **Parc des Buttes-Chaumont** (Ⓜ Buttes-Chaumont). Your reward? A handful of waterfalls, plus excellent views of Montmartre.

Outside the city center, the **Bois de Boulogne** has miles of trails through woods, around lakes, and across grassy meadows. There are 1.8-km (1.1-mi) and 2½-km (1½-mi) loops. The especially bucolic **Bois de Vincennes** has a 14½-km (9-mi) circuit or a 1½-km (1-mi) loop around the Château de Vincennes itself. Maps of routes in both *bois* can be found in *Le Guide du Sport à Paris*.

A number of annual running races, open to the public, are a great excuse to visit the city. The **Paris Marathon** takes place in April and attracts more than 35,000 participants. Subscription details are available from the **Athlétisme Organisation** (☎01–41–33–15–94 ⊕www.parismarathon. com). Spectators also flock to the race, which sets off from the Champs-Élysées and finishes at the top of avenue Foch, near the Arc de Triomphe. Along the route, in spots such as place de la Concorde and place de la République, live music gives the crowds extra energy. **La Parisienne** (⊕ www.la-parisienne.net) is a 6.5-km (4-mi) women's race held every September that attracts more than 5,000 participants. Also in September, the 16.3-km (10-mi) **Paris-Versaille** (☎ 01–30–21–10–25 ⊕ www. parisversailles.com) race draws 20,000 runners. It starts at the Eiffel Tower and ends in Versailles.

Soccer

As in most European cities, *football* (soccer) is the sport that draws Paris's biggest crowds and stokes the strongest sporting passions. See the wildly popular national team play at the **Stade de France** (✉ St-Denis ☎ 01–55–93–00–00 Ⓜ RER: La Plaine–Stade de France), an 80,000-seat, American-style multipurpose stadium with a halo roof to keep spectators dry, built in 1998 for the World Cup. For tickets call early in the season (September) or check the Web site; ticket outlets change occasionally.

Paris St-Germain (✉ 24 rue du Commandant Guilbaud, 16ᵉ, Passy-Auteuil ☎ 01–41–10–71–71 or 08–92–69–21–92 ⊕ www.francebillet.com Ⓜ Porte d'Auteuil), the city's main club, was founded in 1970 and has won various titles. It plays at the 49,000-seat, concrete-fin-ringed Parc des Princes stadium in southwest Paris. Most matches are on Saturday evening at 8; check the Web site for the latest schedule and ticket outlets. You can also try **France Billet**, a ticket service that charges €0.34 per minute for its hotline. Order tickets several months in advance.

Swimming

To swim in a Parisian public pool, know this: everyone must wear a swimming cap; men aren't allowed to wear boxer-type swim trunks or cutoffs (except in more upscale hotels, only tight Lycra swimming briefs are accepted); and most people wear flip-flops around the pool and in the shower area. Once you have that down, swimming in the capital is quite easy—every arrondissement has its own public *piscine* (pool); there are 34 public pools in all. The Paris Tourist Office's *Le Guide du Sport à Paris* lists addresses. For other swimming options, *see* Health Clubs, *above*.

★ The **Piscine St-Germain** (✉ 12 rue de Lobineau, 6ᵉ, St-Germain-des-Prés ☎ 01–43–29–08–15 Ⓜ Mabillon), one of the nicest pools in Paris, combines a bright interior with a parent-perfect observation area and is open Tuesday 7 AM–8 AM, 11:30 AM–1 PM, and 5 PM–7:30 PM; Wednesday 7 AM–8 AM and 11:30 AM–5:30 PM; Thursday and Friday 7 AM–8 AM and 11:30 AM–1 PM; Saturday 7–5:30; and Sunday 8–5:30. Admission is €3.

★ ⚲ **Aquaboulevard** (✉ 4 rue Louis-Armand, 15ᵉ, Montparnasse ☎ 01–40–60–10–00 Ⓜ Balard), the best place to take kids in summer, has an enormous indoor wave pool with water slides and in summer a simulated outdoor beach. It's open Monday–Thursday 9 AM–11 PM, Friday 9 AM–midnight, Saturday 8 AM–midnight, and Sunday 8 AM–11 PM. Last admission each day is at 9 PM. Admission (€20, €10 for kids) buys you a stay for up to six hours.

★ **Paris Plage** brings a beach experience to the Seine in July and August; although you can't jump in the river for a swim, you can still bust out your bathing suit. Thousands of tons of sand get imported, along with musicians, bikes, and bars, to create beaches by the Pont Neuf, Notre-Dame, and the Pont au Change. Arrive early; the three beaches are very popular, especially with locals.

Tennis

One of the highlights of the international tennis circuit is the action on **FodorsChoice** the dusty red-clay courts at the **French Open** (✉ 2 av. Gordon Bennett, ★ 16ᵉ, Bois de Boulogne ☎ 01–47–43–48–00 ⊕ www.frenchopen.com

Ⓜ Porte d'Auteuil), held during the last week of May and the first week of June at **Roland-Garros stadium.** Center-court tickets are often difficult to obtain; try your hotel's concierge or turn up early in the morning (matches start at 11 AM) and buy a general grounds ticket to see early-round matches. Tickets range from €7.50 to €66. The **Bercy Indoor Tournament,** in November at the **Palais Omnisports de Paris-Bercy** (✉ 8 bd. de Bercy, 12ᵉ, Bastille/Nation ☎ 08–03–03–00–31 ⊕ www. bercy.com Ⓜ Bercy, Gare de Lyon), awards one of the largest prizes in the world and attracts most of the top players. The **Open Gaz de France** (Stade Pierre de Coubertin ✉ 82 av. Georges-Lafont, 16ᵉ, St-Cloud ☎ 01–45–27–79–12 ⊕ www.opengazdefrance.com Ⓜ Porte de St-Cloud), every February, is one of the official tournaments on the women's tour. Tickets for the Bercy or Open Gaz tournaments can be purchased at FNAC or a Virgin Megastore, or at their stadiums.

Paris has a number of municipal courts, but getting to play on them can be difficult without reservations. To reserve court time, you must first register and then make reservations online (the site is in French only) at ⊕ www.tennis.paris.fr. You can, however, take a chance, turn up at the public courts, and, if there is one available, play. The best time to go is the middle of the day during the week; you'll have to pay the monitor €5.75 an hour per court for open-air courts, or €11.40 for covered ones. The most central, but crowded, courts are outdoors in the **Jardin du Luxembourg.**

Yoga

Just because you're abroad doesn't mean you have to give up the sticky mat or English-language instruction, though you'll need to call studios ahead since doors open only when there's a class. Caroline Boulinguez, an instructor with over 20 years' experience, oversees **Samasthiti Studio** (✉23 rue de la Cerisaie, 4ᵉ, Bastille/Nation ☎ 01–44–07–31–33 ⊕ www. samasthitistudio.com Ⓜ Bastille/Sully-Morland), a well-lighted neighborhood studio with hardwood floors. It offers fast-flowing Ashtanga and Mysore yoga styles, as well as beginner classes. Visitors pay €20 for one class, €40 for a weekly pass. Private lessons are €80 for up to three people. **Institut Eva Ruchpaul** (✉ 69 rue de Rome, 8ᵉ Champs-Élysées ☎01–44–90–06–70 ⊕www.evaruchpaul.asso.fr Ⓜ Europe) offers Hatha-style yoga—emphasizing breathing and held postures—in a chic studio with skylights. There's a mandatory one-on-one private lesson for €24, after which participants pay a one-time registration fee (€20), then per class (€22).

Shopping

6

WORD OF MOUTH

"Le Marché aux Puces St-Ouen is worth the trip! . . .I do not speak French, but had no trouble going to the markets by myself. If you plan to bargain (and you should!) bring a pen and a small pad of paper . . . ask for the 'best price' and have the dealer write it down. If you want to go lower, write your number and mention cash. . . . I don't regret any of my purchases—only those I passed up!"

—highledge

Updated by
Jennifer Ditsler-
Ladonne

NOTHING, BUT NOTHING, CAN PUSH YOU into the current of Paris life faster or more effectively than a few hours of shopping. Follow the example of Parisians, who slow to a crawl as their eyes lock on a tempting display. Window-shopping is one of this city's greatest spectator sports, and the French call it *lèche-vitrine*—literally, "licking the windows"—which is quite fitting because many of the displays look good enough to eat.

Store owners here play to a sophisticated audience with a voracious appetite for everything from spangly flagship stores to minimalist boutiques to under-the-radar spots in 19th-century glass-roofed *passages.* Parisians know that shopping isn't about the kill, it's about the chase: walking down cobblestone streets looking for things they didn't know they wanted, casual yet quick to pounce. They like being seduced by a clever display and relish the performative elements of browsing. Watching them shop can be almost as much fun as shopping yourself.

With the euro trouncing the dollar, it may seem foolish to even contemplate the latest Chanel handbag or that racy pair of Christian Louboutin stiletto boots. All the more reason to look for things that can be found only in Paris. Travelers can still find a treasure on even the most stringent budget: bottles of fruit-flavor eau-de-vie, a box of jewel-like chocolates, antique filigree picture frames, lacy lingerie. And if you do decide to indulge, what better place to make that once-in-a-blue-moon splurge?

Most stores in Paris—except for department stores and flea markets—stay open until 6 PM or 7 PM, but many take a lunch break sometime between noon and 2. Although shops traditionally close on Sunday, regulations have been greatly relaxed in the past decade, and you'll find a number of stores open then, too, most especially in the Marais. If you're making a special trip somewhere, especially around holidays, it doesn't hurt to call ahead and check the hours. And don't forget to greet and thank the staff everywhere.

Duty-Free Shopping

A value-added tax (V.A.T.) of approximately 19.6%, known by its French-language acronym as the TVA, is imposed on most consumer goods. Non–European Union residents can reclaim part of this tax, known as the *détaxe*. To qualify for a refund, you must purchase the equivalent of €175 of goods in the same shop on the same day; you must have stayed three months or less in the European Union at the time of purchase; and you must have your passport validated by customs within three months following the date of purchase. Don't forget to **ask about your détaxe form at the time of purchase**; smaller stores will fill the form out for you, while department stores have special détaxe desks where the *bordereaux* (export sales invoices) help to streamline the process. **Détaxe forms must be shown and stamped by a customs official before leaving the country**; without this stamp, you will not be refunded. If the refund is substantial, they might want to see the purchases, so be prepared to show them. After you're through passport control, you can seal the form in the envelope provided and post it at an airport mailbox or mail it after you arrive home. The refund can be sent as a check or directly wired to your credit card (the fastest of the two options). Note that there is no refund for food, alcohol, or tobacco products.

SHOPPING BY NEIGHBORHOOD

This is not the place for American-style malls; instead, certain neighborhoods and streets cultivate specific styles and characters, from the couture on avenue Montaigne to the quirky pocket-size boutiques in the Marais. Paris is, however, the birthplace of the modern mall concept. Some of the 19th-century *passages* (glass-roof shopping arcades) are still kicking and are listed in Shopping Arcades below. Reviews for the shops named in boldface can be found in the listings under Specialty Shops.

Avenue Montaigne & Surroundings

Avenue Montaigne is one of the most exclusive shopping streets in the world—it just doesn't get much more *haute* than this, darling. They're all here, all those incredibly expensive, luxurious boutiques that strike fear in the heart of even the most well-padded wallet: **Chanel, Dior,** Nina Ricci, **Celine,** Valentino, Max Mara, Genny, Krizia, Escada, Loewe, **Marni, Emanuel Ungaro, Prada,** Pucci, Calvin Klein, **Louis Vuitton,** and **Dolce & Gabbana.** Many of the boutiques are housed in exquisite mansions with wrought-iron gates in front. On the sidewalks, princess-cum-model-cum-trust-fund types canter along in tiny heeled boots with lacquered packages dangling off their bird-thin wrists. The sales staffs are well trained in dignified-to-chilly reserve, but as they say, "When in Rome . . .." Here you must play by the stringent rules of the purely superficial world: dress well (shopping here is *not* a jeans-and-sneakers day); polish up your greetings for the salespeople; and shop with sangfroid. As any great shopper knows, you don't have to actually buy anything to enjoy the experience. And don't forget neighboring rue François 1er and avenue George V, which also have their share of fine boutiques: Armani, Versace, Fendi, Givenchy, **Balenciaga,** and the must-see **Jean-Paul Gaultier** fantasy.

Champs-Élysées

Cafés and movie theaters keep the once-chic Champs-Élysées active 24 hours a day, but the invasion of exchange banks, car showrooms, and fast-food chains lowered the tone over the past few decades. Nowadays, things are turning back to luxe. True, branches of big chains like the **Virgin Megastore, Sephora,** and the Gap still capture a lot of the retail action. But also of note are the French perfumer **Guerlain,** a major outpost of the jeweler **Cartier,** and the **Louis Vuitton** boutique, whose partnership with American designer Marc Jacobs has turned this institution into the epitome of cool. (The mother-ship Vuitton on the Champs-Élysées proper was closed for renovation at this writing, primed to be relaunched in spring 2005.) Up at the top of the Champs, near the Arc de Triomphe, gleams **Le Drugstore Publicis,** its facade a swirl of glass and steel. Reopened in spring 2004, Le Drugstore has stood here since 1958; in the 1960s it was one of the city's rare late-night stores, so all walks of life ended up in its aisles. Now it spans a pharmacy, a cosmetics area (exclusive lines such as Shu Uemura), a *tabac* (for cigarettes at 1 AM and over a hundred international publications), a café, and a wine cellar.

The Faubourg St-Honoré & Place Vendôme

White-gloved police might politely ask you to pause as the dark-windowed Renaults enter the Palais de l'Élysée—a sign that you are entering the hushed world of diplomats. The Faubourg St-Honoré's shops fit that ambassadorial tone, from the antique galleries of Didier Aaron to the bright prints of **Christian Lacroix** and the chiffon dresses at Lanvin, to the jeweled evening gowns at **Loris Azzaro**. Continue along rue du Faubourg St-Honoré to find **Chloé, Yves Saint Laurent, Hermès,** and **Prada.** As you reach rue de Castiglione, look north into the place Vendôme, ringed with dazzling jewelers' windows: **Cartier,** Boucheron, Chaumet, and the appointment-only JAR.

Louvre & Palais-Royal

Stroll through the atmospheric 18th-century arcades of the Palais-Royal and you'll see everything from military medals and toy soldiers to gorgeous vintage dresses at **Didier Ludot** and a purple-hued parfumier, **Les Salons du Palais-Royal Shiseido.** There are even handmade gardening tools sold by a prince at **Le Prince Jardinier.** Meanwhile, over at the Louvre, an inverted glass pyramid punctures the glossy Carrousel du Louvre underground mall. The Carrousel doesn't have many surprises, but its stores are open every day, unlike most. Worth a visit are **Résonances,** a nostalgia-driven lifestyle shop, and the official Louvre museum boutique, with all manner of posters, cards, reproduction sculptures, and the like.

Le Marais

Fodor'sChoice
★ The Marais scene, a mix of boho-bourgeois, orthodox Jewish, and gay populations, is reflected in its fantastic, varied shops. The quartier's lovely, narrow cobblestone streets have some of the city's most original, individual boutiques, including **Jamin Puech, The Red Wheelbarrow,** and **Sentou Galerie.** Between the pre-Revolution mansions and tiny kosher food shops that characterize this area are dozens of trendy gift and clothing stores, as well as stylish home-decor places. Attention-getting designers like **Azzedine Alaïa** have boutiques within a few blocks of stately place des Vosges and the Picasso and Carnavalet museums. The Marais is also one of the few neighborhoods that has a lively Sunday shopping scene.

Opéra to Madeleine

Two major department stores—**Printemps** and **Galeries Lafayette**—dominate boulevard Haussmann, behind Paris's ornate 19th-century Opéra Garnier. Place de la Madeleine is home to two luxurious food stores, **Fauchon** and **Hédiard.** Lalique and Baccarat crystal also have opulent showrooms near the Église de la Madeleine.

Place des Victoires & Rue Étienne Marcel

The graceful, circular place des Victoires, near the Palais-Royal, is the playground of fashion icons such as Kenzo and Victoire. Seriously avant-garde designers like **Comme des Garçons** and Yohji Yamamoto line rue Étienne Marcel. In the nearby oh-so-charming Galerie Vivienne shopping arcade **Jean-Paul Gaultier** has a shop that has been renovated by Philippe Starck, and definitely is worth a stop. And at 3 rue d'Argout the hottest club-wear emporium in Paris, **Le Shop,** rents retail space to hip, up-and-coming designers.

Rive Gauche

After decades of clustering on the Rive Droite's venerable shopping avenues, the high-fashion houses have stormed the Rive Gauche, and the shopping on this side of the Seine has never been better. The first to arrive were **Sonia Rykiel** and **Yves Saint Laurent,** in the late '60s. Forty years later **Christian Dior, Louis Vuitton,** Emporio Armani, and Cartier have also set up shop in this dynamic area. Rue des Sts-Pères and rue de Grenelle are lined with designer names; the latter is especially known for its excellent shoe stores, such as **Christian Louboutin,** Sergio Rossi, and Stéphane Kélian.

Rue St-Honoré

The cooler-than-thou set makes its way to rue St-Honoré to shop at Paris's trendiest boutique, **Colette.** The street drips with international designers; there's also the delightful vintage jewelry store **Dary's.** On nearby rue Cambon you'll find the wonderfully elegant **Maria Luisa** and the first **Chanel** boutique. A number of hip designers like **Comme des Garçons** have also opened stores on place du Marché St-Honoré.

DEPARTMENT STORES

For an overview of Paris *mode,* visit *les grands magasins,* Paris's monolithic department stores. Size up the sometimes ornate architecture, compare prices, and marvel at the historical value of it all, as some of these stores have been around since 1860. Most are open Monday through Saturday from about 9:30 to 7, and some are open until 10 PM one weekday evening. All five major stores listed below have multilingual guides, international welcome desks, détaxe offices, and restaurants. Most are on the Rive Droite, near the Opéra and the Hôtel de Ville; the notable exception is Le Bon Marché, on the Rive Gauche.

Bazar de l'Hôtel de Ville (✉ 52–64 rue de Rivoli, 4ᵉ, Beaubourg/Les Halles ☎ 01-42-74-90-00 Ⓜ Hôtel de Ville), better known as **BHV,** houses an enormous basement hardware store that sells everything from doorknobs to cement mixers and has to be seen to be believed. There's even a funky, inexpensive café, where how-to demos are held. The fashion offerings are minimal, but BHV is noteworthy for quality household goods, home-decor materials, and office supplies.

Le Bon Marché (✉ 24 rue de Sèvres, 7ᵉ, St-Germain-des-Prés ☎ 01–44–39–80–00 Ⓜ Sèvres Babylone), founded in 1852, has emerged as the city's chicest department store. Long a hunting ground for linens, table settings, and other home items, a face-lift has brought fashion to the fore. The ground floor sets out makeup, perfume, and accessories; here's where celebs duck in for essentials while everyone pretends not to recognize them. Upstairs, do laps through labels chichi (Burberry, Dries van Noten, Sonia Rykiel) and streetwise (Ligne 6 Martin Margiela, A.P.C.). Menswear, under the moniker Balthazar, keeps pace with designers like Zegna, Yves Saint Laurent, and Paul Smith. Best of all, this department store often isn't as crowded as those near the Opéra. Don't miss **La Grande Épicerie** right next door; it's the haute couture of grocery stores. Artisanal jams, nougats, olive oils, and much more make great gifts, and the lustrous pastries and fruit (the staff will measure it out) beg to be chosen for a snack.

Galeries Lafayette (⊠ 35–40 bd. Haussmann, 9ᵉ, Opéra/Grands Boulevards ☎01–42–82–34–56 Ⓜ Chaussée d'Antin, Opéra, Havre Caumartin ⊠ Centre Commercial Montparnasse, 14ᵉ, Montparnasse ☎ 01–45–38–52–87 Ⓜ Montparnasse Bienvenüe) is one of those places that you wander into unawares, leaving hours later a poorer and more humble person. The flagship store at 40 boulevard Haussmann bulges with thousands of designers; a Belle Époque stained-glass dome caps the world's largest perfumery. Don't miss the delectable comestibles department, stocked with the best of everything from herbed goat cheese to Iranian caviar. Just across the street at 35 boulevard Haussmann is Galeries Lafayette Maison. The massive building is devoted to the home, from the kitchenware in the basement to the bedding on the third floor. The Montparnasse branch is a pale shadow of the boulevard Haussmann behemoths.

Printemps (⊠ 64 bd. Haussmann, 9ᵉ, Opéra/Grands Boulevards ☎01–42–82–50–00 Ⓜ Havre Caumartin, Opéra, and RER: Auber) is actually three major stores: Printemps de la Maison (home furnishings), Printemps de l'Homme (menswear—six floors no less), and the brilliant Printemps de la Mode (fashion, fashion, fashion), which has everything from cutting-edge Helmut Lang to the teenagey Free. Be sure to check out the beauty area, with the Nuxe spa, hairdressers, and seemingly every beauty product known to man under one roof. Fashion shows are held on Tuesday (all year) and Friday (April–October) at 10 AM under the cupola on the seventh floor of La Mode and are free. (Reservations can be made in advance by calling 01–42–82–63–17; tickets can also be obtained on the day of the show at the service desk on the first floor.)

La Samaritaine (⊠ 19 rue de la Monnaie, 1ᵉʳ, Louvre/Tuileries ☎01–40–41–20–20 Ⓜ Pont Neuf, Châtelet), a sprawling five-store complex, has a more casual approach to fashion (Antik Batik and Armani Jeans instead of ball gowns) but is especially known for kitchen supplies, housewares, and furniture. Its most famous asset is the Toupary restaurant, in Building 2, from which there's a marvelous view of Notre-Dame and the Left Bank.

Budget

Monoprix (⊠ 21 av. de l'Opéra, 1ᵉʳ, Opéra/Grands Boulevards ☎01–42–61–78–08 Ⓜ Opéra ⊠ 6 av. de la Plaine, 20ᵉ, Bastille/Nation ☎01–43–73–17–59 Ⓜ Nation ⊠ 50 rue de Rennes, 6ᵉ, St-Germain-des-Prés ☎ 01–45–48–18–08 Ⓜ St-Germain-des-Prés), with branches throughout the city, is *the* French dime store par excellence, stocking everyday items like toothpaste, groceries, toys, typing paper, and bath mats—a little of everything. It also has a line of relatively inexpensive basic wearables for the whole family and is, on the whole, not a bad place to stock up on French liqueurs at a reasonable price.

Tati (⊠ 2–28 bd. Rochechouart, 18ᵉ, Montmartre ☎ 01–55–29–50–00 Ⓜ Barbès Rochechouart) is one of Paris's most iconic stores. The ultimate haven for bargain-basement prices, it is certainly not for the fainthearted or claustrophobic. On an average day it is jam-packed with people of all colors, economic levels, and sizes rifling through the jumbled trays in search of a great buy, which they always succeed in finding, since the key word here is cheap—utterly, unabashedly cheap. One of its most famous deals was underwear for just €.15 a pair (they sell 5 million pairs a year). It is also well known for its ridiculously inexpensive bridal store and its chain of cheap jewelry shops, **Tati Or.**

MARKETS

Flea Markets

FodorśChoice The venerable **Le Marché aux Puces St-Ouen** (Ⓜ Porte de Clignancourt
★ ⊕www.parispuces.com), also referred to as **Clignancourt,** on Paris's northern boundary, still attracts the crowds when it's open—Saturday–Monday from 9 to 6—but its once-unbeatable prices are now a relic of the past. This century-old labyrinth of alleyways packed with antiques dealers' booths and *brocante* stalls spreads for more than a square mile. Old Vuitton trunks, ormolu clocks, 1930s jet jewelry, and vintage garden furniture sit cheek by jowl. Arrive early to pick up the most worthwhile loot (like old prints). Be warned—if there's one place in Paris where you need to know how to bargain, this is it!

If you're arriving by métro, walk under the overpass and take the first left at the rue de Rosiers to reach the epicenter of the market. Around the overpass huddle stands selling dodgy odds-and-ends (think pleather, knockoff shoes, and questionable gadgets). These blocks are crowded and gritty; be careful with your valuables. If you need a breather from the hundreds of market vendors, stop for a bite in one of the rough-and-ready cafés. A particularly good pick is **Le Soleil** (⊠ 109 av. Michelet ☎ 01–40–10–08–08).

On the southern and eastern sides of the city—at **Porte de Vanves** (Ⓜ Porte de Vanves) and Porte de Montreuil—are other, smaller flea markets. Vanves is a hit with the fashion set and specializes in smaller objects—mirrors, textiles, handbags, clothing, and glass. It's open on weekends only from 8 to 5, but you have to arrive early if you want to find a bargain: the good stuff goes fast, and stalls are liable to be packed up before noon.

Flower & Bird Markets

Paris's main flower market is in the heart of the city on the Île de la Cité, between Notre-Dame and the Palais de Justice. It's open every day from 8 until 7:30. There's an eye-popping profusion of cut flowers as well as all manner of plants from the usual suspects to the exotic. On Sunday it also hosts a bird market—a great way to spend an hour on an otherwise quiet morning. Parakeets flutter in cages, and you might also spot plumed chickens and exquisite little ducks with teal and mauve markings. What are they for? It's best not to ask. Other colorful flower markets are held beside the Madeleine church (Madeleine, open Monday–Saturday 9–9 and alternate Sundays 9:30–8:30), and on place des Ternes (Ternes, Tuesday–Sunday).

Food Markets

Year-round and in any weather, the city's open-air food markets play an integral part of daily life, gathering together the entire spectrum of Paris society, from the splendid matron, her miniscule dog in tow, to the tobacco-stained regular picking up his daily baguette. While some markets are busier than others, there's not a market in Paris that doesn't captivate the senses. Each season has its delicacies: *fraises des bois* (wild strawberries) and tender asparagus in spring, squash blossoms and fragrant herbs in summer, saffron-tinted chanterelles in autumn, bergamot oranges in late winter. Year-round you'll find pungent *lait cru* (unpasteurized) cheeses, charcuterie, and unfarmed game and fish. Many of the better-known open-air markets are in areas you'd visit for sightseeing. To get a list of market days in your area, ask your concierge or check the markets section on the Web site ⊕ www.paris.fr/EN.

If you're unused to the metric system, you may find it easier to use the following terms: *une livre* is French for a pound; *une demi-livre,* a half-pound. For cheese or meats, *un morceau* will get you a piece, *une tranche* a slice.

Most markets are open from 8 to 1 three days a week year-round (usually the weekend and one weekday, but never Monday) on a rotating basis. Following are a few of the best. On **Boulevard Raspail** (✉ 6ᵉ, St-Germain-des-Prés Ⓜ Rennes), between rue du Cherche-Midi and rue de Rennes, is the city's major *marché biologique,* or organic market, bursting with produce, fish, and eco-friendly products. It's open Tuesday and Friday. The vendors at the **Rue de Buci** (✉ 6ᵉ, St-Germain-des-Prés Ⓜ Odéon) often have tastes of their wares to tempt you—slices of sausage, slivers of peaches. The market's closed Sunday afternoon and Monday. **Rue Mouffetard** (✉ 5ᵉ, Quartier Latin Ⓜ Monge), near the Jardin des Plantes, reflects its multicultural neighborhood; it's a vibrant market with a laid-back feel that still smacks of old Paris. It's best on weekends. **Rue Montorgueil** (✉ 1ᵉʳ, Beaubourg/Les Halles Ⓜ Châtelet Les Halles) has evolved from an old-fashioned market street into a chic, *bobo* (bourgeois bohemian) zone; its stalls now thrive amid stylish cafés and the oldest oyster counter in Paris. **Rue Lévis** (✉ 17ᵉ, Parc Monceau Ⓜ Villiers), near Parc Monceau, has Alsatian specialties and a terrific cheese shop. It's closed Sunday afternoon and Monday. The **Marché d'Aligre** (✉ Rue d'Aligre, 12ᵉ, Bastille/Nation Ⓜ Ledru-Rollin), open until 1 every day except Monday, is arguably the most locally authentic market. Don't miss the wonderful covered hall on the place d'Aligre, where you can stop by a unique olive oil boutique for either prebottled oils from top producers or fill-your-own bottles.

Stamp Market

Philatelists (and fans of the Audrey Hepburn–Cary Grant 1963 thriller *Charade*) will want to head to Paris's unique **stamp market** (Ⓜ Champs-Élysées–Clémenceau,) at the intersection of avenue Marigny and avenue Gabriel overlooking the gardens at the bottom of the Champs-Élysées. On sale are vintage postcards and stamps from all over the world. It is open Thursday, weekends, and public holidays from 10 until 5.

SHOPPING ARCADES

Paris's 19th-century commercial arcades, called *passages,* are worth a visit for the sheer architectural splendor of their glass roofs, decorative pillars, and inlaid mosaic floors. In 1828 they numbered 137, of which only 24 are left. The major arcades are in the 1er and 2e arrondissements on the Rive Droite.

★ **Galerie Véro-Dodat** (⊠ 19 rue Jean-Jacques Rousseau, 1er, Louvre/Tuileries Ⓜ Louvre) was built in 1826. At what is now the Café de l'Epoque, the French writer Gérard de Nerval took his last drink before heading to Châtelet to hang himself. The gallery has painted ceilings and slender copper pillars and shops selling old-fashioned toys, contemporary art, stringed instruments, and leather goods. It is best known, however, for its antiques stores.

★ **Galerie Vivienne** (⊠ 4 rue des Petits-Champs, 2e, Opéra/Grands Boulevards Ⓜ Bourse), between the Bourse and the Palais-Royal, is home base for a range of interesting and luxurious shops; a lovely tearoom, A Priori Thé; and Cave Legrand, a terrific wine shop. Don't leave without checking out the Jean-Paul Gaultier boutique.

Passage du Grand-Cerf (⊠ 145 rue St-Denis, 2e, Beaubourg/Les Halles Ⓜ Étienne Marcel) has most successfully reignited Parisians' interest. La Parisette, a small boudoir-pink space at No. 1, sells fun accessories, while Marci Noum, at No. 4, riffs on street fashion. Silk bracelets, crystals, and charms can be nabbed at Eric & Lydie and Satellite.

Passage Jouffroy (⊠ 12 bd. Montmartre, 9e, Grands Boulevards Ⓜ Grands Boulevards) is full of shops selling toys, antique canes, Oriental furnishings, and cinema books and posters. Try Pain d'Épices, at No. 29, for dollhouse decor, and Au Bonheur des Dames, at No. 39, for all things embroidery.

Passage des Panoramas (⊠ 11 bd. Montmartre, 2e, Grands Boulevards Ⓜ Opéra or Grands Boulevards), opened in 1800, is the oldest arcade still extant; it's especially known for its stamp shops.

Passage Verdeau (⊠ 4–6 rue de la Grange Batelière, 9e, Opéra/Grands Boulevards Ⓜ Grands Boulevards), across the street from passage Jouffroy, has shops carrying antique cameras, comic books, and engravings.

SPECIALTY SHOPS

Some specialty stores have several branches in the city; for these, we list the locations in the busier shopping neighborhoods.

Arts & Antiques

Don't feel shy about visiting the antique and objets d'art dealers and asking questions; most dealers are happy to talk about their wares, and you never know, you might turn up the doorknob from the bedside table of Napoléon's butler's brother. Antiques go through a rigorous evaluation for historical value before they're put on sale, so if you see something in a shop, it's permissible to take it out of the country. Dealers handle all customs forms. For specific art gallery listings, see Nightlife & the Arts.

Fodor'sChoice ★ Museum-quality pieces proliferate in the **Carré Rive Gauche** (⊠ Between St-Germain-des-Prés and Musée d'Orsay, 6ᵉ, St-Germain-des-Prés Ⓜ St-Germain-des-Prés, Rue du Bac) area; head to the streets between rue de Bac, rue de l'Université, rue de Lille, and rue des Sts-Pères to find more than 100 associated shops, marked with a small blue banner on their storefronts. You could find a 13th-century bronze Buddha hand or a hand-carved rocking horse. Several antiques dealers cluster around the **Drouot auction house** (⊠ 9 rue Drouot, 9ᵉ, Opéra/Grands Boulevards Ⓜ Richelieu Drouot,) near the Opéra. The **Louvre des Antiquaires** (⊠ Pl. du Palais-Royal, 1ᵉʳ, Louvre/Tuileries Ⓜ Palais-Royal) is a gleaming mall devoted to antiques of every period and genre. Whether you're a devoted numismatist, hooked on military memorabilia, or just adore collectible posters, vintage estate jewelry, Italian Renaissance paintings, or period French furniture, chances are that with patience (and plenty of cash) you'll find it here. The **Viaduc des Arts** (⊠ 9–147 av. Daumesnil, 12ᵉ, Bastille/Nation Ⓜ Ledru-Rollin) shelters dozens of art galleries, artisans' boutiques, and upscale shops under the arches of a stone viaduct that once supported train tracks. **Village St-Paul** (⊠ Enter from rue St-Paul, 4ᵉ, Le Marais Ⓜ St-Paul) is a clutch of streets with many antiques shops.

Bags, Scarves & Other Accessories

E. Goyard (⊠233 rue St-Honoré, 1ᵉʳ, Louvre/Tuileries ☎01–42–60–57–04 Ⓜ Tuileries) has been making outstanding luggage since 1853. Clients in the past included Sir Arthur Conan Doyle, Gregory Peck, and the Duke and Duchess of Windsor. Today Karl Lagerfeld and Madonna are both Goyard fans. Check out the house's signature chevron monogram, which can be found on everything from polo chests and hatboxes to suitcases and wallets.

★ **Hermès** (⊠24 rue du Faubourg St-Honoré, 8ᵉ, Louvre/Tuileries ☎01–40–17–47–17 Ⓜ Concorde ⊠ 42 av. Georges V, 8ᵉ, Champs-Élysées ☎ 01–47–20–48–51 Ⓜ George V) was established as a saddlery in 1837 and went on to create the eternally chic Kelly (named for Grace Kelly) and Birkin (named for Jane Birkin) handbags. The magnificent silk scarves are legendary for their rich colors and intricate designs, which change yearly. Jean-Paul Gaultier, the latest women's-wear designer, has won raves for his mix of dressage elements and luxe fabrics. Other accessories may not have waiting lists but are extremely covetable: enamel bracelets, intricately patterned silk twill ties, small leather goods. During semiannual sales, in January and July, prices are slashed by up to 50%, and the crowds line up for blocks.

★ **Jamin Puech** (⊠ 43 rue Madame, 6ᵉ, St-Germain-des-Prés ☎01–45–48–14–85 Ⓜ St-Sulpice ⊠ 68 rue Vieille-du-Temple, 3ᵉ, Le Marais ☎ 01–48–87–84–87 Ⓜ St-Paul) thinks of its bags as jewelry, not just a necessity. Nothing's plain-Jane here; beaded bags swing from thin link chains, fringe flutters from dark embossed-leather totes, small evening purses are covered with shells or hand-dyed crochet—all whimsical, unusual, and fun.

Louis Vuitton (✉ 101 av. des Champs-Élysées, 8ᵉ, Champs-Élysées ☎ 08–10–81–00–10 Ⓜ George V ✉ 6 pl. St-Germain-des-Prés, 6ᵉ, St-Germain-des-Prés ☎ 08–10–81–00–10 Ⓜ St-Germain-des-Prés ✉ 22 av. Montaigne, 8ᵉ, Champs-Élysées ☎ 08–10–81–00–10 Ⓜ Franklin-D.-Roosevelt) has spawned a voracious fan base from Texas to Tokyo with its mix of classic leather goods (the striated Epi, the cocoa-brown monograms, the Damier check) and the saucy revamped versions orchestrated by Marc Jacobs. Jacobs's collaborations, such as with Japanese artist Murakami, have become instant collectibles (and knockoffables). At this writing, the Champs-Élysées branch was closed for renovation until at least spring 2005, with a temporary site at 38 avenue George V filling the gap.

Loulou de la Falaise (✉ 7 rue de Bourgogne, 7ᵉ, Trocadéro/Tour Eiffel ☎ 01–45–51–42–22 Ⓜ Invalides) was the original muse of Yves Saint Laurent; she was at his side for more than 30 years of collections and designed his accessories line. Now this paragon of the fashion aristocracy has her own two-floor boutique where you're welcomed by two red dragons. Browse through bracelets in stone, shell, or wood, suede pouch purses, and vibrant scarves, as well as separates in the striking colors (jade green, strong yellow, Chinese red) Loulou pulls off so effortlessly.

Madeleine Gely (✉ 218 bd. St-Germain, 7ᵉ, St-Germain-des-Prés ☎ 01–42–22–63–35 Ⓜ Rue du Bac) is the queen of walking sticks. The late president François Mitterrand used to buy his at this tiny shop, also filled with an amazing range of umbrellas.

Marie Mercié (✉ 23 rue St-Sulpice, 6ᵉ, St-Germain-des-Prés ☎ 01–43–26–45–83 Ⓜ Mabillon, St-Sulpice) is one of Paris's most fashionable hatmakers. Her husband, Anthony Peto, makes men's hats and has a store at 58 rue Tiquetonne.

Miguel Lobato (✉ 6 rue Malher, 4ᵉ, Le Marais ☎ 01–48–87–68–14 Ⓜ St-Paul) is a sweet little boutique with accessories for the girl who wants it all: beautiful high heels by Balenciaga and Pierre Hardy, bags by Jamin Puech and Charlotte Vasberg, and beaded bracelets by Azuni.

Peggy Huynh Kinh (✉ 9-11 rue Coëtlogon, 6ᵉ, Quartier Latin ☎ 01–42–84–83–82 Ⓜ St-Sulpice), a former architect who's now behind the structural line of bags at Cartier, shows her own line of accessories: understated totes, shoulder bags, wallets, and belts in quality leather, as well as a line of office accessories.

Philippe Model (✉ 33 pl. du Marché St-Honoré, 1ᵉʳ, Louvre/Tuileries ☎ 01–42–96–89–02 Ⓜ Tuileries) has been confecting amazing hats for *haute société* for many years and has more recently expanded his creative energy into a successful line of shoes and unusual objects for the home.

Renaud Pellegrino (✉ 14 rue du Faubourg St-Honoré, 8ᵉ, Champs-Élysées ☎ 01–42–65–35–31 Ⓜ Concorde ✉ 8 rue de Commaille, 7ᵉ, St-Germain-des-Prés ☎ 01–45–48–36–30 Ⓜ Rue du Bac, Sèvres Babylone) whips satin, haircalf, suede, and beads into totes, shoulder bags, and evening bags dainty enough to require an outfit (or date) with pockets for the rest of your things. For those who care to match, there are shoes as well.

DISCOUNT **Accessoires à Soie** (✉ 21 rue des Acacias, 17ᵉ, Champs-Élysées ☎ 01–42–27–78–77 Ⓜ Argentine) is where savvy Parisians buy silk scarves and ties in all shapes and sizes. The wide selection includes many big-name designers, and everything costs about half of what you'd pay elsewhere.

Books (English-Language)

The scenic open-air *bouquinistes* bookstalls along the Seine are stacked with secondhand books (mostly in French), prints, and souvenirs. Numerous French-language bookshops—specializing in a wide range of topics including art, film, literature, and philosophy—can be found in the scholarly Quartier Latin and the publishing district, St-Germain-des-Prés. For English-language books and magazines, try the following.

Abbey Bookstore (✉ 29 rue Parcheminerie, 5ᵉ, Quartier Latin ☎ 01–46–33–16–24 Ⓜ Cluny–La Sorbonne) is Paris's Canadian bookstore, with Canadian newspapers (*La Presse* and the *Toronto Globe & Mail*), books on Canadian history, and new and secondhand Québecois and English-language novels. The Canadian Club of Paris also organizes regular poetry readings and literary conferences here.

Brentano's (✉ 37 av. de l'Opéra, 2ᵉ, Opéra/Grands Boulevards ☎ 01–42–61–52–50 Ⓜ Opéra) is stocked with everything from classics to children's titles. It also has a slightly haphazardly arranged international magazine section.

La Chambre Claire (✉ 14 rue St-Sulpice, 6ᵉ, Quartier Latin ☎ 01–46–34–04–31 Ⓜ Odéon) is chockablock with photography books by everyone from Edward Weston to William Wegman. It even stocks instruction manuals and is a favorite with fashion folk.

Comptoir de l'Image (✉ 44 rue de Sévigné, 3ᵉ, Le Marais ☎ 01–42–72–03–92 Ⓜ St-Paul) is where designers John Galliano, Marc Jacobs, and Emanuel Ungaro stock up on old copies of *Vogue, Harper's Bazaar,* and *The Face*. It also sells trendy magazines like *Dutch, Purple,* and *Spoon,* designer catalogs from the past, and rare photo books.

Galignani (✉ 224 rue de Rivoli, 1ᵉʳ, Louvre/Tuileries ☎ 01–42–60–76–07 Ⓜ Tuileries) stocks both French- and English-language books and is especially known for its extensive shelves filled with art books and coffee-table tomes. It also has an excellent selection of French literature and many English translations of the classics.

★ **La Hune** (✉ 170 bd. St-Germain, 6ᵉ, St-Germain-des-Prés ☎ 01–45–48–35–85 Ⓜ St-Germain-des-Prés), sandwiched between the Café de Flore and Les Deux Magots, is a landmark for intellectuals. French literature is downstairs, but the main attraction is the comprehensive collection of international books on art and architecture upstairs. Stay here until midnight with all the other genius-insomniacs.

Ofr (✉ 30 rue Beaurepaire, 10ᵉ, République ☎ 01–42–45–72–88 Ⓜ République) gets magazines from the most fashionable spots in the world before anyone else. In this messy store you can rub shoulders with photo and press agents and check out the latest in underground, art, and alternative monthlies.

★ **Red Wheelbarrow** (✉ 22 rue St-Paul, 4ᵉ, Le Marais ☎ 01–48–04–75–08 Ⓜ St-Paul ✉ 13 rue Charles V, 4ᵉ, Le Marais ☎ 01–42–77–42–17

Ⓜ St-Paul) is *the* Anglophone bookstore—if it was written in English, you can get it here. The store also has a complete academic section and every literary review you can think of. Ask owner Penelope for gift ideas— she has a wonderful collection of special-edition historical reads. The children's branch, just around the corner on rue Charles V, has a great selection of children's books for young teens and under. Check out its fliers for info on English-language readings, given at least once a month; local artists and visiting authors pitch in on events, and sometimes that piano comes into play.

7L (✉ 7 rue de Lille, 7ᵉ, St-Germain-des-Prés ☎ 01–42–92–03–58 Ⓜ St-Germain-des-Prés), a rather minimalist space owned by the book-addicted Karl Lagerfeld, reflects the designer's impressive personal library. Lagerfeld stocks the shelves with his favorite new releases, as well as the books he edits himself.

Shakespeare and Company (✉ 37 rue de la Bûcherie, 5ᵉ, Quartier Latin ☎ 01–43–26–96–50 Ⓜ St-Michel), the sentimental Rive Gauche favorite, is named after the bookstore whose American owner, Sylvia Beach, first edited James Joyce's *Ulysses*. Nowadays it specializes in expatriate literature. You can count on a couple of eccentric characters somewhere in the stacks, a sometimes-spacey staff, the latest titles from British presses, and hidden secondhand treasures in the odd corners and crannies. Poets give readings upstairs on Monday at 8 PM; there are also tea-party talks on Sunday at 4 PM.

Taschen (✉ 2 rue de Buci, 6ᵉ, St-Germain-des-Prés ☎ 01–40–51–79–22 Ⓜ Mabillon) is perfect for night owls, as it's open until midnight on Friday and Saturday night. The Starck-designed shelves and desks hold glam titles on photography, fine art, design, fashion, and fetishes.

Tea & Tattered Pages (✉ 24 rue Mayet, 6ᵉ, St-Germain-des-Prés ☎ 01–40–65–94–35 Ⓜ Duroc) is the place for a bargain: cheap secondhand paperbacks plus new books (publishers' overstock) at low prices. Tea and brownies are served, and browsing is encouraged.

Fodor'sChoice **Village Voice** (✉ 6 rue Princesse, 6ᵉ, St-Germain-des-Prés ☎ 01–46–
★ 33–36–47 Ⓜ Mabillon) is a heavy hitter in Paris's ever-thriving expat literary scene. It's known for its excellent current and classic book selections, frequent book signings, and readings by authors of legendary stature along with up-and-comers, all run by a knowledgeable and friendly staff. There's always a fresh stash of English-language periodicals and magazines.

W. H. Smith (✉ 248 rue de Rivoli, 1ᵉʳ, Louvre/Tuileries ☎ 01–44–77–88–99 Ⓜ Concorde) carries a multitude of travel and language books, cookbooks, and fiction for adults and children. It also has the best selection of foreign magazines and newspapers in Paris (which you are allowed to peruse without interruption—many magazine dealers in France aren't so kind).

Clothing

Children's Clothing

Almost all the top designers make minicouture, but you can expect to pay unearthly prices for each wee outfit. Following are stores for true children's clothing, as opposed to shrunken versions of adult designer outfits.

L'Angelot par Gilles Neveu (✉ 28 rue Bonaparte, 6ᵉ, St-Germain-des-Prés ☎ 01–56–24–21–22 Ⓜ St-Germain-des-Prés) has everything the newborn to one-year-old baby could desire: clothes in white and beige, bed linen, cuddly teddy bears and rabbits. They also specialize in layettes and christening robes with exquisite, frothy designs. Personalized embroideries and engravings are available upon request, as are deliveries to foreign destinations.

Bonpoint (✉ 64 av. Raymond Poincaré, 16ᵉ, Trocadéro/Tour Eiffel ☎ 01–47–27–60–81 Ⓜ Trocadéro ✉ 67 rue Royale, 8ᵉ, Louvre/Tuileries ☎ 01–47–42–52–63 Ⓜ Madeleine) is for the prince or princess in your life (as it is, royalty *does* shop here). Yes, the prices are high, but the quality is truly exceptional. The style ranges from sturdy play clothes—think a weekend at the château—to the perfect emerald-green hand-smocked silk dress or a midnight-blue velvet suit for Little Lord Fauntleroy. Don't even think about just browsing through the collection for newborns—it's irresistible.

FodorśChoice **Calesta Kidstore** (✉ 23 rue Debelleyme, 3ᵉ, Le Marais ☎ 01–42–72–15–59
★ Ⓜ St-Sébastian Froissart) is Paris's hippest destination for children up to eight years old and their parents. A continuous loop of projected cartoons entrances kids while adults browse color-coordinated racks of the latest clothes and a connoisseur's selection of furniture, toys, strollers and those leather-and-shearling baby carriers favored by supermodel moms.

Not So Big (✉ 38 rue Tiquetonne, 2ᵉ, Beaubourg/Les Halles ☎ 01–42–33–34–26 Ⓜ Étienne Marcel) has a great selection of original clothes, toys, and accessories for both children and mom. Favorites include a line of fun T-shirts, funky winter coats, sweet slippers, and the Mexican bola, a sterling-silver necklace made for pregnant women that falls low on the belly and is said to sing the baby to sleep.

Oona l'Ourse (✉ 72 rue Madame, 6ᵉ, St-Germain-des-Prés ☎ 01–42–84–11–94 Ⓜ St-Placide) racks up classic Shetland sweaters, a line of cashmere clothes by aristocrat-cum-model-cum-mommy Stella Tennant, onesies, and tiny shoes ready for first steps.

Ovale (✉ 200 bd. St-Germain, 7ᵉ, St-Germain-des-Prés ☎ 01–53–63–31–10 Ⓜ St-Germain-des-Prés) caters to babies born with the silver spoon (or if not, there are plenty here to choose from). This ebony-and-cream boutique has disposed of color altogether in favor of warm neutrals for their beautifully crafted unisex clothing (newborn to 12 months). All-natural fabrics include undyed linen, cotton, and cashmere. Don't miss their stunning made-to-measure christening gowns in silk damask.

Petit Bateau (✉ 116 av. des Champs-Élysées, 8ᵉ, Champs-Élysées ☎ 01–40–74–02–03 Ⓜ George V ✉ 81 rue Sèvres, 6ᵉ, St-Germain-des-Prés ☎ 01–45–49–48–38 Ⓜ Sèvres Babylone) provides a fundamental part of the classic French wardrobe from cradle to teen and beyond: the T-shirt, cut close to the body, with smallish shoulders (they work equally well with school uniforms or vintage Chanel). The high-grade cotton clothes follow designs that haven't changed in decades—onesies and pajamas for newborns, T-shirts for every season in every color, underwear sets, dresses with tiny straps for summer. Stock up while you're here—if you can find this brand back home, the prices are sure to be higher.

Pom d'Api (⊠28 rue du Four, 6ᵉ, St-Germain-des-Prés ☎01–45–48–39–31 Ⓜ St-Germain-des-Prés) lines up footwear for babies and preteens in quality leathers and wonderfully vivid colors. Expect well-made, eye-catching fashion—bright gold sneakers and fringed suede boots as well as the classic Mary Janes in shades of silver, pink, and gold. There are also standard utility boots for boys and sturdy rain gear.

Wowo (⊠ 4 rue Hérold, 1ᵉʳ, Beaubourg/Les Halles ☎ 01–53–40–84–80 Ⓜ Châtelet Les Halles) is an original line of well-made clothes for children from three months to the preteen. Designer Elizabeth Relin blends her fashion sensibility and love of color with her respect for the world of childhood—no pop tarts here.

Discounted Clothing

Le Dépôt Vente de Passy (⊠ 14 rue de la Tour, 16ᵉ, Trocadéro/Tour Eiffel ☎ 01–45–20–95–21 Ⓜ Passy) specializes in barely worn designer ready-to-wear from all the big names including Chanel, Saint Laurent, Lacroix, Ungaro, and Rykiel. Few shoppers can pass up one of last season's outfits at one-third the price, or can forget to linger over the vast selection of accessories: bags, belts, scarves, shoes, and costume jewelry.

L'Habilleur (⊠ 44 rue de Poitou, 3ᵉ, Le Marais ☎ 01–48–87–77–12 Ⓜ St-Sébastien Froissart) is a favorite with the fashion press and anyone else looking for a great deal. For women there's a great selection from designers like Prada, Barbara Bui, and Martine Sitbon. Men can find suits from Mugler, Strelli, and Paul Smith at slashed prices.

Rue d'Alésia (Ⓜ Alésia), in the 14ᵉ arrondissement, is the main place to find shops selling last season's fashions at a discount. Be forewarned: most of these shops are much more downscale than their elegant sister shops, and dressing rooms are not always provided.

Men's & Women's Clothing

Agnès b (⊠ 2, 3, and 6 rue du Jour, 1ᵉʳ, Beaubourg/Les Halles ☎ 01–42–33–04–13 Ⓜ Châtelet Les Halles) embodies the quintessential French approach to easy but stylish dressing. There are many branches, and the clothes are also sold in department stores, but for the fullest range go to rue du Jour, where she has taken up most of the street (women's wear, at No. 6; children, at No. 2; and menswear, at No. 3). For women, classics include sleek black leather jackets, flattering black-jersey separates, and her trademark wide-stripe T-shirts in gorgeous color combos. Children love the two-tone T-shirts proclaiming their age. And the stormy-gray velour or corduroy suits you see on those slouchy, scarf-clad men? Agnès b.

A.P.C. (⊠ 3–4 rue Fleurus, 6ᵉ, St-Germain-des-Prés ☎ 01–42–22–12–77 Ⓜ St-Placide ⊠ 112 rue Vieille du Temple, 3ᵉ, Le Marais ☎ 01–42–78–18–02 Ⓜ Filles du Calvaire) may be antiflash, but a knowing eye can always pick out their jeans in a crowd. The clothes are rigorously well made with military precision; prime wardrobe pieces include dark indigo and black denim, zip-up cardigans, and peacoats. The women's (No. 3) and men's (No. 4) boutiques face each other; zip around the corner to 45 rue Madame for the discounted "surplus" stock. The boutique in the Marais brings together the men's, women's, and kid's collections.

BARGAIN HUNTING

AN ARSENAL OF BARGAIN SHOPS *is every savvy Parisian's secret for maintaining incredible style without breaking the bank.* Soldéries *offer stacks of low-priced designer labels permanently on sale, while* stocks *are stores that specialize in one label and sell last season's leftovers with prices slashed at least in half.* Dépôts-Vente *are consignment shops that carry barely worn designer outfits in great condition at killer prices. Fashionable* friperies *stock clothes and accessories from the '50s to the '80s and are a constant inspiration to the international design teams that come to Paris during the collections.* Surplus *sell army surplus jackets, pants, and great lace-up boots for nearly nothing. Watch for the word* soldes *(sales). By law, the two main sale seasons are January and July, when the average discount is 30%–50% off regular prices. Sales last six weeks. Also look for goods*

marked dégriffé—*designer labels, often from last year's collection, for sale at a deep discount.*

In addition, there are the fascinating flea markets and brocantes *(secondhand shops), where you'll always have the chance of finding a stray bit of Quimper faience, Art Deco brooches, or evocative old copies of Paris-Match. At such markets, or in antiques stores, bargaining is accepted. So if you're thinking of buying several articles, you've nothing to lose by cheerfully suggesting to the proprietor, "Vous me faites un prix?" ("How about a discount?"). Other bits of lingo to keep in mind:* braderie *or* fin de série *(clearance);* occasions *or* brocante *(secondhand); and* nouveautés *(new arrivals).*

Balenciaga (✉ 10 av. George V, 8ᵉ, Champs-Élysées ☎ 01–47–20–21–11 Ⓜ Alma-Marceau) is now in the hands of Nicolas Ghesquière—guess what inspired him when he designed this boutique? Notice the tile, the wavy line of the store, that slice of turquoise blue, the aloe plants. The clothes are interesting, sometimes beautiful, as Ghesquière plays with volume (bubbling skirts, superskinny pants) and references (military, scuba). The accessories and menswear are often more approachable, like the perfectly tooled leather bags and narrow suits. (You got it, a swimming pool.)

Dolce & Gabbana (✉ 22 av. Montaigne, 8ᵉ, Champs-Élysées ☎ 01–42–25–68–78 Ⓜ Alma-Marceau) serves up a sexy young Italian widow vibe with a side of moody boyfriend. Svelte silk dresses, sharply tailored suits, and plunging necklines are made for drama. The diffusion line, **D&G** (✉ 244 rue de Rivoli, 1ᵉʳ, Louvre/Tuileries ☎ 01–42–86–00–44 Ⓜ Concorde), rocks day wear with white leather, denim, and splashy florals spiked with lingerie details.

L'Eclaireur (✉ 3 rue des Rosiers, 4ᵉ, Le Marais ☎ 01–48–87–10–22 Ⓜ St-Paul ✉ 12 rue Mahler, 4ᵉ, Le Marais ☎ 01–44–54–22–11 Ⓜ St-Paul), splits itself between the women's wear and the men's, around the corner. It maintains avant-garde tastes for designers such as Martin

Margiela, Paul Harnden, and Anne Demeulemeester, plus a smattering of more omnipresent labels like Dolce & Gabbana.

G-Star Store (✉ 46 rue Étienne-Marcel, 2ᵉ, Beaubourg/Les Halles ☎ 01–42–21–44–33 Ⓜ Étienne Marcel) is a haven for fans of raw denim. It uniquely stocks the designs of the Dutch-based label G-Star, whose highly desirable jeans have replaced those of Levi's as the ones to be seen in. There are also military-inspired clothing, bags, and T-shirts.

H & M (✉ 54 bd. Haussmann, 9ᵉ, Grands Boulevards ☎ 01–55–31–92–50 Ⓜ Opéra/Grands Boulevards) pulls everyone in eventually, especially with Karl Lagerfeld now on the designer roster. The young pros, teens, and landed socialites have all dropped a few euros on the fastest, flimsiest spin-offs in town. Good-quality jeans and winter coats are sturdier bets; the lingerie's fun and cheap enough to be nearly disposable. There's even a kids' line. Try to go in the morning, as the lines for the changing rooms stretch out in the afternoon.

Lucien Pellat-Finet (✉ 1 rue Montalembert, 7ᵉ, St-Germain-des-Prés ☎ 01–42–22–22–77 Ⓜ Rue du Bac) cashmeres shake up the traditional world of cable-knits—here, sweaters for men, women, and children come in punchy colors and cheeky motifs. A psychedelic mushroom could bounce across a sky blue crewneck; a crystal-outlined skull could grin from a sleeveless top. The cashmere's wonderfully soft—and the prices are accordingly high.

Maria Luisa (✉ 38 rue du Mont-Thabor, 1ᵉʳ, Louvre/Tuileries ☎ 01–42–96–47–81 Ⓜ Concorde) is one of the most important names in town for cutting-edge fashion. The store at No. 38 is considered a "style laboratory" for young designers for both him and her; No. 2 is the women's shop, stocked by an army of established designers (like Lang and Demeulemeester); No. 4 houses one of the few places in Paris to get über-cool shoes by Manolo Blahnik and chichi bags by Lulu Guinness; No. 19 is the address for *monsieur*.

Martin Margiela (✉ 25 bis, rue de Montpensier, 1ᵉʳ, Louvre/Tuileries ☎ 01–40–15–07–55 Ⓜ Palais-Royal ✉ 23 passage Poitiers, 1ᵉʳ, Louvre/Tuileries ☎ 01–40–15–06–44 Ⓜ Palais-Royal) keeps a determinedly low profile for his shop, his label, and for himself. (The Belgian designer is sometimes known as Mr. Secret.) But the clothing has a devoted following for its cut—sometimes oversize but never bulky—and for its innovative technique, from spiraling seams to deconstructed shirts. Go upstairs for Ligne 6, his secondary line of more casual (and less expensive) clothes. Menswear is just two doors down.

Massimo Dutti (✉ 24 rue Royale, 8ᵉ, Louvre/Tuileries ☎ 01–53–29–92–70 Ⓜ Concorde ✉ 34 rue Tronchet, 8ᵉ, Louvre/Tuileries ☎ 01–49–24–19–20 Ⓜ Concorde), Zara's upscale, higher-quality cousin, trumps the style-to-price quotient. It hasn't yet made its way to the United States, so you can find a bargain your friends won't. Clothes and accessories are ever-changing and catwalk-inspired, pitched to a polished audience. The newer boutique on rue Royale is spacious enough to rarely feel crowded.

Prada (✉ 10 av. Montaigne, 8ᵉ, Trocadéro/Tour Eiffel ☎ 01–53–23–99–40 Ⓜ Alma-Marceau ✉ 6 rue du Faubourg St-Honoré, 8ᵉ, Louvre/Tuileries ☎ 01–58–18–63–30 Ⓜ Concorde ✉ 5 rue de Grenelle, 6ᵉ, St-Germain-des-Prés ☎ 01–45–48–53–14 Ⓜ St-Sulpice) spins gold out of fashion straw. Knee-length skirts, peacock colors, cardigan sweaters, geometric prints . . . and the waiting lists cross continents. The shoes, bags and other accessories for both men and women perennially become cult items.

Shine (✉ 30 rue de Charonne, 11ᵉ, Bastille/Nation ☏ 01–48–05–80–10 Ⓜ Ledru-Rollin) travels the world to find clothes and accessories that embody the store's spirit: chic, glamour, and rock and roll. One-of-a-kind pieces by young designers share the racks with staples like Earl or Levi's jeans. As well as taking in the fashions, check out the fabulous floral wallpaper and sparkly, gold wall displays.

Le Shop (✉ 3 rue d'Argout, 2ᵉ, Louvre/Tuileries ☏ 01–40–28–95–94 Ⓜ Louvre) is the Parisian address for fans of street wear and techno. The industrial-style shop rocks to the beat of resident DJs and carries numerous hip designers as well as skateboards, sports shoes, and flyers for raves and parties. The whole experience is rather like shopping in a nightclub.

Sonia Rykiel (✉ 194 bd. St-Germain, 7ᵉ, St-Germain-des-Prés ☏ 01–45–44–83–19 Ⓜ St-Germain-des-Prés ✉ 175 bd. St-Germain, 6ᵉ, St-Germain-des-Prés ☏ 01–49–54–60–60 Ⓜ St-Germain-des-Prés ✉ 70 rue du Faubourg St-Honoré, 8ᵉ, Louvre/Tuileries ☏ 01–42–65–20–81 Ⓜ Concorde) has been designing insouciant knitwear since the '60s. Her menswear vibrates with colorful stripes. The women's boutiques tempt with sexy keyhole sweaters, lots of opulent furs, accessories dotted with colored rhinestones, and soft leather bags.

Surface to Air (✉ 46 rue de l'Arbre Sec, 1ᵉʳ, Louvre/Tuileries ☏ 01–49–27–04–54 Ⓜ Louvre Rivoli), a garage-like atelier, has an air of counterculture chic. Offbeat items sport glitter-bunnies or cheerful appliquéd skulls; menswear includes unstructured corduroy suits and enigmatic T-shirts. Look for the latest in avant-garde glossies, wacky jewelry, leather goods, and a small selection of sassy undies.

Yazbukey Kokon To Zaï (✉ 48 rue Tiquetonne, 2ᵉ, Beaubourg/Les Halles ☏ 01–42–36–92–41 Ⓜ Étienne Marcel) is a Japanese expression to sum up the concept of opposing extremes (such as hot and cold, young and old). It is also a hip boutique selling the work of more than 40 young designers, including Marjal Pejoski, Bernard Wilhelm, and Raf Simons.

Yohji Yamamoto (✉ 25 rue du Louvre, 1ᵉʳ, Beaubourg/Les Halles ☏ 01–42–21–42–93 Ⓜ Étienne Marcel) brings all three women's lines together for the first time under one roof: couture; Y's ready-to-wear; and Y-3 sportswear. A master of the drape, fold and twist, Yamamoto's predominantly black clothes manage to be both functional and edgy. Pleats, florals, and brilliant colors now punctuate each collection. Menswear, adored by gallerists and hip-hop stars, is nearby at 47 rue Étienne Marcel.

Yves Saint Laurent (✉ 38 and 32 rue du Faubourg St-Honoré, 8ᵉ, Louvre/Tuileries ☏ 01–42–65–74–59 Ⓜ Concorde ✉ 6 pl. St-Sulpice, 6ᵉ, St-Germain-des-Prés ☏ 01–43–29–43–00 Ⓜ St-Sulpice) revolutionized women's wear in the 1970s, putting pants in couture shows for the first time. His safari jackets, "le smoking" suits, Russian-boho collections, and tailored *Belle de Jour* suits are considered fashion landmarks—these are big shoes to fill. Stefano Pilati, successor to the ingenious Tom Ford, started his tenure with a mellow hand with color and cut. The menswear collection, at No. 32 rue du Faubourg St- Honoré, can be relied on for Saint Laurent's classic pinstripes and satin-lapel tuxes.

Zara (⊠ 44 av. des Champs-Élysées, 8ᵉ, Champs-Élysées ☎ 01–45–61–52–80 Ⓜ Franklin-D.-Roosevelt ⊠ 39 bd. Haussmann, 9ᵉ, Opéra/Grands Boulevards ☎ 01–40–98–01–46 Ⓜ Opéra ⊠ 109 rue St-Lazare, 9ᵉ, Opéra/Grands Boulevards ☎ 01–53–32–82–95 Ⓜ St-Lazare) is hyped as the most reasonable place to go for the latest trends for both men and women. Although they do have everything copied and on the racks in record time, the prices aren't as low as you would expect for this type of quality. Choose wisely: check the seams, feel the fabric, and whatever you do, try it on before deciding if it's worth the investment. Oh, and don't worry—it's *not* you; the tops are cut small, the pants smaller.

Men's Clothing

Charvet (⊠ 28 pl. Vendôme, 1ᵉʳ, Opéra/Grands Boulevards ☎ 01–42–60–30–70 Ⓜ Opéra) is the Parisian equivalent of a Savile Row tailor: a conservative, aristocratic institution famed for made-to-measure shirts, exquisite ties, and accessories, for garbing John F. Kennedy, Charles de Gaulle, and the Duke of Windsor, and for its regal address.

Emile Lafaurie (⊠ 11 rue de Birague, 4ᵉ, Le Marais ☎ 01–42–77–97–19 Ⓜ St-Paul) perfects a casual look without going the jeans-and-sneakers route. The simple, affordable clothes include wide-wale corduroys, boxy painter's jackets (wool in winter, linen in summer), and poplin shirts in over twenty colors. The basics look good on virtually anyone from age 21 to 81.

Madélios (⊠ 23 bd. de la Madeleine, 1ᵉʳ, Opéra/Grands Boulevards ☎ 01–53–45–00–00 Ⓜ Madeleine) gathers up all kinds of menswear labels from classy (Dior, Kenzo) to quirky (Paul Smith) to casual (Diesel, Levi's).

Vintage Clothing

Anouschka (⊠ 6 av. du Coq, 9ᵉ, Opéra/Grands Boulevards ☎ 01–48–74–37–00 Ⓜ St-Lazare, Trinité) has set up shop in her apartment (appointment only, Monday–Saturday) and has rack upon rack of vintage clothing dating from the '30s to the '70s. It is the perfect place to find a '50s cocktail dress in mint condition or a mod jacket for him. A former model herself, she calls it a "designer laboratory," and teams from top fashion houses often pop by looking for inspiration.

★ **Didier Ludot** (⊠ Jardins du Palais-Royal, 20 Galerie Montpensier, 1ᵉʳ, Louvre/Tuileries ⊠ 24 Galerie Montpensier, 1ᵉʳ, Louvre/Tuileries ⊠ 125 Galerie de Valois, 1ᵉʳ, Louvre/Tuileries ☎ 01–42–96–06–56 Ⓜ Palais-Royal) is one of the world's most famous vintage clothing dealers and an incredibly charming man to boot. (A tip: be nice to the dogs.) Rifle through the French couture from the '20s to the '70s on the racks: wonderful Chanel suits, Balenciaga dresses, and Hermès scarves. He has three boutiques: No. 20 houses his amazing collection of vintage couture, No. 24 the vintage ready-to-wear, and across the way at No. 125 you'll find his own vintage-inspired black dresses and his coffee-table book aptly titled *The Little Black Dress*.

Réciproque (✉ 88, 89, 92, 95, and 101 rue de la Pompe, 16ᵉ, Trocadéro/Tour Eiffel ☏ 01–47–04–30–28 Ⓜ Rue de la Pompe) is Paris's largest and most exclusive swap shop. Savings on designer wear—Hermès, Dior, Chanel, and Louis Vuitton—are significant, but prices are not as cheap as you might expect, and there's not much in the way of service or space. The shop at No. 89 specializes in leather goods. The store is closed Sunday and Monday.

Scarlett (✉ 10 rue Clément-Marot, 8ᵉ, Trocadéro/Tour Eiffel ☏ 01–56–89–03–00 Ⓜ Alma-Marceau) offers exceptional vintage couture by the likes of Givenchy, Poiret, Schiaparelli, and Vionnet.

Yukiko (✉ 97 rue Vieille du Temple, 3ᵉ, Le Marais ☏ 01–42–71–13–41 Ⓜ Filles du Calvaire), a tiny space, harbors one-of-a-kind vintage treasures. You might score a '70s-era Hermès blouse, a Stella McCartney for Chloé jacket dripping with oversize pearls, or an immaculate pair of original Roger Vivier crocodile stilettos from the 1950s. In 2005 the store added its own vintage-inspired line of ready-to-wear clothes.

Women's Clothing

CLASSIC CHIC **Alberta Ferretti** (✉ 418 rue St-Honoré, 8ᵉ, Louvre/Tuileries ☏ 01–42–60–14–97 Ⓜ Madeleine/Concorde) puts out come-hither designs. Sheer, cutout, and structured by turns, these super-feminine creations seek to enchant—and succeed. Lacquered silk dresses in opulent hues resemble molten candies. Upstairs is the lingerie-inspired secondary line, Philosophy.

Celine (✉ 36 av. Montaigne, 8ᵉ, Champs-Élysées ☏ 01–56–89–07–91 Ⓜ Franklin-D.-Roosevelt) was venerable and dusty before designer Michael Kors showed up with his version of Jackie O, "the Greek magnate years." Now style-watchers await the look of Kors's successor, Roberto Menichetti.

Cotélac (✉ 19 place du Marché St-Honoré, 1ᵉʳ, Louvre/Tuileries ☏ 01–42–86–05–31 Ⓜ Tuileries/Pyramides ✉ 30 rue Montmartre, 1ᵉʳ, Beaubourg/Les Halles ☏ 01–40–28–13–84 Ⓜ Les Halles ✉ 17 rue du Cherche Midi, 6ᵉ, St-Germain-des-Prés ☏ 01–42–84–10–25 Ⓜ Sevres Babylone) gives unabashedly feminine shapes an edge in earthy tones from azure to deep aubergine. The figure-skimming and frillier separates beg to be layered.

Et Vous (✉ 6 rue des Francs-Bourgeois, 3ᵉ, Le Marais ☏ 01–42–71–75–11 Ⓜ St-Paul ✉ 69 rue de Rennes, 6ᵉ, St-Germain-des-Prés ☏ 01–40–49–01–64 Ⓜ St-Sulpice) takes its cue from the catwalk; turning out affordable, extremely well-cut clothing: pants (low waist/slim hip), knee-skimming skirts, chunky sweaters, and classic work wear with individual details.

Paul & Joe (✉ 46 rue Étienne Marcel, 2ᵉ, Beaubourg/Les Halles ☏ 01–40–28–03–34 Ⓜ Étienne Marcel) is designer Sophie Albou's eclectic, girlish blend of modern trends. There's a decidedly retro feeling to the crisp poplin shirts, A-line skirts with matching fitted jackets, and swingy felt coats. In summer she likes to mix in a little hippie chic.

Paule Ka (✉ 20 rue Malher, 4ᵉ, Le Marais ☏ 01–40–29–96–03 Ⓜ St-Paul ✉ 192 bd. St-Germain, 7ᵉ, St-Germain-des-Prés ☏ 01–45–44–92–60 Ⓜ St-Germain-des-Prés ✉ 45 rue François, 1ᵉʳ, 8ᵉ, Champs-Élysées ☏ 01–47–20–76–10 Ⓜ George V) stays youthful yet proper, with springy, knee-skimming dresses in cotton piqué, coats in black, white, or navy with three-quarter-length sleeves, and evening gowns showing just enough décolleté or leg.

Ventilo (✉ 27 bis, rue du Louvre, 2e, Louvre/Tuileries ☎ 01–44–76–83–00 Ⓜ Louvre ✉ 13–15 bd. de la Madeleine, 1er, Louvre/Tuileries ☎ 01–42–60–46–40 Ⓜ Madeleine) brings cool ethnic style to the city. Where else can you find a bright-orange silk-shantung ball skirt with mirror appliqué or a modern Mongol leather coat lined in fur? There is also room for classics to mix and match, such as handmade wool turtlenecks and zippered riding pants that fit perfectly.

COUTURE
HOUSES

No matter, say the French, that fewer and fewer of their top couture houses are still headed by compatriots. It's the creativity, the workmanship, the je ne sais quoi that remain undeniably Gallic. Haute couture, defined by inimitable handwork, is increasingly buoyed by ancillary lines—ready-to-wear, perfume, sunglasses, you name it—which fill the windows of the boutiques. The successes of some houses have spurred the resuscitation of a few more, such as Rochas, now helmed by the young Belgian designer Olivier Theyskens, and Lanvin, with women's wear by Morocco-born Alber Elbaz. Most of the high-fashion shops are on avenue Montaigne, avenue George V, and rue du Faubourg St-Honoré on the Rive Droite, though St-Germain-des-Prés has also become a stomping ground. Following are a few of Paris's haute couture highlights.

★ **Chanel** (✉ 42 av. Montaigne, 8e, Champs-Élysées ☎ 01–47–23–74–12 Ⓜ Franklin-D.-Roosevelt ✉ 31 rue Cambon, 1er, Louvre/Tuileries ☎ 01–42–86–26–00 Ⓜ Tuileries) is helmed by svelte Karl Lagerfeld, who is now so skinny his ears look fleshy but whose collections are steadily vibrant. The historic center is at the rue Cambon boutique, where Chanel once perched high up on the mirrored staircase watching her audience's reactions to her collection debuts. Great investments include all of Coco's favorites: the perfectly tailored tweed suit, a lean, soigné black dress, a quilted bag with a gold chain, a camellia brooch.

Christian Dior (✉ 30 av. Montaigne, 8e, Champs-Élysées ☎ 01–40–73–54–44 Ⓜ Franklin-D.-Roosevelt ✉ 16 rue de l'Abbé, 6e, St-Germain-des-Prés ☎ 01–40–73–54–44 Ⓜ St-Germain-des-Prés) installed flamboyant John Galliano and embarked on a wild ride. Galliano's catwalks are always the most talked-about *evenements* (events) of the fashion season: opulent, crazy shows with strutting Amazons in extreme ensembles, iced champagne, and some of the most beautiful women in the world in attendance (not to mention the men). Despite the theatrical staging and surreal high jinks, his full-length body-skimming evening dresses cut on the bias are gorgeous in whatever fabric he chooses . . . so what if he pairs them with high-tops and a Davy Crockett raccoon hat? It's just fashion, darling.

Christian Lacroix (✉ 73 rue du Faubourg St-Honoré, 8e, Louvre/Tuileries ☎ 01–42–68–79–00 Ⓜ Concorde ✉ 2 pl. St-Sulpice, 6e, St-Germain-des-Prés ☎ 01–46–33–48–95 Ⓜ St-Sulpice) masters color and texture to such an extent that his runway shows leave fans literally weeping with pleasure—and not just Eddy from *Absolutely Fabulous*. Nubby tweeds might be paired with a fuchsia leopard-print blouse and heavy baroque jewels; a tissue-thin dress could dizzy with vivid paisleys. The rue du Faubourg St-Honoré location is the Lacroix epicenter; on the ground floor you'll find the ready-to-wear line "Bazar"; haute couture is through the courtyard.

Fodor'sChoice ★ **Jean-Paul Gaultier** (⊠ 44 av. George V, 8ᵉ, Champs-Élysées ☎ 01–44–43–00–44 Ⓜ George V ⊠ 6 Galerie Vivienne, 2ᵉ, Opéra/Grands Boulevards ☎ 01–42–86–05–05 Ⓜ Bourse) first made headlines with his celebrated corset with the ironic i-conic breasts for Madonna but now sends fashion editors into ecstasy with his sumptuous haute-couture creations. Designer Philippe Starck spun an *Alice in Wonderland* fantasy for the boutiques, with quilted cream walls and Murano mirrors. Make no mistake, though, it's all about the clothes, dazzlers that make Gaultier a must-see.

Loris Azzaro (⊠ 65 rue de Faubourg St-Honoré, 8ᵉ, Louvre/Tuileries ☎ 01–42–66–92–06 Ⓜ Concorde) mastered dramatic dresses: floor-length columns with jeweled collars and sheer gowns with strategically placed sequins. When he saw his 1970s designs, now considered choice collector's items, worn by stars like Nicole Kidman and Liz Hurley, he decided to re-edit his best sellers. The mirrored boutique takes you back to a time when Jane Birkin and model Marisa Berenson wore his slinky gowns.

Ungaro (⊠ 2 av. Montaigne, 8ᵉ, Champs-Élysées ☎ 01–53–57–00–00 Ⓜ Alma-Marceau) tempers sexiness with a sense of fun. Ruffled chiffon, daringly draped dresses, and clinging silk jersey radiate exuberance with their bright floral and butterfly prints, polka dots, and tropical colors (shocking pink, sunset orange).

TRENDSETTERS **Antik Batik** (⊠ 18 rue de Turenne, 4ᵉ, Le Marais ☎ 01–48–87–95–95 Ⓜ St-Paul) has a wonderful line of ethnically inspired clothes. There are row upon row of embroidered velvet dress coats, Chinese silk tunics, short fur jackets, fringed printed shawls, and some of Paris's most popular handbags.

Antoine & Lili (⊠ 95 quai de Valmy, 10ᵉ, République ☎ 01–40–37–41–55 Ⓜ Jacques-Bonsergent ⊠ 90 rue des Martyrs, 18ᵉ, Montmartre ☎ 01–42–58–10–22 Ⓜ Abesses) is a bright fuchsia store packed with eclectic objects from the East and its own line of clothing. The fantasy seems to work for the French because these boutiques are always hopping. There is an ethnic rummage-sale feel, with old Asian posters, small lanterns, and basket upon basket of cheap little doodads, baubles, and trinkets for sale. The clothing itself has simple lines, and there are always plenty of picks in raw silk.

A-POC (⊠ 47 rue des Francs-Bourgeois, 4ᵉ, Le Marais ☎ 01–44–54–07–05 Ⓜ St-Paul) stands for "A Piece of Cloth" (also a play on the word *epoch*). Japanese designer Issey Miyake's concept: a fabrication technique that allows for hundreds of clothes to be cut from one piece of tubular cloth, resulting in clothing that you can customize at will. Contrary to first impressions, Miyake's clothes are eminently wearable. There are even adorable styles for children.

Azzedine Alaïa (⊠ 7 rue de Moussy, 4ᵉ, Le Marais ☎ 01–42–72–19–19 Ⓜ Hôtel de Ville) is one of the darlings of the fashion set with his perfectly proportioned "king of cling" dresses. You don't have to be under 20 to look good in one of his dresses; Tina Turner wears his clothes well, as does every other beautiful woman with the courage and the curves. His boutique/workshop/apartment is covered with artwork by Julian Schnabel and is not the kind of place you casually wander into out of curiosity: the sales staff immediately makes you feel awkward in that distinctive Parisian way.

Chloé (✉ 54–56 rue du Faubourg St-Honoré, 8ᵉ, Louvre/Tuileries ☎ 01–44–94–33–00 Ⓜ Concorde) reinvents the 1970s–80s fox with a sense of humor and a taste for the outré (and the *cher*). The best new interpretation of the poncho and flouncy silk separates under structured jackets or trench coats work a potent if paradoxical magic. Not to mention the accessories: woven leather belts to be worn with chiffon cocktail dresses, and chunky reptile and metallic bags.

★ **Colette** (✉ 213 rue St-Honoré, 1ᵉʳ, Louvre/Tuileries ☎ 01–55–35–33–90 Ⓜ Tuileries) is the address for ridiculously cool fashion par excellence. So the staff barely deigns to make eye contact—who cares! There are ultramodern trinkets and trifles of all kinds: perfumes, an exclusive handful of cosmetics, including Aesop, Kiehls, and François Nars; plus Marie-Hélène de Taillac's jewelry "bar" . . . and that's just the ground floor. The first floor has beautiful clothing from every internationally known and unknown designer (clothes, shoes, and accessories) who oozes trendiness and street cred, and a small library and art display space. The basement has a water bar (because that's what the models eat) and a small restaurant that's actually quite good for a quick bite.

E2 (✉ 2 rue de Provence, 9ᵉ, Opéra/Grands Boulevards ☎ 01–47–70–15–14 Ⓜ Grands Boulevards) houses, by appointment only, three lines by designers Michèle and Olivier Chatenet: their own label of ethnic-influenced fashion inspired by the '30s through the '70s; impeccable vintage couture finds like Pucci, Lanvin, and Hermès; plus clothing remade with their own special customizing method. They take tired fashion and transform it; for example, sewing emerald-green sequins into the pleats of an ordinary gray kilt. With one of these creations in tow, you will be dressed like no one else.

Galliano (✉ 384 rue St-Honoré, 1ᵉʳ, Louvre/Tuileries ☎ 01–53–35–40–40 Ⓜ Concorde), fittingly enough, landed an address with Revolutionary history for his first namesake store. What more can be said about John Galliano, a living hyperbole? Well, the boutique pairs glass and raw stone; a large high-tech plasma screen grabs your eye and a signature Diptyque candle scents the air. The clothes ricochet between debauchery, humor, and refinement. Look past the wackier distractions and you'll find what he does best: flattering long dresses, structured jackets, heels that give the best leg.

★ **Isabel Marant** (✉ 16 rue de Charonne, 11ᵉ, Bastille/Nation ☎ 01–49–29–71–55 Ⓜ Ledru-Rollin ✉ 1 rue Jacob, 6ᵉ, St-Germain-des-Prés ☎ 01–43–26–04–12 Ⓜ St-Germain-des-Prés), a young designer, is a honeypot of bohemian rock-star style. The separates skim the body without constricting it: silk jersey dresses, loose sweaters ready to slip from a shoulder, tight little knitwear sets in cool colors (prune, green, and taupe). Look for the secondary line, Etoile, for a less-expensive take.

Lagerfeld Gallery (✉ 40 rue de Seine, 6ᵉ, St-Germain-des-Prés ☎ 01–55–42–75–51 Ⓜ Mabillon) sells Karl's personal line of sharp-shouldered suits, double-breasted coats, and other elements of the femme fatale arsenal. On the first floor are accessories, perfumes, magazines, and exhibitions of Lagerfeld's own photography.

★ **Marni** (⊠ 57 av. Montaigne, 8ᵉ, Champs-Élysées ☎ 01–56–88–08–08 Ⓜ Franklin-D.-Roosevelt) is an Italian label with a fantastic take on boho chic—retro-ish prints and colors (citron yellow, seaweed green), funky fabrics (striped ticking, canvas), and accessories that suggest wanderlust (hobo bags).

Onward (⊠ 147 bd. St-Germain, 6ᵉ, St-Germain-des-Prés ☎ 01–55–42–77–55 Ⓜ St-Germain-des-Prés) stocks fashion-forward clothes and accessories by the likes of Ann Demeulemeester, Martin Margiela, Jean-Paul Gaultier, Bernhard Wilhelm, and A. F. Vandevorst. It also gives over a space each season to up-and-coming labels like Viktor & Rolf.

★ **Vanessa Bruno** (⊠ 12 rue de Castiglione, 1ᵉʳ, Louvre/Tuileries ☎ 01–42–61–44–60 Ⓜ Pyramides ⊠ 25 rue St-Sulpice, 6ᵉ, Quartier Latin ☎ 01–43–54–41–04 Ⓜ Odéon) stirs up a new brew of feminine dressing: some androgynous pieces (skinny pants) plus delicacy (filmy tops) with a dash of rocker (miniskirts). The handbags have been a favorite since the überpopular sequin-striped canvas totes a few years back.

Zadig & Voltaire (⊠ 42 rue des Francs Bourgeois, 3ᵉ, Le Marais ☎ 01–44–54–00–60 Ⓜ St-Paul ⊠ 1–3 rue Vieux Colombier, 6ᵉ, St-Germain-des-Prés ☎ 01–43–29–18–29 Ⓜ St-Sulpice ⊠ 18–20 rue François 1er, 8ᵉ, Champs-Élysées ☎ 01–40–70–97–89 Ⓜ Franklin-D.-Roosevelt) is the A-list destination for young fashionistas, offering street wear at its funkiest: form-hugging jeans, pointelle cashmere cardigans in offbeat colors, cropped leather jackets, flounced minis in layered organza. The Deluxe store on rue François 1er carries stars such as Alberta Ferretti's Philosophy, See by Chloé, and shoes by Marc for Marc Jacobs.

Cosmetics

When it comes to *maquillage* (makeup), many Parisian women head directly to **Monoprix,** an urban supermarket/dime store and a gold mine for inexpensive, good-quality cosmetics. Brand names to look for are Bourjois, whose products are made in the Chanel factories, and Arcancil. For a great bargain on the best French products, check out the host of "parapharmacies" that have sprung up throughout the city. The French flock here to stock up on pharmaceutical skin-care lines, hair-care basics, and great baby-care necessities normally sold in the more expensive pharmacies. Look for the Roc line of skin products, hair care by Réné Furterer or Phytologie, the popular Caudalíe line of skin care made with grape extracts, or the Nuxe line of body oils and creams infused with a slight gold hue that French actresses swear by, all of which are more expensive back home if you can find them.

Anne Sémonin (⊠ 2 rue des Petits-Champs, 2ᵉ, Beaubourg/Les Halles ☎ 01–42–60–94–66 Ⓜ Palais-Royal ⊠ 108 rue du Faubourg St-Honoré, 8ᵉ, Champs-Élysées ☎ 01–42–66–24–22 Ⓜ Champs-Élysées–Clemenceau) sells exceptional skin-care products made out of seaweed and trace elements, as well as essential oils that are popular with fashion models.

L'Atelier du Savon (✉ 29 rue Vieille-du-Temple, 4ᵉ, Le Marais ☎ 01–44–54–06–10 Ⓜ St-Paul) is a soap addict's delight. There are blocks of chocolate-and-lime soap, mint-and-lemon soap, and others that look strangely like brownies. Fizzy balls for the bath have rose petals and sequins inside, and shampoos come in solid blocks.

By Terry (✉ 36 Galerie Véro-Dodat, 1ᵉʳ, Louvre/Tuileries ☎ 01–44–76–00–76 Ⓜ Louvre, Palais-Royal ✉ 1 rue Jacob, 6ᵉ, St-Germain-des-Prés ☎ 01–46–34–00–36 Ⓜ St-Germain-des-Prés) is the brainchild of Yves Saint Laurent's former director of makeup, Terry de Gunzberg. This small refined store offers her own brand of "ready-to-wear" makeup that is a favorite of French actresses and socialites. Upstairs there is a team of specialists that creates what de Gunzberg calls *haute couleur*, an exclusive made-to-measure makeup line tailored for each client (very expensive and you'd need to book an appointment far in advance).

Codina (✉ 24 rue Violet, 15ᵉ, Trocadéro/Tour Eiffel ☎ 01–45–78–88–88 Ⓜ Dupleix) extracts its organic oils from the oldest oil press in Paris. The French swear by essential oils, and this is where you'll find the best oils around: almond oil to moisturize, argan oil to combat wrinkles, lavender oil to de-stress.

Make Up for Ever (✉ 5 rue de la Boétie, 8ᵉ, Champs-Élysées ☎ 01–53–05–93–30 Ⓜ St-Augustin), at the back of a courtyard, is a must-stop for makeup artists, models, and actresses. The ultrahip selection has a spectrum of hundreds of hues for foundation, eye shadow, lipsticks, and other powders—some of which are parrot bright.

Sephora (✉ 70 av. des Champs-Élysées, 8ᵉ, Champs-Élysées ☎ 01–53–93–22–50 Ⓜ Franklin-D.-Roosevelt ✉ 1 rue Pierre Lescot, in the Forum des Halles, 1ᵉʳ, Beaubourg/Les Halles ☎ 01–40–13–72–25 Ⓜ Châtelet Les Halles), the leading chain of perfume and cosmetics megastores in France, sells its own makeup as well as all the big brands. Choose from 365 colors of lipstick, test a new gloss at the aisle-end mirrors, and browse through the "cultural gallery" at the Champs-Élysées store.

Shu Uemura (✉ 176 bd. St-Germain, 6ᵉ, St-Germain-des-Prés ☎ 01–45–48–02–55 Ⓜ St-Germain-des-Prés) has enhanced those whose faces are their fortune for decades. Models swear by the cleansing oil; free samples are readily proffered. A huge range of colors, every makeup brush imaginable, and a no-pinch eyelash curler keep loyal fans coming back.

Food & Wine

In addition to the establishments listed below, don't overlook La Grande Épicerie in Le Bon Marché department store (*see* above).

À la Mère de Famille (✉ 35 rue du Faubourg-Montmartre, 9ᵉ, Opéra/Grands Boulevards ☎ 01–47–70–83–69 Ⓜ Cadet) is an enchanting shop well versed in French regional specialties and old-fashioned bonbons, sugar candy, and more.

Les Caves Augé (✉ 116 bd. Haussmann, 8ᵉ, Opéra/Grands Boulevards ☎ 01–45–22–16–97 Ⓜ St-Augustin), one of the best wine shops in Paris since 1850, is just the ticket whether you're looking for a rare vintage for an oenophile friend or a seductive Bordeaux for a tête-à-tête. English-speaking Marc Sibard is a knowledgeable and affable adviser.

Debauve & Gallais (✉ 30 rue des Sts-Pères, 7ᵉ, St-Germain-des-Prés ☎ 01–45–48–54–67 Ⓜ St-Germain-des-Prés) was founded in 1800. The two former chemists who ran it became the royal chocolate purveyors and were famed for their "health chocolates, " made with almond milk. Test the benefits yourself with ganaches, truffles, or *pistoles,* flavored dark-chocolate disks.

FodorśChoice
★ **La Dernière Goutte** (✉ 6 rue de Bourbon le Château, 6ᵉ, St-Germain-des-Prés ☎ 01–46–29–11–62 Ⓜ Odéon), an inviting *cave,* focuses on wines by small French producers. Each is handpicked by the owner, along with a choice selection of estate champagnes, Armagnac, and the classic Vieille Prune (plum brandy). The friendly English-speaking staff makes browsing a pleasure. Don't miss Saturday afternoon tastings, a neighborhood event.

L'Épicerie (✉ 51 rue St-Louis-en-L'Île, 4ᵉ, Île St-Louis ☎ 01–43–25–20–14 Ⓜ Pont Marie) sells 90 types of jam (such as fig with almonds and cinnamon), 70 kinds of mustard (including one with chocolate and honey), numerous olive oils, and flavored sugars.

Fauchon (✉ 26 pl. de la Madeleine, 8ᵉ, Opéra/Grands Boulevards ☎ 01–70–39–38–00 Ⓜ Madeleine) remains the most iconic of all Parisian food stores. It's now expanding globally, but the flagship is still right behind the Madeleine church. Established in 1886, it sells renowned pâté, honey, jelly, tea, and private-label champagne. Expats come for hard-to-find foreign foods (U.S. pancake mix, British lemon curd); those with a sweet tooth make a beeline for the *macarons* (airy, ganache-filled cookies) in the patisserie. There's also a café for a quick bite. Prices can be eye-popping—marzipan fruits for €95 a pound—but who can naysay a Fauchon *cadeau.*

Hédiard (✉ 21 pl. de la Madeleine, 8ᵉ, Opéra/Grands Boulevards ☎ 01–43–12–88–88 Ⓜ Madeleine), established in 1854, was famous in the 19th century for its high-quality imported spices. These—along with rare teas and beautifully packaged house brands of jam, mustard, and cookies—continue to be a draw.

Huilerie Artisanale J. Leblanc et Fils (✉ 6 rue Jacob, 6ᵉ, St-Germain-des-Prés ☎ 01–46–34–61–55 Ⓜ Mabillon) corrals everything you need for the perfect salad dressing into its small space: over fifteen varieties of oils pressed the old-fashioned way, with a big stone wheel, from olives, hazelnuts, pistachios, or grapeseed; aged vinegars; and *fleur de sel* (unprocessed sea salt).

★ **Ladurée** (✉ 16 rue Royale, 8ᵉ, Louvre/Tuileries ☎ 01–42–60–21–79 Ⓜ Madeleine ✉ 75 av. des Champs-Élysées, 8ᵉ, Champs-Élysées ☎ 01–40–75–08–75 Ⓜ George V ✉ 21 rue Bonaparte, 6ᵉ, Quartier Latin ☎ 01–44–07–64–87 Ⓜ Odéon), founded in 1862, oozes period atmosphere—even at the new, large Champs-Élysées branch. But nothing beats the original tearoom on rue Royale, with its pint-size tables and frescoed ceiling. They claim a familial link to the invention of the macaron, and appropriately there's a fabulous selection of these cookies: classics like pistachio, salted caramel, and coffee and, seasonally, violet–black currant, chestnut, and lime-basil.

★ **Lavinia** (✉ 3–5 bd. de la Madeleine, 1ᵉʳ, Opéra/Grands Boulevards ☎ 01–42–97–20–20 Ⓜ St-Augustin) has the largest selection of wine in one spot in Europe—a choice of more than 6,000 wines and spirits from all over the world, ranging from the simple to the sublime. On-site there are expert sommeliers to help you sort it all out. A wine-tasting bar, a bookshop, and a restaurant are also here.

La Maison du Chocolat (✉ 56 rue Pierre-Charron, 8ᵉ, Champs-Élysées ☎ 01–47–23–38–25 Ⓜ Franklin-D.-Roosevelt ✉ 8 bd. de la Madeleine, 9ᵉ, Louvre/Tuileries ☎ 01–47–42–86–52 Ⓜ Madeleine ✉ 225 rue du Faubourg St-Honoré, 8ᵉ, Louvre/Tuileries ☎01–42–27–39–44 Ⓜ Ternes) boutiques seem to be steeped in cocoa, down to the ribbons on their boxes. The quality is outstanding, so that even ostensibly simple treats like chocolate-covered almonds reveal complex flavors. Indulge in a cup of thick, intense hot chocolate at the tearooms in the stores on rue Pierre-Charron or boulevard de la Madeleine.

La Maison du Miel (✉ 24 rue Vignon, 9ᵉ, Louvre/Tuileries ☎ 01–47–42–26–70 Ⓜ Madeleine) takes *miel* (honey) seriously—more than 30 varieties are in stock, many sweetly packaged for delicious gift-giving.

Mariage Frères (✉ 30 rue du Bourg-Tibourg, 4ᵉ, Le Marais ☎ 01–42–72–28–11 Ⓜ Hôtel de Ville ✉ 13 rue des Grands-Augustins, 6ᵉ, St-Germain-des-Prés ☎ 01–40–51–82–50 Ⓜ Mabillon, St-Michel), with its colonial *charme* and wooden counters, has more than 100 years of tea purveying behind it. Choose from more than 450 blends from 32 different countries, not to mention teapots, teacups, books about tea, and tea-flavor biscuits and candies. The on-site tearoom serves high tea and a light lunch.

Le Palais des Thés (✉ 64 rue Vieille du Temple, 4ᵉ, Le Marais ☎ 01–48–87–80–60 Ⓜ St- Paul) is a seriously comprehensive experience—white tea, green tea, black tea, tea from China, Japan, Indonesia, South America, and more. Try one of the flavored teas such as Hammam, a traditional Turkish recipe with date pulp, orange flower, rose, and red berries.

Fodor'sChoice ★ **Pierre Hermé** (✉72 rue Bonaparte, 6ᵉ, Quartier Latin ☎01–43–54–47–77 Ⓜ Odéon ✉ 185 rue de Vaugirard, 15ᵉ ☎ 01–47–83–29–72 Ⓜ Pasteur) is the namesake of the man dubbed the "Picasso of pastry." Even notoriously impatient Parisians line up for these pastries: glossy and urbane, they dip into unexpected combinations, like passion fruit and chocolate or lychee and rose. The exotic macarons sparked a major buzz, as more familiar flavors like hazelnut and lemon were joined by white truffle and olive oil.

★ **Pierre Marcolini** (✉ 89 rue de Seine, 6ᵉ, St-Germain-des-Prés ☎01–44–07–39–07 Ⓜ Mabillon) is all seriousness. Belly up to the sleek wooden bar of this Belgian chocolatier for a selection of *palet fins* or *pralines,* chocolates filled with flavored ganache, caramel, or nuts. Mr. Marcolini proves it's all in the bean with his specialty *saveurs du monde* chocolates, which are made with a single kind of cacao from a single location such as Madagascar, Venezuela, or Ecuador.

Ryst-Dupeyron (✉ 79 rue du Bac, 7ᵉ, St-Germain-des-Prés ☎ 01–45–48–80–93 Ⓜ Rue du Bac) specializes in fine wines and liquors, with port, calvados, and Armagnacs that date to 1878. A great gift idea: find a bottle from the year of a friend's birth and have it labeled with your friend's name. Personalized bottles can be ordered and delivered on the same day.

Verlet (✉ 256 rue St-Honoré, 1er, Louvre/Tuileries ☎ 01–42–60–67–39 Ⓜ Palais-Royal) is *the* place in Paris to buy coffee. There are more than 20 varieties, from places as far-flung as Hawaii and Papua New Guinea. Also on sale are teas, jams from the Savoie region, and (in winter) a stunning assortment of candied fruits.

Housewares

Agatha Ruiz de la Prada (✉ 9 rue Guénégaud, 6e, Quartier Latin ☎ 01–43–25–86–88 Ⓜ Odéon) is nothing if not prolific. She designs clothing and accessories for the Spanish department store El Corte Inglés, watches for Swatch, and furniture for Amat. In this small store she also sells her own items, from bags and children's fashions to yo-yos and notebooks. All are typified by naive motifs in primary colors.

Alexandre Biaggi (✉ 14 rue de Seine, 6e, St-Germain-des-Prés ☎ 01–44–07–34–73 Ⓜ St-Germain-des-Prés) is one of the best addresses for 20th-century furniture. He specializes in the period 1910–50 and also commissions the occasional design from such talented contemporary designers as Nicolas Aubagnac and Hervé van der Straeten.

A. Simon (✉ 48 rue Montmartre, 2e, Beaubourg/Les Halles ☎ 01–42–33–71–65 Ⓜ Étienne Marcel) is one of the places where Parisian chefs come to acquire everything they need in the kitchen—from plates and glasses to pans, dishes, and wooden spoons. The quality is excellent and the prices pleasantly reasonable.

Astier de Villatte (✉ 99 rue du Bac, 7e, St-Germain-des-Prés ☎ 01–42–22–81–59 Ⓜ Rue du Bac, Mabillon, St-Sulpice ✉ 173 rue St-Honoré, 1er, Louvre/Tuileries ☎ 01–42–60–74–13 Ⓜ Tuileries) offers its interpretation of 18th-century table settings; live out your baroque or Empire fancies with milk-white china sets.

Avant-Scène (✉ 4 pl. de l'Odéon, 6e, Quartier Latin ☎ 01–46–33–12–40 Ⓜ Odéon) is a good source for original, poetic furniture. Owner Elisabeth Delacarte commissions limited-edition pieces from artists like Mark Brazier-Jones, Franck Evennou, and Hubert Le Gall.

Catherine Memmi (✉ 32–34 rue St-Sulpice, 6e, St-Germain-des-Prés ☎ 01–44–07–22–28 Ⓜ Mabillon, St-Sulpice ✉ 11 rue St-Sulpice, 6e, St-Germain-des-Prés ☎ 01–44–07–02–02 Ⓜ St-Sulpice) sells wonderfully chic bed linens, bath products, lamps, table settings, furniture, and cashmere sweaters—all in elegantly neutral colors and minimalist designs.

Christian Liaigre (✉ 42 rue du Bac, 7e, St-Germain-des-Prés ☎ 01–53–63–33–66 Ⓜ Rue du Bac) ushered in the taste for clean-lined, broad-shouldered furniture made of luxurious materials; no wonder his style has been lapped up by Calvin Klein. Working with feng shui principles, Liaigre produces signally understated, enticing pieces, often in wenge wood, oak, and ebony.

Christian Tortu (✉ 6 Carrefour de l'Odéon, 6e, St-Germain-des-Prés ☎ 01–43–26–02–56 Ⓜ Odéon), a stellar florist, now sells the perfect things to put his flowers in. There are vases in smoked glass, wood, and Plexiglas, plus candles and bath products that mimic the smells of grass and tomato leaves.

Christofle (✉ 24 rue de la Paix, 2e, Opéra/Grands Boulevards ☎ 01–42–65–62–43 Ⓜ Opéra ✉ 9 rue Royale, 8e, Louvre/Tuileries ☎ 01–55–

27–99–13 Ⓜ Concorde, Madeleine), founded in 1830, has fulfilled all kinds of silver wishes, from a silver service for the *Orient Express* to a gigantic silver bed. Come here for timeless table settings, vases, cigarette holders, jewelry boxes, and more.

Compagnie Française de l'Orient et de la Chine (✉ 163 bd. St-Germain, 6ᵉ, St-Germain-des-Prés ☎ 01–45–48–00–18 Ⓜ St-Germain-des-Prés) imports ceramics and furniture from China and Mongolia. On the first floor are vases, teapots, and table settings; in the basement are straw hats, raffia baskets, and bamboo footstools.

Conran Shop (✉ 117 rue du Bac, 7ᵉ, St-Germain-des-Prés ☎ 01–42–84–10–01 Ⓜ Sèvres Babylone ✉ 30 bd. des Capucines, 9ᵉ, Opéra/Grands Boulevards ☎ 01–53–43–29–00 Ⓜ Madeleine) is the brainchild of British entrepreneur Terence Conran. Here you can find expensive contemporary furniture, beautiful bed linens, and items for every other room in the house—all marked by a balance of utility with not-too-sober style. Conran makes even shower curtains fun.

Diptyque (✉ 34 bd. St-Germain, 5ᵉ, St-Germain-des-Prés ☎ 01–43–26–45–27 Ⓜ Maubert Mutualité) is famous for its candles and eaux de toilette in sophisticated scents like myrrh, fig tree, and verbena (these are not inexpensive; the candles, for instance, cost nearly $1 per hour of burn time). The vinegar water can do triple duty, as an after-shave splash, a hair rinse, and, if steamed, as a room purifier.

★ **E. Dehillerin** (✉ 18–20 rue Coquillière, 1ᵉʳ, Louvre/Tuileries ☎ 01–42–36–53–13 Ⓜ Les Halles) has been around since 1820. Never mind the creaky stairs and dust; their huge range of professional cookware in enamel, stainless steel, or fiery copper is so beautiful that cooks have been known to swoon. With an inventory too bountiful to list, suffice it to say Julia Child was a regular and it's easy to imagine her spirit happily lurking about.

Gien (✉ 18 rue de l'Arcade, 8ᵉ, Louvre/Tuileries ☎ 01–42–66–52–32 Ⓜ Madeleine) has been making fine china since 1821. The faience spans both traditional designs, such as those inspired by Italian majolica or blue-and-white delftware, and contemporary looks.

Kitchen Bazaar (✉ Galerie des 3 Quartiers, 23 bd. de la Madeleine, 1ᵉʳ, Opéra/Grands Boulevards ☎ 01–42–60–50–30 Ⓜ Madeleine ✉ 50 rue Croix des Petits-Champs, 1ᵉʳ, Louvre/Tuileries ☎ 01–40–15–03–11 Ⓜ Palais-Royal/Musée du Louvre) gleams with an astonishing array of small culinary essentials. Don't be surprised at the urge to replace every tatty utensil in your kitchen, down to the last pastry brush and pepper mill, with the up-to-the-minute designs here.

Laguiole (✉ 1 pl. Ste-Opportune, 1ᵉʳ, Beaubourg/Les Halles ☎ 01–40–28–09–42 Ⓜ Châtelet) is the name of the country's most famous brand of knives. Today designers like Philippe Starck and Sonia Rykiel have created special models for the company. Starck also designed this striking boutique (note the animal horn sticking out of the wall).

★ **Maison de Baccarat** (✉ 11 pl. des Etats-Unis, 16ᵉ, Trocadéro/Tour Eiffel ☎ 01–40–22–11–10 Ⓜ Trocadéro) was once the home of Marie-Laure de Noailles, known as the Countess of Bizarre; now it's a museum and crystal store. Philippe Starck revamped the space with his signature cleverness—yes, that's a chandelier floating in an aquarium and, yes, that crystal arm sprouting from the wall alludes to Jean Cocteau (a friend of Noailles). Follow the red carpet to the jewelry room, where crystal baubles hang from bronze figurines, and to the immense table stacked with crystal items for the home.

★ **Le Monde Sauvage** (⊠ 11 rue de l'Odéon, 6ᵉ, Quartier Latin ☎ 01–43–25–60–34 Ⓜ Odéon) is a must-visit address for home accessories—reversible silk bedspreads in rich colors, scrumptious velvet throws, hand-quilted bed linens, silk floor cushions, rice-paper lanterns, zinc mirrors, and the best selection of ready-made, hand-embroidered curtains in silk, cotton, linen, or velvet.

★ **Muji** (⊠ 47 rue des Francs Bourgeois, 4ᵉ, Le Marais ☎ 01–49–96–41–41 Ⓜ St-Paul ⊠ 27 and 30 rue St-Sulpice, 6ᵉ, St-Germain-des-Prés ☎ 01–46–34–01–10 Ⓜ Odéon) runs on the concept of *kanketsu*, or simplicity. The resultant streamlined designs for sportswear, housewares, and other supplies are all the rage in Europe. Must-haves include a collection of mini-necessities—travel essentials, wee office gizmos, purse-size accoutrements—so useful and adorable you'll want them all. They're perfect for gifts, but the happy recipient is likely to be you. Consider visiting on weekdays, as the stores get very crowded on weekends.

Le Prince Jardinier (⊠ Pl. Palais-Royal, 1ᵉʳ, Louvre/Tuileries ☎ 01–42–60–37–13 Ⓜ Palais-Royal ⊠ 46 rue du Bac, 7ᵉ, St-Germain-des-Prés ☎ 01–42–22–30–07 Ⓜ Rue du Bac) has a bona fide noble pedigree. The namesake prince is passionate about gardening; disappointed in the available equipment, he set out to find the best artisans to make hand-crafted tools. The Palais-Royal arcade makes the perfect setting for the resulting shop, where you'll find trowels, watering cans, and topiary shears so beautiful you may be tempted to display them instead of use them. The rue de Bac boutique shares space with the famous taxidermist Deyrolles, an amiable partnership.

Résonances (⊠ Carrousel du Louvre, 99 rue de Rivoli, 1ᵉʳ, Louvre/Tuileries ☎ 01–42–97–06–00 Ⓜ Louvre/Palais-Royal) specializes in nostalgic French lifestyle items: 1950s-style soap holders that attach to the wall, everything you need to cook the perfect egg, a neat porcelain figurine called Pierrot le Gourmand that holds lollipops. You can pick up cupboard fillers of honey and chestnut cream, or home scents that duplicate the delicious perfume of waxed wood.

R & Y Augousti (⊠ 103 rue du Bac, 7ᵉ, St-Germain-des-Prés ☎ 01–42–22–22–21 Ⓜ Sèvres Babylone) are two Paris-based designers who make furniture and objects for the home in materials like coconut, bamboo, fish skin, palm wood, and parchment. Also on sale is their line of textiles inspired by peacock feathers. Treat yourself to one of their great hand-tooled leather bags.

★ **Sentou Galerie** (⊠ 24 rue du Pont Louis-Philippe, 4ᵉ, Le Marais ☎ 01–42–71–00–01 Ⓜ St-Paul) knocked the Parisian world over the head with its fresh designs. Avant-garde furniture, spiral staircases, rugs, and a variety of home accessories line this cool boutique. Look for the Spring Vase, old test tubes linked together to form different shapes, or the oblong suspended crystal vases. Be sure to stop by No. 18, a small shop devoted to table settings with charming hand-painted plates, salt and pepper shakers, candleholders, and such.

Ugly Home (✉ 108 rue St-Honoré, 1er, Louvre/Tuileries ☎ 01–40–26–18–51 Ⓜ Louvre Rivoli) is anything but. Love child of two architects, the emphasis is utterly contemporary, with unusual lamps, fanciful limited-edition wallpapers, artist-designed rugs and pillows, and lusterware demitasse sets.

Van Der Straeten (✉ 11 rue Ferdinand Duval, 4e, Le Marais ☎ 01–42–78–99–99 Ⓜ St-Paul) is the lofty gallery-cum-showroom of Paris designer Hervé van der Straeten. He started out creating jewelry for Saint Laurent and Lacroix, designed a perfume bottle for Christian Dior, and also moved on to making rather baroque and often wacky furniture. On show are necklaces, rugs, chairs, and startling mirrors.

Jewelry

Most of the big names are on or near place Vendôme. Designer semi-precious and costume jewelry can generally be found in boutiques on avenue Montaigne and rue du Faubourg St-Honoré.

Agatha (✉ 23 bd. de la Madeleine, 1er, Opéra/Grands Boulevards ☎ 01–45–08–04–56 Ⓜ Madeleine ✉ 45 rue Bonaparte, 6e, St-Germain-des-Prés ☎ 01–46–33–20–00 Ⓜ St-Germain-des-Prés) is the perfect place to buy a moderately priced piece of jewelry just for fun. Agatha's line of earrings, rings, hair accessories, bracelets, necklaces, watches, brooches, and pendants is ever popular with Parisians. Styles change quickly, but classics include nifty charm bracelets and fine gold necklaces with whimsical pendants.

Alexandre Reza (✉ 23 pl. Vendôme, 1er, Opéra/Grands Boulevards ☎ 01–42–96–64–00 Ⓜ Opéra), one of Paris's most exclusive jewelers, is first and foremost a gemologist. He travels the world looking for the finest stones and then works them into stunning pieces, many of which are replicas of jewels of historical importance.

Arthus-Bertrand (✉ 6 pl. St-Germain-des-Prés, 6e, St-Germain-des-Prés ☎ 01–49–54–72–10 Ⓜ St-Germain-des-Prés), which dates back to 1803, carries vitrines full of designer jewelry and numerous objects to celebrate births.

Au Vase de Delft (✉ 19 rue Cambon, 1er, Louvre/Tuileries ☎ 01–42–60–92–49 Ⓜ Concorde) specializes in fine vintage jewelry, ivory sculptures from China and Japan, gold boxes, watches, and Russian-made silverware (some by Fabergé).

Cartier (✉ 23 pl. Vendôme, 1er, Louvre/Tuileries ☎ 01–44–55–32–20 Ⓜ Tuileries, Concorde ✉ 154 av. des Champs-Élysées, 8e, Champs-Élysées ☎ 01–58–18–17–78 Ⓜ George V) flashes its jewels from more than half-a-dozen boutiques in the city. Longtime favorites, such as the Trinity rings and Tank watches, have new competition for your attention in the Asian-inspired Baiser du Dragon jewelry and the colorful Délices de Goa collection.

Chanel Jewelry (✉ 18 pl. Vendôme, 1er, Opéra/Grands Boulevards ☎ 01–55–35–50–00 Ⓜ Tuileries, Opéra) feeds off the iconic design elements of the pearl-draped designer: quilting (reimagined for gold rings), camellias (now brooches), and shooting stars (used for her first jewelry collection in 1932, now circling as diamond rings).

Christian Dior (✉ 28 av. Montaigne, 8ᵉ, Champs-Élysées ☎ 01–47–23–52–39 Ⓜ Franklin-D.-Roosevelt ✉ 8 pl. Vendôme, 1ᵉʳ, Opéra/Grands Boulevards ☎ 01–42–96–30–84 Ⓜ Opéra) got a big dollop of wit and panache when it signed on young designer Victoire de Castellane to create Dior's first line of fine jewelry. She does oversize flowerlike rings, hoop earrings, and bracelets swinging with diamonds, and—lest you forget the amped-up spirit in the Dior house—white-gold death's-head cufflinks.

FodorśChoice ★ **Dary's** (✉ 362 rue St-Honoré, 1ᵉʳ, Louvre/Tuileries ☎ 01–42–60–95–23 Ⓜ Tuileries) crystallizes the best of a Paris shopping experience—a wonderful, family-run, Ali Baba–ish cavern teeming with artists, actors, models, and jewelry lovers. You'll need to take your time though, because the walls are filled with row upon row of antique jewels from every era, more modern secondhand jewelry, and drawer upon drawer of vintage one-of-a-kinds.

Dinh Van (✉ 16 rue de la Paix, 2ᵉ, Opéra/Grands Boulevards ☎ 01–42–61–74–49 Ⓜ Opéra ✉ 22 rue François 1er, 8ᵉ, Champs-Élysées ☎ 01–56–64–09–91 Ⓜ Franklin-D.-Roosevelt ✉ 58 rue Bonaparte, 6ᵉ, St-Germain-des-Prés ☎ 01–47–20–76–10 Ⓜ St-Germain-des-Prés), just around the corner from Place Vendôme's titan jewelers, thumbs its nose at in-your-face opulence. The look here, both in the boutique's design and in the jewelry, is refreshingly spare. Best-sellers include a hammered gold orb necklace and leather-cord bracelets joined with geometric shapes in white or yellow gold, some with pavé diamonds.

Lingerie

Alice Cadolle (✉ 4 rue Cambon, 1ᵉʳ, Louvre/Tuileries ☎ 01–42–60–94–22 Ⓜ Concorde ✉ 255 rue St-Honoré, 1ᵉʳ, Louvre/Tuileries ☎ 01–42–60–94–94 Ⓜ Concorde) has been selling fine lingerie to Parisians since 1889. Ready-to-wear bras, corsets, and sleepwear fill the rue Cambon boutique; on rue St-Honoré, Madame Cadolle offers a made-to-measure service popular with couture clients from nearby Chanel.

FodorśChoice ★ **Chantal Thomass** (✉ 211 rue St-Honoré, 1ᵉʳ, Louvre/Tuileries ☎ 01–42–60–40–56 Ⓜ Tuileries), a legendary lingerie diva, is back with this *Pillow Talk*-meets-Louis XV-inspired boutique. This is French naughtiness at its best, striking just the right balance between playfulness and straight-on seduction. Whisper-thin silk negligees edged in rainbow-hued Chantilly lace and lascivious bra-and-corset sets punctuate the signature line unique to this shop. Upstairs are lingerie-inspired swimsuits and beaded crop tops with Thomass's own sweetly subversive messages.

Erès (✉ 2 rue Tronchet, 8ᵉ, Opéra/Grands Boulevards ☎ 01–47–42–28–82 Ⓜ Madeleine ✉ 40 av. Montaigne, 8ᵉ, Louvre/Tuileries ☎ 01–47–23–07–26 Ⓜ Franklin-D.-Roosevelt) has the most modern line of swimwear and lingerie in town: streamlined shapes in classic colors uncluttered by lace. The lingerie masters the art of soft sheer tones and is comfortable, flattering, and subtly sexy.

Fifi Chachnil (✉ 68 rue Jean-Jacques Rousseau, 1ᵉʳ, Beaubourg/Les Halles ☎ 01–42–21–19–93 Ⓜ Étienne Marcel) girls are real boudoir babes, with a fondness for marabou slippers, quilted-satin bed jackets, and lingerie in candy-land colors. The look is cheerfully sexy, with checkered push-up bras, frilled white knickers, and peach-satin corsets.

SLICE-OF-LIFE SHOPPING

SOME STORES ARE DON'T-MISS experiences even though you may not buy a thing—instead, keep an observant eye out and you'll score a priceless slice of Parisian life. **Deyrolle** (✉ 46 rue du Bac, 7ᵉ, St-Germain-des-Prés ☎ 01–42–22–30–07 Ⓜ Rue du Bac), for instance, is a fascinating 19th-century taxidermist. Head upstairs and you'll be met by a group of zebras, birds seemingly frozen in mid-flight, and exotic mounted insects. Children are usually enthralled by the lion and the trays of shimmering butterflies. **Atelier du Bracelet Parisien** (✉ 7 rue St-Hyacinthe, 1ᵉʳ, Louvre/Tuileries ☎ 01–42–86–13–70 Ⓜ Tuileries/ Pyramides) fits that matchless watch with an equally exceptional band. In-store artisans custom-make small leather items like card carriers and cell-phone cases. Want to browse in the footsteps of the great 20th-century artists? **Sennelier** (✉ 3 quai Voltaire, 7ᵉ, St-Germain-des-Prés

☎ 01–42–60–72–15 Ⓜ Rue du Bac) has been the city's source for artists' supplies since 1887—Cézanne, Modigliani, and Picasso all came here for pigment. This venerable family business is packed with exceptionally high-quality pastels, oils, inks, brushes, and more. You might rub elbows with chefs seeking inspiration at **La Librairie Gourmande** (✉ 4 rue Dante, 5ᵉ, Quartier Latin ☎ 01–43–54–37–27 Ⓜ St-Michel), a nonpareil collection of cookbooks, rare titles on wine and spirits, gastronomic studies, and anything else to do with the pleasures of the table. And at **Paris Accordéon** (✉ 80 rue Daguerre, 14ᵉ, Montparnasse ☎ 01–43–22–13–48 Ⓜ Denfert-Rochereau) you can check out an impressive collection of antique accordions, choose a CD of classic, accordion-driven bal musette music, and perhaps catch an impromptu performance by the owner.

★ **Les Folies d'Elodie** (✉ 56 av. Paul Doumer, 16ᵉ, Trocadéro/Tour Eiffel ☎ 01–45–04–93–57 Ⓜ Trocadéro), a large, lush boutique, can trick you out in anything from a 1950s-style cotton bra and panties à la Bardot to a risqué sheer-silk nightgown with Calais lace insets. Everything is handmade, with an emphasis on the grown-up rather than little-girlish. **Sabbia Rosa** (✉ 73 rue des Sts-Pères, 6ᵉ, St-Germain-des-Prés ☎ 01–45–48–88–37 Ⓜ St-Germain-des-Prés) is a discreet, boudoirlike boutique you could easily walk straight past. It is, however, one of the world's finest lingerie stores and the place where actresses Catherine Deneuve and Isabelle Adjani (and others who might not want to reveal their errand) buy superb French silks. Look for the slips with inset lace.

Music

Record stores here are a terrific source for music from all over, especially Europe and Africa. Be prepared to pay around €12–€20 for a CD, but those seeking vinyl can still find great bargains. Keep an eye out for funky compilation albums, such as those put out by stores like Colette and A. P.C.; these can be cool samplings of edgy or niche musicians.

Afric'Music (✉ 3 rue des Plantes, 14ᵉ, Montparnasse ☎ 01–45–42–43–52 Ⓜ Alésia) is a hub for the city's African population. Tiny it may be, but the store blasts with music from the Congo, Zaire, Senegal, Haiti, the West Indies, and elsewhere. If you're curious about something, the owner will play it for you right off the bat.

Born Bad (✉ 17 rue Keller, 11ᵉ, Bastille/Nation ☎ 01–49–23–98–05 Ⓜ Bastille ✉ 11 rue St-Sabin, 11ᵉ, Bastille/Nation ☎ 01–49–23–98–05 Ⓜ Bastille) is the place to go for rare underground finds—stop by the branch **Born Bad Exotica**, on rue St-Sabin, if you'd like to listen to a sound track of every James Bond movie ever made or check out a host of old records with dancing Hawaiian hula girls on the cover—in other words, you'll find all that is kitsch and underground and otherwise elusive.

★ **Crocodisc** (✉ 40-42 rue des Écoles, 5ᵉ, Quartier Latin ☎ 01–43–54–33–42 Ⓜ St-Michel/Maubert-Mutualité ✉ 64 rue de la Montagne Ste-Geneviève, 5ᵉ, Bastille/Nation ☎ 01–49–23–98–05 Ⓜ Luxembourg/Maubert-Mutualité) cozies up to music lovers of all persuasions. The collection is an impressively large, well-chosen compendium of nearly every modern musical style: rock, world, funk, rap, film music, and more. Even better than the CD racks are the well-priced and plentiful choices on vinyl. The nearby sister store **Crocojazz**, on rue de la Montagne Ste-Geneviève, rounds out the selection with plenty of classics to choose from. (And the bags are cooler than cool!)

FNAC (✉ Forum des Halles, 1ᵉʳ, Beaubourg/Les Halles ☎ 01–40–41–40–00 Ⓜ Les Halles ✉ 74 av. des Champs-Élysées, 8ᵉ, Champs-Élysées ☎ 01–53–53–64–64 Ⓜ Franklin-D.-Roosevelt ✉ 136 rue de Rennes, 6ᵉ, Montparnasse ☎ 01–49–54–30–00 Ⓜ St-Placide) is a high-profile French chain selling music, books, and photo, TV, and audio equipment at good prices—by French standards.

Paris Jazz Corner (✉ 5 and 7 rue de Navarre, 5ᵉ, Quartier Latin ☎ 01–43–36–78–92 Ⓜ Jussieu) covers the market on rare and sought-after jazz recordings on vinyl. Parisians embrace jazz with a passion usually reserved for women and wine; aficionados flock here for a regular fix. If not exactly encouraged, you're welcome to listen to any disc before buying.

Virgin Megastore (✉ 52 av. des Champs-Élysées, 8ᵉ, Champs-Élysées ☎ 01–49–53–50–00 Ⓜ Franklin-D.-Roosevelt ✉ In Carrousel du Louvre, 99 rue de Rivoli, 1ᵉʳ, Louvre/Tuileries ☎ 01–49–53–52–90 Ⓜ Palais-Royal) has acres of albums; the Champs-Élysées store has a large book section, too.

Perfumes

Annick Goutal (✉ 14 rue de Castiglione, 1ᵉʳ, Louvre/Tuileries ☎ 01–42–60–52–82 Ⓜ Concorde) sells its own line of signature scents, which come packaged in gilded gauze purses. Rose, Tuberose, and Sable are sold here exclusively.

L'Artisanat Parfumeur (✉ 32 rue du Bourg Tibourg, 4ᵉ, Le Marais ☎ 01–48–04–72–75 Ⓜ Hôtel de Ville) sells its own brand of scents for the home and perfumes with names like Méchant Loup (Big Bad Wolf).

Comme des Garçons Perfume Shop (✉ 23 pl. du Marché St-Honoré, 1ᵉʳ, Louvre/Tuileries ☎ 01–47–03–15–03 Ⓜ Tuileries) is devoted to the ultraconceptual Japanese label's perfumes, scented candles, and body creams. The shop is worth a visit simply to admire the whiter-than-white store design with pink-tinted lighting.

Creed (✉ 38 av. Pierre 1er de Serbie, 8e, Champs-Élysées ☎ 01–47–20–58–02 Ⓜ George V) concocted exclusive perfumes for Queen Victoria and Princess Grace; today it sells a selection of its own scents and makes personalized perfumes.

★ **Editions de Parfums Frédéric Malle** (✉ 37 rue de Grenelle, 7e, St-Germain-des-Prés ☎ 01–42–22–77–22 Ⓜ Rue du Bac ✉ 140 av. Victor Hugo, 16e, Trocadéro/Tour Eiffel ☎ 01–45–05–39–02 Ⓜ Victor Hugo) is based on a simple concept: take the nine most famous noses in France and have them edit singular perfumes. The result? Exceptional, highly concentrated fragrances to be had nowhere else. Le Parfum de Thérèse, for example, was created by famous Dior nose Edmond Roudnitska for his wife. Monsieur Malle has devised high-tech ways to keep each smelling session unadulterated. At the rue de Grenelle store, individual scents are released within glass columns; stick your head in and sniff (rather *Star Trek* but effective). The avenue Victor Hugo boutique has a glass-fronted "wall of scents"; at the push of a button a selected fragrance mists the air.

Guerlain (✉ 68 av. des Champs-Élysées, 8e, Champs-Élysées ☎ 01–45–62–52–57 Ⓜ Franklin-D.-Roosevelt) boutiques are the only authorized Paris outlets for legendary perfumes like Shalimar, L'Heure Bleue, Vol de Nuit, and their collection of light eaux de toilette. They also have an extremely popular makeup and skin-care line, and Terra Cotta, their bronzing powder, is an eternal French favorite.

Iunx (✉ 48–50 rue de l'Université, 7e, Invalides ☎ 01–45–44–50–14 Ⓜ Invalides) is ancient Greek for "seduction by scent"; this collection's fascination lies in its subtle notes rather than in powerful musks or florals. The scents are light and made with very little alcohol; some of the best combine earthy elements such as wood, rice, and straw. The testing mechanisms are high-tech and fun; be sure to sample the line of bath products.

Parfums de Nicolaï (✉ 69 av. Raymond Poincaré, 16e, Trocadéro/Tour Eiffel ☎ 01–47–55–90–44 Ⓜ Victor-Hugo ✉ 80 rue de Grenelle, 7e, Trocadéro/Tour Eiffel ☎ 01–45–44–59–59 Ⓜ Dupleix) is run by a member of the Guerlain family, Patricia de Nicolaï. Children's, women's, and men's perfumes are on offer (including some unisex), as well as sprays for the home and scented candles.

Fodor's Choice
★ **Les Salons du Palais-Royal Shiseido** (✉ Jardins du Palais-Royal, 142 Galerie de Valois, 1er, Louvre/Tuileries ☎ 01–49–27–09–09 Ⓜ Palais-Royal) douses its old-new *pharmacie* decor in shades of lilac—Aubrey Beardsley would surely feel at home here. Every year Shiseido's creative genius Serge Lutens dreams up two new scents, which are then sold exclusively in this boutique. Each is compellingly original, from the strong *somptueux* scents, often with musk and amber notes, to intense florals (Rose de Nuit).

DISCOUNT The airport duty-free shops are your best bet for minor purchases. But if you're going to spend more than €175, it's worthwhile to seek out the top discounters. Don't forget to claim your détaxe!

Les Halles Montmartre (✉ 85 rue Montmartre, 2e, Opéra/Grands Boulevards ☎ 01–42–33–11–13 Ⓜ Bourse) routinely discounts its great selection of perfumes and cosmetics by up to 20%.

Michel Swiss (✉ 16 rue de la Paix, 2nd fl., 2ᵉ, Opéra/Grands Boulevards ☎ 01–42–61–61–11 Ⓜ Opéra ✉ 24 av. de l'Opéra, 1ᵉʳ, Louvre/Tuileries ☎ 01–42–96–52–86 Ⓜ Pyramides) offers savings of up to 25% on perfumes, designer jewelry, and fashion accessories.

Shoes

Berluti (✉ 26 rue Marbeuf, 8ᵉ, Champs-Élysées ☎ 01–53–93–97–97 Ⓜ Franklin-D.-Roosevelt) has been making fantastically exquisite and expensive men's shoes for more than a century. "Nothing is too beautiful for feet" is Olga Berluti's motto; she even exposes her creations to the moonlight to give them an extra-special patina. One model is named after Andy Warhol, and other famous clients of the past have included the Duke of Windsor, Fred Astaire, and James Joyce.

Fodor'sChoice **Bruno Frisoni** (✉ 34 rue de Grenelle, 7ᵉ, St-Germain-des-Prés ☎ 01–42–
★ 84–12–30 Ⓜ St-Germain-des-Prés) has an impressive pedigree, most lately as art director for Roger Vivier. His first boutique is lined with ultrasexy, ultrasophisticated shoes in vivid colors. The vertiginous tapered heels, lean platforms, and delicately conceived flats mix glamour with a hint of S&M.

★ **Christian Louboutin** (✉ 19 rue Jean-Jacques Rousseau, 1ᵉʳ, Beaubourg/Les Halles ☎ 01–42–36–05–31 Ⓜ Palais-Royal ✉ 38-40 rue de Grenelle, 7ᵉ, St-Germain-des-Prés ☎ 01–42–22–33–07 Ⓜ Sèvres Babylone) shoes carry their own red carpet with them in their trademark crimson soles. Whether tasseled, embroidered, or strappy, in Charvet silk or shiny patent leather, these heels are always perfectly balanced. No wonder they set off such legendary legs as Tina Turner's and Gwyneth Paltrow's.

Un Dimanche A Venise (✉ 318 rue St-Honoré, 1ᵉʳ, Louvre/Tuileries ☎ 01–40–20–47–37 Ⓜ Concorde ✉ 64 rue François 1er, 8ᵉ, Louvre/Tuileries ☎ 01–47–23–04–43 Ⓜ Franklin-D.-Roosevelt) has the best collection of midrange shoes, sandals, and boots in the city. From the worn brown-leather boots with the perfect tooling to the classic pointy-toe two-tone pump, to the high-heeled evening fantasies with sequins and feathers and beads—you just can't go wrong.

Mare (✉ 23 rue des Francs-Bourgeois, 4ᵉ, Le Marais ☎ 01–48–04–74–63 Ⓜ St-Paul ✉ 4 rue du Cherche-Midi, 6ᵉ, St-Germain-des-Prés ☎ 01–45–44–55–33 Ⓜ St-Sulpice) makes the most of its heels. Here you'll find all sorts: square, round, pencil-thin, transparent. The sales are particularly good, with prices on best-selling boots slashed in half and some of the more interesting specimens going for a song.

Michel Perry (✉ 243 rue St-Honoré, 1ᵉʳ, Louvre/Tuileries ☎ 01–42–44–10–07 Ⓜ Tuileries) is known for his polished, slender, mile-high shoes. The rose-color boudoir-style store is a perennial favorite. Patent leather ankle boots in neon colors and lingerie-lace stilettos punctuate the collection.

Rodolphe Ménudier (✉ 14 rue de Castiglione, 1ᵉʳ, Louvre/Tuileries ☎ 01–42–60–86–27 Ⓜ Tuileries) spins a hard-edge sexiness, from its interior design—think sleek black windows, metal cupboards, and a wall covered in white crocodile leather—to its pointy-toe high heels. Stilettos with ankle straps? *Mais oui.*

★ **Roger Vivier** (✉ 29 rue du Faubourg St-Honoré, 8ᵉ, Louvre/Tuileries ☎ 01–53–43–00–85 Ⓜ Concorde) was known for decades for his Pilgrim-buckle shoes and inventive heels. Now his name is being resurrected through the creativity of über-Parisienne Inès de la Fressange and the expertise of shoe designer Bruno Frisoni. The duo had carte blanche, and the results are brilliant: leather boots that mold to the calf perfectly, satin evening sandals, square-toe pumps in crocodile.

DISCOUNT In the know Parisians flock to the République *quartier* to check out the luxury-shoe-lover-on-a-slender-budget boutiques on **rue Meslay.** The discount stores are often jam-packed and the service rather dodgy, but for more than 50% off on last season's collections from the biggest names, it's well worth the visit.

L'Autre Boutique (✉ 42 rue de Grenelle, 7ᵉ, St-Germain-des-Prés ☎ 01–42–84–12–45 Ⓜ Rue du Bac) is a mixed bag with reliably great finds. Among those unsellable gladiator numbers you might turn up delicate silvery-pink pumps or a pair of open-toed brown-leather boots. Season-old collections of Michel Perry shoes are half off; during sales the store practically gives them away. The staff is helpful, down-to-earth, and fun.

Mi-Prix (✉ 27 bd. Victor-Hugo, 15ᵉ, Montparnasse ☎ 01–48–28–42–48 Ⓜ Porte de Versailles) is an unruly jumble of end-of-series designer shoes and accessories from the likes of Rodolphe Ménudier, Prada, Michel Perry, and Goffredo Fantini, priced at up to 70% below retail.

Stationery

Calligrane (✉ 4–6 bis, rue Pont Louis Philippe, 4ᵉ, Le Marais ☎ 01–48–04–31–89 Ⓜ St-Paul) has three adjacent stores in the 4ᵉ arrondissement. Only one sells an Italian paper called Fabriano, another designer office equipment (pens, staplers, and unusual notebooks covered in ostrich skin), and the third accents its different types of paper from India, Japan, and Mexico.

Cassegrain (✉ 422 rue St-Honoré, 8ᵉ, Louvre/Tuileries ☎ 01–42–60–20–08 Ⓜ Concorde) is the last word on beautifully engraved cards and elegant French stationery. The desk accessories and inexpensive glass-nib writing pens make great gifts.

Marie Papier (✉ 26 rue Vavin, 6ᵉ, Montparnasse ☎ 01–43–26–46–44 Ⓜ Vavin) sells extraordinary colored, marbled, and Japanese writing paper and notebooks, plus every kind of posh writing accessory.

Toys

Au Nain Bleu (✉ 408 rue St-Honoré, 8ᵉ, Louvre/Tuileries ☎ 01–42–60–39–01 Ⓜ Concorde) is a high-priced wonderland of elaborate doll-houses, miniature sports cars, and enchanting hand-carved rocking horses.

Bonton (✉ 82 rue de Grenelle, 7ᵉ, St-Germain-des-Prés ☎ 01–44–39–09–20 Ⓜ Rue du Bac) comes from the creators of Bonpoint; check out the selection of fun toys, like special editions of an Andy Warhol coloring book or wooden cars and trucks. Next door there's a hair salon just for kids.

Side Trips from Paris

7

WORD OF MOUTH

"I recommend Chartres as the wonder of France. The cathedral gives one a feeling of entering the middle ages with its cobblestone floor . . . the town is wonderful and there is a tour of the crypts and a great stained glass museum/school across the square from the cathedral."

—laurensuite

"Versailles is the palace to which all others are compared."

—Patrick

"Giverny in season is a thrill (though small and often crowded) . . . riots of color, planted for the sheer joy and beauty of flowers."

—elaine

www.fodors.com/forums

Revised and
updated by
Simon Hewitt

EVEN THOUGH PARIS ITSELF HAS SO MUCH TO SEE, you should plan on taking a short trip outside the city, for just beyond its gates lies the fabled region known as Île-de-France, the ancient heartland of France—the core from which the French kings gradually extended their power over the rest of a rebellious, individualistic nation. Though Île-de-France is not really an island (*île*), it is figuratively isolated from the rest of France by three rivers—the Seine, the Marne, and the Oise—that weave majestic, meandering circles around its periphery. Remarkably, this fairly confined region contains 10 million people—one-sixth of France's population. This type of statistic conjures up visions of a never-ending suburban sprawl, but nothing could be farther from the truth. There are lovely villages here—notably Auvers-sur-Oise, immortalized by Vincent van Gogh, and Giverny, site of Monet's home and garden.

Grand cathedrals and stately châteaux dot the lush, gently rolling landscape: the kings and clerics who ruled France liked to escape from the capital now and then. The region never lost favor with the powerful, partly because its many forests—large chunks of which still stand—harbored sufficient game to ensure even the most indolent monarch an easy kill. First Fontainebleau, in humane Renaissance proportions, then Versailles, on a minion-crushing, baroque scale, reflected the royal desire to transform hunting lodges into palatial residences.

In 1992 Disney wrought its own kind of kingdom here: Disneyland Paris. The magic was slow to take effect. The resort opened with the uninspiring name of EuroDisney and further baffled the French, for whom no meal is complete without wine, with its ban on alcohol. After that ban was lifted in the park's sit-down restaurants and the park's name changed, Disneyland Paris became France's leading tourist attraction. A second park, Walt Disney Studios, opened in 2002.

Getting from the capital to the sights in this region is easy: almost all are within an hour of central Paris and most are easily accessible by train. Contact the Espace du Tourisme d'Île-de-France (open Wednesday–Monday 10–7, www.pidf.com), under the inverted pyramid in the Carrousel du Louvre, in the center of Paris, for general information on the area.

About the Restaurants

Not surprisingly, given its proximity to Paris and its relatively well-heeled population, the Île-de-France has no shortage of good restaurants. Although Île-de-France's fanciest dining rooms can be just as pricey as their Parisian counterparts, prices overall are slightly lower than those in the capital and eating hours a little earlier. Some restaurants will refuse to accept diners who arrive after 9 PM, and lunchers are expected to sit down by 1:15. Be aware that restaurants popular with the locals and not over-reliant on tourist trade often close for a month in July or August.

There are plenty of restaurants in Versailles, Chartres, and Fontainebleau, but fewer in smaller towns like Chantilly or Auvers-sur-Oise. Book ahead if choices are slim, and in summer reservations are recommended everywhere. The dress code here is pretty relaxed, with tie and jacket

expected in only the poshest establishments. On the menus look for game and asparagus in season in the south of the region and the soft creamy cheeses of Meaux and Coulommiers to the east.

WHAT IT COSTS IN EUROS				
$$$$	**$$$**	**$$**	**$**	**¢**
AT DINNER over €30	€23–€30	€17–€22	€11–€16	under €11

per person for a main course at dinner, including tax (19.6%) and service; note that if a restaurant offers only prix-fixe (set-price) meals, we have given it the price category that reflects the full prix-fixe price.

About the Hotels

Although it's easy to visit the Île-de-France region on day trips from the capital, staying overnight enables you to experience the area in greater depth. Lodging in the Île-de-France is invariably less expensive than in Paris, though you may be surprised by just how rustic some country inns remain. Many small hotels with their own restaurant will expect you to dine in, so ask about meal plans. It's essential to book well ahead if you hope to stay in one of the region's larger towns in summer, especially Versailles.

WHAT IT COSTS IN EUROS					
	$$$$	**$$$**	**$$**	**$**	**¢**
FOR 2 PEOPLE	over €225	€151–€225	€101–€150	€75–€100	under €75

Prices are for two people in a standard double room in high season, including tax (19.6%) and service charge.

AUVERS-SUR-OISE

Cézanne, Pissarro, Corot, Daubigny, and Berthe Morisot all painted in Auvers in the second half of the 19th century. But it is Vincent van Gogh whose memory haunts every nook and cranny of this pretty riverside village. Van Gogh moved here from Arles in 1890 to be with his brother Theo. Little has changed since the summer of 1890, which coincided with the last 10 weeks of van Gogh's life, when he painted no fewer than 70 pictures and then shot himself behind the village château. He is buried in the village cemetery, next to his brother in a simple ivy-covered grave halfway along the top wall. The cemetery is still surrounded by the wheat fields where Vincent once painted, and the whole village is peppered with plaques featuring reproductions of his paintings, enabling you to compare them with the scenes as they are today. After years of indifference and neglect, van Gogh's last abode has been turned into a shrine, and the village château is now home to a stunning high-tech exhibit on the Impressionist era. You can also visit the medieval village church, subject of one of van Gogh's most famous paintings, *L'Église d'Auvers,* and admire Ossip Zadkine's powerful statue of van Gogh in the village park.

The Auberge Ravoux, the inn where van Gogh stayed, is now the **Maison de van Gogh** (Van Gogh House). A dingy staircase leads up to the tiny, spartan wood-floor attic where van Gogh stored some of modern art's most famous pictures under the bed in which he breathed his last. A short film retraces van Gogh's time at Auvers, and there is a well-stocked souvenir shop. ⊠ *8 rue de la Sansonne* 🕾 *01–30–36–60–60* 🎫 *€5* ⊗ *Mid-Mar.–mid-Nov., Tues.–Sun. 10–6.*

The elegant 17th-century village château, set above split-level gardens, now houses the **Voyage au Temps des Impressionnistes** (Journey Through the Impressionist Era). You'll receive a set of infrared headphones (English available), with commentary that guides you past various tableaux illustrating life during the Impressionist years. Although there are no Impressionist originals—500 reproductions pop up on screens interspersed between the tableaux—this is still an imaginative, enjoyable museum. Some of the special effects—talking mirrors, computerized cabaret dancing girls, and a simulated train ride past Impressionist landscapes—are worthy of Disney. ⊠ *Rue de Léry* 🕾 *01–34–48–48–40* ⊕ *www.chateau-auvers.fr* 🎫 *€10* ⊗ *Apr.–Sept., Tues.–Sun. 10:30–6; Oct.–mid-Dec. and mid-Jan.–Mar., Tues.–Sun. 10:30–4:30.*

The landscape artist Charles-François Daubigny, a precursor of the Impressionists, lived in Auvers from 1861 until his death in 1878. You can visit his studio, the **Atelier de Daubigny,** and admire the remarkable mural and roof paintings by Daubigny and fellow artists Camille Corot and Honoré Daumier. ⊠ *61 rue Daubigny* ☎ *01–34–48–03–03* 🎫 *€5* ⊙ *Apr.–Oct., Thurs.–Sun. 2–6:30.*

Where to Eat

★ **$$–$$$** ✕ **Auberge Ravoux.** For total van Gogh immersion, have lunch in the restaurant he patronized regularly more than 100 years ago. The €33 three-course menu changes regularly, but it's the spirit of the place that makes eating here special, with glasswork, lace curtains, and wall blandishments carefully modeled on the original designs. A magnificently illustrated book, *Van Gogh's Table,* by culinary historian Alexandra Leaf and Fred Leeman, recalls Vincent's stay at the Auberge and describes in loving detail the dishes served there at the time. ⊠ *52 rue Général-de-Gaulle* ☎ *01–30–36–60–63* 🍴 *Reservations essential* �ͅ *AE, DC, MC, V* ⊙ *Closed mid-Nov.–mid-Mar and Mon. No dinner Sun.*

Auvers-sur-Oise A to Z

To research prices, get advice from other travelers, and book travel arrangements, visit www.fodors.com.

CAR TRAVEL

Auvers is 38 km (24 mi) northwest of Paris. Take highway A1, then A15 toward Pontoise; then head east along N184 to Méry-sur-Oise and pick up the N328, which crosses the river to Auvers.

TRAIN TRAVEL

Two trains depart every hour for Auvers from Paris's Gare du Nord; a change is necessary, usually at St-Ouen-l'Aumône, and the journey time varies from 60 to 90 minutes. A quicker (53 minutes) but less frequent train leaves from Paris's Gare St-Lazare and involves a change at Pontoise. On either route, the one-way fare is just under €5. It's an easy stroll from the station to the town's main sights, although the cemetery is a steepish half-mile walk up from the church.

VISITOR INFORMATION

🚩 **Auvers-sur-Oise Office de Tourisme** ⊠ rue de la Sansonne, opposite the Maison de van Gogh, 95430 Auvers-sur-Oise ☎ 01-30-36-10-06 ⊕ www.auvers-sur-oise.com.

CHANTILLY

Celebrated for lace, cream, and the most beautiful medieval manuscript in the world—*Les Très Riches Heures du Duc de Berry*—romantic Chantilly has a host of other attractions: a faux Renaissance château with an eye-popping art collection, splendid baroque stables, a classy racecourse, and a 16,000-acre forest.

Fodor'sChoice   Before entering the gates of the **Château de Chantilly,** stop to admire one ★   of the grandest panoramas in France. From left to right: the forest; the verdant sweep of the racetrack; the golden-hued stables; the cobbled avenue leading to the town's grand entrance archway; and, nestling within its park behind a gleaming moat, the château itself.

The first château here was built in 1528, but it was two later figures who shaped its destiny. Prince Henri de Bourbon-Condé, known as Le Grand Condé (1621–86), transformed the buildings and gardens into a domain to rival Versailles. His work was razed during the Revolution. Next up to the plate was Henri d'Orléans, Duc d'Aumale (1822–97), great-nephew of the last Duc de Bourbon-Condé and youngest son of France's final king, Louis-Philippe, who rebuilt the château in the 1870s. The Duc d'Aumale furnished it with a magnificent collection of illuminated manuscripts, tapestries, furniture, and paintings, which comprises today's **Musée Condé.**

The museum's most famous room is the tiny **Santuario** (sanctuary), where in hushed reverence visitors peer at two celebrated works by Italian painter Raphael (1483–1520)—the *Three Graces* and the *Orleans Madonna*—and at an exquisite ensemble of 15th-century miniatures by the most illustrious French painter of his time, Jean Fouquet. The largest room, the **Galerie des Peintures** (picture gallery), lighted by a glass roof, is crammed from floor to ceiling with old masters. Nicolas Poussin, Annibale Carracci, and Salvatore Rosa lead the parade. Adjacent rooms are lined with paintings by 18th- and 19th-century French artists, with a noted array of Orientalist paintings set in North Africa, recalling the Duc d'Aumale's stint as Governor General of Algeria in the 1840s. The two-level **Cabinet des Livres,** built in 1877, is lined with more than 11,000 books and 1,500 manuscripts; most can only be consulted by prior arrangement with the curator.

Other highlights of this unusual museum are the **Galerie de Psyché** (Psyche Gallery), with 16th-century stained glass and portrait drawings by Flemish artist Jean Clouet II; the **Cabinet des Gemmes** (Gem Cabinet), with an exquisite array of jewelry, enamels, fans, and miniatures; and the **Chapelle,** with sculptures by Jean Goujon and Jacques Sarrazin. You may also wish to take the €6.50 guided tour of the private apartments decorated by court painter Eugène Lami in the 1840s and gleaming with rococo boiseries, porcelain, and gilt-wood furniture.

The château's park, designed by Versailles's famed landscaper André Le Nôtre, is based on that familiar French royal combination of formality—neatly planned parterres and a mighty straight-banked canal—and a romantic eccentricity: a waterfall and a *hameau,* a mock-Norman village that inspired Marie-Antoinette's version at Versailles. You can take a tour on an electric train (daily July and August; weekends May, June, September, and October) or board a **hydrophile,** an electric-powered boat, for a 30-minute glide down the Grand Canal. ☎ *03–44–62–62–62* ⊕ *www.chateaudechantilly.com* ✉ *€7 including park, €3 park only, €8 with boat, €10 with boat and train; €15 joint ticket including château, park, boat, and train* ☯ *Château and park Mar.–Oct., daily 10–6; château Nov.–Feb., Wed.–Mon. 10:30–12:45 and 2–5; park Nov.–Feb., daily 10:30–12:45 and 2–5.*

Sprawling between the château, the town, and the forest is the manicured, gently rolling turf of Chantilly's racetrack, home to two of Europe's top flat races: the Prix du Jockey-Club (French Derby), on the first Sunday of June, and on the following Sunday the Prix de Diane, for three-year-old fillies. Lording it over the town side of the track, a ★ ☾ short walk from the château, are the palatial 18th-century **Grandes Écuries** (Grand Stables), built in 1719 to accommodate 240 horses and 500 hounds for stag and boar hunts in the forest nearby. The stables are still in use as the home of the **Musée Vivant du Cheval** (Living Horse Museum), with 30 horses and ponies housed in straw-lined comfort, in between dressage demonstrations beneath the awe-inspiring central dome. Half-hour demonstrations are held at 11:30, 3:30, 5:15; special shows are held throughout the year. The 31-room museum has a comprehensive collection of equine paraphernalia: from saddles, bridles, and stirrups to rocking horses, anatomy displays, and old postcards. ⊠ *7 rue du Connétable* ☎ *03–44–57–40–40* ⊕ *www.musee-vivant-du-cheval.fr* 🎟 *€8* ☾ *Apr.–Oct., Wed.–Mon. 10:30–6; Nov.–Mar., Wed.–Fri. 2–5.*

The 5-acre **Potager des Princes** (Princes' Kitchen Garden) was created by André Le Nôtre in the late 17th century. After years of research and replanting it was opened to the public in 2002. Attractions vary from a tropical garden with palms and banana trees to a terrace, flower beds, rose bushes, an herb garden, and a farmyard with goats, rabbits, pigeons, and 15 tasty types of pheasant. ⊠ *Parc de la Faisanderie* ☎ *03–44–57–40–40* ⊕ *www.potagerdesprinces.com* 🎟 *€7* ☾ *Apr.–mid-Oct., weekdays 2–5; weekends 11–12:30 and 2–6.*

The best place to admire Chantilly lace and porcelain is the town's small **Musée du Patrimoine** (Heritage Museum), but be warned: it's open only Wednesday and Saturday. Chantilly porcelain, usually with colorful Japanese motifs, was first made for the Prince de Condé in the 1720s; production continued until 1870. Empress Eugénie led the fashion for fine black Chantilly lace in the 1850s, when more than 3,000 lacemakers were employed locally. One local article you won't find in the museum is *crème Chantilly*. Legend says it was first whipped up by a château cook who had forgotten to order enough *crème fraîche*; by whipping what little fresh cream he had left, its volume was increased sufficiently for the prince to enjoy his just desserts. ⊠ *34 rue d'Aumale* ☎ *03–44–58–28–44* 🎟 *€4* ☾ *Wed. and Sat. 10–11:30 and 3–5:30.*

Where to Eat

$$–$$$ ✕ **Capitainerie.** Adorned with old kitchen utensils, this diverting, vaulted restaurant in one wing of Château de Chantilly serves a five-course feast for €36 as well as such à la carte fare as leg of rabbit stuffed with ewe's cheese, lamb chops with pistachio nuts and apricots, and trout in walnut butter. ⊠ *In Château de Chantilly* ☎ *03–44–57–15–89* ▤ *MC, V* ☾ *Closed Tues.*

Chantilly A to Z

To research prices, get advice from other travelers, and book travel arrangements, visit www.fodors.com.

CAR TRAVEL
Take highway A1 from Paris (Porte de la Chapelle) to Senlis, 50 km (31 mi) away; Chantilly is 10 km (6 mi) west along pretty D924.

TRAIN TRAVEL

Chantilly is about 30 minutes (€6.60) from Paris's Gare du Nord and at least one train departs every hour. The château is just over 4 km (2 mi) from the station, a pleasant, but lengthy, walk through either the town or the forest. If you prefer you can take a taxi or a bus. Call the tourist office to check the bus schedule since buses do not meet all Paris trains. Taxis are generally available at the station, and you can arrange for a return trip with the driver; if there's not a cab on hand, call 03–44–57–10–03.

VISITOR INFORMATION

🛈 **Chantilly Office de Tourisme** ✉60 av. du Maréchal-Joffre ☎03–44–67–37–37 ⊕www.ville-chantilly.fr.

CHARTRES

The noble, soaring spires of Chartres are among the most famous sights in Europe. Try to catch a glimpse of them surging out of the vast, golden grain fields of the Beauce as you approach from the northeast. Although you're probably visiting Chartres chiefly for its magnificent Gothic cathedral and its world-famous stained-glass windows, the whole town is also worth a leisurely exploration. Ancient streets tumble down from the cathedral to the Eure River; the view of the rooftops beneath the cathedral from rue du Pont-St-Hilaire is particularly appealing.

Fodor'sChoice ★ The **Cathédrale de Chartres** is the sixth church to occupy the same spot. It dates mainly from the 12th and 13th centuries; the previous 11th-century structure burned down in 1194. A well-chronicled outburst of religious fervor followed the discovery that the relic kept in the church, a tunic believed to have belonged to the Virgin Mary, had miraculously survived unsinged. Reconstruction went ahead at a breathtaking pace. In only 25 years Chartres Cathedral rose again, and it has remained substantially unchanged ever since.

Worship on the site of the cathedral goes back to before the Gallo-Roman period; the crypt contains a well that was the focus of Druid ceremonies. With the arrival of Christianity the original cult of the fertility goddess merged with that of the Virgin Mary. In the late 9th century King Charles the Bold presented Chartres with what was believed to be the tunic of the Virgin Mary. This precious relic attracted hordes of pilgrims, and Chartres swiftly became—and has remained—a prime destination for the faithful. Though this relic no longer survives, present-day pilgrims still trek on foot from Paris to Chartres.

The lower half of the facade is all that survives from the 11th-century Romanesque church. (The Romanesque style is evident in the use of round rather than pointed arches.) The main door—the **Portail Royal** (Royal Portal)—is richly sculpted with scenes from the life of Christ. The flanking towers are also Romanesque, though the upper part of the taller of the two **spires** (380 feet versus 350 feet) dates from the start of the 16th century, and its fanciful flamboyance contrasts with the stumpy solemnity of its Romanesque counterpart. The **rose window** above the main

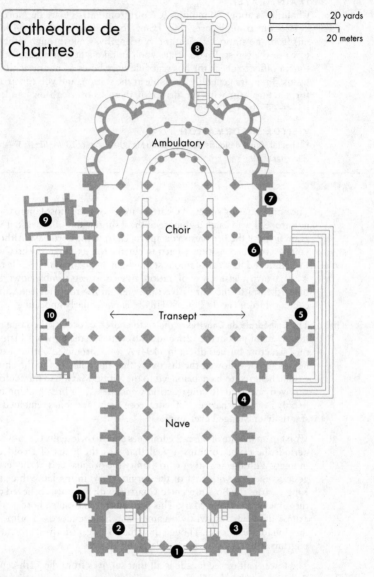

Cathédrale de Chartres

0 — 20 yards
0 — 20 meters

Ambulatory

Choir

← Transept →

Nave

portal dates from the 13th century. The three windows below it contain some of the finest examples of 12th-century stained glass in France.

The interior is somber, so you'll need time to adjust to the dark. Your reward will be a view of the gemlike richness of the stained glass, dominated by the deep "Chartres blue." This incredibly vibrant color is all the more famous because the secret for making it is long lost. The oldest window, and perhaps the most stunning, is **Notre-Dame de la Belle Verrière** (Our Lady of the Lovely Window), in the south choir. It's worth bringing binoculars to pick out the details. If you wish to know more about stained-glass techniques and the motifs used, visit the small exhibit in the gallery opposite the north porch. The vast black-and-white medieval pattern on the floor of the nave is one of the few to have survived from the Middle Ages. The faithful were expected to crawl along its entire length (some 300 yards) on their knees. A longtime Chartres aficionado, Malcolm Miller, gives fabulous tours (€10) in English at noon and 2:45 PM daily except Sundays (he's usually away in December and sometimes in March; you can check by calling 02–37–28–15–58).

Guided tours of the crypt start from the **Maison de la Crypte** (Crypt House) opposite the south porch (where you can also rent a Walkman for a tape-recorded cathedral tour in English). In the crypt itself you'll see Romanesque and Gothic chapels along with a 4th-century Gallo-Roman wall and some 12th-century wall paintings. ⊠ *16 cloître Notre-Dame* ☎ *02–37–21–56–33* 🎫 *Towers €3, crypt €2.60* ☉ *Cathedral daily 8:30–7:30. Guided tours of crypt Easter–Oct., daily at 11, 2:15, 3:30, 4:30, and 5:15; Nov.–Easter, daily at 11 and 4.*

Like the cathedral, the old part of town, studded with picturesque houses and streets, has been preserved in its cloak of mellowing old stone. One of its zanier attractions is the **Maison Picassiette** (⊠ 20 rue du Repos), a house built from bits of glass and crockery by Raymond Isodore, an eccentric local, between 1930 and 1962. Paying tribute to the town's history as a farming center is the **COMPA** museum, in a converted circular train-shed; its thoughtful display of old tools and machinery includes a battalion of tractors dating back to 1816. There's a brochure in English. ⊠ *Pont de Mainvilliers* ☎ *02–37–84–15–00* ⊕ *www.lecompa.com* 🎫 *€4* ☉ *Tues.–Fri. 10–12:30 and 1:30–6, weekends 10–12:30 and 1:30–7.*

The **Musée des Beaux-Arts** (Fine Arts Museum), just behind the cathedral, is a handsome 18th-century building that used to serve as the bishop's palace. Its varied collection includes Renaissance enamels, a portrait of Erasmus by Holbein, tapestries, armor, and some fine, mainly French paintings of the 17th, 18th, and 19th centuries. There is also a room devoted to the forceful 20th-century paintings of Maurice de Vlaminck, who lived in the region. ⊠ *29 cloître Notre-Dame* ☎ *02–37–36–41–39* 🎫 *€2.50* ☉ *May–Oct., Wed.–Mon. 10–noon and 2–6; Nov.–Apr., Wed.–Mon. 10–noon and 2–5.*

The Gothic **Église St-Pierre** (⊠ rue St-Pierre), near the Eure River, has magnificent medieval windows from a period (circa 1300) not repre-

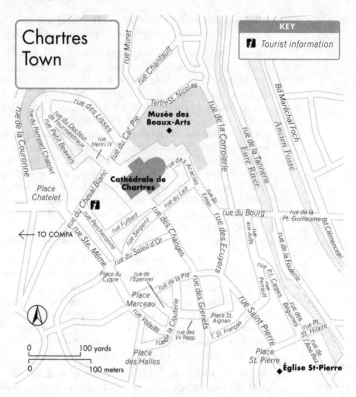

Chartres Town

KEY
🛈 Tourist information

rue Muret

rue Chantault

TertreSt. Nicolas

rue de la Corroierie

rue de la Tannerie Entre River

Bd Maréchal Foch

Ancien Fossé

Musée des Beaux-Arts ◆

rue des Lisses

rue du Docteur de Tourmestraux

rue du Petit Beauvais

rue Henri IV

rue du Cal. Pie.

rue des Acacias

Cathédrale de Chartres

rue de la Couronne

rue du Rampart Chatelet

Place Chatelet

rue du Cheval Blanc

rue Percheronne

rue Ste. Même

rue au Lait

rue St. Eman

rue du Bourg

rue aux Juifs

rue de la Pt. Guillaume

Bd Clémenceau

← TO COMPA

rue Fulbert

rue Serpent

rue des Changes

rue du Soleil d'Or

Place du Cygne

rue de l'Epervier

rue de la Pie

rue des Ecuyers

rue des Grenets

rue Pl. Capes

Perrault

rue de la Foulerie

Place Marceau

rue Volaille

rue de la Clouterie

rue des Vx Rapp.

Place St. Aignan

T. St. François

rue Saint Pierre

rue des Béguines

rue Pt. St. Hillaire

rue de l'Ane Rebe.

0 ___ 100 yards
0 ___ 100 meters

Place des Halles

Place St. Pierre

◆ **Église St-Pierre**

sented at the cathedral. The oldest stained glass here, portraying Old Testament worthies, is to the right of the choir and dates from the late 13th century.

Where to Eat

★ **$$$–$$$$** ✕ **Château d'Esclimont.** One of the most photogenic of all châteaux-hotels in France, this magnificently restored Renaissance estate—part of the Relais & Châteaux group—is frequented by high-profile Parisian businesspeople. Lamb with asparagus, hare fricassee (in season), and lobster top the menu. After dining on the rich cuisine, take a stroll through the luxuriant grounds embellished with regal lawns and a lake. ⊠ *2 rue du Château-d'Esclimont, St-Symphorien-le-Château (6 km [4 mi] west of Ablis exit on A11 and about 24 km [15 mi] from Chartres and Rambouillet)* 🕾 *02–37–31–15–15* ⌂ *Reservations essential* 🏦 *Jacket and tie* ⊟ *AE, DC, MC, V.*

$$$ ✕ **La Vieille Maison.** On a narrow street close to Chartres's cathedral, this intimate spot with a flower-filled patio has a regularly changing menu. Invariably, however, it includes regional specialties such as truffles and asparagus with chicken. Prices, though justified, can be steep; the €29 prix-fixe lunch menu is a good bet. ⊠ *5 rue au Lait* 🕾 *02–37–34–10–67* ⊟ *AE, MC, V* ☺ *Closed Mon. No dinner Sun.*

$–$$ ✕ **Moulin de Ponceau.** In this 16th-century watermill-turned-restaurant ask for a table with a view of the Eure River, with the cathedral looming behind. Choose from a regularly changing menu of French stalwarts such as rabbit terrine, trout with almonds, and tarte tatin. ⊠ *21 rue de la Tannerie* ☎ *02-37-35-30-05* ▤ *AE, MC, V* ☯ *Closed 2 wks in Feb. No lunch Sat., no dinner Sun.*

Chartres A to Z

To research prices, get advice from other travelers, and book travel arrangements, visit www.fodors.com.

CAR TRAVEL
The A10/A11 expressways link Paris to Chartres, 88 km (55 mi) away.

GUIDED TOURS
Cityrama organizes half-day trips to Chartres (€55 per person, €93 per person including Versailles).

🛈 **Cityrama** ⊠ 4 pl. des Pyramides, Paris ☎ 01-44-55-61-00 ⊕ www.cityrama.com.

TRAIN TRAVEL
Trains depart hourly from Paris's Gare Montparnasse to Chartres (50–70 minutes, €12.10 each way). The cathedral is a quarter-mile uphill walk from the station.

VISITOR INFORMATION
🛈 **Chartres Office de Tourisme** ⊠ pl. de la Cathédrale, 28000 Chartres ☎ 02-37-18-26-26 ⊕ www.ville-chartres.fr.

DISNEYLAND PARIS

☾ In 1992 American pop culture secured a mammoth outpost just 32 km (20 mi) east of Paris in the form of Disneyland Paris. On 1,500 acres in Marne-la-Vallée, Disneyland Paris has a convention center, sports facilities, an entertainment and shopping complex, restaurants, thousands of hotel rooms, and, of course, the theme park itself. The park is made up of five "lands": Main Street U.S.A., Frontierland, Adventureland, Fantasyland, and Discoveryland. The central theme of each land is relentlessly echoed in every detail, from attractions to restaurant menus to souvenirs.

Main Street U.S.A. is the scene of the Disney Parades held every afternoon—and during holiday periods every evening, too. Top attractions at **Frontierland** are the chilling Phantom Manor, haunted by holographic spooks, and the thrilling runaway mine train of Big Thunder Mountain, a roller-coaster that plunges wildly through floods and avalanches. Whiffs of Arabia, Africa, and the West Indies give **Adventureland** its exotic cachet; the spicy meals and snacks served here rank among the best in the theme park. Don't miss the Pirates of the Caribbean, an exciting mise-en-scène populated by eerily human computer-driven figures, or Indiana Jones and the Temple of Doom, a breathtaking ride that relives some of our luckless hero's most exciting moments.

Fantasyland charms the youngest park visitors with familiar cartoon characters from such Disney classics as *Snow White* and *Peter Pan*. The focal point of Fantasyland, and indeed Disneyland Paris, is Le Château de la Belle au Bois Dormant (Sleeping Beauty's Castle), a 140-foot, bubble-gum-pink structure topped with 16 blue- and gold-tipped turrets. In the dungeon is a scaly, green 2-ton dragon who rumbles and grumbles in his sleep and occasionally rouses to roar. **Discoveryland** is a futuristic spin on high-tech Disney entertainment. Robots on roller skates welcome you to Star Tours, a pitching, plunging, sense-confounding ride through intergalactic space. Space Mountain's star-bejeweled roller-coaster ride catapults you through the Milky Way.

Walt Disney Studios opened next to the Disneyland park in 2002 and is divided into four "production zones" behind imposing entrance gates. **Front Lot,** with its 100-foot water tower based on the one erected in 1939 for Disney Studios in Burbank, California, contains shops, a restaurant, and a studio recreating the atmosphere of Sunset Boulevard. **Animation Courtyard** has Disney artists demonstrating the various phases of character animation; Animagique brings to life scenes from *Pinocchio* and *The Lion King,* while Aladdin's Genie hosts Flying Carpets over Agrabah.

Production Courtyard incorporates the Walt Disney Television Studios; Cinemagique, a special-effects tribute to U.S. and European cinema; and a behind-the-scenes Studio Tram tour of location sites, movie props, studio design, and costuming, ending with a visit to Catastrophe Canyon in the heart of a film shoot. Highlights of **Back Lot** are Armageddon Special Effects, where you'll fly through a flaming meteor shower aboard the Mir space station; and the Stunt Show Spectacular, involving cars, motorbikes and Jet Skis, at a 3,000-seat, giant-screen, outdoor arena.

The park can be crowded any time, but try to avoid school vacations, summer weekends, and Wednesday, a free day for young French schoolchildren. To avoid the worst of the lines, arrive early and start with the attractions farthest from the entrance. Look into Fastpasses, too, which allow you to reserve your place in line at some of the most popular attractions (only one at a time). Fastpass distributor machines stand in front of key rides. As for avoiding the crowds at lunchtime, have a big breakfast and try to delay lunch until around 1:30, when the restaurants are less congested.

For entertainment outside the theme parks, check out **Festival Disney** (☎ 01–60–45–68–04 for information), a vast pleasure mall designed by celebrated American architect Frank Gehry. Featured are American-style restaurants (crab shack, diner, deli, steak house), a disco, and a dinner theater where Buffalo Bill stages his Wild West Show twice nightly. An 18-hole golf course is open to the public. ⊠ *Marne-la-Vallée* ☎ *01–60–30–60–30* ⊕ *www.disneylandparis.com* ☒ *Disneyland Paris and Walt Disney Studios €40 each, 3-day pass €108 for both* ☉ *Disneyland Paris mid-June–mid-Sept., daily 9 AM–10 PM; mid-Sept.–mid-June, weekdays 10–8, weekends 9–8; Walt Disney Studios daily 10–6 (tickets for Walt Disney Studios are valid for Disneyland Paris for the last 3 hrs before closing).*

Where to Stay & Eat

$–$$$ ✕ **Disneyland Restaurants.** Disneyland Paris is peppered with places to eat, ranging from snack bars and fast-food joints to five full-service restaurants—all with a distinguishing theme. In addition, Disney Village and Disney Hotels have restaurants open to the public. But since these are outside the park, don't waste time traveling to them for lunch. In typical French fashion, Disneyland Paris serves wine and beer in the park's sit-down restaurants, as well as in the hotels and restaurants outside the park. ☎ *01–60–45–65–40* ▤ *AE, DC, MC, V accepted at sit-down restaurants.*

$$–$$$$ ▥ **Disneyland Hotels.** The resort has 5,000 rooms in six hotels, all a short distance from the park, ranging from the luxurious Disneyland Hotel to the not-so-rustic Camp Davy Crockett. Free transportation to the park is available at every hotel. Packages including Disneyland lodging, entertainment, and admission are available through travel agents in Europe. ⊠ *Centre de Réservations, B.P. 100, 77777 Cedex 4 Marne-la-Vallée* ☎ *01–60–30–60–30, 407/934–7639 in U.S.* 🖷 *01–49–30–71–00* ❧ *Restaurant, café, indoor pool, health club, sauna, bar, Internet, free parking* ▤ *AE, DC, MC, V.*

Disneyland Paris A to Z

To research prices, get advice from other travelers, and book travel arrangements, visit www.fodors.com.

BUS TRAVEL

Shuttle buses link Disneyland Paris to Roissy (56 km [35 mi]) and Orly (50 km [31 mi]) airports. Each trip lasts around 45 minutes, and the fare is €15 one-way. There are no direct buses from Paris proper.

CAR TRAVEL

The Strasbourg-bound A4 expressway leads from Paris to Disneyland Paris, at Marne-la-Vallée, a journey of 32 km (20 mi) that in normal traffic takes about 30 minutes. The 4-km (2½-mi) route from the expressway to the entrance of the theme park is clearly marked. Day visitors must head for the PARKING VISITEURS, which costs €8 per car and is 600 yards from the theme-park entrance.

TRAIN TRAVEL

Disneyland Paris's suburban train station (Marne-la-Vallée–Chessy) is just 100 yards from the entrance to both the theme park and Festival Disney. Trains run every 10–20 minutes from RER-A stations in central Paris: Charles-de-Gaulle–Étoile, Auber, Châtelet–Les Halles, Gare de Lyon, and Nation. The trip takes about 40 minutes and costs €14 round-trip (including the métro to the RER). A TGV station next to the RER station at Disneyland Paris offers direct train services to and from Lille, Lyon, and Marseille.

VISITOR INFORMATION

🛈 **Disneyland Paris S.C.A.** ⊠ Central Reservations Office, B.P. 104, 77777 Cedex 4 Marne-la-Vallée, France ☎ 01–60–30–60–30 🖷 01–49–30–71–00 ⊕ www.disneylandparis.com. **Walt Disney World Central Reservations** 🖃 Box 10100, Lake Buena Vista, FL 32830-0100 ☎ 407/934–7639 ⊕ disneyworld.disney.go.com.

FONTAINEBLEAU & VAUX-LE-VICOMTE

Fontainebleau, with its historic château—the favored retreat of King François I and Napoléon—is an ideal day-trip destination. The stately town is ringed by the Forest of Fontainebleau, a great place for hiking and rock climbing. Jean-François Millet and other 19th-century painters who lived in the nearby village of Barbizon captured the area's scenic beauty. The superb baroque château of Vaux-le-Vicomte is also within striking distance. Compared to regal Fontainebleau, Vaux-le-Vicomte feels more intimate, especially on a candlelight visit. The gardens, though, exceed even Fontainebleau's for regimented magnificence.

Fontainebleau

Like Chambord in the Loire Valley and Compiègne to the north of Paris, Fontainebleau earned royal esteem as a hunting base. As at Versailles, a hunting lodge once stood on the site of the current château, along with a chapel built in 1169 and consecrated by exiled (later murdered and canonized) English archbishop Thomas à Becket.

The **Château de Fontainebleau** you see today dates from the 16th century, although additions were made by various royal incumbents over the next 300 years. The palace was begun under flamboyant Renaissance king François I, the French contemporary of England's Henry VIII.

The king hired Italian artists Il Rosso (a pupil of Michelangelo) and Francesco Primaticcio to embellish his château. In fact, they did much more: by introducing the pagan allegories and elegant lines of mannerism to France they revolutionized the realm of French decorative art. Their extraordinary frescoes and stuccowork can be admired in the **Galerie François-I** (Francis I Gallery) and the crown jewel of the interior, the **Salle de Bal.** This ceremonial ballroom, which is nearly 100 feet long, glows with dazzling 16th-century frescoes and gilding. Completed under Henri II, François's successor, it is luxuriantly wood paneled, with a parquet floor whose gleaming finish reflects the patterns on the ceiling above. Like the château as a whole, the room exudes a sense of elegance and style, but on a more intimate, more human scale than Versailles: this is Renaissance, not baroque.

Napoléon's apartments occupied the first floor. You can see a lock of his hair, his Légion d'Honneur medal, his imperial uniform, the hat he wore on his return from Elba in 1815, and one bed in which he definitely did spend a night (almost every town in France boasts a bed in which the emperor supposedly snoozed). There is also a throne room—Napoléon spurned the one at Versailles, a palace he disliked—and the queen's boudoir, known as the Room of the Six Maries (occupants have included the ill-fated Marie-Antoinette and Napoléon's second wife, Marie-Louise). Highlights of other salons include 17th-century tapestries, marble reliefs by Jacquet de Grenoble, and paintings and frescoes by the versatile Primaticcio.

Although Louis XIV's architectural fancy was concentrated on Versailles, he commissioned Jules Hardouin-Mansart to design new pavilions and had André Le Nôtre replant the gardens at Fontainebleau, to which the king and his court returned every fall for the hunting season. But it was Napoléon who made a Versailles out of Fontainebleau, as it were, by spending lavishly to restore it. He held Pope Pius VII captive guest here in 1812, signed the second Church-State Concordat here in 1813, and in the cobbled **Cour des Adieux** (Farewell Courtyard) said good-bye to his Old Guard in 1814 as he began his brief exile on the Mediterranean island of Elba. The famous Horseshoe Staircase that dominates the Cour des Adieux, once the Cour du Cheval Blanc (White Horse Courtyard), was built by Androuet du Cerceau for Louis XIII (1610–43).

Another courtyard—the **Cour de la Fontaine** (Fountain Courtyard)— was commissioned by Napoléon in 1812 and adjoins the Étang des Carpes (Carp Pond). Ancient carp are alleged to swim here, although Allied soldiers drained the pond in 1915 and ate all the fish, and in the event they missed some, Hitler's hordes did likewise in 1940.

The **Porte Dauphine** is the most beautiful of the various gateways that connect the complex of buildings; its name commemorates the dauphin— heir to the throne, later Louis XIII—who was christened under its archway in 1606. ✉ *Pl. du Général-de-Gaulle* ☎ *01–60–71–50–70* ⊕ *www. musee-chateau-fontainebleau.fr* ✍ *Château €5.50, Napoleon's Apartments €3 extra, gardens free* ⊙ *Château Wed.–Mon. 9:30–5. Gardens May–Sept., daily 9–7; Oct.–Apr., daily 9–5.*

Where to Eat

$$–$$$ ✗ **Table des Maréchaux.** Close to the château in the Napoléon hotel, this restaurant serves classic French fare in a plush salon with red-velvet seats and gold wallpaper, around a central patio; specialties include snails in flaky pastry, fried mullet, and rabbit with mushrooms. Prix-fixe menus start at €25. ✉ *9 rue Grande* ☎ *01–60–39–50–50* ⊕ *www. hotelnapoleon-fontainebleau.com* ⌂ *Jacket and tie* ▭ *AE, DC, MC, V.*

Vaux-le-Vicomte

★ The majestic **Château de Vaux-le-Vicomte,** started in 1656 by court finance wizard Nicolas Fouquet, is one of the most impressive buildings in Île-de-France. The construction process was monstrous: villages were razed and 18,000 workmen called in to execute the plans of architect Louis Le Vau, decorator Charles Le Brun, and landscape gardener André Le Nôtre. The housewarming party was so lavish that star guest Louis XIV, tetchy at the best of times, threw a jealous fit, hurled Fouquet in the slammer, and promptly began building Versailles to prove just who was boss. The château subsequently had various owners; it was nearly destroyed during the Revolution, occupied by Russian and Bavarian troops in 1814 after the fall of Napoléon, then abandoned in 1847 after the owner, the Duc de Praslin, murdered his wife here before committing suicide in jail. The estate lay neglected for nearly 30 years before Alfred Sommier, a local industrialist, bought it at an auction in 1875. He spent massively to restore the building and garden; today the domain is tended by his great-grandson, Comte Patrice de Vogüé.

Decoration of the château's landmark feature, the oval cupola of the stately **Grand Salon,** was halted at Fouquet's arrest, and remains depressingly blank. Le Brun's major achievement is the ceiling of the **Chambre du Roi** (King's Bedchamber), depicting *Time Bearing Truth Heavenward.* Le Brun's other masterwork is the ceiling in the **Salon des Muses** (Salon of the Muses), a painted allegory in sensuous colors as vivid as anything he achieved at Versailles. A clever exhibit complete with life-size wax figures explains the rise and fall of Nicolas Fouquet. Although accused by Louis XIV and subsequent historians of megalomania and shady financial dealings, he was apparently condemned on little evidence by a court eager to please the jealous, irascible monarch.

Le Nôtre's stupendous **Jardin,** nearly nearly 2 km (1 mi) long yet seldom more than 200 yards wide, was his first major project and contains statues, waterfalls, and fountains powered by 20 km (12 mi) of pipes, which gush into action between 3 PM and 6 PM on the second and fourth Saturday of the month, April through October. From the domed château, dominating the scene from behind its trim moat, lawns "embroidered" (as the French say) with flower beds (40,000 tulips bloom in April and May) and low-cut box hedge and studded with conical yew bushes resembling giant green molehills extend to the canal which, by a trick of perspective that would become Le Nôtre's hallmark, appears invisible until you draw near. Beyond the canal lies a "grotto" where 17th-century sculptures of bearded river gods loll beneath stone stalactites. A giant nude statue of Hercules gambols up on the hill behind.

There is also a **Musée des Équipages** (Carriage Museum)—stocked with carriages, saddles, and a smithy—near the entrance. Check with the château's office or Web site to see if there are any special events scheduled around the time of your visit—candlelight tours, concerts, and other delights sometimes adorn the Vaux-le-Vicomte schedule. ⊠ *Domaine de Vaux-le-Vicomte, 77950 Maincy* ☎ *01–64–14–41–90* ⊕ *www.vaux-le-vicomte. com* ⊠ *€12; candlelight visits €15; gardens only €7* ⊙ *Château Easter–Nov. 11, daily 10–6. Candlelight visits May–mid-Oct., Sat. 8 PM–midnight.*

Where to Eat

¢–$ ✕ **L'Écureuil.** An imposing barn to the right of the château entrance has been transformed into this self-service cafeteria where you can enjoy fine steaks (insist yours is cooked enough), coffee, or a snack beneath the ancient rafters of a wood-beam roof. The restaurant is open daily for lunch and tea and for dinner during candlelight visits. ⊠ *Château de Vaux-le-Vicomte* ☎ *01–60–66–95–66* ▤ *MC, V.*

Fontainebleau & Vaux-le-Vicomte A to Z

To research prices, get advice from other travelers, and book travel arrangements, visit www.fodors.com.

CAR TRAVEL

From Paris (Porte d'Orléans or Porte d'Italie), take A6, then N7 to Fontainebleau (total distance 72 km [45 mi]). Vaux-le-Vicomte is 21 km (13 mi) north of Fontainebleau via Melun (where you take N36 northeast, direction Meaux, turning right after after 3 km (2 mi) or so along D215). From Paris to Vaux-le-Vicomte, take A6 to Evry, then N104/A5 (following signs to Troyes); leave A5 at exit 15, follow N36 toward Melun, and turn left after 3 km (2 mi) on D215 to Vaux-le-Vicomte.

GUIDED TOURS

Cityrama and Paris Vision run half-day trips to Fontainebleau (including a visit to the nearby painters' village of Barbizon). The cost is €60.

Cityrama ⊠ 4 pl. des Pyramides, Paris ☎ 01-44-55-61-00 ⊕ www.cityrama.com. **Paris Vision** ⊠ 214 rue de Rivoli Paris ☎ 01-42-60-30-01 ⊕ www.parisvision.com.

TRAIN TRAVEL

Fontainebleau is about 50 minutes from Paris's Gare de Lyon; take a bus to complete the 3-km (2-mi) trip from the station (Fontainebleau-Avon) to the château. You can buy a *forfait* (fixed price) pass, including train and bus tickets plus château admission, for €21 at Gare de Lyon. Vaux-le-Vicomte is a 7-km (4-mi) taxi ride from the nearest station at Melun, served by regular trains from Paris and Fontainebleau. Taxis are usually available at the station, but you can book one in advance by calling 01–64–37–13–29; the ride costs around €15 one way (be sure to arrange a return pickup).

VISITOR INFORMATION

Fontainebleau Tourism ⊠ 4 rue Royale, 77300 Fontainebleau ☎ 01-60-74-99-99 ⊕ www.fontainebleau-tourisme.com.

GIVERNY

The village of Giverny has become a place of pilgrimage for art lovers. It was here that Impressionist Claude Monet (1840–1926) lived for 43 years, and next to his house he created the water-lily garden depicted in some of his most memorable paintings. For 50 years after the painter's death the home lay neglected. In the late 1970s, thanks to gifts from around the world and, in particular, from the United States, the site reopened as the **Maison et Jardin de Claude Monet**, with the pretty pink house, the studios, and the garden all restored. Late spring is perhaps the best time to visit, when the apple trees are in blossom and the garden is a riot of color. Try to avoid summer weekends and afternoons in July and August, when the limited capacity of Monet's home and gardens is pushed to the limit by busloads of tourists.

Monet was brought up in Normandy and, like many of the other Impressionists, was attracted by the soft light of the Seine Valley. After several years at Argenteuil, just north of Paris, he moved downriver to Giverny in 1883 along with his two sons, his mistress Alice Hoschedé (whom he later married), and her six children. By 1890 a prospering Monet was able to buy the house outright. Three years later he purchased another plot of land across the lane to continue his gardening experiments, diverting the Epte River to make a pond.

Monet's house has a warm family feeling that may come as a welcome break after visiting stately French châteaux. The rooms have been restored to Monet's original designs: the kitchen with blue tiles, the buttercup-yellow dining room, and Monet's bedroom on the second floor. Reproductions of his own works, as well as some of the Japanese prints Monet avidly collected, are displayed around the house. The garden, with flowers spilling out across the paths, is as cheerful and natural as the house—quite unlike formal French gardens. The enchanting water garden with its water lilies, Japanese bridge, and rhododendrons is across the lane that runs to the side of the house and can be reached through a tunnel. In this setting it's easy to conjure up an image of the grizzled, bearded brushman dabbing at his canvases—capturing changes in light and weather in a way that was to have a major influence on 20th-century art. ⊠ *84 rue Claude-Monet* ☎ *02–32–51–28–21* ⊕ *www.giverny.org* ⊠ *€5.50; gardens only, €4* ⊙ *Apr.–Oct., Tues.–Sun. 10–6.*

The spacious **Musée d'Art Américain** (American Art Museum), endowed by the late Chicago art patrons Daniel and Judith Terra, stages temporary exhibits of American paintings, many by artists who were influenced by—and often studied with—Claude Monet. ⊠ *99 rue Claude-Monet* ☎ *02–32–51–94–65* ⊠ *€5.50* ⊙ *Apr.–Nov., Tues.–Sun. 10–6.*

Where to Stay & Eat

$$–$$$ ✕ **Les Fleurs.** This small, white-walled restaurant in the center of Vernon, 600 yards from the rail station in the direction of the Seine, looks unremarkable inside and out, but the food reveals plenty of personality—try the roast salmon with herbs, or the escargot in a Roquefort sauce. Fresh flowers on the tablecloths add a colorful touch, and service is slick and friendly. ⊠ *71 rue Sadi-Carnot* ☎ *02–32–51–16–80* ▤ *AE, MC, V* ⊙ *Closed Aug., part of Mar., and Mon. No dinner Sun.*

$–$$ ✕ **Les Jardins de Giverny.** This restaurant with a tile-floor dining room overlooking a rose garden is a few minutes' walk from Monet's house. Enjoy the €20 menu or choose from a repertoire of inventive dishes such as foie gras spiked with calvados, duck in cider, or scallops with wild mushrooms. ⊠ *Chemin du Roy* ☎ *02–32–21–60–80* ▤ *AE, MC, V* ⊙ *Closed Mon. and Dec.–Feb. No dinner Sun.–Fri.*

$ ✕ **Ancien Hôtel Baudy.** Back in Monet's day this pretty-in-pink villa was the hotel of the American painters colony. The rustic bar and the luscious rose garden with the studio shed where Cézanne once took up residence, are so enchanting that a recent art book was devoted to La Maison Baudy. The tasteful mise-en-scène makes it easier to forgive the simple cuisine and busloads of tour groups. ⊠ *81 rue Claude-Monet* ☎ *02–32–21–10–03* ▤ *MC, V* ⊙ *Closed Mon. and Nov.–Mar. No dinner Sun.*

¢–$$ ▥ **Giverny B&Bs.** A handful of stylish and affordable bed-and-breakfasts in many of the town's homes makes up for Giverny's dire shortage of hotels. **Le Clos Fleuri** (⊠ 5 rue de la Dîme ☎☎ 02–32–21–36–51) is a Norman manor house set in a lovely garden and run by Claude and Danielle Fouché. Expansive **La Réserve** (⊠ rue Blanche-Hoschedé ☎☎ 02–32–21–99–09), about 2 km (1 mi) outside town, is surrounded by orchards and has gorgeous antiques-adorned and wood-beamed guest apartments, some of which have fireplaces and canopy beds. The home of **Marie-Claire Boscher** (✉ 1 rue du Colombier ☎☎ 02–32–51–39–70) used to be a hotel-restaurant that Monet frequented. It's handily set on the corner of the main village street. ⊕ *www.giverny.org/hotels.*

Giverny A to Z

To research prices, get advice from other travelers, and book travel arrangements, visit www.fodors.com.

CAR TRAVEL
Take expressway A13 from Paris to the Vernon exit (D181). Cross the Seine in Vernon and follow D5 to Giverny (total distance just over 80 km [50 mi]).

GUIDED TOURS
Cityrama runs afternoon tours to Giverny, lasting about five hours, Tuesday–Saturday; the cost is €60.
🚍 **Cityrama** ✉ 4 pl. des Pyramides, Paris ☎ 01-44-55-61-00 ⊕ www.cityrama.com.

TRAIN TRAVEL
Take the train from Paris's Gare St-Lazare to Vernon (50 minutes, €11.10 each way). Giverny is 5½ km (3½ mi) away by bus or taxi, which you can get at the train station. Call the Vernon Tourist Office for information.

VISITOR INFORMATION
🚍 **Vernon Tourist Office** ✉ 36 rue Carnot, 27600 Vernon ☎ 02-32-51-39-60 ⊕ www.ville-vernon27.fr.

VERSAILLES

Numbers in the text correspond to numbers on the Versailles map.

Paris in the 17th century was a rowdy, rabble-ridden city. Louis XIV hated it and set about in search of an alternative power base. He settled on Versailles, 20 km (12 mi) west of Paris, where his father had a small château–hunting lodge.

❶
FodorśChoice
★
Today the **Château de Versailles** seems monstrously big, but it wasn't large enough for the army of 20,000 noblemen, servants, and hangers-on who moved in with Louis. A new city—a new capital, in fact—had to be constructed from scratch to accommodate them. Tough-thinking town planners promptly dreamed up vast mansions and avenues broader than the Champs-Élysées—all in bicep-flexing baroque.

It was hardly surprising that Louis XIV's successors rapidly felt out of sync with their architectural inheritance. Louis XV and Louis XVI preferred to cower in small retreats in the gardens, well out of the mighty château's shadow. The two most famous of these structures are the Petit Trianon, a model of classical harmony and proportion built for Louis XV, and the Hameau, where Marie-Antoinette could play at being a shepherdess amid the ersatz rusticity of her Potemkin hamlet. The contrast

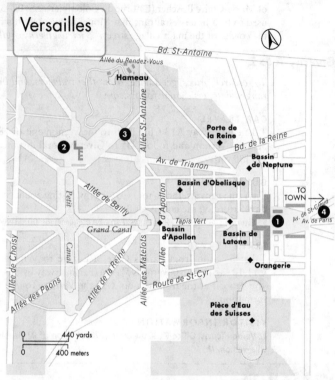

between the majestic and the domesticated is an important part of Versailles's appeal. But pomp and bombast tend to prevail, and you won't need reminding that you're in the world's grandest palace—or one of France's most popular tourist attractions. The park and gardens outside are a great place to stretch your legs while taking in details of formal landscaping.

One of the highlights of the tour is the dazzling **Galerie des Glaces** (Hall of Mirrors). It was here that Bismarck proclaimed the unified German Empire in 1871, and where the controversial Treaty of Versailles, asserting Germany's responsibility for World War I, was signed in 1919. The formal **Grands Appartements** (State Apartments) are whipped into a lather of decoration, with painted ceilings, marble walls, parquet floors, and canopy beds topped with ostrich plumes. The **Petits Appartements** (Private Apartments) where royal family and friends lived are on a more human scale, lined with 18th-century gold and white rococo boiseries. The **Opéra Royal,** the first oval hall in France, was designed for Louis XV. Check out the "marble" loges—they're actually painted wood. The chapel, begun in 1699 to the design of Jules Hardouin-Mansart but only completed in 1710 by his brother-in-law Robert de Cotte, is a study in white-and-gold solemnity. The former state rooms and the sumptuous debate chamber of the **Aile du Midi** (South Wing) are also open to the public, with infrared headphone commentary (available in English) explaining Versailles's parliamentary history.

Despite its sprawl, the palace of Versailles can get stiflingly crowded, especially as visitors are funneled through one narrow side of most of the rooms, with the furniture and objets d'art roped off. The quietest times to visit are weekday mornings from October through May. In 2004 château authorities embarked on a 17-year renovation program that will gradually make the palace—and park—more visitor-friendly. Much of the work will be behind the scenes, related to such mundane matters as drainage and roof insulation. Among the more high-profile projects, the Hall of Mirrors is top priority, with its painted ceiling and parquet floors receiving major restorations. 🖼01–30–83–78–00 ⊕*www.chateauversailles. fr* 🖼 *Château €7.50, parliament exhibition €3 extra* ☉ *Apr.–Oct., Tues.–Sun. 9–6:30; Nov.–Mar., Tues.–Sun. 9–5:30.*

★ After the château's awesome feast of interior decor, the **Parc de Versailles** is a refreshing place to catch your breath. André Le Nôtre's gardens represent classical French landscaping at its most formal and sophisticated. Louis XIV was so proud of them that he wrote a guidebook prescribing the perfect visitor's circuit, starting from the steps behind the château where, as he put it, one should "pause to consider the situation." The vista he considered, unchanged to this day, sweeps past flower beds and the Bassin de Latone, a fountain ringed with giant frogs; down a long narrow lawn called the Tapis Vert; on to the Bassin d'Apollon, where the sun god Apollo gallops out of the water in his chariot; and arrives at the arrow-straight Grand Canal. On either side, down gravel paths lined with trellises and hedges, lurk pools and fountains alive with plump goldfish and gilded statues of gods. Louis XIV's guidebook describes how to do the rounds without retracing your steps, but you'll need many hours to follow the route the Sun King used to take—pushed along, toward the end of his life, by puffing minions in his shiny red three-wheeled thronemobile. Still, it's fun to wander at will. You may get lost, but sooner or later the château will loom back into view.

Because the distances are vast—the Trianons are more than 2 km (1 mi) from the château—you might prefer to climb aboard a horse-drawn carriage (round-trip from the château to Trianon, €8), take the electric train (€3.50 each way, €5.50 round-trip), or rent a bike from the **Grille de la Reine** near the Trianon Palace Hotel (€4.70 per hour) or from the **Petite-Venise** building at the head of the Grand Canal (€5.40 per hour, or €26 for six hours). You can also drive to the Trianons and Canal through the Grille de la Reine (€5.50 per car). You can hire a rowboat (€10 for four) at the head of the Grand Canal, too, and there's a popular restaurant nearby.

An extensive tree-replacement scheme—necessary once a century—was launched in 1998 to recapture the full impact of Le Nôtre's artful vistas. Replantings became all the more necessary after 10,000 trees were uprooted by a hurricane in 1999. The cost of repairing that damage came to some $35 million, and the *American Friends of Versailles* contributed handsomely to the project—as they did to the replanting of Le Nôtre's long-abandoned **Bosquet des Trois Fontaines,** a tiered glade of fountains and yew hedges near the Bassin de Neptune, which reopened in 2004 after two centuries of neglect.

The park is at its golden-leafed best—give or take the odd yew hedge—in autumn but is also enticing in summer, especially on Sunday afternoons from mid-April through mid-October, when the **Grandes Eaux** (fountains) are in full flow. Spectacular son et lumière shows with fireworks, called the **Fêtes de Nuit,** are held on Saturday night in July and September at the Bassin de Neptune (call ☎ 01–30–83–78–88 for details). ⌦ *Park free; gardens €3 Apr.–Oct., free Nov.–Mar.; Sun. fountain displays €6* ☉ *Daily 7 AM–8 PM or dusk.*

At one end of the Petit Canal, about 1½ km (1 mi) from the château, ❷ stands the **Grand Trianon,** a flat-roofed, single-story pleasure palace ringed with pink-marble pilasters. Built by Jules Hardouin-Mansart in the late 1680s, its two wings are linked by an open colonnade. The interior gleams with ormolu-mounted mahogany furniture from Napoléon's time and large malachite ornaments given by Russian czar Alexander I. The finest rooms are the mirror-lined Salon des Glaces overlooking the Petit Canal, and the stately Galerie decorated with 24 paintings of the gardens as they appeared in the days of Louis XIV. ⌦ *€5 (joint ticket with Petit Trianon)* ☉ *May–Sept., Tues.–Sun. noon–6:30; Oct.–Apr., Tues.–Sun. noon–5:30.*

★ ❸ The **Petit Trianon,** close to the Grand Trianon, is a sumptuously furnished neoclassical mansion erected in the 1760s by architect Jacques Gabriel. Louis XV had a superb botanical garden planted here; some of the trees from that era survive today. Louis XVI presented the Petit Trianon to Marie-Antoinette, who spent lavish sums creating an idealized world nearby, the charming **Hameau,** a hamlet of thatch-roof cottages complete with water mill, lake, and pigeon loft. Here the tragic queen played out her happiest days pretending to be a shepherdess tending a flock of perfumed sheep, and here her spirit remains stronger than anywhere else in France, making this a must-do for fans of the hapless Hapsburg. ⌦ *€5 (joint ticket with Grand Trianon)* ☉ *May–Sept., Tues.–Sun. noon–6:30; Oct.–Apr., Tues.–Sun. noon–5:30.*

As you look from the château, on either side of the Avenue de Paris are the Trojan-size royal stables, built by Jules Hardouin-Mansart in the 1680s: to the right, the Petites Ecuries, originally designed for coach horses (and ❹ not open to the public); to the left, the **Grandes Écuries** (Great Stables) built for the horses ridden by the king and his courtiers. The Grandes Écuries now house the **Musée des Carosses** (Carriage Museum)—its array of royal and imperial carriages is open summer weekends only (€2)—and the **Manège,** where legendary horsemaster Bartabas directs 30 gray horses and a dozen apprentice riders in his equine academy (⇨ *see* The Mane Man). You can observe their training every morning (Wednesday–Sunday) on an hour-long visit called the Matinale des Ecuyers, or watch the horses and riders perform to music (much of it from the Sun King's period) at a 50-minute show, the *Reprise Musicale,* held on week-

THE MANE MAN

A FORMER STEEPLECHASE JOCKEY and circus performer may seem an unlikely pick to resurrect the Sun King's stables at Versailles, but the single-monikered Bartabas has done just that.

In 1989 Bartabas launched the Zingaro Theater in Aubervilliers, a northern suburb of Paris, to stage eclectic performances mixing horses, dance, and theater. Since then his horses and equestrians have performed in France and internationally to the accompaniment of Berber chants, Korean singers, the music of Igor Stravinsky, and the bells and rituals of Tibetan monks. This is no horse-whisperer at work; instead, Bartabas says, "I'm the man who listens to them."

When the French government decided to restore the Great Stables in Versailles, Bartabas was the man they summoned to bring them to life. In 2003 he moved in with 30 Lusitanian grays and 15 riders to set up the world's first Academy of Equestrian Theatrical Art. Each rider has a two-year contract, with the best five offered permanent jobs performing for Zingaro and teaching new students in Versailles.

Apart from working with horses, the Bartabas apprentices study dance, singing, and fencing. Bartabas wants them to become multitalented "equestrian artists," following in the hoofsteps of the Sun King and his courtiers. "Noblemen were dancers and fencers as well as riders," he explains. "Louis XIV used horses not just for hunting but for pleasure." This modern-day equestrian artist plans that someday his horses and students will perform "carrousels" in the park of Versailles, just like those staged in Louis's day.

end afternoons. The Manège's 600-seat rectangular hall has giant mirrors along the walls and glass chandeliers shimmering overhead. You are free to wander through the stables after each visit. ☒ *Av. Rockefeller* ☎ *01–39–02–07–14* ⊕ *www.acadequestre.fr* ☒ *Matinales* €7, *Reprise Musicale* €15 ☉ *Mid-Feb.–Dec., Tues.–Thurs., at 9, 10 and 11, weekends at 10, 11 and 2; Jan.–mid-Feb. weekends at 10, 11 and 2.*

The **town of Versailles** is often overlooked, but it's worth strolling along the town's broad, leafy boulevards. The majestic scale of many buildings is a reminder that this was, after all, the capital of France from 1682 to 1789 (and again from 1871 to 1879). Visible to the right, as you look toward the town from the palace, is the dome of the austere **Cathédrale St-Louis** (☒ pl. St-Louis), built from 1743 to 1754; it has a fine organ loft and a two-tier facade.

To the left of place d'Armes, beyond elegant, octagonal place Hoche, is the sturdy baroque church of **Notre-Dame** (☒ at rue Hoche and rue de la Paroisse), built from 1684 to 1686 by Jules Hardouin-Mansart as the parish church for Louis XIV's brand-new town. The street in front of Notre-Dame, rue de la Paroisse, leads up to **place du Marché,** site of a magnificent morning market every Tuesday, Friday, and Sunday.

Where to Stay & Eat

★ **$$$$** ✕ **Les Trois Marches.** One of the best-known restaurants in the Paris area, in the Trianon Palace hotel near an entrance to the château park, serves chef Gérard Vié's creative dishes such as duckling roasted with vinegar and honey. The prix-fixe (€28) two-course weekday business lunch offers the best value. ⊠ *1 bd. de la Reine* ☎ *01–30–84–52–00* ⚭ *Reservations essential* 🏛 *Jacket and tie* ▭ *AE, DC, MC, V* ☉ *Closed Aug.*

$–$$ ✕ **Quai No. 1.** Barometers, sails, and model boats fill this small seafood restaurant. In summer you can enjoy your meal outside on the terrace. Fish with sauerkraut and home-smoked salmon are specialties; any dish on the two prix-fixe menus (€17 and €20) makes for a good, economical choice. ⊠ *1 av. de St-Cloud* ☎ *01–39–50–42–26* ▭ *MC, V* ☉ *Closed Mon. No dinner Sun.*

$–$$$ ✕▥ **Domaine du Verbois.** Greek goddesses set the tone here: bedrooms in this stately late-19th-century mansion are named after them. The larger rooms are at the front; the smaller rooms at the back are quieter and overlook the pretty, tumbling garden. All rooms have reproduction 18th-century furniture and colorful Chinese rugs. The four-course €30 set menu in the pink-walled dining room might include crawfish salad or turbot in champagne sauce. Genial owner Kenneth Boone is half-American and speaks English perfectly. The estate is 21 km (13 mi) from Versailles, a 30-minute drive west of Paris (take A13 from Porte d'Auteuil, then A12/N12). ⊠ *38 av. de la République 78640 Neauphle-le-Château* ☎ *01–34–89–11–78* 🖷 *01–34–89–57–33* ⊕ *www.hotelverbois.com* ➥ *22 rooms* ⚬ *Restaurant, some minibars, cable TV, babysitting, Internet, some pets allowed (fee); no a/c* ▭ *AE, DC, MC, V* ☉ *Closed 2 wks Aug. No dinner Sun.* ⦿ *MAP.*

Versailles A to Z

To research prices, get advice from other travelers, and book travel arrangements, visit www.fodors.com.

CAR TRAVEL
From Paris head west on highway A13 from Porte d'Auteuil (a total distance of 20 km [12 mi]). Allow 15–30 minutes, depending on traffic.

GUIDED TOURS
Many guided-tour companies offer excursions to Versailles. Paris Vision arranges a variety of half- and full-day guided tours of Versailles that cost between €48 and €88. Cityrama is another popular Versailles tour-company option.

🚩 **Cityrama** ⊠ 4 pl. des Pyramides, Paris ☎ 01-44-55-61-00 ⊕ www.cityrama.com.
Paris Vision ⊠ 214 rue de Rivoli, Paris ☎ 01-42-60-30-01 ⊕ www.parisvision.com.

TRAIN TRAVEL
Three train routes travel between Paris and Versailles (20–30 minutes each way). The RER-C to Versailles Rive-Gauche takes you closest to the château (600 yards away via avenue de Sceaux). An all-inclusive forfait pass including round-trip train fare plus château admission costs €16. The other trains run from Paris's Gare St-Lazare to Versailles Rive-Droite (closer to the Trianons and town market but a kilometer from

the château via rue du Maréchal-Foch and avenue de St-Cloud) and from Paris's Gare Montparnasse to Versailles-Chantiers (1 km [½ mi] from the château via rue des États-Généraux and avenue de Paris). From Versailles-Chantiers some trains continue on to Chartres.

VISITOR INFORMATION

🛈 **Versailles Office du Tourisme** ✉ 2 bis, av. de Paris, 78000 Versailles ☎ 01-39-24-88-88 🌐 www.versailles-tourisme.com.

UNDERSTANDING PARIS

CHRONOLOGY

The Merovingian Dynasty (486–751)

507   Clovis, king of the Franks and founder of the Merovingian Dynasty, makes Paris his capital. Many churches are built, including the abbey that will become St-Germain-des-Prés. Commerce is active; Jewish and Asian communities are founded along the Seine.

The Carolingian Dynasty (751–987)

Under the Carolingians Paris ceases to be the capital of France but remains a major administrative, commercial, and ecclesiastical center—and as a result one of the foremost centers of culture and learning west of Constantinople.

845–87   Parisians restore the fortifications of the city, which is repeatedly sacked by Vikings (up to 877).

The Capetian Dynasty (987–1328)

987   Hugh Capet, count of Paris, becomes king. Paris, once more the capital, grows in importance. The Île de la Cité is the seat of government, commerce makes its place on the right bank, and a university develops on the Seine's left bank.

1140–63   The Gothic style of architecture appears at St-Denis: Notre-Dame, begun in 1163, sees the style come to maturity. In the late 12th century streets are paved.

1200   Philippe-Auguste charters a university, builds walls around Paris, and constructs a fortress, the first Louvre.

1243–46   The Sainte-Chapelle is built to house the reputed Crown of Thorns brought by Louis IX (St. Louis) from Constantinople.

1250s   The Sorbonne is founded, destined to become a major theological center.

The Valois Dynasty (1328–1589)

1348–49   The Black Death and the beginning of the Hundred Years' War bring misery and strife to Paris.

1364–80   Charles V works to restore prosperity to Paris. The Bastille is built to defend the new city walls. The Louvre is converted into a royal palace.

1420–37   After the Battle of Agincourt, Henry V of England enters Paris. Joan of Arc leads an attempt to recapture the city (1429). Charles VII of France drives out the English (1437).

1469   The first printing house in France is established at the Sorbonne.

1515–47   François I imports Italian artists, including Leonardo da Vinci, to work on his new palace at Fontainebleau, bringing the Renaissance to

France. François resumes work on the Louvre and builds the Hôtel de Ville in the new style.

1562–98 In the Wars of Religion, Paris remains a Catholic stronghold. On August 24, 1572, Protestant leaders are killed in the St. Bartholomew's Day Massacre.

The Bourbon Dynasty (1589–1789)

1598–1610 Henri IV begins his reign after converting to Catholicism, declaring, "Paris is worth a mass." He embellishes Paris, laying out the Renaissance place des Vosges, the first square in a new style of town planning that would last until the 19th century. In 1610 Henri is assassinated.

1624 Cardinal Richelieu is appointed minister to Louis XIII and concludes the ongoing religious persecution by strictly imposing Catholicism on the country. In 1629 he begins construction of the Palais-Royal.

1635 The Académie Française is founded.

1643–1715 Reign of Louis XIV, the Sun King. Paris rebels against him in the Fronde uprisings (1648–52). Early in his reign he creates a new palace at Versailles, away from the Paris mobs. André le Nôtre transforms the Jardin de Tuileries (Tuileries Gardens) and lays out the Champs-Élysées (1660s). Louis founds the Hôtel des Invalides (1670). Cultural activity abounds, with Molière, Racine, Fragonard, and Rameau reaffirming Paris's reputation as a center of artistic production.

1715–89 During the reigns of Louis XV and Louis XVI Paris becomes the European center of culture and style.

1765 The Western world's first restaurant opens in what is now the rue du Louvre, serving a single dish: sheep's feet simmered in wine.

1783 New outer walls of Paris are begun, incorporating customs gatehouses to control the flow of commerce into the city. The walls, which include new parks, triple the area of Paris.

The Revolution, Empire, and Restoration (1789–1814)

1789–99 The French Revolution begins as the Bastille is stormed on July 14, 1789. The First Republic is established. Louis XVI and his queen, Marie-Antoinette, are guillotined in place de la Concorde. Almost 2,600 others perish in the same way during the Terror (1793–94).

1799–1814 Napoléon begins to convert Paris into a neoclassical city—the Empire style. The Arc de Triomphe and the first iron bridges across the Seine are built. In 1805 he orders the completion of the Louvre.

1815 The Congress of Vienna ensures the restoration of the Bourbon Dynasty following the fall of Napoléon.

1828–42 Urban and political discontent causes riots and demonstrations in the streets. An uprising replaces Charles X with Louis-Philippe's liberal monarchy in 1830. Napoléon's remains are returned to Paris in 1840.

The Second Republic and Second Empire (1848–70)

1848   Economic hardship sparks more turmoil in the capital; barricades go up, brutal street fighting puts casualties in the thousands, and Louis-Philippe abdicates. The brief Second Republic ends with the election of Napoléon's nephew, who seizes power in 1851 and begins his reign as Napoléon III.

1852   Further additions to the Louvre are made. Under Napoléon III the Alsatian town planner Baron Haussmann guts large areas of medieval Paris to lay out broad boulevards linking important squares. Railroad stations and the vast covered markets at Les Halles are built. Au Bon Marché, the first department store in Paris, opens its doors.

1857   Charles-Pierre Baudelaire (1821–67) ignites a literary scandal with the publication of his *Fleurs du Mal*.

1858   Englishman Charles Worth establishes the first haute-couture fashion house in Paris.

1862   Victor Hugo's *Les Misérables* is published in Paris while the liberal author remains in exile by order of Napoléon III.

1870–71   Franco-Prussian War; Paris is besieged by Prussian troops; starvation is rampant—each week during the winter 5,000 people die. The Paris Commune, an attempt by the citizens to take power, in 1871, results in bloody suppression and much property damage (the Tuileries Palace is razed). Hugo returns to Paris.

The Third Republic (1871–1944)

1875   The Paris Opéra is inaugurated after 14 years of construction.

1889   The Eiffel Tower is built for the Paris World Exhibition. The Moulin Rouge opens.

1894–1900   A Jewish Army captain, Alfred Dreyfus, is court-martialed on trumped-up charges of treason and whisked off to Devil's Island. Émile Zola publishes the fiery *J'Accuse* (*I Accuse*), an open letter to the president of the republic; his defense of Dreyfus is one of the most powerful pieces of journalism ever written. The ensuing Dreyfus Affair bitterly divides France, as anti-Semitism, entrenched bureaucratic traditions, and personal loyalties shake the government and society.

1895   The Lumière Brothers introduce their Cinématographe to a paying public, screening a series of 10 short films in the basement of the Grand Café on December 28.

1900   The international exhibition in Paris popularizes the curving forms of Art Nouveau decorating the entrances to the newly opened Paris métro.

1906   Dreyfus is officially exonerated.

1914–18   World War I. The Germans come within 15 km (9 mi) of Paris (so close that Paris taxis are used to carry troops to the front).

1915   The cabaret singer Edith Piaf, known as the Little Sparrow, is born (allegedly under a gaslight) on the rue de Belleville.

1919   The Treaty of Versailles is signed, formally ending World War I.

1925   International decorative art exhibition consecrates the restrained, sophisticated design style now known as Art Deco.

1918–39   Between the wars Paris attracts artists and writers, including Americans Ernest Hemingway and Gertrude Stein. Paris nourishes the philosophical movement existentialism and major modern art movements—Constructivism, Dadaism, Surrealism.

1939–45   World War II. Paris falls to the Germans in 1940. The French government moves to Vichy and collaborates with the Nazis. The Resistance uses Paris as a base. The Free French Army, under Charles de Gaulle, joins with the Allies to liberate Paris after D-Day, in August 1944.

The Fourth and Fifth Republics (1944–Present)

1944–46   De Gaulle moves the provisional government to Paris.

1946   With the arrival of the Fourth Republic women acquire the right to vote.

1958   De Gaulle is elected president of the Fifth Republic.

1959   The European Economic Community, a precursor of the European Union, is established, with France a founding member.

1960s–70s   Paris undergoes physical changes: dirty buildings are cleaned, beltways are built around the city, and expressways are driven through the heart of it. Major new building projects (especially La Défense) are banished to the outskirts.

1962   De Gaulle grants Algeria independence; growing tensions with immigrant workers in Paris and other cities.

1968   Parisian students protest the state's educational policies and clash with the state riot police. In May students build barricades in the Latin Quarter and occupy buildings of the Sorbonne, sparking increasingly violent conflicts with the police. Trade unions forge an alliance with the student groups and begin general strikes. The country stabilizes over the summer, after June elections retain the Gaullist government.

1969   De Gaulle steps down from the presidency; Georges Pompidou (1911–1974) is elected in his place. Les Halles market is moved, and its buildings are demolished.

1977   The Centre Pompidou opens to controversy, marking a high point in modern political intervention in the arts and public architecture.

1981   François Mitterrand (1916–96) is elected president and embarks on a major building program throughout the city.

1986   The Musée d'Orsay opens in the former Gare d'Orsay train station.

1989   Paris celebrates the bicentennial of the French Revolution. The Louvre's glass pyramid, the Grande Arche of La Défense, and the Opéra Bastille are completed.

1994   Paris–London rail link via Channel tunnel becomes operational.

1995   Paris mayor Jacques Chirac replaces François Mitterrand as the president of France.

1998   Amid scenes of popular fervor in Paris not seen since the Liberation in 1944, France hosts and wins the soccer World Cup.

1999   Opening of the Bibliothèque Nationale de France François Mitterrand in southeast Paris, containing 12 million books.

2000   Paris marks the new millennium with a new lighting scheme for the Eiffel Tower, a giant Ferris wheel on place de la Concorde, and a huge statue of Charles de Gaulle on the Champs-Élysées. The facade of the Opéra is cleaned, and the Centre Pompidou reopens after major renovation. A new pedestrian bridge links the Musée d'Orsay to the Tuileries.

2001   Socialist Bertrand Delanoë is elected mayor of Paris, the first left-wing city leader in more than 100 years. To repair the damage caused by a storm at the end of 1999, nine new parks and gardens are planned. The Mediterranean TGV line connecting Paris and Marseille opens.

2002   On February 17 the franc ceases to be legal tender and is officially replaced by the euro. Delanoë inaugurates Paris's annual Nuit Blanche, an all-night cultural festival; during the event an assailant stabs him (Delanoë recovers after minor surgery). On May 5 Jacques Chirac is reelected president in a landslide victory over extreme right-winger Jean-Marie Le Pen.

2003   A brutal summer heat wave kills hundreds in the capital. Chirac stresses the French commitment to secular education by recommending a law forbidding conspicuous symbols of religious faith in public schools.

2004   Lance Armstrong wins his sixth consecutive Tour de France. Delanoë continues to change the face of the city with his plans to renovate Les Halles and to make the center of Paris car-free by 2012. The city's bid for the 2012 Olympics generates buzz. Controversy continues as a number of young Muslim girls are expelled from school for continuing to wear head scarves after they are banned.

BOOKS & MOVIES

Books

Fiction. Think of writers in Paris, and often the romanticized figures of the interwar "lost generation" expats arise: Ernest Hemingway (*The Sun Also Rises*), F. Scott Fitzgerald, Ezra Pound, Djuna Barnes (*Nightwood*), and the overseeing eye of Gertrude Stein (*Paris, France*). But look farther back for some equally compelling reads: Charles Dickens's *A Tale of Two Cities*, an adventure tale set during the Revolution; Jules Verne's *Paris in the Twentieth Century*, with a view from the past of Paris in the future; and Henry James's novels *The American* and *The Ambassadors*.

The Tattered Cloak, by Nina Berberova, revolves around Russian exiles living in Paris just before WWII. James Baldwin's experience in Paris in the 1950s informed his novels, such as *Giovanni's Room*, as well as the nonfiction *Notes of a Native Son*, a breakthrough work of the American civil rights movement. The denizens of the so-called Beat Hotel (Allen Ginsberg, William Burroughs) squeezed in some writing among their less salubrious activities. Mavis Gallant also began her tenure in Paris in the '50s; unfortunately, much of her work is out of print, with the exception of the excellent *Paris Stories*, but look for others in your library.

Recent best-sellers with a Paris setting include *The Da Vinci Code*, a mystery by Dan Brown, Diane Johnson's *Le Divorce* and *Le Mariage*, Anita Brookner's *Incidents in the Rue Laugier*, Kaylie Jones's *A Soldier's Daughter Never Cries*, and Patrick Suskind's *Perfume: The Story of a Murderer*. Paul LaFarge's *Haussmann, or the Distinction* spins historical detail about the ambitious city planner into a fascinating period novel. For literary snacking, look up *Paris in Mind*, which pulls together excerpts from books by American authors.

Food. Patricia Wells's *The Food Lover's Guide to Paris* is a virtual bible for anyone passionate or curious about this topic; Wells covers everything from restaurants and cafés to cheese shops, street markets, and food and wine bookshops. Start reading this before you get on the plane, as there's a lot to absorb. *Remembrance of Things Paris* compiles articles published in *Gourmet* magazine over the past 60 years, with profiles on restaurants, special dishes, and local characters. Daniel Young's *The Paris Café Cookbook* is more than the title suggests; it introduces 50 fantastic cafés, with compelling descriptions of each, tips on café etiquette, and recipes.

For Children. *Madeleine* is the first of a series of long-loved children's books about the namesake heroine; Ludwig Bemelmans whimsically illustrates Paris landmarks such as the Opéra and the Jardins du Luxembourg. *Eloise in Paris*, by Kay Thompson, also has priceless illustrations, these by Hilary Knight (look for his take on Christian Dior). The *Anatole* books by Eve Titus are classics, starring a Gallic mouse. Playful, bright illustrations drive Maira Kalman's *Ooh-la-la (Max in Love)*; the singsong language, smattered with French, is perfect for reading aloud. Joan MacPhail Knight has written a pair of books about an American girl visiting France in the late 1800s: *Charlotte in Giverny* and *Charlotte in Paris*. Engagingly written in a diary style, they're also a good dose of art history, as Charlotte meets artists such as Mary Cassatt. (For another art-related book, seek out *Linnea in Monet's Garden*, by Christina Björk.) *The Inside-Outside Book of Paris*, by Roxie Munro, is a kid-friendly pictorial tour through the city.

History. Recent studies devoted to the capital include: Philip Mansel's *Paris Between Empires: Monarchy and Revolution*; *Barricades: War on the Streets in Revolutionary Paris,* by Jill Harsin; and Johannes Willms's *Paris: Capital of Europe*, which runs from the Revolution to the Belle Époque. Simon Schama's *Citizens* is a good introduction to the French Revolution. Alistair Horne's *Seven Ages of Paris* skips away from standard historical approaches, breaking the city's past into seven eras and putting a colorful spin on the Renaissance, the Revolution, Napoléon's Empire, and other periods. *A Traveller's History of Paris,* by Robert Cole, is a selective, somewhat patchy overview.

Dozens of studies of particular aspects of Parisian history are now out of print and will require library sleuthing. A few of the best general volumes are Otto Friedrich's *Olympia: Paris in the Age of Manet* and Vincent Cronin's *Paris on the Eve: 1900–1914* and *Paris: City of Light 1919–1939.*

Biographies and autobiographies of French luminaries and Paris residents can double as satisfying portraits of the capital during their subjects' lifetimes. Works on Baron Haussmann are especially rich, as the 19th-century prefect so utterly changed the face of the city. For a look at American expatriates in Paris between the wars, pick up *Sylvia Beach and the Lost Generation,* by Noel R. Fitch. Tyler Stovall's *Paris Noir: African-Americans in the City of Light* examines black American artists' affection for Paris during the 20th century; *Harlem in Montmartre,* by William A. Shack, hones in on expat jazz culture. The photographs of Eugène Atget are a sort of visual history; Atget set out to record hundreds of streets, building facades, street vendors, and architectural details at the turn of the 20th century. There are several editions of his work in print. Walter Benjamin's *The Arcades Project* uses the 19th-century passages as a point of intersection for studies on advertising, Baudelaire, the Paris Commune, and other subjects.

Memoirs, Essays & Observations. Ernest Hemingway's taut, engrossing *A Moveable Feast,* the tale of his 1920s expatriate life in Paris as a struggling writer, grips virtually everyone from its opening lines. Gertrude Stein, one of Hemingway's friends, gave her own version of that era in *The Autobiography of Alice B. Toklas.* In *The Se-*

cret Paris of the '30s, Brassaï put into words the scenes he captured in photographs. Joseph Roth gave an exile's point of view in *Report from a Parisian Paradise.* Art Buchwald's funny yet poignant *I'll Always Have Paris* moves from the postwar GI Bill days through his years as a journalist and adventurer. Stanley Karnow also drew on a reporter's past in *Paris in the Fifties.* Henry Miller's visceral autobiographical works such as *The Tropic of Cancer* reveal a grittier kind of expat life. Janet Flanner's incomparable *Paris Journals* chronicle the city from the 1940s through 1970. Julian Green's *Paris* spans even more decades from a near-native's perspective.

No one has yet matched A. J. Liebling at table, as described in *Between Meals.* More recent accounts by Americans living in Paris include: Edmund White's *Our Paris: Sketches with Memory* (White is also the author of a brief but captivating wander through the city in *The Flaneur*); Alex Karmel's *A Corner in the Marais: Memoir of a Paris Neighborhood; The Piano Shop on the Left Bank,* by Thad Carhart; and the hysterically funny *Me Talk Pretty One Day,* by David Sedaris. Adam Gopnik, a *New Yorker* writer who lived in Paris in the 1990s, intersperses articles on larger French issues with descriptions of daily life with his wife and son in *Paris to the Moon.* Gopnik also edited the anthology *Americans in Paris,* a mesmerizing collection of observations by everyone from Thomas Jefferson to Cole Porter.

The Collected Traveller: Paris and *Travelers' Tales Guides: Paris* are two terrific anthologies of articles and essays encompassing dozens of viewpoints within their covers. *A Place in the World Called Paris* samples letters, fiction, poetry, and memoirs about the city. Two unconventional choices are Karen Elizabeth Gordon's witty and surreal *Paris Out of Hand* and Lawrence Osborne's *Paris Dreambook,* which probes the city's outskirts and hidden corners.

Works in Translation. Many landmarks of French literature have long been claimed as classics in English as well—Victor Hugo's great 19th-century novels, for instance, such as *The Hunchback of Notre-Dame* and the sprawling *Les Misérables.* Hugo spun elaborate descriptions of Paris, from its sewers to its spires. Other 19th-century masterpieces include Gustave Flaubert's *Sentimental Education,* set against the capital's 1848 uprisings; Honoré de Balzac's *Human Comedy,* a series of dozens of novels, many set in Paris; *Cyrano de Bergerac,* Edmond Rostand's verse play starring the large-nosed hero; and Émile Zola's *Nana, Thérèse Raquin,* and other novels of passion and ambition played out in Paris's backstreets and bedrooms. The original character of *The Phantom of the Opera* was dreamed up by Gaston Leroux. Alexandre Dumas's *The Count of Monte Cristo* pursues revenge through post-Napoleonic society.

Even more verbose than Victor Hugo was Marcel Proust, whose masterpiece *À la Recherche du Temps Perdu (In Search of Lost Time)* describes fin-de-siècle Paris's parks, glittering aristocratic salons, and dread during the Great War. Viking Press began releasing a fresh English translation in 2003. Colette was another great chronicler of the Belle Époque with her short, bracing works such as *Chéri* and the Claudine stories.

Simone de Beauvoir's *The Prime of Life,* the second book in an autobiographical trilogy, details her relationship with the existentialist philosopher Jean-Paul Sartre in the context of 1930s and '40s Paris, the days when the Rive Gauche cemented its modern bohemian reputation in its cafés and jazz clubs. Georges Simenon's Inspector Maigret mysteries spanned these decades as well and went on for decades more.

Movies

Drama. The heist film *Ronin* (1998) pairs Robert De Niro and Jean Reno with a hyperkinetic chase through the streets of Paris. In *Frantic* (1987) Harrison Ford plays an American doctor visiting Paris when his wife disappears and director Roman Polanski shoots the city to build suspense and dread. The Palais-Royal gets an equally tense treatment in the Audrey Hepburn–Cary Grant thriller *Charade* (1963). (The 2002 remake, *The Truth About Charlie,* doesn't hold a candle to the original.) In *Before Sunset* (2004), Ethan Hawke meets Julie Delpy in the sequel to *Before Sunrise.*

For Children. *Rugrats in Paris* (2000) sends the cartoon kids all over town. Upping the age bracket, the Olsen twins (Mary-Kate and Ashley) live a junior-high student's Paris dream in *Passport To Paris* (1999), shopping at boutiques, chasing French boys, and dining at the Eiffel Tower.

French Films. One of the biggest hits to come out of France in years is *Amélie* (2001), which follows a young woman determined to change people's lives. There's a love angle, *bien sûr,* and the neighborhood of Montmartre is practically a third hero, although Parisians sniffed that it was a sterilized version of the raffish quartier.

Jean-Luc Godard's *Breathless* (1960) and François Truffaut's *The 400 Blows* (slang for "raising hell"; 1959) kicked off the new wave cinema movement. Godard eschewed traditional movie narrative techniques, employing a loose style—including improvised dialogue and handheld camera shots—for his story of a low-level crook (Jean-Paul Belmondo) and his girlfriend (Jean Seberg, memorably picked up as she hawks newspapers on the Champs-Élysées). Truffaut's film is a masterwork of innocence lost, a semiautobiographical story of a young boy banished to juvenile detention.

Catherine Deneuve is practically a film industry in and of herself. Her movies span the globe; those shot in Paris range from *Belle de Jour* (1967), Luis Buñuel's study of erotic repression, to *Le Dernier Métro* (1980), a WWII drama, to *Le Temps*

Retrouvé (1999), an evocation of the last volume of Proust's novel.

Film noir and crime dramas are also highlights, particularly *Rififi* (1955), with an excruciatingly tense 33-minute heist scene; *Le Samouraï* (1967), in which Alain Delon plays the ultimate cool assassin; and Robert Bresson's *Pickpocket* (1959). *La Casque d'Or* (1952) looks back to the underworld of the early 1900s, with Simone Signoret as the title irresistible blonde. French director Luc Besson introduced a sly female action hero with *Nikita* (1990) in which Jean Reno chills as the creepy "cleaner" you don't want making house calls.

Filmed during the Occupation, *The Children of Paradise* (1945) became an allegory for the French spirit of resistance. The love story was set in 1840s Paris, thereby getting past the German censors. Other romantic films with memorable takes on Paris include *Cyrano de Bergerac* (1990), with Gérard Depardieu as the large-schnozzed hero; *When the Cat's Away* (1996); the talk-heavy films of Eric Rohmer; *Camille Claudel* (1988), about the affair between Rodin and fellow sculptor Claudel; and the gritty *The Lovers on the Bridge* (1999), the flaws balanced by the bravado of Juliette Binoche waterskiing on the Seine surrounded by fireworks. *The Red Balloon* (1956) is also a love story of a sort: a children's film of a boy and his faithful balloon.

Musicals. Love in the time of Toulouse-Lautrec? Elton John songs? Baz Luhrmann's *Moulin Rouge* (2001) whirls them together and wins through conviction rather than verisimilitude. Also try John Huston's 1952 film of the same name. Gene Kelly pursues Leslie Caron through postwar Paris in *An American in Paris* (1951); the Gershwin-fueled film includes a stunning 17-minute dance sequence. (Oscar Levant provides the necessary dash of cynicism.) Caron reappears as the love interest—this time as a young girl in training to be a courtesan—in *Gigi* (1958). *Funny Face* (1957) stars Fred Astaire and Audrey Hepburn, and there's an unforgettable scene of Hepburn descending the staircase below the *Winged Victory* in the Louvre.

VOCABULARY

One of the trickiest French sounds to pronounce is the nasal final *n* sound (whether or not the *n* is actually the last letter of the word). You should try to pronounce it as a sort of nasal grunt—as in "huh." The vowel that precedes the *n* will govern the vowel sound of the word, and in this list we precede the final *n* with an *h* to remind you to be nasal.

Another problem sound is the ubiquitous but untransliterable *eu,* as in *bleu* (blue) or *deux* (two), and the very similar sound in *je* (I), *ce* (this), and *de* (of). The closest equivalent might be the vowel sound in "put," but rounded. The famous rolled *r* is a glottal sound. Consonants at the ends of words are usually silent; when the following word begins with a vowel, however, the two are run together by sounding the consonant. There are two forms of "you" in French: *vous* (formal and plural) and *tu* (a singular, personal form). When addressing an adult you don't know, *vous* is always best.

English	French	Pronunciation

Basics

English	French	Pronunciation
Yes/no	Oui/non	wee/nohn
Please	S'il vous plaît	seel voo play
Thank you	Merci	mair-**see**
You're welcome	De rien	deh ree-**ehn**
Excuse me, sorry	Pardon	pahr-**don**
Good morning/ afternoon	Bonjour	bohn-**zhoor**
Good evening	Bonsoir	bohn-**swahr**
Goodbye	Au revoir	o ruh-**vwahr**
Mr. (Sir)	Monsieur	muh-**syuh**
Mrs. (Ma'am)	Madame	ma-**dam**
Miss	Mademoiselle	mad-mwa-**zel**
Pleased to meet you	Enchanté(e)	ohn-shahn-**tay**
How are you?	Comment allez-vous?	kuh-mahn-tahl-ay **voo**
Very well, thanks	Très bien, merci	tray bee-ehn, mair-**see**
And you?	Et vous?	ay voo?

Numbers

English	French	Pronunciation
one	un	uhn
two	deux	deuh
three	trois	twah
four	quatre	**kaht**-ruh

five	cinq	sank
six	six	seess
seven	sept	set
eight	huit	wheat
nine	neuf	nuf
ten	dix	deess
eleven	onze	ohnz
twelve	douze	dooz
thirteen	treize	trehz
fourteen	quatorze	kah-torz
fifteen	quinze	kanz
sixteen	seize	sez
seventeen	dix-sept	deez-**set**
eighteen	dix-huit	deez-**wheat**
nineteen	dix-neuf	deez-**nuf**
twenty	vingt	vehn
twenty-one	vingt-et-un	vehnt-ay-**uhn**
thirty	trente	trahnt
forty	quarante	ka-**rahnt**
fifty	cinquante	sang-**kahnt**
sixty	soixante	swa-**sahnt**
seventy	soixante-dix	swa-sahnt-**deess**
eighty	quatre-vingts	kaht-ruh-**vehn**
ninety	quatre-vingt-dix	kaht-ruh-vehn-**deess**
one hundred	cent	sahn
one thousand	mille	meel

Colors

black	noir	nwahr
blue	bleu	bleuh
brown	brun/marron	bruhn/mar-**rohn**
green	vert	vair
orange	orange	o-**rahnj**
pink	rose	rose
red	rouge	rouge
violet	violette	vee-o-**let**
white	blanc	blahnk
yellow	jaune	zhone

Days of the Week

Sunday	dimanche	dee-**mahnsh**
Monday	lundi	luhn-**dee**
Tuesday	mardi	mahr-**dee**
Wednesday	mercredi	mair-kruh-**dee**
Thursday	jeudi	zhuh-**dee**
Friday	vendredi	vawn-druh-**dee**
Saturday	samedi	sahm-**dee**

Months

January	janvier	zhahn-vee-**ay**
February	février	feh-vree-**ay**
March	mars	marce
April	avril	a-**vreel**
May	mai	meh
June	juin	zhwehn
July	juillet	zhwee-**ay**
August	août	ah-**oo**
September	septembre	sep-**tahm**-bruh
October	octobre	awk-**to**-bruh
November	novembre	no-**vahm**-bruh
December	décembre	day-**sahm**-bruh

Useful Phrases

Do you speak English?	Parlez-vous anglais?	par-lay **voo** **ahn**-glay
I don't speak . . . French	Je ne parle pas . . . français	zhuh nuh parl pah frahn-**say**
I don't understand	Je ne comprends pas	zhuh nuh kohm-**prahn** pah
I understand	Je comprends	zhuh kohm-**prahn**
I don't know	Je ne sais pas	zhuh nuh say **pah**
I'm American/British	Je suis américain/anglais	zhuh sweez a-may-ree-**kehn**/ahn-**glay**
What's your name?	Comment vous appelez-vous?	ko-mahn voo za-pell-ay-**voo**
My name is . . .	Je m'appelle . . .	zhuh ma-**pell** . . .
What time is it?	Quelle heure est-il?	kel air eh-**teel**

How?	Comment?	ko-**mahn**
When?	Quand?	kahn
Yesterday	Hier	yair
Today	Aujourd'hui	o-zhoor-**dwee**
Tomorrow	Demain	duh-**mehn**
Tonight	Ce soir	suh **swahr**
What?	Quoi?	kwah
What is it?	Qu'est-ce que c'est?	kess-kuh-**say**
Why?	Pourquoi?	**poor**-kwa
Who?	Qui?	kee
Where is . . .	Où est . . .	oo ay
the train station?	la gare?	la gar
the subway station?	la station de métro?	la sta-**syon** duh may-**tro**
the bus stop?	l'arrêt de bus?	la-**ray** duh **booss**
the post office?	la poste?	la post
the bank?	la banque?	la bahnk
the . . . hotel?	l'hôtel . . .?	lo-**tel**
the store?	le magasin?	luh ma-ga-**zehn**
the cashier?	la caisse?	la **kess**
the . . . museum?	le musée . . .?	luh mew-**zay**
the hospital?	l'hôpital?	lo-pee-**tahl**
the elevator?	l'ascenseur?	la-sahn-**seuhr**
the telephone?	le téléphone?	luh tay-lay-**phone**
Where are the restrooms? (men/women)	Où sont les toilettes? (hommes/femmes)	oo sohn lay twah-**let** (**oh**-mm/**fah**-mm)
Here/there	Ici/là	ee-**see**/la
Left/right	A gauche/à droite	a goash/a draht
Straight ahead	Tout droit	too drwah
Is it near/far?	C'est près/loin?	say pray/lwehn
I'd like . . .	Je voudrais . . .	zhuh voo-**dray**
a room	une chambre	ewn **shahm**-bruh
the key	la clé	la clay
a newspaper	un journal	uhn zhoor-**nahl**
a stamp	un timbre	uhn **tam**-bruh
I'd like to buy . . .	Je voudrais acheter . . .	zhuh voo-**dray** **ahsh**-tay
cigarettes	des cigarettes	day see-ga-**ret**
matches	des allumettes	days a-loo-**met**
soap	du savon	dew sah-**vohn**
city map	un plan de ville	uhn plahn de **veel**
road map	une carte routière	ewn cart roo-tee-**air**

magazine	une revue	ewn reh-**vu**
envelopes	des enveloppes	dayz ahn-veh-**lope**
writing paper	du papier à lettres	dew pa-pee-**ay** a **let**-ruh
postcard	une carte postale	ewn cart pos-**tal**
How much is it?	C'est combien?	say comb-bee-**ehn**
A little/a lot	Un peu/beaucoup	uhn peuh/bo-**koo**
More/less	Plus/moins	plu/mwehn
Enough/too (much)	Assez/trop	a-say/tro
I am ill/sick	Je suis malade	zhuh swee ma-**lahd**
Call a . . . doctor	Appelez un . . . docteur	a-play uhn dohk-**tehr**
Help!	Au secours!	o suh-**koor**
Stop!	Arrêtez!	a-reh-**tay**
Fire!	Au feu!	o fuh
Caution!/Look out!	Attention!	a-tahn-see-**ohn**

Dining Out

A bottle of . . .	une bouteille de . . .	ewn boo-**tay** duh
A cup of . . .	une tasse de . . .	ewn tass duh
A glass of . . .	un verre de . . .	uhn vair duh
Bill/check	l'addition	la-dee-see-**ohn**
Bread	du pain	dew pan
Breakfast	le petit-déjeuner	luh puh-**tee** day-zhuh-**nay**
Butter	du beurre	dew burr
Cheers!	A votre santé!	ah vo-truh sahn-**tay**
Cocktail/aperitif	un apéritif	uhn ah-pay-ree-**teef**
Dinner	le dîner	luh dee-**nay**
Dish of the day	le plat du jour	luh plah dew **zhoor**
Enjoy!	Bon appétit!	bohn a-pay-**tee**
Fixed-price menu	le menu	luh may-**new**
Fork	une fourchette	ewn four-**shet**
I am diabetic	Je suis diabétique	zhuh swee dee-ah-bay-**teek**
I am vegetarian	Je suis végé-tarien(ne)	zhuh swee vay-zhay-ta-ree-**en**
I cannot eat . . .	Je ne peux pas manger de . . .	zhuh nuh **puh** pah mahn-**jay** deh

I'd like to order	Je voudrais commander	zhuh voo-**dray** ko-mahn-**day**
Is service/the tip included?	Est-ce que le service est compris?	ess kuh luh sair-**veess** ay comb-**pree**
It's good/bad	C'est bon/mauvais	say bohn/ mo-**vay**
It's hot/cold	C'est chaud/froid	say sho/frwah
Knife	un couteau	uhn koo-**toe**
Lunch	le déjeuner	luh day-zhuh-**nay**
Menu	la carte	la cart
Napkin	une serviette	ewn sair-vee-**et**
Pepper	du poivre	dew **pwah**-vruh
Plate	une assiette	ewn a-see-**et**
Please give me . . .	Donnez-moi . . .	doe-nay-**mwah**
Salt	du sel	dew sell
Spoon	une cuillère	ewn kwee-**air**
Sugar	du sucre	dew **sook**-ruh
Waiter!/Waitress!	Monsieur!/ Mademoiselle!	muh-**syuh**/ mad-mwa-**zel**
Wine list	la carte des vins	la cart day vehn

MENU GUIDE

French	English

General Dining

Entrée	Appetizer/Starter
Garniture au choix	Choice of vegetable side
Plat du jour	Dish of the day
Selon arrivage	When available
Supplément/En sus	Extra charge
Sur commande	Made to order

Petit Déjeuner (Breakfast)

Confiture	Jam
Miel	Honey
Oeuf à la coque	Boiled egg
Oeufs sur le plat	Fried eggs
Oeufs brouillés	Scrambled eggs
Tartine	Bread with butter

Poissons/Fruits de Mer (Fish/Seafood)

Anchois	Anchovies
Bar	Bass
Brandade de morue	Creamed salt cod
Brochet	Pike
Cabillaud/Morue	Fresh cod
Calmar	Squid
Coquilles St-Jacques	Scallops
Crevettes	Shrimp
Daurade	Sea bream
Ecrevisses	Prawns/Crayfish
Harengs	Herring
Homard	Lobster
Huîtres	Oysters
Langoustine	Prawn/Lobster
Lotte	Monkfish
Moules	Mussels
Palourdes	Clams
Saumon	Salmon
Thon	Tuna
Truite	Trout

Viande (Meat)

Agneau	Lamb
Boeuf	Beef
Boudin	Sausage
Boulettes de viande	Meatballs
Brochettes	Kabobs
Cassoulet	Casserole of white beans, meat
Cervelle	Brains
Chateaubriand	Double fillet steak
Choucroute garnie	Sausages with sauerkraut
Côtelettes	Chops
Côte/Côte de boeuf	Rib/T-bone steak
Cuisses de grenouilles	Frogs' legs
Entrecôte	Rib or rib-eye steak
Épaule	Shoulder
Escalope	Cutlet
Foie	Liver
Gigot	Leg
Porc	Pork
Ris de veau	Veal sweetbreads
Rognons	Kidneys
Saucisses	Sausages
Selle	Saddle
Tournedos	Tenderloin of T-bone steak
Veau	Veal

Methods of Preparation

A point	Medium
A l'étouffée	Stewed
Au four	Baked
Ballotine	Boned, stuffed, and rolled
Bien cuit	Well-done
Bleu	Very rare
Frit	Fried
Grillé	Grilled
Rôti	Roast
Saignant	Rare

Volailles/Gibier (Poultry/Game)

Blanc de volaille	Chicken breast
Canard/Caneton	Duck/Duckling
Cerf/Chevreuil	Venison (red/roe)
Coq au vin	Chicken stewed in red wine
Dinde/Dindonneau	Turkey/Young turkey
Faisan	Pheasant
Lapin/Lièvre	Rabbit/Wild hare
Oie	Goose
Pintade/Pintadeau	Guinea fowl/Young guinea fowl
Poulet/Poussin	Chicken/Spring chicken

Légumes (Vegetables)

Artichaut	Artichoke
Asperge	Asparagus
Aubergine	Eggplant
Carottes	Carrots
Champignons	Mushrooms
Chou-fleur	Cauliflower
Chou (rouge)	Cabbage (red)
Laitue	Lettuce
Oignons	Onions
Petits pois	Peas
Pomme de terre	Potato
Tomates	Tomatoes

Fruits/Noix (Fruits/Nuts)

Abricot	Apricot
Amandes	Almonds
Ananas	Pineapple
Cassis	Blackcurrants
Cerises	Cherries
Citron/Citron vert	Lemon/Lime
Fraises	Strawberries

Framboises	Raspberries
Pamplemousse	Grapefruit
Pêche	Peach
Poire	Pear
Pomme	Apple
Prunes/Pruneaux	Plums/Prunes
Raisins/Raisins secs	Grapes/Raisins

Desserts

Coupe (glacée)	Sundae
Crème Chantilly	Whipped cream
Gâteau au chocolat	Chocolate cake
Glace	Ice cream
Tarte tatin	Caramelized apple tart
Tourte	Layer cake

Drinks

A l'eau	With water
Avec des glaçons	On the rocks
Bière	Beer
Blonde/brune	Light/dark
Café noir/crème	Black coffee/with steamed milk
Chocolat chaud	Hot chocolate
Eau-de-vie	Brandy
Eau minérale	Mineral water
gazeuse/non gazeuse	*carbonated/still*
Jus de . . .	. . . juice
Lait	Milk
Sec	Straight or dry
Thé	Tea
au lait/au citron	*with milk/lemon*
Vin	Wine
blanc	*white*
doux	*sweet*
léger	*light*
brut	*very dry*
rouge	*red*

INDEX

NOTES

NOTES

NOTES

NOTES

NOTES

FODOR'S KEY TO THE GUIDES

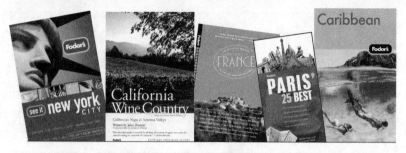

AMERICA'S **GUIDEBOOK LEADER** PUBLISHES GUIDES FOR **EVERY KIND OF TRAVELER**. CHECK OUT OUR MANY SERIES AND FIND YOUR **PERFECT MATCH**.

FODOR'S GOLD GUIDES
America's favorite travel-guide series offers the most detailed insider reviews of hotels, restaurants, and attractions in all price ranges, plus great background information, smart tips, and useful maps.

COMPASS AMERICAN GUIDES
Stunning guides from top local writers and photographers, with gorgeous photos, literary excerpts, and colorful anecdotes. A must-have for culture mavens, history buffs, and new residents.

FODOR'S 25 BEST / CITYPACKS
Concise city coverage in a guide plus a foldout map. The right choice for urban travelers who want everything under one cover.

FODOR'S AROUND THE CITY WITH KIDS
Up to 68 great ideas for family days, recommended by resident parents. Perfect for exploring in your own backyard or on the road.

SEE IT GUIDES
Illustrated guidebooks that include the practical information travelers need, in gorgeous full color. Perfect for travelers who want the best value packed in a fresh, easy-to-use, colorful layout.

FODOR'S FLASHMAPS
Every resident's map guide, with 60 easy-to-follow maps of public transit, parks, museums, zip codes, and more.

FODOR'S LANGUAGES FOR TRAVELERS
Practice the local language before you hit the road. Available in phrase books, cassette sets, and CD sets.

THE COLLECTED TRAVELER
These collections of the best published essays and articles on various European destinations will give you a feel for the culture, cuisine, and way of life.